CRITICAL SURVEY
OF
POETRY

English Language Series

REVISED EDITION
Holm-MacD

4

Edited by
FRANK N. MAGILL

SALEM PRESS
Pasadena, California   Englewood Cliffs, New Jersey

Library of Congress Cataloging-in-Publication Data
Critical survey of poetry. English language series/edited
by Frank N. Magill. — Rev. ed.
   p.   cm.
Includes bibliographical references and index.
  1. English poetry—Dictionaries. 2. American
poetry—Dictionaries. 3. English poetry—
Bio-bibliography. 4. American poetry—Bio-
bibliography. 5. Poets, English—Biography—
Dictionaries. 6. Poets, American—Biography—
Dictionaries.
I. Magill, Frank Northen, 1907-   .
PR502.C85   1992   92-3727
821.009′03—dc20   CIP
ISBN 0-89356-834-1 (set)
ISBN 0-89356-838-4 (volume 4)

LIST OF AUTHORS IN VOLUME 4

OLIVER WENDELL HOLMES

Born: Cambridge, Massachusetts; August 29, 1809
Died: Boston, Massachusetts; October 7, 1894

Principal poetry
Poems, 1836; *Songs in Many Keys*, 1862; *Songs of Many Seasons*, 1875; *The Iron Gate and Other Poems*, 1880; *Before the Curfew and Other Poems*, 1888.

Other literary forms
A remarkably versatile writer, Oliver Wendell Holmes produced not only five volumes of poetry but also three novels (*Elsie Venner*, 1861; *The Guardian Angel*, 1867; and *A Mortal Antipathy*, 1885); several collections of essays, including *The Autocrat of the Breakfast-Table* (1858), *The Professor at the Breakfast-Table* (1860), and *The Poet at the Breakfast-Table* (1872); biographies of John Lothrop Motley (1879) and Ralph Waldo Emerson (1885); and a large number of essays dealing with medicine, including the classic study "The Contagiousness of Puerperal Fever" (1843).

Achievements
Along with William Cullen Bryant, John Greenleaf Whittier, Henry Wadsworth Longfellow, and James Russell Lowell, Holmes has come to be known as one of the so-called "Schoolroom Poets." The label is an unfortunate one: half affectionate and half patronizing, it indicates that for the last 150 years these poets have been regarded as the creators of verse so simplistic in theme, rhyme, and meter that it is ideally suited to memorization and recitation by grade school children; indeed, until recently it was not uncommon to find the portrait of at least one of these five men gracing the wall of the average American grade school classroom. In the final analysis, however, the amenability of a poem to memorization and recitation is not indicative of its intrinsic worth (or lack thereof). An objective reconsideration of Holmes's poetry reveals that he did indeed produce verse worthy of the admiration of serious readers of poetry. Such poems as "Old Ironsides," "The Last Leaf," "Dorothy Q.," "The Deacon's Masterpiece," and "The Chambered Nautilus" are still thought-provoking and entertaining works, and it is doubtful that future generations of poetry readers will find them any less so. In addition, Holmes's collection of essays *The Autocrat of the Breakfast-Table* is still studied, and his novel *Elsie Venner*, so curiously modern in its psychological and ethical dimensions, could very well enjoy a revival of sorts in the present age of Freudian and Jungian approaches to human behavior.

Biography
Oliver Wendell Holmes was born on August 29, 1809, in Cambridge, Mas-

sachusetts, a town which had already become established as a major American cultural center by virtue of Harvard College and nearby Boston—"the hub of the solar system," as Holmes would note only half jokingly in Essay VI of his *Autocrat* papers. Holmes's father, Abiel Holmes (1763-1837), was a Congregational minister in Cambridge who had already established his reputation as a writer with *The Annals of America* (1805; revised 1829), generally regarded as the first attempt at an exhaustive compilation of American historical data beginning with 1492. Holmes's mother, Sarah Wendell, was a descendant of the noted Puritan poet Anne Bradstreet; indeed, like Bradstreet, Sarah Wendell was unusually liberal on religious issues, and her son—far from following in the devout footsteps of his clergyman father—had little patience with religious orthodoxy. From an early age, Holmes was fascinated by natural science, and he is reported to have devoted the playtime of his childhood to analyzing the snails and insects which he found in the family's garden, but his decision to pursue a career in medicine—which, contrary to popular belief, probably was not due to his passion for driving horse carriages at illegal speeds through the streets of Boston—would not come until much later. After a year (1824-1825) at a Calvinist preparatory school, Phillips Academy at Andover, Holmes entered nearby Harvard College and was graduated in 1829 as Class Poet. Still undecided as to how best to use his unusual talents, he entered Dane Law School in Cambridge and remained there for one year (1829-1830); he then enrolled at Boston's Tremont Medical School, which he attended until 1833. This training was followed by two years of intensive study in Paris, a city which in the 1830's was noted for its superb facilities for medical research and which attracted the brightest medical students in the United States. In 1836, Holmes received his M.D. degree from Harvard and immediately commenced his extraordinary career as a physician, research scientist, and teacher. In 1836 and 1837, Holmes won three Boylston Prizes for his essays entitled "The Nature and Treatment of Neuralgia," "Facts and Traditions Respecting the Existence of Indigenous Intermittent Fever in New England," and "The Utility and Importance of Direct Exploration in Medical Practice." His 1843 essay, "The Contagiousness of Puerperal Fever," generated widespread controversy in its day, and it was not until 1861 that the Hungarian obstetrician Ignaz Philipp Semmelweis confirmed Holmes's theory that the deadly "childbed fever" was spread by contagion—that, in fact, it was often transmitted by the midwives and physicians who attended births. Holmes also was a pioneer in the use of microscopes in scientific research, in the establishment of histology as a legitimate branch of science, and in the improvement of surgical procedures; in fact, it was Holmes who in 1846 suggested the name "anesthesia" for the physiological condition induced by Dr. William Morton in a demonstration at the Massachusetts General Hospital in October of that year. Even at this early stage of his career, Holmes was teaching as well as doing extensive research; he was a professor of anatomy at Dartmouth College (1839-1840), and from 1847 to 1882 he served as the Parkman professor of anatomy and physiology at the Harvard Medical School. Between his teaching and research, Holmes tended not to continue his early practice as a family doctor. Part of the problem was his appearance. Boyish-looking and short (five feet four inches), Holmes found it difficult to instill confidence in his patients; more important, they apparently did not much appreciate his lighthearted manner, his sense of humor, or his reputation as—of all things—a poet. Holmes had become famous as a poet at the age of twenty-one when, in response to a newspaper notice that the American frigate *Constitution* was to be demolished, he quickly wrote "Old Ironsides"—an enormously popular poem which is held to have been responsible for saving the famed warship. A collected edition of his poetry appeared in 1836, and Holmes (like Ralph Waldo Emerson) was very successful both as a public lecturer in the 1850's and as the remarkably obliging author of "occasional" verse (including a poem entitled "For the Meeting of the National Sanitary Association").

In the minds of many nineteenth century Americans, however, Holmes was famous not as a physician, college professor, or poet, but as an essayist. When he was only twenty-two years old, Holmes published in the short-lived *New England Magazine* two brief, witty essays entitled "The Autocrat of the Breakfast-Table" (November, 1831; February, 1832). A quarter of a century later, Holmes decided "to shake the same bough again, and see if the ripe fruit were better or worse than the early windfalls" ("The Autocrat's Autobiography"), and so in the first issue (November, 1857) of a new magazine entitled the *Atlantic Monthly*, he printed the third "Autocrat" essay. The twelve essays serialized in the *Atlantic Monthly* were phenomenally popular; collected in book form, they reportedly sold ten thousand copies in three days and have been in continuous print ever since. While his fame as an essayist was spreading, Holmes also tried his hand at long fiction, producing three self-proclaimed "medicated novels": *Elsie Venner*, *The Guardian Angel*, and *A Mortal Antipathy*. Of the three, *Elsie Venner* is the best. Finally, Holmes wrote two biographies. *John Lothrop Motley* (1879) focuses on the noted historian and United States minister to Austria (1861-1867) and to Great Britain (1869-1870); *Ralph Waldo Emerson* (1885) was written for the American Men of Letters series.

By the time Holmes died in 1894, his name was a household word in the United States; in fact, his name lived on well into the twentieth century, not only because of his writings but also because of his distinguished son, Supreme Court Justice Oliver Wendell Holmes, Jr. (1841-1935). In many respects, it would be difficult to appreciate nineteenth century American life and thought without having some understanding of Holmes and his achievements. Not only did he lead a rich and productive life which spanned nearly the entire nineteenth century, helping to train several generations of American physicians, but he also produced half a dozen popular and enduring poems and a series of essays which clearly found responsive chords in the collective American psyche. In fact, it is questionable whether literary scholars and historians have even begun to determine the extent to which Holmes influenced and reflected American thought and literature in the nineteenth century. Although S. I. Hayakawa and Howard Mumford Jones are probably correct in maintaining that Holmes either was unaware of, or simply chose not to acknowledge, the milltowns proliferating in New England, the slums in the larger cities, and the squandering of human and natural resources which made possible the remarkable growth of America in the nineteenth century, it is nevertheless also true that this conservative Boston Brahmin, this American Samuel Johnson, this Renaissance man of medicine and literature was a spokesman for the majority of middle-class Americans of the nineteenth century.

Analysis

Of the hundreds of poems which the prolific Oliver Wendell Holmes produced, at least six are still being given serious attention by students of American literature: "Old Ironsides," "The Last Leaf," "Dorothy Q.," "The Deacon's Masterpiece," "The Chambered Nautilus," and "The Living Temple." The six poems are surprisingly varied in theme, depth, and technical expertise, although generally speaking they do reveal Holmes's lifelong interest in historical, scientific, and spiritual matters.

"Old Ironsides" was written virtually extempore in 1830 when the twenty-one-year-old Holmes read in the Boston *Daily Advertiser* that the American frigate *Constitution* was to be demolished. Launched in 1797, the forty-four-gun *Constitution*—better known as "Old Ironsides" because cannon balls allegedly would bounce off her sides—had served with great distinction in the Tripolitan War and the War of 1812. The *Constitution* was especially honored for its victories over two British vessels, the *Guerrière* (off Newfoundland) and the *Java* (off Brazil), in the War of 1812. Holmes's poem so aroused public sentiment against the demolition of the *Constitution* that the ship was ordered saved and rebuilt. A rather brief poem (three octaves), "Old Ironsides" is still a powerful work which moves organically from a skillfully ironic opening ("Ay, tear her tattered ensign down!") to an impassioned plea to let the ship be destroyed by "the god of storms" rather than by "the harpies of the shore." Generally speaking, the imagery is neither imaginative nor well developed ("the battle shout," "the cannon's roar"), but there are some vivid, highly emotional images ("Her deck, once red with heroes' blood") which tend to compensate for the commonplace nature of so much of the poem. More important, "Old Ironsides" shows Holmes to be a master of psychology: nowhere does he plead overtly that the ship be saved; nowhere does he mention its proper name, or catalog its many victories. Rather, by manipulating tone and imagery, Holmes produced a poem which is above all intensely emotional; indeed, those universal emotions upon which it plays—the honoring of the dead of war, the veneration of the old, the love of military glory—are probably as potent today as they were in the 1830's. It is difficult to imagine that either the poem or the ship—now carefully preserved and lying at anchor in the Charlestown Navy Yard—will be treated with anything less than the deepest respect for generations to come.

The poem "The Last Leaf" also reveals Holmes's tendency to handle aspects of American history in an emotional fashion, although this poem also embodies a more personal dimension. The subject, a "Sad and wan" old man who walks the streets dressed in "the old three-cornered hat,/ And the breeches, and all that," was Major Thomas Melville, the grandfather of Herman Melville. Of "The Last Leaf," Holmes wrote in a prefatory note to the Riverside edition of his writings that it "was suggested by the appearance in one of our streets of a venerable relic of the Revolution, said to be one of the party who threw the tea overboard in Boston Harbor," and that the smile with which Holmes (the poem's persona) greeted him "meant no disrespect to an honoured fellow-citizen whose costume was out of date, but whose patriotism never changed with years." Holmes goes on to note proudly that the poem was copied down by Edgar Allan Poe and memorized by Abraham Lincoln. "The Last Leaf" is not simply of historical or patriotic interest; it focuses upon the resiliency of the human spirit and, more precisely, the need and desire to cling to life despite the loneliness and physical infirmities of old age. In this regard, the poem is something of a tour de force; it is rather remarkable to find someone so young (twenty-two) writing with such tenderness and empathy of old age. On the other hand, the poem may be seen as a reflection of Holmes's extraordinary personality; for only someone as imaginative, compassionate, and observant as the author of "The Last Leaf" would be able to succeed in two such diverse pursuits as medicine and literature. One wonders whether the poem, first published in 1831 when Holmes was a medical student, was reread by him or his son as they approached old age (Holmes lived to be eighty-five; his son died in 1935 at ninety-four). Like Major Melville, each of them "live[d] to be/ The last leaf upon the tree/ In the spring."

"Dorothy Q." also shows Holmes's imaginative response to an actual person of the past, but in this charming poem the subject is one of his own ancestors: Dorothy Quincy, Holmes's great-grandmother on the maternal side. The premise of the poem is simple enough: the poem's persona (Holmes himself) regards a portrait of Dorothy made when she was only thirteen years old. The portrait itself was not painted with exceptional skill, and the canvas had been damaged by "a Red-Coat's rapier-thrust," but the girl, "a lady born," reveals in "her slender shape" the "Hint and promise of stately mien." Holmes realizes that he owes to Dorothy a "Strange" gift, for she gave him "All my tenure of heart and hand,/ All my title to house and land;/ Mother and sister and child and wife/ And joy and sorrow and death and life!" Here Holmes reveals, as he seldom does in his poetry, his deep interest (by both training and temperament) in human heredity; for by her acceptance of Edward Jackson's proposal of marriage (the "tremulous question"), young Dorothy ultimately helped to create not only Holmes but also Amelia Jackson, the distant relative of Holmes whom he married in June, 1840 (hence the paradoxical line "Mother and sister and child and wife"). Holmes speculates on heredity by questioning what he would have been like had she declined Jackson's marriage proposal; "Should I be I, or would it be/ One tenth another, to nine tenths me?"; and, touching upon the rather serious issue of the degree to which people are to be held morally responsible for creating new human life, Holmes wonders, "Shall I bless you, Dorothy, or forgive/ For the tender whisper [that is, her saying "Yes"] that bade me live?" The hint of unhappiness which pervades that final couplet is uncharacteristic of Holmes. It evidently does not reflect Holmes's personal dissatisfaction with being alive, for apparently he was a singularly contented man; however, it does seem to reflect his realization that many people certainly do regret having been born because of their physical or emotional problems. This unfortunate state of affairs, which would have been especially apparent to Holmes in his capacity as a physician, gave rise to two of his most enduring concerns. Is it not true that in large measure we are simply the victims of genetic factors beyond our comprehension or control? Furthermore, as "victims," should we—or our parents, or no one—be held morally responsible for our behavior? Several decades before the rise of naturalism in American literature, Holmes was confronting the power of human sexuality and the problem of determinism. Virtually all of that confrontation took place in Holmes's "medicated novels" (most notably *Elsie Venner*). In such poems as "Dorothy Q.," one sees but a glimmer of Holmes's deep interest in sex and genetic determinism.

More widely known than "Dorothy Q." are "The Deacon's Masterpiece: Or, The Wonderful 'One-Hoss Shay'" and "The Chambered Nautilus," both of which were originally published in Holmes's *Autocrat* papers, but which can be read outside of that context. "The Deacon's Masterpiece," one of Holmes's longest poems (120 lines), is also one of his most controversial. The story line is extremely simple: A deacon in 1755 sets out to build a "one-hoss shay." Mindful of the belief that in building a *chaise* "There is always *somewhere* a weakest spot" which is responsible for its eventual destruction, he constructs the carriage of the finest materials using the soundest technical knowledge available. One hundred years to the day after its creation, this ostensibly perfect carriage literally falls to pieces "in a heap or mound,/ As if it had been to the mill and ground!" The controversy resides in the poem's meaning: Is it a story about logic, a parable suggesting that any theoretically airtight system of beliefs is doomed to collapse simply because it cannot accommodate changes in context, attacks from without, or the passage of time? Or, is the poem (as is believed by many commentators) specifically a parable on the demise of Calvinism? The latter interpretation was first proposed in 1900 by Barrett Wendell, and the details in the poem upon which this reading is based are rather convincing. As Hyatt Waggoner points out in his *American Poets*, the shay is specifically "a 'deacon's' masterpiece, and it disappeared just as the parson got to 'fifthly' in his sermon." The religious element in the poem is insistent, and although Calvinism as such is not mentioned, "those who wanted to take the hint could do so."

Even more convincing is Holmes's emphasis on the fact that the shay was constructed in 1755, a singular year in the history of Calvinism, or, more precisely, in its decline. In 1755 came the death of Jonathan Edwards, the author of the Calvinist tract *The Freedom of the Will* (1754), as well as the great Lisbon earthquake, an event which raised serious questions concerning free will and original sin. Between Edwards' death and the earthquake, Calvinism suffered blows from which it never recovered, and by 1855 that inflexible system of religious beliefs was perceived as being so inappropriate for the rapidly changing American way of life that it was simply rejected wholesale. Further support for this reading of "The Deacon's Masterpiece" is to be found in Holmes's personal attitude toward Calvinism: he felt that it was "not just mistaken but vicious." As Waggoner further reveals, Holmes felt that Calvinism not only

> denied man his dignity, it denied God his sublimity, reducing him to an unjust Oriental potentate. But most of all it offended the moral sense, especially in its doctrine of Election. "Any decent person," he once wrote . . . "ought to go mad if he really holds . . . such opinions."

Several other interpretations of "The Deacon's Masterpiece" have been offered (including the theory that it is an allegory about manufacturing), but in the light of Holmes's personal contempt for Calvinism and various details in the poem, it seems most reasonable to agree with Barrett Wendell's reading. The poem, of course, can be enjoyed even without accepting or rejecting it as a religious allegory. Its rollicking couplets, thick New England dialect, and lively humor still make interesting reading; it helps to explain why Holmes is regarded today as a master of light verse.

Even better known than "The Deacon's Masterpiece" is "The Chambered Nautilus." The controlling image of the poem is the shell of a type of cephalopod native to the South Pacific and Indian oceans. The shell, a "ship of pearl," fancifully believed to sail about in the depths of the ocean, has been washed ashore and split open—"Its irised ceiling rent, its sunless crypt unsealed!" The splitting has revealed the internal structure of the shell: a spiral consisting of the progressively larger chambers which the cephalopod constructed, occupied, and abandoned as it grew to maturity. The image of that broken shell with its spiraling chambers is interpreted as conveying a "heavenly message": "Build thee more stately mansions, O my soul,/ As the swift seasons roll!" The poem, with its carefully controlled movement from poetic fancy (the shell as the "venturous bark" which sails where "the cold sea-maids . . . sun their streaming hair") to science (the observation and analysis of the beached shell) to spiritual faith, demonstrates that the didactic impulse which was so potent a force in early American poetry was still evident in Holmes's verse in 1858.

Evident it was, but not necessarily predominant. Although Holmes was enough of a proper Boston Brahmin not to question anyone else's religious beliefs overtly (witness the veiled allegorical attack on Calvinism in "The Deacon's Masterpiece"), he was much more a man of science than a man of faith, and in that respect he embodied the increasing tendency on the part of nineteenth century Americans to place their trust in technology rather than in religion. True, the persona of "The Chambered Nautilus" sees a "heavenly message" in the structure of the shell, but this does not qualify his obvious interest in conchology.

Holmes's preference for science over faith is especially evident in his poem "The Living Temple" (1858). Working from the biblical statement that "your body is the temple of the Holy Ghost," Holmes provides a surprisingly effective paean to human physiology. It is true that in the first of the seven stanzas he indicates that the poem is intended to prove that God's "Eternal wisdom" may be detected as clearly in man's "wondrous frame" as it is in "the world of light" and "in earth below," but the fact remains that for the next five stanzas God is quite forgotten in the elaborate, neoclassical discussion of the human body and its functions. The second stanza focuses on breathing: "The smooth soft air with pulse-like waves/ Flows murmuring through its hidden caves"; the third deals with the circulatory system, that "woven net" at the center of which is the "throbbing slave . . ./ Forever quivering o'er his task"; the fourth focuses on muscles and bones, the "living marbles jointed strong/ With glistening band and silvery thong"; the fifth discusses vision (the eyes as "lucid globes") and hearing ("Hark how the rolling surge of sound,/ Arches and spirals circling round"); and the sixth deals with the human brain ("the cloven sphere") and, more abstractly, the mind ("Think on the stormy world that dwells/ Locked in its dim and clustering cells").

Holmes's excitement over the wonders of the human body is palpable in this poem, so much so that the final stanza—with its apostrophe to the "Father" to "grant thy love divine/ To make these mystic temples thine," and its request that when the marvelous human body dies its "poor dust" may be "mould[ed] . . . into heavenly forms"—sounds more than a little forced and artificial. One may, in fact, be reminded of the poetry of Holmes's Puritan ancestor, Anne Bradstreet, who often undercut the powerful personal emotions in her verse by introducing religious doctrine (see, for example, "Some Verses Upon the Burning of Our House," where her agony over the loss of her home is ostensibly nullified by the thought that she has "an home on high erect;/ Framed by that mighty Architect"). Even though "The Living Temple" has its origins in a biblical text, and even though the first and last stanzas introduce matters of religious faith, the fact remains that this is far more a poem of physiology than of religious orthodoxy. Unfortunately, the tension generated between the real and the ostensible subject weakens the poem significantly.

By reason of "Old Ironsides," "The Last Leaf," "Dorothy Q.," "The Deacon's Masterpiece," "The Chambered Nautilus," "The Living Temple," the *Autocrat* papers, and the novels and biographies, Oliver Wendell Holmes stands as one of the most popular, prolific, and versatile American writers of the nineteenth century. No serious student of life and letters in the United States can afford to overlook him and his considerable achievements.

Alice Hall Petry

Other major works
LONG FICTION: *Elsie Venner*, 1861; *The Guardian Angel*, 1867; *A Mortal Antipathy*, 1885.
NONFICTION: *The Autocrat of the Breakfast-Table*, 1858; *The Professor at the Breakfast-Table*, 1860; *The Poet at the Breakfast-Table*, 1872; *John Lothrop Motley*, 1879; *Medical Essays, 1842-1882*, 1883; *Ralph Waldo Emerson*, 1885.

Bibliography
Brenner, Rica. *Twelve American Poets Before 1900*. New York: Harcourt, Brace, 1933. In the thirty-page chapter on Holmes, Brenner quotes from a number of Holmes's poems in order to picture his life through his poetry. The author examines the poetry, using it to chart Holmes's growth as a poet and transformations in his method and style. This volume has chapters on Holmes's contemporaries, many of them his friends—Ralph Waldo Emerson, Henry Wadsworth Longfellow, John Greenleaf Whittier, James Russell Lowell, Walt Whitman, and Emily Dickinson—which help situate him in the cultural and literary era he belonged to.
Carter, Everett. "The Typicality of Oliver Wendell Holmes." In *Themes and Directions in American Literature: Essays in Honor of Leon Howard*, edited by Ray B. Browne and Donald Pizer. Lafayette, Ind.: Purdue University Studies, 1969. Carter's premise is that Holmes's work should be examined not in a search for literary originality and uniqueness but using an approach that recognizes his literary virtues as typicality and representativeness of his culture. Holmes's work, though currently unfashionable, Carter says, embodies the conventional beliefs of his times and was given form by these beliefs. Includes notes and bibliographic references.
Howe, M. A. De Wolfe. *Holmes of the Breakfast Table*. 1939. Reprint. Mamaroneck, N.Y.: P. P. Appel, 1972. This 172-page, illustrated biographical study divides Holmes's life into four periods. Each chapter uses his poetry

in part to help describe his endeavors and illuminate his life. Contains an index.

Hoyt, Edwin Palmer. *The Improper Bostonian: Dr. Oliver Wendell Holmes.* New York: William Morrow, 1979. This definitive biography is thorough and well researched, with generous notes on each chapter. All twenty-nine chapters are short, well focused and readable. Holmes as a literary figure is studied primarily in chapters 16-20, which quote a number of poems in full and in part. Supplemented by illustrations and a good index.

Small, Miriam Rossiter. *Oliver Wendell Holmes.* New York: Twayne, 1962. Small looks at Holmes's work in three groups: the Breakfast-Table series, the novels, and the poems for Harvard occasions. Her biocritical study follows a chronology established by the autobiographical echoes in his prose and poetry. In addition to six chapters, the book includes a chronology, references and notes, a select bibliography, and an index.

Sullivan, Wilson. *New England Men of Letters.* New York: Macmillan, 1972. By showing how their lives resulted in their work, Sullivan hopes to bring his ten subjects alive for a contemporary audience. The problems they explored in their work—social, philosophical, moral, religious—are explored for their relevance to current readers. The short chapter on Holmes uses his poetry to enliven an overview of his life and accomplishments.

GARRETT HONGO

Born: Volcano, Hawaii; May 30, 1951

Principal poetry
Yellow Light, 1982; *The River of Heaven*, 1988.

Other literary forms
Nisei Bar & Grill, a play, was written in 1976 and performed in Seattle and San Francisco. Its revised version became a workshop production at the Kilauea Theater (1992). The play depicts interactions among veterans of World War II and the Korean conflict. Garrett Hongo also has written literary essays appearing in *Agni Review, The New York Times Book Review, New England Review*, and *Ohio Review*.

Achievements
Hongo's poetry is notable for its immediacy of voice, clear evocation of place, and poignant negotiation of both ethnic and temporal boundaries. He typically employs memory to compile imagistic pastiches that re-create an emotional state. Many of his poems are quests—for a synthetic cultural identity, for a true personal history, for a unique and satisfactory voice. Traversing landscapes from the volcano of his birthplace to the volcanic experience of living in a mainland metropolis (primarily Los Angeles), Hongo explores the brutality of contemporary life as it assaults the tenderness of the spirit. Alienation, discrimination, cruelty, violence, loss, and isolation permeate the poems as insults to the soul.

Hongo has received high acclaim and support through several prizes and fellowships: the Thomas J. Watson Travelling Fellowship, 1973-1974; the Hopwood Poetry Prize, 1975; the Discovery/*The Nation* Award, 1981; National Endowment for the Arts fellowships, 1982 and 1988; Pushcart Prize selection, 1986; the Lamont Poetry Prize, 1987; and a Guggenheim Fellowship, 1990-1991. In 1989 he was a finalist for the Pulitzer Prize in Poetry and the *Los Angeles Times* Book Award.

Biography
A fourth-generation Japanese-American, Garrett Kaoru Hongo was born in Volcano, Hawaii, in 1951. His parents are Albert Kazuyoshi Hongo, who died in 1984, and Louise Tomiko Kubota Hongo. Until he was six years old, he and his family lived in Kahuku and then Hauula on the island of Oahu. Hongo learned at this time to speak Pidgin English and Japanese. From the ages of six to eighteen, Hongo lived with his family in and around Los Angeles, where he began to experience the harshness of city life (in contrast to the

easy rhythms of life in the rain forest) and the prejudices and injustices of a multicultural society. He attended an inner-city high school that was an integration pilot, combining whites, Asian-Americans, African-Americans, and Hispanic-Americans in the same classes. Some of his poems, "Morro Rock" in particular, evoke conflicts experienced for the first time in his teenage years.

Hongo's beginnings as a poet came when he was eighteen and started writing love poems to a European-American girl, celebrating a relationship that they felt pressured to keep secret. She awakened in him an intellectual camaraderie with "books about adolescent yearning and rebellion, about 'the system' not understanding you," notably William Golding's *Lord of the Flies* (1954), J. D. Salinger's *The Catcher in the Rye* (1951), Hermann Hesse's *Siddhartha* (1951), J. R. R. Tolkien's *The Lord of the Rings* (3 vols., 1954-1955), and Ken Kesey's *One Flew Over the Cuckoo's Nest* (1962). His first serious poetry came when he was twenty and a student at Pomona College. There as a freshman he read the early fiction of James Joyce, who made him aware of links between language and culture and the literary divisions of loyalty that an artist might feel. As a sophomore he progressed to the poetry of Ezra Pound and William Butler Yeats, whom he began to revere as sages who had reinvented English according to their own inner voices. He immersed himself in listening to the language of poets by attending actual readings by Philip Levine (who was to become a mentor), Gary Snyder, Seamus Heaney, and Galway Kinnell. He studied Japanese and Chinese formally, and, as Hongo himself relates, "practiced calligraphy every night, and, afterwards, my mind tight and cluttered with bristling ideograms, read the great translations of T'ang Dynasty Chinese poetry by Pound, Arthur Waley, Witter Bynner, and Kenneth Rexroth." Through this process he began to have confidence in his own authentic voice, what he calls his "inner speech," later encouraged by poet-teachers Bert Meyers, Charles Wright, C. K. Williams, and Philip Levine.

At the age of twenty, Hongo returned to Hawaii and began to try to reclaim that portion of his own past, his heritage. Here he discovered in a garage his father's library, consisting primarily of works of realistic fiction, and he established a connection with his uncle, Robert Hongo, who was a novelist. The first "real" poem Garrett Hongo wrote was called "Issei: First-Generation Japanese American." The poem relates an ancestral explanation of how he received his own middle name and thus reveals the close link between name and identity, between name and heritage. Writing the poem was a turning point for him, a moment that confirmed his calling. Hongo describes this experience in terms that represent the matter and spirit of much of his poetry:

> It was a childhood recollection of my grandfather reading a Japanese book—a sort of bound scroll of folded paper stitched together in a way that reminded me of the lacing on a fishing

pole. It was about descent, heritage, and his injunction to me to remember it. I wrote the lines quickly after practicing ideograms all night once, in cadences I imitated from translations of Chinese poetry. After I was done, I felt my life had changed—that I had said a *true* thing, that I was a *poet*. I remembered the feeling, the new conviction, and tried for it every time I wrote thereafter. It was a standard I used to test authenticity and depth of feeling.

Working to combine the early literary influence of "the fiction of John Steinbeck, the poetry of Dylan Thomas and Robinson Jeffers, the lyrics of Hawaiian songs, and Motown," Hongo entered the Watts Writers' Workshop. There he was primarily an observer while more experienced writers debated many of the same questions that plagued the young Hongo: voice, authenticity, ethnic fidelity and literary sophistication, legitimacy, genuineness. He began to connect the forms and methods of music and poetry, striving for the avant-garde mastery of jazz pianists McCoy Tyner and Cecil Taylor in his own writing, and finding a fascination with the representative possibilities of theater—*Macbeth* with an all-black cast, for example.

After being graduated *cum laude* in 1973 from Pomona College, Hongo journeyed to Japan on a quest for an understanding of where he might belong; he spent a year there, traveling and writing poetry. He then commenced graduate study of Japanese language and literature at the University of Michigan. Returning to the West Coast, Hongo lived in Seattle from 1976 to 1979, where he worked as a professor and a poet. Ultimately he returned to California to study and receive, in 1980, an M.F.A. in English from the University of California at Irvine, where he continued in doctoral study in critical theory for two more years.

Although he finds himself more attuned to dialogue with poets than with professors, more at home in the artistic world than in the academy, Hongo negotiates the common ground with grace and intelligence. His critical training is apparent in his experimentation with various poetic forms, as well as in the metapoetic nature of some of his writings. Hongo is aware of the myriad poetic influences that have helped to define him. He pays homage to his predecessors by emulating their forms and by injecting himself into their situations or embedding their poems within his, as in "To Matsuo Basho and Kawai Sora in Nirvana," where the persona of the poem visits the pond of the famous frog haiku and invites the ghosts of the masters to return to him and speak, "before the fog rolls in." In his later poems Hongo often includes a dedication to other poets in a kind of ongoing literary conversation. His connection to other working poets helps to sustain his own writing; those who have figured in this dialogue include Mark Jarman ("Morro Rock"), Gerald Stern ("Nostalgic Catalogue"), Edward Hirsch ("Ancestral Graves, Kahuku"), and Charles Wright ("Volcano House").

Even though Hongo enjoys thinking critically about his own and others' poetry, he found deconstructionist theory to be debilitating rather than enabling and thus left his doctoral program in 1984, taking a position as an assistant professor of English at the University of Missouri, where he was also poetry editor of *The Missouri Review*. Meanwhile Hongo had married Cynthia Thiessen, a violinist, and his first son, Alexander, was born (a second son is named Hudson). In Missouri, Hongo began daydreaming about Hawaii, about California, about his own and his family's past. Instead of producing a doctoral dissertation, he wrote *The River of Heaven*—a decision that salvaged his spirit in an alien landscape and confirmed his allegiance to creativity rather than to scholarship. After a year's sojourn at the University of Houston, Hongo accepted in 1989 a position as director of the creative writing program at the University of Oregon in Eugene, his wife's hometown; there he tries to instill in his students a poetic discipline analogous to that of the martial arts.

He divides his time between Eugene and Volcano, a place for which his spirit hankers and where the ghost of his grandfather is evident. Hongo has himself become an active literary presence of his hometown and is the leader of a theater group. He speaks of his connection with place, of how the volcano itself informs his poetry:

> My poems speak now of the fragility of all things—culture, inheritances, loyalties—and the great vulnerability of love of them. I look out the window here and see myrtle trees with their red-crest blossoms—*o'hia lehua* in Hawaiian—and feel sad to think that there might only be 60 years left for this forest, for the *apapane* and *i'iwi* honeycreepers which live among these trees. Mostly, though, I still write from an ancient human sadness for existence and for eternity, a feeling Japanese aesthetics defined as *sabi*—a kind of serene worry or melancholy about the universe.

Analysis

The collected volumes of Garrett Hongo's poetry—*Yellow Light* and *The River of Heaven*—offer a chronological narrative of his autobiography and his development as a poet. By reading the poems in the order of their collection, one becomes immersed in the external details of life in the modern metropolis, exotic locales, and a multicultural community, as well as in the resulting internal emotions and reflections of the writer. A recurring theme in his work is the search for a personal identity that is unique, separate, and autonomous but also continuous with one's heritage. There is a sense of the need for separation and then return; the poems trace a journey of discovery.

The title poem of *Yellow Light* sets the tone for the rest of the collection. These earlier poems reflect the writer's concern with the sensibility of his father's soul, which was brutalized by his necessary manual labor and the hardship of making a living in an alien society. The sensations, the impressions, of his father's condition were indelibly etched on the consciousness of the poet as a young child. The conflict and compromise that he knew his father felt become abstracted into larger, less personal issues and then reparticularized into observable details of the environment and projections into the lives of observed people.

In "Yellow Light," a woman returns to her apartment after work and shopping. In her walk through the city, the poet juxtaposes images of nature to the trappings of city life. The contemporary urban environment has as its "natural" images children reenacting war games, sounds of domestic squabbles, noisy machinery, polluted air, and unsightly barriers separating yard from yard, protecting material property. These contrast with vivid sensations of a truly natural environment, appearing here as flowers that would be colorful, fragrant, and profuse.

The contrast continues in descriptions of the light the woman experiences. Light is often used in poetry to indicate truth or clarity of vision. The city offers only ugly, glaring, artificial light—false illumination. It is revealed in searchlights from car lots and the fluorescent and neon lights of commerce and trade. By offering as an alternative to this light the warm and mellow glow of a kitchen lamp, the poet hints that each individual may establish his or her own "natural" territory domestically: a place where one is in control and one's values and priorities are proper. Later poems indicate that poetry itself may be one's private territory, where a corrective vision can be offered as an alternative to the flawed world "out there." Hongo carries forth the kitchen image, and its associations with sustenance and nurturance, in the overpowering natural light of the moon, a larger version of the mellow kitchen lamp, here compared to the rich yellow of onions. The light of the moon proves ultimately victorious, as it blankets the horrors of the city and renders invisible the lesser metropolitan lights. The act of writing poetry, the poet suggests, may itself be redemptive.

The remaining poems in the volume continue with similar themes and may be grouped accordingly. Several of them focus on domestic life, often employing the idea of a return to the haven of home and family. In "Off from Swing Shift," a father returns home from the sapping drudgery of his assembly-line job to the comforts of his humble apartment and the pleasures of the idle pastime of gambling. In "Preaching the Blues," a young man returns from a time away from home to find his brother waiting for him at the airport. They reestablish the patterns of their childhood relationship by enacting the ritual of playing basketball in the parking lot. As they drive home, memories of their youth and the growth and patterns of their relationship engulf the narrator. He is filled with empathy for the life of his brother, which is linked with his, yet of an entirely different essence and identity.

Empathic projection is also apparent in two other domestic poems, "Stay with Me" and "The Hongo Store." In the former, the poet depicts a gesture of kindness between strangers. A woman on a bus is filled with emotional suffering. As she cries silently and unobtrusively, a young black man reluctantly bridges the gap from polite concern to a true sharing of her pain, as he comforts her by holding her. In the latter the poet projects himself into a

photograph taken just after the family home and store had survived the erup-
tion of a volcano, and he recaptures the entire episode from an adult perspective.

Several of the works could be labeled "identity poems," as they reclaim
the poet's personal heritage and ethnic history. "Roots" and "Issei: First-
Generation Japanese American" are obviously in this vein. The poem "Step-
child" moves out of the concern with personal identity to retrace the troubled history of Asian-Americans in the first half of the twentieth century.
The form of this poem is also unique, for it actually incorporates accounts
by other writers of life in the internment camps and after World War II. The
suffering of others like him, the narrator implies, is also part of who he is.

A major work in this collection could be labeled a "quest poem." "Cruising 99" is a poetic version of the influential Beat-generation book *On the
Road* (1955) by Jack Kerouac. In this poem, the narrator and two friends
travel Highway 99 in California, looking for something to make sense of
their lives, but also simply content with movement, at least the illusion of
making progress, of seeking, of "getting there." The poem chronicles the details observed on the trip, again juxtaposing the natural and the artificial;
that made by nature and that produced by humankind. Separate sections in
various experimental forms re-create the human sounds, the sights, and the
events of the trip: a chant to pass the time; a dialogue; a philosophical meditation about the purpose of travel; a palm-reading incident; haikulike versions of postcard messages mailed home; an encounter in a café while the
car is being repaired that leads to a realization of the fleeting nature of the
travelers' youth; the surprising discovery of a Japanese community that brings
them, ironically, back to themselves, back to where they began; and a final
stanza on the patterns of running away and returning, patterns that can be
remedied by a process of incorporation. By the end of this quest, the narrator realizes that one may become a landscape composed of all of one's
heritage and experience: one becomes able to carry the journey within one
rather than to move, constantly seeking something outside of oneself.

Part of the quest in Hongo's case was to return to the ancestral homeland
of Japan. Several of the poems recount the experience as "outsider poems."
The visitor feels part of the culture yet alien to its sources. "Who Among
You Knows the Essence of Garlic?" is an immersion into the culinary details
of the Japanese ecosystem, ultimately becoming a microcosm of Japanese
philosophy and culture that cannot include the American observer. In "To
Matsuo Basho and Kawai Sora in Nirvana," the poet visits a site frequented
by two of the most famous of Japanese poets and attempts to speak with
their ghosts, to become part of their literary tradition. Even if he can recapture their vision for a moment, he still senses that time and his own distance
from their realities will continue to separate them.

The other categories of poems contained in this volume are portraits, meditations, and love poems, as well as an important set of pieces that might be called poems about art. "What For," in particular, reveals Hongo's concern with the value of capturing reality and giving it a name that occurs in writing poetry. This poem traces the child-poet's attraction to work rituals in his early life: the magic of incantation in Hawaiian natural mythology, family oral lore and storytelling, and singing. All of these contributed to the making of the poet, yet they are contrasted to the adult death of the spirit that the child perceives in his father. As he sees the exigencies of modern life drag his parent down, the child-poet desires to use his own word magic to soothe the pain and cure his father's suffering.

Hongo's second volume, *The River of Heaven*, takes its title from a line in "The Unreal Dwelling: My Years in Volcano," which is the death poem of the poet's grandfather. Here he imagines the last year of his ancestor's life in the town of Hongo's own birth. The title indicates the centrality of ancestral heritage and the image of the volcano itself in all the poems. Yet in this collection of poems, much of the restlessness of *Yellow Light* is gone. "Mendocino Rose," a poem of prologue to the collection, establishes a new tone of synthesis, wholeness, and peace. Indeed, the tenor of this poem is the harmonies that one can both find and impose on music, landscape, heritage, and a transplanted identity.

The collection is divided into two distinct parts, the first chronicling the poet's initial return to Hawaii after leaving at the age of six, and the second moving to mainland poems. There is a developmental movement to the first part. At the beginning the narrator simply tries to recapture the experience of coming home in all of its sensuous detail, as in "Nostalgic Catalogue." There follows an immersion into the memories that are stimulated by the new sensuous stimuli, as in "Village: Kahuku-*mura.*" He begins to experience a reclaiming of authentic selfhood in poems such as "Ancestral Graves, Kahuku" and "Hilo: First Night Back" and recognizes his kinship to relatives who remained in Hawaii. Then there is the self-scrutiny that results when he writes poetic stories of his ancestors and applies the lessons to himself, as in "*Jigoku*: On the Glamour of Self-Hate." The center of this section is Volcano itself and its landscape, which is real, as the birthplace of the poet, but also metaphorical, as the representation of fragility, destruction, and re-creation, which occur in poetry as in life.

The mainland poems of the second section are introduced by a quotation from Albert Camus to establish their predominant tone. Camus speaks of "this desire for unity, this longing to solve, this need for clarity and cohesion," at which Hongo has already hinted as being the process of poetry. These poems are more intellectual and literary, such as "Portrait of a Lady" (a title used by other famous writers such as T. S. Eliot, Ezra Pound, and Henry James). Hongo modernizes and individualizes both the form and the content of the tradition, offering a portrait of a contemporary ethnic woman in a free verse style that resembles a prose-poem.

The elements present in both volumes of poetry remain, however they may be transformed or altered in tone. Garrett Hongo's persistent interests in identity, heritage, beauty and sadness, and the power of poetry lend a satisfying unity to the entire body of his work.

Sandra K. Fischer

Other major work

PLAY: *Nisei Bar & Grill,* 1976, 1992.

Bibliography

Hongo, Garrett. "Ancestral Voices." Interview by Bill Moyers for *The Power of the Word.* Public Broadcasting Service, 1989. Television series interview of Hongo by journalist Bill Moyers, produced by WNET-Television of New York. Hongo discusses influences on and concerns of his poetry.

Kaganoff, Penny. Review of *The River of Heaven,* by Garrett Hongo. *Publishers' Weekly,* no. 233 (February 12, 1988): 81. Earliest published review of Hongo's second collection of poetry.

Muratori, Fred. Review of *The River of Heaven,* by Garrett Hongo. *Library Journal,* no. 113 (May 1, 1988): 81-82. Slightly longer review of Hongo's second volume.

Pettingell, Phoebe. Review of *The River of Heaven,* by Garrett Hongo. *The New Leader,* no. 71 (June 13, 1988): 16. Most recent review of Hongo's work.

THOMAS HOOD

Born: London, England; May 23, 1799
Died: London, England; May 3, 1845

Principal poetry

Odes and Addresses to Great People, 1825 (with John Hamilton Reynolds); *Whims and Oddities: In Prose and Verse*, 1826-1827; *The Plea of the Midsummer Fairies, Hero and Leander, Lycus the Centaur, and Other Poems*, 1827; *The Comic Annual*, 1830-1839, 1842 (poetry and prose); *The Epping Hunt*, 1829; *The Dream of Eugene Aram, the Murderer*, 1831; *Hood's Own: Or, Laughter from Year to Year*, 1839; *Miss Kilmansegg and Her Precious Leg*, 1840; *Whimsicalities: A Periodical Gathering*, 1844.

Other literary forms

As a journalist, Thomas Hood contributed prose as well as poetry to such periodicals as the *London Magazine*, *The New Monthly Magazine*, and *Hood's Magazine and Comic Miscellany*, while serving as their editor. He also wrote drama criticism for *The Atlas* for several months in 1826, before trying to write dramatic pieces of his own. In 1828, he wrote an ill-fated farce, *York and Lancaster: Or, A School Without Scholars*, for the theater manager Frederick Henry Yates, and followed this unsuccessful attempt with at least two more burlesques which have been lost in whole or in part. He wrote two closet dramas that were not published until after his death: *Lamia: A Romance* (published in 1852) based on Keats's poem of the same title, and *Guido and Marina: A Dramatic Sketch* (published in 1882), a romantic dialogue.

Hood did numerous etchings and drawings for his publications, and had others executed under his direction. His best-known engraving, "The Progress of Cant," a large Hogarthian-style work published in 1825, shows a rag-tag parade of Londoners bearing signs and banners to proclaim their favorite causes and philosophies, meanwhile exhibiting their contrary actions.

Encouraged by the early success of his first volumes of comic verse, Hood published a two-volume collection of short stories entitled *National Tales* in 1827; unfortunately, just as his attempts to write drama demonstrated his lack of dramatic skill, the stories exhibited that he had no real talent for prose fiction. Hood imitated the Italian *novella* form used by the Elizabethans, without writing a single story of literary value. He also wrote two novels— *Tylney Hall* (1834) and *Up the Rhine* (1840)—with somewhat better popular success, although the novels were nearly as lacking in literary merit. *Tylney Hall* went through numerous printings in England and America, but owed its success to the humorous portions; the serious plot and major characters are rather insipid, manifesting the same contrivance and shallowness that afflicted his short stores. *Up the Rhine* was a success in the bookstalls—in England, America, and, predictably, in Frankfurt. A travelogue-novel similar to Mark Twain's *Innocents Abroad* (1869), *Up the Rhine* draws upon Hood's "exile" years in Germany (1835 to 1839). It is light and enjoyable reading, but far from "quality" fiction. In both novels Hood gave free vent to his punning genius, which adds humor but detracts from the overall temper of both stories. Another novel, *Our Family*, remained incomplete at Hood's death, although several chapters were published serially in *Hood's Magazine* (it was eventually published in 1861). There is no evidence that Hood's aspirations to be a novelist would have produced a better book. His many letters, though often delightful and always sparkling with wit and humor, are difficult to read. Hood's main difficulty as a prose writer was his inability to sustain a smooth, readable text that is not chopped up by distracting wordplay; in addition, he was simply not a good storyteller. Both problems greatly handicapped his ability to write long poetic narratives as well.

Achievements

Hood's position in the generally overlooked period between the end of the Romantic movement and the beginning of the Victorian era has caused his true importance to be greatly underestimated. Although he can scarcely be called one of the giants of English poetry, his achievements are far from insignificant. His primary contributions to English letters have been fourfold: the refinement of English poetic humor, the popularization of poetry, the sympathetic portrayal of common English domesticity, and the arousal of humanitarian sentiments on a popular level.

Hood's comic verse—of which the amount is greater than and the quality superior to the work of any other English or American poet—evolved into what J. C. Reid calls "a highly individual amalgam of the farcical and the sinister, the pathetic and the ghoulish, that has few ancestors but many heirs." Hood's peculiar style did not preclude his diverse experimentation, whereby he often imitated and improved upon earlier comic techniques. He remains without rival in the use of the pun. He left a legacy of humorous poetry so varied that it not only provides a smooth transition from the often acrimonious wit of the eighteenth century—with none of the acrimony—but also often anticipates comic techniques and themes that died with Hood until they were resurrected in the twentieth century, especially in the dark or grotesque humor of writers such as Franz Kafka.

Because Hood made poetry relevant to everyday life and wrote in a highly entertaining style, verse once more became something that the common people could enjoy. Since the death of William Shakespeare, who also catered in his drama to popular tastes, poetry had become an almost purely academic art form. The neoclassical movement isolated poetry from the common man to a great extent through various formulary restraints and elevated diction. The Romantic movement sought to reestablish the language of life as the language of poetry, but the philosophy and ideals of many Romantics were inaccessible to the masses. Hood popularized poetry by brilliantly expressing commonplace ideas in common words.

Writing for a popular audience meant being free to explore popular themes. Hood's treatment of domestic scenes merits special attention. Ordinary housewives and mothers, with their squalling babes in arms, domestic servants, husband-wife or parent-child relations, all of the accoutrements of home and hearth (especially cookery) receive sympathetic treatment from the pen of this devoted family man. Hood takes the reader into mansions, but through the servant's entrance, and takes the butler's perspective or leaves the reader in the kitchen. What William Hogarth did with engraving, Hood did with poetry. Not afflicted by pretension or ambition, but sensitive to both, he remained the poet of the common man throughout his career.

In his later years, this sympathy for the proletariat led to some of the first and finest advocacy of basic human rights ever to be expressed in verse. Hood echoed the faint cries of social protest sounded by William Blake, amplified them, and added his own passionate appeals for reform. Never a revolutionary, Hood sought to inspire the upper middle class to extend a hand of true charity and compassion to the needs of the poor, sought to influence industrialists to pay a decent wage, sought to influence a notoriously competitive society to reassess its values. Hood was a voice crying somewhat in vain in the wilderness, but those he inspired were able to induce many notable social reforms in the second half of the nineteenth century.

On a more mundane level, Hood served in various editorial and journalistic capacities from 1821, when he became a proofreader and contributor for the *London Magazine*, until 1845, when he was still producing material on his deathbed for the magazine he had founded, *Hood's Magazine*. In the years between, he was associated with *The Atlas* (as drama critic, 1826), *The New Monthly Magazine* (as editor, 1841-1843), and a number of annuals, including his own *Comic Annual*.

Biography

Thomas Hood's father, also named Thomas, was a partner in the bookselling and publishing firm of Vernor and Hood, which produced *Poetical Magazine*, *Lady's Monthly Museum*, and the *Monthly Mirror*. His mother, Elizabeth Sands, was the daughter of an engraver. Both occupations determined the future career of Thomas Hood, one of six children in the Hood family to survive infancy. Hood's early education was at an Islington preparatory school, then at the Alfred House Academy at Camberwell Green. The deaths of his father and elder brother in 1811 left Thomas the man of the family, so he took a job clerking to supplement the family income. Poor health forced him to move from clerking to engraving for his uncle, but because his constitution continued to suffer, he was sent in 1815 to live with relatives in Dundee, Scotland, where he continued his apprenticeship in the engraving trade. At Dundee Hood began writing seriously. His health improved, and he returned to London in the autumn of 1817, where he worked as an engraver until he was hired in 1821 by John Taylor, a former employee of Hood's father and then editor of the *London Magazine*. Within a few months his mother died, leaving Hood the responsibility of providing for four sisters, one of whom also died a short time later.

At the *London Magazine* Hood was plunged into the company of many of England's prominent writers—Charles Lamb, Allan Cunningham, T. G. Wainewright, and John Hamilton Reynolds. Hood's friendship with Reynolds brought him into close contact with the circle and work of the recently deceased John Keats, and Hood strove for several years to imitate the great Romantic's lush and effusive style. Indeed, he was thought by many (including Cunningham) to be the logical successor of Keats, but Hood's collaboration with Reynolds on a book of comic verse in 1825 did more to further his literary career than any of his attempts to imitate the Romantics. During the same year, Hood married Reynolds' sister Jane and settled into the domestic life that would later inspire much of his poetry. Since he had ceased to edit the *London Magazine* during the previous year, Hood was obliged to publish in earnest for an income.

Hood's first daughter was born and died in May, 1827, inspiring Lamb's famous elegy "On an Infant Dying as Soon as Born." Hood's repeated exposure to the death of those closest to him was having a profound impact on his poetry, in which death figures so prominently. The following year an attack of rheumatic fever left Hood in the weakened condition that plagued him for the rest of his life. Hood continued writing, even while ill, since it was his sole means of support. He produced the first of his *Comic Annuals* in 1830, the year that his daughter Frances Freeling was born. Although his comic verse was popular, the Hood family never advanced beyond a lower-middle-class life-style. In 1832, they moved into their own home—Lake House in Wanstead—but the failure in 1834 of an engraving firm in which Hood had heavily invested, together with his own financial mismanagement, forced them to relinquish the house and accept the more economical life of the Continent. After the birth of his only son, Tom, Hood moved his family to Coblentz, Germany, to begin an "exile" that lasted until 1840.

In 1841, Hood assumed the editorship of *The New Monthly Magazine*. In and out of illness, financially struggling, and changing residences almost annually, Hood began to write his poems of social conscience. In 1843, he ceased editing *The New Monthly Magazine* to found *Hood's Magazine*, which he edited until early in 1845, although he was seriously ill during the entire period. A Civil List pension was granted his wife in November, 1844, when Hood was confined to what would be his deathbed. He continued writing almost to the very end. He died in May, 1845, and is buried at Kensal Green, London. Perhaps the finest tribute to his poetry is found in a letter from Hood to Frederick Ward, written in the summer of 1844: "Though I may not have reflected any very great honour on our national literature, I have not disgraced it. . . ." Such humility was typical of Thomas Hood.

Analysis

Primarily because he lived to write and wrote to live, Thomas Hood managed to publish a staggering amount of poetry in a relatively short time. Unfortunately, the pressure to keep the creditors at bay and the bacon on his table rendered much of his poetry unworthy of regard; he often failed to edit poems for which he could hardly afford enough time to write. He was seldom more than a hack writer, churning out journalistic doggerel and meanwhile maintaining an apparently voluminous correspondence, editing his annuals and magazines, executing his engravings, and trying to establish a reputation as a novelist. The mystery of his life is that he accomplished all this as a frequently bedridden invalid.

As a consequence of his need to offer original and entertaining poetry to the public on a regular basis, Hood wandered widely through the realm of possibilities to produce a profusion of experiments in form and content, in theme, rhythm, and rhyme—perhaps covering a wider range than any other English poet. In Hood one can find examples of such peculiarities as initial rhyme, various metrical arrangements of anapests and dactyls, all the major English stanza forms, and imitations of numerous styles—from those of Geoffrey Chaucer, Edmund Spenser, John Milton, Alexander Pope, Percy Bysshe Shelley, Lord Byron, Keats, and Shakespeare, to a host of lesser lights. Hood's imitations are often well-executed; his originals are even better. Omitting what is merely topical, trivial, childish, or deplorable, one finds that the remainder of Hood's canon contains a considerable quantity of poetry, some of it brilliant.

Hood began writing poetry as a pastime about 1814, during the period when he supplemented the family income by working as a clerk. In "Literary Reminiscences" (1833), Hood recalls how he stole moments from his employer, uninformatively identified as "Bell & Co.," to "take stray dips in the Castalian pool." A year later, after removing to Dundee, Scotland, to improve his health, Hood started writing a satirical *Dundee Guide*, the manuscript of which was unfortunately lost by 1820, although enough lines survived in a letter to show that it was nothing brilliant. As early as 1816, however, Hood began making anonymous contributions to Dundee periodicals, and thus first began to see his work in print. This fired him with a thirst to sell himself to "that minor Mephistopheles, the Printer's Devil." Hood was at this time being influenced by William Wordsworth and Samuel Taylor Coleridge, Byron, and Shelley; to a lesser extent by Charles Lamb, George Crabbe, Robert Southey, and Leigh Hunt; and most of all by Sir Walter Scott, "The Great Unknown." The narrative manner of Byron's *Childe Harold's Pilgrimage* (1812-1818), *The*

Giaour (1813), *The Bride of Abydos* (1813), *The Corsair* (1814), and *Lara* (1814) tempered by the influence of Scott's *The Lay of the Last Minstrel* (1805), *Marmion* (1808), *The Lady of the Lake* (1810), *Waverley* (1814), and *Rokeby* (1815) combined to foster Hood's first major poem, "The Bandit," probably written between 1815 and 1817 but not published until forty years after his death.

The Bandit is a relatively long poem (some 820 lines divided into three cantos), a narrative about Ulric, the Earl of Glenallen, who, as a result of treacherous circumstances, has been forced into the role of "Chieftain" to a band of outlaws. Although a cunning and brave leader, Glenallen secretly despises the mischievous deeds he has done, yet "Repeated wrongs had turned his breast to steel,/ And all but these he had forgot to feel." In the first canto, Glenallen discloses the plans of his final act as chief of the bandits, "To 'venge the wrongs he suffered from the world!" Heedlessly, he discloses to the outlaws his true identity as Earl of Glenallen, proclaimed a traitor to the throne of Scotland. All the bandits except Wolf, Glenallen's rival, depart with the chieftain to take revenge on Glenallen's former friend, Arden, at the latter's wedding to Glenallen's former betrothed, Adelaide. In the second canto, Glenallen disrupts the wedding and announces his intention of murdering Arden before he can consummate the marriage; but after the pitiful pleadings of "trembling Adelaide," he repents and orders his bandits to disperse. Just at this moment Wolf arrives with another band to take Glenallen for the reward on his head. In the ensuing swordplay, Arden makes several attempts to save the life of Glenallen, who is finally wounded into unconsciousness after killing Wolf. Before the bandits can deal with the wedding guests, however, the castle is mysteriously set afire. The bandits take up the unconscious Glenallen and flee. Canto three opens with Glenallen already in the custody of the authorities, locked away in a tower and awaiting execution. In his bitterness of soul, he eagerly awaits the release that death will bring him. The keeper enters and proves to be a former confederate: "Is it Donald! or a mocking dream?/ Are these things so, or do they only seem?/ Am I awake?" Donald, after failing to convince Glenallen to escape, and in haste for what seems to be the sound of an approaching guard escort, lends his dagger to the captive so that he might dispatch himself honorably. Glenallen perishes just as "Pardon! Pardon!" echoes on the walls and Arden rushes into the cell.

The puerility of the plot and the verse fails to disguise the influences of Romanticism. Glenallen is a typically Romantic hero, arraigned in a stock melodramatic situation, pausing at the appropriate times to brood over his cruel alienation from humanity and life, more ready to die than to live. His is the childish fantasy of "after I'm dead and gone, then they'll be sorry they hurt me," but, after all, it is the same childishness of vision that pervades much of Byron and Shelley. The significance of *The Bandit* lies in Hood's ability to use language well and to exercise a healthy imagination in verse that accommodates at least the superficial elements of Romanticism at a time before he has seriously devoted himself to writing poetry.

Although there were Romantic tendencies in Hood's own writing before Keats's death, one can find in his verse a pronounced identification with the style of Keats that extends about five or six years after 1821, beginning with Hood's introduction to the Reynolds family through his work at the *London Magazine* that same year. John Hamilton Reynolds and his sisters had enjoyed a close friendship with Keats, and entertained fond memories of the young Romantic. Hood entered an atmosphere in the Reynolds household suffused with intimacies from the life and work of the relatively unknown Keats. To this period belongs most of what is often called Hood's "serious" poetry. The Romantic movement had peaked and already begun to decline into the commonplace sentimentality and melodrama from which Robert Browning and Alfred, Lord Tennyson were destined to rescue it momentarily. Shelley and Byron's best works had already been published; indeed, Shelley died soon after Keats. Coleridge had graduated to philosophy, Wordsworth had defected to the establishment. Keats's final volume—*Lamia, Isabella, The Eve of St. Agnes, and Other Poems*—had appeared in 1820 (Hood's closet drama *Lamia*, based on Keats's poem, was written in 1824, but not published until after Hood's death). With friendly critics encouraging and applauding the growing likeness of Hood's poetry to that of Keats, it was an easy time for Hood to begin imagining himself to be Keats's successor.

Perhaps a sense of identification with Keats's illness and death led Hood to give death such a preeminent place in his serious and even in his comic verse. Hood seems to accord death a place of passive acceptance, at times even to embrace it. For example, "The Sea of Death," which appeared first in the *London Magazine* (March, 1822) and later in *The Plea of the Midsummer Fairies*, makes the somewhat trite comparison of death to an "ocean-past" that erases the sand-tracks of life "like a pursuing grave." This idea, however, is developed into a passively beautiful scene, where "spring-faced cherubs" also are asleep in "the birth-night of their peace." For contrast, Hood adds "neighbour brows scarr'd by the brunts/ Of strife and sorrowing"; and with the dead, Time itself "Slept, as he sleeps upon the silent face/ Of a dark dial in a sunless place." It is a typically Romantic eschatology; death is a place of silence and repose, a dreamlike eternity. Although Hood's view of death acquired a more theologically sound dimension during the next twenty years, his attitude of resignation to the inevitable did not change. His awareness of the closeness of death permeates all of his poetry; death, dying, and corruption tinge nearly every poem with sobriety and cause his humor to wax dark. Living in continual ill health as he did, this could hardly be called a Romantic affectation.

Hood's important poems from this period include a number of sonnets, many deserving more attention than they have received. The sonnets also reflect the influence of the Romantic poets. "Midnight," the pair "On a Sleeping Child" (all three in the *London Magazine*, December, 1822), and the eulogistic "Sonnet: Written in Keats's 'Endymion'" (the *London Magazine*, May, 1823) are among his very best. Another, beginning "It is not death . . .," reveals not only Romantic, but also direct Shakespearean influence. It was included, along with most of his other "serious" poetry, in the volume *The Plea of the Midsummer Fairies*.

Most of the poems in this book (twenty-two out of thirty-seven) had been previously published, many in the *London Magazine*. The book constitutes the evidence offered by many that Hood was a thwarted Romantic, so pervasive is the influence of Keats. The title poem consists of 126 Spenserian stanzas (except that the final lines are pentameters), celebrating, "by an allegory, that immortality which Shakspeare has conferred on the Fairy mythology by his *Midsummer Night's Dream*." Hood had previously written a fairly long Romantic allegory, "The Two Swans" (1824), and so had prepared himself to create what he no doubt hoped would be considered his masterpiece. Charles Lamb, to whom the poem was affectionately dedicated, likened the poem to "the songs of Apollo," but few others have felt it to be so. Although the poem abounds in the lush sensual imagery characteristic of Keats, it sags hopelessly throughout, mainly because the story is too skimpy and the monologues too substantial for a narrative of that length. The narrator, who happens upon a circle of accommodating but unhappy fairies (including Titania, Puck, Ariel, and Queen Mab), learns from Titania that they are unhappy because their "fairy lives/ Are leased upon the fickle faith of men." Her complaint lasts through nearly eight stanzas, after which the "melancholy Shape" of Time (Saturn, Mutability) appears with "hurtful scythe" to harvest the wee folk. After an argument between the fairies and Saturn that lasts seventy-five stanzas (nearly sixty percent of the poem), the ghost of Shakespeare arrives just in time to save the fairies, who express their affectionate gratitude by crowning the Bard with a halo "Such as erst crown'd the old Apostle's head." As an allegory defending the importance of imagination (Fancy) above Reason in poetry, the significance of human feeling, the allurements of Nature, and the mysterious, "The Plea of the Midsummer Fairies" fails; seeking to establish the principles of the Romantic movement, Hood offended through employment of its excesses.

The second poem in the volume, *Hero and Leander*, while certainly not lagging as a narrative, nearly approaches *The Bandit* in its tendency toward melodrama. Written in the sestina form of Shakespeare's *Venus and Adonis* (1593), the poem has a loveliness of its own but it is not brilliant. By far the better is the third poem, *Lycus, the Centaur*, first published in 1822. Dedicated to Reynolds, it employs the strikingly unusual rhythm of anapestic tetrameter couplets that give the impression of fast-paced narrative; it is a galloping rhythm, suitable to horses and centaurs. The 430 lines of the poem are rich in sensuous detail, a feature that lies nearly dormant in poetry from Keats to A. C. Swinburne. *Lycus, the Centaur* must be read aloud to be thoroughly appreciated. Admittedly, Hood's poetry did not achieve anything near perfection. The poem has flaws, as when Lycus complains of his loneliness: "There were women! there men! but to me a third sex/ I saw them all dots— yet I loved them as specks"; or when several successive closed couplets begin to give the feel of "The Night Before Christmas," but *Lycus, the Centaur*, for all its faults and its Keatsian imagery, is original and beautiful.

Most critics agree that the best poems in *The Plea of the Midsummer Fairies* are the lyrics, most of which are definitely Keatsian. Hood's "Ode: Autumn" at times provides an interesting contrast to Keat's "Ode to Autumn," but there is more to compare than to contrast. Two other short poems on autumn are included in the volume, as are three poems on the loss of innocence ("Retrospective Review," "Song, for Music," and "I Remember, I Remember"), a decent "Ode to Melancholy," and some of Hood's best sonnets. Pervasive throughout the book is the awareness, without terror, of death and corruption. Although the volume of serious poems caused some readers to see Hood as a worthy successor to Keats, *The Plea of the Midsummer Fairies* met with a generally poor critical and public reception and failed to sell out even a single printing.

The apparent cause of this cool reception is that during the years immediately preceding its publication Hood had captured the public's attention as a writer of comic verse. In 1825 he produced *Odes and Addresses to Great People* (in collaboration with Reynolds), and in the following year the first series of *Whims and Oddities*. The time for humor in poetry had come—not the incisive, often caustic wit of the eighteenth century, but an inoffensive, wholesome humor to help people laugh their way through the oppressively industrial times at the beginning of the nineteenth century. The reading public wanted a humor that appealed to men of low estate without being vulgar. It found in the humorous verse of Thomas Hood exactly what it sought, and came to expect nothing more nor less than that from him.

The success of Hood's early comic publications depended heavily upon his skill as a punster, examples of which are so abundant that they need not be dwelt upon at length. Most commonly cited in this regard are the two ballads, "Faithless Sally Brown" and "Faithless Nelly Gray." In the first, two lovers go out for a walk that is interrupted by an impress gang from the Royal Navy: "And Sally she did faint away,/ While Ben he was brought to." After Ben's tour of duty is finished, he returns to find Sally is another man's sweetheart; he laments, "I've met with many a breeze before,/ But never such a blow." In the opening stanza of the second poem, "Ben Battle was a soldier bold,/ And used to war's alarms:/ But a cannon-ball took off his legs,/ So he laid down his arms!" Although these are not the best examples of his craft, there is no question that Hood was the best punster of his century (perhaps the best in English letters); most of his puns are exceptional. Unfortunately, much of Hood's humor is topical; many of his puns and jokes cannot be grasped by the modern reader without an understanding of the times and a knowledge of the idiom of the 1820's and 1830's. Even so, many of Hood's poems retain an appreciable humor for today because they present general observations on the human condition. The most notable include "An Address to the Steam Washing Company" in *Odes and Addresses*; "A Valentine," "The Fall of the Deer," "December and May," "She Is Far from the Land," "Remonstratory Ode: From the Elephant at Exeter Change. . . ," "The Sea-Spell," and the darkly humorous "The Last Man," all in *Whims and Oddities* (First Series); and "Bianca's Dream," "A Legend of Navarre," "The Demon-Ship," and "Tim Turpin" in *Whims and Oddities* (Second Series). In "The Demon-Ship" Hood does a masterful job of creating a terrifying situation that is reversed in the humor of the closing lines; in "The Last Man," the wry ending cannot shift a much longer poem into the comic mode, so that the overall effect is far from humorous. As a serious poem, "The Last Man" offers a brilliant description of a postapocalyptic world.

Hood continued writing "serious" poetry during the remainder of his life, but until the last few years his comic verse claimed the limelight. With the failure of the engraving firm in 1834, and the subsequent "exile" to Germany, however, financial and physical hardship weighed heavily upon Hood and his family, and his comic verses began to acquire a certain note of sobriety. There had always been a loosely didactic element, a flexible moralizing, in his humor. Without gross distastefulness, Hood amused his audience by good-naturedly ridiculing people and institutions that were newsworthy or offensive to the public—in a way that often seemed to "teach a lesson." One of the most consistent objects of his humor was human greed; another was impoverishment. Employee displacement caused by unjust laws or advancements in technological efficiency also provoked his satirical wit. Since Hood no longer entertained hopes of succeeding Keats, his "serious" poetry began to develop an originality and power of its own, as Hood became a voice of the people's protest against those institutions. Hypocrisy and ambition became primary targets of his comic verse, which also developed a morbid, often sadistic, grotesqueness. Poems such as "Death's Ramble," from *Whims and Oddities*, in which a morality play is effected through pun after pun, led to "Death in the Kitchen" (1828), in which the puns are ingenious but the philosophizing about death unhumorous; to "Gog and Magog" (1830), with its hints of judgment and violence; to "Ode to Mr. Malthus" (1839), wherein the double standard of the well-to-do is satirized; and, finally, to *Miss Kilmansegg and Her Precious Leg* (1840). Each poem outdoes the last in taking a more caustic, albeit humorous, view of humanity or some of its elements.

Beginning with *Miss Kilmansegg and Her Precious Leg*, the serious side of Hood sought to reassert itself again, this time with a vigor and force of wit that it had manifested only in comic verse, but with a simplicity of expression unencumbered by flowery Romantic or Elizabethan rhetoric. During the final years of his life, Hood produced his greatest impact on English poetry in the songs of social protest—*Miss Kilmansegg and Her Precious Leg,* "The Song of the Shirt," "The Bridge of Sighs," and others—and his artistic masterpiece, "The Haunted House," which alone, said Edgar Allan Poe, "would have secured immortality for any poet of the nineteenth century."

Miss Kilmansegg and Her Precious Leg is a long satirical narrative of almost 2,400 lines. The central character is born into a family of great wealth:

> When she saw the light—it was no mere ray
> Of that light so common—so everyday—
> That the sun each morning launches—
> But six wax tapers dazzled her eyes,
> From a thing—a gooseberry bush for size—
> With a golden stem and branches.

After separate passages dealing in detail with her pedigree, birth, christening, childhood, and education, the reader learns that one day, while riding, Miss Kilmansegg lost control of her horse, which bolted at the sight of a ragged beggar, and in the ensuing accident "Miss K" lost her leg. Because she had been educated to a life-style of conspicuous consumption and hatred for the ordinary, she insists fanatically on replacing her natural leg with a golden one: "All sterling metal—not half-and-half,/ The Goldsmith's mark was stamped on the calf." (The pun on "golden calf" is intentional.) After she receives the expensive leg, the poem pursues her through her career as a fashionable debutante, her courtship, and her subsequent marriage to a foreign Count of questionable origin. Their honeymoon is spent at a country estate, where she learns that her husband's sole interest is gambling. After several years of tumultuous living that exhausts all of "Miss K's" resources, the Count murders her in the night, using her expensive leg as a bludgeon. Hood concludes the poem with a moral reminiscent of the "Pardoner's Tale" from Chaucer: "Price of many a crime untold;/ Gold! Gold! Gold! Gold:/ Good or bad a thousand fold!" The poem is very funny throughout, but the humor is accompanied by an undercurrent of bitterness against the rich, and the moralizing stanza at the poem's conclusion seems to affirm its serious didactic intention.

Eight months later *The New Monthly Magazine* published Hood's "A Tale of a Trumpet," another long satirical poem, this time about a deaf woman to whom the Devil supplies a trumpet through which she can hear all manner of scandalous gossip. Again, the poem ends in a moral against rumor-mongering. In November, 1843, *Punch* published Hood's "A Drop of Gin," a poem reminiscent of Hogarth's famous engraving "Gin Lane." The following month *Punch* published "The Pauper's Christmas Carol" and "The Song of the Shirt," poems of social protest which probably better express Hood's mind than any other poems of his last fifteen years.

"The Song of the Shirt," with its driving, mechanical rhythm, is based on the plight of a poor widowed woman with starving infants who was arrested while trying to pawn some of her employer's garments to obtain money for food (she was a seamstress for seven shillings a week). Touched by the newspaper accounts and always sensitive to the exploitation of the poor, Hood wrote what his wife considered to be his finest poem. In it, a woman sits sewing, and as she sews she sings the "Song of the Shirt": "Work! work! work!/ While the cock is crowing aloof!/ And work—work—work,/ Till the stars shine through the roof!" The poem calls to mind the protest movements and revolutions which were soon to plague Europe in the wake of the Industrial Revolution—and the publication of Karl Marx's *Communist Manifesto* in 1848 and *Das Kapital* in 1850. The Woman's lament is a desperate appeal born of the most abject misery: "Oh! God! that bread should be so dear,/ And flesh and blood so cheap!"

"The Haunted House" (*Hood's Magazine*, January, 1844), over which Poe became ecstatic, is indeed a powerful artistic creation: a descriptive, camera-eye narrative that builds an atmosphere of terror—which dissipates in the absolute meaninglessness of the poem. The reader can learn nothing of the source of the mystery, other than that a murder has apparently been committed, and that the house is haunted. The conclusion of the poem could be transplanted to any other part of the poem without disrupting the internal logic. It is as if Hood had left "The Haunted House" unfinished, perhaps to add to the sense of mystery and terror, but more likely through a lack of inspiration.

The artistic achievement represented by this poem notwithstanding, Hood's heart in these last years was more concerned with the suffering of others. Having spent so many years in sickness and pain, laboring feverishly to meet endless deadlines, striving in spite of his own sufferings to make others laugh, he had acquired a true compassion for the poor and unfortunate that sought to be expressed in his verse. His last years of writing produced "The Lady's Dream" (February, 1844), a song of regret for a life not spent ministering to the needs of others; "The Workhouse Clock" (April, 1844), an "allegory" that fires its blistering sermon at a leisurely middle class: "Christian Charity, hang your head!"; and "The Lay of the Labourer" (November, 1844), a panegyric to the working class.

A final volume of comic verse—*Whimsicalities: A Periodical Gathering*—appeared in 1844, but besides "The Haunted House," Hood's most regarded publication of that year is "The Bridge of Sighs." Often anthologized or cited as an example of dactylic verse, it concerns a young woman who commits a desperate suicide by leaping from a city bridge. Journalistic, as most of Hood's verse was, "The Bridge of Sighs" is based on an actual case; whatever the circumstances of the original suicide were, however, Hood turns the incident to good use in expounding a favorite theme:

> Alas! for the rarity
> Of Christian charity
> Under the sun!
> Oh! it was pitiful!
> Near a whole city full,
> Home she had none!

Hood continued to write even as he lay upon his deathbed, where, among other poems and letters, he produced "Stanzas" (March, 1845): "Farewell, Life! My senses swim;/ And the world is growing dim;/ . . . Strong the earthy odour grows—/ I smell the Mould above the Rose!" Hood's farewell to life concludes with the same homely, cheerful philosophy that infused so much poetry written in pain, the same positive outlook that inspired him to ask for reform rather than revolution: "Welcome, Life! the Spirit strives!/ Strength returns, and hope revives;/ . . . I smell the Rose above the Mould!" The juxtaposition of the stanzas intimates that Hood's source of hope and strength was his willingness to embrace death without terror. Nine years after his death, a monument was erected over his grave, paid for by public subscription. Beneath the bust of Hood is engraved a simple coat-of-arms: on the shield is a heart pierced by a sewing needle; under it, the scroll reads, at Hood's request, "He sang the Song of the Shirt."

Larry David Barton

Other major works

LONG FICTION: *Tylney Hall*, 1834; *Up the Rhine*, 1840.

SHORT FICTION: *National Tales*, 1827.

PLAYS: *York and Lancaster: Or, A School Without Scholars*, 1828 (written); *Lamia: A Romance*, 1852; *Guido and Marina: A Dramatic Sketch*, 1882.

MISCELLANEOUS: *The Works of Thomas Hood*, 1869-1873 (Thomas Hood, Jr., and Mrs. Frances Freeling Broderip, editors, 10 volumes); 1882-1884 (11 volumes); 1972 (8 volumes).

Bibliography

Brander, Laurence. *Thomas Hood*. London: Longmans, Green, 1963. Discusses Hood's early and later poems, as well as the public poems, for which Hood is remembered the most. A valuable resource for beginning readers of Hood. The criticism of the public poems is particularly noteworthy.

Bush, Douglas. "Thomas Hood." In *Mythology and the Romantic Tradition in English Poetry*. New York: W. W. Norton, 1963. A perceptive although brief account of Hood's works. The commentary on "Lycus, the Centaur" and

"Hero and Leander" are worth reading.

Clubbe, John. *Victorian Forerunner: The Later Career of Thomas Hood.* Durham, N.C.: Duke University Press, 1968. A scholarly and important contribution to the literary criticism available on Hood's later poems. Clubbe asserts that Hood wrote many of his most memorable poems in the last decade of his life.

Jeffrey, Lloyd N. *Thomas Hood.* New York: Twayne, 1972. This introduction to Hood's poetry argues for the intrinsic value of his work despite his being overshadowed by the Romantics. Views the study of Hood's poems as an important lead into nineteenth century literature. Discusses his poetry selectively and devotes one chapter to the macabre and grotesque in his works.

Jerrold, Walter, ed. *Thomas Hood and Charles Lamb: The Story of a Friendship.* London: Ernest Benn, 1930. The introduction is useful in its appraisal of Hood's "Literary Reminiscences," which reveals much about Hood's contemporaries and his early life.

_____. *Thomas Hood: His Life and Times.* New York: Haskell House, 1968. A full account of Hood's life with critical commentary of his poems. Some inaccuracies about Hood's life are corrected here, particularly in his early period. An important work for Hood scholars.

Reid, J. C. *Thomas Hood.* London: Routledge & Kegan Paul, 1963. A full-length biographical and critical study of Hood. Well researched and sympathetic in its approach to this poet.

A. D. HOPE

Born: Cooma, Australia; July 21, 1907

Principal poetry

The Wandering Islands, 1955; *Poems*, 1960; *A. D. Hope*, 1963; *Collected Poems, 1930-1965*, 1966; *New Poems, 1965-1969*, 1969; *Dunciad Minor: An Heroick Poem*, 1970; *Collected Poems, 1930-1970*, 1972; *Selected Poems*, 1973; *The Damnation of Byron*, 1973; *A Late Picking: Poems, 1965-1974*, 1975; *A Book of Answers*, 1978; *The Age of Reason*, 1985; *Selected Poems*, 1986.

Other literary forms

A. D. Hope has distinguished himself as poet, critic, and editor. His collections of lectures, essays, and reviews include *Australian Literature, 1950-1962* (1963), *The Cave and the Spring: Essays on Poetry* (1965), *A Midsummer Eve's Dream: Variations on a Theme by William Dunbar* (1970), *Native Companions: Essays and Comments on Australian Literature, 1936-1966* (1974), and *The Pack of Autolycus* (1979). In addition, he has published a critical study of a contemporary Australian poet, *Judith Wright* (1975), and a collection of "notes on the craft of poetry," *The New Cratylus* (1979). He has also edited an anthology, *Australian Poetry, 1960* (1960), and, with Leonie Kramer, a selection of poems, prose, and letters by Henry Kendall, the nineteenth century Australian colonial poet.

Achievements

While Australia has yet produced no poet who has had a lasting influence on world literature, Hope has perhaps come closest to attaining an international reputation. Since the publication of his first collection in 1955, he has emerged as the dominant figure in Australian poetry.

Hope stands outside the mainstream of much modern poetry in his rigid formalism and outspoken disdain for much of the poetry and critical theories of his contemporaries, or what he calls in *The New Cratylus* "Heresies of the Age." In his carefully balanced wit and in the lucidity of his use of such neoclassical forms as the heroic couplet, he seems much closer in his attitudes and manner to Alexander Pope than to T. S. Eliot. While early compared to W. H. Auden in his sometimes scathing denunciations of twentieth century life, Hope possesses a distinctive voice with a wide range; his satirical poems have been no less admired than his passionate love poetry. In all of his work, the notion of poetry as a learned craft is preeminent. Unlike many of his contemporaries, he has remained content to express his vision in the traditional patterns of accentual-syllabic meter and rhyme. His poetic conservatism and use of classical learning make him unique among living poets.

Hope's first collection was published when he was nearly fifty; since then, his reputation has grown rapidly. He has been the recipient of numerous awards, including the Arts Council of Great Britain award for poetry (1965), the Ingram Merrill Award for Literature (1969), the Levinson Prize (1969), and the Robert Frost Award (1976). In 1972, he was named Officer, Order of the British Empire, and in 1985, he was elected Ashby Visiting Fellow of Clare Hall, Cambridge, and Honorary Fellow of University College, Oxford. He has traveled and lectured extensively, especially in the United States.

Biography

Alec Derwent Hope was born in Cooma, New South Wales, Australia, on July 21, 1907, the firstborn of the family. His father, Percival Hope, a Presbyterian minister, moved the family to Tasmania when Hope was four years old. In the rural area where Hope's father's new congregation was located, school was rudimentary at best, often being held in the local sheepshearing shed. Hope, like many middle-class children, received much of his primary instruction at home. His mother, who had been a schoolteacher, taught him to read and write, and his father later instructed him in Latin. The family library was large, and the parents took turns reading classics of English literature aloud to the five children. Hope began to write poems in ballad stanzas when he was seven or eight, and by the time he was in his early teens, he had published his first poem, a translation of Catullus' *Phasellus ille quem videstis, hospites.*

When Hope was fourteen, he was sent to the Australian mainland for his secondary education, first at Bathurst High School and later at Fort Street High School, one of the best schools in Sydney. Upon graduation, he was awarded a scholarship designated for sons of Presbyterian clergymen and matriculated at St. Andrew's College of the University of Sydney. He had originally intended to study medicine, but low science marks forced him to read for an arts degree instead. During his undergraduate years, he published poems in university magazines and in the Sydney *Bulletin.* He was graduated in 1928. Hope distinguished himself in his undergraduate work in philosophy and English and won a scholarship for further study in England.

He entered University College, Oxford, in the fall of 1928, shortly after the graduation of Auden, Louis MacNeice, and Stephen Spender. Poor and underprepared, Hope had difficulty with the tedious Oxford English curriculum, which at that time leaned heavily toward philological studies. Despite his admiration for such notable scholars as C. S. Lewis, he managed no better than a third-class degree, which he completed in 1930.

He returned to Sydney just as the Depression was deepening and became a public-school teacher and vocational psychologist for several years before obtaining a position as a lecturer in education at Sydney Teachers' College in 1937. In 1938, he married Penelope Robinson and was appointed lecturer in

English at Sydney, where he remained until 1944. In 1945, he became the Senior Lecturer in English at the University of Melbourne, where he taught courses in English and European literature. In 1951, he became the first Professor of English at Canberra University College (now the Australian National University), a chair which he held until 1969, after which he was Library Fellow for three years and, later, Professor Emeritus. Hope, who is in poor health, still travels occasionally and lives with his wife in Canberra.

Analysis

In his introduction to a selection of his poems in 1963 as part of the Australian Poets series, A. D. Hope stated that "all theories about poetry are inadequate and that good poetry has been written on many assumptions which actually appear to be incompatible with one another." That claim notwithstanding, Hope does admit to several "comfortable prejudices" which allow him to ignore poetical practices with which he has no sympathy. "The chief of these," he says, "is a heresy of our time which holds that by excluding those things which poetry has in common with prose, narrative, argument, description, exhortation and exposition, and that, depending entirely on lyric impulse or the evocative power of massed imagery one can arrive at the pure essence of poetry." This remark is central to any understanding of Hope's work, for he consistently laments the impoverishment of twentieth century poetry when it is compared to the "great variety of forms practised in the past." The remark also reveals the strong influence of Latin studies on Hope's work, for his list includes most of the common topics of classical rhetoric. Of those he mentions, narrative and argumentation are important techniques that he consistently employs in his best poems.

Hope's second complaint is with "the notion that poetry can be improved or its range extended by breaking down the traditional structure of English verse by replacing its rhythms by those of prose." Hope, who studied at Oxford with C. L. Wrenn, editor of *Beowulf*, has written learnedly on the origins of English poetic meter, particularly on the transition from accentual meters to accentual-syllabics that took place in the century after Geoffrey Chaucer's death and on the metrical practices of John Dryden and Pope. Like Robert Frost, Hope credits the tension between meter and sentence rhythm as the key to the successful iambic pentameter line, of which Hope is a master. Indeed, he is perhaps more knowledgeable about meter than any other living poet and, thus, has little patience with theories of "open form" or "projective verse" that have been forwarded in defense of free verse.

According to Hope, another of these modern "heresies" stems from "that irritable personalism which is partly a heritage of the Romantics, the view that poetry is primarily self-expression." Even though Hope has stated his disagreement with the poetical theories of Edgar Allan Poe, he would seem to agree with the primacy of a poem's effect on its audience: "The poem is not a feeling, it is a structure of words designed, among other things, to arouse a certain state of feeling." Similarly, Hope would seem to agree with T. S. Eliot ("a poet whose poetry I cannot bring myself to like at all") in the need for a poet to find "an 'objective correlative' for the transmission of the poet's state of heart and mind to his readers." It should be apparent from these comments that Hope has little sympathy for the confessionalist tendencies of much contemporary poetry, which have provided many poets with "an adoring cannibal audience waiting for the next effusion of soul meat." He adds that the emotions in poems should not necessarily be equated with the emotions of poets: "The delight of creation and invention is their proper emotion and this must be in control of all other feelings."

Finally, Hope comments on his personal preferences in the language of poetry, which he prefers "to be plain, lucid, coherent, logically connected, syntactically exact, and firmly based in current idiom and usage." To a large degree, Hope has remained true to this dictum; his poetry is remarkable for its avoidance of needless obscurity and ambiguity. As he says, "A poem which can be parsed and analysed is not necessarily a good poem, but a poem which cannot is almost certainly bad." He does, however, allow himself the option of a certain elevation of language, what has been disparagingly called "poetic diction" in the twentieth century. With William Wordsworth, Hope agrees that "a poet should certainly be a man speaking to men in a language common to all," but that does not mean that the debased vocabulary of conversational speech should be his sole resource. For Hope, whose learning is catholic, the "word-hoard" of the poet should be ample enough to include terms from a great range of interests which, in his own case, include numerous historical and literary references, classical allusions, and scientific terms.

Australian literature, like all colonial literatures, including that of the United States, has been throughout much of its short history in search of an identity. During the nineteenth century, Australian poets fell into two general classes: those who imitated the poetic styles of the English Romantics and Victorians and those who carried on a lively body of "bush poetry," largely anonymous balladry derived from the folk traditions of Great Britain. Of this first group, Oscar Wilde, reviewing an 1888 anthology of Australian writing, could find "nothing but echoes without music, reflections without beauty, second-rate magazine verses, arid third-rate verse for Colonial newspapers, . . . artless Nature in her most irritating form." Hope makes two revealing comments regarding the situation of the Australian writer of his generation: the first is that his father's library, while amply supplied with the classics of English literature, contained no Australian poets; the other is that, as late as the early 1950's, Hope had to struggle to obtain credit-status for the course in native literature that he instituted and taught at Canberra University College. Thus, the Australian poet is caught in an uncomfortable dilemma: he may wish to create a truly "national" poetry, but he lacks a tradition upon which to build it.

Hope has himself identified, in *Native Companions*, the three main stages of a colonial literature. In the first, the work of colonial writers is simply part of the literary tradition of the homeland. In the second, writers born in the new land but educated in the tradition of the mother country attempt to create a literature of their own. In the final stage, this self-consciousness disappears, and writers emerge who can influence the whole literary tradition, including that of the mother country. Though Hope believes that Australian literature still resides in the middle stage, one could argue, with the novelist Patrick White's winning of the Nobel Prize, the publication of Judith Wright's *The Moving Image* and James McAuley's *Under Aldebaran* in 1946, and the publication of Hope's first collection, *The Wandering Islands*, in 1955, that Australian writing has clearly moved into its maturity.

Though Hope had been publishing poetry and criticism since the late 1930's, *The Wandering Islands*, which appeared when he was forty-eight, was his first full collection. In a cultural climate that was still marked by parochialism and censorship, Hope's first book was something of a *succès de scandale*. The sexual explicitness of the title poem, his lightly worn learning, and his unsparing satire caused many critics to accuse him variously of academism, obscurity, misogyny, and even anti-Australian sentiments. Certainly, "Australia" would not have pleased the nationalistic poets of the Jindyworobak movement, at whose expense Hope had on occasion been mercilessly critical in his reviews. In this outwardly bitter poem, Hope sees his homeland as "without songs, architecture, history." Despite the fact that Hope later characterizes himself as one who turns "gladly home/ From the lush jungle of modern thought" to a country which has not yet been overwhelmed by "the chatter of cultured apes," the poem gave his early critics an abundant supply of ammunition with which to attack him.

In the book's title poem, Hope also delineates another constant theme of his work: the attractions and disappointment of love. For Hope, "the wandering islands" are the isolations of individual sexual identities, which are always, like the sundered beast in Plato's analogy of the two sexes, frustrated in their attempts at complete union: "An instant of fury, a bursting mountain of spray,/ They rush together, their promontories lock/ An instant the castaway hails the castaway,/ But the sounds perish in that earthquake shock." In these brief seconds of orgasmic loss of self lies "all that one mind ever knows of another,/ Or breaks the long isolation of the heart." Commenting on Hope's recurrent motifs in a review of *The Wandering Islands*, S. L. Goldberg notes that "the attitude from which his themes arise is Dionysian or tragic, disturbed, romantic, existentialist at least in its premises; on the other hand, the sense of tradition and order implicit in his art . . . is decidedly Apollonian or classical, and intellectual rather than freely organic." In this sense, Hope seems closest to the tradition of the English Metaphysical poets, John Donne in particular, who saw no divorce between passion and intellect, the "dissociated sensibility," to borrow Eliot's phrase.

A significant number of Hope's best poems deal with the sexual theme, by turns satirically and seriously. In "Conquistador" he sings "of the decline of Henry Clay/ . . . a small man in a little way," who is mashed flat in a sexual encounter with a "girl of uncommon size," who uses "him thereafter as a bedside mat." The poem, which is not without its darker side, bears comparison with Auden's "Ballad of Miss Gee." In "The Brides," Hope, in an impressive piece of social satire, works an extended conceit comparing the bridal and automotive "industries." The prospective groom, shopping for the smartest model in the sexual showroom, is lured to the altar by promises of "every comfort: the full set/ Of gadgets; knobs that answer to the touch/ For light or music; a place for his cigarette;/ Room for his knees; a honey of a clutch." That the majority of contemporary marriages last not much longer than a new car's extended warranty period is at least implicit in this witty poem.

In the other poems Hope expands the sexual theme to include larger observations of nature and human history. "Imperial Adam," one of his most widely reprinted poems, retells the story of the Fall as a sexual fable. Having partaken of the "delicious pulp of the forbidden fruit," Adam and Eve immediately experience the awakening of sexual desire:

> Sly as the snake she loosed her sinuous thighs.

> And waking, smiled up at him from the grass;
> Her breasts rose softly and he heard her sigh—
> From all the beasts whose pleasant task it was
> In Eden to increase and multiply

> Adam had learned the jolly deed of kind:
> He took her in his arms and there and then,
> Like the clean beasts, embracing from behind
> Began in joy to found the breed of men.

In lines that are reminiscent of William Butler Yeats's "A shudder in the loins engenders there/ The broken wall, the burning roof and tower . . . ," Hope foreshadows the whole violent future of humanity in the "sexual lightning stroke" of the first embrace. The poem closes with Adam witnessing the consequences of his act:

> Adam watching too
> Saw how her dumb breasts at their ripening wept,
> The great pod of her belly swelled and grew,

> And saw its water break, and saw, in fear,
> Its quaking muscles in the act of birth,
> Between her legs a pigmy face appear,
> And the first murderer lay upon the earth.

It is significant that Hope, in a later poem entitled "The Planctus," offers "another version of the Fall" in which Eve escapes the Garden and is provided with another helpmate, "While Adam, whose fellow God had not replaced,/ Lived on immortal, young, with virtue crowned,/ Sterile and impotent and justified." In Hope's view, a purely hermetic retreat from the moral perplexities of life is equivalent to a living death.

One other early poem comments, at first satirically, on those who see the "standardization" of the modern age as somehow unnatural, in particular the typical "Nature Poet" who "from his vegetable Sunday School/ Emerges with the neatly maudlin phrase" to protest the "endless duplication of lives and objects" which the American poet Theodore Roethke decried in "Dolor." Against this romantic assumption, Hope weighs the evidence of Earth herself, whose procreative fecundity "gathers and repeats/ The cast of a face, a million butterfly wings." Hope argues persuasively that such "standardization" is, in fact, the essence of the reproductive forces that rule nature and human life. As he says, it is love that "still pours into its ancient mould/ The lashing seed that grows to a man again."

Even in those poems which seem purely lyrical, Hope resists the romantic temptation to find in love any easy solutions. In one of his finest short poems, "As Well as They Can," he combines the twin demands of art and love in lines that ironically echo the conceit of Donne's "The Bait":

> As well as he can, the poet, blind, betrayed
> Distracted by the groaning mill, among
> The jostle of slaves, the clatter, the lash of
> trade,
> Taps the pure source of song.

> As well as I can, my heart in this bleak air,
> The empty days, the waste nights since you went,
> Recalls your warmth, your smile, the grace and
> stir

> That were its element.

Hope's poetry is founded on dialectical premises—between the sexes, between assertion and counterargument, between art and life, even between the living poet and his predecessors. In "Moschus Moschiferus," which is on first glance conventional in its subtitle, "A Song for St Cecilia's Day," he contrasts "the pure, bright drops of sound" of Tibetan hunters' flute music with the ends to which it is put, ensnaring the hapless mouse-deer of the title, hunted almost into extinction for their precious musk glands. As a footnote to the twentieth century which has seen, in Nazi Germany to cite only one example, the powers of music set to evil uses, Hope can offer the saint little more than a sardonic gift: "Divine Cecilia, there is no more to say!/ Of all who praised the power of music, few/ Knew of these things. In honor of your day/ Accept this song I too have made for you."

Similarly, in carrying on a continuing dialogue with the writers and litera-ture of the past, Hope takes a revisionist view of personalities and characters that must now be seen from a contemporary perspective. In "Man Friday" he writes a sequel to Daniel Defoe's *Robinson Crusoe* (1719) in which Friday, having had his fill of life in a country where "More dreadful than ten thou-sands savages,/ In their strange clothes and monstrous mats of hair,/ The pale-eyed English swarm to joke and stare,/ With endless questions round him crowd and press/ Curious to see and touch his loneliness," makes his escape home by a last, suicidal swim. "Faustus," informed by the Devil that "Hell is more up-to-date than men suppose" and that his soul has long since been in hell, "reorganized on the hire-purchase plan," avoids living further in his purely material world by killing both Helen and himself. George Gor-don, Lord Byron, who boasted of thousands of seductions, in "The Damna-tion of Byron" is condemned to a "Hell of Women" where, at last satiated by endless "wet kisses and voluptuous legs agape// He longs for the compan-ionship of men, their sexless friendliness." In all these poems, as well as in many others from *A Book of Answers* and *The Age of Reason*, Hope's collec-tion of verse epistles and narratives concerning leading figures, both histor-ical and fictional from the Augustan Age, one is always aware of an intellect passionately involved in a debate with the past.

Even though Hope has stressed, perhaps ingenuously, that his own poems are "hardly ever 'confessions' and [are] usually written in a spirit of 'as if' highly misleading to any unwary commentator or putative biographer," it would be a mistake to assume that his poetry is impersonal in any sense. Eliot, who said that poetry should be "an escape from personality," went on to .add that one must first have a personality to be able to escape from it. In "Hay Fever," a late poem which is one of the few clearly autobiographical works in Hope's oeuvre, the gentle memory of an Edwardian summer spent mowing hay in rural Tasmania moves the mature poet to speculate on the abundant harvest of a life's work:

> It is good for a man when he comes to the end
> of his course
> In the barn of his brain to be able to romp
> like a boy in the heap . . .
> To lie still in well-cured hay . . . to drift
> into sleep.

A. D. Hope's voice, so distinctive in its ability to match the orchestra's full range, is truly remarkable.

R. S. Gwynn

Other major works

PLAY: *Ladies from the Sea*, 1987.

NONFICTION: *The Structure of Verse and Prose*, 1943; *The Study of English*, 1952 (lecture); *Australian Literature, 1950-1962*, 1963; *The Cave and the Spring: Essays on Poetry*, 1965; *The Literary Influence of Academies*, 1970 (lecture); *A Midsummer Eve's Dream: Variations on a Theme by William Dunbar*, 1970; *Henry Kendall: A Dialogue with the Past*, 1971; *Native Companions: Essays and Comments on Australian Literature, 1936-1966*, 1974; *Judith Wright*, 1975; *The Pack of Autolycus*, 1979; *The New Cratylus: Notes on the Craft of Poetry*, 1979; *Poetry and the Art of Archery*, 1980 (lecture).

EDITED TEXTS: *Australian Poetry, 1960*, 1960; *Henry Kendall*, 1973 (with Leonie Kramer).

Bibliography

Argyle, Barry. "The Poetry of A. D. Hope." *Journal of Commonwealth Literature* 3 (1967): 87-96. One of the early but still relevant studies of Hope, this article places his work outside the Australian poetic tradition. Argyle argues that through its formal style and classical subject matter, the work transcends nationality and is far different from the often parochial verse of Hope's fellow Australians. Argyle concludes that Hope can be read the world over because he "does not demand that the reader be a specialist in Australian botany, marsupials, or [aboriginal] dialects."

Brissenden, R. F. "Art and the Academy: The Achievement of A. D. Hope." In *The Literature of Australia*, edited by Geoffrey Dutton. New York: Penguin Books, 1976. The discussion first corrects the idea that Hope's poetry is primarily satiric in nature. Instead, Brissenden argues, Hope's double role as a professor-poet lends his work learning and clarity. Through the analysis of several poems, Brissenden concludes that Hope invokes through his poetry the entire history and culture of Western civilization, thus making him far more than an Australian poet.

Darling, Robert. "The Mythology of the Actual." In *International Literature in English: The Major Writers*, edited by Robert L. Ross. New York: Garland, 1991. Hope's interest in science and his belief that the poet and the scientist share attributes form the basis of this essay, which analyzes fully several poems making use of scientific imagery. Supplemented by biographical information, a list of Hope's published poetry, drama, and criticism, and an extensive annotated bibliography of secondary sources.

King, Bruce. "A. D. Hope and Australian Poetry." *The Sewannee Review* 58 (1979): 119-141. In this comprehensive discussion of the progress of Hope's poetry, King calls Hope "perhaps the best [poet] writing in English." The essay is of special interest, first, for placing Hope's work within the context of the overall development of Australian poetry, second, for providing an overview of the directions that Australia's contemporary poetry is taking.

Paolucci, Anne, and Henry Paolucci. "Poet Critics on the Frontiers of Literature: A. D. Hope, T. S. Eliot, and William Carlos Williams." *Review of National Literatures* 11 (1982): 146-191. Because Hope is an accomplished poetry critic and theorist, this article is of special interest. It compares the critical and theoretical views of these three major contemporary figures and raises intriguing questions on whether the various English-language national literatures (such as Australian) will someday evolve into an international literature with English the only boundary, an outcome that Hope has long predicted and promoted.

GERARD MANLEY HOPKINS

Born: Stratford, England; July 28, 1844
Died: Dublin, Ireland; June 8, 1889

Principal poetry

Poems of Gerard Manley Hopkins, Now First Published, with Notes by Robert Bridges, 1918; *Poems of Gerard Manley Hopkins,* 1930, 1948, 1967; *The Poetical Works of Gerard Manley Hopkins,* 1990.

Other literary forms

Gerard Manley Hopkins' letters and papers were published in six volumes that appeared between 1935 and 1959: *The Letters of Gerard Manley Hopkins to Robert Bridges* (1935, 1955, C. C. Abbott, editor), *The Correspondence of Gerard Manley Hopkins and Richard Watson Dixon* (1935, 1955, C. C. Abbott, editor), *The Note-books and Papers of Gerard Manley Hopkins* (1937, Humphry House, editor), *Further Letters of Gerard Manley Hopkins* (1938, 1956, C. C. Abbott, editor), *The Journals and Papers of Gerard Manley Hopkins* (1959, Humphry House and Graham Storey, editors), and *The Sermons and Devotional Writings of Gerard Manley Hopkins* (1959, Christopher Devlin, editor). A selection of letters from the three volumes edited by Abbott, *Gerard Manley Hopkins: Selected Letters,* was published in 1990. Edited by Catherine Phillips, the letters include many analyses of the work of other poets and artists; they also reveal his bouts of "melancholy," or depression, and implicitly show his internal struggles between his religion and his work as a poet. In addition to the published material, there are significant unpublished lecture notes and documents by Hopkins at the Bodleian Library and the Campion Hall Library at Oxford University.

Achievements

Although Hopkins saw almost none of his writings published in his lifetime, he is generally credited with being one of the founders of modern poetry and a major influence on the development of modernism in art. Many of his letters reflect a sense of failure and frustration. "The Wreck of the *Deutschland*," which he considered to be his most important poem, was rejected by the Jesuit magazine *The Month.* As a professor of classical languages and literature, he was not a productive, publishing scholar. As a priest, his sermons and theological writing did not find popular success. Yet in 1918, some thirty years after his death, his friend Robert Bridges published a collection of his poems. By 1930, when the second edition of this volume appeared, Hopkins began to attract the attention of major theoreticians of modernism: Herbert Read, William Empson, I. A. Richards, and F. R. Leavis. They acclaimed Hopkins as a powerful revolutionary force in poetry. Interest in his poetry led scholars to unearth his scattered letters and papers. Here, too, modern readers found revolutionary concepts: inscape, instress, sprung rhythm, underthought/overthought, counterpoint. Since about 1930 an enormous amount of scholarly analysis has combed through Hopkins' poetry and prose, establishing beyond doubt that he is one of the three or four most influential forces in modern English literature.

Biography

Gerard Manley Hopkins was the first of eight children born to Manley Hopkins, a successful marine insurance agent who wrote poetry and technical books. The family was closely knit and artistic. Two of Hopkins' brothers became professional artists, and Hopkins' papers contain many pencil sketches showing his own talent for drawing. He was devoted to his youngest sister Grace, who was an accomplished musician, and he tried to learn several musical instruments as well as counterpoint and musical composition. The family was devoutly Anglican in religion. When Hopkins was eight years old, they moved from the London suburb of Stratford (Essex) to the more fashionable and affluent Hampstead on the north edge of the city. From 1854 to 1863 Hopkins attended Highgate Grammar School. Richard Watson Dixon, a young teacher there, later became one of Hopkins' main literary associates. Hopkins studied Latin and Greek intensively, winning the Governor's Gold Medal for Latin Verse, as well as the Headmaster's Poetry Prize in 1860 for his English poem "The Escorial." His school years seem to have been somewhat stormy, marked by the bittersweet joy of schoolboy friendships and the excitement of a keen mind mastering the intricacies of Greek, Latin, and English poetry. He was such a brilliant student that he won the Balliol College Exhibition, or scholarship prize. Balliol was reputed to be the leading college for classical studies at Oxford University in the 1860's. Hopkins attended Balliol from April, 1863, until June, 1867, studying "Classical Greats," the philosophy, literature, and language of ancient Greece and Rome. The first year of this curriculum required rigorous study of the structure of the Latin and Greek languages. This linguistic study terminated with a very demanding examination called "Moderations." Hopkins earned a grade of "First" in his Moderations in December, 1864. The remaining years of "Classical Greats" involved the study of the philosophy and literature of ancient writers in their original tongues, concluding with the "Greats" or final honors examination. Hopkins concluded his B.A. (Hons.) with a "First in Greats" in June, 1867. A double first in Classical Greats is a remarkable accomplishment. Benjamin Jowett, the Master of Balliol and himself a famous classical scholar, called Hopkins "The Star of Balliol" and all who knew him at this period predicted a brilliant career for him. Hopkins loved Oxford—its landscapes and personalities, the life of culture and keen intellectual striving—and always looked back to his college days with nostalgia. His schoolmate there was Robert Bridges, who was to be his lifelong friend and correspondent.

These years were not peaceful, however, for the promising young scholar and poet. The colleges of Oxford University were then religious institutions. Only Anglicans could enroll as students or teach there. For some thirty years before Hopkins entered Balliol, Oxford University had been rocked by the "Oxford Movement." A number of its illustrious teachers had questioned the very basis of the Anglican Church, the way in which the Church of England could claim to be independent of the Roman Catholic Church. Many of the leading figures of the Oxford Movement had felt compelled to leave Oxford and the Church of England and to convert to Roman Catholicism. Among the converts was Cardinal John Henry Newman, whose *Apologia pro Vita Sua*, or history of his conversion from the Anglican to the Roman Church, was published in 1864, the year Hopkins was preparing for his Moderations at Balliol. To follow Newman's lead meant to give up hope of an academic career at Oxford, and perhaps even the hope of completing his B.A. Nevertheless, by 1866 Hopkins was convinced that the only true church was the Roman. In October, 1866, he was received into the Roman Catholic Church by Newman himself. It is hard for modern readers to imagine the pain and dislocation this decision caused Hopkins. His family letters reveal the anguish of his father, who believed that his son's immortal soul was lost, not merely his temporal career. Hopkins was estranged from his family to some degree ever after his momentous conversion. After he had completed his B.A. at Oxford, Hopkins taught in 1867 at Newman's Oratory School, a Roman Catholic grammar school near Birmingham. There he decided to enter a religious order. In May, 1868, he burned all manuscripts of his poems, thinking that poetry was not a fit occupation for a seriously religious person. Fortunately, some of his early writing survived in copies he had given to Robert Bridges. He wrote no further poetry until "The Wreck of the *Deutschland*."

In the summer of 1867 he went on a walking tour of Switzerland. In that September he entered the Jesuit Novitiate, Manresa House, London, for the first two years of rigorous spiritual training to become a Jesuit priest. There he followed the regime of the Spiritual Exercises of St. Ignatius Loyola (1491-1556), taking vows of poverty, chastity, and obedience. From 1870 to 1873 he studied philosophy at St. Mary's Hall, Stonyhurst, in the North of England. Although Hopkins had been a brilliant student of classical philosophy at Oxford, he seems not to have pleased his Jesuit superiors so well. Perhaps part of the problem was an independence of mind which could be disconcerting. At Stonyhurst he first read the medieval philosopher John Duns Scotus, who had an unusually strong influence on Hopkins' ideas. He then returned to Manresa House for a year as Professor of Rhetoric. From 1874 to 1878 he studied theology at St. Bueno's College in Wales. There he began to write poetry again when he heard of the wreck of a German ship, the *Deutschland*, and the death of five Catholic nuns aboard.

It is the custom in the Jesuit order to move priests from one location to another frequently and to try them out in a variety of posts. In the next few years, Hopkins tried many different kinds of religious work without remarkable success. He was assigned to preach in the fashionable Farm Street Church in London's West End, but he was not a charismatic or crowd-pleasing performer. Parish work in the Liverpool slums left him depressed and exhausted. When he was assigned temporarily to the Catholic parish church in Oxford, he seemed to have had trouble getting along with his superior. Finally, he was appointed Professor of Greek and Latin Literature at University College, Dublin, Ireland. He held this post until his death in 1889. The Catholic population of Ireland at that time was in near-revolt against English oppression. Hopkins felt a conflict between his English patriotism and his Catholic sympathies. Although he had been a brilliant student as a young man, the University College duties gave him little opportunity to do gratifying scholarly work. Much of his time was spent in the drudgery of external examinations, grading papers of hundreds of students he had never taught. His lectures were attended by only a handful of students. He projected massive books for himself to write, but never was able to put them together. In this period he wrote many sonnets which show spiritual desolation, unhappiness, and alienation. He died of typhoid in 1889 at the age of forty-five. Not until a generation later did the literary world recognize his genius.

Analysis

In 1875 a number of Roman Catholic religious people had been driven out of Germany by the Falck Laws. In the winter of that year, five exiled nuns took passage on the *Deutschland*, which ran aground in a snowstorm near the Kentish shore of England. The ship gradually broke up in the high seas and many lives were lost, including the nuns.' Their bodies were brought to England for solemn funeral ceremonies and the whole affair was widely reported in the newspapers. At this time Gerard Manley Hopkins was studying theology at St. Bueno's College in Wales. He read the reports in the press and many details in his poem reflect the newspapers' accounts. He seems especially to have noticed the report that, as passengers were being swept off the deck into the icy seas by towering waves, the tallest of the five nuns rose up above the others just before her death and cried out for Christ to come quickly to her. Hopkins discussed this fearful catastrophe with his rector, who suggested that someone should write a poem about it. Taking that hint as a command, Hopkins broke his self-imposed poetic silence and began to write again. The experience of the tall nun at her moment of death captured his imagination. How frightening and cruel it must have been to be on the deck of the shattered ship! Yet she was a faithful Catholic servant of God. How could God torment her so? What did she mean when she cried out for Christ to come to her as the fatal waves beat down on her?

"The Wreck of the *Deutschland*" is a very difficult poem. Unlike the smooth sentences of Tennyson's *In Memoriam* (1850), for example, Hopkins' elegy is contorted, broken, sometimes opaque. When Robert Bridges published the first volume of Hopkins' poems in 1918, he warned readers that "The Wreck of the *Deutschland*" was like a great dragon lying at the gate to discourage readers from going on to other, more accessible poems by Hopkins. The thread of the occasion, however, can be traced in the text. The dedication of the poem to the memory of five Franciscan nuns exiled by the Falck Laws drowned between midnight and morning of December 7, 1875, gives the reader a point of reference. If readers skip to stanza twelve, the story goes ahead, following newspaper accounts of the events reasonably clearly. Stanza twelve relates that some two hundred passengers sailed from Bremen bound for America, never guessing that a fourth of them would drown. Stanza thirteen explains how the *Deutschland* sailed into the wintry storm. Stanzas fourteen and fifteen tell how the ship hit a sandbank and people began to drown. Stanza sixteen depicts an act of heroism in which a sailor tries to rescue a woman, but is killed; his body dangles on a rope for hours before the eyes of the sufferers. Stanzas seventeen through twenty-three are about the tall nun. In stanza twenty-four the poet contrasts his own comfortable setting under a safe roof in Wales with that of the nuns who were in their death struggle on the stormy sea. He has no pain, no trial, but the tall nun is dying at that very moment. Rising up in the midst of death and destruction, she calls, "O Christ, Christ, come quickly." Stanzas twenty-five through thirty-five contemplate that scene and ask, "What did she mean?" when she called out. What was the total meaning of her agony and life? The poem therefore can be divided into three sections: Stanzas one to ten constitute a prologue or invocation, stanzas eleven through twenty-five depict the agony of the shipwreck and the tall nun, and stanzas twenty-five through thirty-five contemplate the meaning of that event. The middle section, describing the shipwreck and the tall nun's cry, is reasonably clear. Difficult details in this section are mostly explained in the notes to the revised fourth edition of *Poems of Gerard Manley Hopkins*. There are some additional perspectives, however, which are helpful in grasping the total work.

"The Wreck of the *Deutschland*" is related to the Jesuit contemplative "composition of place" and "application of the senses." As a member of the Society of Jesus, Hopkins' daily life and devotions were shaped by the *Spiritual Exercises* (1548) of St. Ignatius Loyola. Moreover, at certain times in his career he withdrew from the world to perform the spiritual exercises in month-long retreats of an extremely rigorous nature. One objective of the spiritual exercises is to induce an immediate, overwhelming sense of the presence of Divinity in our world. The contemplative is directed by the *Spiritual Exercises* to employ the technique of "composition." For example, to get a sharper sense of the divine presence, one might contemplate the birth of Christ. First one must imagine, or compose, the scene of the Nativity in all possible detail and precision. When Christ was born, how large was the room; what animals were in the stable; where was the holy family; were they seated or standing; what was the manger like? The imagination embodies or composes the scene. The contemplative then applies his five senses systematically to the composition. What did it look like, sound like, smell like, feel like, and taste like? Such a projection of the contemplative into the very situation induces a very powerful awareness of the religious experience. "The Wreck of the *Deutschland*" is similar to such a contemplative exercise. Hopkins is trying to experience the religious truth of the nuns' sacrifice. The middle of his poem is a composition of the scene where the tall nun died. It is constructed systematically to apply the five senses. Stanza twenty-eight depicts the struggle of the poet to put himself in the nun's place, to feel what she felt, to suffer as she suffered, to believe as she believed. At her death, she saw her Master, Christ, King. The poet tries to participate in her experience. The poem should be read in comparison with other poems of the religious meditative tradition—for example, the poetry of George Herbert, Richard Crashaw, and Henry Vaughan. Louis L. Martz in *The Poetry of Meditation: A Study in English Religious Literature of the Seventeenth Century* (1962) is the best introduction to this aspect of Hopkins' work.

In addition to the religious complexities of the poem, there are aesthetic complexities. Hopkins claimed to have discovered a new poetic form, "sprung rhythm," which he employed in "The Wreck of the *Deutschland*." Despite intense scholarly investigation of Hopkins' metrics, there is no clear agreement as to what he means by "sprung rhythm." "The Wreck of the *Deutschland*" contains thirty-five stanzas, each with eight lines of varying length. If one counts the syllables in each line, or if one counts only the accented syllables in each line, there is a rough agreement in the length of a particular line in each of the stanzas. For example, line one has four or five syllables in almost all stanzas. Line eight is much longer than line one in all stanzas. What makes lines of varying length metrical?

It is sometimes thought that Hopkins was isolated in the Jesuit order and did not know what he was doing when he created unusual poetic forms. That is absurd, for he was a professor of classical literature and in correspondence with leading literary scholars. The best way to look at sprung rhythm is to see what Hopkins' associates thought about meter. Robert Bridges, his college friend and lifelong correspondent, studied the iambic pentameter of Milton and wrote a major book on the prosody of Milton. Bridges thought that Milton built his lines out of iambic feet, units of two syllables with the second syllable pronounced more loudly than the first. An iambic pentameter line therefore had five iambic feet, or ten syllables with the even-positioned syllables stressed more loudly than the odd-positioned ones. Lines in Miltonic pentameter which do not fit this pattern follow a few simple variations defined by Bridges. Bridges' study appears to be accurate for Milton, but clearly

Hopkins is not writing poetry of this sort. The number of unstressed syllables differs widely in his lines, a condition that Bridges shows never occurs in Milton.

Another of Hopkins' correspondents, Coventry Patmore, was a leading popular Catholic poet who wrote a study of English metrics based on time, similar to the prosody of hymns. Hopkins' sprung rhythm seems more consistent with such a musical time-based pattern than with the accentual-syllabic pattern of Milton as defined by Bridges. Hopkins, as a professor of classical languages, knew the advanced linguistic work going on in that area. Greek poetry was thought to be quantitative, based on the length of vowel sounds. As a schoolboy Hopkins had to practice translating an English passage first into Latin, then into Greek poetry, arranging the long and short vowels into acceptable feet. (Some of his Latin and Greek poetry is collected in *Poems of Gerard Manley Hopkins.*) Modern readers are not often trained to understand these models in classical languages and so do not appreciate how important they are to Hopkins' patterns in English verse. In Hopkins' unpublished papers, there are lines of Greek poetry interlined by drafts of his English poems, sometimes with arrows and doodles matching up the English and Greek phrases. It seems possible that Hopkins based his distinctive rhythms on Greek models, especially the odes of Pindar, a topic that has been partially explored in Todd K. Bender's *Gerard Manley Hopkins: The Classical Background and Critical Reception of His Work* (1966). Essentially, however, the key to sprung rhythm remains to be discovered.

"The Wreck of the *Deutschland*" was submitted to the Jesuit magazine *The Month* and, after some delay, rejected for publication. Hopkins said that they "dared not" print it, although there is no need to imagine a dark conspiracy among the Jesuit authorities to silence Hopkins. It is likely that the editors of *The Month* simply found "The Wreck of the *Deutschland*" baffling in form and content. The rejection dramatizes, however, a peculiar condition in Hopkins' life. His unquestionable genius for poetry found almost no encouragement in his immediate surroundings as a Jesuit priest. His poetry is, of course, shaped by Roman Catholic imagery and is mainly devotional in nature. Without his Church and his priestly calling, he never could have written his poems. On the other hand, what he wrote was largely unappreciated by his closest associates. Ironically, this highly religious poet became famous in the twentieth century because of the praise of readers who were frequently anti-Roman Catholic. There was a central anguish in Hopkins life, a conflict between his priestly duties and his artistic creativity. Many scholars have tried to explain how Hopkins' poetry and his priesthood fit together. One of the best such studies is John Pick's *Gerard Manley Hopkins: Priest and Poet* (1942). Roman Catholic critics usually tend to say that the Catholic faith made Hopkins a great writer. Readers who are hostile to Catholicism tend to think that Hopkins was a serious writer in spite of extreme discouragements and restraints placed on him by his faith. The truth is probably somewhere in the middle. If Hopkins had not been severely troubled, he would have had little motivation to write. His poems show all the commonplaces of religious imagery found in much less powerful Catholic poets, such as his friend Coventry Patmore. Hopkins rises above the average religious versifier because of his original genius, yet this originality is what the Jesuit editors of *The Month* did not understand.

Stung by the criticism of his major poem, not only by the Jesuit editors but also by his friend Robert Bridges, Hopkins never again tried to write something so long and elaborate. He retreated into the most traditional form in English prosody, the sonnet. After "The Wreck of the *Deutschland*," Hopkins' most famous work is the sonnet "The Windhover." More has been written about these fourteen lines than about any other piece of poetry of comparable length in English. All of Hopkins' sonnets are related to the Petrarchan model, but he alters the tradition to fit his peculiar genius. The poem employs line-end rhymes abba abba cdcdcd. In addition to the repetition of sound at the end of each line, there is also thickly interwoven alliteration and assonance within each line. This internal rhyme is related to the *cynghanedd* or consonant chime of Welsh poetry. Hopkins tried to learn Welsh when he was a student at St. Bueno's College in Wales and he actually wrote a bit of Welsh poetry in the form called *cywydd*. The meter of "The Windhover" is the so-called sprung rhythm, allowing great variation in the length of lines. The Petrarchan sonnet uses its rhyme scheme to define two parts of the poem: abba abba is the octave or exposition in the opening eight lines, cdcdcd is the sestet or commentary in the concluding six lines. Hopkins explained in his letters that the essence of a sonnet is balance and proportion. The octave asserts a situation or condition and then a surprising commentary comes back in the sestet to reply to the octave. Since the sestet has only six lines, it must be correspondingly "sharper" or more forceful if it is to balance the initial statement. The key to the sonnet is this proportion. Hopkins wrote some sonnets longer than the usual fourteen lines and a few shorter, "curtail" or cut-short, sonnets. In all his sonnets, however, he maintains the proportion of octave to sestet, eight to six, and forces the shorter conclusion to a higher pitch of intensity.

In its octave, "The Windhover" describes the flight of a hawk of a kind commonly used in falconry or hunting circling against the dawn sky. The sestet begins with the description of the hawk diving, plummeting earthward, as it "buckles." The sure, steady circling of the hawk in the octave is astonishing, but the sudden buckling downward is even more thrilling. It is beautiful and breathtaking. In the sestet the increased beauty of the hawk as it dives is compared to a plough made to shine as it is driven through sandy soil, and to an ember coated with ashes that sparkles when it falls and breaks.

"The Windhover" illustrates one of the key terms in Hopkins' aesthetic vocabulary: "inscape," a word he coined for the inner nature of a thing which distinguishes it from everything else in creation. Hopkins' reading of Duns Scotus is pertinent to his concept of inscape. *Qualis* in Latin means *what.* When we look at the *qualities* of things, we examine *what* they have in common with other members of their class. The *qualities* of a good racing horse are those features that it has in common with other good horses. Duns Scotus imagines that there is an opposite to *quality. Haec* means *this* in Latin. Duns Scotus coins the word *haecceitas*, the "thisness" of a thing, which sets it apart from everything else, making it unique and different—the principle of individuation. Hopkins frequently celebrates the rare, unusual, or unique in nature. He turns away from the universal quality and toward the individual. The octave of "The Windhover" can be seen as the poet's description of a natural event: the flight and dive of a falcon. In that movement, he seeks to find the inscape, the innermost shape as evidence of God's presence in the created world. He tries to see into the form of the thing, to find what makes it original, unique, special, strange, striking. Like the sacrifice of the tall nun in "The Wreck of the *Deutschland*," the act of the hawk is "composed" so as to be the object for a religious meditation.

Paradoxically, the only way to grasp the unique inscape of a thing is to compare it with something else. The tension of this paradox is evident in the striking, surprising comparisons which Hopkins employs in "The Windhover," comparing the dive of a hawk with a plough shining in use and a burning coal sparkling as it collapses. The poem says that these three events are comparable or analogous in that in each case when the object *buckles* it becomes brighter and more glorious. When the hawk buckles in its dive, it is a thousandfold more lovely than in its stately circling. When the rusty plough buckles to its work, the abrasion of the sandy soil makes the ploughshare shine in use. When the ash crumbles or buckles, its inner brightness shows through the gray, outer ash-coating. Hopkins gave "The Windhover" the dedication, "To Christ Our Lord." The Jesuit order sees itself as the chivalry or the Knights of Christ. Ignatius advises the novice to buckle on the armor of Christ. To become a Jesuit, to buckle on the armor of a true Christian knight, is the proper and glorious activity of a man who would follow his nature, or unique calling. In like manner, a hawk follows its true nature, it *is* what it was *made to be*, when it sails in the wind and dives. A plough was made to work the earth, a coal to burn, and these things do what they were intended to do when they buckle. The activity of buckling may be painful or dangerous, but it produces glory, brilliance, grace, and beauty. The discipline of accepting the vows of the Jesuits may be painful in some earthly way, but it brings the glory of Christ's service. Christ, too, accepted the pain and duty of his earthly incarnation. He was buckled to the cross. He did what he had to do and so was brought to glory through pain and humiliation. The structure of "The Windhover" appears to be a set of analogies or comparisons all coming together in the word *buckle*. Such a structure is also to be found in the odes of the Greek poet Pindar, which Hopkins studied intensely in school. Pindar's poems praise a great athlete or hero by linking together a series of seeming digressions in one key image or figure, sometimes called a "constellation," such as the "golden lyre," a "beacon fire," a "horse," or a "tree." Hopkins' poetry unites the Christian tradition of anagogical interpretation of the created world and the Classical Greek tradition of the Pindaric ode.

Most of Hopkins' shorter poems are sonnets, yet within the confines of this form, Hopkins displays great originality in his metrical structure, his repetition of sound in alliteration and internal rhyme, and his changes in the length of the sonnet while maintaining the crucial eight-to-six proportion of the octave/ sestet division. Like the form of the sonnet, the subjects of most of Hopkins' poems are extremely traditional: (1) elation at the sight of some particular bit of nature; (2) personal dejection, desolation, and despair; (3) celebration of the inner worth of an outwardly ordinary human being. These three topics are commonplaces of Romantic and post-Romantic literature. Hopkins' originality lies in treating these subjects with unusual power and perception. Romantic poets such as William Wordsworth and Percy Bysshe Shelley often looked at nature and said that they felt their hearts leap up to behold the beauty of spring or autumn. For Hopkins, every little corner of nature was evidence of the divine presence of God. His Christianity reinforces the Romantic sentiment. The confluence of the Romantic and the Christian tradition produces unusually powerful statements.

Consider, for example, the sonnet "Hurrahing in Harvest." Like "The Windhover," this poem is an Italian sonnet, rhymed abba abba cdcdcd. Lines six and seven end with an unusual rhyme device. "Saviour" is rhymed with the next line, but in order to hear the complete rhyme, one must continue to the "r" sound that begins line eight: "gave you a/ Rapturous." This extended rhyme is common in Hopkins and illustrates his predilection for unusual twists within the framework of rigid traditional expectations. The subjects of "The Windhover" and "Hurrahing in Harvest" are also similar. In both poems, the speaker looks up at the sky and finds nature breathtakingly beautiful. "Hurrahing in Harvest" declares that the summer is now ending. The *stooks*, or shocks of bundled grain, are now stacked in the fields. The technical and regional term *stooks* is characteristic of Hopkins' vocabulary. The word is not commonly known, but it is exact. The speaker looks up at the autumnal skies and sees the clouds. With the bold verbal comparisons which the poet prefers, he compares the skies to "wind-walks"—they are like alleyways for the winds. The clouds are like "silk-sacks"; they are soft, dainty, and luxurious. The movement of the clouds across the sky is like "meal-drift" or flour pouring across the heavens. In that soft, flowing beauty, the speaker walks and lifts up his eyes. He sees the glory of the natural scene and then recognizes that beyond the heavens, behind all the created universe, there stands the Savior. He at first rejoices in the sheer beauty of nature, but such earthly beauty leads him to the unspeakable inner beauty of Christ's immediate presence in the natural world. In the sestet, the speaker sees the azure hills of autumn as strong as the shoulder of a stallion, majestic and sweet with flowers, like the shoulder of God bearing the creation in all its glory. The speaker realizes that all this is here for him to see, and the realization makes his heart leap up as if it had wings; his spirit hurls heavenward.

Hopkins wrote many poems celebrating nature in sonnet form. "God's Grandeur" states in the octave that the grandeur of God's creating has been obscured by the industrial revolution, trade and toil. The sestet replies that there is a spark of freshness deep in nature which will spring up like the sun at dawn because God broods over the earth like a bird over its egg. "The Starlight Night" begins with a powerful octave describing the beauty of the stars in the night sky. The sestet replies that the stars are like a picket fence separating us from heaven through which we can glimpse a bit of what is on the other side. "Spring" typically gives an excited picture of the juice and joy of the earth stirring in springtime and compares it to the youthful, primal goodness of children, a hint of sinless Eden.

"Pied Beauty" is one of Hopkins' most important philosophical poems on nature. It reflects his study of Duns Scotus and his notion of inscape. The poem is a "curtail" or cut-short sonnet, only ten and a fraction lines long. Hopkins explained that this poem maintained the eight-to-six ratio, which he felt was the key to the sonnet form. The exposition, which occupies the first six lines, states that God is especially to be praised for the irregular, dappled, serviceable parts of creation. The sestet generalizes that whatever is contradictory, strange, or changeable originates in God. In Platonic thought, a material thing is beautiful insofar as it approaches its unchanging ideal. For example, a beautiful circle is one that approaches—as nearly as possible in our world—the perfection of an ideal circle. Because the things of our world are always struggling to become like their perfect forms, our material world is always changing. It is sometimes called the mutable world of "becoming." The ideal world cannot change, however, because when something is perfect, any change would make it imperfect. The world of Platonic ideals is therefore unchanging. It is sometimes called the world of permanent "being." "Pied Beauty" makes a striking statement about the nature of beauty. It asserts that things are not beautiful because they approach the perfect type, but because they are various, changing, contradictory. Hopkins seems to be praising the very aspect of the material world that Platonic philosophy connects with degeneration and decay. Somehow God, who is perfect and unchanging, has fathered a universe of imperfection, contradiction, and decay. Nevertheless, this created world reflects his praise: Duns Scotus maintained that God's perfection must be manifest somehow in the constant change and variety of his creation.

Hopkins' admiration for Duns Scotus is expressed in "Duns Scotus's Oxford," which combines the nature-sonnet and the celebration of a famous man. Its octave depicts the ancient university town of Oxford. The sestet comments that this was the very city that Duns Scotus knew when the subtle doctor taught there in the thirteenth century. Now Hopkins finds Scotus to have the best insight into philosophical problems, even more comforting to him than Greek philosophers such as Plato, or Italian philosophers such as St. Thomas Aquinas. All of the nature sonnets give an extremely sharp picture of some relatively common event or situation in nature: a hawk in flight, the landscape of Oxford, the rebirth of the countryside in springtime, the clouds and fields of autumn. The poet reflects on the source of all this beauty. The scene itself uplifts his spirits, but the awareness of God's creative force glimpsed behind the material world brings even more elation.

A second group of poems is in the tradition of the heroic sonnet. These poems examine a person's life and define what is noteworthy in an ordinary man's career. "The Lantern Out of Doors" is typical. The octave tells of seeing a lantern moving at night. There must be someone behind that light, but he is so far off that he passes in the darkness and all that can be seen is a little spark. We have trouble knowing other people, and death is soon upon us. The sestet replies that Christ knows every person; Christ is the first and last friend of every man. "Felix Randal," one of Hopkins' best sonnets, is about a blacksmith who fell ill and died. The once powerful man wasted away, but he finally came to accept Christ. Paradoxically, in the weakness of his death he became more blessed than in the pagan power he was so proud of in the days when he forged and fitted horseshoes with his fellow workers. "The Soldier," "Tom's Garland: Upon the Unemployed," and "Harry Plough-man" all fit into the category of poems celebrating the inner worth of ordinary people. Perhaps the pattern of this kind of sonnet is best displayed in "In Honour of St. Alphonsus Rodriguez: Laybrother of the Society of Jesus." Alphonsus Rodriguez performed no noble deeds. For forty years, however, he faithfully carried out his duty and filled his station as doorkeeper. It is not his exploits, but his humanity, that Hopkins celebrates. Humility, obedience, and simple faith have their reward. The poem is in the tradition of Milton's theme of the faithful Christians: "They also serve who only stand and wait."

The third major theme of Hopkins' sonnets is spiritual desolation and terror. These poems constitute the dark, opposite side of Hopkins' view of reality. In the nature poems, the poet looks at some part of the created universe and feels that God is in every corner of our world. His joy, already aroused by the pure beauty of nature, rises to an ecstatic pitch when he realizes that God is behind it all. The poems of desolation, sometimes called the "terrible sonnets," on the other hand, imagine a world without God—all joy, freshness, and promise withdrawn. They depict the dark night of the soul. Many readers think that these poems are directly autobiographical, indicating that Hopkins in the last years of his life was devastated by despair. This view is probably not sound. The sonnet is a highly dramatized form; sonnets are traditionally constructed like little plays. Thus the speaker of one of Shakespeare's sonnets is no more Shakespeare, the man himself, than is Macbeth or Hamlet, and the persona or mask through which a sonneteer speaks is not to be confused with the real author. The *Spiritual Exercises* of Saint Ignatius, moreover, follows a spiritual progression which every Jesuit would imitate in his retreats and private worship. In a long retreat, lasting about a month, the exercitant is called upon to drive himself gradually into a state of extreme desolation into which a renewed sense of God's presence finally bursts like Easter into the dormant world. The sonnets of terror may be as artificial as Elizabethan love sonnets. They may be, to some degree, virtuoso exercises in imagining a world devoid of spirituality and hope. The real feelings of Hopkins may be quite separate from the imagined feelings of the persona who speaks these sonnets. On the other hand, we can hardly imagine that Hopkins could write these poems unless there were some wrenching personal feelings motivating his creative act.

The sonnets of terror appeal to readers in our century because they mirror a cosmic despair or alienation. The feeling that modern man is a stranger in a strange land, that he is alienated from the profit of his own productivity, that he is caught in a meaningless or absurd activity like Sisyphus rolling his stone endlessly up a mountain in Hell, is extremely widespread. It is doubtful that Hopkins felt alienated in exactly this way. His religious belief promised him a future life and salvation. When he speaks of despair, it is always hypothetical: think how unbearable life would be *if* there were not hope. "Carrion Comfort," among the best of Hopkins' dark sonnets, considers despair, which is itself a sin, depicting the struggle of the Christian with his own conscience. It begins a series of six sonnets of unusual power which treat the struggle of the soul. These poems should be read in sequence: (1) "Carrion Comfort," (2) "No Worst, There Is None," (3) "To Seem a Stranger Lies My Lot," (4) "I Wake and Feel the Fell of Dark, Not Day," (5) "Patience, Hard Thing," and (6) "My Own Heart Let Me Have More Pity On." Read in sequence, these sonnets constitute a short psychodrama or morality play. The Christian speaker confronts his own doubt, weakness, and unworth, and is terrified of God. In five scenes he is seen writhing and twisting in mental contortions of guilt and terror. At the conclusion of "My Own Heart Let Me Have More Pity On," the sestet provides the dramatic release, as God's smile breaks through, like sunlight on a mountain guiding the traveler. This sonnet sequence corresponds to the progress of the exercitant through the final stages of his spiritual exercises. The same progress of the mind, through terror to elation at the Resurrection, is outlined in "That Nature Is a Heraclitean Fire and of the Comfort of the Resurrection." The first segment of this poem looks at the changing natural world. Like a bonfire, everything around us is changing, decaying, being consumed. Man seems so pitifully weak and vulnerable among these flames. The only hope is Christ's promise of salvation, which comes to man like a beacon. Man will pass through the fire and, even when all else is destroyed, his soul will endure like an immortal diamond.

A striking characteristic of Hopkins' poetry is his rich vocabulary. As he sought to find the inscape or unique form in the created universe, he also attempted to find in language the original, spare, strange, exactly right word. He was one of the best trained linguists of his age, working at the research level in Latin and Greek, while studying Anglo-Saxon and Welsh. His notes and journals show him repeatedly developing elaborate etymologies of words. He belonged to a widespread movement in the Victorian era, spearheaded by Robert Bridges and his Society For Pure English, which glorified the archaic elements in modern English. He records in his notes dialect words, and the special words used by workers for their tools or by country people for plants and animals. This attention to the texture of language pours forth in his poetry in an unusually rich, eccentric vocabulary.

Despite the orthodoxy of his religious views, Hopkins is known as one of the founders of modernism in literature. He is frequently compared with Walt Whitman, Emily Dickinson, and the French Symbolist poets as a great revolutionary who rebelled against the sterile forms of Victorian verse and brought a new urgency, freshness, and seriousness to poetry. He revolutionized the very basis of English meter with his experiments in sprung rhythm. He revitalized the bold metaphor in the manner of the English metaphysical poets. He created a whole new lexicon, a poetic vocabulary constructed from dialect, archaic, technical, and coined words. The critics who initially praised his work in the 1920's and 1930's tended to see him as a cultural primitive, a man isolated from the corruption of society and so able to return to a state of nature and get to the core of language more easily than writers, such as Alfred, Lord Tennyson, who seemed corrupted by false traditions. Although Hopkins was undoubtedly a great innovator, he was certainly not a cultural primitive. He was a highly trained professor of Latin and Greek language and literature. In addition to his "Double First in Greats" from Oxford University, he undertook years of rigorous philosophical and theological training with the Society of Jesus. He was at the center of a group of correspondents who were as powerful intellectually as any group we can find in his era: Bridges, Dixon, Patmore, and other less frequent scholarly correspondents. Hopkins was not a naïve writer; on the contrary, he was an extremely sophisticated writer. His poetry is revolutionary, not because he was ignorant of tradition, but because he brought together many powerful threads of tradition: the contemplative practice of the *Spiritual Exercises*, with their "composition of place" and "application of the senses"; the conventions of the Petrarchan sonnet; the complicated metrical studies of Bridges, Patmore, and the classical scholars;

the classical philosophical background of Oxford University; and the medieval thought of the Jesuit schools, especially of John Duns Scotus. These traditions met, and sometimes conflicted sharply, in Hopkins. From that confluence of traditions he gave modern readers the unique gift of his poems.

Todd K. Bender

Other major works

NONFICTION: *The Letters of Gerard Manley Hopkins to Robert Bridges*, 1935, 1955 (C. C. Abbott, editor); *The Correspondence of Gerard Manley Hopkins and Richard Watson Dixon*, 1935, 1955 (C. C. Abbott, editor); *The Notebooks and Papers of Gerard Manley Hopkins*, 1937 (Humphry House, editor); *Further Letters of Gerard Manley Hopkins*, 1938, 1956 (C. C. Abbott, editor); *The Journals and Papers of Gerard Manley Hopkins*, 1959 (Humphry House and Graham Storey, editors); *The Sermons and Devotional Writings of Gerard Manley Hopkins*, 1959 (Christopher Devlin, editor); *Gerard Manley Hopkins: Selected Letters*, 1990.

Bibliography

Bergonzi, Bernard. *Gerard Manley Hopkins*. New York: Macmillan, 1977. This volume is one in the Masters of World Literature series. Contains five chapters of biography, followed by a sixth chapter which seeks to give a general account of Hopkins' poetry as linked to his life. Includes a select bibliography and an index.

Bloom, Harold, ed. *Gerard Manley Hopkins*. New York: Chelsea House, 1986. One of the Modern Critical Views series. Includes a number of significant essays on Hopkins, a chronology, a bibliography, and an index.

Gardner, W. H. *Gerard Manley Hopkins, 1844-1889.* 3d ed. 2 vols. New York: Oxford University Press, 1958. This third edition of the first really major study of Hopkins' poetry (originally published in 1944) is still one of the best. The first volume deals extensively with Hopkins' development of the sonnet form, his themes and imagery, and then seeks to place him in relation to Modernism. Volume 2 goes through his poems more chronologically, but also deals with development of rhythm and critical theory. Contains appendices, a bibliography, and indexes.

Robinson, John. *In Extremity: A Study of Gerard Manley Hopkins.* Cambridge, England: Cambridge University Press, 1978. Traces the nature of Hopkins' religious experiences as they receive poetic expression. The latter was intense because the former was out of extremity. The philosophy of Duns Scotus is seen as a vital bridge between experience and expression. Includes notes and an index.

Schneider, Elisabeth W. *The Dragon in the Gate: Studies in the Poetry of Gerard Manley Hopkins.* Berkeley: University of California Press, 1968.

One of the Perspectives in Criticism series, it is still an excellent introduction to Hopkins' major poetry, dealing specifically with the development of style and rhythm. Includes an index.

Sulloway, Alison G. *Gerard Manley Hopkins and the Victorian Temper.* New York: Columbia University Press, 1972. Places Hopkins more firmly in the Victorian context than do many studies. Two appendices refer to the Tractarian wars. Includes notes, a selected bibliography, and an index.

Weyand, Norman, ed. *Immortal Diamond: Studies in Gerard Manley Hopkins.* New York: Sheed & Ward, 1949. Reprint. New York: Octagon Books, 1969. A series of essays by Jesuit scholars that represents the widest and clearest Jesuit commentary on the poet available. Includes appendices and a full bibliography through 1946.

A. E. HOUSMAN

Born: Fockbury, Worcestershire, England; March 26, 1859
Died: Cambridge, England; April 30, 1936

Principal poetry
A Shropshire Lad, 1896; *Last Poems*, 1922; *More Poems*, 1936; *Collected Poems*, 1939.

Other literary forms
A. E. Housman's only work of prose fiction is *A Morning with the Royal Family*, a youthful fantasy printed without his permission in 1882 in the *Bromsgrovian* and unpublished elsewhere. His translations total 102 lines from Aeschylus' *Septem Contra Thebas* (467 B.C., *Seven Against Thebes*), Sophocles' *Oedipus Coloneus* (401 B.C., *Oedipus at Colonus*), and Euripides' *Alcestis* (438 B.C.) and first appeared in A. W. Pollard's *Odes from the Greek Dramatists* in 1890. They have since been included in the *Collected Poems*. Henry Maas has collected more than eight hundred of Housman's letters, which, though not in the great tradition of English letter-writing, shed considerable light on the poet's enigmatic personality.

Achievements
Although Housman's fame today rests on a handful of poems, it was to classical scholarship that he devoted most of his life. For nearly fifty years he was a professor of Latin, first at University College, London, and later at Cambridge University. A profound and prolific scholar fluent in five languages, he published in that time approximately two hundred critical papers and reviews spanning the entire spectrum of classical literature from Aeschylus to Vergil. This work consists mainly of textual emendations of corrupt manuscripts and is highly technical, providing a stark contrast to the lucid simplicity of his poetry. Titles such as "Emendationes Propertianae," "The Codex Lipsiensis of Manilius," and "Adversaria Orthographica" abound in *The Classical Papers of A. E. Housman* (1972), collected and edited by J. Diggle and F. R. D. Goodyear in three volumes. In addition, Housman has left behind editions of Ovid, Juvenal, Lucan, and Manilius and several major lectures, including *The Confines of Criticism* (1969) and *The Name and Nature of Poetry* (1933).

Housman held no illusions either about the power of classical knowledge to influence human character or the extent of its appeal, but he nevertheless placed the highest premium on learning for its own sake and was a relentless seeker after truth using the method of textual criticism, which he defined in *The Application of Thought to Textual Criticism* (1922) as "the science of discovering error in texts and the art of removing it." This was for him "an aristocratic affair, not communicable to all men, nor to most men." The one thing most necessary to be a textual critic "is to have a head, not a pumpkin, on your shoulders, and brains, not pudding, in your head." He applied to others the same rigorous standards of scholarship that he set for himself, and he had no sympathy for incompetence in any form. He was particularly annoyed by the practice of modern criticism of following one manuscript whenever possible instead of weighing the relative merits of alternative manuscripts, a practice, he writes in his Preface to Juvenal (1905), designed "to rescue incompetent editors alike from the toil of editing and from the shame of acknowledging that they cannot edit." His harshest words are reserved for self-complacent and insolent individuals masquerading as sane critics. His vituperative attacks on Elias Stoeber and Friedrick Jacob in his 1903 Preface to Manilius may be taken as typical: "Stoeber's mind, though that is no name to call it by, was one which turned as unswervingly to the false, the meaningless, the unmetrical, and the ungrammatical, as the needle to the pole," and "Not only had Jacob no sense for grammar, no sense for coherency, no sense for sense, but being himself possessed by a passion for the clumsy and the hispid he imputed this disgusting taste to all the authors whom he edited." The extent of Housman's learning and the unbridled candor of his judgments made him a respected and feared polemicist and perhaps the most formidable classicist of his age. W. H. Auden called him "The Latin Scholar of his generation."

Throughout his career Housman repeatedly denied having any talent for literary criticism, and he turned down the Clark Lectureship in English Literature at Trinity College, Cambridge, on the ground that he did not qualify as a literary critic, who, he wrote in *The Confines of Criticism*, is rarer than "the appearance of Halley's comet." When he was at University College, London, he delivered papers on various English poets including Matthew Arnold, Algernon Charles Swinburne, and Alfred, Lord Tennyson, but he refused to allow them to be published and apparently resented the demands the Literary Society made on him, writing in his Preface to Arthur Platt's *Nine Essays* (1927) that "Studious men who might be settling *Hoti's* business and properly basing *Oun* are expected to provide amusing discourses on subjects of which they have no official knowledge and upon which they may not be entitled even to open their mouths." Nevertheless, Housman's several excursions into literary criticism reflect a great sensitivity to such central concerns as the integrity of literary texts and the debasement of language. In its emphasis on the numinous intractability of great poetry, *The Name and Nature of Poetry* is an oblique repudiation of the intellectualism of T. S. Eliot and I. A. Richards. Housman's criticism shows the influence of Matthew Arnold, but the importance he attached to the undergirding of impressionistic judgments with sound scholarship goes beyond that Victorian sage.

As a poet, Housman was successful to the point of celebrity. *A Shropshire Lad* was initially slow to catch on with the reading public, but after Grant Richards took over as Housman's publisher, it became a great success on both sides of the Atlantic. Its moody *Weltschmerz* caught the *fin de siècle* mood, just as *Last Poems* captured the ennui of a war-weary generation. Today the inevitable reaction has set in and Housman's poetry is not as highly regarded as it once was. The melancholy of his poems too often seems uninformed by spiritual struggle, but the plaintive lyricism of his best work has a universal and enduring appeal.

Biography

Alfred Edward Housman was born on March 26, 1859, in Fockbury, Worcestershire, into an ancient family of preachers and farmers whose English roots extended back to the fourteenth century. His great-grandfather on his father's side, an evangelical preacher who lived out his life with a wife and eight children in genteel poverty, was shy and unassertive in manner but inwardly tough, capable of bearing up under the hardships of life with manly fortitude. Housman was able to observe at first hand that stoicism which informs so much of his mature poetry in his own mother, Sarah, whose prolonged suffering and death after bearing seven children was a model of quiet courage. In the words of George L. Watson, "With his grimly stoical demeanor, Housman often recalled some ancestral farmer, glowering at the inclement weather" (*A. E. Housman: A Divided Life*, 1957). No such family precedent exists for Housman's career as a scholar unless it be a distant cousin on his father's side who was a lecturer in Greek and Divinity at Chichester College, and still less exists for the poet's rejection of the Church within a year of his mother's death.

The death of Housman's mother on his twelfth birthday brought a traumatic end to his childhood and left him with a profound sense of loss from which he never fully recovered. He had adored the witty, intelligent woman who took pride in her descent from Sir Francis Drake, and her death created a vacuum which could not be filled by his father, Edward, a lackluster solicitor who took increasingly to drink during Sarah's illness and who, two years after her death, married his cousin Lucy and began a long slide into poverty, dying after many years of broken health in 1894. Alfred was never close to his father. He regarded his drunkenness and general improvidence as intolerable weaknesses and held him in barely concealed contempt. He was, however, close to his six brothers and sisters during his early life and, as the oldest, conducted literary parlour games for them, taking the lead in writing nonsense verse, a practice that continued during summer vacations through his college years.

Sarah's death was not permitted to interrupt for long Housman's studies at nearby Bromsgrove School, where he had enrolled on a scholarship in the fall of 1870. Bromsgrove was an old and reputable public school and provided an excellent foundation in the classics, English, and French. As a student, Housman was introspective and shy and was known as "Mouse" by his classmates. Throughout his childhood, he was afflicted with a nervous disorder and while a student at Bromsgrove he had violent seizures which the headmaster attributed to St. Vitus's dance (chorea). Later in life this nervous condition took the form of occasional facial contortions which might "incongruously reappear in the course of the most impersonal lectures, as he read aloud one of the odes of Horace, leaving his astonished students 'afraid the old fellow was going to cry,'" in the words of George L. Watson. His nervous affliction notwithstanding, Housman seemed to thrive on the rigorous eleven-hour-a-day regimen at Bromsgrove School. In 1874, he appeared for the first time in print with a poem in rhymed couplets about the death of Socrates for which he won the prize for composition in English verse and which he delivered on Commencement Speech Day. It was published in the *Bromsgrove Messenger* on August 8, 1874, much to his later chagrin. In adult life, Housman was always jealous of his reputation and forbade the publication of his juvenilia and occasional addresses, which he felt did not meet the high standards he set for himself.

Housman's career at Bromsgrove School ended in triumph as he won the Lord Lyttelton prize for Latin verse, the honorarium for Greek verse, and the Senior Wattell prize, along with a generous scholarship to St. John's College, Oxford. At least some of Housman's success at this time can be attributed to Herbert Millington, who became headmaster at Bromsgrove School in 1873. A man of keen intellect, Millington presented a formidable figure to the students, and Housman felt some hero-worship for him, referring to him much later as a good teacher for a clever boy. Millington was the most important role model of Housman's youth.

In the fall of 1877, Housman entered Oxford and within a few days was writing irreverently to his stepmother about the solemn Latin ceremony of matriculation. He joined the Oxford Union, and although he was inactive he was "an avowed member and staunch champion of the Conservative faction" (Watson). Generally, however, Housman remained uninvolved in the life of the university. He was unimpressed by its professors and attended only one lecture by the illustrious Benjamin Jowett. Housman came away disgusted by Jowett's disregard for the "niceties" of scholarship. A lecture by John Ruskin also left Housman unimpressed. Housman later wrote that "Oxford had not much effect on me." This was not entirely the case, for it was at Oxford that he began to develop in earnest his capacity for classical scholarship. Passively resisting the conventional curriculum, Housman early in his Oxford career decided to devote his energies to the text of the Latin poet Propertius, whose garbled works required extensive editorial attention. He continued to work on Propertius for the remainder of his time at Oxford.

George Watson writes that Housman was already "embarking on those problems of conjectural emendation which are the acme of classical learning." It
was also at this time that Housman began keeping a commonplace book of
his favorite quotations, which tended toward the sepulchral, as one might
expect of a young man whose only adornments for his college rooms were
Albrecht Dürer's "Melancholia" and "The Knight, Death and the Devil."
Housman's favorite poem during his early Oxford years was Arnold's *Empe-
docles on Etna* (1852), which he said contained "all the law and the prophets."
He was attracted to Thomas Hardy's early novels for their gloomy stoicism.
For a time Housman flirted with the poetry of Swinburne and wrote an
antiecclesiastical poem, "New-Year's Eve," modeled on Swinburne's style.

Clearly the most important thing that happened to Housman during these
years was his friendship with Moses Jackson, which had a deep and lasting
effect on him. Among the first people he met at Oxford were A. W. Pollard
and Jackson. He liked them both, but he was especially attracted to the latter.
Jackson was everything that Housman was not: sociable, handsome, athletic,
charismatic. A brilliant student of engineering, he excelled with ease at everything he did. The three became fast friends, and in 1879, Housman won a
first class in Moderations but his failure to win either the Hertford Classical
Scholarship or the Newdigate Prize for English verse was an omen of worse
to come. In his last year at Oxford, Housman shared rooms with Pollard and
Jackson and according to Watson this "was to be the most perturbed and
momentous period of his life." There is convincing evidence that at this time
Housman developed a passionate attachment for Jackson, which he kept
hidden from everyone at great psychic cost to himself. He became irritable
and moody, but his friends apparently suspected nothing. He failed his
examination in Greats, and in the summer of 1881, he returned to his family
in disgrace. Andrew S. Gow in his *A. E. Housman: A Sketch* (1936) attributes
Housman's failure to the nature of the curriculum, which emphasized history
and philosophy at the expense of literature, but the weight of more recent
opinion, including that of Watson and Maude M. Hawkins (*A. E. Housman:
Man Behind a Mask*, 1958) places the blame on Housman's changed feelings
for Jackson.

Housman returned to Oxford in the fall of 1881 to qualify for the lowly
pass degree. He worked occasionally as a tutor in Greek and Latin at his old
school and studied intensively for the Civil Service Examination. In December, 1882, he moved to London to share lodgings with Jackson and Jackson's
younger brother, Adalbert, and went to work in the Patent Office, where he
spent the next ten years registering trademarks. From this point until 1885,
not one letter emerged from Housman and not even a brother and sister could
gain access to him when they came to live in London. In 1886, Housman,
seeking the peace of solitude, took private rooms in Highgate, and from this
time on, his "invariable mode of life," according to Watson, would be

"monastic seclusion." Only the Jackson brothers were encouraged to intrude upon his privacy.

In 1888 Housman broke upon the scholarly world with an avalanche of brilliant critical articles that won for him an international reputation (and would secure for him the Chair in Latin at University College, London, in 1892). When one remembers that these early scholarly publications were researched in the evenings at the British Museum after a full day at the Patent Office, his accomplishment must be seen as nothing short of heroic. His *Introductory Lecture* (1937) was given on October 3, 1892, at University College and earned for him the lasting respect of his colleagues. Housman's scholarly writing continued unabated during his years there. He continued to work on the manuscripts of Propertius, edited works by Ovid and Juvenal, and in 1897 came out with a brilliant series of papers on the *Heroides*. In the meantime, Moses Jackson had gone to live in India and Adalbert had died, plunging Housman into near suicidal gloom which was to persist at intervals for the rest of his life and which could be relieved only by creative activity. In 1896, *A Shropshire Lad* appeared, published at his own expense, and 1899 saw the first paper on Manilius, the poet who was to become the object of Housman's most important work of scholarship. His edition of Manilius appeared in five books over a twenty-seven-year period, "a monument of incomparable skill and thankless labour."

The eventual success of *A Shropshire Lad* and Housman's recognized position as a scholar of the first rank made him something of a celebrity, and during his last ten years at University College, he would dine at the Café Royal with a select circle of friends that included his brother Laurence, his publisher Grant Richards, his faculty colleague Arthur Platt, and a few others. By now Housman was a connoisseur of fine food and wine and an accomplished dinner conversationalist. He remained aloof from the London literary scene, however, and had little appreciation for the serious writers of his day, including the poet William Butler Yeats. On a lesser level, he intensely disliked the novels of John Galsworthy, and when James Joyce's *Ulysses* (1922) was published, Housman sniffed, "I have scrambled and waded through and found one or two half-pages amusing." Nor did he display any interest in music or painting. About such composers as Ralph Vaughan Williams and Charles Butterworth, who set some of his poems to music, Housman remarked, "I never hear the music, so I do not suffer."

In October, 1911, Housman was elected Kennedy Professor of Latin at Cambridge University and a Fellow of Trinity College. His brilliant inaugural lecture on *The Confines of Criticism* remained unpublished during his lifetime because he was unable to verify a reference in it to Percy Bysshe Shelley. At the university, Housman became a member of a select group of the faculty known as "The Family," which met twice a month for dinner. At these ritual banquets Housman proved a good raconteur and was a well-accepted member of the group, but according to Gow, he held himself back from intimate friendships with his colleagues for fear of rejection or disappointment. He was equally distant toward his students; and his lectures, which he gave twice weekly in all three academic terms, were sparsely attended both because of the highly technical nature of his subject matter and the coldness of his demeanor on the platform. Throughout his twenty-five years at Cambridge, Housman continued to publish widely, directing his major efforts to the edition of Manilius. He was both respected as a great scholar and feared as a devastating polemicist. *Last Poems*, which appeared in 1922, was a great success. In the spring of 1933, Housman was prevailed upon to give the Leslie Stephen Lecture. He delivered *The Name and Nature of Poetry* on the twenty-second anniversary of his inaugural lecture as Kennedy Professor of Latin. In the summer of 1935, an ill Housman rallied enough strength for one last trip to France, where he had vacationed regularly since 1897. Weakened by heart disease, he died in Cambridge on April 30, 1936. In the words of Watson, he "wore in absolute repose a look of 'proud challenge.' "

Analysis

A. E. Housman once remarked with that scathing condescension of which he was a master that Swinburne "has now said not only all he has to say about everything, but all he has to say about nothing." Actually, when Housman was at Oxford he fell under Swinburne's powerful spell. His "New Year's Eve" (*Additional Poems*, XXI), written about 1879, celebrates the death of the gods in a labored imitation of the "Hymn to Proserpine": "Divinities disanointed/ And kings whose kingdom is done." The poem is interesting but uninspired and it is well that Housman early rejected Swinburne as a model. Still, one wishes that Housman had possessed more of the older poet's exuberance of imagination and richness of rhetoric, for it is in these qualities that his poetry is most deficient. Practically all of his poems are variations on the related themes of mortality and the miseries of the human condition; while a close reading reveals considerably more variety than at first appears, it is nevertheless true that the body of Housman's poetry is slighter than that of any other English poet of comparable reputation. The authorized canon consists of only three small volumes which were published separately: *A Shropshire Lad*, *Last Poems*, and the posthumous *More Poems*. The twenty-three *Additional Poems* and three verse translations have been added to the *Collected Poems* for a total of 175 original poems. All are short, some no more than a stanza in length. The predominant form is the lyric. The tone is characteristically mournful and the mood elegiac. It is useless to look for any kind of development, either of substance or technique, in these poems, for most of them were written in the 1890's when Housman was under great psychological stress. They are intensely autobiographical inasmuch as they spring from the deep well of Housman's psyche, but few refer to specific events in his life. Housman's passion for privacy was as great as Robert Browning's, and he was attracted to the lyric as a verse form largely because of its essential impersonality. The emotion of his poems is usually general, an undifferentiated *Weltschmerz*, and such dramatic elements as may occur as persona and setting are characteristically undefined. The extremely personal and revealing "The world goes none the lamer" (*More Poems*, XXI) and "Because I liked you better" (*More Poems*, XXXI) are exceptional.

In the world of Housman's poetry, which is more obviously consistent than that of more complex poets, youth fades into dust, lovers are unfaithful, nature is lovely but indifferent, and death is the serene end of everything. These great archetypal themes have given rise to some of the world's finest poetry, from Sir Walter Raleigh's "The Nymph's Reply to the Shepherd" to William Butler Yeats's "Sailing to Byzantium." What makes them interesting in Housman's poetry are the particular forms in which they are cast. "With rue my heart is laden" (*A Shropshire Lad*, LIV), a poem sometimes set to music, may be taken as exemplary of his lyricism:

> With rue my heart is laden
> For golden friends I had,
> For many a rose-lipt maiden
> And many a lightfoot lad.
> By brooks too broad for leaping
> The lightfoot boys are laid;
> The rose-lipt girls are sleeping
> In fields where roses fade.

In this lyric of studied simplicity there is a classical blending of form and substance. The simple and inventive diction; the Latinate syntax, parallelism, and balance; the alternating seven- and six-syllable lines restrain still further the already generalized emotion; and while the poem is cold and artificial, it has a kind of classical grace. A comparison with William Wordsworth's "A Slumber Did My Spirit Seal" will reveal the power of a great sensibility working through the constraints of classical form to convey a sense of profound personal feeling.

In too many of Housman's lyrical poems, including the well-known "When I was one-and-twenty" (*A Shropshire Lad*, XIII) and "When first my way to fair I took" (*Last Poems*, XXXV), the feeling is severely attenuated by a mannered flatness, and the passion that the poet undoubtedly experienced is swallowed up by the generalization of the emotion. At worst, the feeling degenerates into the bathos of "Could man be drunk for ever" (*Last Poems*, X) or the histrionic posturing of "Twice a week the winter thorough" (*A Shropshire Lad*, XVII), but at their best there is a genuine communication of feeling, as in "Yonder see the morning blink" (*Last Poems*, XI) and "From far, from eve and morning" (*A Shropshire Lad*, XXXII). There is a thin line between the expression of the poignancy of existence and sentimentality, and it is a tribute to Housman's tact that he so seldom crosses it.

Housman's poems work best when the emotion is crystallized by a dramatic context, as in some of the love pieces and the poems about soldiers in which the oracular pronouncements about the miseries of living which so easily lapse into an unacceptable didacticism are subordinated to more concrete situations. "Oh see how thick the goldcup flowers" (*A Shropshire Lad*, V) is a clever and humorous dialogue between a young blade and a girl who spurns his advances, but beneath the surface gaiety there is the slightest suggestion of the mortality and faithlessness of lovers. In "Delight it is" (*More Poems*, XVIII) the youthful speaker addresses the maiden in words of reckless honesty—"Oh maiden, let your distaff be/ And pace the flowery meads with me/ And I will tell you lies"—and one is to assume that he is a prototype of all young lovers.

In "Spring Morning" (*Last Poems*, XVI), the idyllic beauty of an April morning and the universal renewal of life in the spring place in ironic relief the "scorned unlucky lad" who "Mans his heart and deep and glad/ Drinks the valiant air of dawn" even though "the girl he loves the best/ Rouses from another's side." The speaker of "This time of year" (*A Shropshire Lad*, XXV) is more fortunate, but only because the former lover of his sweetheart has died. "Is my team ploughing" (*A Shropshire Lad*, XXVII) dramatizes a similar situation in which the surviving youth has taken his dead friend's girl. In a dialogue that extends beyond the grave, the living lover tells his dead friend: "I cheer a dead man's sweetheart/ Never ask me whose." One of the most effective of Housman's love poems is "Bredon Hill" (*A Shropshire Lad*, XXI), in which the sound of the church bells reminds the speaker of the untimely death of his sweetheart. The poem ends ambiguously with the distraught lover saying to the humming steeples: "Oh, noisy bells, be dumb/ I hear you, I will come." Also with death in mind is the speaker of "Along the field" (*A Shropshire Lad*, XXVI), who a year before had heard the aspen predict the death of his sweetheart. The prediction fulfilled, he now walks beside another girl, and under the aspen leaves he wonders if they "talk about a time at hand/ When I shall sleep with clover clad/ And she beside another lad."

In all of these poems love is doomed to transience by infidelity or death. This, they say, is the human condition. In virtually all of them, death has supplanted sex as the major ingredient, making them unique in English love poetry.

Death is also, less surprisingly, the main element in most of Housman's military poems. The poems about soldiers, with the exception of the frequently anthologized "Epitaph on an Army of Mercenaries" (*Last Poems*, XXXVII), are not as well known as some of Housman's other poetry. At first sight they may seem somewhat out of place, but it is not surprising that an introverted classical scholar of conservative convictions should glamorize the guardians of the Empire. The attitude toward the soldier is consistently one of compassion and respect and the poems convey a depth of sincerity not always felt elsewhere. The prospect of young men going to die in foreign lands in the service of the Queen takes on an added poignancy from the death of Housman's younger brother, Herbert, who was killed in the Boer War. On another level, a soldier's death is an honorable form of suicide and a way to attain lasting fame. "The Deserter" (*Last Poems*, XIII) and "The Recruit" (*A Shropshire Lad*, III) may be taken as typical. In the first, the lass, rejected by her lover so that he may rejoin his comrades, upbraids him and others like him for scouring "about the world a-wooing/ The bullet to their breast"; in the second, the lad is promised eternal fame either as a returning hero or as a slain comrade. In "Lancer" (*Last Poems*, VI), the speaker affirms his coming death with the ringing refrain of *"Oh who would not sleep with the brave?"* In these poems Housman succeeds in investing Thanatos, characteristically an enervated and sterile attitude, with a singular vitality. The placid stoicism of the soldiers makes these ultimately the least melancholy of all of Housman's poems.

The melancholy that permeates virtually every line of Housman's poetry is a matter of temperament more than of a well-wrought metaphysics. He affirms the existence of the soul in such poems as "The Immortal Part" (*A Shropshire Lad*, XLIII) and "Be still, my soul" (*A Shropshire Lad*, XLVIII) even as he denies its immortality, the agnostic "Easter Hymn" (*More Poems*, I) notwithstanding. Such monologues to the dead as "To an Athlete Dying Young" (*A Shropshire Lad*, XIX) and "Shot? so quick, so clean an ending?" (*A Shropshire Lad*, XLIV) are intended as no more than poetic license. Death is seen as the final, desirable release from the Sisyphean exhaustion of living. Thanatos ultimately leads to suicide, which in several of the poems is prescribed as the best antidote for the illness of life. Other strategies for coping with the suffocating consciousness of "our long fool's-errand to the grave" are hedonism and, more logically, stoicism.

In Housman's hedonistic poems, the traditional sexuality of the *carpe diem* theme has been eliminated. In his most rousing invitation to pleasure, "Think no more lad" (*A Shropshire Lad*, XLIX), the lad is told to "be jolly/ Why should men make haste to die?" Such pleasures as "jesting, dancing, drinking" stave off the darkness, since "'tis only thinking/ Lays lads underground." The other exercises in hedonism are more subdued. The speaker of "Loveliest of trees" (*A Shropshire Lad*, II), aware of his limited time, will go about the woodlands "To see the cherry hung with snow," and "The Lent Lily" (*A Shropshire Lad*, LXXIX) invites anyone who will listen to enjoy the spring and gather all the flowers that die on Easter day. In "Reveille" (*A Shropshire Lad*, IV), the lad is enjoined to rise and enjoy the morning, for "Breath's a ware that will not keep/ Up, lad: when the journey's over/ There'll be time enough to sleep." "Ho, everyone that thirsteth" (*More Poems*, XXII) makes an effective use of the living waters of Scripture as a metaphor of fulfillment. The poem concludes that "he that drinks in season/ Shall live before he dies," but the "lad that hopes for heaven/ Shall fill his mouth with mold."

Stoicism is a more satisfying way of coming to grips with the human condition, and it provides the basis for several of Housman's most rewarding poems, including "The Oracles" (*Last Poems*, XXV), "The Sage to the Young Man" (*More Poems*, IV), and "The chestnut casts his flambeaux" (*Last Poems*, IX). In this last poem, an embittered young man drinking in a tavern deplores the passing of another spring and curses "Whatever brute and blackguard made the world" for cheating his "sentenced" soul of all that it has ever craved. Then with dramatic suddenness, he sees that "the troubles of our proud and angry dust/ Are from eternity," and this leads to his stoic affirmation that "Bear them we can, and if we can we must." The idea here that human misery is both certain and universal is the central focus of such powerful poems as "The First of May" (*Last Poems*, XXXIV), "Westward on the high-hilled plains" (*A Shropshire Lad*, LV), and "Young is the blood" (*More Poems*, XXXIV). In "Young is the blood," the speaker identifies his own pain in a youth he espies whistling along the hillside highway and proclaims in the succession of the generations "that the sons of Adam/ Are not so evil-starred/ As they are hard." This is the heart of Housman's stoicism, and this is one of his more honest and successful poems.

In a number of Housman's poems, the universalization of the existential predicament embodies a vision of the remote past that suggests the ultimate insignificance of everything. The speaker of "When I watch the living meet" (*A Shropshire Lad*, XII) is reminded by the moving pageant filing through the street of the dead nations of the past where "revenges are forgot/ And the hater hates no more," just as the speaker of "On Wenlock Edge" (*A Shropshire Lad*, XXXI) is put in mind by a storm of "the old wind in the old anger" threshing the ancient Roman city of Uricon. He knows the storm will pass even as "the Roman and his trouble," both now "ashes under Uricon." The perspective shifts to the future in "I wake from dreams" (*More Poems*, XLIII) and "Smooth between sea and land" (*More Poems*, XLV), which present visions of apocalyptic dissolution.

The poetry of Housman is the poetry of negation. Most of it is shot through with a nameless melancholy and much of it is pessimistic. His lyrics invite comparison with Hardy's, with which they are often included in anthologies, but they reflect none of Hardy's moral depth. They are closer in spirit to those of Heinrich Heine, whom Housman mentioned as one of the three major influences on his work, along with the English ballads and the songs of William Shakespeare. Housman's *Weltschmerz* struck a deep chord in two generations of English readers, making *A Shropshire Lad* and *Last Poems* two of the most popular volumes of poetry of their period. Today, Housman's reputation is tempered by the knowledge that his poetry, though capable of creating haunting moods, neither expands nor deepens one's self-awareness nor one's awareness of life, despite his claim in "Terence, this is stupid stuff" (*A Shropshire Lad*, LXII) that it prepares one for life's rigors. For this reason Housman must be considered a minor poet.

Robert G. Blake

Other major works

NONFICTION: *The Application of Thought to Textual Criticism*, 1922; *The Name and Nature of Poetry*, 1933; *Introductory Lecture*, 1937; *Selected Prose*, 1961 (John Carter, editor); *The Confines of Criticism*, 1969; *The Letters of A. E. Housman*, 1971 (Henry Maas, editor); *The Classical Papers of A. E. Housman*, 1972 (J. Diggle and F. R. D. Goodyear, editors).

MISCELLANEOUS: *M. Manilii Astronomicon Liber Primus*, 1903 (edited); *Ivnii Ivvenalis Satvrae*, 1905 (edited); *M. Manilii Astronomicon Liber Secundus*, 1912 (edited); *M. Manilii Astronomicon Liber Tertius*, 1916 (edited); *M. Manilii Astronomicon Liber Quartus*, 1920 (edited); *M. Annaei Lvcani Belli Civilis Libri Decem*, 1926 (edited); *M. Manilii Astronomicon Liber Quintus*, 1930 (edited).

Bibliography

Graves, Richard Perceval. *A. E. Housman: The Scholar-Poet*. London: Routledge & Kegan Paul, 1979. A fine, balanced biography, drawing on material previously unpublished from public and private sources. Especially significant is Graves's reconciliation of Housman's romantic poetry and classical scholarship. Extensive notes and a bibliographical essay make this volume an especially useful study.
Haber, Tom Burns. *A. E. Housman*. Boston: Twayne, 1967. A biographical study of the poet with separate chapters on his major collections of poetry, two chapters on "literary tastes and influences," and a "retrospect and summing-up." Extensive notes, references, and an annotated bibliography make this book a valuable introductory work, although superseded, in some respects, by later biographies.
Leggett, B. J. *Housman's Land of Lost Content: A Critical Study of "A Shropshire Lad."* Knoxville: University of Tennessee Press, 1970. Contending that *A Shropshire Lad* contains most of Housman's enduring poems, Leggett provides a painstaking analysis of its structure and its theme ("the problem of change"). Leggett aims to shift discussion away from Housman's personality. The bibliography is especially helpful in bringing together the fragmentary and scattered commentary on Housman.
_____. *The Poetic Art of A. E. Housman*. Lincoln: University of Nebraska Press, 1978. A useful study divided by topics: the use of metaphor,

nature poetry, structural patterns, Housman, T. S. Eliot, and "critical fashion in the thirties." Leggett devotes two chapters to Housman's theory and practice of poetry, since this has been a contested point in literary criticism. Supplemented by extensive notes but no bibliography.

Page, Norman. *A. E. Housman: A Critical Biography*. New York: Schocken Books, 1983. A succinct account drawing on published and unpublished sources, with separate chapters on Housman's classical scholarship and the development of his poetry. The introduction is especially helpful on the biographer's method, on his evaluation of previous biographies, and on his decision to separate discussions of the life and the work.

Ricks, Christopher, ed. *A. E. Housman: A Collection of Critical Essays*. Englewood Cliffs, N.J.: Prentice-Hall, 1968. The learned introduction concentrates on the quality and critical reception of the poet's work. The collection includes several fine essays by distinguished poets and critics. The list of important dates in Housman's life is sketchy, and the brief bibliography is out of date.

SUSAN HOWE

Born: Boston, Massachusetts; June 10, 1937

Principal poetry

Hinge Picture, 1974; *The Western Borders*, 1976; *Secret History of the Dividing Line*, 1978; *Cabbage Gardens*, 1979; *The Liberties*, 1980; *Pythagorean Silence*, 1982; *Defenestration of Prague*, 1983; *Articulation of Sound Forms in Time*, 1987; *A Bibliography of the King's Book: Or, Eikon Basilike*, 1989; *The Europe of Trusts*, 1990; *Singularities*, 1990.

Other literary forms

Susan Howe has also published several reviews and *My Emily Dickinson* (1985). This last, a book-length consideration of Dickinson's work, elucidates the poetry not only of its subject but also of its author, and it is central to an understanding of her oeuvre.

Achievements

In the years since she began to publish her poetry, Howe has established herself as a poet of profound engagement with the problematic of Being in the era she confronts. Her work also addresses the meaning of being American and being a woman, in order to strip away obsolete ideas concerning both America and Woman, the better to discover the realities of these conditions in the present.

Because her poetry is engendered both by a close attention to the minims of language and by a constant examination of the ground from which the language stems, Howe has come into association with the group known as the Language Realists, publishing in the magazines of that movement as well as in several anthologies predominantly or wholly of Language Realism: *The L = A = N = G = U = A = G = E Book* (1984), *21 + 1 American Poets Today* (a bilingual edition, 1986), *In the American Tree* (1986), and *Language Poetry* (1987).

Howe has twice received the American Book Award of the Before Columbus Foundation, in 1982 for *Pythagorean Silence* and again in 1985 for *My Emily Dickinson*. In 1980, she received a Pushcart Prize for "The Art of Literary Publishing," an interview she conducted with James Laughlin; in 1986, she was awarded a Writer's Fellowship by the New York State Arts Council; in 1989, she received a second Pushcart Prize. In 1985, she participated in the Colloquium on New Writing held by the Kootenay School for Writers in Vancouver, Canada, and in that same year was writer-in-residence at New College in San Francisco. In 1986, she spoke on Emily Dickinson to a conference on H. D. and Emily Dickinson held at San Jose State University. In

1989, a complete issue of a journal called *The Difficulties* was devoted to discussion of her work.

Biography

Susan Howe was born in Boston, Massachusetts, on June 10, 1937. With the exception of a relatively brief period in Buffalo, New York, her childhood and adolescence were spent in Boston and Cambridge, where she attended the Beaver Country Day School, from which she was graduated in 1955. Also in 1955, she began a year's study at the Gate Theater, Dublin, Ireland, acting and designing sets. From 1957 to 1961, she attended the Museum School of Fine Arts in Boston. She next took up residence in New York City, working as a painter and exhibiting her paintings at a number of galleries, including the Kornblee. In 1961 she married Harvey Quaytman, and their daughter Rebecca was born that same year. When her marriage ended in 1966, Howe began living with the sculptor David von Schlegell, and in 1967, their son Mark was born. The couple was married in 1976.

In 1971, Howe moved to Guilford, Connecticut, which she made her residence for nearly twenty years. From 1975 to 1980, she produced the program *Poetry* for WBAI, New York City's Pacifica Radio station. In 1988-1989, she was Butler Fellow at the State University of New York, Buffalo, where she stayed on to teach; in 1990-1991, she was a visiting professor of writing at Temple University in Philadelphia.

Analysis

Susan Howe's poetry challenges habitual assumptions on many levels, but the level the reader is most likely to notice first is the syntactic; what Howe says of Dickinson can with equal force be applied to herself: "In prose and poetry she explored the implications of breaking the law just short of breaking off communication with a reader." Generally, Howe's poems make much use of the page, where the white space is allowed to interrupt the sequence of print, so that a variety of statements may be derived from relatively few phrases, and the overall thrust of the syntax is continually thwarted. Denied easy access to an overarching meaning, the reader must work with smaller units (phrase, line, couplet) and can only gradually constitute the meaning of the whole. This process parallels the approach to Being advocated both explicitly and implicitly in Howe's work. The presumptions of categorical value which modern Western culture persists in advocating are resisted at every turn, for Howe sees (and reveals) just how damaging such presumptions and categories can be. Often, she labors to construct a fresh view of her subject, be it Esther Johnson (known to Jonathan Swift's readers as Stella), Emily Dickinson, or Jonathan Edwards. To this end, Howe employs the various devices of deconstruction, notably the fracturing of sentence, phrase, or even word.

Such a project inevitably must challenge received notions of the poetic. It is for this reason that traditional forms are absent from Howe's poetry. Such forms by their very ease of recognition would defeat her purpose. To arouse the critical faculties in her reader, Howe must abjure whatever constructions might encourage a reader to glide effortlessly onward: the work must be difficult, not only to reflect accurately the difficulty of living but also to remind the reader at each turn of his or her preconceptions concerning the nature of reality, art, and the very act of reading. For Howe, as for other poets wedded to this task, the question then becomes, What portion of the inherited conceptions of beauty, truth, and the good ought to be retained (as inherent to the art of poetry), and what portion uprooted and discarded (as inimical to a faithful representation of the present)? Language, derived from Being, comes then to govern Being; the reader projects back onto the world expectations previously drawn therefrom: yet the world is always in process, always changing, always endangering our assumptions and rendering them obsolete. It is therefore to language itself, argue poets who share Howe's address, that the poet ought to draw attention; the reader must be kept aware of the ways in which language governs not only one's concepts but also one's perceptions, and it is for this reason that Howe through "parataxis and rupture" never lets her readers forget the effect of words and phrases on content. Content, in fact, always includes the agony of choice, whether it be the deliberations as to formal procedure or their counterparts in other modes of action.

"The lyric poet," Howe writes in *My Emily Dickinson*, "reads a past that is a huge imagination of one form," and while the labor of precursors in one sense is enormously beneficial, providing as it does countless elucidations of Being, in another sense it becomes a mighty burden, because of the irresistible nature of preexisting formulations, whether to the poet or to her audience, formulations which nevertheless demand to be resisted if one is to come to a personal definition of one's epoch. Howe, then, in her determination to "make it new," aligns herself with such high modernists as Ezra Pound, Gertrude Stein, and William Carlos Williams, although she must also—for the reasons given above—keep her project distinct from theirs. The world in the 1970's and 1980's is far from the world of the 1910's and 1920's; Howe is among those who see the poet's calling as a demand to make forms consonant with her own day.

The analysis provided during the 1960's and 1970's of dominant patriarchal elements in Western society is one example of this altered ideology to which Howe would be responsible. Therefore *The Liberties*, a book of poetry whose sufficient cause is the largely masculine-engendered version of Esther Johnson, known—and it is the commonality of this means of recognition Howe intends to attack—as Dean Swift's Stella. Howe would liberate from this patriarchal version another picture of this historical personage. As she writes in another context (in her analysis of the received idea we termed "Emily

Dickinson"): "How do I, choosing messages from the code of others in order to participate in the universal theme of Language, pull SHE from all the
myriad symbols and sightings of HE?" In *The Liberties*, Howe begins by
providing a prose sketch, "Fragments of a Liquidation," whose import can
best be summarized by repeating the last two sentences of its first paragraph:
"Jonathan Swift, who gave allegorical nicknames to the women he was romantically involved with, called her 'Stella.' By that name she was known to
their close friends, and by that name she is known to history." The poems
that follow spring from Howe's desire to liberate Esther from Stella and, by
extension, Howe's own self from equally pernicious assumptions. In practice,
it is not always possible to distinguish from each other these twin liberations,
and so a composite woman, struggling to be freed from the roles provided
for her by men and a male-dominated history, becomes the shadow heroine
of Howe's pages.

   If the method is to question in this manner, and to reconstitute a truer
history, the technique that Howe develops and that is consonant with her
method is to call meaning into question not only at the level of the sentence
(these poems are so severely underpunctuated that the reader usually must
decide the limits of the sentence) but also at the level of the phrase or even
the word. One poem, for example, begins "and/ she/ had a man's dress mad/
e/ though her feet ble/ d/ skimming the surf/ ace," a series of ruptures which
militates against any "skimming of the surface" on the reader's part.

   In a subsequent section of *The Liberties*, Howe extends her attention to
William Shakespeare's Cordelia, surely attractive to Howe for her refusal to
accede to the patriarchal demand to accord with the picture of herself her
father wished to perpetuate. This section, titled "White Foolscap," puns on
"fool's cap" and thus reminds the reader that Cordelia is a dramatic character whose only "real" context is the play *King Lear*, complete with Fool. Yet
the title also refers to the blank page that the writer addresses: metaphorically, the nothingness into which she throws herself, composing. In the next
section, "God's Spies," a playlet, Stella and Cordelia meet, together with
the ghost of Jonathan Swift; the women are dressed as boys in their early
teens. The action is fragmented, the dialogue sparse, truncated, enigmatic.
The longest speech is Stella's, a poem the historical Stella wrote, very much
in the manner of Swift: When it is done, Stella shoots herself. To so sink
herself in the style of another, Howe is saying, is tantamount to suicide.

   The third and final section of *The Liberties*, "Formation of a Separatist,
I," is prospective, as the previous sections were retrospective. Howe has composed these poems of isolated words—single words with white space between
each, arranged in blocks—and celebrates their individual tones, rather than
their syntactic possibilities. There are, however, other poems in this section
which depend upon phrases and sentences; in fact, the book ends with these
lines: "Tear pages from a calendar/ scatter them into sunshine and snow." The

nightmare of history disperses into a present which is subject to elements in their own nature.

Pythagorean Silence is also divided into three sections: the first, "Pearl Harbor," opens with a poem titled "Buffalo, 12.7.41" and the announcement of the cataclysm that has unleashed such terrible forces upon the second half of the century, the cataclysm that has so thoroughly trammeled survivors and inheritors in an ethical dilemma that becomes, for the artist, an aesthetic dilemma as well. Theodor Adorno, the German theoretician of art and society, averred that it has become impossible, since Auschwitz, to write poetry; the tens of millions murdered since 1941 cry out whenever Being is addressed. A character in Howe's poem, who is called TALKATIVE, "says we are all in Hell": Howe suggests that a truer use of language, one less suspect (in Howe's world and work, all talking *about* things is seen as vitiated by its own remove), can be found in biblical Rachel's inconsolable cry: "her cry/ silences/ whole/ vocabularies/ of *names*/ for *things.*" The problem with the declaration that we are all in Hell arises from the clichéd nature of the phrase, which works against an experience of its meaning. Howe's "negative poetry" would undo prior namings where these have become impenetrably familiar. This is why she nudges her poems along through puns: in the pun, other meanings break through the intended singularity of usage, the law of logical syntax is transgressed by the play of several possibilities. "Connections between unconnected things are the unreal reality of Poetry," she asserts in *My Emily Dickinson*.

In section 2, the title section of *Pythagorean Silence*, the initial poem opens with a pun arising from the fracturing of a single word: "He plodded away through drifts of i/ ce." "Drifts of i" suggests the accumulation of personal, even egocentric, experience, with "drifts" implying the contingent nature of such accumulations, accrued as "the wind listeth." The line's extension equates "i" with "ice"—a frozen lump of such subjectivity. Yet Pythagoras broke through the amassed subjectivity of his experience to accomplish, with his theorem, the objective; to the extent that he is the hero of this sequence and this book, Howe implicitly urges emulation of his persistence. The "silence" of her title—which Howe discovered in a footnote in E. R. Dodd's *The Greeks and the Irrational*—refers to the silence maintained by initiates of the Pythagorean rites prior to their more active worship, a form of meditation. Indeed, the impression of her poetry is of (to echo William Butler Yeats) "speech after long silence," a use of language directly opposed to unthinking, unfeeling chatter.

Notice should be taken, however, of Howe's statement in *My Emily Dickinson:*

at the center of Indifference I feel my own freedom . . . the Liberty in wavering. Compression of possibilities tensing to spring. Might and might . . . mystic illumination of analogies . . . instinctive human supposition that any word may mean its opposite. Occult tendency of opposites to attract and merge.

Taking this as a rule of thumb and applying it to the claim that Pythagoras is the hero in her book, the reader will consider the possibility that he is also the villain, capable of leading the unsuspecting into frozen wastes of abstruse speculation. Nor will this afterthought annul the previous reading, but rather coexist with it. Howe's greatest clarity lies in her ability to imply and exemplify the insupportable partiality of any single answer.

Single answers, after all, like universal concepts, are acts of enclosure, a delimiting of the possible; historically, they have been imposed by men upon women and children, by imperialists upon territories hitherto regarded as "unknown," terra incognita, full of hidden terrors—even as women and children for the dominant male. Howe herself, in an article published in *Politics and Poetic Form* (edited by Charles Bernstein; New York: Segue, 1989), addresses these issues, remarking that that sum of single answers, knowledge, "no matter how I get it, involves exclusion and repression." She continues

National histories hold ruptures and hierarchies. On the scales of global power what gets crossed over? Foreign accents mark dialogues that delete them. . . . When we move through the positivism of literary canons and master narratives, we consign our lives to the legitimation of power, chains of inertia, an apparatus of capture.

It has become part of the burden of Howe's poetry to make plain enough these concerns, to confront, although at oblique angles, readers with modes of capture and unfreedom of which they may have been unaware. Her method is to locate the mortmain of the past in documents—demotic narratives of escape and capture, for example—of the past, and in instanced persistence of past patterns into the conduct of the present. In this second endeavor, she may take herself as instance, although the work never resembles autobiography in any of its conventional senses. When all is said and done, however, a poem itself is a form of enclosure, even as the choice of a place of one's own, an affirmation of belonging (as in Howe's case, being a New Englander). Clearly, then, such acceptance of limitation can be a source of strength, succor, and enabling. Even though Howe admits that all power is unstable, she does not deny its existence. There is a push-pull in her poetry, then, between the need for limits and a suspicion of them: Are they freely elected? Or are they imposed from without?

Inescapably, Howe is, by birth and gender, both American and a woman, subject to the assumptions of those categories, and at once in revolt against such predications and eager to discover their underlying realities. In *My Emily Dickinson*, she would rescue the Dickinson of her particular vision from the several inadequate characterizations which prevent, to Howe's view, a full experience of the poetry. To this end, Howe, in a work that is cousin to both

William Carlos Williams' *In the American Grain* (1925) and Charles Olson's *Call Me Ishmael* (1947), rereads the contribution of figures vital to Dickinson's production: Elizabeth Barrett Browning and Robert Browning, James Fenimore Cooper, Emily Brontë, Charles Dickens, Jonathan Edwards, Ralph Waldo Emerson, Cotton Mather, Mary Rowlandson, William Shakespeare, Henry David Thoreau, and Thomas Wentworth Higginson. Howe finds that, approached from this rich assortment of angles, Dickinson's poetry yields a wealth of information about Being in general, but also about being American and being a woman, and about how a poetry grows consanguineously. Howe is severe with certain feminist critics who, while lauding Dickinson, laud a Dickinson who is essentially the creation of patriarchal vision, swallowing whole this distortion. Toward the end of *My Emily Dickinson*, Howe observes: "Victorian scientists, philosophers, historians, intellectuals, poets, like most contemporary feminist literary critics—eager to discuss the shattering of all hierarchies of Being—didn't want the form they discussed this in to be shattering." Howe's poetic practice is the negation of this widespread and persistent error.

David Bromige

Other major works

NONFICTION: *Religious Literature of the West*, 1971 (with John Raymond Whitney); *My Emily Dickinson*, 1985.

Bibliography

Campbell, Bruce. "Ring of Bodies/Sphere of Sound." *The Difficulties* 3, no. 2 (1989). According to Campbell, Howe "is a kind of post-structuralist visionary." He explains that this "means that, while attuned to a transcendental possibility, she is fully aware of how mediated both language and consciousness are." While she must therefore explore history, she mistrusts it, and cannot "accept it as truth."

Chamberlain, Lori. Review of *Defenestration of Prague*, by Susan Howe. *Sulfur* 9 (1984). A useful look at this book—a sound, informal approach, which is the one that yields the best results for this poet. Chamberlain sees heterogeneity as always threatening to undermine unity in this work. Howe, Chamberlain notes, overlays self-remembering via various allegories with her remembering of Ireland. Chamberlain finds the final section "the most uneven," containing "lists of words that do not invite the reader's participation in this archeology of memory."

DuPlessis, Rachel Blau. "'Whowe' On Susan Howe." In *The Pink Guitar*. New York: Routledge, Chapman & Hall, 1990. A comprehensive review of Howe's work, from a feminist viewpoint: "Howe appears to be on the cusp between two feminisms: the one analyzing female difference, the other 'feminine' difference. For the latter, she is close to Julia Kristeva, who evokes marginality, subversion, dissidence as antipatriarchal motives beyond all limits." DuPlessis is a thoroughly informed adjudicator of postmodern poetry; this is an excellent essay.

O'Brien, Geoffrey. "The Way We Word." *The Village Voice Literary Supplement*, December, 1990. Deeper than most journalistic notices, this article provides some firm handles for raising Howe's work to consideration. "The complex structures, images and narratives Howe evokes [are] not written down; they exist in the margins of what *is* written down." O'Brien notes Howe's use of "runes, scratches, accretions of speech" and a vocabulary that "restores an awareness of the immensity of a single word."

Quartermain, Peter. "And The Without." *The Difficulties* 3, no. 2 (1989). Finds Howe more subject to language than master thereof—approvingly, for this brings her poetry nearer to experience, creating a reality that culture seldom acknowledges. Quartermain reads text meticulously and succeeds in giving the impression that this is an excellent way to read Howe's poems.

LANGSTON HUGHES

Born: Joplin, Missouri; February 1, 1902
Died: New York, New York; May 22, 1967

Principal poetry

The Weary Blues, 1926; *Fine Clothes to the Jew*, 1927; *Dear Lovely Death*, 1931; *The Negro Mother*, 1931; *The Dream Keeper and Other Poems*, 1932; *Scottsboro Limited*, 1932; *A New Song*, 1938; *Shakespeare in Harlem*, 1942; *Jim Crow's Last Stand*, 1943; *Lament for Dark Peoples*, 1944; *Fields of Wonder*, 1947; *One Way Ticket*, 1949; *Montage of a Dream Deferred*, 1951; *Selected Poems of Langston Hughes*, 1959; *Ask Your Mama: Or, 12 Moods for Jazz*, 1961; *The Panther and the Lash: Or, Poems of Our Times*, 1967.

Other literary forms

In addition to his prolific production of poetry, Langston Hughes wrote, translated, edited and/or collaborated on works in a number of other genres. He wrote two novels, *Not Without Laughter* (1930) and *Tambourines to Glory* (1958), and produced several volumes of short stories, including *The Ways of White Folks* (1934), *Laughing to Keep from Crying* (1952), and *Something in Common and Other Stories* (1963). Hughes's short fiction also includes several collections of stories about his urban folk philosopher, Jesse B. Semple (Simple): *Simple Speaks His Mind* (1950); *Simple Takes a Wife* (1953); *Simple Stakes a Claim* (1957); *The Best of Simple* (1961); and *Simple's Uncle Sam* (1965).

Hughes published several works for young people, including the story *Popo and Fifina: Children of Haiti* (1932), with Arna Bontemps; biographies of black Americans in *Famous American Negroes* (1954), *Famous Negro Music Makers* (1955), and *Famous Negro Heroes of America* (1958); and a series of "first book" histories for young people, such as *The First Book of Negroes* (1952), *The First Book of Jazz* (1955), and *The First Book of Africa* (1960). Hughes's histories for adult readers include *Fight for Freedom: The Story of the NAACP* (1962) and two pictorial histories in collaboration with Milton Meltzer, *A Pictorial History of the Negro in America* (1956) and *Black Magic: A Pictorial History of the Negro in American Entertainment* (1967). Other experimental volumes of photo essays are *The Sweet Flypaper of Life* (1955), with photographs by Roy De Carava, and *Black Misery* (1969), with illustrations by Arouni.

Major translations by Hughes include *Cuba Libre* by Nicolás Guillén (1948), with Ben Carruthers; *Gypsy Ballads*, by Federico García Lorca (1951); and *Selected Poems of Gabriela Mistral* (1957).

Hughes was also productive as a playwright, although his plays did not enjoy much critical or financial success. They include *Mulatto* (1935); *Little*

Ham (1936); *Simply Heavenly* (1957), based on the characters in his Simple stories; and *Tambourines to Glory* (1963), adapted from his novel. The last play was billed as a "gospel song-play," and Hughes created four other plays in that category: *Black Nativity* (1961), *Gospel Glory* (1962), *Jerico-Jim Crow* (1964), and *The Prodigal Son* (1965). These productions are of interest mainly because they underscore Hughes's heartfelt sympathy with the black folk life of America, a love affair he carried on throughout his works.

Hughes wrote the libretti for several operas, a screenplay—*Way Down South* (1942), with Clarence Muse—radio scripts, and song lyrics. His most famous contribution to musical theater, however, was the lyrics he wrote for Kurt Weill and Elmer Rice's musical adaptation of Rice's *Street Scene* (1947).

Over the years, Hughes also wrote several nonfiction articles, mainly focused on his role as a poet and his love of black American music—jazz, gospel, and the blues. Perhaps his most important article was his first: "The Negro Artist and the Racial Mountain," published in *The Nation* on June 23, 1926, in defense of the idea of a black American literary style, voice, and subject matter.

Anthologies of Hughes's work include *The Langston Hughes Reader* (1958), and *Five Plays* (1963), edited by Walter Smalley. Hughes himself edited many volumes of work by black American writers, including *The Poetry of the Negro, 1746-1949* (1949), with Arna Bontemps; *The Book of Negro Folklore* (1959), also with Bontemps; *New Negro Poets: U.S.A.* (1964); *The Book of Negro Humor* (1966); and *The Best Short Stories by Negro Writers: An Anthology from 1899 to the Present* (1967).

Finally, there are the two volumes of autobiography, *The Big Sea: An Autobiography* (1940) and *I Wonder as I Wander: An Autobiographical Journey* (1956). A planned third volume was not completed.

Achievements

All of his works illustrate the depth of Hughes's commitment to a celebration of black American life in all its forms and make immediately evident the reason why he has been proclaimed "The Poet Laureate of Black America." As a young poet he won prizes in contests sponsored by *The Crisis* and *Opportunity*, and his first two volumes of poetry, *The Weary Blues* and *Fine Clothes to the Jew*, won critical acclaim. Hughes also won a Harmon Gold Award for his novel *Not Without Laughter*, as well as a Rosenwald Fund Fellowship in the early 1930's, which enabled him to make his first cross-country reading tour.

His stature as a humorist grew from his creation of Jesse B. Semple, also known as Simple, a Harlem barstool philosopher in the tradition of American folk humor ranging from Davy Crockett to Mr. Dooley. Hughes wrote about Simple in columns published in the *Chicago Defender*, begun in the 1940's and continuing into the 1960's. His Simple columns also appeared in the *New*

York Post between 1962 and 1965. Publication of his five books of Simple sketches increased the readership of that sage of Harlem with his views on life in white America.

Although Hughes never had any one big seller, his efforts in so many fields of literary endeavor earned for him the admiration and respect of readers in all walks of life. Certainly, too, Hughes is a major poetic figure of his time and perhaps the best black American poet.

Biography

James Mercer Langston Hughes (the first two names were soon dropped) was born in Joplin, Missouri, on February 1, 1902. His parents, James Nathaniel and Carrie Mercer Langston Hughes, separated when Hughes was young; by the time he was twelve, he had lived in several cities: Buffalo, Cleveland, Lawrence and Topeka, Kansas, Colorado Springs, and Mexico City (where his father lived). Until 1914, however, Hughes lived mainly with his maternal grandmother in Lawrence.

Hughes began writing poetry during his grammar school days in Lincoln, Illinois. While attending Cleveland's Central High School (1916-1920), Hughes wrote his first short story, "Mary Winosky," and published poems in the school's literary publications. The first national publication of his work came in 1921, when *The Crisis* published "The Negro Speaks of Rivers." The poem had been written while Hughes was taking a train on his way to see his father in Mexico City, a visit that the young man dreaded making. His hatred for his father, fueled by his father's contempt for poor people who could not make anything of themselves, actually led to Hughes's being hospitalized briefly in 1919.

Hughes's father did, however, send his son to Columbia University in 1921. Although Hughes did not stay at Columbia, his experiences in Harlem laid the groundwork for his later love affair with the city within a city. Equally important to Hughes's later work was the time he spent at sea and abroad during this period of his life. His exposure to American blues and jazz players in Paris nightclubs and his experiences in Europe, especially in Africa, although brief, provided a rich source of material that he used over the next decades in his writing.

The years between 1919 and 1929 have been variously referred to as the Harlem Renaissance, the New Negro Renaissance, and the Harlem Awakening. Whatever they are called, they were years of rich productivity within the black artistic community, and Hughes was an important element in that Renaissance. While working as a busboy in the Wardman Park Hotel in Washington, D.C., in 1925, Hughes showed some of his poems—"Jazzonia," "Negro Dancers," and "The Weary Blues"—to Vachel Lindsay, who read them during one of his performances that same evening. The next day, Hughes was presented to the local press as "the busboy poet." With that introduction, and with the aid of people such as writer Carl Van Vechten and Walter White (of the NAACP), Hughes's popularity began to grow. He published *The Weary Blues* in 1926 and entered Lincoln University in Pennsylvania, where he completed his college education. The 1920's also saw the publication of his second volume of poems, *Fine Clothes to the Jew*, and the completion of his first novel, *Not Without Laughter*.

During much of the early 1930's, Hughes traveled abroad. He went to Cuba and Haiti during 1931-1932 and joined a group of young writers and students from Harlem on a film-making trip to Russia in 1932-1933. Publishing articles in Russian journals enabled him to extend his own travels in the Far East; he also began to write short stories during that time. By 1934, he had written the fourteen stories that he included in *The Ways of White Folks*.

During the mid-1930's, several of Hughes's plays were produced: *Mulatto* (1935), and *Little Ham* were among them. In the course of having these plays performed, Hughes started the Harlem Suitcase Theatre in 1938, the New Negro Theatre in Los Angeles (1939), and the Skyloft Players of Chicago (1941).

After the publication of his first autobiographical volume, *The Big Sea*, Hughes spent time in Chicago with the group he had founded there. When America entered World War II, Hughes produced material for the war effort, ranging from "Defense Bond Blues" to articles on black American participation in the war. In addition, during the 1940's, he began work on his translations of the poetry of Nicolás Guillén, wrote essays for such diverse magazines as the *Saturday Review of Literature* and *Negro Digest*, wrote the lyrics for *Street Scene*, and published three volumes of poetry: *Shakespeare in Harlem*, *Fields of Wonder*, and *One Way Ticket*.

Also in the 1940's, Hughes "discovered" Jesse B. Semple. Drawing inspiration from a conversation he had in a bar with a worker from a New Jersey war plant—during which the man complained to his nagging girl friend, "You know white folks don't tell colored folks what cranks crank"—Hughes developed the framework for his Simple stories. He combined his own authorial voice, the voice of Simple's learned interrogator (eventually named Boyd), and the voice of Simple himself to weave a mixture of folk humor that has direct ties back to the "old southwest" humor of Mark Twain and his contemporaries.

The next decades saw continued production of poetry and other writing by Hughes. He wrote his pictorial histories and his "first books" for children. He continued his public readings, often accompanied by piano and/or jazz orchestra—a prototype of the Beat poets. His second volume of autobiography, *I Wonder as I Wander*, was published in 1956, and *The Langston Hughes Reader*, an extensive collection of his work in several genres, appeared two years later. The last two volumes of his poetry, *Ask Your Mama* and *The Panther and the Lash*, continued his experimentation with incorporating jazz and folk elements in his poetry.

Hughes spent the last years of his life living and working in Harlem. He encouraged younger black writers, publishing several stories by newcomers in his *The Best Short Stories by Negro Writers*, as well as including works by established older writers such as Ralph Ellison and Richard Wright. Hughes died on May 22, 1967, in Harlem, the city that so inspired and informed his best work. No one caught the magic that Harlem represented during his lifetime in quite the way that Hughes did.

Analysis

Langston Hughes often referred to three poets as his major influences: Paul Laurence Dunbar, Carl Sandburg, and Walt Whitman. If one were to assay which qualities of Hughes's poetry show the influence of which poet, one might say that Hughes got his love of the folk and his lyric simplicity from Dunbar, his attraction to the power of the people—especially urban dwellers—and his straightforward descriptive power from Sandburg, and his fascination with sensual people—people of the body rather than the mind—and his clear sense of rhythm from Whitman. No one would draw such a clear delineation, but the elements described are essential elements of Hughes's poetry. His work explores the humor and the pathos, the exhilaration and the despair, of black American life in ways that are sometimes conventional and sometimes unique. He explored the blues as a poetic form, and he peopled his poems with Harlem dancers, as well as with a black mother trying to explain her life to her son. He worked with images of dreams and of "dreams deferred"; he looked at life in the middle of America's busiest black city and at the life of the sea and of exploration and discovery. Always, too, Hughes examined the paradox of being black in mostly white America, of being not quite free in the land of freedom.

Hughes's first collection of poetry, *The Weary Blues*, contains samples of many of the poetic styles and themes of his poetry in general. The collection begins with a celebration of blackness ("Proem") and ends with an affirmation of the black American's growing sense of purpose and equality ("Epilogue: I, Too, Sing America"). In between, there are poems that sing of Harlem cabaret life and poems that sing the blues. Some of the nonblues poems also sing of a troubled life, as well as an occasional burst of joy. Here, too, are the sea poems drawn from Hughes's traveling experiences. All in all, the sparkle of a love of life in these poems was that which caught the attention of many early reviewers.

The titles of some of the poems about cabaret life suggest their subject: "Jazzonia," "Negro Dancers," "The Cat and the Saxaphone (2 a.m.)," and "Harlem Night Club." "The Cat and the Saxaphone (2 a.m.)" is especially intriguing because it intersperses a conversation between two "jive" lovers with the first chorus of "Everybody Loves My Baby," producing the effect of a jazz chorus within the song's rhythmic framework.

Part of the controversy which flared in the black community during the Harlem Renaissance involved whether an artist should present the "low-life" elements or the more conventional middle-class elements in black American life. Hughes definitely leaned toward the former as the richer, more exciting to portray in his poetry.

Because the blues tradition is more tied to the common folk than to the middle-class, Hughes's interest in the possibilities of using the blues style in his poetry is not surprising. He took the standard three-line blues stanza and made it a six-line stanza to develop a more familiar poetic form; the repetition common in the first and second lines in the blues becomes a repetition of the first/second and third/fourth lines in Hughes's poems. As in the traditional blues, Hughes varies the wording in the repeated lines—adding, deleting, or changing words. For example, here is a stanza from "Blues Fantasy":

> My man's done left me,
> Chile, he's gone away.
> My good man's left me,
> Babe, he's gone away.
> Now the cryin' blues
> Haunts me night and day.

Often exclamation points are added to suggest more nearly the effect of the sung blues.

There are not as many blues poems in this first collection as there are in later ones such as *Fine Clothes to the Jew* and *Shakespeare in Harlem*. (The latter contains a marvelous seven-poem effort entitled "Seven Moments of Love," which Hughes subtitled "An Un-Sonnet Sequence in Blues.") The title poem of his first collection, "The Weary Blues," is an interesting variation because it has a frame for the blues which sets up the song sung by a bluesmaker. The poet recalls the performance of a blues singer/pianist "on Lenox Avenue the other night" and describes the man's playing and singing. Later, the singer goes home to bed, "while the Weary Blues echoed through his head." Over the years, Hughes wrote a substantial number of blues poems and poems dealing with jazz, reflecting clearly his love for the music that is at the heart of the black American experience.

Some of the poems in *The Weary Blues* are simple lyrics. They are tinged with sadness ("A Black Pierrot") and with traditional poetic declarations of the beauty of a loved one ("Ardella"). The sea poems are also, by and large, more traditional than experimental. Again, their titles reflect their subject matter: "Water-Front Streets," "Port Town," "Sea Calm," "Caribbean Sunset," and "Seascape."

A few of these early poems reflect the gentle but insistent protest that runs through Hughes's poems; they question the treatment of black Americans and search for a connection with the motherland, Africa. The last section of the book is entitled "Our Land," and the first poem in the section, "Our Land: Poem for a Decorative Panel," explores the idea that the black American should live in a land of warmth and joy instead of in a land where "life is cold" and "birds are grey." Other poems in the section include "Lament for Dark Peoples," "Disillusion," and "Danse Africaine." Perhaps the most poignant poem in the book is also in this last section: "Mother to Son." The poem is a monologue in dialect in which a mother encourages her son to continue the struggle she has carried on, which she likens to climbing a rough, twisting staircase: "Life for me ain't been no crystal stair./ It's had tacks in it . . . And places with no carpet on the floor—/ Bare." The collection's final poem, "Epilogue" ("I, Too, Sing America"), raises the hope that some day equality will truly be reached in America for the "darker brother" who is forced "to eat in the kitchen/ When company comes." Taken together, the poems of *The Weary Blues* make an extraordinary first volume of poetry and reveal the range of Hughes's style and subject matter.

The next two principal volumes of poetry, *Fine Clothes to the Jew* and *The Dream Keeper and Other Poems*, present more of Hughes's blues poems (the latter volume is primarily in that genre) and more poems centering on Harlem's night life. The final two volumes, *Ask your Mama* and *The Panther and the Lash*, continue the experiment of combining musical elements with poetry and offer some of Hughes's strongest protest poetry.

Ask Your Mama is dedicated to "Louis Armstrong—the greatest horn blower of them all." In an introductory note, Hughes explains that "the traditional folk melody of the 'Hesitation Blues' is the leitmotif for this poem." The collection was designed to be read or sung with jazz accompaniment, "with room for spontaneous jazz improvisation, particularly between verses, when the voice pauses." Hughes includes suggestions for music to accompany the poetry. Sometimes the instructions are open ("delicate lieder on piano"), and sometimes they are more direct ("suddenly the drums roll like thunder as the music ends sonorously"). There are also suggestions for specific songs to be used, including "Dixie" ("impishly"), "When the Saints Go Marchin' In" and "The Battle Hymn of the Republic." As a final aid, Hughes includes at the end of his collection "Liner Notes" for, as he says, "the Poetically Unhep."

Throughout, the poems in *Ask Your Mama* run the current of protest against "the shadow" of racism that falls over the lives of the earth's darker peoples. Shadows frequently occur as images and symbols, suggesting the fear and the sense of vague existence created by living in oppression. "Show Fare, Please" summarizes the essence of the poet's feeling of being left out because he has not got "show fare," but is also suggests that "the show" may be all illusion anyway. Not all the poems are so stark; the humor of Hughes's earlier work is still very much in evidence. In "Is It True," for example,

Hughes notes that "everybody thinks that Negroes have the *most* fun, but, of course, secretly hopes they do not—although curious to find out if they do."

The Panther and the Lash, the final collection of Hughes's poetry, published the year he died, also contains some of his most direct protest poetry, although he never gives vent to the anger which permeated the work of his younger contemporaries. The collection is dedicated "To Rosa Parks of Montgomery who started it all . . ." in 1955 by refusing to move to the back of a bus. The panther of the title refers to a "Black Panther" who "in his boldness/ Wears no disguise,/ Motivated by the truest/ Of the oldest/ Lies"; the lash refers to the white backlash of the times (in "The Backlash Blues").

The book has seven sections, each dealing with a particular part of the subject. "Words on Fire" has poems on the coming of the Third World revolution, while "American Heartbreak" deals with the consequences of "the great mistake/ That Jamestown made/ Long ago"; that is, slavery. The final section, "Daybreak in Alabama," does, however, offer hope. In spite of past and existing conditions, the poet hopes for a time when he can compose a song about "daybreak in Alabama" that will touch everybody "with kind fingers."

The poetry of Langston Hughes is charged with life and love, even when it cries out against the injustice of the world. He was a poet who loved life and loved his heritage. More than any other black American writer, he captured the essence of the complexity of a life that mixes laughter and tears, joy and frustration, and still manages to sing and dance with the spirit of humanity.

Edward E. Waldron

Other major works

LONG FICTION: *Not Without Laughter*, 1930; *Tambourines to Glory*, 1958.

SHORT FICTION: *The Ways of White Folks*, 1934; *Simple Speaks His Mind*, 1950; *Laughing to Keep from Crying*, 1952; *Simple Takes a Wife*, 1953; *Simple Stakes a Claim*, 1957; *The Best of Simple*, 1961; *Something in Common and Other Stories*, 1963; *Simple's Uncle Sam*, 1965.

PLAYS: *Mulatto*, 1935; *Little Ham*, 1936; *Don't You Want to Be Free?*, 1938; *Freedom's Plow*, 1943; *Simply Heavenly*, 1957; *Black Nativity*, 1961; *Tambourines to Glory*, 1963; *Five Plays*, 1963; *Jerico-Jim Crow*, 1964; *The Prodigal Son*, 1965.

NONFICTION: *The Big Sea: An Autobiography*, 1940; *The First Book of Negroes*, 1952; *The First Book of Rhythms*, 1954; *Famous American Negroes*, 1954; *Famous Negro Music Makers*, 1955; *The First Book of Jazz*, 1955; *The First Book of the West Indies*, 1955; *A Pictorial History of the Negro in America*, 1956; *I Wonder as I Wander: An Autobiographical Journey*, 1956; *Famous*

Negro Heroes of America, 1958; *The First Book of Africa*, 1960; *Fight for Freedom: The Story of the NAACP*, 1962; *Black Magic: A Pictorial History of the Negro in American Entertainment*, 1967; *Arna Bontemps—Langston Hughes Letters*, 1980.

TRANSLATIONS: *Masters of the Dew*, 1947; *Cuba Libre*, 1948; *Gypsy Ballads*, 1951; *Selected Poems of Gabriela Mistral*, 1957.

MISCELLANEOUS: *Troubled Island*, c. 1930 (opera libretto); *Popo and Fijina: Children of Haiti*, 1932 (with Arna Bontemps); *Street Scene*, 1947 (lyrics); *The Poetry of the Negro, 1746-1949*, 1949 (with Arna Bontemps); *The Langston Hughes Reader*, 1958; *The Book of Negro Folklore*, 1959 (with Arna Bontemps); *Simply Heavenly*, c. 1959 (opera libretto); *New Negro Poets: U.S.A.*, 1964; *The Book of Negro Humor*, 1966; *The Best Short Stories by Negro Writers: An Anthology from 1899 to the Present*, 1967.

Bibliography

Berry, Faith. *Langston Hughes: Before and Beyond Harlem*. Westport, Conn. Lawrence Hill, 1983. The first biography based on primary sources and interviews, which sets out to re-create the historical context in which Hughes lived and worked. Berry quotes an unusual number of poems in their entirety and includes extensive discussions of his poetry throughout the biography.

Bloom, Harold, ed. *Langston Hughes*. New York: Chelsea House, 1989. An up-to-date collection of some of the best literary criticism of Hughes's works, with several articles on his poetry. Unfortunately, these reprinted essays do not have notes. Bloom's introduction is perfunctory. Supplemented by a useful bibliography and an index.

Emanuel, James A. *Langston Hughes*. Boston: Twayne, 1967. A concise overview of Hughes's extraordinary career as a poet, playwright, literary critic, dramatist, and man of letters. Emanuel takes a thematic approach, showing how Hughes's concerns with his race, prejudice, Harlem, and his own past figure in his individual works. Contains a chronology, an annotated bibliography, and notes.

Miller, R. Baxter. *The Art and Imagination of Langston Hughes*. Lexington: University Press of Kentucky, 1989. Divides Hughes's imagination into the "autobiographical," the "apocalyptic," the "lyrical," the "political," and the "tragicomic." Baxter carefully examines Hughes's technique and style, and each chapter focuses on a poem or other work central to an appreciation and understanding of Hughes's imagination.

Mullen, Edward J., ed. *Critical Essays on Langston Hughes*. Boston: G. K. Hall, 1986. Very useful for its generous selection of contemporary reviews of the poet's work. Separate sections are devoted to articles and essays on Hughes's poetry, prose, and drama. An extensive and well-documented introduction surveys and analyzes the critical reception of the poet's work.

The index is especially useful in sorting through this heterogenous material.

Onwuchekwa, Jemie. *Langston Hughes: An Introduction to the Poetry.* New York: Columbia University Press, 1976. Treats Hughes's poetry in thematic terms, with separate chapters on his "black esthetic," the blues, jazz and other musical forms, his social protest verse, his evocation of the ideal ("the dream"), and the poet's place in the "evolution of consciousness in black poetry." Includes an extensive bibliography and an index.

Rampersad, Arnold. *The Life of Langston Hughes, 1902-1941: I, Too, Sing America.* Vol. 1. New York: Oxford University Press, 1986. Situating the poetry and other works in the context of the times and tracing the development of the writer, Rampersad provides acute interpretations of both Hughes's character and career. Distinguished by its fine style and balance, this volume is the definitive biography of the poet.

TED HUGHES

Born: Mytholmroyd, Yorkshire, England; August 17, 1930

Principal poetry

The Hawk in the Rain, 1957; *Lupercal*, 1960; *Wodwo*, 1967; *Crow*, 1970, revised 1972; *Selected Poems 1957-1967*, 1972; *Cave Birds*, 1975 (revised as *Cave Birds: An Alchemical Cave Drama*, 1978); *Gaudete*, 1977; *Remains of Elmet*, 1979; *Moortown*, 1979; *Selected Poems 1957-1981*, 1982; *River*, 1983; *Flowers and Insects: Some Birds and a Pair of Spiders*, 1986; *Wolfwatching*, 1989.

Other literary forms

Ted Hughes has written many works for children, including *Meet My Folks!* (1961), *The Earth-Owl and Other Moon-People* (1963), *How the Whale Became* (1963), *Nessie the Mannerless Monster* (1964), *The Iron Man: A Story in Five Nights* (1968), *The Coming of the King and Other Plays* (1970), *Moon-Whales and Other Moon Poems* (1976), and *Moon-Bells and Other Poems* (1978). He has several stage and radio plays to his credit; they include *The House of Aries* (1960), *The House of Donkeys* (1965), and *Seneca's Oedipus* (1968), an adaptation.

Hughes is also a prolific editor and anthologist, having edited several volumes by Sylvia Plath and other poets. He has collaborated on translations of works by János Csokits and Yehuda Amichai.

Achievements

Ted Hughes is undoubtedly one of the major British poets of the twentieth century, and probably the most influential English poet of the post-World War II era. His writing began as a reaction to "The Movement" poetry of the 1950's—a poetry marked by understatement, classical restraint, and a refusal to go beyond everyday reality. By contrast, Hughes signed himself as a poet who distrusts the intellect and the narrow conformity of ordinary activity. His poetry embraces the violent life of nature, particularly as exemplified by animals and birds, but also by persons who allow instincts and drives to reveal a language of the heart. He has thus returned English poetry to a romantic tradition, critical of the materialism and soullessness of contemporary society.

He has produced poetry regularly, besides editing and dramatizing, particularly for radio. In 1982 he brought out a significant selection of his poetry. He has also written extensively for children, using fablic, comic, and dramatic genres. He became poet laureate on December 19, 1984—a largely honorary role, but one that carries considerable prestige and bespeaks his acceptance by the British literary establishment.

Biography

Edward James Hughes was born in a small Yorkshire town on the edge of the moors, only a few miles from where the Brontës had lived. His father, William, a carpenter, had been badly wounded in World War I during the Gallipoli landings. Hughes was the youngest of three children. His brother briefly became a gamekeeper; his sister, Olwyn, became an executrix and literary agent for the estate of Sylvia Plath. When Hughes was seven, the family moved to a mining town in south Yorkshire called Mexborough. From the grammar school there, he won an award to the University of Cambridge, and he went to Cambridge in 1951 after two years of national service in the British Air Force. Having changed his major from English to archaeology and anthropology, he was graduated in 1954.

He then did a number of jobs, including teaching. Although he had been writing poetry from the age of fifteen, he wrote little at Cambridge and only attempted to publish locally at first. In 1956 he met Sylvia Plath, who was two years younger than he and was in Cambridge on a Fulbright Fellowship. At the time of their meeting, she was already a published poet. She began to send his poems to magazines and also entered him for a competition in New York for a first volume of poetry. He won with *The Hawk in the Rain*, and through publication his name quickly became known.

Plath and Hughes were married within four months of meeting. He returned with her to the United States in 1957, where they earned their living by teaching and wrote prolifically together. In 1959 they returned to London, Hughes having completed *Lupercal*, helped by a Guggenheim Fellowship. The next year their daughter, Frieda, was born, and the year after that they moved to Devon, in the southwest part of England. Soon after the birth of their second child, Nicholas, in 1962, the marriage collapsed. Plath returned to London and filed for divorce, but during a bitterly cold winter she fell into a deep depression and committed suicide on February 11, 1963.

For some time after Plath's suicide, Hughes wrote only for children. In March, 1969, his new partner, Assia Gutsmann, and her child, Shura, both died tragically. Hughes dedicated *Crow*, a volume that marked a new direction for his poetry, to them. In 1970 he was married to Carol Orchard, the daughter of the Devon farmer whose farm he was leasing. *Moortown* has a large section about his experiences there and shows Hughes returning somewhat to the subject matter of his earlier poetry. Apart from periods in London and Yorkshire, he has continued to live in Devon.

Analysis

Ted Hughes's poetic career has been somewhat cyclical. His first volumes of verse contain individual poetic statements on the nature of the created world, focusing on particular animals, plants, people, and seasons. These poems are intended as explorations of identity, of the thing in itself—following closely the late Victorian poet Gerard Manley Hopkins, whose emphasis in much of his nature poetry was on the "this-ness" or "selfhood" of each created being.

While Hopkins saw such creation as manifestations of the variety and infiniteness of the Creator, Hughes denies the existence of divinity. In the earlier poetry his metaphysical claims are very limited; at most he acknowledges some sort of unconscious inspiration, in the manner of Robert Graves, whose concept of a "White Goddess" as poetic inspiration and creative spirit influenced him heavily, and also of Dylan Thomas, though at first Hughes lacked the exuberance of these poets.

Yet Hughes increasingly felt the need for some sort of philosophical expression for his romanticism. That expression, when it came, was as surprising as it was forceful. The themes of violence that characterize the early poetry are transformed in the cycle of mythological poems *Crow* and *Gaudete* to an anarchic energy that subverts the organizing institutional principles of humankind, as expressed in religion, culture, and rationality. Hughes's need for a mythology to advance his personal poetic development is akin to that of William Butler Yeats, a poet he much admires (he claims that at Cambridge he knew all of Yeats by heart).

Again like Yeats, having established a mythology in the middle part of his career and having made some very powerful poetry out of it, Hughes felt free to leave it to one side. Thus, from *Moortown* onward, his poetry has tended to return to a more specific focus, based on the natural life surrounding him. He has also returned to poems of personal reminiscence and of the ritualized violence of war.

Most of Hughes's poetry has been first published in various poetry magazines and in literary and other journals, although some has been commissioned for specific projects. Critical work on Hughes has been growing steadily since the publication of *The Hawk in the Rain*, which was widely recognized from the first as showing great promise. The poems in this volume can be taken alongside those of *Lupercal*, since their composition must be seen as overlapping. One volume contains forty poems, the other forty-one. Rather more from *Lupercal* find their way into Hughes's 1982 *Selected Poems 1957-1981*. Many of Hughes's most anthologized poems are to be found here—for example, "The Thought Fox," "Hawk Roosting," "Esther's Tomcat," "Six Young Men," "View of a Pig," "An Otter," and "Pike."

Most of these are animal poems that in their specificity, brilliance of imagery, and originality of viewpoint are immediately striking and reasonably accessible. It has been pointed out, as a caution, that only a very limited number of poems in *The Hawk in the Rain* are real animal poems. In fact, to believe that the animals presented are real is to misunderstand the poetry, epitomized in "The Thought Fox," which explicitly states that the place of such animals' existence is in Hughes's imagination, for which memory and observation have only provided the raw materials. The majority of his poems are in fact infused with animal imagery. For example, the protagonist of "Famous Poet" is a monster, the subject of "Secretary" is "like a starling under the bellies of bulls," and "A Modest Proposal" is built around the extended simile of two wolves.

Lupercal is perhaps more obviously about animals, and here the nearest influence is D. H. Lawrence. Lawrence, however, develops more moral sympathy for his creatures than does Hughes, whose attitude is far more ambivalent. Hughes frankly admits to terror at times—for example, in "Pike," whose pond he "fished/ With the hair frozen on my head/ For what might move." The pike, like the hawk and the thrushes, is a perfect killing instrument; this reality both fascinates and horrifies Hughes. He recognizes in these creatures depths of darkness that exist within himself. The Jungian idea of a personal shadow is never far distant. In a number of his poems, including "Pike," "An Otter," and "To Paint a Water Lily," the dualism of natural life is vividly portrayed in terms of the surface and depths of water.

In a more ambitious poem, "Mayday on Holderness," this idea is combined with a geographical image of concentric circles. Starting with "the furnace door whirling with larvae" on a pond, through the generating life of the country in springtime, he sees all such draining into the North Sea, beneath which the dead soldiers of Gallipoli lie still, crying, "Mother, Mother!" The "Mother" is profoundly ambiguous, since it is "motherly summer" that moves on the pond in the apparently endless cycle of regeneration ending in (violent) death.

Few of the other poems in these first two volumes—apart from "Pennines in April" and "Wind," in both of which the landscape is seen in terms of the sea—are what might be called regional. Nevertheless, the sense of a northern English countryside is very strong, especially in its bleakness, its mud, and the sheer struggle required to survive there. A number of poems deal with humans who can survive such conditions—"Roarers in a Ring," "Dick Straightup," and "Crag Jack's Apostasy." More significantly, other survivors are praised, though somewhat enigmatically, in "The Retired Colonel" and the powerful "The Martyrdom of Bishop Farrar." What the characters of these poems possess is a physical courage drawn from the deep wellsprings of natural life. Farrar's courage, therefore, is not so much religious or moral as spiritual, in the Lawrentian sense Hughes later developed.

The title poems of both volumes were omitted from *Selected Poems 1957-1981.* "The Hawk in the Rain," perhaps too reminiscent of Hopkins' "The Windhover," contrasts the earthbound poet, drowning in "the drumming ploughland," to the hawk that "effortlessly at height hangs his still eye." The poet is aware of "the master-/ Fulcrum of violence where the hawk stands still," but the violence emanates not only from the hawk but also toward the hawk, which ultimately crashes to the ground. This awareness of the continuity of forces running through nature, destructive yet energy-giving, is one of the central features of these two volumes. The other title poem, "Lupercalia," celebrates a Roman festival of fertility, Lupercus being a god of prophecy also. The poet perhaps sees himself as a priest celebrating both prophetically and ritualistically the mystery of the fertility of nature, giving birth by sacrificing.

The other group of poems not mentioned so far is the war poems: not of World War II, as might be expected from a poet whose boyhood was spent in that period, but of World War I, in which his father fought (William Hughes was one of the few survivors of a regiment otherwise wiped out). Later poems, such as "Out" (from *Wodwo*) and "Dust As We Are" (from *Wolfwatching*), explain how the young boy heard his father reenacting these traumatic experiences. Clearly, he entered deeply into his father's sufferings, and the impact of the violence of humankind in war must have shaped his perceptions of universal violence.

Between 1960 and 1967 Hughes concentrated on children's poetry and poetic drama. The births of his own two children during these years seem to have moved him to channel his creative effort into working his animal poetry into comic and fablic material. Hughes did a number of school broadcasts, including a reworking of the Orpheus and Euridice myth. This echoes poignantly Hughes's own personal tragedy at this time, the breaking up of his marriage and his wife's subsequent suicide. Undoubtedly, these sad events affected his poetic output immediately, and in the longer term acted as catalysts for radical changes in style and manner.

The volume that collects Hughes's adult poetry of the period, *Wodwo*, reflects this upheaval. Some critics see it as a pivotal volume in Hughes's development; certainly it must be seen as transitional. In this, and in its overall layout, it is very similar to Robert Lowell's *Life Studies* (1959), published not long before. Like Lowell's volume, *Wodwo* contains two sections of poetry sandwiching several prose pieces, some of which are autobiographical. Although Hughes's stay in the United States had brought him into touch with such American poets as Wallace Stevens, Hart Crane, and Lowell, the differences remain striking. The open confessional style that Lowell (and John Berryman) developed is the very opposite of Hughes's private manner of creating poems from which autobiographical details must be excavated skillfully, fragment by fragment.

Wodwo again contains some forty poems, to which a few others were added later. Although the poetry is transitional, Hughes selected a greater proportion of it for his 1982 selection than of any other volume. It moves toward a fablic, allegorical, or mythic approach to animals and plants, as in "The Bear," "The Green Wolf," and "The Howling of Wolves." Each creature in these poems manifests some aspect of a life force, certainly, but in a more ritualistic and metaphysical way than in earlier poems. The title poem tells of some legendary animal seeking its identity, full of questions, exploring the dualism of intention and instinct, of self and not-self. Though still in the romantic tradition, many of the poems seem explicitly antiromantic in sentiment; in "Skylarks," for example, Hughes denies the truth-beauty equation. Despite critical claims to unity, the volume is more a collection of parts: Hughes is still searching for a belief system for his poetic. The arrangement of poems within the volume seems somewhat random, and their internal logic appears arbitrary. The title of one poem, "You Drive in a Circle," is rather apt for the whole collection.

Nevertheless, a number of poems in *Wodwo* do point forward to Hughes's next volume, *Crow*. "Logos," "Reveille," and "Theology" reorder the Adam and Eve story in the simplistic, demotic comic style that typifies *Crow*. The powerful "Pibroch" suggests the medieval sense of the chain of being, while it denies medieval teleology—leaving a bleakness and pessimism caught also in "Wings" and "Gnat Psalm." Hughes's verse, too, is far more experimental in *Wodwo*, ranging from the tight balladlike form of "The Bear" to the loose "Wodwo," in which punctuation and line structures have almost collapsed. Particularly, Hughes is moving away from poetic rhetoric toward the direct speaking voice (as did Lowell), and the isolation of the single line or phrase is exploited as an alternative to stanza form. Thus, even if *Crow* did come as a shock, there had been hints of it previously.

The cycle of *Crow* actually began as a response to an invitation from the American artist Leonard Baskin to write poems to accompany his drawings of mythic animals, particularly a crow that was half bird, half human. Hughes was already aware of the crow in various Native American legends as a trickster figure, and he saw in this image an "object correlative" on which to construct the mythology he needed for his poetic. The volume is subtitled *From the Life and Songs of the Crow*, suggesting that the original intention was, as it had been for Yeats, to construct a full mythology. The complete mythology failed to materialize, however—possibly because of certain irresolvable contradictions in the enterprise—and thus there is very much of a provisional feel to the volume. Later editions have added several more poems, and there seems to be no internal reason that other poems should not be added, deleted, or rearranged. Nevertheless, *Crow* came as a new, powerful, and quite shocking voice in British poetry in the early 1970's, a voice that most reviewers did recognize as once and for all establishing Hughes as a major poet, if not the major poet of his generation.

Hughes's need for myth springs from two explicit causes, with probably two unstated factors also involved. First is his stated rejection of Christianity, its account of creation and of the Creator, and the nature of its spirituality—a rejection arising from his encounter with narrow fundamentalism in the village chapel of his boyhood. His rejection is in some sense reactionary: he still needs Christian myth, especially the account of the Fall. Many of his poems in *Crow* and elsewhere rework the figures of Adam, Eve, and the serpent, introducing Crow as a "wild card" element to suggest a creative principle separate from the God of the Genesis account (see, for example, "Crow's Theology," "Crow Communes," and "Crow's First Lesson").

Second is his rejection of demythologizing rational humanism and the preeminence of the word as logical utterance and rational discourse. In this he follows William Blake and Robert Graves, as he does stylistically. He sees modern Western civilization as having lost its primitive energies through its superficial materialism and its denial of the spirit. For him, though, the spirit is out of nature, not out of Christianity—there is nothing holy about it, nor any moral necessity to it ("A Disaster" and "Crow's Account of St. George" are illuminating in this regard).

These rejections are explicit. Not openly explored yet clearly influential in Hughes's life are the nuclear threat that hung heavily over the world in the 1960's and 1970's and the tragic deaths of two women close to him. There also seems to have been a difficult, unresolved relationship with his mother. At a psychological level, *Crow* could be interpreted as an attempt to exorcise these tragedies and to resolve his feelings toward the women involved (as in "Criminal Ballad," "Song for a Phallus," "Crow and Mama," and "Lovesong"). On a political level, the nuclear threat could be seen as a subtext, underlining for him the urgency for Western civilization to find new roots to draw upon, however primitive or pagan.

A new influence on Hughes's style in this period was contemporary East European poetry, especially that of Vasko Popa, whose work he helped to make known in the West. Like Popa, Hughes was interested in colloquial, folktale-like myths as images of survival, and he used poem cycles to build up such mythology. The trickster figure is basically a survivor, although the central contradiction is that usually he stays unchanged, whereas Hughes wants Crow to develop and to take on different roles and guises—as victim, helper, rebel, humankind, even Hughes himself as poet.

Crow is anarchic; so is the verse form. Words mean what Hughes wants them to mean. His rejection of rational discourse is exhilarating, creative, and unpredictable; it is also arbitrary, exasperating, and sometimes sheer nonsense, a total poetic joke. Hughes at times seems bardic, the shaman, willing to be possessed by spiritual forces in order to speak wisdom or healing; at other times he seems a naughty boy writing rude words. Yet "the song was worth it," as he writes in the final enigmatic "Two Eskimo Songs." Here also water finishes up "utterly worn out   utterly clear." The cycle is meant ultimately as a purification of the will to live: what it does not give is a purpose for living.

Gaudete (meaning "rejoice") seeks to resolve some of the contradictions of *Crow* by positing a hero and his shadow (to use a Jungian term), or double. This double is, in fact, the protagonist—the Reverend Nicholas Lumb, acting as substitute vicar for a village (Lumb Bank is actually the name of Hughes's house in Yorkshire). In fact, he sets himself up as high priest of a pagan fertility cult and spends his time bringing to life the latent sexuality of the village women by making love to them. In a climactic scene, a young woman is ritually initiated into the pagan cult but is killed by its priestess (or witch), who is jealous of Lumb, since she suspects that he is human enough to want to elope with the girl. Meanwhile, the village men, out of jealousy and anger, pursue Lumb in a semiritual stag hunt and shoot him. The bodies of the girl, Lumb, and the priestess, who has stabbed herself, are then burned by the men to hide the evidence.

All this main part of the narrative is told in some fifty-five sections of a new, flexible, and pulsating narrative verse, interspersed with passages of poetic prose. The narrative is enfolded by a prologue and an epilogue, which deal with the real vicar, abducted by dark forces out of a dead world in order to heal a woman. For his inability to do this, he is violently beaten in a purgatorial ritual and then resurrected. The fruits of his resurrection, which takes place on the west coast of Ireland, are some forty short, gemlike poems, centering on the theme of suffering and emptying self.

The whole volume is quite extraordinary. Unlike previous volumes, it must be read as a unity—it is impossible to extract, reorder, or add. It is clearly an achieved work: response is one of purgation or catharsis. The mythic basis is Dionysus and his female followers, the Bacchantae, though ritualistic patterns from other fertility cults are also used. In an interview given in 1971, Hughes called his poetry "a war between vitality and death . . . [which] celebrates the exploits of the warriors on either side." In a reworking of Graves's *White Goddess*, he links Venus with Sycorax, a female figure tamed by the Middle Ages into the figure of Mary, and now lost. Western humanism has served Adonis, the god of rationality. *Gaudete* then becomes the reinstatement of Dionysus—and Venus—as the new spiritual force, Adonis having brought a general death.

In this release, however, men and women become totally separated—the men into their violence, their killer instincts, and the women into their unconscious fertility. Normal men-women relationships necessarily break down. The end is destruction and harm, as damaging as anything Adonis brings. Yet by creating Lumb as a duality, Hughes is able to avoid the dichotomy that he elsewhere describes as possible responses to the energy "of the elemental power circuit of the Universe": refusal brings death, but acceptance brings destruction. To escape the dichotomy, one needs the purgatorial experience—not the naked instinctual one, though it is necessary to recognize and embrace the shadow within oneself—and through it to come to some sort of resurrection of spirit. Both Lumbs undergo a death. Out of this comes, at the end, a Dickinsonian distillation of regenerative and intuitive wisdom, cryptically and allusively personal. It rounds off a poem that seeks a way forward (not merely a subversion), as an alternative to both Christianity and modern secularism.

Between *Crow* and *Gaudete*, Hughes produced a number of other volumes, two of which were done in close conjunction with Leonard Baskin. *Cave Birds* was based, like *Crow*, on a series of Baskin drawings of various fablic birds. Hughes then wrote further poems, for most of which Baskin did drawings—some thirty in all. The volume represents a reworking of *Crow* in a much more positive and orderly fashion. A bird—a cockerel to start with— is drawn into the underworld into a Kafkaesque trial scene. As it realizes the guilt of its rationalism, it takes on a series of shifting guises to reach its own hidden psyche. It refuses easy answers, going through execution, a dying to self, until finally it meets (in Jungian fashion) an anima, a female counterpart. Their marriage in "Bride and Groom Lie Hidden for Three Days" suggests renewal through love, reversing poems such as "Lovesong" and "The Lovepet," in which sexual love is shown as purely destructive and possessive. Finally comes resurrection—as a falcon, the Egyptian Horus, a sky god. Thus the book contains a complete cycle of dying and rising, showing the need to die in order to live spiritually. Hughes's final question is "But when will he land on a man's wrist?" At their best, the poems have a beautifully cadenced sensitivity; at worst, they are perhaps too tied to Baskin: Hughes's rhetoric begins to establish itself too easily.

Season Songs was also done with Baskin, but this time Baskin was merely Hughes's illustrator. The pieces in this book were intended for children primarily, but they manifest a delightful marriage of traditional seasonal poetry and the vivid children's poetry of a few years earlier. A number of the poems seem assured of a place in the many anthologies produced for schools. Nature is not romanticized here, but neither is it full of the instinctual violence and bleakness of *Lupercal* or the chaos of *Crow*. "Swifts" and "The Harvest Moon" are good examples of the suppleness of style of which Hughes was now master, and also of his mixing of modern and traditional imagery.

Another volume, *Remains of Elmet*, was produced at this time, in conjunction with the photographer Fay Godwin. A later volume, *River*, was done in the same way. *Remains of Elmet* is a portrait of the region of Hughes's youth, whereas *Season Songs*, anticipating *Moortown*, reflects the Devon countryside and farm where he had settled.

Moortown is a mixed volume, almost an anthology in itself. It incorporates a large section of poems centering on the Devon farm, but written over a period of time as a "verse farming diary," and then several separate sequences or mini-cycles. One of these, "Prometheus on His Crag," had been published separately in 1973, the result of an invitation to take part in a drama festival in Persepolis, Iran. For this occasion Hughes had written a drama, *Orghast*, centered partly on the Prometheus myth. The cycle of poems emerged indirectly from this play as a sort of meditation. For inclusion in *Moortown*, several more were added, making a total of twenty-one. They trace the sufferings of Prometheus from his first awakening to his agony, chained to a rock, as part of his punishment for stealing fire from the gods (though he does not remember doing so), to his trying to identify the full suffering (the vulture pecking at his liver, the heat and the cold, the permanence of the enchainment), to his coming to terms with it. The vulture is even admired for its being a perfect instrument of punishment. The sequence ends with a poem as full of questions as "Wodwo," but also with a sense of acceptance that the poet's humanity is made up of pain and endurance. The poems themselves are in tightly controlled yet very flexible stanzas, with a typical disintegration at the end into isolated lines and phrases. The imagery, again typically, is startling, violent yet lyrical in its dramaticity.

The second sequence is "Adam and the Sacred Nine." Here again, an originally mythic figure holds this shorter cycle together. Each poem describes a different bird that comes to present itself to Adam—not for him to name, as in the Genesis account, but for him to learn from. One or two poems, such as "The Dove Came," are in the *Crow* style; each bird is symbolic or allegorical; and all are far removed from the *Lupercal* treatment. Further sequences are entitled "Earth-Numb" and "Seven Dungeon Songs."

The farming poems are more relaxed and personal, focusing largely on the sufferings and joys of the farm animals in creating new life; births and miscarriages are detailed, almost gratuitously at times, along with deaths and partings of mothers and infants. Certainly the treatment suggests that creation, even with human intervention, works poorly. Nevertheless, the quality of felt experience is powerfully portrayed. In this antipastoral, the reader comes to see Hughes as a compassionate, sensitive farmer.

The farming poems, like *Season Songs*, show Hughes moving away from mythic statements toward more lyrical and personal ones. This tendency continues in *Flowers and Insects* and *Wolfwatching*. In the latter, myth remains in "Two Astrological Conundrums" and "Take What You Want But Pay for It," but "Wolfwatching" is a more orthodox zoo poem, and "The Black Rhino" has an ecological message. Perhaps the most attractive poems here are those of reminiscence, especially concerning his father. The violence of the war poems of *The Hawk in the Rain* is now counterbalanced by a small boy's watching of a shell-shocked father.

Hughes's verse has perhaps lost some of its energy and freshness, but his remarkable productivity and skill are still impressive. Even if neither Christianity nor humanism is on such shaky or bankrupt ground as Hughes perceives them to be, his commitment to the universal human condition and his ability to establish a poetic language for the late twentieth century will ensure for him a central place in an ongoing romantic tradition.

David Barratt

Other major works

SHORT FICTION: *The Threshold*, 1979.

PLAYS: *The House of Aries*, 1960; *The Calm*, 1961; *The Wound*, 1962; *Epithalamium*, 1963; *The House of Donkeys*, 1965; *Seneca's Oedipus*, 1968; *Orghast*, 1971; *Eat Crow*, 1971; *The Story of Vasco*, 1974 (music by Gordon Crosse; adaptation of a play by Georges Schehadé).

RADIO PLAYS: *The House of Aries*, 1960; *A Houseful of Women*, 1961; *The Wound*, 1962; *Difficulties of a Bridlegroom*, 1963; *Dogs*, 1964; *The House of Donkeys*, 1965.

NONFICTION: *Shakespeare's Poem*, 1971; *Henry Williamson: A Tribute*, 1979.

CHILDREN'S LITERATURE: *Meet My Folks!*, 1961; *The Earth-Owl and Other Moon-People*, 1963; *How the Whale Became*, 1963; *Nessie the Mannerless Monster*, 1964 (also as *Nessie the Monster*, 1974); *Poetry in the Makkkilng: An Anthology of Poems and Programmes from "Listening and Writing,"* 1967 (revised as *Poetry Is*, 1970); *The Iron Man: A Story in Five Nights*, 1968 (also as *The Iron Giant*, 1968); *Five Autumn Songs for Children's Voices*, 1969; *The Coming of the King and Other Plays*, 1970 (augmented as *The Tiger's Bones and Other Plays for Children*, 1974); *Orpheus*, 1971 (play); *Spring, Summer, Autumn, Winter*, 1974 (revised as *Season Songs*, 1975); *Earth-Moon*, 1976; *Moon-Whales and Other Moon Poems*, 1976; *Moon-Bells and Other Poems*, 1978; *The Pig Organ: Or, Pork with Perfect Pitch*, 1980 (play; music by Richard Blackford); *Under the North Star*, 1981; *What Is the Truth: A Farmyard Fable*, 1984.

TRANSLATIONS: *Selected Poems*, by Yehuda Amichai, 1968 (with Amichai); *Selected Poems*, by János Pilinszky, 1976 (with János Csokits); *Amen*, by Amichai, 1977 (with Amichai); *Time*, by Amichai, 1979 (with Amichai).

EDITED TEXTS: *New Poems 1962*, 1962 (with Patricia Beer and Vernon Scannell); *Here Today*, 1963; *Five American Poets*, 1963 (with Thom Gunn); *Selected Poems*, by Keith Douglas, 1964; *Ariel*, by Sylvia Plath, 1965; *A Choice of Emily Dickinson's Verse*, 1968; *With Fairest Flowers While Summer Last: Poems from Shakespeare*, 1971 (also as *A Choice of Shakespeare's Verse*, 1971); *Crossing the Water*, by Plath, 1971; *Winter Trees*, by Plath, 1971; *Johnny Panic and the Bible of Dreams, and Other Prose Writings*, by Plath, 1977, augmented 1979; *New Poetry 6*, 1980; *The Collected Poems of Sylvia Plath*, 1981; *The Journals of Sylvia Plath*, 1982 (with Frances McCullough); *1980 Anthology: Arvon Foundation Poetry Competition*, 1982 (with Seamus Heaney); *The Rattle Bag: An Anthology*, 1982 (with Heaney); *Selected Poems*, by Plath, 1985.

Bibliography

Faas, Ekbert. *Ted Hughes: The Unaccommodated Universe*. Santa Barbara, Calif.: Black Sparrow Press, 1980. This is a selection of Hughes's critical writings, including extracts from his introductions to his editions of other poets. There are also two interviews conducted by Faas.

Gifford, Terry, and Neil Roberts. *Ted Hughes: A Critical Study.* London: Faber & Faber, 1981. A very thorough study of Hughes's poetry through his *Moortown* volume. There are particularly full chapters on *Crow, Gaudete,* and *Cave Birds.* Includes a full bibliography and indexes.

Robinson, Craig. *Ted Hughes as Shepherd of Being.* Basingstoke, Eng.: Macmillan, 1989. Robinson examines Hughes in the light of Heidegger's philosophy, seeking his "redefinition of human maturity in our time." He places Hughes firmly in the Romantic tradition, especially of Blake, in his desire for freedom from Enlightenment rationalism. The study covers all Hughes's writings through *Flowers and Insects.* Features a bibliography and an index.

Sagar, Keith. *The Art of Ted Hughes.* 2d ed. Cambridge, Eng.: Cambridge University Press, 1978. One of the earliest admirers of Hughes, Sagar has updated an earlier study to include a consideration of the *Moortown* sequences. Still a definitive study. Its very full bibliographies include citations of translations of Hughes. There is also an index.

Scigaj, Leonard M. *The Poetry of Ted Hughes: Form and Imagination.* Iowa City: Iowa University Press, 1986. This study explores the Oriental influences in Hughes, and how Hughes has sought to augment the modern Western consciousness. Contains a bibliography and an index.

Walder, Dennis. *Ted Hughes.* Philadelphia: Open University Press, 1987. One of the "Open Guides to Literature," this book is written specifically to accompany *Selected Poems, 1957-1981.* It is basically thematic, focusing on Hughes's myths of violence and masculinity, but seeing these tempered by more recent "feminine" poems. Offers suggestions for further reading and includes an index.

RICHARD HUGO

Born: Seattle, Washington; December 21, 1923
Died: Seattle, Washington; October 22, 1982

Principal poetry
A Run of Jacks, 1961; *Death of the Kapowsin Tavern*, 1965; *Good Luck in Cracked Italian*, 1969; *The Lady in Kicking Horse Reservoir*, 1973; *What Thou Lovest Well, Remains American*, 1975; *31 Letters and 13 Dreams*, 1977; *Selected Poems*, 1979; *White Center*, 1980; *The Right Madness on Skye*, 1980; *Making Certain It Goes On: The Collected Poems of Richard Hugo*, 1984.

Other literary forms
Richard Hugo's fiction and essays share the basic concerns of his poetry. *Death and the Good Life* (1982), a detective novel in the Dashiell Hammett-Raymond Chandler tradition, re-creates the familiar landscapes and character types of Hugo's West. Combining psychic exploration and social commentary, Hugo compensates for a somewhat melodramatic plot with an active sense of humor tinged with self-parody. Many of the vignettes in *Death and the Good Life* reveal an affinity with the method of poetic composition described in *The Triggering Town: Lectures and Essays on Poetry and Writing* (1979). The collection serves as both an excellent practical guide to teaching creative writing and an introduction to Hugo's own poetry. Emphasizing sound as a means of overcoming psychological blocks and discovering meaning, Hugo discusses his method of imaginatively reconstructing particular scenes. Before his death, Hugo had published several segments of his autobiography; the book was published posthumously as *The Real West Marginal Way: A Poet's Autobiography* in 1986. Several recordings of his exceptional public readings are available.

Achievements
Hugo's importance derives from his ability to uncover the rich diversity of human experience generated by the alternately barren and breathtaking landscape of the American West. For many younger Western writers, Hugo occupies a position similar to that of William Faulkner in the South. Like Faulkner, Hugo confirms his region's unique identity, exploits the hidden poetry of its idiom, and commands the attention of the national literary community. His regional importance was recognized in 1966 when he won the Northwest Writers Award. He subsequently received a Rockefeller Foundation grant (1967) and a Guggenheim Fellowship (1977-1978). Two of his collections, *The Lady in Kicking Horse Reservoir* and *What Thou Lovest Well, Remains American*, have been National Book Award finalists. The latter volume also received the Theodore Roethke Memorial Poetry Prize in 1976.
Hugo's poetry incorporates modes developed by writers associated with

highly diverse forms. Responding to the call of Walt Whitman and William Carlos Williams for a specifically American poetic language, Hugo's distinctive personal voice also echoes the music of Theodore Roethke and Wallace Stevens. A much less philosophical poet, Hugo shared Stevens' sense of the multiplicity of possible perceptions of any given scene. Hugo's choice of scenes and development of possibilities, however, accords with the emphasis of the Whitman-Carl Sandburg strain of populist poetry. The resulting voice attains a balance of social and aesthetic intensity which establishes Hugo's claim to recognition as one of the leading poets of his generation. Hugo communicated his vision of the emotional complexity of ordinary life with a directness and integrity accessible to both academic and nonacademic readers.

Biography

Richard Franklin Hugo's parents separated when he was twenty months old. His mother, who was about eighteen at the time, had no means to support the child, so left him with her parents, who reared him in the working-class neighborhood of White Center just outside Seattle, Washington. He was born Richard Hogan; his mother remarried in 1927, and he began using the name he is known by when he entered the eighth grade in 1936. Growing up during the Depression, Hugo was surrounded by the poverty which set White Center apart from the more affluent nearby neighborhoods of West Seattle. After serving in the United States Army Air Corps as a bombardier during World War II, Hugo attended the University of Washington, earning his B.A. degree in 1948 and his M.A. in 1952. During these years, he was taught by Theodore Roethke, who exerted a strong influence on Hugo. Following graduation, Hugo worked at the Boeing Aircraft Corporation in Seattle for thirteen years and married for the first time.

Publishing his first volumes while still at Boeing, Hugo left Seattle, spent a year in Italy, then joined the faculty at the University of Montana in 1964. He subsequently taught at Colorado University, the University of Iowa, and the University of Arkansas at Little Rock. While at Iowa in 1970-1971, he suffered the near-breakdown which provides the background of *31 Letters and 13 Dreams.* Hugo also spent several periods abroad. The poems of *Good Luck in Cracked Italian*, the "Scotland" sections of *The Lady in Kicking Horse Reservoir*, and *The Right Madness on Skye* draw on these travels. While living in Missoula with his second wife Ripley, Hugo encouraged the development of many young writers, including Native Americans such as James Welch, while directing the creative writing program at the University of Montana. In 1977, he was appointed editor of the Yale Series of Younger Poets. Hugo died in Seattle in 1982.

Analysis

Richard Hugo's poetry centers on two types of madness: a "wrong madness" of isolation, and a "right madness" of community. Paradoxically, the experience of dispossession provides the foundation for both types. Those who perceive their dispossession—economic, sexual, or psychologial—as purely individual can only talk to themselves or remain silent. Only by recognizing dispossession as a shared experience can they form a community with a language capable of expressing either rage or compassion. Identifying closely with the dispossessed, Hugo seeks to develop a voice embodying his vision of emotionally intense connections with other people, with the land, with his own past, and with the language which allows him to escape the wrong madness of inarticulate disintegration. The origins, though not the boundaries, of this vision are in the American West. Concentrating on specific places and scenes, Hugo emphasizes that their meaning derives as much from the observer's state of mind as from intrinsic elements. Though the scenes themselves, especially in his early poetry, are Western, the states of mind recur throughout the world. Ultimately, Hugo seeks a voice like that of Gilleasbuig Aotram in "The Semi-Lunatics of Kilmuir," a poem set on the island of Skye. Himself "crazy like a dolphin," Aotram leads a band of "lunatics" rejecting the insane economic system where "You pay and pay and own nothing." Encountering a "real crazy" capable only of raving, Aotram addresses him in a voice which connects psychological orientation with social salvation: "'Had you the right madness bread would be secure.'" Directly addressing the reader (whose madness, like that of the "crazy," provides the potential base for an expanded community), the concluding lines reiterate the saving power of place and affirm Hugo's populist faith: "Have the right madness. This land has always passed on/ and, like you, is still here." Connection with the land offers hope, however mad it may seem, for an enduring social and psychological security.

Hugo's distinctive stylistic signatures reflect this emphasis on place, concern with shared experience, and struggle to overcome the wrong madness in the individual. Although many poems vary from the details of the pattern, a typical Hugo lyric describes a specific scene, frequently the social landscape of a town, to an implied audience who may be someone familiar with the scene, an aspect of the persona, or a potential reader such as the one addressed at the end of "The Semi-Lunatics of Kilmuir." Investing the scene with an initial emotional meaning, often derived from some disquieting realistic detail, he explores its psychological implications, frequently leading to a transformation of the original emotional tone. Hugo typically writes in a loosely iambic four- or five-stress line organized into verse paragraphs around shifts in time, scene, or tone. Rarely employing end-rhyme, he uses numerous internal rhymes and sound echoes both to establish prosodic coherence and to reveal emotional possibilities. In his early poems Hugo in fact pledged himself to repeating "interesting" sounds within eight syllables, thereby creating a richness of sound texture which remains in his later work. By concentrating on sound rather than meaning as such, Hugo argues in *The Triggering Town*, he was able to discover emotional connections which had been consciously repressed. This connection between sound and psychological release recurs frequently in Hugo's poetry, where transformed perceptions of the original scene occur in connection with new clusters of sounds.

This basic pattern can be seen clearly in "Degrees of Gray in Philipsburg," perhaps Hugo's finest, and certainly his most widely anthologized single poem. The first line, "You might come here Sunday on a whim," places the persona in Philipsburg and addresses the listener. The next sentence, "Say your life broke down," establishes both the initial tone attached to the scene and the importance of the "you" in relation to the thematic and emotional impact of the poem. This second person exists on two levels, one psychological (as an aspect of the persona) and one social (as a person with whom the persona ultimately shares the experience). Only by coming to terms with the psychological "you" can the persona free himself to react to the red-haired waitress of the final stanza and to communicate with the social "you." Hugo structures the poem around this movement toward increased freedom, especially as it interacts with the persona's changing perception of his immediate surroundings.

Initially, the persona creates a Philipsburg reinforcing the sense of emotional breakdown that he projects onto the second person. Assuming a stance of total dispossession ("The last good kiss you had was years ago"), he perceives only manifestations of the wrong madness. Walking "streets/ laid out by the insane," he imagines only one human inhabitant, a prisoner in jail "not knowing what he's done." Emblems of social isolation are everywhere; two "dead kilns" overlook the town. The persona contemplates a "defeat/ so accurate, the church bell simply seems/ a pure announcement: ring and no one comes." The acceptance of this defeat, simultaneously sexual and social ("no one comes"), culminates in the final stanza in the old man who threatens to "go to sleep and not wake up." Confronted with death as the ultimate price of resignation, however, the persona rebels against this madness which he now sees in himself: "You tell him no. You're talking to yourself." The negation paradoxically effects a transition to an affirmative vision. Where previously the persona encountered only a gray ghost town where "the best liked girls/ . . . leave each year for Butte," he now recognizes the redemptive presence of the slender girl whose "red hair lights the wall." Previously blinded by his memory of sexual dispossession ("the ancient kiss still burning out your eyes"), the persona now sees the sexually charged potential of his surroundings.

Before reaching this epiphany, however, he must come to terms with his own responsibility for the emotional grayness of his initial perception. At first he attempts to evade this responsibility by refusing to identify clearly the broken-down "you" with himself and by focusing only on the aspects of the landscape which indulge his depression. Gazing out at the inaccessible pastures which contrast sharply with "the various grays/ the mountain sends," the persona accepts "rage" as "the principal supporting business of Philipsburg" and "hatred" of the mill that no longer provides economic sustenance but "won't fall finally down." His perception of economic dispossession is accurate but his resignation to isolation is only one of the possible "degrees of gray." Hugo emphasizes the hopelessness of the response with a texture of sound in the second stanza which reinforces the quiescent tone. An almost unbroken flow of extended vowel sounds (rage, hatred, grays, gaze, green, eat, town, down) is accompanied by soothing consonants. Particularly prominent are "l" (mill, bill, repeal, liked, girls, leave), "w" (now, mountain, wipe, known, town, down) and "m" (mountain, mill, mines, memory). The only contrasting sounds occur when the persona describes the 1907 silver boom with a cluster of "b," "v," and "z" sounds. The boom, however, remains in the irrecoverable past. The syntax of the description breaks down—no verb follows the apparent subject "boom"—and the persona's memory "resolves itself in gaze," returning to the dominant sound texture of the stanza. The interlude introduces the sounds which will spur the regeneration of the final stanza, but Hugo leaves them dormant. The sequence of end-rhymes and slant-rhymes of the stanza (now, out, town, down) works in conjunction with the other sounds to emphasize the passive acceptance of dispossession. At no point does the sound pattern allow a break from the flow of depressed perceptions or encourage an emotionally intense response to dispossession.

The persona's movement toward renewed intensity begins with his moment of total despair at the beginning of the third stanza. Seeing nothing but external desolation, he embraces internal isolation and longs for blindness: "Isn't this your life? That ancient kiss/ still burning out your eyes?" The question, despite its attempt to distance the agony by projecting it onto the ambiguous "you," introduces the new pattern of sound and rhythm which reawakens the persona's sense of emotional and sexual possibility. The kiss that existed only "years ago" at the start of the poem similarly assumes a new emotional presence. In essence, the key to this renewal is the persona's discovery of a new voice, one capable of directly expressing the rage which seemed abstract and distant in the second stanza.

In the third stanza, dispossession no longer *sounds* inevitable. The transformed language frees the persona for a clearer perception of psychological and social connections. Consisting of five questions, the stanza phrases each in terms of negation: "Isn't this your life," "Isn't this defeat," "Don't empty houses." Even those not beginning with negatives include negative phrases: "no one comes," "never let you have." Rather than implying deeper resignation, these anticipate the affirmative negations of the final stanza: "Say no to yourself," "You tell him no." In addition, Hugo carefully controls the rhythm of the questions (four, eight, eighteen, four, and thirty-six words long), building from an implied acceptance of "the ancient kiss" to the explicit outrage of: "Are magnesium/ and scorn sufficient to support a town,/ not just Philipsburg, but towns/ of towering blondes, good jazz and booze/ the world will never let you have/ until the town you came from dies inside?" The sound texture of the questions extends that of the preceeding stanza, particularly with the consonants "m" (simply, seems, comes, empty, magnesium) and "w" (town, towns, towering, world, will, town). In order to effect the psychological transition, however, Hugo introduces new patterns of shorter vowels (which allow the tempo to speed up) and sharper consonants, particularly "f" (life, defeat, sufficient, Philipsburg), "s" (this, kiss, isn't, so, simply, seems, scorn, sufficient, dies, inside) and, most important, the thematically crucial "z's." Thinking of "jazz" and "booze," the persona realizes that the "world," the source of his dispossession, ultimately demands total psychic and social isolation. The powerful rhythm combines with the difficult syntax of the question to create a sense of emotional urgency centering on the persona's relationship with his own psychological and social past ("the town you came from").

The climactic negations, therefore, take on an intricate complex of meanings. The determination to "say no" spurs the persona's recognition of the internal level of his conversation/soliloquy: "You're talking to yourself." Rejecting the social madness which offers "magnesium and scorn" as the basis of community, he simultaneously rejects the wrong madness of the old man/ prisoner's resignation to death. These refusals generate a new vision of the landscape he had previously seen as entirely gray. Seeing the "silver" of his money (significantly, the first bright color is also a degree of "gray") and the "red hair" of the girl, the persona achieves new economic and personal awareness. By accepting the isolated "you" as himself, he provides an image of the process of regeneration which paradoxically expands the "you" to include all readers sharing the initial feeling of dispossession.

This complex interdependence of internal and external realities is a leitmotif of Hugo's poetry. Feelings of psychological alienation and social isolation frequently reinforce one another, as in "Helena, Where Homes Go Mad," "Port Townsend," and "Montana Ranch Abandoned." Conversely, psychological recovery, usually based on a deeper confrontation with the past, is normally accompanied by an expanded vision of community, as found in "What Thou Lovest Well, Remains American," and "Missoula Softball Tournament." The volumes *White Center* and *The Right Madness on Skye* (both published in 1980) exemplify the pattern. *White Center* marks Hugo's return to "the town he came from," his refusal to let his experience die. *The Right Madness on Skye* demonstrates his vision of a community extending beyond the bars and softball fields of the West. Of course it would be too simple to say that one volume is internal, the other external. *White Center* returns to Hugo's social, as well as his psychological, roots. The vision of community in *The Right Madness on Skye* clearly has its foundation in Hugo's personal perception. Together the two volumes provide a complex gloss on Hugo's basic insight that "All cause is local, all effect" ("A Snapshot of Uig in Montana"). Far from being limiting, Hugo's regionalism becomes the source of his encompassing vision. Grounding himself firmly in the local causes of dispossession, he develops a vocabulary capable of revealing the immediate dispossession as a bond with communities everywhere.

This continuing struggle for a common vocabulary can be seen in the contrast between "A Map of Montana in Italy" in *The Lady in Kicking Horse Reservoir* and "A Snapshot of Uig in Montana" and "A Map of Skye" in *The Right Madness on Skye*. Hugo's fascination with representations, particularly maps and photos, testifies to a certain interest in the nature of perception and the relationship between art and reality. Rather than concentrating on the self-reflexive aspects of the question, however, Hugo meditates on the relationship between individual attitude and social context. Where "A Map of Montana in Italy" emphasizes the difficulty of overcoming the social constraints on individual recovery, the later poems present a more hopeful vision of renewed social connection.

"A Map of Montana in Italy" explores the roots of the Western sense of dispossession in a mythology of violence which threatens to engulf the larger community; even the relatively gentle Italians cheer the movie violence at the poem's conclusion. Although he begins with images of coldness and violence, Hugo stresses that Montana is colored white "on *this* map" (emphasis added). Intimating an awareness of other possibilities, he explicitly recognizes that the emotional implications of the map are projected rather than intrinsic: "Glacier Park's green with my envy." Similarly, he maintains an awareness of potential freedom, of maps of places where "antelope sail/ between strands of barbed wire and never/ get hurt." Spatially removed from Montana, Hugo continues to share the Western sense of psychic dispossession: "It's white here too." Rather than resigning himself, however, he attempts to find freedom from paralysis, reinterpreting the whiteness of the map as a call for a desperate compassion: "This map is white, meaning winter, ice/ where you are, helping children who may be already frozen." The only hope lies in reaching those who may already be lost.

Although the Montana weather provides his physical image, Hugo clearly identifies the American mystiques of monetary success and macho toughness as the real sources of the emotional dispossession. He characterizes Montana's "successful" towns as narrow-minded and dull, dedicated to making money. Conversely, the "interesting" towns "have the good sense to fail." Throughout the state, the immature macho stance represses any admission of vulnerability: "There's too much/ schoolboy in bars—I'm tougher than you—/ and too much talk about money." With no foundation for human connection, the tensions are internalized in dreams of "jails and police." These in turn are denied through projection onto a mythical "Poland." Again the American myth precludes recognition of shared dispossession; only Eastern Europeans live in communist-imposed chains. Like the jail of "Degrees of Gray in Philipsburg," however, the prison is more internal than external. Unable to free themselves, the psychic prisoners become social jailers, working against the possibility of the community which might liberate them: "With so few Negroes and Jews we've been reduced/ to hating each other, dumping our crud/ in our rivers, mistreating the Indians." The "whiteness" of the Montana map assumes racial and cultural dimensions, reinforcing the refusal to admit connection with other communities of the dispossessed (and ultimately with the landscape itself). Trapped by insufficient myths reflecting the wrong madness of American culture, the Western community remains ignorant of the existence of alternative maps.

Where "A Map of Montana in Italy" reconsiders realities Hugo had previously experienced, both "A Snapshot of Uig in Montana" and "A Map of Skye" project possibilities onto a largely unknown landscape. As their titles imply, they "revise" the earlier poem. The new statements reflect Hugo's increasing concentration on specific forms of the right madness. "A Snapshot of Uig in Montana" begins with a relatively optimistic, though by no means facile, restatement of an image from "A Map of Montana in Italy": "Children take longer to die there." Speaking in a "we" voice implying connection and community, Hugo identifies a "music all moan dispossessed." This music unites the "failed" Montanans lasting out yet another white winter ("April and our snow hangs on") with the crofters on Skye whose island has been ravaged by historical invasions. In "A Map of Skye," Hugo pursues this sense of connection which involves new communities, new landscapes, and new languages.

Fascinated by the Nordic and Gaelic place names on Skye (much as he is fascinated by the Indian place names in the West), Hugo connects them with the history of dispossession: "It is all here/ in the names, the sound of broken bone and blood." This connection in turn sparks a vision of "slow recovery" generating "a continuum of song." Like the moan of the dispossessed, this continuum of song implies a community based on the acceptance of past pain, whether social or individual. The specific sources of dispossession will inevitably differ: "All cause is local, all effect" ("A Snapshot of Uig in Montana"). The resulting expressions, however, will share a vocabulary. By recognizing this connection, the dispossessed can discover new passages, internal and external. Contrasting sharply with the roads which were "red veins full of rage" on the map of Montana, the roads on the map of Skye promise connection with a "wider world beyond." The transformation testifies not to an essential difference between Montana and Skye but to Hugo's increased determination to provide new emotional maps.

Hugo develops the search for new connections and community most comprehensively in *31 Letters and 13 Dreams*, presenting a full cycle of personal and social disintegration and recovery. Written in Hugo's typical four- to five-stress line but unusually elusive in image and voice, the dream poems concentrate on the experience of an unnamed "you." The letter poems, written mostly in seven-stress Whitmanesque lines, focus directly on Hugo's relationship with specific people and places. The volume was arranged by Ruth Whitman, who brilliantly revealed the underlying unity evident in the thematic and Imagistic connections within sequences of dreams and letters. The early poems, for example, reflect a wrong madness shared by Hugo and the "you" of the dreams. Letters concerning Hugo's flight from Iowa City and his war experiences are juxtaposed with "In Your Fugitive Dream" and "In Your War Dream." Gradually, the volume progresses to the warmth of "Letter to Kathy from Wisdom," the reassurance of "Letter to Oberg from Pony," and the right madness of the concluding "In Your Good Dream." Ultimately *31 Letters and 13 Dreams* develops a vocabulary of dispossession in response to a "country where a wealthy handful/ of people tear down anything you could possibly love,/ break your affectionate connections with yourself by whim/ for profit" ("Letter to Oberg from Pony"). Only by recognizing the shared isolation of self and others can individuals rebuild these connections.

The stylistic tension between the dreams and the letters mirrors this thematic tension. While the dreams exist in a world of shifting Stevensesque images, the letters draw their vitality from shared social experience. If the dreams are "poetic" in the traditional sense, the letters are somewhat prosaic. The prosaic quality, however, is like that of the catalogs in "Song of Myself." Out of the unshaped experiences with which each letter begins, Hugo derives an intensity of perception which enables him to reforge the shattered connections between internal and external reality. The poetic intensity wells up out of ordinary details—concerning food, car trouble, weather—for Hugo's aesthetic is based on revealing the emotional intensity of everyday experience. "Letter to Peterson from Pike Place Market" exemplifies this process:

> Sorry. Got carried away. But you know, Bob, how
> in the smoky recess of bars all over the world, a man
> will suddenly dance because music, a juke box, a Greek taverna band, moves him, and
> how when he dances we
> applaud and cry go. That's nobility of blood, a recognition
> by those who matter that in special moments
> we are together facing the brute descent of the sun
> and that cold brittle star we know already burned out.

Just as the bar scene becomes an emblem of human connection, Hugo's colloquial language ("Got carried away") rises suddenly to the poetic power of the speeding rhythm and the repeated sounds, particularly "b" (blood, brute, brittle, burned) and "t" (moments, brute, descent, brittle, out). Typically the letters return to the colloquial diction, implying the reintegration of poetic insight into the ordinary social context. In contrast, the dreams begin with intensely charged details such as the "seven ultra-masculine men" explaining "the bars of your cage are silver/ in honor of our emperor" ("In Your Bad Dream"). Developed emotionally rather than logically, the images maintain their intensity throughout, reflecting the manner in which the mind obsessively reworks external experience—in this case involving sexual and political dispossession—and establishes the basis for the perception of subsequent experience.

For Hugo, style—whether elusive or direct—involves an intensity of experience which is not limited to writing. In "Letter to Mantsch from Havre," he emphasizes the importance of style in all aspects of life: "So few of us are good at what we do, and what we do,/ well done or not, seems futile. I'm trying to find Monty Holden's barber shop. I want to tell him style in anything,/ pitching, hitting, cutting hair, is worth our trying even if we fail." The prosaic segments of the letter-poems link the poetic intensity with the actual experience of "those who matter," providing the barbers and pitchers with access to the world of Hugo's "Good Dream."

What Hugo offers this populist community is esssentially an outline of the process of finding the right madness. First, he traces individual alienation to a nearly unconscious acceptance of the social madness which devalues individuals in order to advance commercial and material interests. Second, he implies that resisting these forces demands recognition of the connections between isolated individuals and acceptance of the primacy of local truth. Finally, he insists that these local truths be shared.

The early letters in *31 Letters and 13 Dreams* concentrate almost entirely on Hugo's sense of isolation and, significantly, are relatively lacking in the poetic intensity which reflects shared experience. Only with the "Letter to Simic from Boulder" does his social vision begin to take shape. In this poem Hugo perceives himself, a bombardier, and Simic, a potential target on the ground, as victims of the same "mindless hate." The war, the social embodiment of mindless hatred, establishes the base for a common vocabulary even while rendering direct communication impossible:

> And what did your mind
> do with the terrible how of bombs? What is Serb for 'fear'?
> It must be the same as in English, one long primitive wail
> of dying children, one child fixed forever in a dead stare.

Hugo attributes his wartime actions to a "willing confusion" which he traces back to a belief in "Heroics," recalling the corrupt white myths in "A Map of Montana in Italy." This belief is even more clearly revealed as corrupt in the "Letter to Matthews from Barton Street Flats," which concentrates on the internment of Japanese-Americans during the war.

Rejecting the generalized heroics of the war, Hugo turns to the more legitimate, because more local, heroic figure of softball player Mike Mantsch. Comparing his own poetry with Mantsch's hitting, Hugo restates the parallel between various types of experience:

> The ball jumps
> from your bat over and over. I want my poems to jump
> like that. All poems. I want to say once to a world that feels
> with reason it has little chance, well done. That's the lie
> I cannot shout loud as this local truth: Well done, Mike.

Significantly, Mantsch resembles the figure of Buss in the "Dream on the Eve of Success," the psychological turning point of the volume. Buss, also a softball star, speaks with the "you" while the "president" speaks an incomprehensible gibberish which no longer distorts the persona's self-image: "You cannot understand his claim." Again, the local emphasis helps to counter the isolating social forces. Hugo deliberately turns away from the grand, the universal truth, which, however well-intentioned, can only be a "lie." In the face of massive social pressure, he affirms only that which is within his experience. The local poetry, the solid hit, and the dance in the bar carry far more importance than any generalized expression of "Heroic" bravado in the light of a "brute descending sun."

Building on this awareness, Hugo probes for the precise nature of "local truth." Increasingly, he focuses on the difficulties of personal identification with other dispossessed and alienated individuals, such as the mentally retarded Kenny in "Letter to Wagoner from Port Townsend." Although he used to fish with Kenny when they were young, Hugo eventually came to see him as "subnormal," repressing his knowledge of shared experience: "finally we saw each other/ in passing in White Center and didn't speak." Accepting the social definition of "normality" enforces separations. Not yet able to establish a realistic connection with Kenny, Hugo projects the impulse onto the tide which is "washing the remains of crippled fish back deep to the source,/ renewing the driftwood supply and the promise of all night/ fires on the beach, stars and dreams of girls, and that's/ as rich as I'll ever get. We are called human." Turning from the social to the personal definition of "richness," Hugo recognizes that the crippled Kenny shares his origin and his dreams, his humanity. The imaginative act assumes populist significance.

Perhaps the most powerful poem in the volume, "Letter to Levertov from Butte" emphasizes the profound social consequences of the wrong madness. Its intense outrage immediately precedes "In Your Dream on the Eve of Success," which includes the imaginative destruction of the "president" who stands apart from the dispossessed. In Butte, "where you choose sides/ to die on, company or man, and both are losers," Hugo contemplates his own "inadequate" labor, rejecting the materialistic identification of "salary or title" with human worth. This sense of shared isolation leads to a clearer perception of the difficulty of communicating with precisely those who most need connection: "the wife who has turned/ forever to the wall, the husband sobbing at the kitchen/ table and the unwashed children taking it in and in and in/ until they are the wall, the table." This emphasis on the dehumanizing impact of industrial forces makes it clear that Hugo is not romanticizing poverty. As in the "Letter to Simic from Boulder," he stresses that the unresisting individual ultimately merges with the dehumanizing machinery which enforces the wrong madness: "hate takes over, hippie, nigger, Indian, anyone you can lump/ like garbage in a pit, including women." This ability both to accept his connection with the poverty of Walkerville and to understand the extent to which this poverty further isolates the impoverished underlies Hugo's resolve to shape a communal vocabulary of dispossession. Hugo clearly perceives this vocabulary as necessary for his internal as well as his social survival: "And I want my life/ inside to go on long as I do, though I only populate bare/ landscape with surrogate suffering, with lame men/ crippled by more than disease, and create finally/ a simple grief I can deal with, a pain the indigent can find/ acceptable." Ultimately, Hugo commits himself to creating a poetry of the man dancing in the darkness of the bars, the lost friend crippled by a social structure that denies his humanity, the women and children becoming the wall.

This resolve is far more than a poetic pose. The style of Hugo's poetry, as well as its content, attests to his desire to reach "the people who matter," to realize the populist ideal of direct communication. Seeking a renewed sense of connections, Hugo refuses to separate himself from his past, his people, or his poetry. In "Letter to Kathy from Wisdom," he insists that "old towns we loved in matter, lovers matter, playmates, toys/ and we take from our lives those days when everything moved,/ tree, cloud, water, sun, blue between two clouds, and moon,/ days that we danced, vibrating days, chance poem." Overcoming his sense of isolation, Hugo extends himself to his community. "Letter to Oberg from Pony," one of the greatest of American populist poems, rings with the right madness of Hugo's hard-won local truth:

> This is only to assure you, Art,
> that in a nation that is no longer one but only an
> amorphous collection of failed dreams, where we have been told
> too often by contractors, corporations and prudes that
> our lives don't matter, there still is a place where the soul
> doesn't recognize laws like gravity, where boys catch trout
> and that's important, where girls come laughing down the dirt road
> to the forlorn store for candy.

Craig Werner

Other major works

LONG FICTION: *Death and the Good Life*, 1981.

NONFICTION: *The Triggering Town: Lectures and Essays on Poetry and Writing*, 1979; *The Real West Marginal Way: A Poet's Autobiography*, 1986.

Bibliography

Allen, Michael S. *We Are Called Human: The Poetry of Richard Hugo.* Fayetteville: University of Arkansas Press, 1982. A full-length story of Hugo with critical commentary on his major works. Contains valuable information about Hugo, his poems, and his Western roots, written with ease and clarity.

Gerber, Frederick. "On Richard Hugo and William Stafford." *The American Poetry Review* 9, no. 1 (1980): 16-18. Considered an important review of Hugo's *31 Letters and 13 Dreams*, which illustrates how the Pacific Northwest landscape is a metaphor for the spaciousness of the self.

Gerstenberger, Donna. *Richard Hugo.* Pamphlet no. 59. Boise, Idaho: Boise State University, 1983. A brief but authoritative introduction to the life and work of Hugo. Contains critical commentary on *A Run of Jacks, The Lady in Kicking Horse Reservoir,* and *Death of the Kapowsin Tavern,* among others. Includes a useful select bibliography.

Lindholt, Paul J. "Richard Hugo's Language: The Poem as 'Obsessive Musical Deed.'" *Contemporary Poetry* 16, no. 2 (Fall, 1983): 67-75. A technical review that examines Hugo's fondness for local idiom and contemporary slang.

Pinsker, Sanford. *Three Pacific Northwest Poets: William Stafford, Richard Hugo, and David Wagoner.* Boston: Twayne, 1987. A concise, useful overview of Hugo's works, noting that for Hugo, "landscape and poem are interchangeable." Discusses his major works, his use of language, and applauds him as a champion of American contemporary poetry.

LEIGH HUNT

Born: Southgate, England; October 19, 1784
Died: Putney, England; August 28, 1859

Principal poetry
Juvenilia, 1801; *The Feast of the Poets*, 1814; *The Story of Rimini*, 1816; *Foliage*, 1818; *Hero and Leander, and, Bacchus and Ariadne*, 1819; *The Poetical Works of Leigh Hunt*, 1923 (H. S. Milford, editor).

Other literary forms
Leigh Hunt was a poet, familiar essayist, critic, political commentator, playwright, and translator. While he wrote well in all of these genres and with occasional brilliance in some, his reputation as an essayist has best endured. The critical essays reveal a keen sense for what is good in literature; they quote extensively from the works being considered. The familiar essays are famous for their quiet good humor. They are seldom as polished as the essays of Charles Lamb or as perceptive as those of William Hazlitt; still, a few—such as "Getting Up on Cold Mornings" and "Deaths of Little Children"—continue to be anthologized as classics.

Achievements
In his own time, the general reading public respected Hunt as an important literary figure, one whose opinions on literature and the political scene were both valid and influential. His role as editor of several periodicals afforded him an effective means of voicing those opinions to a great many readers, far more than expensive books could reach. Thus Hunt was the great popularizer of the Romantic movement in England. Later critics, however, concluded that several of his contemporaries, though then of less influence and popularity, were actually better artists and more profound thinkers. The common twentieth century attitude has tended to ignore Hunt's individual achievements, rather viewing him as the comparatively less important hub of an illustrious literary circle: John Keats, Percy Bysshe Shelley, Lord Byron, Charles Lamb, and William Hazlitt, in particular. More recently, critics have again begun to assess Hunt's own achievements, and while few would allow that he was as fine a poet as Keats, as graceful an essayist as Lamb, or as profound a critic as Hazlitt, still his work does not merit oblivion. His translations are among the finest in English, and he must be credited with increasing the English-speaking world's awareness of Italian literature. His countless journalistic pieces reflect wide reading and high standards of scholarship, and he deserves recognition for his contribution to the quality of popular journalism. A fair assessment of Hunt's literary achievement would have to include his positive influence on the several young poets who went on to surpass their

mentor, but that assessment should also not overlook the quality of his own work as a journalist and translator.

Biography

Leigh Hunt was the son of a Philadelphia lawyer who had returned to England at the time of the American Revolution. The father was a highly principled if rather impractical man who changed his profession from lawyer to Unitarian minister and occasional tutor. At seven years of age, young Hunt was sent to school at Christ's Hospital, where Charles Lamb and Samuel Taylor Coleridge had also been students. Hunt's *The Autobiography of Leigh Hunt* (1850) reveals that from his earliest years he was instilled with a hatred of all that is evil. He detested violence, was shocked by profane language, and opposed tyranny by defending his weaker schoolmates with passive resistance of schoolyard bullies. Hunt stayed at Christ's Hospital until he was fifteen. At seventeen he published a volume of juvenile verse.

In 1808, Hunt became the editor of a journal, *The Examiner*, owned by his brother John. *The Examiner* championed a number of liberal causes: abolition of slavery, freedom of the press, an end to imprisonment for debt. In their catalog of social evils, the Hunts did not hesitate to include even the Prince Regent of England. Their description of the Prince as "a violator of his word, a libertine over head and ears in debt and disgrace, a despiser of domestic ties, the companion of gamblers" resulted in a libel case and two years' imprisonment for both brothers. Prison was not very hard on Leigh Hunt. He had a decent room, which he decorated with flowered wallpaper, and in which he received such notable visitors as Byron, Shelley, and Hazlitt. After his release, Hunt published his major poem, *The Story of Rimini*, and became the literary mentor to young Keats. The Tory critics, however, could not forgive the slanderer of the Prince and viciously attacked Hunt. In 1817, *Blackwood's Magazine* coined the term "cockney school" to describe Hunt's frequently colloquial style, and the appellation was to plague him for many years.

In 1822 Hunt and his family arrived in Italy. Shelley invited him to assume editorship of *The Liberal*, a periodical conceived by Byron and Shelley as a vehicle for their own writings. Shelley drowned soon thereafter, and when Byron, upon whom the Hunts had depended for financial support, left Italy, the family was stranded until 1825, when Hunt borrowed enough money to return to England. He naturally felt that Byron had done him an injustice and in 1828 he published *Lord Byron and Some of His Contemporaries*, presenting a most unfavorable picture of Byron's personal fears and dishonesties. Hunt maintained in the face of widespread adverse criticism that he had included nothing which he did not believe to be entirely true. True or not, few considered it proper to write so about a man who had recently gone to a heroic death.

With the exception of the embarrassment resulting from his identification with the character Harold Skimpole in Charles Dickens' *Bleak House* (1852) (Dickens insisted that any similarity was unintentional), the remainder of Hunt's life was rather uneventful. He wrote voluminously in all literary forms and on countless topics. The concise *Cambridge Bibliography of English Literature* (1965) estimates that a complete edition of his prose works alone would fill forty volumes. He lived to see his liberal ideas become the popular thought of the day and himself a respected figure in the literary community. Hunt's productive life ended peacefully in 1859 while he was visiting one of his oldest friends, the printer Charles Reynell, in Putney.

Analysis

Leigh Hunt's three-volume *The Autobiography of Leigh Hunt* has remained the single most important source of information on both the facts of his life and those personal attributes which influenced his writings. There is, in fact, comparatively little in *The Autobiography of Leigh Hunt* dealing exclusively with Hunt; it is more a series of recollections and examinations of his many literary friends. This fact is of some importance in understanding Hunt the man, for it reflects a total lack of selfishness and a genuine sympathetic concern for the many fortunate people who won his friendship. These friendships were treasured by Hunt, and in the accounts of his youthful infatuations is reflected the simple kindheartedness and romantic idealism which were noted by his contemporaries and by later critics. *The Autobiography of Leigh Hunt* does not follow a strict chronology but is rather a series of units. For example, he describes his parents' lives until their deaths before he discusses his own early years. In fact, Hunt's father lived to see his son a successful editor. This organizational method may well be a result of Hunt's reliance on personal taste. His taste of course was selective; he extracted from his experience what he considered excellent and showed little regard for the organizational coherence of the whole. His literary criticism, indeed even his poetry displays the same fondness for selection found in his autobiography.

Most critics agree that Hunt's greatest contribution to poetry was not the poetry he himself wrote but his fine criticism of the poetry of others. Again, Hunt's criticism is based on his own excellent taste, but his taste was far more useful in recognizing good literature than in distinguishing what was specifically bad and forming a thoughtful critical opinion as to the nature of the faults. In practice, Hunt the critic was a selector; he chose those passages from a work which especially appealed to his taste and quoted them at length. Thus he assumed that the works would speak for themselves. He did not conceive of a critic as one who thinks for the reader and locks literature into a single interpretation. If Hunt has survived as a critic, it is because his personal taste was so good. At the same time, his natural sensitivity to what is fine in literature may be said to have worked against his ever achieving a place among the very greatest critics. He had no need for detailed analysis to tell him what was fine in art, and he created no aesthetic concepts approaching the sophistication of some of his contemporaries, notably Coleridge. Thus, Hunt cannot be numbered among the important literary theoreticians. His reputation as a quite respectable critic is dependent on the fact that he was perhaps the greatest appreciator of literature in the history of English letters.

The same quality of taste that enabled Hunt to select what was best in the writings of others also influenced his own poetic compositions. That selective talent, however, did not serve Hunt the poet quite so well. In the composition of his own verse, he was inclined to combine lines and passages reflective of specific poetic principles without a view to the appropriateness of the principle in relation to the poem as a whole. For example, Hunt as the great popularizer of Romantic literary ideas did more than William Wordsworth to bring home to the nineteenth century reader the notion that poetry should reflect the language really used by people. Another aim of the Romantics was to make a place in literature for the experiences of the lower classes, comprising that whole stratum of society that neoclassical writers generally ignored. Hunt's conviction that it was the business of poetry to do these things led him, much more than Wordsworth, Coleridge, and his other illustrious contemporaries who shared these ideas, to overlook yet another major principle of composition that had so concerned the neoclassicists: decorum.

Decorum demanded that all of the various elements of a work of art contribute to the unified effect of the work as a whole. Thus, diction must be appropriate to character and action; a king suffering tragedy should not speak like the common man in the street. Decorum made the poet responsible to the propriety of the particular work. Hunt too often forced the work to comply with principle, and while the principle of natural poetic language suited certain poems, lines such as "The two divinest things this world has got,/ A lovely woman in a rural spot" are jarring. The many critics who have viewed Hunt's poetry with disfavor have really played variations on a single theme: the unevenness of the work. The tone is inappropriate for the subject; good writing is not maintained throughout; the central idea is lost for the digressions. These are all pitfalls into which a reliance on personal taste might lead one, and though Hunt is guilty of all this, it must also finally be acknowledged that this same disregard for uniformity resulted in an important contribution to English poetry of the nineteenth century.

The unfortunate couplet just quoted is from *The Story of Rimini*, a retelling of Dante's tragic story of Paolo and Francesca and Hunt's most ambitious poetic effort. At the time of its composition, Hunt found John Dryden "The most delightful name to me in English literature." In *The Autobiography of Leigh Hunt* he confesses that while *The Story of Rimini* was intended to reflect the vigor and music of Dryden's natural style, his personal taste produced some variations, such as a more simple diction and less vigorous versification. Obviously the results of these liberties were not always happy. The effect of *The Story of Rimini* on English poetry, however, was certainly positive. The poem contributed greatly to the breakup of the highly polished closed couplet perfected by Alexander Pope; Hunt called for a less rigid couplet structure making use of run-on lines and feminine endings. The poem had a marked influence on the styles of several of his contemporaries. Some of Keats's most important early pieces, such as "I Stood Tip-toe Upon a Little Hill" and "Sleep and Poetry," show the influence of Hunt's couplet. Indeed, the motto for "I Stood Tip-toe" was borrowed from *The Story of Rimini*.

Still, the vicious political critics from *Blackwood's Magazine* and the *Quarterly* who dubbed Hunt the leader of the so-called Cockney School of poetry were not completely wrong in their identification of the poem's faults. The freer couplet form resulted in an easy, almost conversational tone which was only aggravated by colloquial diction. Hunt simply did not recognize that some of the ingredients he selected to mix in this noble experiment were not appropriate to the dignity of the subject. Regardless of particular theories of poetic composition or the unique tastes of any age, a character such as Francesca deserves better than "She had strict notions on the marrying score."

Despite its several flaws, *The Story of Rimini* does contain passages of natural grace and elegance. Clearly Dryden's lesson was not completely lost on Hunt. Moreover, the canon of Hunt's poetry includes some astonishingly pure gems that prove the truth of the judgment of *The Cambridge History of English Literature* (1916) that Hunt's best poetry is better than his best prose. These best efforts are short—sonnets and brief narratives. The rigid structure of the sonnet seems to have provided the direction that Hunt was likely to lose sight of in his longer experiments, and brief narratives prevented those digressions which he was likely to engage in for their own sake and at the expense of the clarity of his theme. The sonnet on "The Nile" is an example of Hunt at his best. Critics have generally praised it over the sonnets on the same topic by Keats and Shelley. Here, Hunt achieves smooth versification with natural rhymes and diction reflective of the tranquil progress of the river through an ancient and glorious landscape. Very unobtrusively, in only the last one and a half lines, meditation on the river is allowed to slide gracefully into a metaphor for meditation on human experience. Had Hunt more often shown the sense of dignity and decorum obvious in "The Nile," his place as an important English poet would be secure.

The best of the brief narratives is also Hunt's most famous poem. "Abou Ben Adhem" first appeared in Samuel Carter Hall's *The Amulet* (1835) and is certainly one of the most frequently anthologized poems in the English language. The poet relates a simple tale, and while an incident of angelic visitation might seem to demand the most heroic language, Hunt wisely understood that the point of the tale is not so much the magnificence of the angel as it is the intimacy that exists between a good person and the divine.

The character of Abou Ben Adhem, then, is most important; that character had to be made to appeal to human readers. Thus, Abou Ben Adhem, secure in his knowledge of what he is, is not intimidated by the angel. His address is respectful but relaxed and touched by humor. He does not disagree with the angel's omission of his name from the list of those who love God but politely suggests an alternative: "I pray thee then/ Write me as one that loves his fellow-men." In this poem of only eighteen lines, Hunt successfully drew a quite sophisticated character and suggested a relationship between God and human beings more subtle than the implied message that God loves people who love their neighbors. In the hands of a lesser poet, "Abou Ben Adhem" might have been an undistinguished exercise in lofty language and baroque figures; the theme would allow such an approach. Indeed, in the hands of Hunt it might have been a hodgepodge of styles and words at war with themes, but in this poem and several others he managed to keep his eye on the poem itself rather than on assorted notions about poetry.

In his *An Essay on Criticism* (1711), Alexander Pope describes two kinds of literary genius: the genius to create the material of poetry, the rhetorical figures, the variety of styles, and the genuis to know how to arrange the material into a unified whole. In this latter respect Hunt too often showed himself deficient. When he managed to overcome that deficiency, as he often did, he showed himself the worthy companion of Keats, Shelley, and the many immortal Romantics who loved him so well.

William J. Heim

Other major works
PLAY: *A Legend of Florence*, 1840.
NONFICTION: *Lord Byron and Some of His Contemporaries*, 1828; *Imagination and Fancy*, 1844; *Wit and Humour*, 1846; *Men, Women and Books*, 1847; *The Autobiography of Leigh Hunt*, 1850; *Leigh Hunt's Dramatic Criticism, 1808-1831*, 1949 (Carolyn W. Houtchens and Lawrence H. Houtchens, editors); *Leigh Hunt's Literary Criticism*, 1956 (Carolyn W. Houtchens and Lawrence H. Houtchens, editors).

Bibliography
Blainey, Ann. *Immortal Boy: A Portrait of Leigh Hunt*. New York: St. Martin's Press, 1985. This biography adds further dimension to the usual perception of Hunt as a cheerful character by emphasizing the infuriating and melancholic sides of the man. Blainey's brief, well-written portrait focuses on Hunt's vulnerable, human qualities. Includes several illustrations, an extensive bibliography, and an index.
Johnson, Brimley. *Leigh Hunt*. 1896. New York: Haskell, 1970. This 152-page work examines Hunt's major works in great detail, assessing the writer's

ability separately as a journalist, poet, and critic. Johnson suggests that "gratitude" to Hunt for his service to liberalism and his "popularization" of taste should persuade critics to overlook his "shallow" intellect and weak style. Supplemented by an index.

Kendall, Kenneth E. *Leigh Hunt's "Reflector."* Paris: Mouton, 1971. Examines Hunt's first literary periodical as a reflection of contemporary thought and times. Although the short 183-page book looks at other contributors from the Hunt circle, Hunt receives most of the attention. Kendall suggests that *The Reflector* was very important to the literary development of Hunt. Complemented by a bibliography, an index, and appendices.

Marshall, William H. *Byron, Shelley, Hunt, and "The Liberal."* Philadelphia: University of Pennsylvania Press, 1960. This 269-page work examines the literary partnership and friendship between George Gordon, Lord Byron, Percy Bysshe Shelley, and Hunt. The work analyzes each number of *The Liberal* in separate chapters and offers a critical study of Hunt as both a writer and an editor. Appendices include a parody of *The Liberal* called *The Illiberal.* Supplemented by a bibliography and an index.

McCown, Robert A., ed. *The Life and Times of Leigh Hunt: Papers Delivered at a Symposium.* Iowa City: Friends of the University of Iowa Libraries, 1985. A collection of critical essays covering various aspects of Hunt's writings. Titles included are "Leigh Hunt in Literary History: A Response," "Inter Pares: Leigh Hunt as Personal Essayist," and "Leigh Hunt's Dramatic Success: A Legend in Florence." These essays marked the bicentennial of Hunt's birth.

DAVID IGNATOW

Born: Brooklyn, New York; February 7, 1914

Principal poetry

Poems, 1948; *The Gentle Weight Lifter*, 1955; *Say Pardon*, 1961; *Figures of the Human*, 1964; *Rescue the Dead*, 1968; *Earth Hard: Selected Poems*, 1968; *Poems 1934-1969*, 1970; *Selected Poems*, 1975 (Robert Bly, editor); *Facing the Tree*, 1975; *Tread the Dark*, 1978; *Sunlight: A Sequence for My Daughter*, 1979; *Whisper to the Earth*, 1981; *Leaving the Door Open*, 1984; *New and Collected Poems, 1970-1985*, 1986; *Shadowing the Ground*, 1991.

Other literary forms

David Ignatow has published several volumes of prose, including *The Notebooks of David Ignatow* (1973), *Open Between Us* (1980), a collection of lectures, interviews, essays, and reviews, and *The One in the Many: A Poet's Memoirs* (1988). In addition, Ignatow published a substantial number of short stories in various little magazines in the 1940's and 1950's.

Achievements

Because of his deliberate eschewal of traditional poetic techniques, including rhyme and meter, and his firm insistence upon the "plain style" in contradiction to prevailing modes of the day, Ignatow has endured a long period of public and academic neglect, not unlike that endured by his idol and warm supporter, William Carlos Williams. Also like Williams, he was an early victim of T. S. Eliot's extraordinary success, which has tended to cast much modern American poetry in a convoluted Donne-shadowed mold, despite Eliot's own sympathetic openness to free verse.

Ignatow's first two collections, *Poems* and *The Gentle Weight Lifter*, were decidedly the work of a poet at odds with the dominant mandarin sensibility of the period. The first collection occasioned an enthusiastic review by Williams in *The New York Times* (November 21, 1948), a review that led to a friendship between the two men. Although conversational in style, the poems' simplicity of diction and syntax, their almost clumsy rejection of conventional lyricism, and their steadfast metaphoric sparseness placed them outside the mainstream of contemporary aesthetics, causing more than one critic to label their author a "naif" or "primitive." Randall Jarrell's more accurate review of *The Gentle Weight Lifter* in the *Yale Review* (Autumn, 1955) characterized Ignatow's poetry as "humane, unaffected, and unexciting," noting that he lacked Williams' "heights and depths."

From the beginning, Ignatow has proclaimed himself "a man with a small song," identifying most strongly with Walt Whitman and Williams in terms of wanting to articulate the travails and tragedies of the ordinary citizen in his own language. A strong chord of social and political protest inevitably accompanied such a program, and not a little of Ignatow's value resides in his willingness to confront the inequities he has seen all around him.

Yet, it must have become increasingly evident to Ignatow that very few of the poems in his first two books were clear successes, for all their integrity of purpose and manner, and that something more was needed if he hoped to achieve the same sort of understated suggestiveness that Ernest Hemingway, an admired fellow writer, had achieved in his best short stories. He had to find a method that could weld Hemingway's lean but loaded sentences to the plain style learned from Williams and the kind of parabolic structures encountered in the Bible (an important source); that is, he needed to use narrative as metaphor but he needed to free it from the innate limitations of a prose mode by more direct confrontations with unconscious forces. Allegory was an obvious answer, as in Stephen Crane's neglected verse, but the specific modernist approach was found in the nightmare revelations of the Surrealists, which seemed to complement perfectly readings in Charles Baudelaire and Arthur Rimbaud.

Consequently, beginning with *Say Pardon*, Ignatow's deceptively modest story-poems started to illuminate deeper, darker undercurrents, started to probe Freudian streams with relentless innocence. In "The Dream" a stranger approaches "to fall down at your feet/ and pound his head upon the sidewalk" until "your life takes on his desperation," even after waking. Like Baudelaire, Ignatow remained a poet of urban landscapes, committed to a moral exploration of man's most ambitious and ambiguous invention, yet he has never lost his spiritual roots in a Jewish past in his search for godhead and ideal certitudes. In the book's title poem, for example, he advises, "Say pardon/ and follow your own will," but two poems later, "The Complex" addresses the dilemma of a father whose "madness is to own himself/ for what he gives is taken," while another poem, "And I Said," envisions "God" behind "my enemy."

The tension energizing his strongest poems, an ethical and psychological matrix of contending defiance and guilt, often entails a transformation of public material into family dramas, spotlighting an ambivalent father figure, a wronged wife, a victimized son. A prolific writer intent upon processing every vagrant bit of daily experience, however trivial, Ignatow has published more poems than he should, far too frequently lapsing into sententious whimsy or belaboring the obvious. This has contributed, no doubt, to his dismissal by many academics. It was not until the 1970's and the publication of *Poems 1934-1969* and the *Selected Poems* that the true extent of his contribution to American literature was appreciated, climaxing in the award of the prestigious Bollingen Prize and reconfirming the truism that risk-taking and pratfalls are ever the hallmarks of the serious artist.

Fellow poets have been more ready to concede and celebrate the sly art beneath Ignatow's rough surfaces—at least poets who share his concern for establishing an alternative aesthetic closer to the Whitman-Williams line of descent, ranging from Charles Reznikoff to the "deep image" school of Robert Bly, James Wright, and Diane Wakoski. They have helped bring Ignatow's verses to the forefront of contemporary American poetry—Bly in particular, through his choices for the *Selected Poems.*

In recent years, belying his age, Ignatow has continued to evolve, another sign of genuine talent, and has relaxed enough, at last, to appreciate poetic stances at the opposite end of the scale, including a growing comprehension of Eliot's technical radicalism and intelligence. If *Tread the Dark* exhibited symptoms of possible fatigue, compulsive reiteration of death threats and near self-parodies, these have since been denied in the moving *Sunlight: A Sequence for My Daughter* and *Whisper to the Earth*, in which the concluding "With Horace" epitomizes Ignatow's determination to dig for rocks, to strike off "his fire upon stone."

Ignatow has received the National Institute of Arts and Letters Award (1964), two Guggenheim Fellowships (1965 and 1973), the Shelley Memorial Award (1965), and the Bollingen Prize (1977).

Biography

Born February 7, 1914, in Brooklyn, New York, the son of Russian immigrant parents, Max and Yetta (née Reinbach) Ignatow, David Ignatow had the misfortune to graduate from New Utrecht High School in 1932: "I stepped out of high school into the worst economic, social, and political disaster of our times, the Great Depression." He did enroll at Brooklyn College but lasted only half a semester, subsequently schooling himself in literary matters by reading Hemingway, Whitman, Friedrich Nietzsche, Arthur Schopenhauer, Søren Kierkegaard, the Russian novelists, the French poets of the previous century, and the Bible. He worked in his father's commercial pamphlet bindery, running a machine or delivering the finished pamphlets by hand-truck, and wrote stories and poems in his spare hours. Oppressed by the tedious labor, and by an ambivalent, often heated relationship with a hard-driving father, Ignatow envisioned literature as an escape. With his mother's aid, he managed to secure an appointment as a reporter for the WPA Newspaper Project. The year before, his short story "I Can't Stop It" had appeared in *The New Talent* magazine, earning a place on Edward J. O'Brien's Honor List in his *The Best American Short Stories* annual in 1933.

Ignatow was finally able to leave the family business and home in 1935, when he found a cheap apartment in Manhattan's East Village, where he became a part of the literary scene and met artist Rose Graubart, whom he married two years later. Their son David was born in 1937. Financial difficulties harassed the young couple, and in the period from 1939 to 1948 Ignatow was forced to work at a series of low-paying jobs, as night clerk at the Sanitation Department, as a Health Department clerk, as an apprentice handyman in the lathe workshop at the Kearny Shipyards in New Jersey, and, for five years, as night admitting clerk at Beth Israel Hospital in New York. It was during his last year at Beth Israel that his first collection, *Poems*, appeared and garnered an enthusiastic review from William Carlos Williams. Williams, in fact, emerged as a friend, as did Charles Reznikoff, and these two poets probably exerted the most enduring influence upon Ignatow's career.

The year 1955 proved to be crucial in Ignatow's life. *The Gentle Weight Lifter* was published; he was asked to edit the Whitman Centennial issue of the *Beloit Poetry Journal*; and his son began to exhibit the signs of mental illness that would eventually result in his being institutionalized. A daughter, Yaedi, was born the next year, and Ignatow became closely associated with *Chelsea* magazine. In 1961, his third volume of poetry, *Say Pardon*, was published by Wesleyan University Press—destined to remain his publisher for almost two decades—but money was still a pressing problem, and Ignatow worked as a paper salesman in the years between 1962 and 1964, also serving as an auto messenger for Western Union on the weekends. During the same interval, he spent a year as poetry editor of *The Nation* and gave a poetry workshop at the New School for Social Research.

The publication of *Figures of the Human* helped to earn him an award from the National Institute of Arts and Letters in 1964, his first significant token of recognition. This was followed by a Guggenheim Fellowship a year later. In 1965 he also won the Shelley Memorial Award and was Visiting Lecturer at the University of Kentucky. Other academic posts came his way: at the University of Kansas in 1966 and at Vassar College from 1967 to 1969. He then accepted positions as Poet-in-Residence at York College (CUNY) and as adjunct professor at Columbia University. Editorial assignments included extended stints with *Beloit Poetry Journal* and *Chelsea*, and in 1972 he was among the first associate editors connected with the founding of *The American Poetry Review*, a connection that was dissolved near the decade's end when he and a group of fellow editors resigned in protest over what they perceived as implicit unfairness in the magazine's attitude toward women and minority groups.

In 1973 Ignatow was granted a second Guggenheim Fellowship, but the award that had the most to do with bringing his name before a broader audience was the Bollingen Prize of 1977. The publication of *The Notebooks of David Ignatow*, selections from his journals which the poet hoped, in vain, would result in a wider readership for his poetry, had made clear the terrible cost of being a writer, particularly an antiestablishment writer, in America, while also demonstrating with high principle, brutal candor, and almost claustrophobic narcissism, the ultimate advantages and limitations of constantly translating self into *res*. Ignatow's career achieved ironic completeness with his election to the presidency of the Poetry Society of America in 1980.

Analysis

In his poetry written in the 1930's and 1940's, later gathered in the first section of *Poems 1934-1969*, David Ignatow projected an abiding concern for both the well-made poem, however occasionally denuded of conventional lyric devices, and a reformer's vision of realistic life, in the city, in the streets, in the homes of the poor and outcast, who are romantically linked with the artist's difficult lot. The subjects were traditional—marriage, murder, sex, love's complexities, adolescence, the death of Franklin D. Roosevelt—but their treatment exhibited a diverting ability to make sudden leaps from the banal to the profound, always in language direct enough to disarm. "Autumn Leaves," for example, moves skillfully from an ordinary image of the leaves as Depression victims to a vivid figure of God sprawling beneath a tree, gaunt in giving, "like a shriveled nut where plumpness/ and the fruit have fed the worm." This kind of dramatic shift epitomizes Ignatow's focus on social injustice and his often bitter struggle with a religious heritage and the questionable place of deity in a scheme of things so geared to grind down human hopes.

Surprisingly, many of the early poems betray a professional smoothness and a reliance on metaphor and balanced lines that one might not expect from a disciple of Williams; there is scant sense in these poems of a language straining for experimental intensities. "The Murderer," an undeniable failure, marked by simplistic psychology but true to its author's identification with the underclass, can only express love for "those who cart me off to jail" in easy prose: "I love them too/ for the grief and anger/ I have given." More relevant, the murderer had killed with a knife, that most intimate of weapons, which reappears again and again in the Ignatow canon, a reflection of the menace and death lurking behind every scene of ordinary existence, as well as symbolic reminder of murderous impulses and contrary fears of castration by the father and his capitalistic society.

In *Poems*, which is a bundle of furies, rage against America's hunger for money, "our masterpiece" (according to a poem of that title), and frustration at being caught in its fatal web—"Keep me from doing what I want/ and I shall harm someone,/ including myself"—the obsession with creating a "small song" rarely escapes self-imposed boundaries. Occasionally, as in "At the Zoo," a quiet pathos gives modest dimensions their proper subject; an elephant trapped and separated from his real self, like the poet of course, in "stingy space and concrete setting." Repeatedly, however, as in "Come!" and "The Poet Is a Hospital Clerk," Ignatow underestimates his audience, wherein lies the innate danger of such songs, and settles for either blatant self-abasement—"I have said it before, I am no good"—or political invective:

"Come, let us blow up the whole business;/ the city is insane." At his best, he can produce "Europe and America," merging anger against world ills with ambivalence toward his father, the knife resurfacing in a climax of fused violences:

> My father comes of a small hell
> where bread and man have been kneaded and baked together.
> You have heard the scream as the knife fell;
> while I have slept
> as guns pounded offshore.

Working with a larger canvas and a surer touch, *The Gentle Weight Lifter* evinces a growing dependence on narrative means and on verbal portraits and mirrors of the people who define Ignatow's imagination. The collection is not unlike Edgar Lee Masters' urbanized *Spoon River Anthology* (1915), although it is brightened by exotic historic additions and splashes of darker Kafka-esque tones. In its quest for parallel lives and allegorical configurations, the collection ranges back in time to ancient Greece, to Oedipus at Colonnus in "Lives II"—tellingly centered on the father, not Antigone, his head in her lap as "he thought surely some cover/ could be found for him"—to Nicias in "The Men Sang," a parable about the poet's generic function, and to the Old Testament in "The Pardon of Cain," which captures Cain in the "joy" of having freed himself from death's insidious allure.

Though not yet prevalent, surrealistic perspectives, when they do appear, tend to be founded upon absurd juxtapositions of mythic and modernist elements, as in "News Report," where "a thing" arises from a sewer to run amok among urban females—primeval sexuality rampant in a city field. Each victim describes her special view, "one giving the shaggy fur, the next the shank bone/ of a beast." In the end, the creature is an obvious refugee from Greek mythology, "the red teeth marks sunk into the thigh/ and the smell of a goat clinging tenaciously." Throughout the book, there is a stubborn quest for philosophic truths at variance with contemporary culture, and the governing voice, confounding Ignatow's own aesthetic, often resounds with a pedant's dense lexicon, as in "The Painter," a sensitive inquiry into a particular artist's world, which has a fourth stanza beginning: "These are not dreams, and the brush stroke is the agent./ At the hour of appropriate exhaustion, leaving the field/ of canvas, she ravens on the transient bread and cheese."

This is far from streamlined narrative terseness, far from the language of the man in the street, and it points up *The Gentle Weight Lifter*'s uneasy transitional quality, despite several remarkable poems, and its abrupt swings between simple allegorical spareness and thicker meditative measures. In *Say Pardon*, much of the uncertainty has disappeared, carrying Ignatow's main voice and means closer to the spare slyness that distinguishes his final style. In *Babel to Byzantium* (1968), James Dickey salutes the collection's "strange,

myth-dreaming vision of city life" and isolates, with acute accuracy, its basic
modus operandi as "an inspired and brilliantly successful metaphysical repor-
tage." Since it announces a greater willingness to accept a surrealistic path
to unconscious resources, without jettisoning conversational immediacy and
treasured social and moral concerns, one of the key poems is "How Come?"
A naked, unpretentious self funnels the experience into Everyman's tale:
"I'm in New York covered by a layer of soap foam." The conceit, whimsey
in service of darker designs, is logically developed, radio newscasts informing
him of the foam's spread to San Francisco, Canada, and the Mexican border,
climaxing with "God help the many/ who will die of soap foam." Light fantasy
has suggested the paradox of drowning in cleanliness, next to American god-
liness, the pollution of scientific and commercial advances against nature.

   The relaxed speech is matter-of-fact, contrasting scaffolding for a surreal
flight, not quite as jagged as it will later become in Ignatow's continued effort
to simulate urban realities, and the situation adeptly yokes "what if" fantasy
to persistent reformist despair. More touching, though no less characteristic,
are two poems about the author's institutionalized son, "In Limbo" and "Sunday at the State Hospital," the former a brief statement of grief, insisting that
"there is no wisdom/ without a child in the house," and the latter recounting
a visit in which the son cannot eat the sandwich his father has brought him:

> My past is sitting in front of me
> filled with itself
> and trying with almost no success
> to bring the present to its mouth.

A poem called simply "Guilt" lays bare the emotional core of these and other
family verses: "Guilt is my one attachment to reality."

   Jewish guilt, the anxiety bred of childhood training in a context that conditions love to obedience, outsider status, and unresolved Oedipus complexes,
must forever seek release not only in the past, but in a specific religious ethos
as well. Thus, the last section of *Say Pardon* is a procession of spiritual selves
that assumes a living godhead, who proffers salvation (from guilt, rage,
hatred) through the act of loving fatherhood, the "Lord" claiming "you will
win your life/ out of my hands/ by taking up your child." These lines are from
"I Felt," second in the series of twelve poems, after "The Mountain Is
Stripped," where the poet had conceded, "I have been made frail with righ-
teousness:/ with two voices. I am but one person." Because of its inveterate
opposition to his rational espousal of liberal dogma and experimental openness, this conservative streak in Ignatow's consciousness, which helps to fuel
his moral indignation, generates the lion's share of the tension in some of his
strongest poetry. It also explains how such a cosmopolitan individual could,
as revealed in *The Notebooks of David Ignatow*, react with abhorrence to

homosexuality, viewing it as a degeneration into self-love. "And I Stand," third in the series, ostensibly a declaration, has the impact of a prayer in its speaker's avowal not to kill his enemy, standing and gazing, instead, past "my enemy at Him." Noah, Samson, and Job, three personifications of a volatile man-god fulcrum, are considered for antithetical urges, their stories rephrased, until the final poem, "The Rightful One," confronts a divine visitation, a New Testament Christ to replace the Old Testament's paternal fierceness, full of forgiveness, "his hair long, face exhausted, eyes sad," with pardon again based on selfless parenthood: "Bless your son . . . / . . . And the Rightful One/ was gone and left a power to feel free." Redemption is not the reader's, however, ideal or otherwise, since boredom is the normal response when any dramatic conflict flattens out into a species of George Santayana's "animal faith," intimating that belief, in this case, is either forced or without sufficient doubt.

Figures of the Human is free of such overt metaphysical gestures toward mental entropy, and more potent as a result. Its first section concentrates on those human figures whose crimes and tragedies populate the daily tabloids; it is tuned to the violence, urban and sudden, that Ignatow deems typical of modern life. A victim, for example, of a random, fatal assault in his own home is elegized in "And That Night." The poem's attitude is one of primitive awe: "You bring up a family in three small rooms,/ this crazy man comes along/ to finish it off." Note how the language refuses mandarin remoteness, and savors instead the vernacular tongue of victim and reporter. Another victim, a nine-year-old girl raped and thrown off a tenement roof, is the voice in "Play Again," which enables Ignatow to grant her (at the brink of poor taste) a sacrificial mission:

> The living
> share me among them. They taste
> me on the ground, they taste me
> in the air descending.

Salvation comes, saving the poem, with a beautiful death plea, as the child and author ask readers to play again "and love me/ until I really die, when you are old/ on a flight of stairs." A poem called "Two Voices," echoing Alfred, Lord Tennyson, underscores the almost schizophrenic division in self of which the poet is always aware; the retreat into "Baudelaire, Whitman, Eliot" versus the need for active involvement in a present tense is translated into a suicidal leap into a winter lake, which is daring, if deadly, because it challenges "the weather," nature itself.

The rest of *Figures of the Human*, three further sections, varies its approach with frequent recourse to personal days and ways—"My mind is green with anxiety/ about money"—and surreal fantasies, one of which, the brief "Earth Hard," has a delicious Blakean air:

Earth hard to my heels
bear me up like a child
standing on its mother's belly.
I am a surprised guest to the air.

Childhood is an issue in the title poem also, questing after "the childhood spirit" of a maddened beloved for the impulse that impels art as well: "Then are we loved, hand drawing swiftly/ figures of the human struggling awake." This is mission and theme combined, dream explicating experience, and a reply to the savage urge that brings back the "knife" in other poems.

Whatever else it accomplishes, *Figures of the Human* demonstrates the firm command Ignatow had obtained over his unique aesthetic, culminating, four years later, in *Rescue the Dead*, his finest, most consistently effective volume of verse, which is, at times, his most autobiographical. As the title avers, the major goal of the book is to revive the past, the personal dead and strangers and the dead in spirit. A handful of its poems have already been recognized for the virtuoso performances they are, among them "The Boss" and "The Bagel," first and last in the initial section, which is introduced by a "Prologue" that offers up parents "who had small/ comfort from one another." The larger arrangement of the section, which evolves from a bitter portrait of a sinning father into the playful absurdity of a man turning into a rolling bagel, has the additional weight of a small sequence about the father: five poems, beginning with the "Prologue" and concluding with his "Epitaph," which prays: "Forgive me, father,/ as I have forgiven you/ my sins."

The Freudian chain has thus been broken, at least for the moment, at least within the limits of the poem, and "Nourish the Crops," the next poem, can proceed to the other father, God, realizing self as the "product of you to whom all life/ is equal." The proposition here is the same frightening one, minus deity, facing Albert Camus and Jean-Paul Sartre in the 1950's, modern man's existential dilemma vis-à-vis an indifferent cosmos. In spite of conflicting religious restraints, for Ignatow the pivotal answer must be imagination, ceaseless reworkings of the Romantic heritage he had forsworn, and an alter ego in pursuit of a bagel, sounding like Williams and Wright, tumbling head over heels, "one complete somersault/ after another like a bagel/ and strangely happy with myself." In the title poem, the climb to redemption is pitted against paradox—"Not to love is to live"—and has the poet conceding his incapacity to choose love over life (survival, materialist wants) and asking that you "who are free/ rescue the dead." A powerful poem at the end of the second section, "The Room," reconfirms the crucial role of imagination in the battle against loneliness, emotional and physical, again seeking, with fluid lyricism, escape from loss of self and others—his bed constructed from "the fallen hairs/ of my love, naked, her head dry"—through a magical transformation, the persona flying around his dark room like a bat or angel.

The fourth section of *Rescue the Dead* is the weakest by far, its lapses made glaring by the general excellence of section three, which focuses on rituals of survival in breathless contrast to the violence of the real world (inner and outer), circling from the murder of innocence in England to a derelict, who returns, like "a grey-haired foetus," to his mother while asleep, and two ignored children in the "East Bronx," sharpening their "knives against the curb." The failure of the section stems from a stubborn determination to fashion vehicles of protest, blunt weapons to combat what is perceived as massive public wrongs, such as the Vietnam War and the Medgar Evers incident, and even contains a poem about "Christ" and dares add the coda of "In My Childhood," a facile memory of a yellow canary and a boy with an air gun. Returning to more complex private visions to tap a wellspring, the fifth section recoups some of the lost poetic energy, humming appreciations, never without saving shadows, of a put-upon wife, a foraging bum, an old love, and so on. It peaks with "Omen," a sentimental grab for love from sylvan nature that beats false, but provides a smooth thematic entry to the sixth and final section of eleven poems about poetry, three of which are dedicated to admired fellow craftsmen, Denise Levertov, Marianne Moore, and Williams.

Like Stanley Kunitz, whom he closely resembles in his search for paternal, mystical salvation amid alien corn, Ignatow summons up Dante for validation in "Anew," commencing, "Dante forgot to say,/ Thank you, Lord, for sending me/ to hell." The apex of the sequence is "Walk There," an allegorical walk in a dark wood, full of fear, before a heaven is glimpsed: "Ahead, is that too the sky/ or a clearing?/ Walk there." The desire is credible and is honestly earned by prior struggles with private and public demons, but the poetry that inevitably concludes an Ignatow collection, mirroring Dante's *Paradiso*, never equals in intensity and metaphoric convolutions the engrossing journey through infernal regions that got him there.

Facing the Tree is more of a mixed bag than its predecessors, sure of its technique and confident in voice, and including a growing fondness for prose poems, that most dangerous invitation to self-indulgence. The voice of "Reading the Headlines" mates, typically, personal and social anguish: "I have a burial ground in me where I place the bodies/ without fuss or emotion." Whimsy alternates with stark tragedy as the naïve but shrewd narrator reacts to an evil world by laboring to extract some psychological and spiritual truths from its surface madness, filtered, always, through the mesh of a receptive self. The poems that work efficiently, such as "Letter to a Friend," "My Own Line," "The Refuse Man," "Autumn," "In Season," and several untitled prose poems, are those which remember to keep near the taut edge of the parabolic methodology that Ignatow has perfected, avoiding the glibness and rhetorical excess that ruin so many others in the book, notably where they are attached to political frames, such as "My President Weeps" and "Now

Celebrate Life and Death."

Tread the Dark is similarly confident in style and speech, but its obsession with death and the absence of adequate counter-moods numb the reader to its occasional brilliance and successes, such as "The Abandoned Animal," "Death of a Lawn Mower," "The Dead Sea," "The Forest Warden," "An Account in the Present Tense . . . ," "Midnight," and two untitled pieces, numbered 46 and 80. All the poems are numbered, stressing their author's conception of them as a series structured upon the leitmotif of death. In treading the dark, fighting off oblivion with imagination, the poet too often treads familiar waters, flounders into pretentiousness and embarrassing arch-ness, appropriately reaching a nadir in "Epilogue," a short coda that has the persona, aware of being watched by trees ("tall gods") in his study, bow over his typewriter and start "the ceremony/ of a prayer." A year later, the publication of the highly charged *Sunlight* sequence demonstrated that the decline signaled by *Tread the Dark* was temporary.

Although not equal to Ignatow's strongest volumes, *Whisper to the Earth* is ripe with readiness, open to new modes, and at peace with the softer hues of twilight and autumn and the death they prefigure. Divided into five sec-tions, the collection's first group of poems, with a single exception, approach nature directly, forsaking urbanscapes in favor of garden meditations upon apples and trees and stones, a strategy for resolving death fears, so that en-tering the grave will "be like entering my own house." In a poem for his daughter, "For Yaedi," Ignatow claims that when he dies he wants it said, "that I wasted/ hours in feeling absolutely useless/ and enjoyed it, sensing my life/ more strongly than when I worked at it." Elegies fittingly dominate the next two sections, but the ones for his father and mother—"Kaddish," "The Bread Itself," "A Requiem," and "1905"—can be counted among the most evocative poems he has ever written, regardless of their mellow reor-dering of the past to concentrate upon his parents' genuine gifts to him. The father is forgiven by way of a comprehension of his own harsh youth in Rus-sia, and the mother is celebrated as the "bread" that sustained him. Tension here is less important than the positive electricity of love heightening the language out of itself and its narrative solidity.

The fourth section, "Four Conversations," is the weakest series in the book, a sequence of dialogues that seems to lead toward Wallace Stevens, but its experimental boldness reflects credit upon Ignatow's resolve not to surrender to old age's penchant for self-parody and safe repetitions. In the final sec-tion, the prose poem holds sway, at its tightest in "I Love to Fly," which uses a dream to good effect. The climax is in "With Horace," an identifica-tion with the Roman poet that accepts the Sabine Farm wisdom of his retreat from the city to use the experience of his late years as a new tool for pen-etrating nature's rock hardness.

Edward Butscher

Other major works

NONFICTION: *The Notebooks of David Ignatow*, 1973; *Open Between Us*, 1980; *The One in the Many: A Poet's Memoirs*, 1988.

Bibliography

Emanuel, Lynn, and Anthony Petrosky. "It's Like Having Something in the Bank: An Interview with David Ignatow." *American Poetry* 3 (Winter, 1986): 64-85. This interview offers valuable insights into Ignatow's poetic philosophy. Ordinary life is his subject, and he tries to show it in a new way. Essential to understanding Ignatow.

Ignatow, David. *The Notebooks of David Ignatow*. Chicago: Swallow Press, 1973. Ignatow allows the reader into his creative process by means of these journals. He offers biographical details as well as insights into his philosophy of writing poetry.

_____. *The One in the Many: A Poet's Memoirs*. Middletown, Conn.: Wesleyan University Press, 1988. Ignatow presents his essays on poetry written over a period of four decades. In them, he reveals that he has been obsessed with a single artistic quest: to uncover the human dimension beneath the technical structure of poetic theory. Valuable for any student of Ignatow.

Mazzaro, Jerome. *Postmodern American Poetry*. Urbana: University of Illinois Press, 1980. Mazzaro outlines Ignatow's work, as well as that of six other modern American poets. He includes biographical references and an index. A good, quick overview useful to any student.

Sjoberg, Lief. "An Interview with David Ignatow." *Contemporary Literature* 28 (Summer, 1987): 143-162. Ignatow explains to Sjoberg the influence of Walt Whitman and William Carlos Williams on his poetry. Whitman, he says, wrote about everyday life, and Williams wrote in everyday speech. These two influences were Ignatow's salvation in the 1930's and through the 1950's, when the fashion in poetry was lofty abstraction.

Wakoski, Diane, Linda M. Wagner, and Milton Hindus. "David Ignatow: Three Appreciations." *American Poetry* 3 (Winter, 1986): 35-51. Wakoski praises Ignatow's use of simple American language, as opposed to a more stylized British idiom. Wagner points out that Ignatow achieves the rhythms of spoken speech through idiomatic phrasing rather than colloquial word choice. Hindus explains the reason that Ignatow and his literary predecessors, William Carlos Williams and Walt Whitman, have been so rarely anthologized.

RANDALL JARRELL

Born: Nashville, Tennessee; May 6, 1914
Died: Chapel Hill, North Carolina; October 14, 1965

Principal poetry
"The Rage for the Lost Penny," in *Five Young American Poets*, 1940; *Blood for a Stranger*, 1942; *Little Friend, Little Friend*, 1945; *Losses*, 1948; *The Seven-League Crutches*, 1951; *Selected Poems*, 1955; *The Woman at the Washington Zoo*, 1960; *The Lost World*, 1965; *The Complete Poems*, 1969.

Other literary forms
An important critic and teacher of literature as well as a poet, Randall Jarrell published critical essays, translations, children's books, and a novel. His first book of criticism, *Poetry and the Age* (1953), examines the function of the poet in modern society, the nature of criticism, and the work of John Crowe Ransom, Wallace Stevens, Marianne Moore, and William Carlos Williams. Direct, witty, and sometimes harsh commentary in these essays aims at expanding the appreciative faculty in its broadest sense. The next collection, *A Sad Heart at the Supermarket* (1962), examines values and literature, including the American obsession with consumption. *The Third Book of Criticism* (1969), collected posthumously, includes discussions of Wallace Stevens, Robert Graves, W. H. Auden, Robert Frost, Russian novels, and American poetry since 1900. Close reading, Freudian analysis, myth interpretation, and religious considerations are features of Jarrell's method. His translations include *The Golden Bird and Other Fairy Tales of the Brothers Grimm* (1962) and *Faust, Part I* (1976), as well as other works for children and adults. Jarrell's novel, *Pictures from an Institution* (1954), presents life in an academic community from a satirical point of view. His children's books are *The Gingerbread Rabbit* (1964). *The Bat-Poet* (1964), and *The Animal Family* (1965).

Achievements
Jarrell's reputation as an artist and critic spans a writing career of thirty-three years. Initially recognized as a poet of World War II, Jarrell received a Guggenheim Post-Service Award in 1946. He also served as literary editor of *The Nation*, visiting lecturer at the Salzburg Seminar, and visiting fellow in creative writing at Princeton. Awarded a second Guggenheim Fellowship in 1963, he served as a chancellor of the Academy of American Poets and a member of the National Institute of Art and Letters. One of his collections of poetry and translations, *The Woman at the Washington Zoo*, won the National Book Award in 1960.

Jarrell's chief contribution to the poetry of the twentieth century is his insistence that the experience of ordinary people is worth exploring to discover truth. His work reflects a determination to communicate everyday experience in a language and a form that speak to the general reader as well as to the literary scholar.

Biography

Randall Jarrell spent his youth in Tennessee and California, living with his grandparents in Hollywood for a time when his parents separated. Although his family expected him to go into his uncle's candy business, Jarrell enrolled in psychology at Vanderbilt University, where he met the poet and critic John Crowe Ransom and, through him, other members of the waning Fugitive movement, including Robert Penn Warren, Allen Tate, and Donald Davidson. In 1937, Jarrell and his associate Peter Taylor followed Ransom to Kenyon College, where Jarrell began a lifelong association with Robert Lowell. During this period, Jarrell also completed work for his M.A. degree in literature, including a critical thesis on A. E. Housman under the direction of Donald Davidson.

Jarrell began his career as a professor at the University of Texas in Austin, where he met Mackie Langham, who became his wife in 1940. He enlisted in a ferry-pilot training program soon after Pearl Harbor, but actually began his military career as a private in the Army Air Corps. He served as a celestial navigation tower operator at Chanute Field in Illinois and Davis-Monthan Field in Arizona. After the war he taught at Sarah Lawrence College and then at the Women's College of the University of North Carolina in Greensboro. In the summer of 1948, Jarrell traveled to Europe, teaching American civilization at the Salzburg Summer Seminar. In 1951 Randall and Mackie Jarrell separated, and in 1952 they were divorced. Jarrell married Mary von Schrader late in 1952.

Jarrell was hospitalized briefly for a nervous disorder in 1965. He continued to teach at the University of North Carolina in Greensboro until October of that year, when he was struck and killed by an automobile in Chapel Hill, North Carolina.

Analysis

Randall Jarrell's poetry speaks with intelligence and humanity about the problem of change as it affects men and women in the twentieth century. Often using the motif of a dreamer awakening in an unfamiliar world, Jarrell probes the experience of each speaker to discover enduring truths, however bleak they may be. Although the speakers in his poems learn that the difference between innocence and experience is often bewilderment and pain, they also express a sense of dignity and affirmation. Whether the focus is on a soldier facing death, a mother relinquishing her son, or a lonely woman wandering in a zoo, Jarrell's poems achieve a balance between the common experience of humanity and the suffering of the individual.

From the beginning of his career, Jarrell confronted the necessity that opposes human desires. In early works such as "For an Emigrant" and "The Refugees," he acknowledges the enormous isolation that engulfs hopeful arrivals gaining their freedom only to endure without identity in their new homeland. On a larger scale, Jarrell also anticipates the self-destructive force of mankind in poems such as "The Automaton" and "The See-er of Cities," in which archetypal death figures hover on the horizons of civilization. Jarrell's lasting concern, however, is the individual's search for meaning in a world of change and death. In "90 North," a poem following the pattern of the dreamer awakening to the world of experience, a child secure in bed at night dreams of discovering the North Pole. Envisioning himself as an adult explorer, the lone survivor of his party, the child reaches his goal only to find darkness and cold. This experience of emptiness and death becomes for him the truth he sought: "Nothing comes from nothing . . ./ Pain comes from the darkness/ And we call it wisdom. It is pain." Next, the child's dream is juxtaposed with an adult's dream in which North has no meaning, for the adult realizes that the dark world of dream is the final reality of man's experience, the meaninglessness acceptable only to the unconscious and terrifying to the conscious explorer of existence. A deep-sea diver makes a similar journey in "The Iceberg," finding ultimate annihilation in the "sick ambiguous wisdom of the sea" and surfacing to observe the many faces of the great berg melting as he loses consciousness.

In his second collection, *Little Friend, Little Friend*, Jarrell's presentation of those affected by World War II reflects the same concern with the extremes of psychological experience, whether at first hand or vicariously. In the war poems, specific characters and settings provide a structural basis and blank verse provides the medium for the voices. In "2nd Air Force," a mother visiting her son at an air base senses the necessary detachment of the young soldiers preparing their bombers, "hopeful cells/ heavy with someone else's death." She knows that her son, like the others, may as easily be a victim, and she ponders whether all her years of hope and care "meant this?" In the course of her meditation, she sees in her imagination the crash of her son in a burning plane; the distress call "little friend," Jarrell's title for the book, is repeated without hope of the young pilot's survival. "Losses," one of the most famous poems in the collection, voices the confusion of young soldiers for whom death has yet no personal meaning. They are amazed when members of their group disappear during training, since ordinary accidents lack the heroism expected in wartime. In their view, "it was not dying: everybody died," and surely they expected more of the experience than to die "like aunts or pets or foreigners." Even in battle over the unfamiliar cities of the enemy, the youths still fail to comprehend the meaning of their end. The problem, as Jarrell's simple, colloquial speaker addresses it, is that "When we left high school nothing else had died/ For us to figure we had died like." Their dream of life failed to allow for personal experience of death; the cities they bomb are no more to them than names studied in geography class at school.

Jarrell's awareness of the child within each fighting man appears also in "The State" and "The Death of the Ball Turret Gunner," often anthologized for their dramatic appeal. The speaker of the first understands the power of government through the loss of his family. He begins, "When they killed my mother it made me nervous," continuing to lament the loss of his sister, and finally his cat; their disappearance causes the death of his consciousness, underscored by the simple frantic expression of a child. The speaker of "The Death of the Ball Turret Gunner" endures a cycle of birth to death in the course of his service to the "State." Awakening to discover himself in the rotating turret of a fighting plane "six miles from earth, loosed from its dream of life," his nightmare of reality ends violently as it began, but his voice persists: "When I died they washed me out of the turret with a hose." A poem recording a similar awakening with greater detail and tension, "A Pilot from the Carrier," describes a flier's escape from his burning plane and his lengthy parachute descent. Imagery of fire and ice effectively captures the intensity of his struggle to free himself from the "blazing wheel" of the cockpit. As the ball turret gunner falls into the belly of the State, so the pilot descends toward the warmth of earth, its sunlight and stillness contrasting with his frenzied escape. As he hangs suspended over the sea, his new perceptions, "the great flowering of his life," create a sense of detachment and calm. The brilliant gleam of his burning plane as it reaches the water reveals his location to an enemy plane so that he recognizes the approach of death as clearly as if he were "reading a child's first scrawl." In his last moments he learns the lesson of his own vulnerability in the unreasoning natural world. As a bombardier realizes in "Siegfried," death simply comes: "It happens as it does because it does."

The difficulty of reconciling a moral perspective with the life of war is the subject of "Eighth Air Force," one of Jarrell's best-known poems. Civilian life and battle merge for the men of this force that bombed continental targets from bases in Britain. Having the opportunity for some domestic comforts, the men groom themselves, keep pets, and even cut flowers. As they lounge, playing cards and counting up their missions, are they murderers because they have fulfilled their duty the day before? The persona delivers no harsh judgment on these whom he observes, for he has been one of them and has survived. As Pilate offered Christ, so he offers these figures for whom he has suffered and lied in his dreams. As he sees it, the guilt must be widely shared: "Men wash their hands, in blood, as best they can." Actor and victim become arbitrary designations once the process of war begins. In this view, to "behold the man" carries complex contradictory associations. The men are saviors of Europe, sinners against their own consciences, and scapegoats for others' blame. As the speaker shares their role, the reader must evaluate the speaker's final judgment that he "finds no fault in this just man," a composite symbol for the Eighth Air Force and humanity itself.

Jarrell also deals with the problems of accepting violence and death as a part of life in "Burning the Letters," portraying the wife of a pilot killed in the Pacific. Her husband died a fiery death, and now, several years later, she burns his letters as a sign of relinquishment. Jarrell notes that she was once a Christian, and, in her meditation, imagery of her husband's death mingles continually with imagery of Christ as she struggles to reconcile the paradox of life exchanged for death. In the context of her loss, Christ appears as a flame and a bird of prey seeking the hidden lives of those who dwell in darkness; then they turn on him, drawing from his life both bread and blood. Entering her dream, the woman sees herself as an aging child, clutching at the Christ figure who devours his own body before flickering away in the darkness. In addition to identifying the death of her husband with the death of Christ, she also recalls the sea burial of her husband in terms of the secretive burial of Christ's body. Like those who buried Christ, and those who bury the dead at sea, she attempts to bury her dead in flames. Although she chooses life for herself, her final prayer is addressed to the grave. Her acceptance of the death of her husband points toward a final emptiness and negation; in this nightmare of experience she acknowledges the same end discovered by the dreaming child in "90 North."

If human experience converges ultimately in isolation, emptiness, and darkness, where is the life men expect to have lived? Dreams also carry out this function in Jarrell's poems. "Absent with Official Leave" records the dreamlife of a soldier who finds his only protection from painful experience in sleep. There he achieves identity beyond his number and enjoys relationships not controlled by authority. After the lights dim, he enters the larger world "where civilians die/ Inefficiently, in their spare time, for nothing." Curved roads, contrasting sharply with the grids of army life, lead into a pastoral atmosphere where hunters seek birds in sporting fashion. In a cottage, the soldier visualizes the careful work of loving women "tending slow small fires." Their presence signals a transition to the "charmed" world of a fairy tale, where the soldier becomes a bear sheltered by Snow White and Rose Red as snow falls in the form of gentle blossoms. Negative forces appear, also, in the shape of accusing eyes and "grave mysterious beings" from his past, who represent the causes that justify war. Although they mourn his fate hypocritically at best, in his dream they grant him justification, signifying the love that he longs to experience. The poem reflects Jarrell's interest in the fairy tale and myth as a means of wish-fulfillment connected with the unconscious. The dreamer awakes, however, to the darkness of his fellow soldiers. A fuller development of the conflict between the fairy-tale world of dream and the painful nature of reality is "The Marchen," dramatizing men's desires to live and rule over an obstacle-filled environment.

While many critics believe that Jarrell found his most effective subject in the turmoil of war, his interest in the folktale stimulated a series of meditative poems in the collection *The Seven-League Crutches*. In the well-known poem "A Girl in a Library," Jarrell considers the outlook of a modern young coed napping in the library. Although she is no intellectual (her subjects are home economics and physical education), she too is a dreamer, with the simplicity of a kitten. Unaware of the power that the library offers in terms of art or science, she rests secure in the method of her modern studies of function and technique. The speaker who observes her, however, recognizes her potential as a woman of virtue and intelligence such as Alexander Pushkin's Tatyana Larina, if she should ever awake from her "sleep of life." Her courses in food preparation and exercise will surely not arouse the soul within her, which "has no assignments/ neither cooks/ Nor referees." The mythic self locked within her, however, balances the speaker's judgment of her superficial dreams and pursuits. Two earlier poems that reflect similar needs among young students are "Children Selecting Books in a Library" and "The Carnegie Library, Juvenile Division." In these poems, children seek intellectual transformation, unknowingly, in the imaginative world of myth and fairy tale, in contrast with the older girl, who will never be significantly changed by anything in the library. She will, however, carry out the rituals of love and suffering that the speaker anticipates in his allusions to the Corn King and Spring Queen of the ancient myths.

Jarrell's interest in the psychology of the fairy tale also appears in several reworkings of well-known works. "A Quilt Pattern" incorporates the plot of "Hansel and Gretel" in a child's dream that forms the narrative line of the poem, enriched with allusions to the Fall of Genesis. Hansel and Gretel are renamed "Good Me and Bad Me" to underscore the psychological aspects of the story. Similarly, Jarrell's version of "Cinderella" portrays her as an ash girl rejecting the world in favor of an "imaginary playmate," the godmother. This Cinderella indulges herself in fantasies that are destructive in the end. She moves from the fireside of her childhood to the furniture of marriage and family life, then finally into the fires of Hell, where she is again happy in isolation from reality. In like manner, Jarrell deals with the other side of fairy tales in "The Sleeping Beauty: Variation of the Prince" and "La Belle au Bois Dormant." In the first reworking of the tale, Jarrell proposes a new ending in which the prince does not awaken the princess with his kiss, but determines to sleep on eternally with her, thus achieving a truly permanent union. The story also embodies a death wish—the desire for an unbroken peace—and a rejection of sexual fulfillment. In "La Belle au Bois Dormant," Jarrell uses the sleeping beauty story in a perverse way to present a woman who has been murdered and dismembered by her lover. The poems are characteristic of Jarrell in the theme of a lonely death without transcendence or hope, but the characters lack the grounding in a human context that enhances Jarrell's best work.

"The Woman at the Washington Zoo," one of Jarrell's most powerful treatments of human loneliness, reflects the intensity of experience typical of his poetry. An aging woman finds herself envying the caged specimens she observes for the attention they receive, while she remains invisible among the sightseers. Women pass her in brightly colored saris corresponding to the dramatic clothing of the leopard in his cage. The navy print she wears, however, receives no attention, no complaints, and entraps her as surely as iron bars imprison an animal body. The tall columns of Washington serve the same function, in fact, separating the lonely woman from the other workers whom she passes. Her inner cries burst out in frustration at the world's indifference to her suffering. In desperation she covets the experience of violence she sees as the animals devour their meat. Identifying with the offal rejected by all but the vulture, the old woman imagines the hope of a magical transformation and release. Calling out to this ugliest of birds, she visualizes herself among the animal kingdom with man as the ruler: "You know what I was,/ You see what I am: change me, change me!" In the impossibility of her outward renewal is the necessity that frustrates hope; in the expression of her need is release and affirmation of self. Jarrell's poem gives utterance to the suffering of the woman as a type and as an individual, providing a wider recognition of her existence and of the human need for inner change and transformation through love.

Jarrell's last volume of poetry, *The Lost World*, emphasizes the themes of his maturity: aging, loneliness, loss, and the dreamworld where every man is a child. "Next Day," for example, is narrated by a lonely middle-class woman who has suddenly recognized her passage into old age. Her material and social success far surpass that of the woman at the zoo, but she is equally unhappy. The title of the poem refers to the woman's vision of herself in the mirror the day after attending the funeral of a friend her age. In plain language and a contemporary American setting Jarrell presents ordinary experience with great psychological intensity.

The poems of the final collection also treat the experiences of pain and loss with an affirmative note, for especially in these poems Jarrell develops the power of the dreamworld as real, if only in a metaphorical sense. In "The Lost Children," "The Lost World," and "Thinking of the Lost World," the experience of reality attains for some a magical, mythical quality in its own right. "The Lost Children" originated as a dream recorded by Jarrell's wife and develops a wish-fulfillment sequence found in "They" by Rudyard Kipling. While Kipling's story involves the recovery of a man's beloved child among several who have returned to earth after death, Jarrell's poem uses this dream as a background for a mother's contemplation of the possession and loss of a child as it matures. Each stanza then presents a stage in the process of separation and maturity. Eventually the parent exchanges the parental bond for friendship with the child as an adult, but the initial relationship lives on in the mother's consciousness. The mother compares the persistence of memory to a hide-and-seek game that the little girls still require her to play. The thought of them brings sadness at their separation, but the richness of the association remains.

"The Lost World" recovers portions of Jarrell's own past, using sensory impressions as Marcel Proust uses them in *Le temps retrouvé* (1927, *The Past Recaptured*). The poem is Jarrell's own, however, although it may have been stimulated by his interest in Proust's *À la recherche du temps perdu* (1913-1927, *Remembrance of Things Past*). Jarrell employs the effective strategies of his thirty years' writing experience to create impressions of his life in Hollywood in the 1920's, combining the world of his neighborhood with the world of art and filmmaking. Although the poem is narrated in the present tense, a sense of the struggle of re-creating time appears periodically as a conflict. Images of Hollywood, boyhood fantasies, and intense moments of pleasure or fear interweave in a journey undertaken to establish relationships between the past and the meaning of the present. "Thinking of the Lost World" considers the importance of the quest for the lost world of childhood. In keeping with the meditative intent of the poem, Jarrell returns from the formalistic use of terza rima that structures "The Lost World" to the conversational free verse characteristic of his later work. The flavor of chocolate tapioca evokes memories for the speaker of the poem as did the taste of the madeleine in Proust's great work of memory, but Jarrell's narrator finds the way into the past more difficult. "The sunshine of the Land/ Of Sunshine is a gray mist now," he admits, and the atmosphere is as polluted as that of an area given up to industry. In the realm of memory he constructs a compensating fantasy, an "undiscovered/ Country between California and Arizona," where his past resides. He longs, too, for the objects of the past: his "Mama's dark blue Buick" or "Lucky's electric" surely could transport him back. His late aunt reappears to him often in the guise of other women, and in this regard his past sustains itself in awakening memory.

The changes in his own body also testify to some remarkable ongoing process that persists despite the attempts of his memory to conserve the lost world of childhood and maturity. For the speaker as for the mother in "The Lost Children," the paradox is that while nothing remains, all of the past belongs to the rememberer. As he says, "My soul has memorized world after world," and in this memory he finds not merely an acceptable end, but happiness. For him, an awareness of the loss is assurance of some existence in the past that transcends time and death. The awareness itself is a "reward," a way of coming to terms with change in human experience, perhaps the central concern of Jarrell's poetry.

Tremendous sensitivity, critical insight, and human concern characterized the work of Jarrell throughout his career. The vigor of his last poems suggests that his work had not reached its end, although much of his talent had fulfilled itself in his last books. Jarrell wrote poetry with a human focus, poetry that is lasting and influential in its attempt to communicate the nature of experience in the modern world.

Chapel Louise Petty

Other major works

LONG FICTION: *Pictures from an Institution*, 1954.

SHORT FICTION: *The Golden Bird and Other Fairy Tales of the Brothers Grimm*, 1962 (translation).

PLAY: *Faust, Part I*, 1976 (translation).

NONFICTION: *Poetry and the Age*, 1953; *A Sad Heart at the Supermarket*, 1962; *The Third Book of Criticism*, 1969; *Kipling, Auden, & Co.: Essays and Reviews, 1935-1964*, 1981; *Randall Jarrell's Letters: An Autobiographical and Literary Selection*, 1985.

CHILDREN'S LITERATURE: *The Gingerbread Rabbit*, 1964; *The Bat-Poet*, 1964; *The Animal Family*, 1965.

Bibliography

Bryant, J. A. *Understanding Randall Jarrell.* Columbia: University of South Carolina Press, 1986. An easy book to read. Contains biographical information and an overview of Jarrell's writings, including a breakdown of his earlier poems, his criticism and essays, his children's poems, and his later poetry. Supplemented with a bibliography and an index.

Ferguson, Suzanne. *The Poetry of Randall Jarrell.* Baton Rouge: Louisiana State University Press, 1971. This excellent book stresses Jarrell as first a teacher and second a poet. Ferguson gives a solid, in-depth analysis of his major works, taking selections from all of his different areas of interest. Complemented by a select bibliography and an exhaustive index.

Flynn, Richard. *Randall Jarrell and the Lost World of Childhood.* Athens: University of Georgia Press, 1990. Flynn addresses the importance of Jarrell redetermining the "child's set face" in the tumultuous life-style of modern-day society. The critical analysis that he offers is very insightful in this neglected genre of children's poetry, as he sets Jarrell up as one of its masters. Contains a good bibliography and an index.

Hoffman, Frederick. *The Achievement of Randall Jarrell.* Glenview, Ill.: Scott, Foresman, 1970. This short book concentrates on an analysis of Jarrell's poetry, centering on one of his characteristic themes, that of a dreamer being awakened into a reality which is somehow parallel or connected to the dream. Although not comprehensive in the scope of all Jarrell's poetry, it provides excellent coverage within that parameter.

Lowell, Robert, et al., eds. *Randall Jarrell: 1914-1965*. New York: Farrar, Straus & Giroux, 1967. In this book of assorted essays, Jarrell's life is reflected on by many of his friends and scholars. Offers excellent coverage of his dreams, aspirations, and writings as seen from diverse individuals, but gives little critical analysis of his works.

Meyers, Jeffrey. *Manic Power: Robert Lowell and His Circle*. New York: Arbor House, 1987. Investigates the relationships between Robert Lowell, John Berryman, Theodore Roethke, and Jarrell. Meyers gives an in-depth study of the influences these men had on Jarrell and sheds light on the foundations from which his poetry emerged. Supplemented by a select bibliography and an index.

ROBINSON JEFFERS

Born: Pittsburgh, Pennsylvania; January 10, 1887
Died: Carmel, California; January 20, 1962

Principal poetry

Flagons and Apples, 1912; *Californians*, 1916; *Tamar and Other Poems*, 1924; *Roan Stallion, Tamar, and Other Poems*, 1925; *The Women at Point Sur*, 1927; *Cawdor and Other Poems*, 1928; *Dear Judas and Other Poems*, 1929; *Descent to the Dead: Poems Written in Ireland and Great Britain*, 1931; *Thurso's Landing and Other Poems*, 1932; *Give Your Heart to the Hawks and Other Poems*, 1933; *Solstice and Other Poems*, 1935; *Such Counsels You Gave to Me and Other Poems*, 1937; *Poems Known and Unknown*, 1938; *The Selected Poetry of Robinson Jeffers*, 1938; *Be Angry at the Sun and Other Poems*, 1941; *Medea*, 1946 (verse drama, translation); *The Double Axe and Other Poems*, 1948; *Hungerfield and Other Poems*, 1954; *The Beginning and the End*, 1963; *Selected Poems*, 1965; *The Alpine Christ and Other Poems*, 1973; *Brides of the South Wind*, 1974; *What Odd Expedients and Other Poems*, 1980; *Rock and Hawk: A Selection of Shorter Poems by Robinson Jeffers*, 1987; *The Collected Poetry of Robinson Jeffers: Volume I, 1920-1928*, 1988; *The Collected Poetry of Robinson Jeffers: Volume II, 1928-1938*, 1989; *The Collected Poetry of Robinson Jeffers: Volume III, 1939-1962*, 1991.

Other literary forms

Robinson Jeffers explained his own work and expressed his ideas on society and art in some detail in the forewords to the Modern Library edition (1935) of his *Roan Stallion, Tamar, and Other Poems* and his *Selected Poetry of Robinson Jeffers* (1938). Other important prose statements are "Poetry, Gongorism and a Thousand Years," *The New York Times Book Review*, Jan. 18, 1948, pp. 16, 26; *Themes in My Poems* (1956); and *The Selected Letters of Robinson Jeffers, 1897-1962* (1968, Ann N. Ridgeway, editor).

In addition, the poet William Everson has collected, from various forgotten pages, two volumes of poetry that Jeffers had discarded. These volumes reconstitute the work of the transitional period from 1916 to 1922. They are *The Alpine Christ and Other Poems* (1973) and *Brides of the South Wind* (1974).

Achievements

Many years after his death, Jeffers remains probably the most controversial American poet, with the exception of Edgar Allan Poe, who has ever been termed "major." A number of important writers and critics have ranked him with Walt Whitman and invoked the Greek tragedians in trying to suggest his somber power. In the early years of his fame his books typically went into several editions, and he was the subject of a *Time* magazine cover story. In 1947 his free translation of *Medea* for the New York stage brought him new acclaim as a dramatic poet. Since the early years of his fame, however, some critics, few but influential, were hostile, and others found Jeffers merely uninteresting as the subject of critical examination. The deep division over Jeffers' importance as a poet is seen today in college anthologies: he is given generous space in some, and omitted entirely from others. The weight of criticism, however, has been consistently on the positive side. In relatively recent years, a number of serious studies have been published which, while strongly favorable, avoid the extravagant praise of some of Jeffers' early admirers. All but the most hostile critics are agreed that he had an unmistakably original voice, strong dramatic talents, and great descriptive ability. He is the only American poet of note since Edwin Arlington Robinson— who praised him highly—to write a large quantity of narrative poetry. Some of Jeffers' short lyrics, moreover, notably "Hurt Hawks," "The Eye," "The Purse-Seine," and "Shine, Perishing Republic," seem destined to become classics. In addition to his poetic gifts, and indeed inseparable from them, is the force of a worldview that is unusual, coherent, and challenging, a set of reasoned attitudes that justifies classifying him as a philosophical poet of unusual interest. Jeffers' radical skepticism about the human race, embodied in his doctrine that man should "uncenter himself" from the universe, is expressed in poetry that draws on considerable scientific and historical study, on thorough knowledge of religious and classical literature, and on deep resources of myth and ritual. It is the combination of poetic power and philosophical stance that argues strongly for Jeffers' place in a twentieth century pantheon of American poets.

Biography

John Robinson Jeffers' life, milieu, and work are of one piece. From his early adulthood, one can see him choosing a place of living and a way of life that are strongly reflected in his poetry and in his occasional prose statements about his work.

When Jeffers was born in Pittsburgh in 1887 his father was forty-nine, his mother twenty-seven. His father's occupation as well as his age set the boy apart; the senior Jeffers had been a Presbyterian minister and was Professor of Old Testament Literature and Exegesis at Western Theological Seminary. Young Robin was an only child for seven years, and he spent much of his time in solitary wandering or reading on the relatively isolated family property. He was later educated in Switzerland for nearly four years, in schools in which the language of instruction was either French or German. His father had introduced him to Greek at the age of five, and he also acquired Latin and some Italian. After his parents moved to Los Angeles, he entered Occidental College, where he continued his classical and literary education and supplemented his childhood religious training with courses in biblical literature and theology.

Although popular with his fellow students, Jeffers already was establishing the pattern of his life through his interest in camping and mountain climbing on the one hand, and in reading and writing on the other. Graduating at eighteen, he then pursued medical studies at the University of Southern California, and later studied forestry, hoping to find a way to support himself amid nature that would permit him time for poetry. A small legacy, however, enabled him to settle, with his bride Una Call Custer, in Carmel, California, in 1914. The whole area, then uncrowded, had a dramatic beauty, and Jeffers called it his "inevitable place." He was profoundly affected by its massive simplicity of elements: huge, treeless mountains plunging directly into the Pacific, broken by occasional narrow canyons in which grew at that time little groves of redwoods; the constant pound and swirl of the sea against bare granite shore-rocks; hawks soaring above the cattle-pasturing headlands. In this setting, Jeffers helped masons to construct a simple stone house on Carmel Point, looking directly seaward; and, later, he built with his own hands, using boulders that he laboriously rolled up from the shore, his famous "Hawk Tower." Evoking with its name the fierce independence of the birds that were one of his favorite subjects, the tower became symbolically for him a place beyond time, a psychological vantage point for his often apocalyptic and prophetic stance in the world.

With his wife, to whom he was devoted, Jeffers reared twin sons (a daughter, born previously, lived only a day), and lived quietly in Carmel, departing only for vacations in Taos, New Mexico, and for rare trips to the East Coast or the British Isles. With a very few exceptions, he did not participate in the round of readings, book reviews, or campus appearances that characterizes the life of so many American poets. He won a number of important awards, including the Academy of American Poets prize; he was never given the Pulitzer Prize, even though Edna St. Vincent Millay and Louis Untermeyer, among others, repeatedly pressed his case.

When Jeffers died in 1962, it was in the seaward bedroom of his own house. There, in the poem "The Bed by the Window," he had many years earlier envisioned the day when a ghostly figure would appear, rap with his staff, and say, "Come, Jeffers."

Analysis

Robinson Jeffers' central concept of the universe and of mankind's place in it, all-important in understanding his poetry, is grounded in his respect for scientific thought and in his own historical observations, but strongly colored in its expression by emotion. From science, he took a cool, analytical view of the human race as one species that evolved in one stage of an ever-evolving, dynamic universe—a mere "fly-speck" in the scheme of things. Perhaps because of his interest in astronomy (his younger brother, Hamilton, was for many years a scientist at the Lick Observatory in California), he took an extraterrestrial view even of the earth. The first photograph taken by the astronauts of the earth from the vicinity of the moon represented a view that Jeffers had achieved in his imagination long before: "It is only a little planet/ But how beautiful it is. . . . " In "The Double Axe," Jeffers paid tribute to one of the scientists who helped him to achieve this view, Copernicus, hailing him as the first who "pushed man/ Out of his insane self-importance. . . . "

A second factor which influenced Jeffers' outlook was his study of history. From the British archaeologist Flinders Petrie and the Italian philosopher Giovanni Battista Vico, Jeffers drew the concept of cultural cycles and the conviction that cultural or national groupings are inherently unstable and social progress temporary. This view, again, was bolstered by his observations of the inevitable cycles of growth, flowering, and decay in nature. It was given special force by Jeffers' belief, influenced by Oswald Spengler, that Western civilization was already on the downgrade.

Many scientists share Jeffers' objective view of the world but not the intensity of his feeling for the insignificance of humanity or the "beauty of things," his often-used phrase for natural loveliness. The roots of Jeffers' feeling seem to be in the Calvinistic teachings of his father's religion, which proclaimed the glory of God and the nothingness of man. Rejecting his father's Christian God, Jeffers transferred his religious feeling to a new object, a universe whose parts are all "expressions of the same energy," a dynamic universe, ever in strain and struggle, and ever in that process discovering its own nature. In a letter outlining his views, Jeffers wrote, "This whole is in all its parts so beautiful, and is felt by me to be so intensely in earnest, that I am compelled to love it, and to think of it as divine." He went on to say that he felt there was "peace, freedom, I might say a kind of salvation, in turning one's affections toward this one God, rather than inward on one's self, or on humanity, or on human imagination and abstractions. . . . " Jeffers' sole admission of the possibility that humans could have a positive effect was to say that one may "contribute (ever so slightly) to the beauty of things by making one's own life and environment beautiful. . . . " While he granted that such action could include moral beauty, which he called one of the qualities of humanity, for the most part the weight of his emotions was on the side of sad resignation where the human race was concerned, or actual disgust with its frequent moral ugliness.

Jeffers' intensity of feeling for natural beauty and especially for the dynamism of nature was profoundly affected by his lifelong residence on the spectacular Carmel coast. The area is not only ruggedly beautiful, but is also wracked by periodic events reminding one of the awesome power of nature and of man's uncertain tenure on earth: brush fires that sweep the dry hills in late summer and sometimes destroy farms and homes; earthquakes that shudder along the San Andreas fault; fierce winds that torture the pictur-esque Monterey cypresses; drenching rains that bring floods and dangerous mudslides. These natural events, recalling the fire, earthquake, wind, and deluge of the biblical apocalypse, appear as major instruments of destruction in many of the narratives, and are centrally important, too, in some of the lyrics. Most important, probably, was the sheer beauty of the surroundings, beauty which Jeffers identified as one of the six major themes in his poems in a talk given in 1941 at the Library of Congress. It is possible to imagine Jeffers living on the coast of Ireland, or in the Scottish Hebrides, or on a mountainside, but not in a quiet New England meadow or an industrial city. He chose his landscape, his "inevitable place," and it in turn formed him and became a major actor in his dramas. Today the Carmel/Big Sur area is known as "Jeffers country."

The expression of his basic attitudes, to which Jeffers eventually gave the name "Inhumanism," took three major forms in poetry: dramatic, narrative, and, loosely considered, lyric. The dramatic poetry includes not only a play primarily intended for stage production, Euripedes' *Medea*, but also dramas primarily intended to be read, a Japanese Noh play, and a masque. The nar-ratives and dramas range in length to well above one hundred pages. The lyrics include some poems that are of substantial length—several pages or more. Some poems are mixtures of elements and defy classification.

The narratives and dramas reveal metaphorically—and occasionally through interposed comments—Jeffers' preoccupation with the self-concern and so-lipsism of the human race. At the same time, they express the poet's sense of the historical cycles of human behavior and of the larger cycle of death and rebirth that Jeffers called, in "Cawdor," the "great Life." To embody these attitudes, Jeffers chose a number of often shocking subjects: incest, murder, rape, self-mutilation because of guilt, suicide, and the sexual feel-ings of a woman for a horse.

One of the best of the long narratives, the one which caused the greatest initial sensation when it was published with other poems in 1924, is *Tamar.* The setting is an isolated part of the California coast, where the Cauldwell family lives. Circumstances lead the daughter, Tamar, and her brother, Lee, into incest. Later, Tamar learns that her father had committed the same sin with his sister, now long dead. In one strange scene on the beach at night Tamar is possessed sexually by the ghosts of the Indians who once occupied the area; the scene is a kind of descent into death, and after it Tamar is a "flame," self-destructive and demonic, feeling herself doomed because of her breaking of natural laws. She then tempts her father sexually, as if to prove her depravity, although she commits no sexual act with him. Finally, the entire family is consumed in a fire from which they could have saved themselves had not Tamar, her brother, and her suitor, Will Andrews, been acting out the climax of fierce sexual jealousy.

This seemingly fantastic and occasionally lurid drama was based on one or both of the two biblical Tamar stories, and on Percy Bysshe Shelley's *The Cenci* (1820), all of which include incest. These tales in turn, however, are overshadowed by the Greek myth of the creation of the human race: the incest of Heaven and Earth to produce Titan, and Titan's ensuing incest with his mother, Earth, to produce a child. Thus Jeffers has created a modern story based on layers of myth, reminding readers of the powerful libidinal forces that have been repressed by millennia of taboos but never, as Sophocles and Sigmund Freud noted, eliminated from human nightmares. Further, the isolated home of the Cauldwells on Point Lobos allegorically suggests the entire world, and the initial incest has strong overtones of Adam's fall. Thus man's failure to relate himself humbly to his environment, obeying natural laws such as the ban on incest, is comparable to Adam and Eve ignoring God's command to know their place in the scheme of things. The expulsion of Adam and Eve from paradise is comparable to the troubles visited on the little world of the House of Cauldwell. The story, moreover, is a chapter of apocalypse, with fire—persistently invoked throughout as an agent of cleansing destruction—accomplishing the destruction of Judgment Day. It is prophecy inasmuch as it warns against man's self-concern. It is also persistently evocative, as Robert J. Brophy has pointed out (*Robinson Jeffers: Myth, Ritual, and Symbol in His Narrative Poems*, 1973), of the monomyth of the seasonal cycle of death and rebirth. Yet only in relatively recent years have critics paid systematic attention to the complexity of *Tamar* and Jeffers' other narratives.

Those other narratives similarly explore recurrent patterns of human conduct as expressed in folklore, myth, or religion. "Roan Stallion," the poet's most powerful short narrative, is a modern version of the myth of God uniting with a human. This pattern is seen not only in the Christian story of the fatherhood of Jesus, but also in myths from various cultures, especially the Greek tales of Zeus and his sexual encounters—with Leda, when he took the form of a swan; with Antiope, as a satyr; with Europa, as a bull; and others. "The Tower Beyond Tragedy," one of Jeffers' most successful long poems, is a free adaptation of the first two plays of Aeschylus' *Oresteia* (458 B.C.). In "Cawdor," the poet reworks the Hippolytus story of Euripides, adding an element—self-mutilation—from Sophocles' *Oedipus the King* (429-401 B.C.). "The Loving Shepherdess," another relatively early narrative that was well received, is imaginatively based on the Scottish legend of "Feckless Fannie." "Such Counsels You Gave to Me" is built on suggestions from the Scottish ballad "Edward, Edward," which in turn, like all true ballads, invokes deep folk memories. Other narratives explore age-old problems. "Give Your Heart to the Hawks" explores the question of who should administer justice; "Thurso's Landing" considers when, if ever, it is right to take another's life out of pity.

In one of his early long poems—the longest, in fact, at 175 pages—Jeffers did not base his story on myth or folklore, but created a poem that has become itself a kind of literary legend of magnificent failure: *The Women at Point Sur*. It is a violent, brilliant, chaotic, and difficult-to-comprehend story of a mad minister who collects disciples by telling them that there are no more moral rules and that they can do as their hearts, or bodies, desire. The poem did not generally achieve one of its main purposes, which, as Jeffers put it, was to show "the danger of that 'Roan Stallion' idea of 'breaking out of humanity,' misinterpreted in the mind of a fool or a lunatic." The prologue and other parts are impressive, nevertheless, and the poem has a curiously prescient character. Barclay, who commits an incestuous rape to prove that he is beyond good and evil himself, leads his followers into sex orgies. Not very many years later, the Big Sur area of the poem was the scene of sometimes tragic experimentation in sexual behavior amid some of the more extreme communes and "sensitivity institutes." Further, Barclay's corrupting influence on those around him prefigured the monstrous sway that Charles Manson held over the young women who went out from his remote California hideaway to do murder at his bidding.

The nature of the narratives and dramas changed somewhat through the years. In Jeffers' first mature period (his youthful work, when he produced two volumes of conventional verse, is of interest only to specialists), the concentration was on writing modern versions of myths, such as *Tamar*. In the second period, ranging from the late 1920's to about 1935, the narratives were realistic, though still based on older stories. Such scenes as the violation of Tamar by ghostly Indians were no longer written. "Cawdor," "Thurso's Landing," and "Give Your Heart to the Hawks" were in this vein, while "Dear Judas," chronologically a part of the period, a play in the Japanese Noh form, was based on myth and religion. In the late 1930's, Jeffers again concentrated on myth. In two of his least successful narratives, "Solstice" and "Such Counsels You Gave to Me," he focused on what Frederick I. Carpenter (*Robinson Jeffers*, 1962) has called "case histories in abnormal psychology." In the same period Jeffers wrote "At the Birth of an Age," a philosophical poem, partly in dramatic form, which has as a central figure a self-torturing Hanged God of the universe. One of the most interesting of Jeffers' poems, it is also one of the most complex and difficult, often appealing primarily to the mind, and having some of the same virtues and faults as Shelley's *Prometheus Unbound* (1820).

Jeffers again ventured into the mythic and the supernatural in "The Double Axe," a two-part poem published in 1948. In the first part, "The Love and the Hate," he took an idea from his earlier "Resurrection," a short narrative (1932) about a World War I soldier returned miraculously from the grave. In "The Love and the Hate," Hoult Gore has similarly returned from death in World War II. His denunciation of war and his presentation of the facts about who actually suffers for the pride of patriots and politicians are sometimes eloquent, but the ghoulishness of the central figure, the walking corpse, is so naturally repellent that it is difficult for the reader to sympathize with the hero emotionally, much less to identify with him. Additionally, there are moments when the writing comes close to unintentional humor, as when Gore's widow, first seeing him, says he looks "dreadful." The violence of the action, even though it is meant to be cleansing, is not properly prepared for by the buildup of emotions, so that it seems exaggerated and gratuitous. The second half of the poem, "The Inhumanist," is much more successful. In this poem Jeffers creates a new mythical hero, an old man armed with Zeus's double-bitted axe, which is a symbol both of divine destruction and procreation. This Inhumanist has various adventures in the course of a complex and sometimes supernatural story. Despite its flaws, which include prosy passages of bitter political ranting, it is one of the essential poems for anyone wishing to achieve a full knowledge of Jeffers' thought.

"The Double Axe," which dealt a heavy blow to Jeffers' reputation, was succeeded by one other major narrative, another excursion into the supernatural, but this time a generally successful one—"Hungerfield." Written after the crushing blow of Una Jeffers' death, "Hungerfield" tells the story of a man who wrestled with death to save his mother from cancer. This violation of natural laws causes all kinds of other natural disasters to occur, recalling the way that the "miracle drugs" and chemical sprays with which people and farmlands are treated cause unforeseen and often disastrous side effects. The Hungerfield story, which also has mythic references (Hungerfield is a Hercules figure), is framed by Jeffers' personal meditation on the death of his wife, and ends with his reconciliation with it. These framing passages lack the compactness and intense poetic power of Jeffers' best lyrics, but their directness, tenderness, and simplicity carry them past the danger of sentimentality and make them moving and effective.

The lyric poems, which are here taken to include all the shorter poems that are not basically narratives or dramas, celebrate the same things and denounce the same things as the narratives. Being primarily meditations on one subject, they are more intense and unified, and are free of the problems of multilayered poems such as *The Women at Point Sur.* Typically, a Jeffers lyric describes an experience and comments upon it; and it does this in the simple, declarative voice that stamped every poem with his unique signature.

"The Place for No Story," although exceptionally short, is an excellent example. Jeffers opens with a simple description: "The coast hills at Sovranes Creek:/ No trees, but dark scant pasture drawn thin/ Over rock shaped like flame." Then he describes the "old ocean at the land's foot, the vast/ Gray extension beyond the long white violence." Jeffers describes a herd of cattle on the slope above the sea, and above that "the gray air haunted with hawks. . . . " Ending this section with a colon, he draws, figuratively and spiritually, a deep breath and simply states:

> This place is the noblest thing I have ever seen
> No imaginable
> Human presence here could do anything
> But dilute the lonely self-watchful passion.

There are many qualities to notice in this simple poem, qualities that will stand for those of scores of other lyrics, meditations, mixed-mode poems, and sections of the narratives and dramas. First, there is the voice. It is simple and colloquial, as characteristically attuned to the rhythms of everyday American speech as anything by Robert Frost. The word order is natural. The diction is simple and dignified, but not formal. It reflects Jeffers' conscious decision to focus on things that will endure. It would have been easily comprehensible in sixteenth century England, and will almost certainly be so for centuries to come. The poem is written in the typical style of the mature Jeffers: no rhyme, no regular metrical pattern. As Jeffers explained, however, he had a sense of pattern that made him disagree with those who called his lines free verse. His feeling, he once wrote, was for the number of beats to the line and also for the quantitative element of long and short syllables. Most of his poems break up into recurring patterns of beats per line—ten and five, six and four, five and three alternations being common. In this poem, less regular than many, there is still a recurrence of four-beat lines, culminating in a pair at the end to make a couplet effect. The longer lines run mostly to six stresses, depending on how the poem is read. Binding the whole together is a subtle pattern of alliteration, a device that Jeffers used with full consciousness of his debt to the strong-stress lines of Anglo-Saxon verse. In the first few lines, for example, the hard "c" of "coast" is repeated in "Creek" (and picked up much later in another stressed word, "cows"); the "s" in "Sovranes" reappears in "scant" and "shaped"; the "d" in "dark" reappears in "drawn"; the "f" of "flame," in "foot"; the "v" of "vast" in "violence"; the "h" in "hills" appears five lines later in "herd," six lines later in "hardly," seven lines later in "haunted" and "hawks." A notable assonance is "old ocean," which works to slow down its line with its long syllables.

In this short lyric, too, are embodied some of Jeffers' key ideas. The ocean's "violence" reminds the reader of the struggle ever-present in the natural world. The contrast between rock, a symbol of endurance, and flame, a symbol of violent change, suggests that even rocks undergo change from the same process of oxidation that produces flame. Above, the hawks are Jeffers' preferred symbol of independence and of the inexorable violence of nature. The poem simply and unaffectedly celebrates beauty, and at the end reminds the reader of the insignificance of human beings in a universe still discovering itself in the "passion" of its dynamic life.

The qualities found in this short lyric are found in abundance in many other poems of varying length. Among the most notable of the short poems not already cited are "To the Stone-Cutters," "Night," "Boats in a Fog," "Noon," "Rock and Hawk," "Love the Wild Swan," "Return," "All the Little Hoofprints," "Original Sin," "The Deer Lay Down Their Bones," and "For Una."

Among the longer lyrics, several are important for a full understanding of the poet. Chief among these is *Apology for Bad Dreams*, Jeffers' *ars poetica*. "Meditation on Saviors" and "De Rerum Virtute" are also important philosophical poems, as is "Margrave," a short narrative framed by an approximately equal amount of meditative lyric. Two large sections of "Cawdor" contain particularly powerful lyric sections. These, "The Caged Eagle's Death-Dream" and "The Old Man's Dream After He Died," have been reprinted in *The Selected Poetry of Robinson Jeffers* (1938).

After passing through a period (1938-1948) during which many of his poems were bitter political harangues, Jeffers achieved a quieter tone in the poems that were posthumously printed in *The Beginning and the End* (1963). They lack the close texture and the intensity, however, of his better poems from earlier years, and tend to become prosy. At the same time, in their increasing concern with astrophysics, the origins of human life, and the terrible prospect that all may end in a nuclear catastrophe, they explore new territory and provide a fitting, relatively serene end to an enormously productive career.

In seeking to place Jeffers in the continuum of American poets, one is drawn to generalizations that often apply surprisingly well to Walt Whitman, who was temperamentally and sometimes philosophically Jeffers' polar opposite. Like Whitman, Jeffers was a technical innovator, developing a typically long, colloquial line and a voice that can be mistaken for no other. Like Whitman, he was often charged, with some justification, with using inflated rhetoric and exaggeration to achieve his effects, and with repetitiveness. Like Whitman, he was a poet of extremes, and for that reason perhaps he will be best appreciated when some of the political and social passions which he stirred have been forgotten. Like Whitman, too, Jeffers had a well-developed set of attitudes toward society and the world. These views put both men in the prophetic stance at times. Like Whitman, Jeffers was deeply religious in a pantheistic way, and so profoundly conscious of the cycle of birth and regeneration that he thought of death as a redeemer.

Many of these characteristics are those of a public poet, a person in a dialogue with his nation and the world about its life and the right way of living. Beyond these qualities, Jeffers had other attributes of the public poet. He was not only prophetic, admonishing and seeking reform in attitudes and behavior, but also apocalyptic, standing apart and reminding his readers of the immanence and possible imminence of worldly destruction. He was historical, reminding them that cultures and nations had risen and fallen before them. He was an early environmentalist, reminding Americans that they were part of a complex cycle of life, and castigating them for their sins against the earth. He was an explorer of the depths probed by Freud and Carl G. Jung—and thus a psychological poet. He was also a mystical poet—the "Caged Eagle's Death-Dream" constituting a supreme illustration.

The process of sifting out and properly appraising the poems in which Jeffers succeeded in his various roles has begun. No single long narrative has been acclaimed by all favorable critics as entirely successful, but it is certain that at least half a dozen, probably led by "Roan Stallion," will survive. Many lyrics and shorter mixed-mode poems, however, are generally esteemed, and it is these poems that already have assured Jeffers a place among the honored writers of the century. Finally, the quality that seems most likely to ensure Jeffers' future stature is his very lack of timeliness. His references are not to ephemera but to rock, hawk, sea, and mountain—things that will be with the world as long as humans are there to perceive their beauty and their significance.

Edward A. Nickerson

Other major works
PLAYS: *Medea*, 1946 (translation); *The Cretan Woman*, 1954.
NONFICTION: *Themes in My Poems*, 1956; *The Selected Letters of Robinson Jeffers, 1897-1962*, 1968 (Ann N. Ridgeway, editor).

Bibliography
Bennett, Melba Berry. *The Stone Mason of Tor House: The Life and Work of Robinson Jeffers.* Los Angeles: Ward Ritchie Press, 1966. Although this is the only book-length biography of Robinson Jeffers, it was written by a personal friend of the poet and is therefore rather uncritical of his views. Supplemented with an index, illustrations, and bibliographies of works by and about Jeffers.
Brophy, Robert J. *Robinson Jeffers: Myth, Ritual, and Symbol in His Narrative Poems.* Reprint. Hamden, Conn.: Archon Books, 1976. This basic study, often referred to by critics, thoroughly establishes the grounding of Jeffers' narrative works in—among others—Judeo-Christian, Greek, Norse, and Hindu mythologies. Contains illustrations, an index, notes, and a bibliography.
_____, ed. *The Robinson Jeffers Newsletter: A Jubilee Gathering, 1962-1988.* Los Angeles: Occidental College, 1988. A collection of the best articles from the first twenty-five years of the journal devoted to the poet and his works. Includes illustrations.

Everson, William. *The Excesses of God: Robinson Jeffers as a Religious Figure.* Stanford, Calif.: Stanford University Press, 1988. The author, himself a poet, sees Jeffers as a bardic and prophetic man and relates him to the thought of such modern theologians as Mircea Eliade. Contains notes and an index. Everson is also the author, under his previous pen name of Brother Antoninus, of an earlier study on the same subject, *Robinson Jeffers: Fragments of an Older Fury*, Berkeley, California: Oyez, 1968.

Nolte, William H. *Rock and Hawk: Robinson Jeffers and the Romantic Agony.* Athens: University of Georgia Press, 1978. Relates Jeffers to the traditions of European, English, and American Romantic philosophy and poetry. Supplemented with notes and an index.

Vardamis, Alex A. *The Critical Reputation of Robinson Jeffers: A Bibliographical Study.* Hamden, Conn.: Archon Books, 1972. A chronological annotated bibliography of all the books, articles, and reviews about Jeffers from the beginning of his career to 1971. Contains a critical introduction.

Zaller, Robert. *The Cliffs of Solitude: A Reading of Robinson Jeffers.* New York: Cambridge University Press, 1983. An interpretation of Jeffers' entire career, with particular emphasis on the long narratives. Combines the psychoanalytic and mythic viewpoints. Complemented with a chronology, an index, notes, and a bibliography.

RONALD JOHNSON

Born: Ashland, Kansas; November 25, 1935

Principal poetry

A Line of Poetry, A Row of Trees, 1964; *Assorted Jungles: Rousseau,* 1966; *Gorse/Goose/Rose and Other Poems,* 1966; *Sunflowers,* 1966; *Io and the Ox-eye Daisy,* 1966; *The Book of the Green Man,* 1967; *The Round Earth on Flat Paper,* 1968; *Reading 1 and 2,* 1968 (two volumes); *Valley of the Many-colored Grasses,* 1969; *Balloons for Moonless Nights,* 1969; *The Spirit Walks, The Rocks Will Talk,* 1969; *Songs of the Earth,* 1970; *Maze/Mane/Wane,* 1973; *Eyes and Objects,* 1976; *RADI OS I-IV,* 1977; *Ark: The Foundations 1-33,* 1980; *Art 50: Spires 34-50,* 1984.

Other literary forms

In addition to his poetry, Ronald Johnson has published several cookbooks, including *The Aficionado's Southwestern Cooking* (1968), *The American Table* (1984), his culinary magnum opus, *Southwestern Cooking, New and Old* (1985), *Simple Fare* (1989), and *Company Fare* (1991).

Achievements

A disciple of Charles Olson, Johnson has followed Olson's intuition that a poem must find the form necessary to its fullest expression. For Johnson, this has meant the writing of poems which by conventional measures of poetry do not seem to be poems at all. As well, under the pull of energies initially mobilized during the concrete poetry movement in the early 1960's, Johnson has explored the poetic possibilities of typography and the visual presence of a poem as a kind of sign. At the root of his attention is the natural world, its sounds and sights. Out of his deference to this phenomenal world, Johnson has devised techniques to register it in a new way. In some of his poems, where his manipulation of typography and instinct for the suggestibility of individual letters is working, the poem becomes a wholly novel visual experience.

From his early concrete poems to his Ark series, Johnson has sought to bind the world of poetry to the world of made things. Thus, his work is a rare and refreshing turn-away from the hypersubjectivity typical of much post-modern poetry. Against the ramblings of selfhood he erects a bright vision, directing one toward the complex and beautiful universe.

Prizes awarded to Johnson for his poetry include the Boar's Head Prize for Poetry, in 1960; *Poetry's* Inez Boulton Award, in 1964; National Endowment for the Arts awards, in 1969 and 1974; and the National Poetry Series Award, in 1983.

Biography

Ronald Johnson was born and grew up in Ashland, Kansas. He briefly attended the University of Kansas before spending two years in the United States Army, earning as a result the post-Korea veterans' benefits which allowed him to attend and be graduated from Columbia University, New York, in 1960. During the years in New York, he became acquainted with many other artists, poets, and scholars, including the people associated with Black Mountain College in North Carolina. In the early 1960's, Johnson traveled in England with the poet and publisher Jonathan Williams, and he received inspiration from the country for many of his most memorable poems. During this time he participated in the concrete poetry movement and became a close friend of Ian Hamilton Finlay, one of the best-known poets in the movement.

In 1968, Johnson moved to San Francisco, where, with the exception of two teaching jobs, he was to make his permanent home. In 1971, he taught creative writing at the University of Kentucky, and in 1973 he held the Roethke Chair for Poetry at the University of Washington.

Analysis

In his book *Valley of the Many-colored Grasses*, Ronald Johnson quotes Ralph Waldo Emerson in an epigraph to one of his poems. The quotation attributes to Nature the power to use creation as a means of expressing itself: "The air is full of sounds; the sky, of tokens; the ground is all memoranda & signatures." These signs speak to "the intelligent," or human beings with eyes and ears. If "the intelligent" are not suitably articulate to pass on the language Nature speaks, it "waits & works, until, at last, it moulds them to its perfect will & is articulated." Reading the poem following the epigraph, one discovers that it is simply the words of the epigraph "aired out" in free-verse lines, Johnson's spacial arrangement of the words serving to arrest the flow of Emerson's prose and emphasize key perceptions. A poem has been found in Emerson's text.

This poem, titled "Emerson, on Goethe," exemplifies two characteristics of Johnson's thought and writing. The first is his preoccupation with nature, or everything that makes up the cosmos, from ants to stars and not exclusive of what an architect designs or a composer composes. A man is subservient to nature, inhabiting nature, dependent upon nature. Nature produces patterns of order and sentient secretaries, artists of various kinds, who are not justified in feeling alienated from a world so animated and willful. Pervading Johnson's poetry is the idea that a poet is someone who brings nature to the ears and eyes of nonpoets under the command of nature itself. This mission puts Johnson as a poet outside the trend of contemporary poetry, where the poet seems more often the secretary of himself, that subjective complex which utters forth from deep within its private and often obscure consciousness. Johnson's heritage as a writer is much more old-fashioned. His poems frequently refer to writers and painters, for whom the real show is the world outside the self. The Johnson heritage includes, along with the transcendentalist Emerson, the poet William Blake, who saw everything in a grain of sand. It embraces the records Henry Thoreau left of his daily eyework along Walden Pond and the paintings of Joseph Turner, who had himself roped to a ship's mast during a storm, the better to know what he was painting. It welcomes the visionary eye of the painter Samuel Palmer, as in Johnson's poem on Palmer, in which the eye is "covered with fire after every immersion/ in the air" and is taken by nature's leading beyond the horizon, where "it gathers to itself all light/ in visionary harvest." It is the same heritage which guided the poet Ezra Pound, in his World War II prison cage, to find in the wasps and midges in the grass a vision of the highest order, an order uncreated by humans but requiring gifts of sensitivity and vision to recognize.

The second characteristic that Johnson's Emerson "poem" demonstrates is Johnson's unconcern about what is actually a poem. None of its words is Johnson's, but the perception of the words is Johnson's. Perception, attention, and observation are of more value to the poet than so-called originality, not that Johnson as a writer is simply copying down what others have written. His attention is arrested by nature and by other writers who testify to similar devotion, so, if in the course of writing a poem Johnson remembers that "to Coleridge, the Marigold,/ Monk's-hood, Orange-lily & Indian pink/ flash with light—" the poem is not spoiled by borrowing. On this poet's mind, Johnson's, happened to be the working of another poet's mind, Samuel Taylor Coleridge's. Appropriately, then, the line that follows the one just quoted tells about Charles Darwin's ability to see phosphorus in a horse's eyes. Perhaps the poetic spell is ruined by telling about what a scientist can do, but Johnson is not particularly concerned about "the poem"; he seeks to evoke dazzling examples of human eyesight working in the real world.

Yet Johnson is also concerned about the "the poem." He wants his poems to be new, bright, as dazzling as the source of inspiration. To readers familiar with what T. S. Eliot and Ezra Pound did to the form of a poem, Johnson's poetry does not seem unpoetic at all. What does seem uncommon is Johnson's persistent belief in a nature which speaks to human beings. Johnson is not interested merely in objectivity, but in seeing through the objectivity. He pursues the calling of seer, or hearer: A tree and its leaves are never ordinary; commonplace objects speak and establish intimacy, an intimacy which is the vision. Thus, a suite of Johnson's poems in another early book, *The Book of the Green Man*, have sweetly innocent titles: "What the Earth Told Me," "What the Air Told Me," and "What the Leaf Told Me." In this book, Johnson mentions the "skiey influences" which entered into the poet William Wordsworth's pores, sustaining his poetic vision of countryside and lakes. Johnson desires such a relationship. He longs to hear the earth speak, to "issue some dark, meditated/ syllable perhaps—/ something more/

than this inarticulate warble and seething." The earth writes to the poet instead: "Today I saw the word written on the poplar leaves./ It was 'dazzle.'/ As a leaf startles out/ from an undifferentiated mass of foliage,/ so the word did from a leaf—." The poet is Adam in a garden which has not yet been seen with language. Nature continues to educate Adam in this garden, beyond declaring the adjectives through which it is known, with basic scientific facts: "For the tree forms sun into leaves, & its branches & saps/ are solid & liquid states of sun." Johnson would have his reader respond to photosynthesis as a visionary entity, while still bringing along a knowledge of electrochemical force and the laws of physics. When the earth tells the poet that "nothing is allowed to stand still," the commonplace law becomes marvelous in its numberless examples, poplar leaves in the wind being only one in the countless manifold. "In the homage of attentions 'all things/ are in flux,'" Johnson writes, and, throwing a stone into a pond, observes "its circles interlacing/ & radiating out to the most ephemeral edge." Again, the high school physics experiment becomes an occasion for religious meditation.

Writing of Johnson's poetry, Guy Davenport notes that "his every poem has been to trace the intricate and subtle lines of force wherein man can discern the order of his relation to the natural world." Thus, Johnson's desire to make nature have a voice is to regather the modern ear to a hearing of what it has been taught is dead. In his poems, the goal of registering the voice of phenomena is reached by pruning away conventional poetic rhetoric and extruding lines of gnomic brevity. In *The Book of the Green Man*, the theme is that a man desires to enter the green world and be taught by it. The man of the title is that mythical figure from England who, in one of his guises, has leaves growing on his face like a beard and foliage for hair. This man bespeaks that intimacy of botany and humanity which for Johnson is the substratum of his art of writing a poem: "Poems beginning germinal in the instant/ —reeling out, unravelling, tendril & silken, into the air—/ ethereal growths,/ sudden, & peculiar as mushrooms?/ Uncrumpling/ as moths from cocoons—." The poet marvels at the relationship between the world and the mind and understands the relationship as something ethereally botanical, biological. In this light, Johnson assembles a corps of writers, from Alexander Pope to Wordsworth to William Klivert, who sensed the heavenly abode which nature suggested. Pope dreamed of planting a cathedral from poplar trees; Johnson dreams in a poem of entering "the architecture of bees" and the mole's passages and the lizard route through "scrolls of leaves." Dominant in all Johnson's work is this urging to go *into* nature, and to recall those writers who attempted the same kind of entry and union.

In a slender volume published in 1970 titled *Songs of the Earth*, Johnson continued his efforts to listen to the world. He said of the poems: "These songs are listenings, as poems must listen and sing simultaneously." One of the poems is simply the word "earth" repeated without spacing three times in one line, this one line repeated seven times: "earthearthearth." The eye picks out significant terms hiding in the bushes: art, ear, hear, heart, hearth. Another poem spaces out the first and last "s" in the word "stones" to reveal "tone." Yet another places the word "wane" in a square grid, the word printed with spaces between the letters and the lines. Within the square thus formed of capital letters the word "anew" appears in lowercase letters. As in nature, there is no waning that leads to nothing; all waning is, rather, a kind of reprocessing, so in the poem the recycling of letters displays new meaning. Such a poem cannot be spoken, and such poetry to Johnson is "a magical world where all is possible and an 'o' can rise, like the real moon, over the word *moon.*" Such writing is sign-making and emphasizes the dominance of the eye as the ruling mode of perception for Johnson. His *Songs of the Earth* was written in response to Gustav Mahler's symphony of the same name. The concrete poems which resulted may have been the product of the poet's listening, but they exist for the reader solely as mute visual patterns, for the eye alone. Johnson considers this not a drawback but a revolution: "We can now make a line of poetry as visible as a row of trees." In a later volume of poetry, titled *Eyes and Objects*, Johnson defines a self as the things it sees: "You are what you look for/ zeroing out on the light-and-dark,/ the X of eyes." His need and intuition as a poet have been to make visible objects for pairs of eyes to converge upon and see.

Johnson has continued to marvel at the products of the universe and to erect structures to hold his marvellings. A book titled *RADI OS I-IV* is a rewriting by excision of John Milton's *Paradise Lost* (1667, 1674). Milton's text, like his title, undergoes a rereading by Johnson, and what is left after the cutting is a modern poem, both in appearance and in ideas. One theme is energy, a familiar twentieth century concern. The radii of the sun energize men and also enable them to see. A fragment of the poem reads: "Too well I see/ :for the mind/ swallowed up/ entire, in the heart/ to work in fire,/ words The Arch." The poet takes his vocation, a commitment not without risk, from the energy mysteriously generated by his capacity to be impassioned by the world. *RADI OS I-IV* is one part of a longer work titled *Ark: The Foundations 1-33*, in which the analogy between writing poetry and creating physical structures is declared in the subsection's titles: "The Foundations," "The Spires," and "The Outworks." In a note on *Ark*, Johnson says that he wrote the poem "with stones of words and mortar of song." Individual poems in the work are "Spires," and the reader is impressed by Johnson's unique ability to *arrest* language, whether single words or phrases:

> to say then head wedded nail and hammer to the
> work of vision
> of the word
> at hand
> that is paradise

"Ark" is that structure so literally prescribed for Noah by God in which he would leave behind the old world and find a new, a terrestrial paradise. It, the ark, is also the arc, the curve of the globe, one segment of which is America, the last promised land humanity was vouchsafed and from which humanity managed to fall, ignoring and persecuting the original inhabitants. Artificers, builders, poets, remain, however, Johnson a member of the host, and they project their various visions. The vision is work, Johnson reminds the reader: "for if hell indeed rein time stood still/ and paradise thus daily fall/ unlikely wings/ on usual shoulders." Johnson clearly views writing poetry as a religious quest, as the establishment of a testimonial edifice which will inspire belief in the hearts of nonartificers. Behind this poem stand Johnson's predecessors for whom nature was the first place to look for inspiration—William Blake, Walt Whitman, Henry David Thoreau, and Samuel Palmer. It is a vision which sees swarms of mayflies as bands of angels and an ear for which "even the humble fly/ buzz anthem/ Christ."

The poetry of Ronald Johnson is inimical to despair and gloom. It derives from a mandate, clearly religious, to make the world seen and heard. In vain a reader will search for confirmations or investigations of the popular twentieth century focus: the self. In abundance, however, the reader will find things for that self to study and see, and constant reminders of what powers of perception a human possesses, and what he or she is supposed to do with them:

> Let us grasp at
> the gate, unhinge the dark
>
> clear lake
>
> (moon to sky's edge)
>
> awake! awake!

Bruce Wiebe

Other major works

NONFICTION: *The Aficionado's Southwestern Cooking*, 1968; *The American Table*, 1984; *Southwestern Cooking, New and Old*, 1985; *Simple Fare*, 1989; *Company Fare*, 1991.

TRANSLATION: *Sports and Divertissments*, 1965 (of notes by Erik Satie for his piano pieces under the same title).

Bibliography

"California and the West." *Library Journal* 102 (December 15, 1977): 2469. This article evokes the spirit of Guy Davenport, who wrote about Johnson in his collection of essays *The Geography of the Imagination*, in asserting the importance of Johnson's poem *RADI OS I-IV*. It also reiterates the ultimate payoff to the reader who perseveres through this difficult and fragmented poem which is based on John Milton's work.

Harmon, William. "The Poetry of a Journal at the End of an Arbor in a Watch." *Parnassus: Poetry in Review* 9 (Spring/Summer, 1981): 217-232. For the Johnson scholar, this work represents an apex in the canon of critical evaluations of the poet's works from *A Line of Poetry, A Row of Trees* to *Ark: The Foundations 1-33*. Harmon's ambitions often make his writings as complex and dense as the work he is examining. This is a rewarding essay that requires perseverance and determination.

Jaffe, Dan. "Voice of the Poet." *Saturday Review* 52 (September 6, 1969): 29. This review of *Valley of the Many-colored Grasses* illustrates Johnson's devotion to nature, the inspiration provided by Walt Whitman and the Black Mountain poets, and his decidedly unfashionable language. Jaffe observes that "Grasses" blends the intentions of the Symbolist poets with the imagery of the naturalists to create an energetic expression of the universe.

Johnson, Ronald. *The American Table*. New York: William Morrow, 1984. Although an unconventional source of information, this book provides a fascinating perspective on Johnson's travels throughout America and his ruminations on the country and its diverse communities and life-styles. Offers glimpses of the significant impact Johnson's travels and exposure to different cultures—from the Shakers to the Southwest and Wyoming to the east coast—have had on his poetry.

Metzger, Linda, and Deborah A. Straub, eds. *Contemporary Authors*. Vol. 20. New Revision series. Detroit: Gale Research, 1987. The entry on Johnson contains valuable biographical information concerning this poet who is rarely written about. Includes a list of his writings, his contributions to anthologies, his awards, extensive quotes from reviews of his work, and a bibliography.

SAMUEL JOHNSON

Born: Lichfield, Staffordshire, England; September 18, 1709
Died: London, England; December 13, 1784

Principal poetry

London: A Poem in Imitation of the Third Satire of Juvenal, 1738; *The Vanity of Human Wishes: The Tenth Satire of Juvenal Imitated*, 1749; *Poems: The Yale Edition of the Works of Samuel Johnson*, 1965 (E. L. McAdam, Jr., and George Milne, editors, volume 6).

Other literary forms

Samuel Johnson was a journalist, essayist, critic, scholar, lexicographer, biographer, and satirist. Early in his career, he wrote reports on the debates in Parliament for *The Gentleman's Mazagine*. Until 1762, when he received a pension from the British government, Johnson was a professional writer and wrote what publishers would buy. The most important results of his efforts, in addition to his poetry, were his *A Dictionary of the English Language* (1755), his essays in *The Rambler* (1750-1752) and *The Idler* (1758-1760), and *Rasselas, Prince of Abyssinia* (1759). *A Dictionary of the English Language* remains one of the outstanding achievements in the study of language. Johnson contracted in 1746 with a group of publishers to write the first comprehensive dictionary of the English language. Nine years later, with the help of only six assistants, he produced a work that is notable for its scholarship and wit. Although scholars fault its etymological notes, its definitions are generally apt and often colored by Johnson's wit, biases, and sound understanding of English usage. *The Rambler* and *The Idler* are composed of periodical essays, which, when combined with those that Johnson wrote for *The Adventurer* (1753-1754), number more than three hundred. The essays discuss literature, religion, politics, and society. They were much admired in Johnson's day, but are less so in the modern era. They are often grave, but rarely dull, and represent some of the finest prose in English. Another important prose work, *Rasselas, Prince of Abyssinia* is Johnson's major contribution to fiction. Like Voltaire's *Candide: Or Optimism* (1759), *Rasselas, Prince of Abyssinia* features a naïve young protagonist whose adventures gradually strip away his illusions. Johnson's work is the less harsh of the two, but is similar in tone.

Johnson's work as a biographer and scholar began early. In 1740, he wrote biographies of Admiral Robert Blake, Sir Francis Drake, and Jean-Philippe Barretier. These works are unoriginal in content. In 1744, he published *An Account of the Life of Mr. Richard Savage, Son of the Earl Rivers*, which was later included in *The Lives of the Poets* (1779-1781), although it was often published separately. Savage was a bitter and angry man; Johnson emphasized with dramatic narrative the wrongs society had visited on him. Many years after *An Account of the Life of Mr. Richard Savage, Son of the Earl Rivers*, Johnson agreed to write a series of prefaces to the works of English poets for a group of booksellers. The result was *The Lives of the Poets* (four volumes in 1779 and an additional six volumes in 1781). These essays are marked by Johnson's critical insight and immense knowledge of literature; many are still standard references. Johnson was also an editor, and produced an important edition of Shakespeare with commentary. Some critics have denigrated Johnson's lack of appreciation of Shakespeare's poetry, but his appraisal of the plays is well considered, and his defense of the plays against dogmatic neoclassical criticism is notable for its good sense.

Among Johnson's other significant writings are the political essays *Thoughts on the Late Transactions Respecting Falkland's Islands* (1771) and *Taxation No Tyranny* (1775), and the account of his travels in Scotland with his young Scottish friend, James Boswell, entitled *A Journey to the Western Islands of Scotland* (1775). In these works Johnson displays his hatred of war and political profiteering and his acuteness of observation.

Achievements

The diversity of Johnson's writings can be daunting; he was a novelist, playwright, essayist, journalist, editor, critic, scholar, biographer, lexicographer, etymologist, moralist, social and political commentator, philosopher, and poet. His poem *London* (1738) was published at least twenty-three times during his lifetime, and the popularity of his poetry contributed much to his reputation as the quintessential *man of letters*. In his era, no one had read more of the world's literature than he, and few equaled his literary achievements. Johnson seems to have so dominated the literary life of England that the period from 1750 to 1784 is often called the Age of Johnson.

"Poet" was a term of honor in eighteenth century England. The poet was at the apex of literature, and Johnson took pleasure in being referred to as one. After his death, his reputation as a poet fell from the high esteem of his contemporaries to a level of near disregard. His best-known poetry is the product of intellectual work, not inspiration. The Romantics and their nineteenth century descendants valued emotional and inspirational verse. Johnson's verse is well organized, often satirical, filled with social commentary and moralizing, and more realistically observational than metaphorical; his poetry is well within the Augustan style. Modern readers have begun to rediscover Augustan satire, and interest in Johnson's poetry is growing.

He was among the best poets of his day, his verse being dynamic and rich in thought. He believed that poetry should emphasize the contemporary language of the poet; it should be accessible to the poet's contemporary readers. In this belief he is in the same tradition as John Donne, John Dryden, Alexander Pope, and even poets as recent as Karl Shapiro. The language of Johnson's verse is still accessible to readers; it is distinctive in its combination of precision, nearly explosive anger and contempt, and acute observation of the human condition.

Biography

Many writers have suffered, and many more have pretended to suffer, for their art. Samuel Johnson's own suffering in fact made his art necessary. He was born on September 18, 1709 to Michael Johnson, a bookseller, and Sarah (née Ford), who was then forty years old. The labor had been difficult, and Samuel Johnson was, by his own account, born nearly dead. While he was a child he contracted scrofula and smallpox; he was horribly scarred by the diseases and became deaf in one ear and partially blind in one eye. Although his father was a respectable citizen and even gained a small degree of prominence in 1709 as Sheriff of Lichfield, Johnson's ancestors were of humble background. His parents were unhappy with each other, and their mild mutual hostility contributed to the miseries of their son's life.

In spite of his ugliness, poor background, and unhappy family life, Johnson became a leader among his schoolmates. He was not an ideal student; he would neglect his studies, then in great bursts of energy apply himself to learning. He wrote much as he had studied; for example, *An Account of the Life of Mr. Richard Savage, Son of the Earl Rivers* was written in as little as thirty-six hours, and it has been claimed that *Rasselas, Prince of Abyssinia* was completed in a week. He aspired to be almost anything but a writer. With a small savings he paid for more than a year at Oxford, from October, 1728 to December, 1729, but lack of money forced him to leave. After his father's death in 1731, he tried teaching. He was temperamentally unsuited for teaching; he gesticulated wildly when lecturing, and his bizarre antics confused his students. David Garrick, the actor, was among his pupils, and later helped Johnson have the verse play *Irene: A Tragedy* (1749) produced. Johnson's next ambition was to become a lawyer, but his poverty and physical infirmities inhibited his studies and his ability to pursue strenuous professions. He turned to writing in order to support himself and his wife.

He married Elizabeth Jervis, the widow of Harry Porter, in 1735. She was nineteen years his senior, but provided him with love, a home, and companionship that helped to stabilize his passionate and explosive personality. Acutely aware of his responsibilities as a husband, Johnson took work where he could find it. He moved to London and persuaded the publisher of *The Gentleman's Magazine*, Edward Cave, to allow him to write for the periodical. During this period of his life he wrote and sold the poem *London*, and tried to interest theater owners in a rough version of *Irene*. As a professional writer who sought to meet the needs of publishers, Johnson wrote essays, reports, poetry, and biographies—whatever would earn him money. *London* was a success and greatly advanced his reputation, but he sold the copyright and profited little from it. His literary labors earned enough for food and a place to live, but he endured bitter poverty.

A group of London publishers contracted with him in 1746 for *A Dictionary of the English Language*, which he completed its compilation seven years later and which was published in 1755. The loyal support of the syndicate of publishers provided him with some small financial security, although his life remained hard. While writing the dictionary with the help of six secretaries, Johnson wrote *The Rambler*, which was published twice weekly from 1750 to 1752. The periodical's reputation was great, but its sales were small. Such was the reputation of the dictionary and *The Rambler* that Johnson became known as "Dictionary Johnson" and "Author of *The Rambler*." In 1749, the poem *The Vanity of Human Wishes* was published. Today it is probably the best known of Johnson's poetic works. Also in that year, David Garrick, Johnson's onetime pupil, by then a famous actor, produced *Irene* at the Drury Lane Theatre. The play lasted for nine nights, a respectable run, and Johnson earned almost two hundred pounds from the production. Subject to depressions in the best of times, Johnson was greatly saddened by the death of his wife in 1752.

From 1755 to 1762, Johnson's most important literary efforts were *The Idler*, which was published from 1758 to 1760 in the *Universal Chronicle*, and *Rasselas, Prince of Abyssinia*. In 1759, Johnson's mother died. Perhaps her illness and death inspired Johnson to contemplate his youth and its disillusionments. The evident result was *Rasselas, Prince of Abyssinia*. Some biographers assert that *Rasselas* was written to pay for his mother's funeral, but most scholars disagree. In 1762, Johnson was awarded an annual pension of three hundred pounds, enough to free him from the necessity of labor.

In 1763, Johnson met James Boswell, a young Scot who would become a favorite companion. It is because of Boswell's *The Life of Samuel Johnson, LL.D.* (1791) that scholars know more about the last twenty years of Johnson's life than they know of the previous fifty-five. Free from financial cares, and afflicted by a variety of physical complaints, Johnson did not write at the prodigious rate that he had when he was younger. His principal literary efforts were *The Lives of the Poets*, a series of prefaces to English poets written for a consortium of booksellers, and *A Journey to the Western Islands of Scotland*, an account of a tour in 1773 with Boswell. Johnson's poetry during his last years consisted primarily of parodies and burlesques written for friends, and Latin verse, composed mostly for his own contemplation. Always a moody and introspective man, his poetry became private and contemplative in his last years. In public, of course, he sought companionship and good conversation, relishing his status as England's leading man of letters. In private, he had an almost morbid dread of death. He believed that people should, at the peril of their souls, fulfill all of their talents; he was acutely aware of his own superior intellectual powers, and believed that he had not properly made use of them. Once in February, 1784, the dropsy that afflicted him disappeared while he prayed, and he took the relief to be a sign from God and spent the last months of his life in spiritual peace. He died on December 13, 1784, and was buried on December 20 in Westminster Abbey, as befitted a poet.

Analysis

Samuel Johnson wrote two major poetic works: *London* and *The Vanity of Human Wishes*. The remaining verse divides into the play *Irene*, poems in Latin, miscellaneous verse in English, and translations from Greek and Latin. *London* was the most popular of Johnson's poems during his life, and it remains the most accessible to modern audiences. Its language is clear and its images straightforward. Like *London*, *The Vanity of Human Wishes* is an imitation of the satires of Juvenal, a Latin poet of the first and second centuries. It is widely regarded as Johnson's poetic masterpiece and is Johnson's effort to convey the essence of the Christian ethos through verse and imagery. The density of its images and ideas makes *The Vanity of Human Wishes* difficult to interpret even for experienced critics. *Irene*, on the other hand, yields readily to interpretation through its strong plot, although its verse, while competent, is unremarkable.

Johnson customarily composed his poems mentally before committing them to paper. *London* was composed in this manner; it was written on large sheets of paper in two columns—the left being for the first draft and the right for revisions. Johnson's poetry is firmly in the Augustan tradition, typified in the eighteenth century by the works of Alexander Pope, Jonathan Swift, and Joseph Addison; *London* is characteristically Augustan in its dependence on a Latin model, in this case Juvenal's third satire. When the poem was published, the passages that were derived from Juvenal were accompanied by Juvenal's original lines, which were included at Johnson's request—a common practice at the time. A good edition of *London* will include the relevant Juvenalian passages.

Juvenal's third satire, Johnson's model for *London*, focuses on Rome. In general, Juvenal's satires attack what he perceived to be the immorality of Roman society. In his third satire he cites particulars in the city of Rome itself. Johnson focuses his poem on the city of London and, like Juvenal, cites particulars. He also includes translations from Juvenal's poem and updated versions of some of Juvenal's sentiments. As the accompanying Latin verse shows, Johnson's borrowings are only part of the whole and tend to illustrate the universality of some of the poem's ideas. Too much of *London* is original for it to be simply a translation. For example, Juvenal writes from the point of view of a conservative Roman who believed that his countrymen had grown soft from lack of war and sacrifice, while Johnson writes from the point of view of an eighteenth century Christian who believed that the vices of his age stemmed from his countrymen's failure to recognize the importance of the soul. Johnson was a man of ideas, and his ideas make *London* his own work—

a statement of his views of the city when he was a young man of twenty-eight. *London* is written in rhyming iambic pentameter couplets. Johnson believed that blank verse could be sustained only by strong images; otherwise, verse needed clear structure and rhyme. His best poetry exemplifies his ideas about prosody; *London*'s heroic couplets follow the model established by Pope. The poem's language is lively and its ideas flow rapidly. Johnson's condemnations are sharply expressed:

> By numbers here from shame or censure free,
> All crimes are safe, but hated poverty.
> This, only this, the rigid law pursues,
> This, only this, provokes the snarling muse.

The city is portrayed as rife with crime, folly, and injustice. King George II is said to be more interested in Hanover than England and London; learning is said to be unrewarded (a favorite theme of Juvenal); government is said to be grasping while the nation sinks; and the city is characterized as architecturally in bad taste. The satire makes London seem bleak and ugly, but the language is exuberant and makes London's faults seem exciting.

The poem's persona (the speaker) is named Thales, who intends to leave London for Cambria (Wales); he craves solitude and peace. Some scholars have identified Thales as the personification of Richard Savage, who had suffered poverty and indignities in London; he left London in 1739 for Wales. Other scholars maintain that Johnson had not yet met Savage, and that *London* was, after all, published in 1738, a year before Savage's migration. This dispute over seeming minutiae represents a major problem that infects much criticism of Johnson's works. Those who support the notion that Savage is the original for Thales sometimes cite Johnson's assertion that anyone who is tired of London is tired of life. They maintain that the poem's point of view is not representative of Johnson but of Savage. Even some critics who do not assert that Savage was the model for Thales dismiss *London* as insincere— as an exercise that does not reflect Johnson's true love for the city.

Students new to the study of Johnson should be wary of reasoning based on Johnson's views in Boswell's *The Life of Samuel Johnson, LL.D.* Boswell's work is monumental; it has helped to shape the modern view of eighteenth century England. Johnson's opinions as reported by Boswell are forcefully expressed and seemingly permanently set, and even knowledgeable scholars have sometimes read into Johnson's early works the views he held when he was a conservative old man. In fact, like most writers who have been fortunate enough to have long careers, Johnson changed his views as he matured, as he read new works, and as he gained new experiences. As a young man, Johnson was rebellious and angry. He was learned and poor; he disliked the Hanoverian monarchy; and the architecture of London in 1738 could be not only ugly but downright dangerous—poorly built walls sometimes collapsed into the streets. The crowding, poverty, and crime of London would probably have shocked any young person from the country who was experiencing it for the first time; Johnson arrived in London in 1737, and the poem appeared in 1738.

The Vanity of Human Wishes, on the other hand, was written when Johnson was in his middle years. Juvenal's satires still interested him, as they did, according to Boswell, in his late years; and *The Vanity of Human Wishes* is an imitation of Juvenal's tenth satire. In this satire, Juvenal shows that people are unable to perceive their own best interests. Some people wish to be eloquent, even though Cicero was doomed by his own eloquence; others seek power, even though Alexander the Great was undone by power. Wise people, Juvenal says, would let the gods choose what is best for them. Typical of the Latin poet, the tenth satire expresses a conservative Roman's disgust with the foolishness of society in the Empire. The dominant themes in the satire would have appealed to Johnson: anger at a people who neglect the ideals that made them great, dismay at the successes of fools at the expense of supposedly intelligent people, and the notion that society's values were distorted, with learning and wisdom ranking below ignorance and vice.

The ethos of *The Vanity of Human Wishes* is Christian. Johnson replaces Juvenal's notion that people do not choose to do what will do them good with the idea that people choose vainly when they choose material and worldly success. Johnson also replaces Juvenal's notion that wise people let the gods choose for them with the idea that wise people put their lives in God's hands. The tenth satire of Juvenal was popular during the Middle Ages because preachers could convert its criticisms of vice into homilies on the dangers of materialism, and it provides ready material for Johnson's portrait of human life gone astray. Nearly 350 lines of his poem are devoted to discussing how people who seek wealth, power, or other earthly pleasures and rewards, fail to find happiness. The poem is thick with images and requires close reading; it is in large part depressingly negative. Much of human life seems hopeless. Even so, Johnson's scope is remarkable; he reaches beyond the range of *London* and beyond the range of Juvenal's satire; he discusses all human beings, everywhere. He cites Thomas Wolsey's power and wealth, Charles XII of Sweden's ambition, the miserable fates of John Churchill Marlborough, who was debilitated by strokes, and Jonathan Swift, who suffered from a disease similar to senile dementia. Neither power, wealth, ambition, honor, nor intellect mean much in the great scheme of life, and none are proof against misery and humiliation.

Johnson leaps back and forth through time, and from one part of the world to another, in his effort to convey the vastness of his topic and universality of his theme. He asserts:

Unnumber'd suppliants crowd Preferment's gate,

Athirst for wealth, and burning to be great,
Delusive Fortune hears th' incessant call,
They mount, they shine, evaporate, and fall.

A host of examples are mustered to support Johnson's contention that all earthly human wishes are vain; a reader can feel overwhelmed by the images and arguments that Johnson presents. If one does not read the poem carefully, one might interpret it as a despairing depiction of human endeavors and of lives without hope. Some critics call the poem "stoic," as if the only response to the hopelessness of life as depicted by Johnson were withdrawal and endurance. Such a reading misses the poem's fundamental point and fails to recognize Johnson's rejection of stoicism: "Must helpless man, in ignorance sedate,/ Roll darkling down the torrent of his fate?" No, Johnson answers, because "petitions yet remain,/ Which heav'n may hear, nor deem religion vain." God is the solution to the vanities of humanity. Stoicism demands a retreat into one's self; Johnson advocates that one reach outside himself. An important teaching of Christianity in Johnson's day was that one needed to seek beyond the material world for happiness—that unselfishness would bring enduring rewards. Johnson notes the "goods for man the laws of heav'n ordain," "love," "patience," and "faith." He says, "With these celestial wisdom calms the mind." Just as folly is universal, so too is the answer to folly. God responds to anyone who is devoted to Him.

The Vanity of Human Wishes is grim; the poem reflects Johnson's personality and his concerns, and his unhappy view of the disorder of an unfair world is expressed in relentless images. He was also a Christian, holding out hope for himself and the rest of humanity. His poetic skill is revealed in his shift from a lengthy account of the failures of even the best of people to the simple assertion of God's ability to ease the misery of anyone. He uses the heroic couplet, as in *London*, to give his poem a clear structure. Within that structure he maneuvers ideas with seeming ease and resolves the complex problem of the vanity of human wishes with the poetically elegant answer of the Christian ethos.

Johnson's play *Irene* was begun while he was still a teacher, before he moved to London in 1737, and he continued to work on it sporadically until 1749, when David Garrick produced it under the title *Mahomet and Irene*. The primary source for the play was the *Generall Historie of the Turkes* (1603), by Richard Knolles. The story is filled with intrigue: Mahomet, the Turkish Sultan, falls in love with a Greek Christian, Irene. He offers her wealth, power, and marriage, if she will renounce Christianity and convert to Islam. His followers are unhappy that their leader, who has conquered Constantinople, would fall for a conquered infidel, and they plot his overthrow. Greeks join in the plotting as well. After some soul-searching and passionate scenes, Irene yields to Mahomet and becomes a victim of the play's intrigues. The plot of *Irene* is surprisingly good, given its neglect by modern readers. Its weakness is in its blank verse, which, as Donald Greene notes in *Samuel Johnson* (1970), has a "sledgehammer monotony." Although the play made money during its run as Garrick's production and was reprinted three times while Johnson lived, it was not a critical success. Its verse is unimaginative and dull, unequal to the strengths of both plot and characters. Johnson reveals insight into his characters, particularly the spiritually struggling Irene, and an ability to present an interesting story.

Although *London* and *The Vanity of Human Wishes* are justifiably rated by critics as his best poems, much of Johnson's lesser verse is rewarding. His *Prologue Spoken at the Opening of the Theater in Drury-Lane* (1747), for example, discusses the merits of drama. In addition to writing prologues that are superior to most others, Johnson was a master of the epitaph and elegy. His "Epitaph on Hogarth" is representative of his ability to evoke pathos in a short poem with such lines as: "Here death has clos'd the curious eyes/ That saw the manners in the face." The poem on William Hogarth, the painter, was something of an exercise for Johnson, written as it was in response to Garrick's request for advice on an epitaph requested by Mrs. Hogarth. His "On the Death of Dr. Robert Levet" comes more from his heart. The elegy was written in 1782 after the death of the friend and surgeon who had been living in Johnson's home. The poem presents a picture of a man who was "Officious, innocent, sincere,/ Of ev'ry friendless name the friend." Johnson makes the poem a comment on life in general, both its sorrows and glories, and makes the seemingly humble Levet a representative of the best virtues: sacrifice for others, modesty in material desires, and selfless working to improve the lot of humanity. The poem is united by metaphor ("mine" and "caverns") and theme.

The somber themes of the elegy and epitaph and the weighty themes of the prologues and major poems might suggest that Johnson's verse is devoted exclusively to the unhappy aspects of life. Such a view, however, would be unbalanced. Even in the bitterness of *London* there is witty wordplay; and Johnson had a remarkable taste for stinging humor. He sent to Mrs. Thrale in 1780 a poem about her scapegrace nephew, John Lade, entitled "A Short Song of Congratulation." Lade had recently come into his inheritance, and Johnson lists the various ways that the young man could waste his money. The wit is pointed and accurate; Lade wasted his fortune. Most of Johnson's light verse is extemporaneous, being meant for his friends, rather than for the public, lacking the careful structure of Johnson's other poetry. His Latin poetry, on the other hand, is usually very well-constructed.

Johnson's stature as a poet has varied according to critical fashion. The critics of the Romantic and Victorian periods often dismissed his work as heavy-handed; they favored spontaneity and image over calculation and idea. Johnson was a man of ideas; he thrived on them and loved to toy with them, but his work was also emotional. The critics of the nineteenth century favored lyric poetry over satire and often missed the merits of the poetic tradition in which Johnson's best verse belongs. Twentieth century critics have, in general, rediscovered the virtues of Johnson's prosody. At his best, he fashions his verse with persuasive naturalness. His poetry conveys a powerful vision of the universality of the human condition. *The Vanity of Human Wishes* rightly ranks as one of the best and most important poems of world literature; with *London* and some of the minor poems, taken as a group, it argues powerfully for Johnson's status as a significant poet.

Kirk H. Beetz

Other major works

LONG FICTION: *Rasselas, Prince of Abyssinia: A Tale by S. Johnson*, 1759 (originally published as *The Prince of Abissinia: A Tale*).

PLAY: *Irene: A Tragedy*, 1749.

NONFICTION: *Marmer Norfolciense*, 1739; *A Compleat Vindication of the Licensers of the Stage*, 1739; *The Life of Admiral Blake*, 1740; *An Account of the Life of John Philip Barretier*, 1744; *An Account of the Life of Mr. Richard Savage, Son of the Earl Rivers*, 1744; *Miscellaneous Observations on the Tragedy of Macbeth*, 1745; *The Plan of a Dictionary of the English Language*, 1747; essays in *The Rambler*, 1750-1752; essays in *The Adventurer*, 1753-1754; *A Dictionary of the English Language*, 1755; essays in *The Idler*, 1758-1760; preface and notes to *The Plays of William Shakespeare*, 1765 (8 volumes); *The False Alarm*, 1770; *Thoughts on the Late Transactions Respecting Falkland's Islands*, 1771; *The Patriot: Addressed to the Electors of Great Britain*, 1774; *Taxation No Tyranny: An Answer to the Resolutions and Address of the American Congress*, 1775; *A Journey to the Western Islands of Scotland*, 1775; *Prefaces, Biographical and Critical, to the Works of the English Poets*, 1779-1781 (10 volumes; also known as *The Lives of the Poets*); *The Critical Opinions of Samuel Johnson*, 1923, 1961 (Joseph Epes Brown, editor).

TRANSLATIONS: *A Voyage to Abyssinia*, 1735; *Commentary on Pope's Principles of Morality*, 1739.

MISCELLANEOUS: *The Works of Samuel Johnson*, 1787-1789.

Bibliography

Bate, Walter Jackson. *Samuel Johnson*. New York: Harcourt Brace Jovanovich, 1979. This Pulitzer prize-winning biography has shrewd psychological assessments of Johnson's early and major poems.

Eliot, T. S. Introduction to *London* and *The Vanity of Human Wishes*, by Samuel Johnson. London: Etchells and Macdonald, 1930. Reprinted in *English Critical Essays: Twentieth Century*, edited by Phyllis M. Jones. London: Oxford University Press, 1933. One of Eliot's most brilliant critical pieces, this groundbreaking essay is an indispensable introduction to Johnson's poetry. More than fifty years ago, Eliot proclaimed Johnson's excellence as a poet and declared that *London* and *The Vanity of Human Wishes* were among the finest verse satires in any language.

Greene, Donald. *Samuel Johnson.* 2d ed. Boston: Twayne, 1989. This updated biography offers a vigorous summing-up of Johnson's poetic genius.

Hinnant, Charles H. "The Decline of the Heroic: From *London* to *The Vanity of Human Wishes.*" In *Samuel Johnson: An Analysis.* New York: St. Martin's Press, 1988. This chapter discusses the different approaches of Johnson's two major poems and the changes in artistic vision behind the differences. This essay is a detailed, usually reliable interpretation of both works in relationship to his literary canon.

Johnson, Samuel. *The Poems of Samuel Johnson.* Edited by David Nichol Smith and Edward L. McAdam, Jr. 2d ed. Oxford, England: Clarendon Press, 1974. This pioneering collection arranges all Johnson's poems in chronological order. The editorial and explanatory scholarship is of the highest order. Supervised by J. D. Fleeman in the second edition of 1974, the text is one of the major printings of Johnson's poetry. Prefaces for individual poems provide useful explanations of meaning and any editorial problems.

_____. *Samuel Johnson: The Complete English Poems.* Edited by J. D. Fleeman. Harmondsworth, England: Penguin Books, 1971. Another fine chronologically arranged collection of Johnson's poetry. This convenient edition includes Johnson's Latin poems, with English prose translations. Contains excellent editorial scholarship, with incisive endnotes.

_____. *Samuel Johnson: Poems.* Edited by Edward L. McAdam, Jr. Vol. 6 in *The Works of Samuel Johnson.* New Haven, Conn.: Yale University Press, 1958- . This standard edition offers a chronological arrangement of Johnson's English and Latin poetry, with English translations and solid critical and editorial commentary in footnotes. Based on newly discovered manuscripts and current literary research, this collection is a reliable addition to the modern publication (still in progress) of all Johnson's literary canon. Unlike the above two editions of Johnson's poetry, the Yale collection indulges in some standardization of the original manuscript texts and reduces capitalized common nouns to lower case, in accordance with the guidelines of the Yale Editorial Committee for this project. Prefaces for individual poems provide useful explanations of meaning and any editorial problems.

Lascelles, Mary M. "Johnson and Juvenal." In *New Light on Dr. Johnson: Essays on the Occasion of His 250th Birthday,* edited by Frederick W. Hilles. New Haven, Conn.: Yale University Press, 1959. This essay is an important study of the poetic transformation of Juvenal's *Satires III* and *X* in, respectively, Johnson's *London* and *The Vanity of Human Wishes.* A comparison of the Latin and English poems demonstrates Johnson's genuine originality, unique Christian vision, and distinctive moral and political concerns.

Naugle, Helen Harrold, and Peter B. Sherry. *A Concordance to the Poems of Samuel Johnson*, Ithaca, N.Y.: Cornell University Press, 1973. This is an alphabetical index of the principal words in Johnson's poetry, citing the passages where they appear. Helpful for identifying both his works and his opinions on issues.

BEN JONSON

Born: London, England; June 11, 1573
Died: London, England: August 6, 1637

Principal poetry

Poems, 1601; *Epigrams*, 1616; *The Forest*, 1616; *Underwoods*, 1640; *Ben Jonson*, 1925-1952 (C. H. Hereford, Percy Simpson, and Evelyn Simpson, editors; includes *Ungathered Verse*).

Other literary forms

Ben Jonson's fame has rested mainly on his comic drama, especially on the masterpieces of his maturity, *Volpone* (1605), *Epicœne: Or, The Silent Woman* (1609), *The Alchemist* (1610), and *Bartholomew Fair* (1614). Surviving earlier comedies are *The Case Is Altered* (1597), *Every Man in His Humour* (1598, 1605), *Every Man out of His Humour* (1599), *Cynthia's Revels* (1600-1601), *Poetaster* (1601), and *Eastward Ho!* (1605, with George Chapman and John Marston). Later comedies are *The Devil Is an Ass* (1616), *The Staple of News* (1626), *The New Inn* (1629), *The Magnetic Lady* (1632), and *A Tale of a Tub* (1633). Jonson wrote two tragedies, *Sejanus* (1603) and *Catiline* (1611). Two uncompleted works date apparently from the end of his life: the pastoral *The Sad Shepherd* and the tragedy *Mortimer His Fall* (only a few pages).

Jonson's court masques and entertainments may conservatively be said to number about thirty, differing tallies being possible depending on whether minor entertainments of various kinds are counted. Important titles include *The Masque of Blackness* (1605), *The Golden Age Restored* (1616), and *The Gypsies Metamorphosed* (1621). Besides plays, masques, and original nondramatic verse, Jonson wrote and translated a few other works which help to place him in the Renaissance humanistic tradition; all were first published in the 1640-1641 *Works*. As a vernacular humanist, Jonson wrote *The English Grammar* (1640); he translated Horace's *Ars Poetica* (as *Horace His Art of Poetry*) in 1640; finally, he compiled and translated extracts from classical and modern authors, mostly having to do with ethics, education, and rhetoric; the collection is entitled *Timber: Or, Discoveries Made upon Men and Matter* (1641).

Achievements

Jonson's achievements as a writer of verse can best be summarized by saying that he founded English neoclassicism. Jonson, of course, wrote several decades before what is usually thought of as the neoclassic age, but his work clearly foreshadows that of John Dryden and Alexander Pope. His, like theirs, was a mode of poetry generally imitative of ancient Roman forms, concerned, as important Roman writers had been, with behavior on a specifically human stage of action, and sometimes heroic, often satirical, in tone and stance.

Biography

Benjamin Jonson's father, a minister, died a month before his son's birth. Ben's mother remarried, apparently fairly soon thereafter, the stepfather being a master bricklayer of Westminster. "A friend" enrolled Jonson at Westminster School, but (as he told William Drummond) he was "taken from" school at about the age of sixteen and "put to" a "Craft," presumably brick-laying. Unable to "endure" this occupation, Jonson escaped briefly into the wars with The Netherlands. The next few years (roughly, his early twenties) are the most obscure of Jonson's life. At some point during this time he married and began having children, although practically nothing is known about his wife or family.

Jonson reappears in the late 1590's in theatrical records as an actor and part-time playwright. In these years Jonson was repeatedly at odds with the law, usually because of his involvement with satirical or political drama. He also attracted the authorities' hostility through his conversion to Roman Catholicism. (Eventually he returned to the Church of England, and later in life expressed, above all, distaste for those who claimed complete theological certainty.) In the series of comedies of "humours" beginning with *Every Man in His Humour*, Jonson coined an original form of satirical comedy based on the caricature of psychological types. In 1600 to 1601 he temporarily abandoned the open-air "public" playhouses to present his "comical satires" at the more fashionable indoor "private" theater at Blackfriars. The move was part of the provocation of the "stage quarrel" or "war of the theaters," in which Jonson, Thomas Dekker, and John Marston traded plays lampooning one another. Jonson's earliest datable nondramatic poetry also belongs to these years. From the first, Jonson wrote occasional and panegyric verse addressed to the aristocracy, invoking their patronage.

The first decade and a half of the seventeenth century were the years of Jonson's superb creativity and greatest popularity as a playwright. During those years he was in social contact with fellow playwrights such as William Shakespeare, and also with scholars such as William Camden and John Selden. Jonson's associations, however, were not limited to the theatrical and the learned; he was steadily employed as the writer of court masques throughout the reign of James I. Both the King and the aristocrats at the court responded to Jonson's work for many years with notable offers of support. The years from 1616 through 1624 probably marked the height of his prestige. In 1616 he published his *Workes* in folio. A royal pension came in the same year and, in 1619, an honorary degree from Oxford. Also gratifying was the gathering around Jonson of the "Tribe of Ben," a circle of poetic "sons," including Thomas Carew and Robert Herrick, who adopted him as their mentor.

The accession of Charles I to the throne in 1625 ended Johnson's tenure as regular writer of masques for the court, and in other respects also the last dozen years of Jonson's life contrast with the preceding successful decades. At some points during these last years, he was clearly in financial need, and in 1628 he suffered a stroke. He was writing comedies again for the popular stage, but none of them won much acclaim. Against such bleak circumstances, however, stands a persistence of poetic energy, embodied in much outstanding verse attributable to these years. Jonson held the regard of his "Sons" until his death in 1637, and beyond: one of them, Sir Kenelm Digby, finally assembled and published Jonson's later, along with his earlier, *Works* in 1640-1641.

Analysis

Until the last few decades, attention to Ben Jonson's poetry focused largely on the famous songs and the moving epitaphs on children. Such choices were not ill-advised, but they are unrepresentative. The works in these modes certainly rank among Jonson's most successful, but they differ in tone from Jonson's norm.

Songs such as "Kiss me, sweet: the wary lover" and "Drink to me only with thine eyes" evoke emotions beyond the world of reason or fact, partly through reference to extravagant gestures and implausible experiences: hundreds and thousands of kisses, a wreath that will not die after the beloved has breathed on it. Through rhythms that are stronger and less interrupted than Jonson usually created, the songs activate the capacity to respond sensually and irrationally to language. Some of them create magical secret worlds where sense and emotion are to be experienced in disregard of troubling or qualifying context (the "silent summer nights/ When youths ply their stol'n delights" in "Kiss me, sweet: the wary lover"). Exactly such worlds are created, but also subjected to critique, in *Volpone* and *The Alchemist*.

The epitaphs, particularly those on Jonson's own children ("On my First Son," "On my First Daughter") are so effective because in them subjective emotions strain against rational conviction. Jonson's statement in each of these poems is doctrinal and exemplary, involving resignation to the will of God, but part of the power of the affirmation of belief arises from Jonson's undertone of grief over which faith has won out. Regret and despair have not been reasoned away but are being rationally controlled; consolation is not easy.

Such richly concentrated poems obviously deserve attention; that they should have received exposure to the virtual exclusion of Jonson's less lyrical or emotive verse, however, perhaps represents a holdover from Romantic or Victorian taste for rhapsodic expressions of feeling and imaginative vision in poetry. In fact, the renewal of contact with the Metaphysical sensibility achieved by T. S. Eliot and other critics in the 1920's and 1930's, which brought about the displacement of Victorian approaches to a number of seventeenth century writers, did not do so, immediately or directly, in the case of Jonson as a nondramatic poet. Some of Jonson's works are recognizably close to the secular reaches of John Donne's writing, but the speaker's psychological self-discovery through metaphor, so often the business of a Donne poem, is only occasionally Jonson's way. The contrast is especially clear between Jonson's poetic range and the realm of the meditative, intense, often all-but-private Metaphysical religious lyric. Jonson wrote very few strictly devotional poems; the ode "To Heaven" is probably the only strikingly successful work that could bear that label. In poems such as the ode to Sir Lucius Cary and Sir Henry Morison and the funeral elegies, where the afterlife is mentioned, the relation of humanity as such to divinity is not the real focus of attention. The poems involve tensions mainly between diverse human levels, between more ordinary experience on the one hand and, on the other, an excellence or superiority of nature which Cary, Morison, Lady Jane Pawlet, and the other exemplary figures achieve.

At most, only on the peripheries of Jonson's nondramatic verse can it be seen to approximate pure emotive lyricism, or can it be cast in Metaphysical terms. Only in the late twentieth century did criticism achieve a modern re-understanding of Jonson's achievement, involving a strongly positive evaluation of his central, typical poetic work. Jonson emerges in this criticism as decisively a neoclassic artist, the intellectual background of whose poetry is Renaissance humanism.

Jonson appears as a humanistic thinker in his *Timber*, and his career reflected humanistic motivations and aspirations. Fundamentally, Jonson conceived of learning, thought, and language as phases of the active life of man. Humanists conceived of education as the initiation of patterns of wise and effective behavior in the student's life. Humanistic education was largely linguistic, because of the traditional importance of the persuasive linguistic act, the centrality of oratory (or, for the Renaissance, the counseling of the prince and nobles) in the repertory of practical, political skills. Patterns both of moral behavior in general and of speech specifically were normally learned through imitation of the deeds and words of figures from the past; for most humanists, and very definitely for Jonson, this did not mean that modern men were supposed to become mere apes of their predecessors, but rather that, through first following models, men should exercise and organize their own capacities to a point where they could emulate and rival the ancients, becomeing effective on their own terms as the ancients were on theirs.

As a nonaristocratic humanist in a stratified society, Jonson essentially followed a pattern marked out since the time of Thomas More and Thomas Elyot early in the preceding century when he attached himself to noble households and the court. Debarred by birth from directly wielding the largest measure of power in his society, he engaged in action obliquely by speaking to the powerful, counseling and offering praise to encourage the elite in the wise conduct of life and authority. This was the light in which Jonson saw his masques, not only as celebrations, but also as reminders of ideals, such as justice, which should inform the court's activity. A great many of Jonson's moralizing poems addressed to noblemen and others also clearly exhibited actual hortatory intent.

Jonson's thought includes, as one might expect, special factors that set it off somewhat from humanism as it appears in other contexts. For one thing, while Jonson was not an unbeliever, it is certainly true that his humanism does not merge clearly and continuously into moralistic, pastoral Christianity, as had that of Desiderius Erasmus a hundred years before. The ethical universe of *Timber* is one of Roman, not obstrusively Christian, virtues; if anything, Jonson looks forward to later secular rationalism. Another characteristic of Jonson's humanism is the trace of influence from Seneca and Roman Stoicism, apparent in his writing, as elsewhere in early seventeenth century English expression. A main effect of Senecan influence on Jonson seems to have been to encourage a concern with and regard for what can best be called integrity; that is, the correlation of an individual's behavior with his inner nature rather than with outward circumstance. Such concern naturally belonged with the Senecan concept of specifically linguistic behavior which *Timber* expresses—a heightened awareness of style as emerging from and conveying an image of the "inmost" self.

Jonson's neoclassic verse is the poetic cognate of his quite secular, somewhat Senecan version of humanism. Splitting the relation into separate aspects only for the sake of analysis, one can say that in form Jonson's poems are above all linguistic acts, the talk of a persona to an implied (often, a designated) human audience. In content, the poems are orderings of levels or modes of human behavior.

Jonson's "An Epistle answering to One that asked to be Sealed of the Tribe of Ben" is identified by its title in terms of the act of communication that it imitates, the letter. Relatively few of Jonson's titles actually include the word "epistle," but many of them involve, or even simply consist of, the designation of an addressee—"To Katherine Lady Aubigny," "To Sir Robert Wroth," and so on. Thus the reader is asked to be aware of many of Jonson's poems not primarily in terms of any myths they may relate or images they may invoke, but as linguistic action, the linguistic behavior of a human speaker toward a human audience.

The fiction of speaker and audience is not an inert element but has an impact on the poem's other aspects. Many qualities of style are conditioned by the character of the addressee and his relation to the speaker. In the "Epistle to Master John Selden," the speaker states that he feels free to use a curt, "obscure," at times almost telegraphic style because "I know to whom I write": he knows that Selden is not only intelligent but also at home with the speaker's ways of thinking. Generally, the grandiloquence, expansiveness, and elaborate structure of public oratory will rarely be appropriate for an epistle or other poem addressed by one person to another.

Jonson's style in "An Epistle answering to One that asked to be Sealed of the Tribe of Ben" is fairly typical of that in a number of his poems. His diction is generally colloquial; Edmund Bolton's characterization of Jonson's "vital, judicious and practicable language" (in Bolton's *Hypercritica,* c. 1618) is an excellent general description of the style. Syntactic units in Jonson's poems are by and large brief and stopped abruptly so that one jumps (or stumbles) from clause to clause rather than making easy transitions. Units are typically not paired or otherwise arranged symmetrically in relation to one another. The effect in "An Epistle answering to One that asked to be Sealed of the Tribe of Ben" is one of rather blurting, unpremeditated speech, propelled by some emotional pressure. Structurally, too, the poem seems unpremeditated, beginning with appropriate introductory comments to the would-be disciple to whom Ben is writing, then falling away into contemptuous griping about phony elements in Jonson's society, circling down into what reads like underlying anxiety about Jonson's personal situation—and coming through this human situation to a now almost heroic assertion of what it means to be Ben or one sealed of his tribe.

In other poems, the style varies, within a generally informal range. Jonson's meaning can in fact be obscure when the syntax is very broken or a great deal of meaning is concentrated in one phrase; the effect is often that of a rather impatient intelligence, not using more words than it needs to communicate meaning to its immediate addressee. In extreme cases, the reader may feel like an outsider reading a communication not meant for him (see, for example, the "Epistle to Sir Edward Sackville"). Such privacy, immured by style, sets Jonson off somewhat from Augustan neoclassic writers such as Alexander Pope, who usually engage in smoother and more public address.

Entitling the poem an "Epistle," besides drawing attention to its character as a linguistic act, also of course associates it with a generic tradition. Seneca was the most influential classical practitioner of the moral epistle as a prose form, Horace of the form in verse. Jonson's epistles and many of his other poems evoke these authors' works in content and style, sometimes through specific allusion. Clearly related to classical tradition, yet utterly topical and personal (with its references to the politics of "Spain or France" and to Jonson's employment as a writer of masques), "An Epistle answering to One that asked to be Sealed of the Tribe of Ben" is a successful act of humanistic imitation. Overt reference to tradition reveals the moral statement of Jonson's poetry in relation to the whole body of classical moral wisdom—and implies that Jonson is not afraid of the juxtaposition.

The particular wisdom of this poem is conveyed most clearly in the description of the course of conduct Jonson has "decreed" for himself, which comes after the middle of the poem's descriptions of a social environment of indulgence of appetite, empty talk, and illusory "Motions." Jonson's resolve is to

"Live to that point . . . for which I am man/ And dwell as in my Center as I can." The image is one of withdrawal from concern for meaningless external situations; it is also a picture of a life standing in relation to some firm, definite principle, as opposed to the poem's earlier images of unfounded judgments and groundless chatter.

The ideas of withdrawal and of a "Center" within the personality are clearly reminiscent of Seneca and Horace. The most characteristic aspect of the poem's meaning is that it consists of definitions not so much of the ideal principle itself as of the behavior which is or is not oriented to it. Jonson is not much concerned with describing the Center except as such, as a point from which surrounding space takes orientation. He is concerned with describing centeredness, and distinguishing it from shapeless and unfocused conditions; or, to return from geometry to humanity, with describing what it is like to operate on a firm moral basis, and distinguishing this from the "wild Anarchy" in which those outside the Tribe of Ben live.

The focus on behavior which is or is not guided, rather than on the available guiding transcendent principle, corresponds to the specifically secular emphasis of Jonson's humanism. There is an almost (though certainly not quite) agnostic quality in Jonson's almost interchangeable references to the "point," the "Center," "heaven," and "reason" as the source of his wisdom and strength. Clearly it is the exemplification of those qualities in life that interests him. Such an interest makes Jonson stand out as strikingly modern against the backdrop, for example, of the highly articulated ideal world of Edmund Spenser; it links Jonson forward to the essence of English neoclassicism, such as in Pope's ethically oriented satires and moral essays.

It should be noted that the movement toward the Center involves choice and effort: Jonson must decree it to himself, and even those who have been once sealed to the tribe of Ben have still to fear the shame of possibly stumbling in reason's sight. For good or evil, no destiny holds Jonson's human beings in place. The ideal principle is only vaguely defined; it is merely an available, not a controlling, factor.

Like the epistles and other more or less epistolary longer poems, Jonson's epigrams are, in form, primarily linguistic acts. They are comments "on" or "to" someone. They are self-consciously brief remarks, aiming to capture or essentialize a character—sometimes, implicitly, to reduce an object to its true dimensions (many of Jonson's epigrams are satirical).

The epigrammatic mode is closely related to the epistolary in Jonson's practice and in the tradition out of which he writes. Martial, the Roman epigrammatist whom Jonson regularly imitated, conceived of his works as epistles in brief. Jonson's style has the same constituents. The broken syntax sometimes seems part of epigrammatic compression; sometimes it promotes a casualness which is part of Jonson's reduction and dismissal of a satirized personality, as in Epigram 21 ("On Reformed Gamester").

The pentameter couplets in which Jonson writes not only the epigrams but the great bulk of his neoclassic verse are derived partly from normal English practice for nonlyric poetry going back through Geoffrey Chaucer. They are also, however, influenced by a classical form, the elegiac distich—a prosodic vehicle used by, among others, Martial. Readily recognizable and essentially symmetrical, the form tends to stand as a strong balancing, controlling, ordering presence in the poetry in which it appears. Part of its potential is as a structure for concentrated, gnomic, almost proverbial utterance, easy for the reader to carry away in his mind; this potential is best realized when the couplet is a tightly closed unit, as is normally the case in Pope.

Jonson uses the form in the several ways just mentioned. Couplet order underscores orderly, almost (for Jonson) patterned, praise of a firmly centered man in Epigram 128 ("To William Roe"). Some epigrams consist of single gnomic couplets (Epigram 34, "Of Death"), and others are memorable for neat, closed-couplet wit (Epigram 31, "On Banck the Usurer"). Both Jonson's prestige and his virtuoso skill in testing the couplet's range of uses were important in establishing it as the standard neoclassic prosodic structure. Jonson's most characteristic way of exploiting the couplet, however, was not simply to employ, but simultaneously to violate, its order, to write across the prosodic structure as if in disregard of it. Actually, more often than not, in Jonson's verse, syntactic and phrasal breaks do not come at such points within a line as to facilitate the prosodic caesura, nor are they matched with line endings or even the ends of the couplets themselves (see for example Epigram 46, "To Sir Luckless Woo-all"). The couplet may be opposed by meaning, along with grammar: antitheses and other logical and rhetorical structures work at cross purposes with the prosody (Epigram 11, "On Some-Thing, that Walks Some-Where").

In such circumstances, the couplet does not cease to be an obtrusive form. Jonson maintains the reader's awareness of it, precisely as a structure that is not managing to control or limit the autonomy of his grammar, rhetoric, and logic. The latter, of course, are the elements of the oratorical presence in the poetry—of Jonson's voice or speech. The net effect is to enhance the sense of the independent liveliness of the speaking persona, his freedom to move about, to understand and to explain in his own way, on his own terms. Jonson's handling of the couplet implies through form a quite radical version of secular humanism, a sense of the detachment of linguistic action (and of man the linguistic actor) from any containing structure.

Many of the same kinds of content are present in the epigrams as in the epistolary writings. The epigrammatic image of William Roe's stable personality, mentioned earlier, is obviously cognate with Ben's self-image in "An Epistle answering to One that asked to be Sealed of the Tribe of Ben," as are such portrayals as those of Sir Henry Nevil (Epigram 109), William, Earl of Pembroke (102), and Sir Thomas Roe (98). (The latter contains one of

Jonson's more gnomic statements of the concept of the inner-directed and self-sufficient man: "Be always to thy gathered self the same/ And study conscience, more than thou would'st fame.") Satire, often a phase in the epistles, can fill entire epigrams. Something, that Walks Somewhere, Sir Voluptuous Beast (Epigrams 35 and 36) and Don Surly (Epigram 38) are incisively but fully realized satiric characters, clearly inhabitants of the same world as the "humour" characters Corbaccio and Epicure Mammon in Jonson's plays. Something, that Walks Somewhere, the lord who walks in "clothes brave enough," "buried in flesh, and blood," unwilling to do and afraid to dare, is one of Jonson's most powerful pictures of pointless, disorganized life—almost of disorganized protoplasm. Jonson suggested in many indirect ways that he regarded Horace as his mentor, and his work certainly has many Horatian traits, but his satire sometimes seems to belong less in the Horatian than in the harsher Juvenalian category.

"To Penshurst," one of Jonson's most famous poems, celebrates a different kind of relatedness from the internal centering discussed so far. Here human life is benign because it stands within what men have recently learned to call an ecosystem: a web of connections between elements that feed and feed off one another and through interaction perpetuate one another's well-being. At Penshurst, the Sidney family's country estate, nature freely delivers its supply into the Sidneys' hands; fish and birds "officiously" serve themselves up; but here and even more in the very similar poem "To Sir Robert Wroth," one feels that the humans could have a harvesting function, culling what sometimes seems almost like a glut of natural abundance. In any case, the human lords of Penshurst themselves stand as the basis of further relations, providing a social center to which neighbors from a whole community and guests from farther away "come in." The neighbors bring even more food, and the "provisions" of Penshurst's "liberal board" flow back to them. The system yields more than it can use, and the superflux passes to the unenvied guest and is there, ready to be offered to the king, the regulator of a larger system and community, when he happens into this particular sphere. The system, though nature flows through it, is not mindless. From Penshurst's lady's "huswifery" up through "The mysteries of manners, arms and arts" which the house's children are learning, specifically human roles and human activities have their place in this strong and ample natural and human network; in fact, the sophisticated culture of an ancestral figure of the house, Sir Philip Sidney, can be alluded to without seeming out of place here.

A close modern analog to "To Penshurst" is W. H. Auden's "In Praise of Limestone," where man also meshes with landscape in a perfect way; Auden's description of the limestone system, however, is interrupted by accounts of less pleasing, more technological adjustments of the relation. In "To Penshurst," on the other hand, contrasting satiric pictures or references have less share than in almost any of Jonson's works. Only a few lines, mainly at the poem's beginning and end, succinctly insert Jonson's usual distinctions. Penshurst is Edenic. One is left with the uneasy feeling that the poem's being so much anthologized may be bound up with its being, for Jonson, atypically untroubled.

Jonson's ode "To the Immortal Memory and Friendship of that Noble Pair, Sir Lucius Cary and Sir H. Morison" stands near the beginning of the history of English efforts to imitate Pindar's odes. It has a complex and stately stanzaic structure. Nevertheless, many traits are carried over from Jonson's epigrammatic and epistolary style, in particular the tendency toward syntax that is at odds with prosodic divisions, of which the poem contains egregious examples: for instance, a stanza break comes in the middle of the name "Ben/ Jonson." An epic, "Heroologia," which Jonson planned, would probably have represented another extension to a new genre of his characteristic manner and ethical matter. The epic was to be in couplets and was to deal with "the Worthies of his country, roused by fame" (reports William Drummond). Like Pope, Jonson actually wrote a mock-epic rather than the serious one; Jonson's work is the "merdurinous" "On the Famous Voyage" (Epigram 133).

The ode to Cary and Morison is extreme in imagery as well as in syntactic-prosodic tension. It opens with a notorious image, that of the "infant of Saguntum" who retreated back to the womb before it was "half got out," appalled by the horror and devastation of wartime scenes into which it was being born. Jonson goes on to surprise conventional taste even further by suggesting that this vaginal peripety represents a "summ'd" "circle . . . of deepest lore, could we the Center find." References to circle and center of course bring along a whole train of important imagery and structure in Jonson, as well as alluding to the structure of the whole poem, with its repeated peripeteia of "Turn," "Counter-Turn," and "Stand."

The will to shock, or at least to write in uncompromisingly extraordinary ways, may indirectly express the speaker's grief and sense of loss (the poem's occasion is Morison's death). It is certainly connected with a larger demand to see life in an unconventional way, which is the poem's essential consoling strategy. (Jonson speaks of the "holy rage" with which Morison "leap'd the present age"; readers are asked to do the same thing, in the same mood.) The distinction that Jonson insists on is between visions of life as "space" and as "act." In terms of the former—sheer duration—Morison's life was indeed lamentably cut off: he lived barely into his twenties. In terms of "act," Morison's life was perfect:

> A Soldier to the last right end
> A perfect Patriot, and a noble friend,
> But most a virtuous Son.
> All Offices were done
> By him, so ample, full and round,
> In weight, in measure, number, sound

As, though his age imperfect might appear,
His life was of Humanity the Sphere.

This is, notably, purely secular consolation. There are later references to a "bright eternal day," but it has less to do with Christian Paradise than with a pagan heaven of commemoration, in which Morison (and Cary) may persist as an "Asterism," a constellation. The poem's contrast with "Lycidas" marks the distance between John Milton's more old-fashioned Christian humanism and Jonson's untheological mind.

Jubilation, rather than lamentation, over Morison's perfection of "act" is, like most of Jonson's higher choices, not easy to maintain. The speaker's own "tongue" "falls" into mourning at one point. Cary, Morison's great friend who survives him and to whom the poem is at least in part addressed, is exhorted to "call . . . for wine/ And let thy looks with gladness shine"—and to maintain connection. Like the centered men of the epigrams and epistles, and like the Sidneys of Penshurst, Cary is to act in relation, to "shine" on earth in conjunction with Morison's now heavenly light. The function of the poem vis-à-vis Cary is to establish this relation for him, and the broken but single name of Ben Jonson bridges over precisely the two stanzas where the relation of the two friends is most fully discussed.

The poem includes a satirical picture. Contrasting with the vital life of act, the vacuous life of space is personified as a futile careerist, "buoy'd . . . up" in the end only by the "Cork of Title." More than by alternation of satiric and positive images, however, the poem works by a tension constant throughout: the tension between the naturalistic sense of death as an end, which is never really lost, and the other vision which Jonson is insisting upon. The poem is a celebration of secular heroism. It depicts that quality in its subjects ("Nothing perfect done/ But as a Cary, or a Morison"), enacts it in its language, and demands it of its readers. The tension and energy which the poem displays are the reasons for reading Jonson's verse.

John F. McDiarmid

Other major works

PLAYS: *The Case Is Altered,* 1597; *The Isle of Dogs,* 1597 (with Thomas Nashe); *Hot Anger Soon Cold,* 1598 (with Henry Chettle and Henry Porter); *Every Man in His Humour,* 1598, 1605; *Every Man out of His Humour,* 1599; *The Page of Plymouth,* 1599 (with Thomas Dekker); *Robert the Second, King of Scots,* 1599 (with Henry Chettle and Thomas Dekker); *Cynthia's Revels,* 1600-1601; *Poetaster,* 1601; *Sejanus,* 1603; *The King's Entertainment in Passing to His Coronation,* 1603 (masque); *The Masque of Blackness,* 1605; *Eastward Ho!,* 1605 (with George Chapman and John Marston); *Volpone,* 1605; *The Masque of Beauty,* 1608; *The Masque of Queens,* 1609; *Epicœne: Or,*

The Silent Woman, 1609; *The Alchemist*, 1610; *Catiline*, 1611; *Oberon, the Fairy Prince*, 1611 (masque); *Bartholomew Fair*, 1614; *The Devil Is an Ass*, 1616; *The Golden Age Restored*, 1616 (masque); *Pleasure Reconciled to Virtue*, 1618 (masque); *Conversations*, 1619, 1711; *The Gypsies Metamorphosed*, 1621 (masque); "To the Memory of My Beloved, the Author, Mr. William Shakespeare, and What He Hath Left Us," 1623; *The Staple of News*, 1626; *The Fortunate Isles and Their Union*, 1626; *The New Inn*, 1629; *Chloridia*, 1630 (masque); *The Magnetic Lady*, 1632; *A Tale of a Tub*, 1633; *The Sad Shepherd*, 1640.

NONFICTION: *The English Grammar*, 1640; *Horace His Art of Poetry*, 1640; *Timber: Or, Discoveries Made upon Men and Matter*, 1641.

MISCELLANEOUS: *The Workes of Benjamin Jonson*, 1616; *The Works of Benjamin Jonson*, 1640-1641 (2 volumes).

Bibliography

Bamborough, J. B. *Ben Jonson*. London: Hutchinson University Library, 1970. A good standard scholarly biography and literary analysis, fact-filled but not overwhelming. Particularly revealing in placing Jonson in his historical context. Complete with basic index and bibliography.

Barton, Anne. *Ben Jonson, Dramatist*. Cambridge, England: Cambridge University Press, 1984. Barton's approach is comprehensive and magisterial. She covers all aspects of Jonson's life and writing with grace, style, insight, and perception. For a scholarly study, this is hard to put down. Includes a chronology, notes, and an index.

Brock, D. Heyward. *A Ben Jonson Companion*. Indianapolis: Indiana University Press, 1983. This long-awaited volume provides everything that was promised: a thorough and multifold first reference work with substance and range. Contains illuminating introductions to all the standard topics related to Jonson. The chronologies, indexes, and bibliography are easy to follow.

Chute, Marchette. *Ben Jonson of Westminster*. New York: E. P. Dutton, 1953. An old standard that has not been surpassed, Chute's biography for the general reader is genial, enthusiastic, and bewitching. A good index makes it easier to cross-relate various topics, although the bibliography is badly dated.

Miles, Rosalind. *Ben Jonson: His Life and Work*. London: Routledge & Kegan Paul, 1986. Miles's volume is a fine standard biography-study, especially for the literary background and Jonson's position in Jacobean courtly society. The scholarly apparatus is thorough: a chronology, an index, a select but extensive bibliography, notes, and an appendix.

Riggs, David. *Ben Jonson: A Life*. Cambridge, Mass.: Harvard University Press, 1989. This is a full-scale biography rather than a literary biography such as Miles's; here the works illuminate the life rather than vice versa.

The illumination is brilliant. Riggs reviews all the facts and assembles them in memorable order. He includes all the standard scholarly attachments; but the book deserves to be read simply for the revelations it contains for Jonson and his age, most of which are illustrated.

JAMES JOYCE

Born: Rathgar, Dublin, Ireland; February 2, 1882
Died: Zurich, Switzerland; January 13, 1941

Principal poetry

Chamber Music, 1907; *Pomes Penyeach*, 1927, "Ecce Puer," 1932; *Collected Poems*, 1936.

Other literary forms

Although James Joyce published poetry throughout his career (*Chamber Music*, a group of thirty-six related poems, was in fact his first published book), it is for his novels and short stories that he is primarily known. These works include *Dubliners* (1914), a volume of short stories describing what Joyce saw as the moral paralysis of his countrymen: *A Portrait of the Artist as a Young Man* (1916), a heavily autobiographical account of the growing up of a writer in Ireland at the end of the nineteenth century and the beginning of the twentieth; *Ulysses* (1922), a novel set in Dublin in 1904, recounting the day-long adventures of Leopold Bloom, a modern-day Odysseus who is both advertising man and cuckold, Stephen Dedalus, the young artist of *A Portrait of the Artist as a Young Man* now grown somewhat older, and Molly Bloom, Leopold's earthy wife; and *Finnegans Wake* (1939), Joyce's last published work, not a novel at all in the conventional sense, but a world in itself, built of many languages and inhabited by the paradigmatic Earwicker family.

Achievements

Joyce's prose works established his reputation as the most influential writer of fiction of his generation and led English prose fiction from Victorianism into modernism and beyond. To this body of work, Joyce's poetry is an addendum of less interest in itself than it is in relationship to the other, more important, work. At the same time, in the analysis of Joyce's achievement, it is impossible to ignore anything that he wrote, and the poetry, for which Joyce reserved some of his most personal utterances, has its place along with the play *Exiles* (1918)—now seen as more important than it once was—and the essays, letters, and notebooks.

Biography

The life of James Joyce is interwoven so inextricably with his work that to consider one requires considering the other. The definitive biography of Joyce, by Richard Ellmann, is as strong in its interpretation of Joyce's work as it is of his life. If Joyce, as Ellmann suggests in that biography, tended to see things through words, readers must try to see him through *his* words—the words of his work—as well as through the facts of his life.

Joyce was born into a family whose fortunes were in decline, the first child to live in the match of a man who drank too much and accumulated too many debts and a woman whose family the Joyces considered beneath them. John Joyce, James's father, became the model for Stephen's father both in *A Portrait of the Artist as a Young Man* and in *Ulysses*, where he is one of the most memorable characters, and also a model for H. C. Earwicker in *Finnegans Wake*. If Joyce's father seemed not to understand his son's work or even to show much interest in it during his lifetime, that work has become a surer form of immortality for him than anything he ever did himself.

Joyce was educated at Clongowes Wood College, a Jesuit school not far from Dublin which he memorialized in *A Portrait of the Artist as a Young Man*, and then later at Belvedere College, also Jesuit, in Dublin. In 1898, upon his graduation from Belvedere, he entered University College, Dublin. At this point in his life, increasingly rebellious against the values of his home and society, Joyce did his first writing for publication. He was graduated from the university with a degree in modern languages in 1902 and then left Dublin for Paris to study medicine. That, however, quickly gave way to Joyce's real desire to write, and he entered a difficult period in which he turned to teaching to earn a living. The problems of the father had become the problems of the son, but during this period Joyce wrote some of his best earlier poems, including what is now the final piece in the *Chamber Music* sequence. With the death of his mother imminent in April, 1903, Joyce returned to Dublin, where, the following winter, he began to write the first draft of *A Portrait of the Artist as a Young Man* (known as *Stephen Hero*).

By far the most important event after Joyce's return to Ireland, however, was his meeting in June, 1904, with the woman who was to become his mate for the rest of his life, Nora Barnacle, whose roots (like those of the family Joyce) were in Galway, the westernmost county in Ireland. If Joyce's mother's family had seemed too low for the Joyces, Nora's family was even lower on the social scale, but Joyce, like Stephen Dedalus, was to escape the net of convention and take the woman he loved away from Ireland to live in a succession of temporary residences on the Continent while he established himself as a major writer. The model, at least in part, for Molly Bloom and also for Anna Livia Plurabelle, Nora, not Joyce's legal wife until 1931, was the mother of their two children—Giorgio, born in 1905, and Lucia, born in 1907—and Joyce's main emotional support for almost four decades.

From the time Joyce and Nora moved to the Continent until the outbreak of World War I, they lived chiefly in Trieste, a port city in northeastern Italy which in appearance seemed more Austrian than Italian; there Joyce taught English in a Berlitz School, and wrote; he returned to Ireland only twice, in 1909 and again in 1912, for what turned out to be his last visit. With the outbreak of the war, Joyce and his family moved to Zurich, which was neutral ground, and in 1920—after a brief sojourn once again in Trieste—moved to Paris, where they were to remain until the fall of France twenty years later.

Paris in the 1920's, Ernest Hemingway was to write years later, was a "moveable feast," but Joyce, as always, was a selective diner, an integral part of the literary life of Paris at that time, yet aloof from it, imaginatively dwelling in the Dublin of 1904, the year he had met Nora. Having published *Chamber Music*, *Dubliners*, *A Portrait of the Artist as a Young Man*, and *Exiles*, Joyce had embarked on his most ambitious project to date—a treatment in detail of one day in Dublin—June 16, 1904—and the adventures of a modern-day Odysseus, Leopold Bloom, ultimately to be his greatest single achievement in characterization. The serialization of *Ulysses* had begun in 1918; its publication in book form waited until Joyce's fortieth birthday, on February 2, 1922. Because of publication difficulties resulting from censorship, Joyce did not realize much financially from the book until later in his life, and remained dependent upon a succession of patrons and subscribers not only for its initial publication but also for his livelihood. With its publication, however—difficult though it was to achieve—came the recognition of Joyce as the greatest living novelist in English, a master stylist who had managed (as such major figures as T. S. Eliot and Ezra Pound were quick to see) to give the modern experience a historical dimension which so many realistic novels had lacked.

As recognition of *Ulysses* came, Joyce characteristically moved on to something different (in a sense, in his published work he almost never repeated himself, in style or in form, though he dealt continuously with certain themes), publishing in 1924 the first portion of what for years was termed "Work in Progress" and then ultimately became *Finnegans Wake*. This novel broke new ground in the same way *Ulysses* did, in its rendering of unconscious universal experiences and in its use of language; but it took much longer for it to achieve general recognition as a masterpiece. Plagued throughout his lifetime by financial problems, health problems (especially with his eyes), and family problems (his daughter's mental health was always fragile, and she has lived most of her life in a sanatorium), Joyce remains the prime example of the artist as exile.

Analysis

Chamber Music appeared in 1907, but James Joyce had been working on the poems which comprise the volume for some time before that date. As early as 1905 he had worked out a plan for the poems, different from the one finally devised for the 1907 version but perhaps more revealing of the thematic content of the poetry. With the addition of several poems not in the 1905 scheme, *Chamber Music* came to thirty-six poems of varying lengths and forms, the work of a young man who had already largely abandoned poetry in favor of prose fiction.

In many ways the poems of *Chamber Music* are typical of the period in which they were written. The poetry of the late nineteenth century in English has a hothouse quality; like the French Symbolist, who—next to the English

Romantics—provided the chief inspiration throughout this period, the poets of the *fin de siècle* eschewed ordinary life in favor of an aesthetic ideal. This was in fact the final flowering of the ideal of art for art's sake so important to nineteenth century literature and art, an attitude which the young Joyce flirted with and ultimately abandoned, satirizing it in the pages of *A Portrait of the Artist as a Young Man*. In the poems of *Chamber Music*, however, the satire is less easy to detect, and *fin de siècle* themes provide the basis of many of the poems in the sequence. The dominant note of the poetry of the *fin de siècle* is one of weariness or sadness, the favorite time dusk or night, the favorite stance one of retreat; in Joyce's *Chamber Music* poems, as later in *A Portrait of the Artist as a Young Man*, such favorite attitudes are questioned but not totally rejected. If the final note is one of anger or bitterness rather than simply of sadness or despair, there is still a strong enough taste of the latter to mark the poems—even the celebrated number XXXVI—as the work of a young man who has grown up in the last important moment of aestheticism. Even so, the experience of the young man who is the principal speaker of the sequence of poems seems ultimately to toughen him in a way more typical of Joyce than of the poetry of the *fin de siècle*.

In Joyce's 1905 sequence, the personae of the poems are more easily perceived, the themes developed in them clearer, as William York Tindall was first to point out at length in his 1954 edition of *Chamber Music*. In that sequence there are thirty-four poems, designated first in the following list, with the numbers from the 1907 edition in Roman numerals in parentheses immediately after: 1 (XXI), 2 (I), 3 (III), 4 (II), 5 (IV), 6 (V), 7 (VIII), 8 (VII), 9 (IX), 10 (XVII), 11 (XVIII), 12 (VI), 13 (X), 14 (XX), 15 (XIII), 16 (XI), 17 (XIV), 18 (XIX), 19 (XV), 20 (XXIII), 21 (XXIV), 22 (XVI), 23 (XXXI), 24 (XXII), 25 (XXVI), 26 (XII), 27 (XXVII), 28 (XXVIII), 29 (XXV), 30 (XXIX), 31 (XXXII), 32 (XXX), 33 (XXXIII), and 34 (XXXIV).

This sequence has certain important features. Poem 1 (XXI) introduces the young man of the sequence, a sort of romantic rebel in the tradition of the Shelleyan hero, a "high unconsortable one" more in love with himself than with anyone else. This theme of aloofness and narcissism is struck in several poems following this one—in 2 (I), 3 (III), and 4 (II)—but by 5 (IV) the young man has not only become the speaker of the poem, but he has also found someone to love. Poem 6 (V) gives her a name—"Goldenhair"—and establishes the theme of the next group of poems: the young man in pursuit of Goldenhair, in the traditional rites of courtship. In 7 (VIII) he pursues her through the "green wood" and in 8 (VII) he sees her among the apple trees, vernal settings for these ancient rites. In 9 (IX), however, he cannot find her, and 10 (XVII) explains why: here the third persona of the sequence is introduced—the rival who is a friend of the young man and who, at the same time, is threatening his relationship with Goldenhair: "He is a stranger to me now/ Who was my friend." Poem 11 (XVIII), addressed both to Goldenhair and to the rival, complains of the failure of friends and suggests that another woman may well give the young man succor. As the poems proceed, this other woman takes on a variety of connotations, until finally, in 17 (XIV) the young man imagines his union with her in terms suggesting that she has combined characteristics, in Tindall's words, "of church, mother, muse, nation, and soul." After 17, the poems do variations on the themes of separation and lost love, ending in 33 (XXXIII) and 34 (XXXIV) on a decidedly wintry note: "The voice of the winter/ Is heard at the door./ O sleep, for the winter/ Is crying, 'Sleep no more.'"

This pattern of love challenged by a rival and ending in bitter or mixed feelings occurs elsewhere in Joyce's work, most notably in *A Portrait of the Artist as a Young Man* and in the play *Exiles*, where, as a test of a relationship, it provides the major theme. *Chamber Music* thus becomes an early working out of this theme, though Joyce ultimately agreed to an ordering of the poems (devised by his brother Stanislaus) different from the one of 1905—allowing for an ending on a much stronger note with poem XXXVI, beginning "I hear an army charging upon the land," which was not part of the 1905 sequence at all and which suggests an attitude that is more than simply passive or accepting on the part of the young man. These little poems, while carrying the weight of themes developed more completely in Joyce's later work, are also lyrics light and fresh enough to serve as the basis of songs. Joyce himself set a number of them to music, and over the years they have been set by many other composers as well.

Poem 16 (XI) illustrates the technique of the lyrics of *Chamber Music*. The diction is simple but frequently archaic—note the use of "thee" and "thy," "hast" and "doth," in keeping with much of the lyric poetry of the 1890's—and the tone light and songlike, with touches of irony apparent only in the last few lines of the second stanza. This irony is heralded in line 9 by the verb "unzone," which stands out in a poem of otherwise simple diction. Like many such words in these poems, "unzone" is unusual for the accuracy with which it is used (compare, for example, "innumerous" in poem 19 [XV]), Joyce returning to its original meaning of "encircle" or "surround," derived by way of the Latin *zone* from Greek *zona*, or "girdle." What is frequently most distinctive about Joyce's choice of words, in prose as well as in poetry, is their accuracy. In this context, the contrast between the formality of "unzone" and the "girlish bosom" of the next line, reinforced by the irony in other poems of the series dealing with the wooing of Goldenhair, makes the reader question her innocence if not the young man's intentions.

The repetition of the opening lines of 16 is another notable feature of the series. In 12 (VI) one can see the same quality on a somewhat larger scale, the final line pointing back to the beginning of the poem. If the poems of *Chamber Music* are relatively simply lyrics, they have their own complexities and ambiguities, as this poem shows. The "bosom" of the first stanza is conceivably Goldenhair's, but may also be interpreted as that of mother or church. "Austerities," like "bosom" used twice in the poem, in particular leads the reader to think so, the bosom or heart leading to an ascetic, not hedonistic, form of satisfaction for the young man. In this poem the young man flees from the relationship with Goldenhair and seeks other means of satisfaction. The language of the poem creates irony through repetition, forcing the reader to reexamine the premises of the relationship described. If this technique is much simpler than the one Joyce employed in his prose masterpieces, it is certainly a technique of the same order.

In 1927, Joyce published a second volume of poetry with the unassuming title *Pomes Penyeach*. The occasion for the volume was largely negative; stung by criticism of "Work in Progress" from people such as Ezra Pound, who had been so supportive of *Ulysses*, Joyce wished to show that he could also produce a relatively simple volume of lyrics. Unfortunately, for the taste of the time the lyrics were too simple and the volume went largely ignored; Pound himself suggested that Joyce should have reserved the poems for the Bible or the family album. This criticism now seems unfair, or at least out of proportion. The thirteen poems of *Pomes Penyeach* do not in any sense break new ground in English poetry, but they provide a kind of personal comment on Joyce's private life which is not easy to find in the prose works, and some of them are also simply good lyrics in the manner of *Chamber Music*.

The poems represent work of a period of approximately twenty years, beginning with "Tilly," composed in 1903 just after Joyce's mother's death, and ending with "A Prayer" of 1923, though stylistically they are of a piece. In this poetry Joyce favored a diction and tone which seemed archaic by the late 1920's, and did so without any of the irony apparent or at least incipient in certain poems of *Chamber Music*. If the mood of these poems did not suit the times in which they appeared, neither did it seem to suit the style of the supreme punster of "Work in Progress." They provide the single instance in Joyce's published work of an anachronism—a work which looks back in style and tone, in this case to the poetry of Joyce's youth and young manhood, rather than forward in time—and this accounts in part for their unenthusiastic reception.

In *Pomes Penyeach* the poems occur in roughly chronological order, in the order of their composition, and may be grouped according to subject matter. Some celebrate Joyce's feelings toward his children, as in "A Flower Given to My Daughter" or "On the Beach at Fontana," while others refer to feelings provoked in him by women he fancied himself to be in love with, either in the Trieste period or in Zurich during World War I. Some poems suggest certain of the prose works, such as "She Weeps over Rahoon" with its echoes of the long story "The Dead," written some five years before the poem. The final poem of the group, "A Prayer," returns to the mood of the darker poems in *Chamber Music* and to the image of woman as vampire which occurs so frequently in the poetry and art of the *fin de siècle*. It also suggests the strain of masochism which shows itself so often in Joyce's work in connection with sensuous pleasure. All in all, these lyrics provide an engaging record of various moods of Joyce as he passed into middle age, tempered by the public reputation he had acquired by that time.

"A Flower Given to My Daughter" and "A Prayer" illustrate the extremity of mood and variety of technique of these poems. In the first, the inverted word order and quaint diction of the poem—"sere" is the best example of the latter—do not keep the last line from being extremely touching, in part because it is so realistic a description. Joyce manages in the best of *Pomes Penyeach* to find just such a strong line with which to end, establishing a kind of contrast between the somewhat antique technique of the poem and conclusions remarkable for their simplicity and strength. "A Prayer" is far more dramatic in tone, but here the long lines and the rolling words ("remembering" followed by "pitying") also carry the reader into the joy become anguish of the final lines. In these poems as in others of the group, Joyce seems to be using the style and tone of another time with sometimes deadly effect—a conscious archaism rather than the more distanced irony of some of the poems of *Chamber Music*.

In 1932, Joyce published his last poem, "Ecce Puer," a touching commemoration of two occasions—the death of his father and the birth of his grandson and namesake Stephen James Joyce, the son of Giorgio and his wife Helen. "Tilly," the first item of *Pomes Penyeach*, was written on the occasion of the death of his mother and is in many ways the strongest of the group; "Ecce Puer"—written just after the death of John Joyce—is even stronger. For felt emotion conveyed, it has no equal among Joyce's works in this form, and its concluding stanza is all the more touching for its echoes of the theme of paternity so important to *Ulysses*—"A child is sleeping:/ An old man gone./ O, father forsaken,/ Forgive your son!" In fact, the poem was completed not many days after the tenth anniversary of the publication of *Ulysses*, which provides yet a third occasion for its composition.

In addition to *Chamber Music*, *Pomes Penyeach*, and "Ecce Puer," Joyce also published occasional broadsides—satiric poems to express his unhappiness over various literary matters. These include "The Holy Office" (1904) (now the rarest of all the published works of Joyce), an attack on the Irish literary movement by a young writer who already knew that his work was to be essentially different from theirs, and "Gas from a Burner" (1912), an attack on the Dublin publisher who ultimately burned the proofs of *Dubliners* rather than print what he considered an indecent book.

Finally, in *A Portrait of the Artist as a Young Man*, one of the crucial moments occurs (in the final part of the book) when Stephen Dedalus composes a poem in the form of a villanelle. This poem, while technically not Joyce's, represents as sure a comment as Joyce ever made on the aestheticism

of the 1890's, and thus stands in contrast with *Pomes Penyeach*, which echoes the themes and tones of that time.

Joyce's poetry was ultimately expressed most fully in his prose works, where the traditional distinctions between poetry and prose are effectively blurred. Perhaps in the end, his lyric poetry is best viewed as a minor expression— almost a form of relaxation—of a master stylist in prose.

Archie K. Loss

Other major works

LONG FICTION: *A Portrait of the Artist as a Young Man*, 1914-1915 (serial), 1916; *Ulysses*, 1922; *Finnegans Wake*, 1939; *Stephen Hero*, 1944.

SHORT FICTION: *Dubliners*, 1914.

PLAY: *Exiles*, 1918.

NONFICTION: *Letters of James Joyce*, 1957 (Stuart Gilbert, editor); *Letters*, 1957-1966 (3 volumes); *The Critical Writings of James Joyce*, 1959; *Selected Letters of James Joyce*, 1975 (Richard Ellmann, editor); *The James Joyce Archives*, 1977-1979 (64 volumes).

Bibliography

Boyle, Robert, S. J. "The Woman Hidden in James Joyce's *Chamber Music.*" In *Women in Joyce*, edited by Suzette Henke and Elaine Unkeless. Urbana: University of Illinois Press, 1982. Boyle describes the woman in the early poems to be an "ideal woman" created out of Joyce's imagination. She is, however, narcissistic and capable of malice. One of the best essays on the poems.

Ellmann, Richard. *James Joyce*. New York: Oxford University Press, 1959. Ellman discusses the background, contexts, publication, and reception of all Joyce's poems and includes critical discussions of each book. Indispensable for the study of Joyce.

Howarth, Herbert. "*Chamber Music* and Its Place in the Joyce Canon." In *James Joyce Today: Essays on the Major Works*, edited by Thomas F. Staley. Bloomington: Indiana University Press, 1966. An excellent discussion of the technique of the poems and the technique's purpose. Howarth feels that Joyce's purpose was music and that he partially achieved that. He also finds similar structures in the poems that are found in the major works.

Tindall, William York. Introduction to *Chamber Music*, by James Joyce. New York: Columbia University Press, 1954. The best introduction to the poems available. Tindall explains the background and publishing history of the poems and makes some cogent critical comments on their nature and value. Joyce disdained his earliest work, but Tindall quotes friends who knew how "precious" the poems were to him.

Wilson, Edmund. "Review." In *James Joyce: The Critical Heritage*, edited by Robert H. Deming. 2 vols. New York: Barnes & Noble Books, 1970. Wilson's review of *Pomes Penyeach* praises Joyce's advance in skill and power from *Chamber Music*. The creation of such lyrics is, he suggests, "difficult and rare." *Pomes Penyeach* is a slim volume, but Wilson finds it to be "real poetry" and among the "purest of our time."

DONALD JUSTICE

Born: Miami, Florida; August 12, 1925

Principal poetry

The Summer Anniversaries, 1960, 1981; *A Local Storm*, 1963; *Night Light*, 1967, 1981; *New Poetry of Mexico*, 1970 (includes ten poems translated by Justice, Mark Strand, editor); *Sixteen Poems*, 1970; *From a Notebook*, 1972; *Departures*, 1973; *Selected Poems*, 1979; *The Sunset Maker*, 1987.

Other literary forms

Best known for his poetry, Donald Justice has also written plays, short stories, critical essays, reviews, and the libretto for Edward J. Miller's opera *The Young God*. His stories "The Lady" and "Vineland's Burning," first published in *The Western Review*, were included in the O. Henry Awards *Prize Stories* of 1950 and 1954. Both portray characters who are locked inside themselves; like a number of Justice's poems, these stories discover the humanity of people who might be overlooked as uninteresting or dismissed as insane. The nonfiction *Platonic Scripts* (1984) is a collection of essays and interviews; Justice's criticism and reviews demonstrate the same concern for craftsmanship that characterizes his own poetry and fiction.

Achievements

Justice is a consummate craftsman. His carefully polished work demonstrates the power and beauty of the appropriate form. He deals with his major themes, change and loss, by fashioning poems which allow him and the reader to contemplate things that cannot stay. He is a literary, some would say academic, poet. If his range is limited, he does not overextend or repeat himself. His voice is quiet, nostalgic but not sentimental, and sometimes ironic. Whether he is writing about artistic activity or more ordinary experiences and people, his personae and other characters are "real," humanly significant. Instead of saying, "This is the way I feel," he says that "This is how things go."

His first book was the Lamont Poetry Selection for 1959, and his *Selected Poems* was awarded the Pulitzer Prize in 1980. Among his other awards are the Harriet Monroe Memorial Prize, grants in poetry from the Rockefeller and Guggenheim Foundations, and a grant in theater from the Ford Foundation. His work is respected by fellow poets.

Biography

Born and reared in Miami, Donald Justice was graduated from the University of Miami in 1945. He received an M.A. degree from the University of North Carolina in 1947 and a Ph.D. from the University of Iowa in 1954.

From 1948 to 1949, he attended Stanford University to study with Yvor Winters. Among his other teachers were Karl Shapiro, Robert Lowell, and John Berryman. He married Jean Ross in 1947 and has one son.

Justice has taught at various universities, including Syracuse, the University of California at Irvine, Princeton, and the Universities of Iowa and Virginia. He joined the faculty of the University of Florida at Gainesville in 1982.

Analysis

The character of Donald Justice's work is most clearly seen against the background of major developments in contemporary poetry. Like most American poets of the 1950's, he worked within the formalist tradition. In the next decade he became involved in the translation of contemporary French and Mexican poets. Following this immersion in the "new surrealism," he began to use suggestive images and freer forms. He has not, however, reacted against T. S. Eliot's ideal of the impersonal poet, nor has he repudiated meter, rhyme, and other traditional artifices; he values them because they provide aesthetic distance during the composing process and an intelligible, satisfying shape for the completed poem.

Justice has observed that "one of the motives for writing is surely to recover and hold what would otherwise be lost totally—memory or experience." He regards the poem not as an expression of the writer's personality but as an artifact which registers a significant perception ("The Effacement of Self: An Interview with Donald Justice," in *Ohio Review*, XVI, no. 3, 1975). In "Meters and Memory" he argues that it is technical skill that makes a subject "accessible to memory, repeatedly accessible, because it exists finally in a form that can be perused at leisure, like a snapshot in an album" (*The Structure of Verse*, 1979, Harvey Gross, editor). Artifice, then, is not incompatible with genuine expression; it is one of the "fixatives" that constitute art—indeed, that make it possible.

Justice's mastery of literary forms and commitment to pattern are evident in *The Summer Anniversaries*, which includes syllabic and accentual poems, sestinas, and sonnets. More than a third of the poems in this collection are rhymed, and most of the others use repetition, assonance, or consonance in place of end-rhyme. No slave to convention, Justice varies traditional forms as he explores his major themes: childhood, loss, and memory. "Sonnet to My Father" pays respects to the Italian sonnet, but Justice substitutes repetition for rhyme. It is fitting that the second, third, sixth, and seventh lines end with "mine," for the poem is about the speaker's participation in his father's dying. The end-words of lines nine through eleven—"die," "place," and "there,"—are mirrored at the ends of the poem's final lines—"there," "place," "die." This repetition represents the son's identification with the father, made explicit in the last line: "while I live, you cannot wholly die." As in most of Justice's early work, the diction, while not elevated, is elegant. The poem is a carefully controlled expression of emotion. Justice uses archaic diction in the remarkable "Tales from a Family Album," a syllabic poem of five nine-line stanzas. The speaker feels constrained to speak of his family's "doom," the effect, or cause, of their "acquaintance/ Not casual and not recent with a monster." Although their ancestral tree might be represented by an ordinary Georgia chinaberry, they have known uncommon tragedy. Even now there lives a cousin with a paw print on his forehead, and the speaker vividly recalls the fate of another "kinsman" who attempted to write the family history: he "perished,/ Calling for water and the holy wafer,/ Who had, ere that, resisted much persuasion." With characteristic gentle irony, Justice uses old-fashioned vocabulary and syntax to portray an imaginative Southerner who longs to be respected as a gentleman.

"In Bertram's Garden," a poem concerned with a young woman's loss of innocence, best illustrates Justice's use of convention and allusion. As Michael Rewa has shown in " 'Rich Echoes Reverberating': The Power of Poetic Convention" (*Modern Language Studies*, IX, no. 1, 1978-1979), the poet examines Jane's fall ironically but not unsympathetically by alluding to Ben Jonson's celebration of chastity in "Queen and Huntress, chaste and fair." (Justice's poem uses the same rhyme scheme as Jonson's and, in the third stanza, the same meter.) Jane's seducer, Bertram, reminiscent of the cynical lover in William Shakespeare's *All's Well That Ends Well* (c. 1602-1604), is also associated with corruption and Cupid, the antitheses of chastity. By placing his poem within a tradition, Justice provides a moral basis for assessing the seduction. As is true of many of his works, "In Bertram's Garden" will be most appreciated by a highly literate audience, but even the reader unaware of its references to Jonson, Shakespeare, Alfred, Lord Tennyson, and perhaps Andrew Marvell will understand why Jane is to "lie down with others soon/ Naked to the naked moon." Toyed with and cast aside, she can no more recover her belief in love than she can retrieve her virginity.

During the 1960's, a number of American poets were making statements on public issues and writing about personal tragedies. *Night Light* includes a few poems critical of the pragmatism, conformity, and latent authoritarianism he saw in mid-twentieth century America. "Memo from the Desk of X" and "For a Freshman Reader" anticipate a not-too-distant time when poetry will become extinct, to be replaced by a "more precise" statement. The undergraduate is advised not to "bother with odes," not to risk "singing": "The day will come when once more/ Lists will be nailed to the door/ And numbers stamped on the chest/ Of anyone who says No" ("For a Freshman Reader"). "To the Hawks," dated February, 1965, sees the escalation of American involvement in Southeast Asia as the beginning of the end of the world. The poet's vision of dawning horror is held in place by sixteen pairs of five-syllable lines. Only the title and dedication ("*McNamara, Rusk, Bundy*") mark the poem as an occasional piece: it might have been written yesterday.

While Robert Lowell, John Berryman (both had been Justice's teachers), and other "confessional poets" probed their traumas and anxieties, Justice wrote guardedly and ironically about the self. "A Local Storm" mocks the ego that takes a storm as a personal threat. In "Heart," Reason speaks to Passion: after urging that "we" should behave maturely, "more becomingly," the speaker finally admits that self-indulgence is irresistible. "We will take thought for our good name"—after one more revel. "Early Poems" comments on Justice's work: "How fashionably sad my early poems are!" he exclaims. "The rhymes, the meters, how they paralyze." Such manicured structures attract "no one" now; it is time for renewal. After a "long silence" comes "the beginning again." Written at (and about) a time when many poets were avoiding rhyme, meter, and logical structure, "Early Poems" is neatly rhymed and carefully ordered. Although responsive to contemporary developments, Justice is not a trend-setter or camp-follower. "Early Poems" is followed by two blank pages and then "The Thin Man," thirty syllables spoken by a persona who relishes "rich refusals"; Justice, beginning again, departed from the beautiful intricacies of formalism and developed a plainer style.

There are no sonnets or sestinas in *Night Light*; there are two prose poems. Rhyming infrequently, Justice experiments with varying line lengths and minimal punctuation. "Dreams of Water" consists of three short lyrics linked by subject and mood; reluctant to relinquish the unifying power of symmetry, Justice gives each poem the same shape: three three-line stanzas followed by a single line.

Most of *Night Light* is concerned with neither the self nor poetry but with obscure people—an anonymous servant and artist who lived centuries ago; the man at the corner who might be a salesman, a tourist, or an assassin; people in bus stops; the stranger whose lights are burning at 3:00 A.M.; men turning forty; a woman whose letters are sold at auction. Imagining what their lives might be like, Justice conveys a sense of their humanity and, in some cases, their otherness. "The Man Closing Up," free verse "improvisations on themes from Guillevic," is unified by images of decay and enclosure. Cutting off all outside influences, the title character climbs up into himself like someone ascending the stairs of a lighthouse. Still more unreachable and mysterious are the suicides, once regarded as friends, who refused to show themselves in life and now must always be strangers ("For the Suicides of 1962").

Night Light, written in the early and middle 1960's, is a transitional book. Still committed to the polish and detachment favored by T. S. Eliot and the New Critics, Justice did not reject, as some contemporaries did, the patterned regularity of meter and rhyme, but he more frequently allowed his forms to "make themselves up as the poems get written."

The aptly named *Departures* deals with endings, partings, and other moments when one realizes the futility of trying to deflect time. Several of Justice's speakers and characters are weary or broken. "A Letter" sketches the desperation of a woman in an asylum. Depressed, disoriented, and troubled by painful memories, she thinks of exposing her "wounds" and her bosom to "the young doctor/ Who has the power to sign prescriptions, passes." Reading her letter, the speaker in the poem understands that she cannot escape her sadness. If she is released, she will return to the city (itself a sanatorium, Justice suggests) to resume her former habits—and find herself "suddenly/ Ten years older, tamed now, less mad, less beautiful." In "A Dancer's Life," neither neurosis nor sex obscures a celebrated dancer's vision of the emptiness of her life. Although she is still famous and beautiful enough to attract young men, she realizes that she has already passed her peak and thinks, "*How disgusting it always must be to grow old.*"

The title *Departures* also reflects a change in Justice's style. There are few signs of formalism. Some pieces are fragments, bits from a notebook. Two consist entirely of questions, two of riddles. Justice uses occasional rhyme, assonance, consonance, and other means of structuring his poems. "Absences," an evocation of subtle, evanescent things and experiences, is composed of related images. The dreamlike companion poem "Presences" uses repetition and association to convey the paradoxical constancy of loss and change. Most of the key words and end-words in "Presences" are repeated; departures, disappearances, and transitions are dreams and drifting clouds, "going away in the night again and again," yet they persist in the mind as they do in the poem. Justice's statement that he likes a poem "to be organized," "to have an apprehensible structure," is not surprising. His typical poem is not contained by, but *is*, its structure. Often it further defines itself in relation to other works of art.

By identifying various sources (including Rafael Alberti, Eugene Guillevic, César Vallejo, and Ingmar Bergman) and noting that some of his poems "come, in part, from chance methods," he asks the reader to consider the way in which the individual poem develops and its relation to other compositions. For this unromantic writer, poetry is a tradition and a craft, not just the pronouncement of a personal vision. Justice presents even first-person narratives as things composed, not manifestations of his unique sensibility. A poem based on the premise that "Donald Justice is dead" and buried under "the black marl of Miami" is entitled "Variations on a Text by Vallejo." Poets, human beings—not just "I"—find ways to deal with mortality. Justice has explained his use of chance methods as "a further means of keeping [himself] distant" from his materials. By shuffling cards on which he had written sentences and words that interested him, then exercising "esthetic choice," he formed some lines and images that he was able to develop into poems (*Ohio Review*, XVI).

A third of the poems in *Departures* are concerned with artists and art, especially with poetry. "Self-Portrait as Still Life" distinguishes two kinds of artists: those who wish to come, singing and playing guitars, "into the picture," and those who say, "Myself, I'm not about to/ Disturb the composition." Two other poems assess contemporary poetry and Justice's relation to it. The "I" of "The Telephone Number of the Muse" dryly but with some regret chronicles the end of his affair with the mistress who now wishes to be "only friends." He still calls her sometimes, long distance, "And she still knows my voice, but I can hear,/ Always beyond the music of her phonograph,/ The laughter of the young men with their keys." Youths who barge unprepared and uninvited into the muse's presence are satirized in "Sonatina in Green" (*"for my students"*). The young anticipate ecstasy; they do not think of work. The ironic poet, an experienced teacher of writing and literature, also looks askance at "[The] few with the old instruments,/ Obstinate, sounding the one string"— limiting themselves to the music of another time instead of responding to the requirements of the present. The poem argues that there is too much performance, too much publication, too little craftsmanship: "There has been traffic enough/ In the boudoir of the muse." Justice himself is a relatively reticent poet, publishing only ninety-eight titles (some poems have two or more parts) in his first three books.

Selected Poems includes seventy-six poems from the previous collections, arranged, as he puts it, "in fair chronological order." He revised many poems as he prepared this book. A group of sixteen previously uncollected titles, also arranged chronologically, once again demonstrates his stylistic virtuosity. As Dana Gioia has observed, *Selected Poems* "reads almost like an anthology of the possibilities of contemporary poetry" (*Southern Review*, XVII, Summer, 1981). The earliest poem is a Shakespearean sonnet; there are several free-verse poems, while other compositions, including some of the most recent ones in the collection, are rhymed.

In the middle and late 1970's Justice continued to observe ordinary people and seemingly insignificant incidents and places, sometimes drawing upon memory, as he had done at the beginning of his career. "Childhood," set in Miami in the 1930's, is narrated in the present tense. Justice represents the texture of the child's "long days": the Sunday boredom, his delight in the starry ceiling of the Olympia Theater, the exhilarating crime of using a drinking fountain for "colored" people. This personal poem is placed, as Justice tends to do, in relation to tradition: there is an epigraph from Arthur Rimbaud, and the work is dedicated to William Wordsworth, Rimbaud, Hart Crane, and Rafael Alberti, "the poets of a mythical childhood."

"First Death," a narrative in tetrameter couplets, uses concrete details to re-create the child's loneliness, restlessness, and fear in the three days following his grandmother's death. Justice comments on the poem's subject and form in *Fifty Contemporary Poets: The Creative Process* (1977). This essay elucidates what might be called his philosophy of composition. As he recalls,

"First Death" began with his writing couplets about "nothing" until an image activated boyhood memories. Writing in a tight form about the child he was in 1933 provided "the illusion of distance" that makes him a craftsman. Although the poem is easily paraphrased, Justice remarks that its form—the shaping and cadences and rhymes that "*fix* the poem, as the right solution fixes the snapshot"—gave its maker the pleasure of finding an appropriate form and enables the reader to experience the child's misery. Justice concludes that he likes the poem "because it records something otherwise lost."

All of Justice's poems are attempts "to keep memorable what deserves to be remembered." He captures the essence of a fantasy, experience, or memory in a vivid detail or image—funeral flowers "sweating in their vases," the "clean blue willowware" prayed over in Depression Miami, the pianist rapt in his finger exercises, Death's extended hand "a little cage of bone"—and "fixes" it with a form appropriate to it, using free verse, metrics, syllabics, rhyme, or any device or convention that helps to make it durable. Much of his work develops by alluding to or departing from other poems or art forms, European and Latin American as well as Anglo-American. For Justice, the choice to make craft, not the self, his chief concern has meant freedom to develop his individual talent.

Mary De Jong

Other major works
NONFICTION: *Platonic Scripts*, 1984.
ANTHOLOGIES: *The Collected Poems of Welden Kees*, 1960, 1975; *Contemporary French Poetry*, 1965 (with Alexander Aspel).

Bibliography
De Jong, Mary Gosselink. "Musical Possibilities: Music, Memory, and Composition in the Poetry of Donald Justice." *Concerning Poetry* 18 (1985): 57-66. De Jong explores the influences of music upon the structures, techniques, and metaphors in Justice's work. The work is both specific (citing the poet's references to Mozart and Thomas Higgins) and general (indicating the poet's use of musical qualities such as rhyme, assonance, and repetition). The extensive footnotes also contribute to this essay's value.
Ehrenpreis, Irvin. "Boysenberry Sherbert." *The New York Review of Books* 22 (October 16, 1975): 3-4. Ehrenpreis explores Justice's stylistic relationships and similarities with such poets as John Ashbery and Wallace Stevens. He also examines the poet's themes including lovers, children, the aged, and the weak. Other subjects covered are the creative process, his distinct refinement of syntax, and his new technique that abandons regular meters for free verse.
Hamilton, David, and Lowell Edwin Folsom. "An Interview with Donald

Justice." *The Iowa Review* 10 (Spring/Summer, 1980): 1-21. This extensive interview features Justice discussing a wide range of subjects, from the qualifications for selecting poems to explorations of specific imagery in a particular poem, such as "The Bridge." So extensive and thorough is this interview that it is difficult to imagine a topic not covered. An accessible and valuable source for all students of Justice's work.

Howard, Richard. *Alone with America: Essays on the Art of Poetry in the United States.* New York: Atheneum, 1950. The extensive chapter on Justice reviews the poet's focused interests, his singular artistic identity, the distinct elegance of his voice, and the "major resolution of the minor" in Justice's poetry. Howard justifies his assertions and assists the reader's comprehension by extensively quoting the poetry he discusses.

St. John, David. "Scripts and Water, Rules and Riches." *The Antioch Review* 43, no. 3 (1985): 309-319. An excellent, in-depth review of Justice's "Platonic Scripts" combined with quotations from an interview with Justice and a lucid interpretation of his work and evaluation of his importance in the world of poetry. This essay is extremely accessible, well written, and essential to anyone with an interest in Justice and his work.

PATRICK KAVANAGH

Born: Inniskeen, Ireland; October 21, 1904
Died: Dublin, Ireland; November 30, 1967

Principal poetry
Ploughman and Other Poems, 1936; *The Great Hunger*, 1942; *A Soul for Sale*, 1947; *Recent Poems*, 1958; *Come Dance with Kitty Stobling and Other Poems*, 1960; *Collected Poems*, 1964; *Complete Poems*, 1972 (Peter Kavanagh, editor).

Other literary forms
Three fictional autobiographies—*The Green Fool* (1938), a collection of short stories and sketches, and the novels *Tarry Flynn* (1948) and *By Night Unstarred* (1977)—are based on Patrick Kavanagh's early years in County Monaghan. The latter part of *By Night Unstarred* pursues his life into Dublin. Various prose essays and occasional pieces can be found in *Collected Pruse* (1967) and *November Haggard* (1971). *Kavanagh's Weekly*, a magazine which published thirteen issues between April 12 and July 15, 1952, contains a variety of fiction, commentary, and verse which was written under various pseudonyms but is almost all Kavanagh's own work (reprinted, 1981). *Lapped Furrows* (1969) and *Love's Tortured Headland* (1978) reprint correspondence and other documents between 1933 and 1967. Since the poet's death, his brother Peter has been editing and publishing his work, and Peter's biography, *Sacred Keeper* (1980), contains a number of previously unpublished or unreprinted documents. Despite the claims of various titles, Kavanagh's work remains uncollected. A poem ("The Gambler") was adapted for ballet in 1961, and *Tarry Flynn* was dramatized in 1966; each was performed at the Abbey Theatre.

Achievements
Despite handicaps of poverty, physical drudgery, and isolation, Kavanagh became the leading figure in the "second generation" of the Irish Literary Revival. He practically reinvented the literary language in which rural Ireland was to be portrayed. Bypassing William Butler Yeats, J. M. Synge, and Lady Gregory, he returned for a literary model to a fellow Ulsterman, William Carleton, and to his own experience of country life as a subject. He invested his fiction and poetry with fresh regional humor which did not sentimentalize or condescend to its characters. His vision is fundamentally religious, imbued with a Catholic sacramental view of nature. His various criticisms of Irish life and institutions arise from an unrefined but genuine spirituality. The quality of Kavanagh's work is uneven, and his public attitudes are inconsistent. Even so, the sincerity of his best work, its confidence in its own

natural springs, its apparent artlessness, its celebration of local character, place, and mode of expression, make him the most widely felt literary influence on the poets of contemporary Ireland, most significantly on those with similar backgrounds, such as John Montague and Seamus Heaney.

Biography

Patrick Kavanagh was the fourth of the ten children of James Kavanagh, a shoemaker, and his wife Bridget. The Kavanagh home is in Mucker, a townland of Inniskeen, County Monaghan, near the Armagh (and now Northern Ireland) border. The boy attended Kednaminsha National School until he was thirteen, when he was apprenticed to his father's trade. Later, he worked a small farm purchased in the nearby townland of Shancoduff. His first literary influences were the school anthologies which featured Henry Wadsworth Longfellow, Charles Kingsley, William Allingham, Alfred, Lord Tennyson, Robert Louis Stevenson, and Thomas Moore, and his earliest poems were written in school notebooks. As he worked on his small farm, he nurtured his taste on magazines picked up at fairs in the town of Dundalk. His keen observations of country life, its customs, characters, and speech patterns, together with his growing awareness of his sensitivity which set him apart from his peers, are well set forth in his account of his early life, *The Green Fool*. Many of his early poems appeared in the 1930's in *The Irish Statesman*, whose editor, Æ (George William Russell), was the first to recognize and cultivate the peasant poet. Æ Russell introduced him to modern world literature, providing him with books, advice, payment, and introductions to the Irish literary establishment. Of the books given him by Russell, *Gil Blas of Santillane* (1715, 1724, 1735), *Ulysses* (1922), and *Moby Dick* (1851) remained the classics most revered by Kavanagh.

After he moved to Dublin in 1939, he supported himself as a journalist. Throughout the 1940's he wrote book and film reviews, a range of critical and human interest pieces, city diaries, and various pieces for *The Irish Press* (as "Piers Plowman"), *The Standard*, *The Irish Times*, and *Envoy*. During that time, the long poem *The Great Hunger*, his second poetry collection, *A Soul for Sale*, and the novel *Tarry Flynn* appeared, so that following the deaths of Yeats (1939) and James Joyce (1941), he emerged as the central figure in Irish literary life. His most ambitious journalistic venture was in 1952 when, with his brother's financial and managerial assistance, he produced *Kavanagh's Weekly*, which ran for thirteen issues (April 12-July 5). This production comprises the fullest expression of Kavanagh's "savage indignation" at the mediocrity of Irish life and letters. It is useful as a document of the Dublin ethos in the early 1950's and in reading Kavanagh's poetry of the same period. In October, 1952, *The Leader* responded—in a spirit typical of the infamous factionalism of Dublin's literary politics—with a malicious "Profile," which prompted Kavanagh to file suit for libel. Following a celebrated trial, which

Kavanagh lost, he fell dangerously ill with lung cancer.
He made a dramatic physical recovery, however, which in turn revivified
his creative powers. This second birth resulted in a group of poems—mainly
sonnets—written in 1955 and 1956—set in and around the Rialto Hospital
and by the Grand Canal, Dublin, and published in *Recent Poems* and *Come
Dance with Kitty Stobling and Other Poems.* Thereafter he went into a slow
decline, physically and creatively. In April, 1967, he married Katherine Mo-
loney, but he died the following November. He is buried in Inniskeen.

His brother Peter (twelve years his junior) was Kavanagh's constant correspondent, financier, confidant, critic, and promoter. He edited and published
many works arising from this fraternal collaboration, including *Lapped Furrows; November Haggard; Complete Poems,* which supersedes and corrects
Collected Poems; a bibliography, *Garden of the Golden Apples* (1972); and a
documentary biography, *Sacred Keeper.* Despite its title, *Collected Pruse* contains only a sampling of Kavanagh's prose works.

Analysis

Although he frequently and vehemently denied it, Patrick Kavanagh was a
distinctively Irish poet. He had already formed his own voice by the time he
discovered—or was discovered by—the Revival and became a leading figure
in the "second generation." Kavanagh was not a Celtic mythologizer such as
W. B. Yeats, a conscious dialectician such as J. M. Synge, a folklorist such as
Lady Gregory, an etymologist such as James Joyce, or a Gaelic revivalist
such as Douglas Hyde. He felt and wrote with less historical or political
consciousness than his progenitors. His gifts and temperament made him an
outsider in Inniskeen, his lack of formal education and social grooming excluded him from Dublin's middle-class literary coteries, and his moral sensibility excluded him from Bohemia.

Yet in retrospect, Kavanagh emerges as the dominant Irish literary personality between 1940 and 1960. Although he admired each of the Revival's pioneers for particular qualities, he regarded the Irish Literary Revival in the
main as an English-inspired hoax. The romanticized peasant, for example,
he considered the product of Protestant condescension, and he felt that too
many writers of little talent had misunderstood the nature of Yeats's and
Joyce's genius and achievements, so that the quality of "Irishness" replaced
sincerity.

Against a pastiche of literary fashions which misrepresented the peasant,
attempted the revival of the Irish language, promoted nationalism in letters
and in politics, Kavanagh posited his own belief in himself, in his powers of
observation, and his intimate knowledge of the actual lives of country people.
Kavanagh's subsequent popular success in Ireland and his influence on the
"third generation" are attributable to several distinct characteristics: his parochialism, which he defined as "confidence in the social and artistic validity

of his own parish"; his directness, the apparent off-handedness of his work, and his freedom from literary posing; his deep Catholicism, which went beyond sentimentality and dogma; his imaginative sympathy for the ordinary experiences of country people; his comedy; his repose; his contemplative appreciation of the world as revelation; and his sincerity, his approval of feelings arising only from a depth of spirit. Although he has often been admired for one or more of these virtues, and although his manner often masked these qualities, they must be taken as a whole in accounting for his character as a poet. He disdained the epithet "Irish poet," yet shares with each of the pioneers of the Revival one or more signally "Irish" characteristics.

Kavanagh's creative development followed three stages: first, the works of intimacy with and disengagement from the "stony grey soil" of parochial Monaghan; second, the works which show his involvements with Dublin or national cultural issues; and third, his "rebirth" in the post-1955 reconciliation of public and private selves, when rural parish and national capital find mutual repose.

His two most successful fictional works, *The Green Fool* and *Tarry Flynn*, provide a rich lode of documentation of their author's country background and the growth of his sensibility. Some of his finest lyrics come from this period, along with his *magnum opus*, *The Great Hunger*. All of these works are set in the same few townlands, and the theme is the revelation of grace in ordinary things and tasks. Through these poems, and from *The Green Fool* to *Tarry Flynn*, the poet's confidence in his own visionary gifts progressively deepens, even though the expression is often uncertain. In a handful of lyrics, however, such as "Ploughman," "Inniskeen Road: July Evening," "A Christmas Childhood," "Spraying the Potatoes," "Shancoduff," and "Epic," Kavanagh's technique realizes his intentions. In each of these, the chance appearances belie the deft design, and the natural voice of the countryman is heard for the first time since Carleton in Irish literature.

"Shancoduff" (*Complete Poems*) is one of Kavanagh's most successful expressions of his parochial voice and is a representative early poem. The small farmer's pride in his bare holding is seemingly disquieted by a casual comment from passing strangers: "By heavens he must be poor." Until this uninvited, materialistic contrast with other places intrudes, this little world, although uncomfortable, has been endurable. Now it may not be so.

Before the cattle drovers assess the farm, the readers have seen it through the eyes of its owner, and they do not need to be told that he is a poet. With him they have first observed these hills' exemplary, incomparable introspection (lines 1-7). Even as his readers are being invited to contemplate the hills' ontological self-sufficiency, however, the poet, by necessity a maker of comparisons, introduces mythological and geographical allusions from the larger world. Even though these references—to Lot's wife, the Alps, and the Matterhorn—ostensibly imply his sympathy with his property's self-justification, their very statement admits some kind of comparison and betrays the principle it proposes. This and the irony in "fondle" arrange the scene for the dour pragmatism of the jobbers. Shancoduff is very poor land, poets do make poor farmers, or farmers make poor poets, and the eavesdropping owner-farmer-poet seems disconcerted. The question in line 16 is slyly rhetorical, however; the poet's evident disdain for the jobbers implies that his heart may not be quite so "badly shaken."

The poem operates by a set of contrasts which set the cold, wet, dark, ungainly native places against apparently more positive reflections from the outside. Earth and water oppose air and fire; St. Patrick's see of Armagh (and/or ancient Ulster's adjacent capital of Emhain Macha) is a counterattraction to the foreign cities of dubious renown—Sodom, Rome, London, even perhaps Tokyo. The gauche place-names of Kavanagh's parish do not seem to invite tourists, yet they combine in shaping the poet's attitude to these humble townlands and the design of the poem (see also "Old Black Pocket"; "Glassdrummond," "Streamy/Green Little Hill"; "Featherna," "Streamy"; with the "Big Forth" they compose an ancient, native estate).

The poem uses seasonal, biblical, and religious images to suggest his parochial independence from urban cultures, while foreshadowing several motifs which run through Kavanagh's later works: his distrust of cities and critics, his investment of local dialect or commonplace phrases with larger, often mystical, reference, his disdain for positivist assessments, and his cutting irony. Yet, despite the representative nature of its content, it must be admitted that by its total coherence and clarity this poem stands out from most of his work.

The Great Hunger is Kavanagh's most ambitious poem and is one of signal importance in the literature of modern Ireland. First published in 1942, it is 756 lines long, in fourteen sections. It narrates the life of Patrick Maguire, a peasant farmer whose life is thwarted by physical poverty, Jansenism, and the lack of imagination. The poem is Kavanagh's most extensive rebuke to the idealization of the peasant: a report "from the other side of the ditch," it has great reportorial force. For just as it describes the degradation of the rural poor, it also projects Maguire sympathetically as a figure of keen self-awareness and spiritual potential. Maguire's anguish is muffled and extended by his procrastination, the dull round of gossip, gambling, and masturbation. The Church distorts his natural religious sensibilities into patterns of guilt, which, together with his mother's hold on the farm, conspire to justify his pusillanimity. Woman is the embodiment of life's potentialities, and Maguire's failure to marry is thus the social expression of his spiritual retardation.

The title recalls the potato famine of 1845 to 1847, when starvation and disease ravaged the population and caused long-term psychological and social harm. The mood of the people turned pessimistic as they accepted the disaster as a judgment from an angry deity, and they turned penurious and late-marrying. This historical catastrophe had a deeply depressing effect on rural life, enlarged the power of the Church, reduced national self-confidence, and led to the disuse of the native language and the loss of the gaiety and spontaneity for which the Irish had been renowned. Kavanagh's poem reflects several of these effects with unflinching honesty.

The poem is a *tour de force* of descriptive writing, technical variation, and complex tonal control. In the modernist mode, it utilizes the rhythms and idioms of jazz, nursery rhymes, ballads, the Hiberno-English dialect, the Bible, the pastoral, and the theater, with only occasional lapses in momentum. The poet stands at very little distance from his subject; the tone is somber to bitter. Kavanagh shows compassion rather than condescension toward his protagonist; the humor is grim and restrained. *The Great Hunger* suffers by its occasional stridency, but its urgency and commitment do not diminish it as much as its author would have readers think when he later disowned it as "lacking the nobility and repose of poetry" (*Self-Portrait*).

By the time Kavanagh had made that statement, he had gone through some important changes in spirit. Even though *The Great Hunger* established his reputation in Dublin's literary life, he suffered from lack of patronage and managed to survive only by journalism. That activity he undertook with zest and courage—witness *Kavanagh's Weekly*—but it brought to the fore some of his insecurities which found expression in flailing abuse of his rivals and in sententious dogma on a range of public issues. As the objects of his satirical verses changed, the central vision began to disintegrate. The bitter libel suit against *The Leader* was a personal disaster. His bout with lung cancer took him close to death, and his creative energies had reached their nadir. His remarkable physical recovery, however, led to a spiritual revivification on the banks of the Grand Canal, Dublin, in the year following the summer of 1955.

This reinvigoration of spirit is reflected in a group of sonnets published in *Recent Poems* and *Come Dance with Kitty Stobling*, notably the title poem of the latter, along with "Canal Bank Walk," "The Hospital," and "Lines Written on a Seat on the Grand Canal." As his various accounts (notably in *Self-Portrait*) of this experience testify, Kavanagh rediscovered his original capacities to see, accept, and celebrate the ordinary. In these poems, the original innocence of the Monaghan fields graces his experience of Dublin, mediated by his hospitalization and the repose offered by the environment of the Grand Canal. Kavanagh purged these poems of many defects which had marred his previous work—contentiousness, self-pity, shrill engagement in passing events, messianic compulsions—all of which arose from relative shallows. In "Lines Written on a Seat on the Grand Canal," for example, there is a nicely balanced irony in the mock-heroic view of self, which is deftly subsumed by the natural grace observed in the setting. The artificial roar is drowned by the seasonal silence. The well-tempered voice of the poet commands original simplicities with easeful assurance. The poet's memorial, "just a canal-bank seat for the passer-by," summarizes Kavanagh's testament: his acknowledgment of Yeats, his self-definition as observer, namer, and diviner, and his humility as no more than a "part of nature." The countryman, the poet, the visionary, the Irishman, and the citizen are finally reconciled to one another. Although the poem appears to mirror the persona's affection of indifference, its taut conclusion indicates that casualness has not been easily won.

The accomplishment of these late poems notwithstanding, Kavanagh retained a sense of defeat to the end of his career. He never overcame a defensiveness arising from his deprived youth. He rarely reconciled his feelings for his Monaghan sources and his need for a Dublin audience. His *Complete Poems* show how small a proportion of his total production is truly successful. Nevertheless, his impact on Irish cultural life is large, and this is attributable to the color of his personality, the humor of his prose, and his unsentimental social criticism, as much as to his poetic oeuvre.

Cóilín Owens

Other major works
LONG FICTION: *Tarry Flynn*, 1948; *By Night Unstarred*, 1977.
SHORT FICTION: *The Green Fool*, 1938.
PLAY: *Tarry Flynn*, 1966.
NONFICTION: *Lapped Furrows*, 1969 (Peter Kavanagh, editor); *Love's Tortured Headland*, 1978.
MISCELLANEOUS: *Kavanagh's Weekly*, 1952, 1981; *Self-Portrait*, 1964, 1975; *Collected Pruse*, 1967; *November Haggard*, 1971 (Peter Kavanagh, editor).

Bibliography
Garratt, Robert F. *Modern Irish Poetry: Tradition and Continuity from Yeats to Heaney*. Berkeley: University of California Press, 1986. The chapter devoted to Kavanagh is divided into four parts: his criticism of the Irish Literary Revival and revisionist reading of William Butler Yeats, his early poetic realism, his poetic rebirth in the "Canal Bank" poems, and the development of his influential poetics of the local and familiar, which influenced the next generation.
Heaney, Seamus. *The Government of the Tongue*. New York: Farrar, Straus & Giroux, 1988. This collection of prose by Kavanagh's most famous successor contains a lecture in which Kavanagh's poetry is seen in two stages: the "real topographical presence" of the early poems, followed by the "luminous spaces" of the late poems. The essay shows the importance of Kavanagh for younger Irish poets in the words of one of the best.
Kavanagh, Peter. *Sacred Keeper: A Biography of Patrick Kavanagh*. The Curragh, Ireland: Goldsmith Press, 1980. This partisan biography by the poet's

devoted brother claims to avoid the lies and legends of "the eccentric, the drunkard, the *enfant terrible* of Dublin" in favor of the facts, lovingly recorded in a pastiche of letters, poems, photographs, articles, and reminiscences.

Nemo, John. *Patrick Kavanagh*. Boston: Twayne, 1979. Like other volumes in the Twayne series, this study provides a useful overview of Kavanagh's life and work, along with a chronology and a bibliography. The examination of the poetry is thorough and authoritative.

O'Brien, Darcy. *Patrick Kavanagh*. Lewisburg, Pa.: Bucknell University Press, 1975. This brief book in the Irish Writers series sketches the poet's career, dwells somewhat on the libel action, examines the poetry, and speculates on his stature and influence. Contains a chronology and a select bibliography.

Ryan, John. *Remembering How We Stood: Bohemian Dublin at Mid-Century.* New York: Taplinger, 1975. A chapter of this colorful, if respectful, memoir captures "Paddy Kavanagh," the picturesque eccentric and pub crawler, in the local atmosphere of literary Dublin from 1945 to 1955. Entertaining, anecdotal, but not thoroughly reliable.

Warner, Alan. *Clay Is the Word: Patrick Kavanagh, 1904-1967.* Dublin: Dolmen Press, 1973. The first full-length study and the best introduction to Kavanagh, Warner's book is engaging in tone, discursive in method, and speculative in its conclusions. Makes use of reminiscences of those who knew the poet, as well as literary analyses of the poems. Includes a checklist of publications by and about Kavanagh.

JOHN KEATS

Born: Moorfields, London, England; October 31, 1795
Died: Rome, Italy; February 23, 1821

Principal poetry

Poems, 1817; *Endymion: A Poetic Romance,* 1818; *Lamia, Isabella, The Eve of St. Agnes, and Other Poems,* 1820; *Life, Letters, and Literary Remains,* 1848; *The Fall of Hyperion: A Dream,* 1856.

Other literary forms

In *The Use of Poetry* (1933), T. S. Eliot referred to the letters of John Keats as "the most notable and the most important ever written by any English poet," primarily because "there is hardly one statement of Keats about poetry, which . . . will not be found to be true." The letters also offer an important gloss on specific poems and have thus become important for understanding Keats. Besides many passing comments of brilliance, the central concept of the letters is "negative capability." As defined by Keats, it is the capability to remain "in uncertainties, Mysteries, doubts, without any irritable reaching after fact & reason" (I, 193), which implies a disinterestedness that permits even competing ideas full play to reach their potential. In his letters, Keats often carried an idea to its extreme with extraordinary intellectual flexibility; another day, its opposite will surface to be worked out, as all things "end in speculation" (I, 387). The concept is also taken to include Keats's understanding of the poetical character, or the ability to surrender one's personal self to create characters and objects with independent life. Keats believed that the artist's first responsibility was to create beauty, which implies that the artist's personally held ideas and beliefs should be temporarily suspended or treated only partially so as to realize fully the work's aesthetic potential. Through the use of sympathetic imagination, Keats attempted.to become the thing he was creating, to intensely identify with its life, not to find his personal life reflected in it. The standard edition of Keats's letters is *The Letters of John Keats, 1814-1821* (1958, Hyder Edward Rollins, editor, 2 volumes). Text citations are to that edition.

Achievements

Without being facetious, one could identify Keats's greatest achievement as becoming one of the greatest poets of the English language in twenty-five years, three months, and twenty-three days of life, for Keats died before the age of twenty-six. Douglas Bush has said that no other English poet would rank as high as Keats if he had died as young—not William Shakespeare, John Milton, or Keats's greatest contemporary, William Wordsworth. Whereas other poets, especially his Romantic contemporaries, have gone in and out of critical fashion, Keats's reputation has endured since shortly after his death.

Keats followed the Shakespearean model of impersonality in art; that is, the surrendering of self to the fullest development of character and object, and it is this impersonality, coupled with intensity, that makes his poetry readily accessible to a wide range of modern readers. The reader does not have to re-create Keats's time, empathize with Romantic norms and beliefs, or identify with the poet's unique biographical experiences, to appreciate his poetry fully. Keats is sane, honest, and open; his art is varied, intense, and rich in texture and experience. As he said of his poetic model, Shakespeare, Keats was as little of an egotist as it was possible to be, in the Romantic period, at least, in the creation of art.

Biography

Though the events of John Keats's life are meager, his biography has fascinated many. Keats did not have a single physical, social, familial, or educational advantage in life, nothing to prepare for or enhance the development of his genius. Internally, however, he was afire with ambition and the love of beauty. Even at that, he did not discover his poetic vocation until late, given the fact that he died at the age of twenty-five and spent the last eighteen months of his life in a tubercular decline. His career lasted from 1816, when Keats renounced the practice of medicine, to the fall of 1819, when he stopped working on his last great, though incomplete, poem, *The Fall of Hyperion: A Dream* (1856). One almost has to count the months, they are so few and precious. In fact, in a single month, May, 1819, he wrote four of his great odes—"Ode to a Nightingale," "Ode on a Grecian Urn," "Ode on Melancholy," and ironically, "Ode on Indolence."

This remarkable and courageous poet, the oldest of four children, was born to keepers of a London livery stable. His father was killed in a fall from a horse when John was eight; his mother died from tuberculosis when he was fourteen. His relatives arranged for schooling and apothecary training so that he might make a living, but the year he received his certificate, 1816, he began to devote himself to poetry. He wrote some good, but mostly bad, poetry, or at least poetry that does not add much to his reputation, until the summer of 1818. His reward was a brutal review of his major early work, *Endymion*, in a leading magazine of the day. Keats was criticized so severely that Percy Bysshe Shelley speculated that the review began Keats's physical decline.

Actually, the truth was much worse. Keats was nursing his brother Tom, who was dying from tuberculosis, when the reviews came out. Though he was too strong in character to be deeply affected by criticism, especially when he was a more astute critic of his poetry than his readers, a contagious illness could hardly be thwarted with character. In the fall of 1818, Keats also fell deeply in love with Fanny Brawne. They intended to marry, but his illness soon made their future together impossible. Sadly, the futility of their love and passion offered important inspiration to Keats's poetry. By late fall, 1819, in the same year that he had written "The Eve of St. Agnes," the odes, *Lamia*, and *The Fall of Hyperion*, his illness was severe enough to arouse his deep concern. In July, 1820, his influential volume *Lamia, Isabella, The Eve of St. Agnes, and Other Poems* was published. Keats, however, now separated from Fanny, ill, in desperate need of money, and unable to achieve his major ambition of writing a "few fine Plays" in the manner of Shakespeare, was utterly despondent. He later spent a few months under the care of the Brawnes, but left England for Italy in September, 1820, in an attempt to save his life in the milder Italian weather. Joseph Severn, a dear friend, nursed him until his death in Rome in February, 1821.

Forever thinking aloud in his letters about the central concerns of existence, Keats once found purpose in this earthly life as "a vale of soul-making"; that is, while every human being perhaps contains a spark of divinity called soul, one does not attain an identity until that soul, through the medium of intelligence and emotions, experiences the circumstances of a lifetime. Thus the world has its use not as a vale of tears, but, more positively, as a vale of becoming through those tears. Keats's soul flourished as rapidly as his genius, and the poetry is evidence of both.

Analysis

Lieben und arbeiten—to love and to work—are, psychologists say, the principal concerns of early adulthood. In John Keats's case, they became, as well, the dominant themes of his most important poetry. The work theme includes both the effort and the love of creating beauty and the immortality Keats longed for as recompense. Once, perhaps exaggerating, Keats wrote that "the mere yearning and fondness" he had "for the Beautiful" would keep him writing "even if [his] night's labours should be burnt every morning and no eye ever shine upon them." Not passing, however, was the tenacity of his ambition: "I would sooner fail than not to be among the greatest." Keats's quest for immortality takes several forms: it appears openly, especially in the sonnets and in "Ode on Indolence" and "Ode to Psyche" as the anxieties of ambition—being afforded the time, maintaining the will and energy, and, not least, determining the topic, or territory, for achievement. It includes a metamorphosis fantasy, whereby the young poet, whether immortal as in *Hyperion: A Fragment* or mortal as in the revised *The Fall of Hyperion*, becomes deified or capable of immortal poetry through absorption of divinely granted knowledge. The ambition/work theme also takes a self-conscious turn in *The Fall of Hyperion*, questioning the value to a suffering mankind of the dreamer-poet's life and work.

The love theme explores dreams of heterosexual bliss, but it also moves into the appropriate relationships to be had with art and nature. The imagination is the ally of love's desires; reality and reason are their nemeses. In "The Eve of St. Agnes," a better lover, in *Lamia*, a better place, are dreams which dissipate in the light of reality and reason. "Ode to a Nightingale" attempts a flight from reality through identification with beautiful song rather than through dream, but the result is an intensification of distress. "Ode on Melancholy," "To Autumn," and "Ode on a Grecian Urn," however, suggest perspectives on the human condition, nature, and art that can be maintained with honesty and deeply valued without recourse to dream. One could say that Keats's love theme moves toward the understanding and acceptance of what is.

Concomitant with the maturation of theme and perspective is Keats's stylistic development. Like most poets, Keats went through phases of imitation during which he adapted the styles and themes he loved to his own work and ambitions. Leigh Hunt, Edmund Spenser, John Milton, and always Shakespeare, provided inspiration, stylistic direction, and a community of tradition. Regardless of origin, the principal traits of Keats's style are these: a line very rich with sound pattern, as in "with brede/ of marble men and maidens overwrought," which also includes puns on "brede" ("breed") and "overwrought" (as "delicately formed on" and as "overly excited"); synaesthetic imagery, or imagery that mingles the senses ("soft incense," "smoothest silence"); deeply empathic imagery ("warmed jewels," "all their limbs/ Locked up like veins of metal, crampt and screwed"); stationing or positioning of characters to represent their dramatic condition (so Saturn after losing his realm, "Upon the sodden ground/ His old right hand lay nerveless, listless, dead,/ Unsceptered; and his realmless eyes were closed"); the use of the past participle in epithets ("purple-stained mouth," "green-recessed woods"); and, of course, as with every great writer, that quality which one can only describe as *Je ne sais quoi*—I know not what—as in the lines from the sonnet "Bright Star": "The moving waters at their priest-like task/ Of pure ablution round earth's human shores."

Themes of ambition and accomplishment inform many of Keats's sonnets. The claiming of territory for achievement is the focus of "How Many Bards Gild the Lapses of Time," "On First Looking into Chapman's Homer," "Great Spirits Now on Earth Are Sojourning," and the great "Ode to Psyche." In "On First Looking into Chapman's Homer," for example, Keats recounts the discovery of Homer's "demesne." The extended metaphor of the sonnet is narrator-reader as traveler, poet as ruler, poem as place. The narrator, much-traveled "in the realms of gold," has heard that Homer rules over "one wide expanse," yet he has never "breath[ed] its pure serene." During the oration of Chapman's translation, however, he is as taken as an astronomer "When a new planet swims into his ken" or as an explorer, such as "stout Cortez," when "He stared at the Pacific—and all his men/ Looked at each other with a wild surmise—/ Silent, upon a peak in Darien." The complementary images of the distant planet and the immense ocean suggest both the distance the narrator is from Homeric achievement and its epic proportions. His reaction, though, represented through the response of Cortez, is heartening: while lesser beings look to each other for cues on what to think, how to react, the greater explorer stares at the challenge, with "eagle eyes," to measure the farthest reaches of this new standard for achievement.

Following the lead of his contemporary William Wordsworth, though with a completely original emphasis, Keats's territory for development and conquest became the interior world of mental landscape and its imaginings. Wordsworth had defined his territory in his "Prospectus" to *The Recluse* (1798) as "the Mind of Man—/ My haunt, and the main region of my song." Whereas Wordsworth believed that mind, "When wedded to this goodly universe/ In love and holy passion," could create a vision of a new heaven and a new earth, Keats initially sought to transcend reality, rather than to transform it, with the power of the imagination to dream. "Ode to Psyche" explores Keats's region and its goddess, who was conceived too late in antiquity for fervid belief. While Wordsworth asserts in "Lines Composed a Few Miles Above Tintern Abbey" (1798) that "something far more deeply interfused" could sanctify our experience with nature, Keats locates days of "holy . . . haunted forest boughs" back in a past that precedes even his goddess of mind. The only region left for her worship must be imagined, interior. As priest, not to nature, but to mind, the poet says he will be Psyche's "choir" to "make delicious moan/ Upon the midnight hours," her voice, lute, pipe, incense, shrine, grove, oracle, her "heat/ Of pale-mouthed prophet" dreaming in "some untrodden region of [his] mind." In the "wide quietness" of this sacred microcosm, "branchèd thoughts, . . ./ Instead of pines shall murmur in the wind"; a "wreathed trellis of working brain" will dress "its rosy sanctuary"; the goddess' "soft delight" will be all that "shadowy thought can win." In keeping with the legend of Cupid as lover of Psyche, a casement will remain open at night "To let the warm Love in!" Keats's topic becomes, then, how the mind is stimulated by desire to create imagined worlds, or dreams, rather than, as in Wordsworth's case, how the mind is moved by love to re-create its perception of the real world.

Besides finding his territory for achievement, Keats struggled as well with the existential issues of the artist's life—developing the talent and maintaining the heart to live up to immense ambitions. It is to be doubted whether poets will ever be able to look to Shakespeare or to Milton as models without living in distress that deepens with every passing work. The "writing of a few fine Plays," meaning Shakespearean drama, remained Keats's greatest ambition to the end. Yet the achievement of *Paradise Lost* (1667) haunted him as well, and the first *Hyperion* was an attempt in its mold. Keats became more critical of Milton's achievement during the course of composing *Hyperion*, however, for it was, "though so fine in itself," a "curruption [sic] of our Language," too much in "the vein of art," rather than the "true voice of feeling." In fact, Keats gave up *Hyperion* because Milton's influence weighed so heavily that he could not distinguish the poem's excessively self-conscious artistry from its true beauty derived from accurate feeling.

Aesthetic considerations aside, a recurring theme in Keats's works of epic scope was the fantasy of poetic metamorphosis. The sonnet "On Sitting Down to Read King Lear Once Again" introduces the wish for transformation that will enable the poet to reach Shakespearean achievement. The metaphor is consumption and rebirth through fire, as adapted from the Egyptian legend of the phoenix bird, which was said to immolate itself on a burning pile of aromatic wood every five hundred years to engender a new phoenix from its ashes. The narrator-poet lays down his pen for a day so that he might "burn through" Shakespeare's "fierce dispute/ Betwixt damnation and impassion'd clay." To "burn through" must be read two ways in the light of the phoenix metaphor—as reading passionately through the work and as being burned through that reading. He prays to Shakespeare and the "clouds of Albion" not to let him "wander in a barren dream" when his long romance, *Endymion*, is concluded, but that "when . . . consumed in the fire" of reading *King Lear*, he may be given "new phœnix wings to fly at [his] desire." Out of the self-immolating achievement of reading will arise a poet better empowered to reach his quest.

The transformation theme of *Hyperion* exceeds the passionate wishfulness of "On Sitting Down to Read King Lear Once Again" by stressing the need for "knowledge enormous," as befits the poem's epic ambitions. *Hyperion* is a tale of succession in which the Titans are supplanted by the Olympians as the reigning monarchs of the universe, with focus upon Hyperion the sun god being replaced by Apollo, the new god of poetry and light. It has been suggested that *Hyperion* becomes Keats's allegory for his own relationship with his poetic contemporaries, especially Wordsworth. Keats had said that Wordsworth was Milton's superior in understanding, but this was not owing to "individual greatness of Mind" as much as to "the general and gregarious advance of intellect." *Hyperion* embodies this hypothesis of progress in its succession and transformation themes.

The poem opens with Saturn, who was the supreme god of the Titans, in a position of perfect stasis—the stationing referred to above—stupefied by his loss of power—"His old right hand lay nerveless, listless, dead,/ Unsceptered." Thea, the bewildered wife of the as-yet-undeposed Hyperion, visits to commiserate. She informs Saturn that the new gods are wholly incompetent; Saturn's "sharp lightning in unpracticed hands/ Scorches and burns our once serene domain." The question is: Why, with the world running perfectly, was there a need for change? Saturn, an image of pomposity and egotism, perhaps inspired by Wordsworth's character, knows only of his personal loss:

> I have left
> My strong identity, my real self,
> Somewhere between the throne, and where I sit
> Here on this spot of earth.

"Thea, Thea! Thea!" he moans, "where is Saturn?" Meanwhile, Hyperion is pacing his domain in the region of the sun, wondering: "Saturn is fallen, am I too to fall?" In his anxiety he overreacts, attempting to wield more power than he ever possessed by making the sun rise early. "He might not," which dismays him tremendously. The first book of this unfinished three-book epic ends with Hyperion sailing to earth to be with his fallen peers.

At the same time, Saturn and Thea also reach those "regions of laborious breath" where the gods sit

> Dungeoned in opaque element, . . .
> Without a motion, save of their big hearts
> Heaving in pain, and horribly convulsed
> With . . . boiling gurge of pulse.

The Titans receive their deposed king with mixed response—some groan, some jump to their feet out of old respect, some wail, some weep. Saturn, being unable to satisfy their need to know why and how they have fallen, calls upon Oceanus, the former god of the sea, for not only does he "Ponderest high and deep," he also looks content! Oceanus then reveals a law of succession particularly appropriate for the early nineteenth century: "We fall," he says, "by course of Nature's law, not force/ Of thunder, or of Jove." Blinded by sheer supremacy, Saturn has not realized that, as he was not the first ruler, so he will not be the last. Nature's law is the law of beauty. Just as heaven and earth are more beautiful than chaos and darkness, and the Titans superior in shape and will to heaven and earth, so the new gods signal another significant advance in being; "a fresh perfection treads,/ A power more strong in beauty, born of us/ And fated to excel us," Oceanus explains, "as we pass/ In glory that old Darkness." In short, the eternal law is that "first in beauty should be first in might."

On Apollo's isle the important transformation is about to begin. Apollo, as a good Keatsean poet, can make stars throb brighter when he empathizes with their glory in his poetry; yet he is inexplicably sad. Mnemosyne the muse seeks to assist her favorite child, who aches with ignorance. She emits what he needs to know and he flushes with

> Names, deeds, gray legends, dire events, rebellions,
> Majesties, sovran voices, agonies
> Creations and destroyings, all at once
> Pour[ing] into the wide hollows of [his] brain.

Apollo shouts, "knowledge enormous makes a God of me" and "wild commotions shook him, and made flush/ All the immortal fairness of his limbs." It is like a death pang, but it is the reverse, a dying into life and immortal power. The poem ends incomplete with Apollo shrieking, Mnemosyne arms in air, and the truncated line—"and lo! from all his limbs/ Celestial * * *." No one has been able to conjecture to the satisfaction of anyone else where the poem might have gone from there, although the result of Apollo's transformation seems inevitable. He would replace Hyperion, effortlessly, in this pre-Darwinian, pre-Freudian, universe where sons, like evolving species, acquire power over the earth without conscious competition with their fathers. As Oceanus indicates, the Titans are like the

> forest-trees, and our fair boughs
> Have bred forth . . .
> . . . eagles golden-feathered, who do tower
> Above us in their beauty, and must reign
> In right thereof.

However timorously, it would follow that Keats, bred on Spenser, Shakespeare, Milton, and Wordsworth, would have to live up to, if not exceed, their accomplishments.

This myth of progress would necessarily still require the superior poem to be written to support its prophetic validity. Keats knew that he needed deeper knowledge to surpass Wordsworth, but there was not much he could do about it. Though it was an attractive imagining, no god was likely to pour knowledge into the wide hollows of his brain. "I am . . . young writing at random—straining at particles of light in the midst of a great darkness," he wrote with characteristic honesty, "without knowing the bearing of any one assertion of any one opinion." Ironically, his dilemma brought out the strength his modern readers prize most highly, his courageous battling with, to use his favorite phrase of Wordsworth's, "the Burthen of the mystery." Caught in this impasse between noble ambition and youthful limitation, Keats's spirit understandably failed in weaker moments. His self-questioning was exacerbated when he reflected upon the frailty of earthly achievement. Such is the torment in "On Seeing the Elgin Marbles," the Grecian ruins brought to England by Lord Elgin.

The narrator opens feeling "Like a sick eagle looking at the sky" in the face of the magnificent architectural ruins. Ironically, they are only the "shadow of a magnitude" that once was, an insubstantial image emphasizing how much has been lost rather than how much was once achieved. Human achievement wasted by time brings the narrator a "most dizzy pain" born of tension between body and soul over committing one's life to mortal achievement. In "Ode on Indolence," Keats enjoys a temporary respite from his demons—love, ambition, and poetry—in a state of torpor in which the body temporarily overpowers spirit. One morning the shadows come to him: love the "fair Maid"; "Ambition, pale of cheek,/ And ever watchful with fatiguèd eye"; and, "the demon Poesy." At first he burns to follow and aches for wings, but body prevails: even poetry "has not a joy—/ . . . so sweet as drowsy noons,/ And evenings steeped in honeyed indolence." The victory is transitory outside the poem; within it, a respite from ambition, love, and work is accepted.

All of these issues—the quest for immortality; the region of quest as dream; the transformation essential to achieve the quest; the spiritual weakness inevitably felt in the face of the challenge to be immortal; and, beyond all these, an altruism that seeks to distinguish between the relative value of humanitarian works and poetry in behalf of suffering humanity—are melded in Keats's second quest for epic achievement, *The Fall of Hyperion*. Following a brief introduction, the poem moves to a dream arbor reserved for the dreamer, who "venoms all his days,/ Bearing more woe than all his sins deserve." Remnants of a feast strew the ground; the narrator eats, partakes of a draught of cool juice and is transported through sleep and reawakening to a second dream kingdom. He finds himself this time amid remnants of an ancient religious festival. These dream regions represent Keats's aspirations to romance and epic respectively. Off in the west, he sees a huge image being ministered to by a woman. The image is Saturn; the minister is Moneta, Mnemosyne's surrogate. Moneta's face is curtained to conceal the immense knowledge her eyes can reveal to those worthy of receiving her immortal knowledge. She challenges the narrator to prove himself so worthy by climbing the altar stairs to immortality, or dying on the spot. Cold death begins to mount through his body; in numbness he strives to reach the lowest step— "Slow, heavy, deadly was my pace: the cold/ Grew stifling, suffocating, at the heart;/ And when I clasped my hands I felt them not." At the last moment, he is saved; his "iced feet" touch the lowest step and "life seemed/ To pour in at the toes." He learns that he has been saved because he has felt for the suffering of the world, though he is only a dreamer, without hope for himself or of value to others. True poets, Moneta tells him, pour balm upon the world; dreamers increase the vexation of mankind.

Although in his letters Keats gave precedence to "fine doing" over "fine writing" as "the top thing in the world," the poem does not clarify whether humanitarians are above the poets of mankind, though both are unquestionably above the dreamers. The poem then moves to the metamorphosis that will make the dreamer a poet through the acquisition of knowledge. Moneta's bright-blanched face reveals the immortal sorrow she has endured for aeons; her eyes hold the narrator enthralled with the promise of the "high tragedy" they contain, for their light and the sorrowful touch of her voice reveal deep knowledge. He begs to know and she relates the fall of the Titans. The revelation begins the narrator's transformation: "Whereon there grew/ A power within me of enormous ken./ To see as a God sees." His vision opens with the "long awful time" Saturn sat motionless with Thea at his feet. In anguish the narrator sits on a tree awaiting action, but the pain must be endured, for knowledge does not come easily or quickly, not even in a dream. The narrator curses his prolonged existence, praying that death release him from the vale, until Saturn moves to speak and the narrator witnesses scenes of the beginning of things from *Hyperion*. The poem continues but this version also ends incomplete, with Hyperion flaring to earth.

It is a poignant fact that Keats never believed that his poetry, his work, had come to anything, his epic endeavors left incomplete, no "few fine Plays" written. Writing to Fanny Brawne in February, 1820, he said that he had frequently regretted not producing one immortal work to make friends proud of his memory. Now frighteningly ill, the thought of this failure and his love for Fanny were the sole two thoughts of his long, anxious nights. Quoting Milton's lines on fame from "Lycidas," Keats wrote to her: "Now you divide with this (may *I* say it) 'last infirmity of noble minds' all my reflection."

Their love had earlier spawned his most important love poems, though he refused his created lovers the bliss of unreflecting love. It would seem unfortunate that dreams do not outlast the act of dreaming, but Keats's romances, "The Eve of St. Agnes" and *Lamia*, approach wish-fulfillment more critically. "The Eve of St. Agnes" permits a love dream to become flesh to provoke a dreamer's response to the contrast between dream and reality, though they are, in person, the same; *Lamia* permits a too-ordinary mortal to enter the love dream of a lovely immortal to elicit the likely response of the nondreamer to the experience of continuous, in this case, carnal, perfection. Together the poems serve to show that lovers cannot have it either way: either reality will not be good enough for the dreamer, or the dream will not satisfy the extra-romantic desires of the nondreamer.

"The Eve of St. Agnes" presents an array of wish-fulfilling mechanisms that seek to alter, control, or purify reality—praying, suffering, drinking, music, ritual, dance, and, at the center, dreaming. This poem with a medieval setting opens with a holy beadsman, "meagre, barefoot, wan," praying to the Virgin in the castle's icy chapel. Though he is fleetingly tempted to walk toward the music dancing down the hall from a party within, he turns to sit among "rough ashes" in recompense for his and others' sins. Among others praying this frigid night is Madeline, who follows the ritual of St. Agnes: if a maiden refrains from eating, drinking, speaking, listening, looking anywhere, except up to heaven, and lies supine when she retires, she will be rewarded with the vision of her future husband. The irony of the patron saint of virgins inspiring a heterosexual vision is lost on the young girl, panting as she prays for all "the bliss to be before to-morrow morn." Meanwhile, Porphyro, her love, is in reality racing across the moors to worship his Madeline. As Madeline works on her dream, Porphyro will act on his desired reality—

getting into Madeline's bedroom closet where "he might see her beauty unespied,/ And win perhaps that night a peerless bride."

The lovers' stratagems provide a weird culmination, though they move in complementary pattern. While Madeline is undergoing her ritualistic deprivations, Porphyro is gathering, through the assistance of her wily old nurse, Angela, a banquet of delights to fulfill deliciously her sensual needs; while she undresses, he gazes, of course, unseen; while she silently sleeps, he pipes in her ear "La belle dame sans merci." When she awakens to find the man of her dream at her side, however, the seemingly perfect solution is shattered. Madeline's dream of Porphyro was better than Porphyro and she tells him so: "How changed thou art! how pallid, chill, and drear!" She implores that he return to her as the dream. Porphyro arises, "Beyond a mortal man impassioned far/ At these voluptuous accents" and

> like a throbbing star
> . . . .
> Into her dream he melted, as the rose
> Blendeth its odor with the violet—
> Solution sweet.

The moon of St. Agnes, which has been languishing throughout the poem, sets as Madeline loses her virginity. Madeline, however, comes out of the experience confused; she wanted a dream, not reality, and apparently she could not distinguish between them at their climax. Now bewildered, and feeling betrayed and vulnerable to abandonment, she chides Porphyro for taking advantage. He assures her of his undying devotion and the two flee the sleeping castle into the storm, for he has prepared a home for her in the southern moors. The drunken revelers from the party lie benightmared; Angela soon dies "palsy-twitched"; and the loveless beadsman, after thousands of Aves, sleeps forever among his ashes.

A skeptical reading of the poem has found Porphyro a voyeur and (perhaps) a rapist, Madeline a silly conjurer whose machinations have backfired; an optimistic reading has Madeline and Porphyro ascending to heaven's bourn. The language, imagery, and structure allow both interpretations, which is the way of complex ironic honesty. The dream experience, for example, has two parts: the first when Madeline awakens to find Porphyro disappointingly imperfect; the second when the two blend into "solution sweet." It would seem that dream and reality have unified in the second part, but the first part is not thereby negated. Rather, the lovers are lost in sensory intensity, which, according to Keats, makes "all disagreeables evaporate." Whether the moment of intensity is worth the necessary conjuration before or the inevitable disillusionment afterwards is a judgment on the nature of romance itself, down to this very day.

Lamia provides the nondreamer, Lycius, with much more than the two ordinary lovers of "The Eve of St. Agnes" are permitted; but the question is whether more is better. T. S. Eliot wrote that mankind cannot stand very much reality; Keats suggests in *Lamia* that neither can we bear very much dreaming. Lamia, as imagination incarnate, provides her lover Lycius with a realized dream of carnal perfection that extends continuously until he tires of her adoration. When Lamia, once bound in serpent form, was capable of sending her imagination abroad to mingle among the mortals of Corinth, she saw Lycius in a chariot race and fell in love. After being released from her serpent prison house by another immortal, Hermes, in an exchange of wish-fulfillments, she assumes a glorious woman's body to attract Lycius. She is successful, but a series of compromises must be made to win him and satisfy his desires. Those compromises are the record of imagination's degeneration. Because Lycius is so overwhelmed by her beauty, he believes she must be immortal and loses his confidence. She "throws the goddess off" to encourage his masculinity. When he tires of the carnal pleasure she provides in the "purple-lined palace of sweet sin," she begs on her knees that he might preserve the privacy of their dream, for she knows of her vulnerability to reason. The sight of her begging brings out the sadist in Lycius, who "takes delight in her sorrows, soft and new." His passion grown cruel, Lamia plays the complementary masochist, burning, loving the tyranny. She grants his wish that they should be married before all of Corinth, and creates a feast and a vision of palatial splendor for the "gossip rout." The philosopher Apollonius, tutor to Lycius, crashes the party to destroy the dream with his "keen, cruel, perceant, stinging" eye. Apollonius is reason to Lamia's imagination, and in the confrontation between them, Lamia dissipates; Lycius the scholar-lover dies because he is incapable of balancing reason and imagination; and Apollonius is left with a Pyrrhic victory, for he has lost his pupil whom he intended to save.

Ironically, the loss of the dream, the dreamers, and the battle is not even tragic because not one was worthy of salvation. Lycius risks his dream so that his friends will look with admiration, but his friends choke over his good fortune; Lamia concedes to this foolish vanity; and Apollonius, the brilliant sophist, mistakes the whole situation, feeling that Lycius has become the prey of Lamia. More than saying that dreams cannot mix with reality, *Lamia* warns that imagination cannot be prostituted to the pleasure principle. Dreams are pure and sensitive constructs inspired by love, created for the psyche by the imagination. The eye of self-consciousness; participation with others, including loved ones; the dictates of forces less pure than love—all cause dissolution of the ephemeral dream.

"Ode to a Nightingale" leaves the medium of the dream for empathic identification with a natural being that seems to promise transcendence of the human condition. Again, a transcendence of self is fleetingly achieved, leaving the poet, *in propria persona*, more isolated and bewildered thereafter. He opens the poem having returned from identification with the bird's "happiness" that causes and permits it to sing "of summer in full-throated ease." The poet, however, is now drowsy and numb, so far has he sunk from that high experience of unself-conscious joy. He wishes for any wine, human or divine, that might effect a dissolution of consciousness and a return to the bird; for among men, "but to think is to be full of sorrow/ And leaden-eyed despairs." The transience of the physical splendor of beauty, of the psychological heights of love; the tragedy of early death, the indignity of aging to death; participation in human misery—all have thwarted any love or hope he might feel for the human condition.

In the fourth stanza the poet seems to join the bird, but ambiguously. After exhorting his imagination and/or the bird to fly "Away! away!" where he will reach it on "the viewless wings of Poesy," he seems to achieve the connection: "Already with thee! tender is the night." The eighth and final stanza supports the interpretation of his extended identification, for it has the poet being tolled back from the bird "to my sole self." Before the identification in stanza four, however, he has qualified the power of those viewless wings to keep him in stable flight, for "the dull brain perplexes and retards." Consequently, throughout the poem, he is neither entirely with the bird, nor entirely in his metaphysical agony, but rather in a state of mixed or split consciousness that leads to the poem's concluding questions: "Was it vision, or a waking dream?/ Fled is that music:—Do I wake or sleep?" In the sixth stanza, for example, as he sits in his "embalmèd darkness" in the arbor, he says, "Darkling I listen; and, for many a time/ I have been half in love with easeful Death." Shortly, he seems to be lost in the ecstasy of the bird's song. Yet immediately he retracts, for common sense tells him that, if he were dead, his ears would be in vain, and "To thy high requiem" of the bird, he would "become a sod."

The seventh stanza distinguishes the immortality of the bird's song from the mortality of the poet, and for another passing moment he seems to experience identification as he slips into empathy with those through time who have also heard the immortal song, especially Ruth of the Old Testament: "Perhaps the self-same song that found a path/ Through the sad heart of Ruth, when, sick for home,/ She stood in tears amid the alien corn." This song that flows through time sparks both the poet's identification with it and his empathy for fellow beings. He is not as explicit as Walt Whitman would be in defining immortality as empathy for all beings and experiences of all times, but his revealed feeling for others is the eternal human counterpart to the song that eternally elicits the feeling. Still, the great divider between the bird and poet is the poet's self-consiousness. The bird, unaware of its individuality and coming death, is more a medium of the song of its species than a being in its own right. The poet withdraws completely in the final stanza to his "sole self." The imagination cannot support the identification with a dissimilar being for very long. The bird's song fades until it is metaphorically dead to the poet, "buried deep/ In the next valley glades." The stimulus for experience now fled, the poet recognizes the division he has undergone between empathy and identity, being in and out of self, with neither strain coming to resolution. The bewilderment of the conclusion reflects perfectly the imperfect resolution of his experience.

The "Ode on Melancholy" offers perhaps the most positive perspective possible to one who appreciates this tragedy of the human condition. Its psychology is a variant of Satan's from *Paradise Lost*: "Evil, be thou my good." The poet advises that when the "melancholy fit shall fall," as fall it must, one should not seek to escape with "poisonous wine," "nightshade," or other agents that would "drown the wakeful anguish of the soul," for that very anguish is the catalyst for more intensely valuing transient beauty, joy, and love. Even the anger of a loved one will reach a value transcending relationship, if we "Emprison her soft hand, and let her rave,/ And feed deep, deep upon her peerless eyes." The glow fired by her passion, the beauty, joy, and pleasure that accompany love, all must dwindle, die, depart, sour; but if one holds an awareness of their end while indulging in their prime, the triumph of deep inclusive response will reward the sensitive soul with ultimate mortal value. It will be among Melancholy's "cloudy trophies hung," which is to say, the "sadness of her might" will hold him forever sensitive to the richness of transience.

In like manner, "To Autumn" offers a pespective on nature in the ultimate richness of its condition. It has always been difficult for poets to look upon nature without moralizing its landscape for human edification. The Romantic period especially sought its morality from nature and its processes. Keats, however, describes nature without pressing metaphor out of it; his goal is to offer it as worthy in itself so that we might love it for itself. If there are analogues between human nature and nature, they are not the subject, concern, or purpose of the poem. As several critics have noted, the stanzas move from the late growth of summer to the fulfillment of autumn to the harvested landscape; correspondingly, the imagery moves from tactile to visual to auditory in an ascension from the most grossly physical to the most nonphysical. The sun and the season are in league to load and bless the vines with fruit, and in a string of energetic infinitives, the push of life's fulfillment is represented: "To bend with apples the mossed cottage trees," to "fill all fruit with ripeness to the core," "To swell the gourd, and plump the hazel shells," "to set budding more,/ And still more, later flowers for the bees." An image of surfeited bees, who think summer will never end, their "clammy cells" are so "o'er-brimmed," concludes the first stanza.

Stanza two presents the personification of autumn "sitting careless on a granary floor"; sound asleep "Drowsed with the fume of poppies" in the fields; "by a cyder press, with patient look," watching the "last oozings hours by hours." The harvested stubble plains of stanza three provoke the poet's question, "Where are the songs of spring?" Even so, the question is raised more to dismiss it as irrelevant than to honor its inevitability. Autumn has its own music and the poem softly presents it: as the stubble plains are covered with the rosy hue of the dying day, the "small gnats mourn," "full-grown lambs loud bleat," "Hedge crickets sing," "with treble soft/ The red-breast whistles from a garden-croft," and "gathering swallows twitter in the skies." The suggestion of animate life singing unconsciously in its joy, while just as unconsciously readying for winter, signals the end of the natural year. Unlike Shelley, however, who in "Ode to the West Wind" looks through the fall and coming winter to spring as an analogue of rebirth for mankind, Keats allows not more than a suggestion of what is to follow, and that only because it belongs to the sound and action of the season. Autumn is accepted for itself, not as an image, sign, or omen of spiritual value. Ripeness is all.

As "Ode on Melancholy" and "To Autumn" established perspectives on the human condition and nature, so "Ode on a Grecian Urn" establishes a relationship with art. This ode begins and ends by addressing the urn as object, but the subject-object duality is dissolved in the third of the five stanzas. The experiential movement of the poem is from ignorance through identification to understanding. The poet addresses the urn as a "bride of quietness," "still unravished" by passing generations. It is a "foster child of silence and slow time." Once the child of the artist and his time, the urn belongs not to eternity, for it is vulnerable to destruction, but to the timeless existence of what endures. It is a sylvan historian, containing a narrative relief of the beings and scenes of its surface. The poet asks questions of it as historian; what gods, music, bacchanalian frenzy it images. All is silent; but that is best, we learn, for "Heard melodies are sweet, but those unheard/ Are sweeter," free to become as flawless as imagination can wish. The second stanza finds the poet moving close, addressing the urn's individuals. The "Fair youth" who pipes the song so softly that only the spirit hears, the "Bold lover" who has neared the lips of his maiden, both arouse the poet-lover's empathy.

In the third stanza, the poet participates fully in the urn's existence as he inspires scenery and youths with imaginative fervor. The "happy, happy boughs! that cannot shed/ [their] leaves, nor ever bid the spring adieu"; the "happy melodist, unwearied,/ Forever piping songs forever new"; and, above all, "more happy love! more happy, happy love!/ Forever warm and still to be enjoyed,/ Forever panting, and forever young"—none of it can pass. Nature, art, and love remain in the glow of their promise. The love on the urn arouses a special contrast with "breathing human passion . . ./ That leaves a heart high-sorrowful and cloyed,/ A burning forehead, and a parching tongue." The fourth stanza begins to pull out of intense identification, with questions on the urn's religious scene: "Who are these coming to the sacrifice?" To what "green altar" does the priest lead his sacrificial heifer? What town do they come from that will be emptied of its inhabitants forever? Stanza five again addresses the urn as object, but with increased understanding over stanza one. She is now "Attic shape! Fair Attitude! with brede/ Of marble men and maidens overwrought." The bride, though unravished and wed to quietness, has her breed of beings, themselves passionately in pursuit of experience. She is a "silent form" that "dost tease us out of thought/ As doth eternity: Cold Pastoral!" If her silence provokes participation so that viewers lose self-consciousness in her form, then truly they are teased out of thought, as the poet was in stanza three. Why, though, is she a "Cold Pastoral!"

Critics have taken this to be the poet's criticism of the urn in her relationship with those who contemplate her; perhaps it is best, however, that the urn remain cold, if she is to encourage and reward the viewers' empathy. Stanza three criticized human passion for its torrid intensity in contrast with the urn's image of love "Forever *warm* and [thus] still to be enjoyed." The urn remains a cold object until it is kindled by the viewers' passion. When the mortals of the present generation have been wasted by time, the urn will continue to exist for others, "a friend to man," to whom it (or the poet) has this to say: "Beauty is truth, truth beauty—that is all/ Ye know on earth, and all ye need to know."

Much ink has been spilled over these final lines of the "Ode on a Grecian Urn" and the technicalities of this famous problem for criticism must be at least briefly addressed. The difficulty is in determining who is saying what to whom; the issue has a mundane origin in punctuation. According to the text of the *Lamia* volume, the lines should be punctuated with the quotation marks enclosing only the beauty-truth statement: "'Beauty is truth, truth beauty'— that is all. . . ." If the lines are punctuated thus, the urn makes the beauty-truth statement, and the poet himself offers the evaluation of it, either to the urn, to the figures on the urn, or to the reader. Many scholars, however, see the matter differently; they would place the entire aphorism within quotations, based upon manuscript authority: "Beauty is truth . . . need to know." With this punctuation, the urn is talking to man. Both choices lead to problematic interpretations. In the former case, it does not make much sense for the poet to speak to the urn or to its images about "all ye know on earth," as if there were someplace else for the urn to know something. There might be an afterlife where things can be known, but not for the urn. On the other hand, it would be odd for the poet to speak to the reader in that way, too. The inconsistency in tone would be especially awkward. Several lines earlier, he had joined his reader in saying to the urn: "Thou . . . dost tease us out of thought." To refer now to "us" as *ye*, as in "that is all/ Ye know on earth," is out of tone. On the other hand, the argument against the urn speaking the entire aphorism is directed against its sufficiency. It has been argued that human beings need to know a great deal more than "Beauty is truth, truth beauty," no matter how one tries to stretch the meanings of the terms to make them appear all-inclusive. There is no way to resolve this critical problem with confidence, though trying to think through it will provide an exercise in Keatsean speculation at its best.

To agree that the experience the poet undergoes is entirely satisfactory might be enough, though there is not critical unanimity about this, either. Lovers about to kiss, rather than kissing; trees in their springtime promise, rather than in fruition; a song that has to be imagined; a sacrifice still to be made, rather than offered—all can suggest experience short of perfection. Yet, like Keats's dreams which surpass reality, these figures are safely in their imaginative prime. The kiss, after all, may not be as sweet as anticipated; the fruit may be blighted; the song may be tiresome or soon grow so; the sacrifice may be unacceptable.

In fact, a reader comes to Keats's poetry as the poet himself came to the urn. Like all great art, Keats's poetry is evocative; it leads its readers' emotions and thoughts into and then out of its formal beauty to teach and delight. One can stand back and examine its formal perfection; one can ask questions of it about human nature and its desires for being and loving. Yet only through the experience of it can one learn what it has to teach; only after one goes through the empathy of Keats's narrator in stanza three can one speak with confidence of its meaning.

Richard E. Matlak

Other major works
NONFICTION: *The Letters of John Keats, 1814-1821*, 1958 (Hyder Edward Rollins, editor, 2 volumes).
MISCELLANEOUS: *Complete Works*, 1900-1901 (edited by H. B. Forman, 5 volumes).

Bibliography
Bate, Walter Jackson. *John Keats*. Cambridge, Mass.: Harvard University Press, 1963. If there is one single book that students of Keats's life and poetry should have at their side, it is this superb critical biography. Bate is accurate with biographical details, subtle in his analyses of Keats's psychology and how it influenced his poetry, and always reliable when discussing the style and themes of the poems.
Bloom, Harold, ed. *John Keats: Modern Critical Views*. New York: Chelsea House, 1985. Eleven essays, most of them reprinted from longer works, which make up a representative collection of modern approaches to Keats. Some of the essays are difficult, and familiarity with the poems and earlier critical approaches to them is recommended. Individual poems discussed are *Endymion* (Stuart Sperry), "To Autumn" (Geoffrey Hartman), *Hyperion* (Paul Sherwin), *Lamia* (Leslie Brisman), "Ode on Indolence" (Helen Vendler), and the two *Hyperions*. Contains several general essays,

including Paul de Man's frequently cited overview of Keats's poetry.
Dickstein, Morris. *Keats and His Poetry: A Study in Development.* Chicago:
University of Chicago Press, 1971. Studies the development of Keats's attitude to consciousness, defined as "self-awareness and awareness of the
world that surrounds, nurtures, and conditions the self." Dickstein argues
that Keats's poetry developed from early escapism to self-awareness and
awareness of the tragic dimension to existence. Provides detailed analysis
of *Endymion*, the odes, and some of the minor poems that have received
less critical attention.
Evert, Walter H. *Aesthetic and Myth in the Poetry of Keats.* Princeton, N.J.:
Princeton University Press, 1965. An important and frequently cited study
of Keats's aesthetic ideas and his use of a mythic structure to express
them. Argues persuasively that the Greek myth of Apollo gave Keats a vision of human life operating in harmony with the cycle of life and growth
in nature. The longest discussion is of *Endymion*, but Evert also provides
illuminating readings of most of the other major poems.
Sperry, Stuart M. *Keats the Poet.* Princeton, N.J.: Princeton University Press,
1973. One of the most respected studies. In the first chapter, Sperry discusses the importance of "sensation" to Keats and the philosophic and
aesthetic theories underlying it. The second chapter discusses analogies between chemical processes as known in Keats's day and Keats's descriptions of the poetic process. Readings of all the major poems follow in
chronological order, as Sperry traces Keats's intellectual and poetic development, with emphasis on Keats's view of the poetic process.
Van Ghent, Dorothy. *Keats: The Myth of the Hero.* Princeton, N.J.: Princeton University Press, 1983. This unusual book, which was completed in
the 1960's and published posthumously, applies mythic and archetypal criticism to Keats. Although this approach is not currently fashionable, Van
Ghent's readings of all the major poems in terms of the quest myth of the
hero, as described by mythologist Joseph Campbell, are fresh and insightful.
Waldoff, Leon. *Keats and the Silent Work of Imagination.* Urbana: University
of Illinois Press, 1985. A psychoanalytic study of the role of imagination
in Keats's poetry and development. Waldoff extends earlier studies by taking into account the "unconscious dimension" of imagination, how it functions to give expression to the deepest images, feelings, and thoughts in
Keats's psyche and art. The psychoanalysis is Freudian, but it is not applied dogmatically, and the result is some thought-provoking close readings of the major poems that reveal the recurring conflicts in Keats's mind.

WELDON KEES

Born: Beatrice, Nebraska; February 24, 1914
Died: San Francisco, California; July 18, 1955

Principal poetry
The Last Man, 1943; *The Fall of the Magicians*, 1947; *Poems, 1947-1954*, 1954; *The Collected Poems of Weldon Kees*, 1975 (revised).

Other literary forms
While the poetry of Weldon Kees eventually dominated his literary career, he began by publishing more than three dozen short stories in little magazines, such as *The Prairie Schooner*, that were scattered throughout the Midwest. From his first published story in 1934 (while still an undergraduate) to his last one in 1940 ("The Life of the Mind"), Kees's reputation grew steadily and impressively. He was frequently cited in annual anthologies such as those published by New Directions. Edward J. O'Brien designated twenty of his stories as "distinctive" in his *Best Short Stories*, an annual distillation from thousands of stories published in English; indeed, O'Brien's 1941 volume was dedicated to Kees. Kees's commitment to short fiction, however, had already waned by then.

In addition to Kees's short stories, he also published a number of reviews in prestigious periodicals such as *Poetry*, *The Nation*, and *The New York Times Book Review*. His interests were astonishingly diverse, and he reviewed books of poetry, fiction, music, art, criticism, and psychology. In 1950, Kees served as art critic for *The Nation*, publishing an important series of articles on the "abstract expressionists." He also wrote the essay "Muskrat Ramble: Popular and Unpopular Music," based on his study of jazz, which was anthologized for its insights into popular culture. Kees also tried his hand at writing plays, and he left behind an experimental, off-Broadway sort of play, *The Waiting Room*, that remains unpublished despite its commendation by Kenneth Rexroth.

Besides writing, Kees managed to make, or help to make, several short "art films" that are representative of American expressionist cinematography of the period. Notable are *The Adventures of Jimmy*, for which he wrote a jazz score, and *Hotel Apex*, his own psychological study of urban disintegration. His filmmaking extended to studies in child and group psychology that led to an association with the psychiatrists Gregory Bateson and Jurgen Ruesch; with the latter, Kees coauthored *Nonverbal Communication: Notes on the Visual Perception of Human Relations* (1956), which contains a stunning series of still photographs taken by Kees himself. Published after his disappearance in 1955, this volume and *The Collected Poems* are essential for an understanding of Kees's poetry.

Achievements

While Kees was fairly well-known and critically acclaimed by reviewers such as Rexroth in his own time, his work is now all but forgotten. A thorough assessment of his place in American poetry remains to be done, yet one senses that Kees has been influential and important in unacknowledged quarters of contemporary poetry. The inclusion of Kees in *The Norton Anthology of Modern Poetry* (1973) would expand his audience. His editor, Donald Justice, saw fit to revise *The Collected Poems* fifteen years after initial publication. Larry Levis, whose first three books have each won a major national award, includes the eulogy "My Only Photograph of Weldon Kees" in his book *The Dollmaker's Ghost* (1981).

If, as Rexroth has suggested, Kees was "launched" into poetry by Conrad Aiken, T. S. Eliot, and W. H. Auden, he also assimilated the objectivist viewpoint of William Carlos Williams, the incremental method of Ezra Pound, the prose rhythms of Kenneth Fearing, and the proletarian realism of James T. Farrell, in moving far beyond those early influences. Kees may, indeed, yet be seen as an important figure in the transition from modernist poetics to the postmodern sensibility, with its preoccupation with loss, fictions of the self, and parody of older forms.

More than as an unknown link in the history of poetics or as an artist of amazing versatility, Kees's achievement is a poetry that is singularly voiced in its blunt honesty and articulate despair over the loss of Walt Whitman's American idealism. There is no poet in all of American literature more bitter than Kees; yet that "permanent and hopeless apocalypse" (Rexroth) in which he lived does not hinder his eloquence, nor does it erode an eerie serenity that constantly seems to accept certain doom. Kees even seems to anticipate the now-familiar despair of the nuclear age in his poem "Travels in North America," in which he declares that "the sky is soiled" by the "University of California's atom bomb." Had he been publishing in the 1960's or the 1970's, Kees might be read widely. As Rexroth has concluded, the poems of Kees may simply have been "just a few years too early."

Biography

Weldon Kees remained in his birthplace, the small town of Beatrice in rural Nebraska, until he attended the University of Nebraska. His childhood and adolescence appear typical of the era and place. By the time Kees had been graduated from a liberal arts curriculum in 1935, he had made a sufficient impression on Professor L. C. Wimberly to become a regular contributor and reviewer for *The Prairie Schooner*. After serving as an editor for the Federal Writers' Project in Lincoln, Kees moved to Denver in 1937 to work as a librarian, eventually becoming director of the Bibliographical Center of Research for the Rocky Mountain Region. His first published poem, "Subtitle," appeared that year in an obscure little magazine called *Signatures*; from then on, Kees turned increasingly toward poetry for the expression of his artistic vision.

By 1943, Kees had moved to New York, where he worked as a journalist for *Time* and became involved in documentary film-making. That year also saw the publication of his first book of poems, *The Last Man*, by the Colt Press in San Francisco. Midway through the 1940's, Kees took up painting, choosing to identify himself with what was to be known as the abstract expressionist movement. He exhibited his work in one-man shows at the Peridot Gallery; at least once, his paintings were shown with those of Hans Hofmann, William de Kooning, Jackson Pollock, and Robert Motherwell—the major artists of the movement. Kees also found time to continue writing poems, and they appeared in *Poetry*, *The New Yorker*, and *Harper's*, among other leading journals. His second collection of poems, *The Fall of the Magicians*, was published in 1947.

Kees abandoned New York for San Francisco sometime in 1951. There he began serious study of jazz piano and jazz composition. He continued his work in cinematography and made several movies himself. Kees also began exploring nonverbal signs with Jergen Ruesch and interpersonal cues with Gregory Bateson in an attempt to grasp the commonplace, to exploit it, and to express it immediately and directly by a method that was "spare, rigorous, and clinical." Meanwhile, he continued to paint and write; in 1954, his last book, *Poems, 1947-1954*, was published in San Francisco.

Aside from Kees's far-ranging activities and multitalented pursuits, his life to this point, in the words of Justice, seems to have been "a fairly typical career for any writer reaching manhood in the depression and passing through a time of political crisis and war." On July 18, 1955, however, Kees's car was found abandoned on the approach to the Golden Gate Bridge. In a review that appeared that same day in *The New Republic*, Kees had written of "our present atmosphere of distrust, violence, and irrationality" that led to "so many human beings murdering themselves—either literally or symbolically. . . ." Justice reports that in the weeks before his car was found, Kees had spoken to friends both of suicide and of going away to Mexico to begin a new life. His disappearance, it seems, was not an act of sudden or impulsive desperation, but rather the culmination of nearly two decades in which his poetry shows an increasing despair that grew deeper with his avid scrutiny of humanity in contemporary society and his insistent denial of those superficial values by which human beings sought to order their lives. Whether Kees did commit suicide or whether he simply fled from any previous social context in his life, his disappearance was the ultimate symbolic act against what he perceived to be an indifferent society seized by the doldrums of pervasive mediocrity.

Analysis

Perhaps the neglect that Weldon Kees's poetry has suffered results from the lack of a single, brilliant "masterpiece." There is no long poem, no ambitious project or sequence like those on which many modern and contemporary poets have founded their reputations. There is no pretentious, gaudy innovation of form that would assure him a place in debates on "technical craft." Many of Kees's poems suffer from flaws such as awkward allusions or tedious repetitions, but despite all such deficiencies his work is original for its soft voice that expresses a tone of hard bitterness. That voice is not especially pleasing in its barrage of satiric details, yet it retains a unique capacity to haunt the memory of anyone who has read his poems. Donald Justice is surely correct in asserting that Kees's poetry "makes its deepest impression when read as a body of work rather than a collection of isolated moments of brilliance," for "there is a cumulative power to the work as a whole to which even the weaker poems contribute."

In Kees's early poems such as "The Speakers," one detects the unmistakable echoes of T. S. Eliot, while a poem such as "Variations on a Theme by Joyce" employs a Joycean "war in the words." Even in those first poems, however, Kees comes quickly to his own sense of rhythm and tone. While he played with formalism by using the villanelle and the sestina, and while he experimented with form in such poems as "Fuge" and "Round," Kees settled in to a rhythmic prose line that was more flexible than traditional meter and more restrictive than free verse. Possessing a naturally good ear, Kees successfully wed form and content by starting with facts and things and then consummated them by placing the right words in the right order—in short, a wholly natural proselike but lyrical style. The consequent unobtrusive tone of the poems is the very heart of Kees's poetic vision.

Kees chose as an epigraph to his final book a passage from Nathaniel Hawthorne's *The Marble Faun* (1860) that reveals much about Kees's own perspective in his poetry. His quest was to enter "those dark caverns into which all men must descend, if they would know anything beneath the surface and illusive pleasures of existence." Hawthorne's novel itself is a study of ambivalent meaning in a world scattered among the fragments of tradition and the incomprehensible debris that is left to the artist. Seeing himself in a similar world, but facing an even more painful disintegration than Hawthorne had perceived, Kees sought to enter his own "dark caverns" by explicating and disclosing the ironies of the "surface" and satirizing the "pleasures of existence." Whatever hope marks that quest—and it does not appear with any frequency—can be found in the intense scrutiny of both personal and public experience, capable not only of recognizing and accepting continuous despair, but also of remaining detached from its implications. Kees proposes a self-protective hope, simple, isolated, solitary, and stationary, out of which, with absolute denial, the self can create a system of values by which it can survive—honestly and naturally—with perhaps its greatest pleasure being in art itself.

The pervasive anguish and bitterness that runs through Kees's poetry like grain through wood appeared in his earliest work. In the early poem "For My Daughter," as the speaker gazes into his "daughter's eyes," he perceives "hintings of death" which he knows "she does not heed." Continuing his contemplation of the destruction of her youth, he fears that she will be subjected to the "Parched years that I have seen" and intensifies his dread by assuming that she will be ravished by "lingering/ Death in certain war." Worse yet, the speaker bemoans the possibility—even probability—that his daughter will be "fed on hate" and learn to relish "the sting/ Of other's agony" in which the masochism of self-destruction overwhelms the tenderness of love. In the midst of such bleak projection, Kees undermines the speaker's fearful uncertainties. "These speculations," says the speaker, "sour in the sun." Just as the reader begins to applaud the father for coming to his senses and rejecting his indulgent morbidity, Kees delivers an excruciating shock in the last line: "I have no daughter. I desire none." The reader now realizes that the despair is even greater than he had supposed; the speaker has already chosen not to have children, because he sees nothing but betrayal and suffering in his vision of the future. He chooses to withhold his own "procreative urge," viewing it as his own inevitable complicity in the suffocation of the unborn generations.

That rather private sense of futility gives way in other poems to a dramatic rendering of an equally futile sense in interpersonal relationships. In "The Conversation in the Drawing Room," Kees creates a dialogue between Hobart, a young man aghast at a "spot of blood" that is "spreading" on the room's wall, and Cousin Agatha, who refuses to acknowledge his hysteria as anything but the result of reading *The Turn of the Screw* (Henry James, 1898) before bedtime. Agatha sees herself as compassionate and progressive; she remarks that the "weather is ideal" and ruminates on joining "a new theosophist group"as Hobart announces that the spot is "growing brighter." When he urges her to examine it, she dismisses it as an "aberration of the wallpaper" and suggests that he suffers from indigestion. When Hobart points out that the spot has become "a moving thing/ That spreads and reaches from the wall," Agatha's response denies even his presence: "I cannot listen to you any more just now." After treating her lily with "another aspirin" and finding her own "barbital," Agatha leaves Hobart twitching, "rather feebly," in the aftermath of a convulsion "on the floor," while speculating that his "youthful animal spirits" and "a decided taste for the macabre" have been responsible for his disconcerting "gasping and screaming." Declaring that it is "a beautiful afternoon," Agatha anticipates her evening dinner party and rejoices smugly that "everything is blissfully quiet now" so that she can depart for her routine afternoon nap. Quite apart from her perception of herself, Kees portrays a drastic indifference on Agatha's part that is the result of her mundane, trivial allegiance to and affirmation of the social and spiritual contexts that she unquestionably accepts as her own. Her unexamined, callous optimism has, in fact, destroyed not only her cousin Hobart, but also her own ability to see beyond the surface of a superficial value system. Agatha has not the slightest notion of the presence of evil in the world. Her refusal to acknowledge it is her constant contribution to its growth.

Kees was later to extend his satirical attack on the shallow values of society in a more mature series of poems that center on Robinson, an archetypal ordinary man who has little idea who he is, what he is doing, or where he has been. In the Robinson poems, however, Kees offers sympathy with ridicule, compassion with condemnation, and self-irony with parody. These poems, "Robinson," "Aspects of Robinson," "Robinson at Home" and "Relating to Robinson," show a curious use of the persona in that Robinson is usually absent or nearly absent from the poems. Kees writes primarily of the things or places that once affirmed his existence: the remnants of his life and actions are all that remain of him. When Robinson is present, he is isolated by a room, a hallway or a stairway, or he is insulated from the world to which he attempts to relate by a deep and troubled sleep. When Robinson looks into a "mirror from Mexico," he finds that it "reflects nothing at all." The pages in his books are blank. He attempts to telephone himself at his own empty house. His existence consists solely of traces of himself that he can no longer discern. Throughout the poems, Robinson speaks only once—and then out of a nightmare: "There is something in this madhouse that I symbolize—/ This city—nightmare—black. . . ." Hardly capable of such a statement in his waking state, Robinson speaks here as much for Kees as for himself. What Kees has sought to use as a device, the persona of absence, has resulted, because of his empathy with that persona, in the presence of his own voice. Kees's satire has become self-irony. The shallow life that he had wished to parody has become all too much a part of his own life.

By the final poem in the series, "Relating to Robinson," Kees's pretense of the persona itself has dissolved: "We were alone there, he and I,/ Inhabiting the empty street." The speaker confesses freely that Robinson is a fiction of himself: "His voice/ Came at me like an echo in the dark." As the creator of the persona, the poet must now accept those aspects of himself that he has sought to keep at a distance by his use of the device. Consequently, he must now accept the paradox that he himself is as much the creation of Robinson as Robinson is the product of his art, for he has now "no certainty,/ There in the dark, that it was Robinson/ Or someone else." In his exploration of "surfaces" and his analysis of "illusive pleasures," Kees has successfully overcome the phenomenological alienation between subject and object, but the intensity of his involvement in doing so has left him hopelessly entangled in the very shallowness he had hoped to overturn. His success is his failure.

In the wake of this tendency to undermine his own quest (his villanelles and sestinas fail precisely because they cannot contain his blunt confrontation with experience without seeming stillborn themselves), Kees developed a poetic technique that embodies his denial of false values, perhaps best illustrated in "A Salvo for Hans Hofmann," which reveals a good deal more about Kees than it does about the painter. Kees's antagonistic method intends to enter "the slashed world traced and traced again" so that by his entry it is "enriched, enlarged, caught in a burning scrutiny" which will illuminate "like fog-lamps on a rotten night" the decay and debris of contemporary civilization. He sifts through the surfaces, "the scraps of living," that continuously "shift and change," with the hope that by that very act, those fragments can be "shaped to a new identity" for both the self and the world. He seeks a path through the rubble where "the dark hall/ Finds a door" and, purging the pain, "the wind comes in." The search itself, however, remains suspect; the last line of the poem comments on the momentary fragility of any new identity: "A rainbow sleeps and wakes against the wall." If a splendid, euphoric new identity has been rekindled from the debris, then in all probability it too will be contained by experience and thus contaminated just as it has been before. The greater terror, however, is that the "rainbow" itself, while apparently new in its radiant beauty, may not be even a new identity of elusive quality but merely one more delusion grounded in the shallow pleasure of a two-dimensional painting. Once again, Kees finds himself turned back upon himself, just as he did in the Robinson poems.

It is this insistent turning back upon itself of the poem (and the poet) that crushes the faint hope of the self-protecting solipsism such as that found in "The Turtle." In this poem, probably written in the late 1940's, Kees seems to cling to a hope that serene detachment can shelter him from his excavations of despair. As he watches a turtle "beside the road," he is also aware of the "smells/ Of autumn closing in." His sense of dormancy, decay, and death, however, are not merely those associated with seasonal change, for there is little that would foreshadow rebirth in spring. The ominous smells are qualified by the din of "night traffic roaring by" on the superhighway that marks a civilization moving too fast to keep up with itself. His inner response is to feel "a husk . . . inside me, torpid, dry," like stale air "from a long-closed room" that "drifts through an opening door" into a tentative, fragile freedom from the indifferent rush of the world. His hope, at best, is to move "as a turtle moves/ Into the covering grass"; that is, Kees seeks a Whitman-like union with the earth that offers little distinction between life and death. The tenuous, plodding movement away from both the psychological turmoil and the speeding reality of "night traffic" is a denial both of the artifacts of civilization and of the human beings who have allowed such disintegration to occur. That denial undermines even an illusion of hope, for it implies the further denial of one's own life and art.

The slow retreat of the hard-shelled self seen in "The Turtle" into a place "far in the woods, at night" could not be sustained when the creature and its creations began to consume themselves. Kees fell prey to his own methods and convictions, for they carried him to a point of moral dilemma beyond which he could not return. His only choice, then, would seem to have been either the ultimate denial of suicide, or a purgative flight from the self-entangled surfaces to a possibility of a new identity. Many suicides by American poets seem ironically to have confirmed their stature in a world that they rejected. The very ambiguity of Kees's disappearance withholds the rather twisted fascination of the "poet and his suicide" from the shallowness of a society that he denied. Kees's art contains the prophecy that art must move beyond itself to some form of pure action. That was to mean for Kees that he would leave his readers with a mystery that would "cleanse/ What ever it is that a wound remembers/ After the healing ends."

Michael Loudon

Other major works

SHORT FICTION: *Best Short Stories of 1941*, 1941 (Edward J. O'Brien, editor; contains twenty of Kees's stories).

PLAY: *The Waiting Room*, unpublished.

NONFICTION: *Nonverbal Communication: Notes on the Visual Perception of Human Relations*, 1956 (with Jurgen Ruesch; includes photographs by Kees).

Bibliography

Elledge, Jim. *Weldon Kees: A Critical Introduction*. Metuchen, N.J.: Scarecrow Press, 1985. The first book-length study of Kees's work, this volume collects nearly fifty essays and reviews—all of the important criticism published before 1985. Eleven previously "lost" poems, a bibliographic checklist, and an index to Kees's works are also included.

Knoll, Robert E., ed. "The New York Intellectuals, 1941-1950: Some Letters by Weldon Kees." *Hudson Review* 38 (Spring, 1985): 15-55. After a brief biography, Knoll quotes and comments on some of Kees's correspondence from the 1940's. This focused collection of letters provides a fascinating glimpse of intellectual society at the time.

_____. *Weldon Kees and the Midcentury Generation: Letters, 1935-1955*. Lincoln: University of Nebraska Press, 1986. Consists mostly of extracts from letters written by Kees and contains lengthy and useful commentaries by the editor. Begins with a chapter on Kees's early life and goes on to assemble a satisfying biography of the poet/musician/filmmaker from his letters. Includes more than thirty illustrations.

Nelson, Raymond. "The Fitful Life of Weldon Kees." *American Literary History* 1 (Winter, 1989): 816-852. This brief but informative biographical essay shows the similarities between Kees's life and death and those of his unhappy contemporaries John Berryman, Randall Jarrell, Robert Lowell, and Delmore Schwartz. The essay is sensitive to Kees's dreams and failures, and appreciative of his successes.

Nemerov, Howard. "On Weldon Kees: An Introduction to His Critical Writings." *The Prairie Schooner* 61 (Winter, 1987): 33-36. This is a personal reminiscence and evaluation by a man who was a close friend and correspondent of Kees during the 1940's. Nemerov is pleased that Kees's poetry has received such high acclaim and makes a case for further study and appreciation of his critical essays and reviews.

Smith, William Jay. "A Rendezvous with Robinson." *Sequoia*, Spring, 1979, 9-11. This brief reminiscence describes Kees's generosity and encouragement toward Smith when both were young writers in the 1940's. Smith's article is one of several in this special issue of *Sequoia*, which addressed the question "Is Weldon Kees America's Greatest Forgotten Poet?"

ROBERT KELLY

Born: Brooklyn, New York; September 24, 1935

Principal poetry

Armed Descent, 1961; *Her Body Against Time*, 1963; *A Joining: A Sequence for H. D.*, 1967; *Twenty Poems*, 1967; *Axon Dendron Tree*, 1967; *Finding the Measure*, 1968; *Songs I-XXX*, 1968; *Sonnets*, 1968; *The Common Shore, Books I-V: A Long Poem About America in Time*, 1969; *Kali Yuga*, 1970; *Flesh, Dream, Book*, 1971; *Ralegh*, 1972; *The Pastorals*, 1972; *The Mill of Particulars*, 1973; *The Loom*, 1975; *The Lady of*, 1977; *The Convections*, 1978; *The Book of Persephone*, 1978; *The Cruise of the Pnyx*, 1979; *Kill the Messenger Who Brings Bad News*, 1979; *Spiritual Exercises*, 1981; *The Alchemist to Mercury*, 1981; *Under Words*, 1983; *Not This Island Music*, 1987; *The Flowers of Unceasing Coincidence*, 1988; *Oahu*, 1988.

Other literary forms

Although Robert Kelly is known primarily for his poetry, it is his fiction that has generated the most enthusiastic reviews. The fiction consists of one novel, *The Scorpions* (1967), a fanciful travelogue, *Cities* (1971), and two collections of stories, *A Transparent Tree* (1985) and *Doctor of Silence* (1988). Kelly has consented to more than half a dozen published interviews, has written prefaces for eight books by other authors, and has contributed occasional statements on film, poetry, and related topics to numerous periodicals since the early 1960's. One collection of such writings was published in 1971, *In Time*, and this book has taken its place as the most significant summation of Kelly's poetics.

Achievements

Kelly has written and published abundantly since his first book appeared in 1961. Recognized at once as one of the most gifted poets of his generation, he has subsequently lived up to his potential by deviating from his original promise over and over again. The first twenty-five years of Kelly's career saw the publication of more than three thousand pages of poetry and nearly one thousand pages of prose. What is remarkable is the consistency of the work and the variety of its forms. It seems certain that Kelly's contribution to the long poem will itself command respect for some time to come. At the same time, he is an adroit miniaturist, a most elegant prose stylist, and a discerning commentator on the work of other poets.

Kelly's prolific body of work is predicated on the fundamental commitment to poetry as a grand project, shared among all of its practitioners. His work is keenly motivated by a sense of poetry as a monumental structure, like a cathedral, arising through centuries of sustained craftsmanship—involving generations and entire communities. The sense of the poem as an addressing of communal concerns is evident throughout Kelly's collections.

On a more private level, Kelly's work is of considerable interest as the daily registration of poetry as process. Because there has been no slackening of energy as the decades have gone by, Kelly's poetry is an invaluable testimony to a demystification of the Romantic legacy of inspiration and divine election. The Kelly poem is a distinct engagement with vision and plenitude as daily obligations. Failure is as inextricably written into the work as success, given the improvisatory legacy of sheer dailiness as a modus operandi.

As several critics noted in a special issue of *Vort* devoted to Kelly in 1974, he is possessed by a rare gift of prosody. This has helped make even his minor efforts seem virtuous in comparison with the preponderance of bad habits prevalent in contemporary free-verse practice. This is all the more astonishing considering Kelly's staggering productivity. The size of his oeuvre has, almost from the beginning, kept his work from being as widely read as that of some of his parsimonious contemporaries. Read even in patches, however, it leaves a lasting impression of energy and eloquence, colloquial ease, and formal grace—a combination rare in the poetry of any period.

Biography

Robert Kelly was born and reared in Brooklyn, in a stimulating urban environment that nourished much of his early poetry. Quite precocious, Kelly entered the City College of New York at age fifteen and entered Columbia at nineteen as a graduate student of medieval studies. The stability of his life as a professor at Bard College since 1962 has afforded Kelly a reliability of circumstance to devote himself to poetry on a prodigious scale. Furthermore, the professorial role at a small college has meant that his daunting intellectual fortitude has been at the service of his poetry rather than diverted into formal scholarship as such.

At the beginning of his career, in the late 1950's and early 1960's, Kelly was associated with a circle of poets that included Paul Blackburn, David Antin, Jerome Rothenberg, Armand Schwerner, George Economou, Diane Wakoski, and Clayton Eshleman. Kelly and Rothenberg in particular rose to some prominence as exponents of "deep image," a short-lived but effective stance for young unknown poets to take, insofar as their manifestos commanded respect and their poetry was taken to be a rich demonstration of the theory. Kelly edited two ephemeral magazines in the early 1960's—*Trobar* and *Matter*—which helped establish him as a proponent of the free-verse line of poetry indebted to Charles Olson, Robert Duncan, and Louis Zukofsky among then-living masters.

From 1967 to 1973, Kelly served as associate editor for Clayton Eshleman's widely influential magazine *Caterpillar.* Kelly's involvement ensured that such contemporaries as Kenneth Irby and Gerrit Lansing were regularly featured in the magazine, as well as students and young protégés such as Thomas Meyer, Charles Stein, Richard Grossinger, Harvey Bialy, and Bruce McClelland. This was a period of extraordinary productivity for Kelly himself, making *Caterpillar* a showcase for his many forays into the long poem, culminating in the magazine's final issues with glimpses of the masterwork *The Loom.*

The demise of *Caterpillar* marked the end of a certain burgeoning of public poetry in the United States, not only for Kelly but also for his generation. Kelly subsequently became more involved at Bard College on administrative levels, continuing to teach but also becoming director of the writing program of the Avery Graduate School of the Arts. Kelly has been a recipient of a fellowship from the National Endowment of the Arts. His collection *Kill the Messenger Who Brings Bad News* was awarded the first annual prize in poetry at the Los Angeles Times Book Awards in 1980. In 1981, his archives were acquired by the Poetry/Rare Books Collection of the University Libraries, State University of New York at Buffalo.

Analysis

Robert Kelly's first book, *Armed Descent*, showed some indebtedness to Ezra Pound's balance of line, presentation of a numinous world through direct images, and rhythmically modulated musicality. Most striking, however, was not the debt but the originality and the confidence. It was a sensuous poetry, a demonstration of Kelly's proclamation that the fundamental rhythm of a poem was the rhythm of images. Each poem contended in its own way for the proposition that visible realities be read as spiritual clarities. The spirit made flesh was the manifest mystery, but there was a practical injunction as well: "The gateway is the visible; but we must go in."

Kelly's imaginistic skills might have easily been directed toward the production of autonomous free association. It was within his means to become a giant among American surrealist poets. He was engaged in a quest which could not rest comfortably on surfaces, however, nor reside in a simple succession of images. In his 1968 retrospective pamphlet *Statement*, Kelly stressed that the significant term in "deep image" had been the word *deep*: it was depth that was striven for in poems. Images were simply material agencies and were to be regarded as cues, clues, tangible signs of spiritual intensity.

The sense of depth, in conjunction with the concept of the image, led Kelly to postulate a location "behind the brain" where human lives as experienced through sense and image are "slain/ minute by minute." The Catholicism of Kelly's childhood has persisted in his poetry in the form of guiding images. This epiphany of "the place of the death of Images" is, suitably, from the poem "In Commentary on the Gospel According to Thomas" (in *The Alchemist to Mercury*), and it should be noted that the epigraphs to *Armed*

Descent are also drawn from that apocryphal gospel. Kelly was fascinated with the image as something that is born or appears (is a *phenomenon*, from the Greek word for "to appear," *phaino*), dies or lapses, and then reappears or is resurrected. Kelly's Christian roots go deep in this image cycle, of which Christ and the grail chalice that holds his life's blood are the sustaining images. Kelly's is a patently antiauthoritarian Christian vision, however, informed by pagan rites, gnostic and neoplatonist philosophy, heretical sects, and alchemy.

The sense of depth for which Kelly was striving in his early poetry soon became associated with what he called "The Dream Work" (in *In Time*). By linking the production of images in a poem with that productive energy of the dream world, Kelly was able to ground his poetics in a mode of psychic creation going on all the time. This certainly facilitated his orientation to poetry as daily practice. Unlike such previous poetics as that of the French Surrealists, who were fascinated with dream imagery, Kelly's was concerned with drawing psychic energy from the depths from which dreams speak, *not* using the poem as a means of reporting on or approximating dream states. Kelly's success is most evident in the narrative passages of *The Loom*, where such dreamlike images as the detached skull or a notch of coffin-shaped sunlight seen through a keyhole become the stimulus for meditations which are somnambulistic yet acutely conscious at the same time.

Given Kelly's training as a medieval scholar, it is no surprise that his poems evoke the world of the books of hours, the body as a zone of astrological inscriptions and humours, and the spirit as a vehicle for ascent through the plectrum of the harmoniously organized stars and planets. "Finding the measure" (the title of his most acclaimed book), in its literal sense, refers to the process of modulating the rhythms of attention to the shape of the language in its shapely apparition as a poem. Finding the measure for Kelly has all the force of a cosmological prescription as well: "Finding the measure is finding the/ specific music of the hour,/ the synchronous/ consequence of the motion of the whole world." At this level, finding the measure is a mode of tuning or attunement, a means of "keeping in touch" with a cosmos that is intimate (a microcosm) despite its infinitude (a macrocosm). "In the burgeoning optimism of unlimited desire, I reach out for universal intimacy" wrote Kelly in "An Alchemical Journal" (in *The Alchemist to Mercury*). In various ways, the poety has clearly manifested such unlimited desire in the forms of both sacred and profane yearning. Much of the best work of the late 1960's and early 1970's chronicles this reaching out for universal intimacy in the images provided by alchemy.

Because alchemy is a lapsed language of science, there have been complaints of esotericism directed at Kelly. It is true that much of the work of *Songs I-XXX* and *Flesh, Dream, Book* is densely allusive. Some simple reminders, however, are in order. Kelly's skills as an image maker have always been prodigious. Even the poems most saturated with arcane lore are guided by the familiar Christian cycle of personal redemption. For Kelly, alchemy was of use in clarifying the concept of the grail. Alchemy was an allegorical presentation of quest motifs intrinsic to the grail legend; in fact, the fundamental concept in alchemy is that of the *vessel*.

In Kelly's work, the experience of being *embodied*—being subjected to growth and decay—is the essence of the alchemical work. The body is the vessel, and the experience is oracular: "Every orifice is a sybil's cave." Every vessel is a chalice or grail, a body that fills, overflows, spills, and is emptied out. This is the cycle of redemption written into Kelly's work from his earliest long poem "The Exchanges" (in *The Alchemist to Mercury*) to "The Emptying" (in *Spiritual Exercises*), passing through such large mediating epiphanies as "Arnolfini's Wedding" and "The World" in *The Mill of Particulars* and *The Loom*.

There are not so much difficulties in Kelly's work as there are mysteries, because Mystery is at the heart of it. Kelly's is the *mysterium tremendum* of sanctity and grace; his single most abiding theme (and the most exacting single pronouncement of his poetics) is the "nonstop imagery of making love salvation." It is Christian in its overall motivation, while allowing for the nonstop profanity of image-making and of "making love." In one of his poems, in fact, Kelly toys with the notion that images are to the eyes what sex is to the body. Both are engaged in a quest for depth, an inkling of that place where images and bodily energies are quelled.

It seems plausible that, in the long run, Kelly's most acclaimed book will be the four-hundred-page poem *The Loom*. This poem oscillates between meditations and narrative, coiling images and insights around the slender axis of the very short line, often consisting of only three or four words. In *The Loom*, Kelly has not so much found his measure as returned to it, in that one of his most compelling early poems was the short-lined, book-length *Axon Dendron Tree*. *The Loom* is a book in which all Kelly's obsessions (sex, death, pain, revelation, transfiguration) are ceaselessly recycled toward a resolution of metabolism, a quieting in which a "sacred language" can be "known best/ when you're hardly listening." Readers of *The Loom*, in fact, can come to know the specific cycle of the alchemical Great Work through the poem, for it duplicates the prescribed stages of alchemical transmutation of base metal into gold without drawing any attention to this as such. The reader not privy to alchemical lore can be satisfied by *The Loom* without even knowing that an immense catalog of occult data is circulating through the text, in the form of narratives and precise images, all of which seem "natural" and not imposed. This is a singular achievement, to transmit secret information in the form of a transparent, lucid text which can be comprehended on an initial (aesthetic, psychological, and philosophic) level without reference to the underlying allegory.

Kelly's work enacts a quest for attaining spiritual intensities in the world of physical forms and forces. It is continually resourceful at generating images that aid the contemplation of this enduring contradiction. The reader's gratitude and perplexity are registered in the image of the poet going into a hardware store to buy a pair of needle-nosed pliers and spark plugs, "as if I were a man on earth": One is moved or unsettled or both, according to one's lights, by the stubborn grace of Kelly's *as if.*

Jed Rasula

Other major works
LONG FICTION: *The Scorpions,* 1967; *Cities,* 1971.
SHORT FICTION: *A Transparent Tree,* 1985; *Doctor of Silence,* 1988.
NONFICTION: *In Time,* 1971.

Bibliography
Barne, Dennis. "Nothing but Doors: An Interview with Robert Kelly." *Credences,* n.s. 3 (Fall, 1985): 100-122. This interview focuses on Kelly's involvement with the periodicals *Chelsea, Trobar,* and *Maller.* Kelly comments on many of his contemporaries, their work, and the influences that shaped his own verse and thought. Gives a good portrait of the poet's career and personality.
Ossman, David. *The Sullen Art.* New York: Corinth Books, 1963. This collection contains a conversation with Robert Kelly covering his notions on what poetry is and how it works. Kelly is approached from his position as editor of the poetry magazine *Trobar* discussing other poets, but for the most part, the interview focuses on his thoughts regarding his own work in relation to his contemporaries. A very interesting interview.
Rasula, Jed. "Robert Kelly: A Checklist." *Credences,* n.s. 3 (Spring, 1984): 91-124. Books, pamphlets, broadsides, separate publications, and contributions to books and periodicals make up this list. An excellent source showing the considerable extent of Kelly's output.
_____. "Ten Different Fruits on One Different Tree: Reading Robert Kelly." *Credences,* n.s. 3 (Spring, 1984): 127-175. A review of Kelly's career and a publishing history that sorts through and presents the scope of the poet's works. Helpful parts of this guide are a list of select poems to introduce the novice to Kelly's verse, a discussion and chronology of the longer poems, analyses of several books (*Finding the Measure, The Loom*), and a look at Kelly's craft as a formalist.
Vort 5 (1974). This special issue periodical dedicated to Kelly predates the publication of *The Loom.* Contains critical appraisals and personal tributes to Kelly.

X. J. KENNEDY

Born: Dover, New Jersey; August 21, 1929

Principal poetry

Nude Descending a Staircase, 1961; *Growing into Love,* 1969; *Bulsh,* 1970; *Breaking and Entering,* 1971; *Emily Dickinson in Southern California,* 1974; *Celebrations After the Death of John Brennan,* 1974; *Three Tenors, One Vehicle,* 1975 (song lyrics in sections by Kennedy, James Camp, and Keith Waldrop); *One Winter Night in August and Other Nonsense Jingles,* 1975 (juvenile); *The Phantom Ice Cream Man: More Nonsense Verse,* 1979 (juvenile); *Did Adam Name the Vinegarroon?,* 1982 (juvenile); *French Leave: Translations,* 1983; *Hangover Mass,* 1984; *The Forgetful Wishing Well: Poems for Young People,* 1985 (juvenile); *Cross Ties: Selected Poems,* 1985; *Brats,* 1986 (juvenile); *Ghastlies, Goops and Pincushions,* 1989 (juvenile); *Fresh Brats,* 1990.

Other literary forms

Although X. J. Kennedy is best known for his poetry, he has also written reviews, several highly successful textbooks, and one novel for children, *The Owlstone Crown* (1983). Kennedy established himself as a witty and discriminating judge of contemporary poetry through a series of book reviews published in *Poetry* magazine from 1961 through 1966. The lively and lucid style developed in these essays played an important part in the success of his various textbooks and anthologies, which include *Mark Twain's Frontier* (1963, edited with James Camp), *An Introduction to Poetry* (1966, 1982, 1990), *Pegasus Descending: A Book of the Best Bad Verse* (1971, edited with James Camp and Keith Waldrop), *Messages: A Thematic Anthology of Poetry* (1973), *An Introduction to Fiction* (1976, 1979, 1987), *Literature* (1976, 1979, 1987), *Tygers of Wrath: poems of hate, anger and invective* (1981), and *The Bedford Reader* (1982, edited with Dorothy Kennedy).

Achievements

Kennedy's literary reputation rests almost exclusively on four volumes of poetry: *Nude Descending a Staircase, Growing into Love, Emily Dickinson in Southern California,* and *Cross Ties.* Of his other published volumes, *Bulsh* has been unpopular and difficult to find in libraries; the title poem (reprinted in *Breaking and Entering*) is an entertaining but unimportant satire skewering a modern pretender to sainthood. Most of the poems in *Breaking and Entering* are reprinted from Kennedy's other volumes. *Celebrations After the Death of John Brennan* is a series of memorial verses inspired by the death of one of Kennedy's former students; it was published in a very limited edition. *Three Tenors, One Vehicle* includes only a few song lyrics by Kennedy, most of which are available in his major collections.

The remaining volumes are intended for children. Over the years, Kennedy has always remained interested in the challenge of composition for an audience that demands nothing more than clarity, wit, and fun. Indeed, he once described children's verse as a form of escape for poets "suffering psychic hangovers from excess doses of Kierkegaard and Freud" and longing to return to "a cosmos where what matters is whether a rabbit can find its red balloon again." Although Kennedy has written a juvenile novel (*The Owlstone Crown*) and several volumes of children's verse, his literary achievement is measured largely in terms of his serious poetry. The poems in *Nude Descending a Staircase* won for him both the Lamont Award from the Academy of American Poets and the Bess Hokin Prize from *Poetry* magazine. The publication of *Growing into Love* brought him the Shelley Memorial Award for 1970; and *Emily Dickinson in Southern California* and *Celebrations After the Death of John Brennan* in 1974 brought the Golden Rose from the New England Poetry Club. He has been a Bread Loaf Fellow in poetry (1960), a winner of a National Council on the Arts grant (1967-1968), and a Guggenheim Fellow (1973-1974).

Although Kennedy is often dismissed as a witty minor poet—a self-described "whittler of little boats in bottles"—he may in time be awarded higher stature. He has published sparingly and slowly. More prolific contemporary poets naturally tend to attract more frequent attention and thus are more likely to attain a loftier status in the hierarchy of living poets. Kennedy's verse, however, is of astonishing technical proficiency. Most likely, a large percentage of the poems in his volumes will withstand the test of time. Indeed, they have had to wear well before Kennedy himself would consent to their publication in book form; their appeal to other readers is demonstrated by their frequent inclusion in anthologies.

Kennedy has lived by his "Prayer to an Angry God" that in rereading his own words he should "Not spare,/ But smite." If there is justice in heaven or value in such textbook advice, he should eventually reap his reward.

Biography

The only child of a Roman Catholic father and a Methodist mother, Joseph Charles Kennedy (who later assumed the nom de plume X. J. Kennedy) must have sensed early in childhood the atmosphere of spiritual tension and uncertainty that is the most distinguishing and thought-provoking aspect of his poetry. A probable self-portrait of the youthful Kennedy occurs in "Poets," a brilliant and ironic sketch of the sensitive, dithering, bespectacled youths who, like stupid swans trapped in ice, can sometimes be freed to soar in dazzling glory. When only twelve, Kennedy published mimeographed science-fiction fan magazines entitled *Vampire* and *Terrifying Test-Tube Tales.*

He was graduated from Seton Hall University (1950) and took a master's degree from Columbia University (1951) before enlisting in the Navy. After his tour of duty, he spent a year studying in Paris, where he received a *certificat* in 1956. From 1956 to 1962 he pursued doctoral studies at the University of Michigan and came into contact with an elite coterie of young poets from the Detroit-Ann Arbor area. Among his friends of the period were Keith Waldrop, James Camp, Donald Hall, John Frederick Nims, and W. D. Snodgrass. He left Ann Arbor without completing work for his degree, spent one year teaching at the Woman's College of the University of North Carolina, and then joined the faculty of Tufts University, where he eventually rose to be a full professor. In 1979 he left Tufts and became a free-lance writer.

From 1961 to 1964 Kennedy was the poetry editor of the *Paris Review*. In 1971 he and his wife founded *Counter/Measures, a Magazine of Rime, Meter, and Song*, to counter the trend toward poetry in "open forms"—the kind of free verse that Kennedy has satirically described as "Disposable stuff, word-Kleenex." The last issue of the magazine appeared in 1974, and Kennedy's later verse has itself occasionally been written in open forms.

Analysis

During a memorable exchange of opinions in the *Saturday Review*, John Ciardi insisted to X. J. Kennedy that poets writing in traditional forms strive to create artifacts for posterity and must therefore believe that there *will be* some posterity. In contrast, those writing casual, formless free verse "reject the idea of the artifact" as the result of a belief "that there is no world to follow, or none worth addressing." Kennedy disagreed. Not only did he contend that a poet such as Gary Snyder, who writes in open forms, manifestly believes in an Oriental concept of human continuity, but he also argued that the effort to create a permanent artifact in traditional poetic form does not necessarily imply a belief in any posterity to enjoy that artifact. Instead, he insisted that, "Even if it all goes blooey tomorrow, the act of trying to write a poem as well as possible is a good way of living until then."

The exchange illuminates the ethical as well as the artistic views of X. J. Kennedy. Recognizing the unsettling changes in art and life, and looking ruefully upon the weakening social and literary conventions, Kennedy continually seeks to resolve the tension between the traditional and the trendy, reactionary and radical. Through the course of his three major books of poetry, his world view shifts from a militant traditionalism (implying belief in God, in ever-renewing life, and in conventional verse forms) into a tolerant uncertainty. His recent poems display a lack of faith in traditional values, combined with a lack of trust in the new. Thus, he seems to stand on shifting ground, offering brilliant satirical insights into the modern world, but little advice about how best to live in that world. Indeed, he no longer seems as certain as he once was that traditional values offer "a good way of living until then."

A number of poems in Kennedy's first book, *Nude Descending a Staircase*, express his belief that the time is out of joint. In its very title, for example, "B Negative" suggests the dehumanizing effect of modern urban life. The poem's protagonist is given no name. Instead, he is identified only by his blood type and by an abbreviated description of his characteristics: "M/ 60/ 5 FT. 4/ W PROT." His monologue depicts the sterile environment of the city, where he discovers that it is spring by the increased litter of coughdrop boxes and "underthings cast off," rather than by daisies in the grass. Spring makes little mark on the city, "No bud from branches of concrete." The city is an unnatural, artificial place where pigeons too fat to stand peck shoelaces and eat sacks of corn as if they "grew on a stalk." It is a place so costly that grown men sleep on subways "tucked in funny sheets" taken from the daily newspaper. It is so dense that the sun cannot penetrate to the street level, and so frigid that spring has no "abiding heat." Here a man's virility can wither to impotence after years pronging litter, or shabbily sustained through steamy musings over the gaudy pages of a movie magazine. In the city the seasons have scant significance, and human life, stripped of its own seasonal qualities, becomes scanty too. The city blocks and cubic rooms create human integers that "wake one day to find [themselves] abstract." In cementing over human roots and rhythms, modern urban life generates abnormal beings who become either suicidal or sadistic.

The poem's diction and imagery are especially effective in suggesting the violence inherent in city surroundings. The daisies, for example, are described as "white eyeballs in the grass." The pick with which the speaker prongs litter is called a "stabpole." The subway riders are observed by "guards." The radio is turned off with a "squawk as if your hand/ Had shut some human windpipe with a twist." In this menacing environment the "routed spirit flees" or looks around "for a foothold—in despair." What comfort life is capable of offering lingers only as a memory of the past. In lines futilely addressed to a lost lover, the speaker laments that he can no longer remember "the twist that brought me to your street," nor can he summon up her face or recall her "outline on the sheet." At least for this speaker, the warmth of the past is irretrievable and the future offers only an increasingly frigid isolation.

Elsewhere in this first book of verse, however, Kennedy is confident that survival and sanity can be maintained in the changing modern world. Procreation can assure survival and continuity between past and future, while religion can provide the same sort of guidelines for a sane life that the rules of rhyme and meter provide for a sane poetry. Thus, after surveying various signs of foreboding (slips in the hangman's knot and the price of stocks, movement of mountains, proliferating madness), the poem "All-Knowing Rabbit" concludes with consolation. The rabbit, who eats voraciously to feed the offspring growing in her womb, smugly ponders "All secrets of tomorrow, of the Nile . . . And munches on, with giaconda smile." The rabbit, the Nile, and the giaconda smile are symbols of fecundity. At this stage in his career, it does not occur to Kennedy that exceptional fertility is itself one of the dangers of the mad world he inhabits. Furthermore, in this book Kennedy perceives only dimly the chinks in the armor of conventional religious faith. His poem "In Faith of Rising" sounds more like Gerard Manley Hopkins or George Herbert than the work of a man reared in an era when one catchphrase was, "God is dead." Kennedy's poem is a pious statement of trust that after death God will "cast down again/ Or recollect my dust."

The confident reverence of "In Faith of Rising" is, however, atypical even in Kennedy's early poetry. "First Confession" is much more representative of his general approach, in both content and style. The first confession inspires awe in the child who perceives the priest as a "robed repositor of truth," burns in his guilt while awaiting penance, and later kneels to take communion in "seraphic light." From the more experienced retrospective of the adult, however, the events take on comic overtones. He sees ludicrous elements coexisting with sanctity. The child "scuffed,/ Steps stubborn" to the confessional. His list of sins included the "sip snitched" from his father's beer and a bribe paid his girl friend to pull down her pants. He zealously said his penance twice to "double-scrub" his soul.

Kennedy emphasizes the disjunction between the holy and the humorous by deliberate incongruity in his choice of words. Formal language exuding a dusty odor of sanctity mingles with the stale stench of street speech. The "curtained portal," the "robed repositor of truth," and the dignified priest's "cratered dome" are somewhat sullied by contact with a diminutive sinner who snitches from his "old man's beer" and who bribes his girl "to pee." The priest himself becomes the object of mirth when he doles out penance "as one feeds birds." Even the sacrament of communion is trivialized at the end when the child sticks out his tongue at the priest: "A fresh roost for the Holy Ghost."

The mood that unfolds through "First Confession" is less skeptical than satirical. Modern humans—both priest and penitant—seem out of place within the ancient traditions of the Roman Catholic Church, just as the poem's use of contemporary slang seems to desecrate its setting. This sense of disjunction, of times out of joint, is characteristic of Kennedy's subsequent poetry.

By the time *Growing into Love* appeared in 1969, Kennedy's faith in the traditions of Roman Catholicism had weakened to the point where he could write in "West Somerville, Mass.": "My faith copped out. Who was it pulled that heist?" Here again one sees the bizarre verbal incongruity that had characterized "First Confession," but Kennedy has moved from satire of tottering traditions to outright skepticism and agnosticism. Nevertheless, he clearly feels a loss in abandoning his faith. A number of poems in the volume show his longing for the solidity of the past and his loathing of the impermanence of the present.

In "Cross Ties," for example, the speaker, walking along a railroad track "where nothing travels now but rust and grass," says, "I could take stock in something . . . Bearing down Hell-bent from behind my back." Figuratively, the speaker's situation is also Kennedy's. Uncomfortable in the present, Kennedy walks a track deserted by others. His poems rhyme and scan and he is predisposed toward tradition. In one sense, then, the speaker, like Kennedy, longs for a return to the past when trains served functions now taken over by semitrucks, superhighways, and motels. Both Kennedy and the speaker also long to believe in their lost religious faith with its freight of forces for good and evil. The speaker hears this phantom train's whistle in the "curfew's wail," sees its headbeam in the full moon, and hears the screech of "steel wrenched taut till severed" (the train's brakes?) in the hawk's cry. He explains the fact that no Hell-bent force strikes him down by hypothesizing that he is "Out of reach/ Or else beneath desiring," and he concludes by observing that when he spills the salt he throws some to the devil and he still allows the priest to bless his child.

The superficial appearance of faith in God and Satan is undercut, however, by closer analysis. The speaker begins by saying that he "could take stock in" this malign force. A statement beginning "I could take stock in . . ." normally continues with a conditional clause: for example, "I could take stock in purple people-eaters if someone could show me their lairs." The absence of the expected conditional clause implies that the speaker cannot state the conditions that must be met before he really *believes*. Moreover, it is clear that the speaker willfully imagines the malign force behind his back. He knows that the tracks are deserted, and he knows too that the curfew's wail, the moon's headbeam, and the hawk's cry are wholly natural phenomena. He uses these aspects of everyday reality in an attempt to scare himself into a faith in Satanic evil, for if there is a devil to fear there must also be a deity to love. He is, however, unsuccessful. As he walks along, "tensed for a leap" and trying to imagine some evil behind him, he declares himself "unreconciled/ To a dark void all kindness." This neatly ambiguous phrase could mean that he is unreconciled to an indifferent universe, a malign universe, or a Godless universe, but, whatever it means, it falls far short of positive faith in God. It is a phrase, then, that hedges its bets just as the speaker does with a pinch of salt and a mist of holy water.

The poem's title, "Cross Ties," has a similar multiplicity of meanings. In a naturalistic sense, the poem is about walking on railroad ties, and the title reflects that subject. Yet the poet's central interest is in the ties of emotion between the longing for the past years when engines rode the tracks and the longing for the faith in God that typified those years. Indeed, the poem's title, by suggesting the form of the crucifix, itself links the literal, historical, and religious implications of the poem.

Kennedy's consciousness of the disjunction caused by changes in the modern world finds expression in several poems in *Growing into Love* that deal with the American landscape. In "Main Road West," the television set in a motel room suddenly goes dead, and the speaker, left with "No magazines, no book but the Good Book," is forced to observe and reflect. He finds himself in a denatured environment. Although trees with leaves are few and "The wind's turned off," a sign for used cars burns brightly, keeping out the starlight, "As though stars will be foresworn, or stared down." Thus, the traveler sees that natural resources are being displaced by mechanical artifice.

"Driving Cross-country" makes the parallel point that imaginative resources are also being destroyed through mass-produced mediocrity. The poem begins with a series of baffling and discontinuous allusions to twentieth century counterparts of fairy-tale figures (Jack the Giant-killer, Cinderella, Sleeping Beauty). Collectively, these allusions illustrate how meager is the spirit of the present in comparison with the traditional legends of the past. The Jack the Giant-killers of today sing to cornstalks in Keokuk, and contemporary Cinderellas (with names like Ella Ashhauler) try to scrounge free meals in the Stoplight Lounge. The only magic of the age is that which has filled the nation with identical motel rooms—each deloused and designed by computer to offend no one. Victims of "Some hag's black broth," Americans hurtle down endless highways knowing that "We had a home. It was somewhere./ We were there once upon a time."

In these poems, as in "Cross Ties," there is a longing for a return to a better past—where nature reigned unchained and where natural man indulged in fantasy and belief. Similar points are made in "Peace and Plenty." Pine-clad hills lie stunned and bound by chains of motels; the river is so choked with debris that it cannot choose its course; the new-fallen snow must "Lay bare her body to the Presto-Blo"; and the blown rose finds her "quietus . . . inside the in-sink waste-disposer." By personifying and feminizing the hills, river, snow, and rose, Kennedy creates an image of nature ravished by the vile artificial constructions of man—the motels, engines, chemical wastes, snowblowers, and disposals.

Kennedy's rejection of mechanized and plasticized society is, however, refreshingly apolitical and unpredictable. In 1961, in apparent reaction to the space flights of Yuri Gagarin and Alan Shepard, Kennedy published "The Man in the Manmade Moon," a scathing satire on space flight and those who seek to promote it. Yet by 1969 his views had begun to change. In "Space," he reflects on man's increasing power over nature, a power bemoaned in "Main Road West," "Driving Cross-country," and "Peace and Plenty." He finds that the ability to escape from earth and let the unweighted heart beat freely has appeal, and the whole process of sending massive projectiles careening through the heavens at the flick of a switch makes Kennedy wonder what life will be like after this power spreads and increases: "Who will need long to savor his desire . . . when acts, once dreamt, transpire?" Will man return to the womb? Indeed, is the fetal crouch of the astronauts on takeoff and the fixation with landing on the moon (a traditional symbol of femininity) a disguised attempt to return to the womb? Kennedy explores these questions with sensitivity. Ultimately, he finds that he shares the same desires for escape that have moved men with slide rules to "Render our lusts and madnesses concrete." In a bar or at the wheel of a car, he too attempts to "shrug the world's dull weight" and is surprised to find himself, "Out after what I had long thought I'd hate."

Similarly, in "The Medium Is the Message" Kennedy contemplates the music-oriented youth of America, "transistors at their brains,/ Steps locked to rock." He concludes that "The rude beast slouches"—that Yeats's second coming is at hand and that "words in lines" will soon be obsolete. The modern age rejects the traditional iambic rhythms of the heart and insists instead on a rock music that beats to the "rush-hour traffic's fits and starts." So much is vintage Kennedy—rejecting contemporary changes in favor of the traditional past—but he surprises the reader when he admits that he would drop out only if he could pack along his own high-technology conveniences: "my hi-fi set,/ Electric light, a crate of books, canned beer. . . ."

Kennedy continues to explore his sense of disjunction between past values and present vicissitudes in *Emily Dickinson in Southern California* (1974), but the acute sense of impending disaster that had prompted earlier allusions to Yeats's "The Second Coming" is here replaced by his bemused transplantation of Emily Dickinson into Southern California. Although the title series of poems, like so much of Kennedy's verse, develops in part through incongruity, here the incongruities are more amusing than upsetting. The whole idea of observing the laid-back, let-it-all-hang-out California scene from the perspective of a wry and reclusive nineteenth century spinster is itself incongruous and delightful. Unfortunately, Kennedy does relatively little with this idea. Seven of the nine poems in the series are simple imitations of Dickinson's style and make no effort to force her approach into a confrontation with the modern world.

Kennedy's "Two Views of Rime and Meter" are written in free verse, a form that Kennedy rarely used in his earlier volumes. The first poem compares meter with the repetitious thud of a carpetbeater, and rhyme with the glittering dust. The second compares meter with the rhythm of copulation, and rhyme with the pleasure of simultaneous orgasm. The implications of the first metaphor are that meter and rhyme are monotonous, routine, and stale, while the implications of the second are that both devices are human, primal, delightful, and creative. The two views are incompatible and incongruous; as elsewhere, Kennedy's own position remains unresolved.

To the extent, however, that the debate about meter and rhyme is part of the larger debate about tradition and change, other aspects of the volume suggest Kennedy's increasing sympathy with the twentieth century. There is, for example, the fact that eight of the seventeen pieces in the volume can be classified as free verse. Furthermore, "Categories," a poem that specifically examines modern changes, concludes that one must come to understand transformations and adapt to circumstances. Although species collide, styles expire, and the century clots or collapses, man can begin to understand if "through the tip of his tongue he hear bright red." If this incongruous and paradoxical advice means anything at all, it certainly demands breaking free of perceptual limitations in the effort to grasp a new reality. Similarly, the poem's very last lines show that one must break free of the limitations of tradition. A novice Buddhist monk, "a scrubber of pots," is capable of teaching his master that, having "hatched from names" and lacking clean plates, one can "Serve cake on a shut fan." Thus, the old must learn from the young and the tradition-bound mind must hatch into a new freedom in order to adapt to difficulties.

Appropriately, the poem starts out with six lines of fairly standard iambic pentameter but becomes increasingly free from formal metrical constraints as it proceeds. If anything, this poem is even more sensitive to the rhythms and sounds of poetic language than many of Kennedy's rigorously metrical compositions. Fifteen of the poem's twenty lines can be classified as loose iambic pentameter, but Kennedy repeatedly alters the iambic rhythm to correspond with his rhetorical emphases. Thus, three of the poem's first four syllables are stressed in making the point that "Nothing stays put." An extra accented syllable is packed into the third line, making the description of the "too-close-following cars" onomatopoeic. The century's collapse through the "mind's pained hour-glass" throbs more forcefully because of the series of strong stresses, as does the need to "hear bright red." Perhaps, however, the last line of the poem is the finest example of Kennedy's liberation. Not only is the assertion that one can "Serve cake on a shut fan" an apt imagistic summary of the change in Kennedy's views and the point of the whole poem, but it is also impossible to scan. It has two stresses, two rests, and two more stresses. What could be more rhythmical and yet further from traditional meter?

This change in Kennedy's attitudes toward traditional thinking and traditional poetics was also reflected in a changed view of the American landscape. Perhaps man's creations do litter the land, but Kennedy has moved far from the depressed mood of the collector of debris in "B Negative" and the discouraged travelers of "Main Road West" and "Driving Cross-country." Now he is capable of writing a poem entitled "Salute Sweet Deceptions," in which he observes that in certain lights bare bricks turn amber, beer cans resemble stars, and raindrops clinging to telephone wires look like a "seed-pearl necklace."

In 1985 Kennedy published *Cross Ties: Selected Poems,* an ample and accurate sampler from his poetic oeuvre—though the back cover of the book is inaccurate in claiming that it includes "every poem that the poet cares to save." Kennedy explains, "That blurb was read to me over the phone for approval, one sleepy morning, and that devastating claim buzzed right on by. There are many poems I couldn't put in *Cross Ties* that I wouldn't destroy just yet, including nearly everything in the books of verse for children." Indeed, the bulk of Kennedy's verse in the 1980's was addressed to children. *Hangover Mass* 1984 was a notable exception.

Kennedy's poetic output in the 1980's demonstrates his continuing interest in standard verse forms, and a number of the poems reflect nostalgia for the past. In "Hangover Mass," for example, he reminisces about his youthful attendance at late-morning Mass with his father; in "One-Night Homecoming" he writes about a brief visit to his aging parents and his emotions as he once again lies in "childhood's bed"; and in "The Death of Professor Backwards" he writes an amusingly sentimental epitaph for a murdered vaudeville performer whose chief claim to fame was an ability to speak backwards: "Transposed perfectly them at back hurl he'd/ Out called crowd the hecklers any whatever." Could it be that this praise of the curmudgeonly Professor Backwards, written in cross-rhymed iambic pentameter, is partially motivated by Kennedy's own desire to go backwards and to cling to the old forms still? If so, this is an instance in which form is closely matched to substance and yet another indication of Kennedy's remarkable skilfulness.

Kennedy's poetry, as it always has been, is dominated by incongruity, but the intense longing for tradition has been modified by a mellow toleration of the times, and the intense commitment to meter and rhyme has been balanced by an interest in exploring the many forms of modern poetry. Kennedy once said, "Writing in rhythm and rhyme, a poet is involved in an enormous, meaningful game not under his ego's control. He is a mere mouse in the lion's den of the language—but with any luck, at times he can get the lion to come out."

Jeffrey D. Hoeper

Other major works

CHILDREN'S LITERATURE: *The Owlstone Crown*, 1983.

ANTHOLOGIES: *Pegasus Descending: A Book of the Best Bad Verse*, 1971 (with James Camp and Keith Waldrop); *Messages: A Thematic Anthology of Poetry*, 1973; *The Bedford Reader*, 1982 (with Dorothy Kennedy); *Knock at a Star: A Child's Introduction to Poetry*, 1982 (with Dorothy M. Kennedy).

MISCELLANEOUS: *Mark Twain's Frontier*, 1963 (edited with James Camp); *An Introduction to Poetry*, 1966, 1982, 1990; *An Introduction to Fiction*, 1976, 1979, 1987; *Literature*, 1976, 1979, 1987; *Tygers of Wrath: poems of hate, anger and invective*, 1981; *The Bedford Guide for College Writers*, 1987 (with Dorothy M. Kennedy).

Bibliography

Bjork, Robert E. "Kennedy's 'Nothing in Heaven Functions as It Ought.'" *Explicator* 40 (Winter, 1982): 6-7. This explication develops the premise that the poem "exploits the concept of norm and deviation . . . to deal with the nature of heaven and hell, questioning our conventional notions about each." Bjork argues that Kennedy cleverly deviates from the reader's expectations of a Petrarchan sonnet in order to demonstrate that "Nothing in heaven, or in this sonnet, functions as it ought."

Ciardi, John. "Counter/Measures: X. J. Kennedy on Form, Meter, and Rime." *Saturday Review* 4 (May 20, 1972): 14-15. Ostensibly, John Ciardi (who was a major poet in his own right) was interviewing X. J. Kennedy about the purpose of Kennedy's literary magazine, *Counter/Measures*. In fact, however, the interview presents both poets with opportunities to formulate their ideas about the merits of form in poetry and the possibility that poems can be enduring "artifacts."

Collins, Michael. "The Poetry of X. J. Kennedy." *World Literature Today* 61, no. 1 (1987): 55-58. This essay provides an overview of Kennedy's poetic achievement. Its main thesis is that Kennedy writes in a way that characteristically fuses "the serious and playful" and that "Kennedy is a poet of contemporary middle-class America."

Kennedy, X. J. "The Poet in the Playpen." *Poetry* 105 (December, 1964): 190-193. In this review of children's books by Marianne Moore, Rumer Godden, and J. R. R. Tolkien, Kennedy formulates a defense of juvenile literature. He observes that "Randall Jarrell and John Ciardi of late seem to write more books for children than for the rest of us" and comments, "It is almost as if we were back in the days when a Blake or a Smart could expect nobody but children to listen to him."

Prunty, Wyatt. *"Fallen from the Symboled World": Precedents for the New Formalism.* New York: Oxford University Press, 1990. In arguing for the existence of a new formalism that takes "doubt as its starting point" and "builds relation from the ground up," Prunty briefly cites Kennedy as a poet of particular power. Kennedy's "On a Child Who Lived One Minute" is called a "little masterpiece" because the contrasts between gentleness and harshness in rhythm, rhyme, and diction "match Kennedy's attitude toward the infant girl's death," creating "the fusion of an abiding absurdity with which we all live."

Sharp, Ronald A. "Kennedy's 'Nude Descending a Staircase.'" *Explicator* 37 (Spring, 1979): 2-3. Sharp largely ignores the similarities between Kennedy's poem and Marcel Duchamps' painting entitled *Nu descendant un escalier*, but he does demonstrate that "the poem turns on an implicit analogy between beautiful women and beautiful poems: both are composed of individually beautiful parts but their unity is dynamic."

HENRY KING

Born: Worminghall, England; baptized January 16, 1592
Died: Chichester, England; September 30, 1669

Principal Poetry

Poems, Elegies, Paradoxes, and Sonnets, 1657; *Poems and Psalms,* 1843; *Poems,* 1965 (Margaret Crum, editor).

Other literary forms

Henry King's significant literary remains other than poetry are his Latin verses and his surviving sermons, which span almost a half-century and provide an excellent record of his ministerial concerns. They have not, however, been collected.

Achievements

A full assessment of King's poetic stature has been slow to evolve. It appears that among his contemporaries, King was renowned less as a poet than as a churchman, as an eminent preacher and respected Bishop of Chichester, and there is no evidence to suggest that King would have preferred to be viewed in any other way. It was only in the period during which for political reasons he was forcibly denied his bishopric that King, at a rather advanced age, published his poetry, and his output is relatively modest—by the reckoning of his most modern editor, Margaret Crum (*Poems,* 1965), only eighty-six poems, exclusive of his little-read and little-esteemed metrical transcriptions of the Psalms. Though the widespread appearance of a number of King's poems in various manuscripts both during his life and for several decades after his death would attest to some popularity, King's poetic achievement as a whole was left to rest in oblivion throughout the eighteenth and much of the nineteenth centuries.

Newly edited and republished in 1843, King's poems attracted some of the attention paid in the late nineteenth and early twentieth centuries to England's poetic antiquities and seventeenth century divines, and when King's good friend and religious associate John Donne came to be "rediscovered" and reacclaimed as one of England's great poets, King's poetic canon began to receive its first sustained critical study. Comparisons with Donne's verse have been inevitable and not wholly to King's advantage. King's personal association with Donne and a general resemblance between the cerebral and sometimes recondite imagery that King employs and the ingeniously involved "conceits" made famous by Donne have led to King's being labeled one of the lesser disciples of Donne's "school," or what Samuel Johnson dubbed the "metaphysical" mode of poetry. That King's imagery is less "knotty" and philosophically adventurous than Donne's and that King's verse lacks the dramatic impact so conspicuous in Donne's have made it easy to confuse difference with inferiority and to view King, not as a poet with his own concerns and idiom, but simply as Donne's unsuccessful imitator. Moreover, the high percentage of his verse which is "occasional," that is, which was prompted by and composed for a particular event, may suggest that his poetry lacks the spontaneity and originality the modern reader demands of poetry.

With closer scrutiny, however, has come the recognition not only that King may owe as much to Ben Jonson as he does to Donne, but also, and more important, that, far from being anyone's servile imitator, King studied and emulated the example of older contemporaries such as Donne and Jonson, while fashioning a poetic style through which he spoke with his own distinctive, ever thoughtful, frequently meditative, voice. In the evolution of poetic techniques and tastes in the seventeenth century, King's volume of published verse is a valuable document, encompassing as it does a period of forty-five years (1612-1657), and at once reflecting the poetic practices of the Elizabethan period and presaging those of the Restoration and neoclassicism. To the epigrammatic plainness and conciseness of Jonson's iambic pentameter and tetrameter rhymed couplets, King brings a refinement of expression that heralds the lapidary smoothness cultivated by practitioners of the rhymed couplet form in the middle and later decades of the century, and if some of King's images recall the kind of imagery brought into vogue by Donne near the beginning of the century, the polished trenchancy of some of King's more satiric and polemical pieces foreshadows the great heroic verse satires of John Dryden near the end of the century.

Above all, King's poetry is of immense interest as a lucid record of a poet's response to a most turbulent and critical period in English history, a period which brought fundamental changes to England's political, social, and religious institutions, and which challenged the perceptive poet to examine the purposes and value of his art. Like the actors Hamlet so esteemed, King's poems are "the abstract and brief chronicles of the time," and King himself a diligent poetic chronicler of the significant literary-historical events of his lifetime: the deaths of great poets, the births and deaths of princes and heirs to the throne, the travails and deaths of monarchs. To these subjects King brought the unifying perspective of a poet nurtured in the Renaissance view of the cosmos and disposed to see in the events of the world—no matter how great or small—the workings of a divinely ordered universe. Thus, side by side in King's poetic "Kalendar" stand poems on affairs of state and affairs of the heart; and in the upheavals of the politic body and the death of a king, as in personal disruptions and the death of a wife, King is prepared to read the hints of a greater disorder and the portents of a world with, in Donne's words, "all cohaerance gone." It is in its power to illuminate these correspondences between the "greater" and "lesser" worlds, and between the poet's private self and his public role, that the signal achievement of King's poetry lies.

Biography

Even a cursory examination of the poet's background will suffice to show that Henry King's art is very much a reflection of the life that produced it. Born in 1592, King was the eldest of five sons of John King, scion of an aristocratic family and renowned Anglican divine and eventual Bishop of London. Since John King intended each of his sons to enter the ministry, Henry received an education befitting a man of learning. As a youngster, he attended the Westminster School, where Ben Jonson, among many other notables, had studied, and where, as part of his classical training, he became practiced in the techniques of versification. After he left Westminster he proceeded to Oxford, where he took his B.A. degree in 1611, his M.A. in 1614, and his B.D. and D.D. in 1625.

The oldest son of an influential clergyman, King came into contact as a child and young man with some of the most distinguished churchmen and courtiers of the time, among whom was John Donne. Donne was a good friend of John King and, according to Donne's early biographer, Izaak Walton, grew to be no less fond of Henry. In 1616, as a young student of divinity, King was named to the clerical office of Prebendary of St. Paul's Church, where several years later Donne would become Dean. Their relationship remained close, and shortly before his death in 1631, Donne made King his legal executor. King's final service for Donne came in the form of the funeral elegy he composed, "Upon the Death of my ever Desired friend Dr. Donne Deane of Pauls."

From the example of his father, from his formal education, and, not improbably, from his acquaintance with Donne would emerge the intellectual cast of mind and the religious and political propensities that would permanently shape King's life, his career, and, no less so, his poetry. From all that is known of it, King's life appears to have been a genuinely religious one, predicated on a belief that God's ordinances were embodied in two temporal institutions: the Church and the Crown. Thus, religious orthodoxy and political conservatism were the mainstays of his thought and colored almost everything he wrote. No personal loss—not even the death of his young wife in 1624—could overturn his religious convictions, and, while in his verse he acknowledges the pain of loss most frankly, as he does in the celebrated elegy he wrote for his wife, "An Exequy to his Matchlesse never to be forgotten Freind," his affirmation of the triumph of the immortal soul over death is nonetheless assured.

Nor did the tribulations of the civil tumult weaken his adherence to either Church or monarch, despite the considerable privations his loyalty cost him. In 1643, a victory of the forces representing the Parliamentary and Puritan factions over the Royalist army led to the ejection of King from the bishopric of Chichester to which he had been elevated only a year before. Stripped of almost all of his property and personal papers, King existed on rather modest means—apparently not without some harassment—for the next seventeen years, until, with the Restoration of the monarchy in the person of Charles II, King returned to his church in Chichester. In the years immediately following his ejection, King wrote his most staunchly partisan and pro-Royalist verse, culminating in by far his longest and most passionate pieces, the elegies written just after the execution of Charles I in 1648, "A Deepe Groane, fetch'd at the Funerall of that incomparable and Glorious Monarch," and "An elegy upon the most Incomparable King Charls the First."

Yet, as strong as King's personal convictions were, his best verse is curiously undogmatic. The depth of King's learning and belief manifests itself not in a welter of information to be presented as absolute truth, but in a self-assured spirit of inquiry. If King shares anything with Donne, it is the pleasure he takes in exploring an idea through the play of language and metaphor. Like Donne, King seems often to be probing, discovering the essential likenesses in things that have ostensibly little in common, between an emotional state or religious point, for example, and the physical properties of the universe. Thus, when King takes a position on an issue, he does not presume its correctness but demonstrates it carefully and seriously, yet imaginatively. It is the depth of both his convictions and intelligence that leaves the reader with the sense of having shared or worked through with the poet the experience he presents in his verse. King's poetic corpus may be relatively small, but a survey of his poems gives one the impression of having learned a good deal about their author precisely because King shows so much, not only of what he thinks, but how he thinks as well.

Analysis

Like most of the technically accomplished poets of his era, Henry King was proficient in a wide range of forms and styles. Yet the form which seems to have been most congenial to his poetic temper, and in which he wrote his most memorable pieces, was the elegy. Constituting a significant part of his rather compact volume, elegies punctuate King's entire poetic career, accounting for his first datable poem, "An Elegy Upon Prince Henryes Death" (1612), and his last, "An Elegy Upon my Best Friend L. K. C." (Lady Katherine Cholmondeley, 1657). Indeed—though it is unlikely that King himself would have coveted this distinction—the list of notable personages memorialized so eloquently in his funeral poems might well give King claim to the title of elegiac poet laureate of the seventeenth century.

That what King calls the "Elegiack Knell" peals so resonantly in his verse is in part a measure of the "occasional" and "public" character much of his poetry assumed. For King, as for many of his contemporaries, private experience and public events were not inimical as poetic subjects, but complementary; in both lay hints of universal significance for the discerning poet to interpret and elucidate. Thus, a poem called forth by a particular "occasion"—

the birth of a child or the death of a celebrated war hero—could serve as a vehicle for recording, for solemnizing, the significance of an event for both the poet and the world at large. No "occasion," though, fulfills this purpose more ably than that of death, for no event is at once so private and so public, and when, in turn, death deprives the world of an individual of special importance, a "Matchlesse" wife, or a "most Incomparable" monarch, for example, the scope of the loss is all the more conspicuous, its implications all the more universal. The "weeping verse" and funeral rites invoked in King's elegies are in part, then, a literary convention by means of which King affirms and reaffirms the common basis of experience that he as a poet shares with the public about whom and for whom he writes.

Still, to suggest that the elegiac strain in King's verse is in some sense "conventional" is not to impugn or belittle what it may reveal about the innermost concerns of King's poetic psyche. In her seminal discussion of "The Laureate Hearse" in *Studies in Seventeenth Century Poetic* (1950), Ruth Coons Wallerstein has persuasively argued that the response to death in the elegiac poems of the seventeenth century crystallized the deepest spiritual and poetic preoccupations of the era, a thesis to which King's elegies prove no exception. For King the "occasion" of death subjected the aspirations of life and art to their most intense scrutiny. In metaphoric terms, King conceived of death as a literary text, the "Killing rhetorick" and "Grammer" of which contained lessons about human experience that King seems never to have tired of reading.

Just how tireless this reading was is suggested not only by the sheer frequency with which elegiac themes appear in King's verse but also by their appearance in poems that are not explicitly funereal pieces and have little ostensibly to do with the issues of death and mourning. A conspicuous example is the poem King wrote in honor of the newly born Prince Charles, entitled "By Occasion of the young Prince his happy birth. May 29-1630." No subject, one would think, has less to do with death than does birth, and, in an ethos in which the divine right of kings was a respected principle, no birth would be a source of as much public rejoicing as would that of a prince and heir apparent. Yet, at the outset of the poem, the reader finds King laboring, not to express his joy but to explain why he has hesitated to write, why at first, in fact, he "held it some Allegiance not to write." What has tempered King's celebrative mood is the recognition that everything that makes the arrival of Prince Charles a welcome event entails a sobering reflection about his father, King Charles. In the advent of a child abides the hope of immortality, along, unfortunately, with the acknowledgement of mortality. Hence, even a newly born child is a *memento mori*, and in that book of harsh lessons by which King metaphorically conceived of death, children form "The Smiling Preface to our Funerall." The arrival of a prince, connoting as it does the hope of a smooth succession and continuity in the royal line, underscores the inevitability of the death of the monarch; to acclaim the birth of Charles the Prince is, King fears, to anticipate and make seem all the more imminent the passing away of Charles the King.

Such insights bring King to something of a dilemma. As a loyal Englishman he would like to use his poetic gifts to frame a compliment to the Crown. Yet his poetic vision enables, obliges, him to see the infant prince both for what he is and for what he represents. The apprehension of mortality and the rhetoric of death force King to see and say things inappropriate to the ostensibly complimentary occasion; but to excise his elegiac concerns, King implies, is to render his compliment hollow and poetically false.

King's solution, both in this poem and in many others, is to reconcile his elegiac presentiments with his religious convictions and to turn the occasion of paying a compliment into an opportunity for teaching a salutary lesson. True, the birth of an heir is a tacit intimation of mortality, but mortality itself is but a milestone on the soul's journey to immortality, and but the last instance of finitude before all time is transformed into the infinitude of life everlasting. To pretend to ignore death, to be obsessed with prolonging life on earth, is to repudiate a fundamental article of faith: "And wee in vaine were Christians, should wee/ In this world dreame of Perpetuitye." Rather deftly, King pays the royal father the ultimate compliment of eschewing flattery and appealing, instead, to wisdom and Christian humility to accept a wholesome truth: "Decay is Nature's Kalendar; nor can/ It hurt the King to think He is a Man." With these reflections articulated, and with the fullest implications of the Prince's birth understood, King can with more genuine enthusiasm acclaim the happy event and even look forward to that time when young Charles will "lead Succession's goulden Teame" and ascend to his father's throne.

The poem on "the young Prince" exemplifies the pattern of argumentation that King pursues in much of his verse, wherein, with varying degrees of success and conviction, he strives to achieve a synthesis in which elegiac sadness and pessimism over the transience of this world is answered by religious belief in the permanence of the next. Nowhere, perhaps, is this religious elegiac vision more moving and more triumphant than in King's most frequently anthologized piece, the poem he wrote upon the death of his young wife Anne, "An Exequy To his Matchlesse never to be forgotten Freind." What at first seems peculiar about this poem, which deals with so emotionally charged an experience, and which ultimately manages to be so moving, is that it at first appears so distanced, so oddly impersonal. Little is learned about Anne herself, and one wonders at first whether King is merely making use of the death of his wife as a pretext for a philosophical discourse. One has only to read a little way into the poem to discover that it is delivered as a meditation in which Anne is a rather abstracted presence. The title of the poem may promise that it is addressed "*To* his Matchlesse never to be forgotten Freind" [italics added], but the poem opens with the poet apostrophizing a burial monument, "Thou Shrine of my Dead Saint." To the extent that Anne herself is addressed at all within the first ten lines of the piece, it is not as a person but as "Deare Losse." It is this "Losse" that consumes all the poet's emotional energy, but that energy has been subsumed in study, in a commitment to do nothing but "meditate" on the loss itself. It is the "Deare Losse" which forms "the Book,/ The Library whereon I took."

Although the poet at first seems to be distanced from Anne, it is precisely this distancing that establishes the emotional tension and intensity within the poem. The poet must turn to the study of his loss because that is all that is left him; all that remains of Anne, after all, is the "Lov'd Clay" lying in the tomb. In the discipline of meditation, then, the poet finds a method of coping with death and a means by which he may explore the psychology of grief and "compute the weary howres/ With Sighes dissolved into Showres."

Initially, at least, meditation enables the poet, not so much to allay his grief, as to define its scope. The emotional void left by the death of Anne makes existence as a whole a desolation because it was Anne who gave existence its meaning. Here the influence of Donne upon King becomes readily apparent, for in attempting to define the impact of his wife's loss, King employs the kind of imagery used by Donne to illustrate the experiences of separation and loss in poems such as "A Valediction: Forbidding Mourning" and "A Nocturnal upon Saint Lucy's Day." The extinction of Anne's life is like the extinction of the sun, since it was she who brought "Light and Motion" to the poet's now darkened "Hemispheare." Yet this is a "straunge Ecclipse," one "As ne're was read in Almanake," because it was not caused by the obstruction of the moon but by the earth itself, which in reclaiming Anne's "Lov'd Clay" has "interposed" itself between the poet and his sun.

What makes this "Ecclipse" especially "straunge" is not merely its provenance but its duration. Unlike a "normal" solar eclipse, this one is not transitory, but will endure as long as the earth endures. The eclipse of the poet's world is not an extraordinary phenomenon but a systemic and all too ordinary condition. With the recognition of this fact comes the realization of the immensity of the poet's loss. In depriving the poet of his wife, mortality has made earthly existence at once a void and a barrier to their reunion that can only be surmounted by the extinction of existence itself.

Still, implanted in the depths of King's sorrow are the very seeds of his remission, although King's recognition and articulation of this truth proceed as much from the promptings of his faith as from the workings of his intellect. If by dying, Anne has succumbed to the mortality inherent in her earthly nature, it follows that all things earthly, including the earth itself, must inevitably succumb as well. Thus, the onerous sentence of King's grief bears with it the promise of a terminus, and King can look forward to that apocalyptic "Day" when a "fierce Feaver must calcine/ The Body of this World," even as a more localized fever has already consumed the body of Anne, "My Little World."

The expectation of the world's dissolution would not be much of a source of comfort to the poet were it not coupled with his unqualified belief in a universal Resurrection. On this premise turns the argument—and the mood—of the latter parts of the poem. Death becomes, then, less a boundless condition than a transitional event: the death of the body brings about the liberation of the soul, while the death of earthly existence is the purificatory and regenerative mechanism by which "our Bodyes shall aspire/ To our Soules blisse." So it is that no hint of equivocation mars the confidence with which the poet envisions that endless day on which "wee shall rise,/ And view our selves with cleerer eyes/ In that calme Region, where no Night/ Can hide us from each other's sight." Moreover, that the poet begins to use pronouns such as "wee" and "us" suggests that the reunion with Anne to be attained in the general Resurrection is already under way, and that the gulf created by death which had so tormented the poet at the outset of the piece has already been bridged by the poetic process of meditation. Death becomes less an insuperable foe than a functionary accountable to a higher power. Anne's tomb is less a devourer of her flesh than a temporary custodian whose duty will be to return on the day of the Resurrection an accurate "reck'ning" of "Each Grane and Atome of this Dust." Nothing has been, or will be, lost.

At the same time, it is a measure of the complexity and artistry of King's vision that no matter how assured his faith leads him to be about the ultimate implications of death, its immediate reality remains no less horrid. Although King's quickened religious insight may enable him to think of Anne now, not as someone gone forever, but as his temporarily sleeping bride, there is something chillingly reminiscent of Juliet's entombment in the Capulets' charnel house in the picture of King's young wife, enfolded with "Black Curtaines," lying on "Thy cold bed/ Never to be disquieted." Death seems no less importunate, no less an interloper, and when the poet poignantly takes "My last Goodnight" he forcibly acknowledges that he is still very much wedded to the things of this world, "to that Dust/ It so much loves." Indeed, the poet's resounding triumph in the conclusion of the poem takes the form of a paradox: the more fully he affirms his mortality the more clearly he beholds the date of his transcendence, the very rapidity with which mortality encroaches setting the pace by which immortality approaches. It is this image of mortality fused with immortality in one relentless motion that resonates in the cadences of King's parting assurance to his wife that "My pulse, like a soft Drum/ Beates my Approach, Tells Thee I come," while the resolute stroke of eight monosyllabic words underscores the poet's final promise that "I shall at last sitt downe by Thee."

Elegiac sadness for the human condition merges with religious conviction in King's poem to his wife to produce an illusion of poise and inner assurance which make the poem one of the great elegies of the language and, not surprisingly, his most highly esteemed work. In other poems, King's vision is more darkly elegiac, his remorse over the fragility of human existence less evenly tempered by the consolation of faith. One striking instance is the twelve-line epigram entitled, "Sic Vita," a poem very much in the *memento mori* tradition, the very compression and conciseness of which give dramatic immediacy to its familiarly elegiac theme that existence is transitory and all too peremptorily brief. In the first six lines of the poem, King presents a series of six exquisite and ephemeral natural phenomena whose exquisiteness, in fact, arises from their ephemeral character and from the teasing hope they engender that somehow they can be preserved, frozen in time. The space is very small, but King manages to select examples that are representative of the diverse operations of the natural world, both great and small: a falling star, a soaring eagle, the fecundity of spring, a gust of wind on the sea, some dew drops, some bubbles on the surface of water. All of these are introduced as terms of one extended simile, and in the seventh and eighth lines one discovers that what draws them together, besides their ephemeral attractiveness, is that they are emblems of man. Man is but one more image of transience, and, like the other entities of nature, he too has a life and "Light" that are "borrow'd" and will be "streight Call'd in, and Pay'd to Night."

If it took only one eight-line sentence to establish the common bond between man and the other elements of his universe, it takes only one four-line sentence to make the implications of this bond briskly and brusquely clear. Swept up in the annihilative rush of time, mortality, and King's swiftly paced iambic tetrameter verse are all the things of nature, including man and, worse, all traces of man's life: "The Dew dryes up: The Starr is shott:/ The Flight is past: And Man Forgott."

For King, the brevity of existence is, however, often only a catalyst for other, even more somber, ruminations about the human condition. Indeed, the importunity of death would hold little but terror for King did he not see it as the culmination of the sorrows that afflict and waste a man's life. "What is th' Existence of Man's Life?" King asks rhetorically at the outset of "The Dirge," only to answer the question immediately: "open Warr, or Slumber'd Strife," from which "Death's cold hand" alone provides a reprieve. What makes this "strife" most pernicious is that it arises from the disorders that original sin has wrought upon the human soul and psyche, effectively making man his own implacable foe, in whom "each loud Passion of the Mind/ Is like a furious gust of Wind."

It is this perception that makes King, at his most pessimistic, a satirist in the vein of the writer of Ecclesiastes, a scourge of vanity, of the delusions and emptiness that are the inveterate accessories of one's existence. Such is certainly the stance King assumes in "The Dirge," in which he concludes by employing one of William Shakespeare's recurrent metaphors, likening man's existence to a play, "a weary Enterlude," the acts of which are consumed by man's "vaine Hope and vary'd Feares," and the only fitting "Epilogue" to which is "Death." Even more stridently contemptuous is the assessment of man and his aspirations that King offers in "An Elegy Occasioned by Sicknesse." Here illness becomes a meditative device to turn one's attention inward and "Make Man into his proper Opticks look,/ And so become the Student and the Book." What this self-inventory reveals is rather deflating. From conception and birth man is ordained to emerge as little else but "complicated Sin." At the height of his pretensions he is merely "Poore walking Clay," fated to be "a short-liv'd Vapour upward wrought,/ And by Corruption unto nothing brought."

In the face of these dour appraisals of man's worth, the value and role that King allots in his poetry to meditation and the self-scrutiny entailed in meditation become clear. Central to King's excoriation of human vanity is the premise that man's intellect is a casualty of his spiritual defects, that vanity prevents man, for all his apparent intellectual attainments, from knowing himself and what conduces to his own good. Thus, the meditative strain so recurrent in King's poems has, in part, a hortatory function and invites man to lay aside the studies of the external world with which he is so preoccupied in order to study himself, his "proper Opticks," the better to confront and dispel, if possible, the mists impairing his vision.

Such is the challenge posed in "The Labyrinth," which opens with the proposition that "Life is a crooked Labyrinth" in which man is "dayly lost" and then proceeds to draw the reader into a scrutiny of the conundrums that lie at the heart of human conduct. How can it be that man can know what is good, resolve to do the good, and then lapse and relapse into wrong, ever erring, never extricating himself from the labyrinth his will has created? "Why is the clearest and best judging Mind/ In her own Ill's prevention dark and blind?" What contrition can possibly be effective when the mind has become so practiced at begging forgiveness while rationalizing the commission of sin, when, like the usurper King Claudius in Hamlet, the sinner cannot in good conscience seek to undo what he has done since he knows that he would do it again? The more thoughtfully the reader ponders these questions, the more surely he is drawn into the labyrinth the poet is describing, for in posing these questions the poet has been appealing to the reader's intellect; and the more the reader acknowledges the intellectual validity of the questions, the more deeply he identifies himself as an intellectual and implicates himself in the cycle of rationalization and recrimination that the labyrinth comprises.

Are there answers to these questions? None, King implies, that can be provided by human intellection, even as there are no strategies the intellect can devise on its own for coping with the experience of death. The intellect is part of the problem, and, unaided, it cannot provide a solution to what King calls "this home-bred tyranny." Instead, King can only abjure his intellectual pretensions and appeal to God for the insight which the human mind lacks. With a nod to Ezekiel (11:19), King calls upon God in his redemptive power to soften man's heart and "imprint" upon his "breast of flint" the marks of true contrition, for it is only through the genuine conversion of the heart that the mists clouding the mind will be dispersed. For King, as for his contemporaries, there was no inherent dichotomy between the mind and the emotions, the affections of the mind following directly from the disposition of the heart and soul. Thus, God is beseeched to provide not merely emotional reassurance but intellectual clarity, or "thy Grace's Clew," with which King, like some latter-day, Christianized Theseus, may aspire to thread his way through "this Labyrinth of Sinne/ My wild Affects and Actions wander in."

The skepticism with which King regards the powers of the human intellect very much affects the attitude he brings to the intellectual activity of writing poetry. If the intellect is impaired by its own frail mortality, then the verse that the intellect produces will be similarly inept, incapable of dealing satisfactorily with the experiences and paradoxes of the human condition. Indeed, in depicting the phenomenon of death, for example, as a text, as a book with its own lessons to impart, King explicitly calls attention to the deficiencies of his own text, his verse. Thus, in his early "Elegy Upon Prince Henrye's Death," King not only laments the passing of the young prince, but wonders how his own verse can ever do justice to the occasion or presume to vie in eloquence with the succinctly "Killing rhetorick" of death, which manages to embody "Woe's superlative" in only two words: "Henry's dead." Again and again, King's poetry runs a poor second either to the experience to which it responds or to the emotion it is intended to express. "And think not," he hastens to assure his deceased friend in "The Departure: An Elegy," that "I only mourne in Poetry and Ink." Rather, the "melancholy Plummets" of his pen "sink/ So lowe, they dive where th'hid Affections sitt." So impatient does King ultimately profess to become with the inadequacy of his verse that in his last datable poem, "An Elegy Upon my Best Friend, L. K. C." (Lady Katherine Cholmondeley, 1657), King announces his "long Farewell" from his poetry, "That Art, where with our Crosses we beguile/ And make them in Harmonious numbers smile"—a valediction in which King strives for that elusive fusion of art and life by burying his verse with his friend.

It is not to impugn King's sincerity to suggest that his insistence upon the deficiencies of his poetry owes a good deal to convention. As an apt student of poetry and poetic tradition, King would have been quite aware of the innumerable writers of and before his time who displayed their eloquence by lamenting their ineloquence, who emblazoned the depth of their passion or sense of loss by artfully expressing their inability to express their passion or loss. With King, however, the convention acquires something of the force of a personal signature. Loath to divorce his poetic craft for his life, he was even less willing to excise his verse from the principles and beliefs that gave his life

its purpose. Convinced of the contingency and vulnerability of human existence, King could not consider his poetic exercises as anything but reflections of his own limitations. King would not have minded very much the
gentle irony that the very powers he denigrated in his verse helped to ensure
the continued survival and appeal of that verse.

Thomas Moisan

Bibliography
Berman, Ronald. *Henry King and the Seventeenth Century.* London: Chatto
& Windus, 1964. King is presented in this study as embodying some of
the paradoxes of the seventeenth century. It includes a biography and an
in-depth look at King's world, his political and social philosophies, as well
as an analysis of his poetry. Examples are used extensively and notes and
bibliography follow the text.
Crum, Margaret, ed. *The Poems of Henry King.* Oxford, England: Clarendon
Press, 1965. The introduction to this collection provides a biography, a short
discussion of the poems, and notes on the original texts. The poems themselves are followed by notes and appendices.
Tuve, Rosamund. *Elizabethan and Metaphysical Imagery.* Chicago: University
of Chicago Press, 1947. This is a study of the imagery employed by the
Elizabethan and metaphysical poets of the English Renaissance. The analysis stresses the intellectual, sensual, and charming aspects of the imagery. King and other poets as recent as William Butler Yeats are covered in
the discussion.
Wallace, John M., ed. *The Golden and the Brazen World: Papers in Literature
and History, 1650-1800.* Berkeley: University of California Press, 1985. This
collection contains an essay by Cleanth Brooks on King's "The Exequy"
and "The Legacy" entitled "Need Clio Quarrel with Her Sister Muses?
The Claims of Literature and History" (p. 1-15). The essayist takes a biographical approach and gives a close reading of "The Exequy." He discusses seventeenth century theological beliefs, burial customs, and King's
life and literary career in order to illuminate the poem on the light of its
historical roots.

GALWAY KINNELL

Born: Providence, Rhode Island; February 1, 1927

Principal poetry

What a Kingdom It Was, 1960; *Flower Herding on Mount Monadnock,* 1964; *The Poems of François Villon,* 1965 (translation); *On the Motion and Immobility of Douve,* 1968 (translation); *Poems of Night,* 1968; *Body Rags,* 1968; *Lackawanna Elegy,* 1970 (translation); *First Poems, 1946-1954,* 1970; *The Book of Nightmares,* 1971; *The Avenue Bearing the Initial of Christ into the New World: Poems 1946-1964,* 1974; *Mortal Acts, Mortal Words,* 1980; *Selected Poems,* 1982; *The Fundamental Project of Technology,* 1983; *The Past,* 1985; *When One Has Lived a Long Time Alone,* 1990.

Other literary forms

Black Light (1966) is a fablelike novel, set in Iran, that chronicles how a carpet maker's act of heinous murder propels him into a dark journey toward spiritual awakening. In *Walking Down the Stairs: Selections from Interviews* (1978), Galway Kinnell offers his opinions about other poets and his own work, gleaned from interviews of himself between 1969 and 1976. *How the Alligator Missed Breakfast* (1982) is a children's book. Kinnell has also published numerous translations: *Bitter Victory* (a novel by René Hardy, 1956), *The Poems of François Villon* (1965, 1977), *On the Motion and Immobility of Douve* (poems by Yves Bonnefoy, 1968), and *Lackawanna Elegy* (by Yvan Goll, 1970). He was editor of *The Essential Whitman* (1988). Numerous magazines and literary journals have published articles by Kinnell, several of which have been reprinted as book chapters.

Achievements

Kinnell's poetry has garnered an ever-increasing and appreciative audience among both critics and the public. In 1974 he received the Shelley Prize from the Poetry Society of America, followed in 1975 by the Medal of Merit from the National Institute of Arts and Letters. For *Selected Poems,* Kinnell was awarded both the Pulitzer Prize and the American Book Award in 1983. He has been a Fulbright professor, president of the International Association of Poets, Playwrights, Editors, Essayists, and Novelists (PEN), and a MacArthur Fellow, and is currently the state poet of Vermont and the Samuel F. B. Morse Professor of Fine Arts at New York University.

Biography

Born the fourth of four children to immigrant parents (his mother was from Ireland, his father from Scotland), Galway Kinnell spent most of his youth in Pawtucket, Rhode Island, where his father, James Scott Kinnell, earned his living as a carpenter and woodworking teacher. Kinnell left home his senior year of high school to attend Wilbraham Academy in Massachusetts on scholarship. From there he entered Princeton University, where for two of his undergraduate years he was a member of the U.S. Navy, training as an officer, and where he also met W. S. Merwin and Charles Bell. Bell became Kinnell's mentor. In 1949, following his graduation from Princeton *summa cum laude*, Kinnell received his M.A. from the University of Rochester. Between 1951 and 1964, Kinnell spent two years at the University of Grenoble in France as an instructor of American literature, two years in Iran as a lecturer and journalist, periods of teaching in Chicago and New York City, and retreats to an abandoned farm he purchased in 1961 in northern Vermont. Kinnell's commitment to social justice during the period was evidenced both in his poetry and his membership in the Congress of Racial Equality. Later he would be an active participant in Poets Against the Vietnam War.

Marriage to Ines Delgado de Torres in 1965, and the subsequent arrival of a daughter, Maud, in 1966, and a son, Finn Fergus, in 1968, temporarily stinted Kinnell's wanderlust; in 1969, following two years in Spain and then short-term teaching engagements in California, Colorado, and Iowa, the Kinnells set up housekeeping in New York City for eight years. During this time the Kinnells hosted frequent gatherings, at both their New York apartment and the Vermont farm, at which friends such as James Wright, Saul Galin, Betty Kray, Mary Kaplan, and Etheridge Knight were known to converse, argue, and read their work aloud. In 1978, having been offered new teaching engagements, the Kinnells began globetrotting once again, this time from Nice, France, to Sydney, Australia, to Hawaii. In 1982 they resettled in New York City. In the years following, *Selected Poems* was awarded the Pulitzer Prize and was cowinner of the American Book Award, Kinnell and his wife were divorced, and Kinnell became the Samuel F. B. Morse Professor of Fine Arts at New York University—his first tenured position.

Analysis

Galway Kinnell's earliest poems demonstrate his ability to express himself in traditional poetic forms governed by rhyme and meter. "A Walk in the Country," "The Feast," and "First Song," among others, have each been critically acclaimed for their tenderness and delicacy. Citing constrictions on creative expression, however, Kinnell came to reject rhyme and meter—a position in agreement with Ezra Pound, T. S. Eliot, William Carlos Williams, and Walt Whitman, all of whose influences can be traced in Kinnell's poetry—and espoused free verse as the exclusive suitable medium for modern American poetry. Even in his "pre-enlightened" days, however, when the influence of William Butler Yeats was most evident, there was evidence of his preoccupation with secular sanctification of the material world and with humankind's hope for regeneration after death, though he rejected the possibility of bodily resurrection; these themes would continue to mark his later work, though the form of that work would change considerably.

The last stanza of "First Song" carries suggestions of Kinnell's more dramatic, mature voice found in his monumental achievement "The Bear":

> It was now fine music the frogs and the boys
> Did in the towering Illinois twilight make
> And into dark in spite of a shoulder's ache
> A boy's hunched body loved out of a stalk
> The first song of his happiness, and the song woke
> His heart to the darkness and into the sadness of joy.

Boy and frogs playing together become, in their primitive (or perhaps primeval) communication, as one. The boy's "frogness" can be seen in his "hunched body," emphasized by the mention of "a shoulder's ache" and the "towering Illinois twilight." Clearly not as visceral or brutal in vocabulary and imagery as the later narrative, this poem nevertheless suggests that it is the animal nature of human beings that accesses the unconscious (here referred to as "the darkness") and brings wholeness to experience ("the sadness of joy").

Here, too, is an inkling that the boy's song flows from a place of suffering, just as the song that "blows across" the "sore, lolled tongue" of the dreaming poet of the "The Bear" flows from his wounded lurching across the tundra. "The Bear," oozing gustatory imagery, takes a darker, lonelier route than "First Song," but the two poems arrive at a similar life- and art-affirming destination.

Many of Kinnell's most celebrated poems keenly observe the animal kingdom. Besides the odoriferous he-bear splashing a trail of blood, there is a hen killed by weasels ("The Hen Flower"), a porcupine gutted while falling, wounded, from a tree branch ("The Porcupine"), a sow with fourteen suckling piglets ("St. Francis and the Sow"), and a mutating bird ("The Gray Heron"). The graphic descriptions of all these creatures are intended as heuristic paradigms to expand the reader's understanding of what it means to be an individuated human being.

Documenting humanity's moments of wholeness is essential to Kinnell's mode. His universe, absent a Father God on whom to heap blame or credit for what has happened, what is happening, and what will happen, is lit instead by death's ever-burning candle. While Kinnell displays a rudimentary knowledge of Christian myth and ritual—using concepts such as "grace" and "agape" in some poems, and making reference to Christ to provide a framework for a series of images, as he does in "To Christ Our Lord"—the hope and comfort he offers are based not in Christian orthodoxy but in a spirituality born of New Age pantheism. Christianity serves merely as fodder for irony.

Kinnell's evident belief in a vast, mystical union of all things existing, tangible and intangible, stretches from the "dark afternoons" that precede "a bright evening" in his early poem "Westport," to the fire blossoming out of wood that is "not *things dying* but just the *dying*," in "Flower of Five Blossoms" (*When One Has Lived a Long Time Alone*). It is from an acceptance of life as a brief journey that ends in nothingness—the loss of human identity and consciousness beyond the last breath, then a return into the creative essence of which all things earthly are derived—that Kinnell seems to draw the courage to live and die.

In "These Are Things I Tell To No One," from *Mortal Acts, Mortal Words*, Kinnell describes his "God" (his own quotation marks) as a "music of grace" that plays "from the other side of happiness." This music triggers worship of a "backward spreading brightness." In his 1972 essay "The Poetics of the Physical World," he attributes to "something radiant in our lives" the human ability to "invent the realm of eternity." Yet he celebrates "another kind of glory," one that is connected to people's inability to enter the paradise they have invented.

> That we last only for a time, that everyone around us lasts only for a time, that we know this, radiates a thrilling, tragic light on all our loves, all our relationships, even on those moments when the world, through its poetry, becomes almost capable of spurning time and death.

Besides reducing twentieth century divinity to human proportions, Kinnell's formula for earthbound transcendence formulates a modern reply to the argument, voiced as early as 1820 by Thomas Love Peacock, that poetry has no intellectual place in a society committed to scientific progress. Through his form and content, Kinnell seems to say that postmodern poetry—the kind that employs frank language to describe common, everyday occurrences and objects in order to point to the sacredness of every part of creation—is necessary precisely *because* contemporary society is committed to scientific progress. Kinnell's poetics are grounded in a philosophy that affirms Percy Bysshe Shelley's *A Defense of Poetry* (wr. 1821, pb. 1840), which was written in response to Peacock's *The Four Ages of Poetry* (1820). Shelley pointed out that scientific discoveries could very well lead to a worsening of social inequities, absent humanitarian considerations.

Kinnell nurtures his readers' admiration for and identification with nature's workings through the use of metaphor. Through an intermingling of images—those that represent humans' inner struggle to transcend the suffering that comes with being mortal with those, both gentle and grisly, that represent outward processes drawn from nature, the city landscape, or his ordinary domestic routine—Kinnell formulates the argument that human transcendence comes in fleeting moments of surrender to primitive instincts arising from the unconscious.

Aesthetic considerations rank high for Kinnell; his poems overflow with provocative imagery. He often communicates with his readers through the medium of song—not using the notes of the musical scale, but arranging his words in indefinite verbal melodies, and even sometimes deliberately organizing his poems in accord with musical structures. Thus he appeals to his readers' inner rhythms without resorting to what he considers to be the inadequate patterns of formal meter and rhyme.

"The Avenue Bearing the Initial of Christ into the New World" and "Vapor Trail Reflected in the Frog Pond" typify yet another of Kinnell's approaches, an approach heavily Whitmanesque, designed to facilitate awakenings. Both address a social issue by painting a graphic picture of a spoiled environment. In terms of music, both reverberate with auditory descriptions. The former is a long poem, organized in fourteen sections, incorporating onomatopoeia, one of Kinnell's preferred techniques. The three brief sections of "Vapor Trail Reflected in the Frog Pond," like musical suites all organized around a central theme, describe the reflection left by a bomber flying over a frog pond and move on to ruminate on the American involvement in the Vietnam War. The first suite introduces the scene: The speaker tells what he sees at the frog pond. The second suite branches away to record the speaker's mental journey, suggested by impressions of sounds from the racially torn South and a battlefield. The final suite, a wrenching tour de force, focuses on the anguish war brings, the violence it does to spirit as well as to flesh. Nevertheless, the poem suggests an ultimate triumph of nature in the cycle of life and death. "They gaze up at the drifting sun that gives us our lives," says Kinnell, "seed dazzled over the footbattered blaze of the earth."

Such images of light and fire—"the drifting sun," "seed dazzled," "blaze of the earth"—are characteristic of Kinnell. Secular glory shines throughout his poetry in variations on these two symbols of a mystic earthly presence awaiting recognition. In his poems things flash, sparkle, glisten, glitter, glimmer, glow, smolder, or burn.

In "That Silent Evening," the speaker tells how he and a lover once talked in bed in flickering firelight. Their talk is "low, silent," like the snowfall outside and the firewood's giving up its ghosts "without a cackle," and suggestive of intimacy rather than conversation. The speaker knows that he will remember the closeness of that fragment of time. Tracks the two have made in the snow become a metaphor for their relationship's journey, the weaving together and apart marking stretches of alienation interrupted by moments of completeness and bliss.

Branches "*scritch, scritch, scritch,*" a chickadee "*dee, dee, dees*"—small sounds that suggest noumenal communications from the creative mystic fire that underlies everything. All the happenings of the world are reduced to a

scratch in a field of snow. These auditory and visual images of impermanence are reminders of the ultimate insignificance of individual actions and
the futility of ignoring the "end" built into the "beginning" of everything.
The speaker muses that words come close to easing the worry over the inevitable loss of relationship ahead, by death if not by fracture, for whichever of
the two lovers comes in need of reassurance. Yet it is in the anticipated remembering of the unspoken, loving oneness, that time past, present, and future overlaps. "The light/ that lives inside the eclipse doubles and shines/
through the darkness the sparkling that heavens the earth." Once again, Kinnell's "backward spreading brightness" penetrates the modern gloom to provide transcendence.

Kinnell has been criticized for "pseudo-shamanism," repetition of devices,
overuse of certain tag words, and sentimentality. Yet few modern writers
command such widespread respect among their peers, and almost none can
match his skill in creating bold and beautiful endings. His mastery of the
graphic, emotion-laden image and his ability to marshal language to create
subtle yet powerful music ensure his place among American poets of the
twentieth century.

Virginia Starrett

Other major works
LONG FICTION: *Black Light*, 1966, 1980; *Bitter Victory*, 1965 (translation).
SHORT FICTION: "The Permanence of Love," 1968.
NONFICTION: *"The Poetics of the Physical World,"* 1971; *Walking Down the
Stairs: Selections from Interviews*, 1978; *Thoughts Occasioned by the Most
Insignificant of Human Events*, 1982.
CHILDREN'S LITERATURE: *How the Alligator Missed Breakfast*, 1982.

Bibliography
Bly, Robert. "Galway Kinnell: The Hero and The Old Farmer." In *American
Poetry: Wildness and Domesticity*. New York: Harper & Row, 1990. This is
a revised version of the essay that originally appeared in Howard Nelson's
On the Poetry of Galway Kinnell: The Wages of Dying (see below). The
changes from its earlier form clarify meaning, and Bly's introductory chapters in the book set the stage for his thoughtful analysis of Kinnell's poetic
voice.
Goldensohn, Lorrie. "Approaching Home Ground: Galway Kinnell's *Mortal
Acts, Mortal Words." The Massachusetts Review* 25 (Summer, 1984): 303-
321. After unraveling several of Kinnell's captured moments, Goldensohn
lays them beside his professed philosophy and finds serious conflicts. Especially problematical, she points out, are the deficiencies in Kinnell's treatment of women. Goldensohn's feminist perspective provokes new questions

and provides new insights.

Kleinbard, David. "Galway Kinnell's Poetry of Transformation." *The Centennial Review* 30 (Winter, 1986): 41-56. While Kleinbard focuses exclusively on Kinnell's *The Book of Nightmares*, exploring its relationship with Whitman's "Song of Myself" and Rainer Maria Rilke's *Duineser Elegien* (1923, *Duino Elegies*, 1930), his explication of language and image provides a paradigm to follow in reaching under Kinnell's surface rhythms for the unifying context of meaning.

Nelson, Howard, ed. *On the Poetry of Galway Kinnell: The Wages of Dying.* Ann Arbor: University of Michigan Press, 1987. This indispensable book is a collection of excerpts from previously published book reviews and articles together with essays—overviews, appraisals, analyses of specific poems, and a particularly insightful reminiscence—written specifically for the project. Writers include Charles Molesworth, Louise Bogan, Harold Bloom, Donald Davie, Joseph Bruchac, and Tess Gallagher. A chronology as well as an extensive bibliography provides interesting and useful information.

Taylor, Granville. "From Irony to Lyricism: Galway Kinnell's True Voice." *Christianity and Literature* 37 (Summer, 1988): 45-54. Taylor explores Kinnell's emphasis on immanence over transcendence and the evolution of his form of grace. For readers interested in reconciling Kinnell's rejection of traditional Christian myths with orthodoxy, Taylor offers a solution.

Zimmerman, Lee. *Intricate and Simple Things: The Poetry of Galway Kinnell.* Chicago: University of Illinois Press, 1987. Zimmerman's study is divided into five chapters and an epilogue, each of which focuses on one of Kinnell's collections, ending with *The Past.* Especially helpful are the author's discussions of the oppositions that form the heart of Kinnell's work, the literary context in which the work has evolved, and the effect on his message of the gradually increasing distance of the poet from his subject. An index facilitates use of this book for researching specific topics.

THOMAS KINSELLA

Born: Dublin, Ireland; May 4, 1928

Principal poetry

The Starlit Eye, 1952; *Three Legendary Sonnets,* 1952; *The Death of a Queen,* 1956; *Poems,* 1956; *Another September,* 1958, revised 1962; *Moralities,* 1960; *Downstream,* 1962; *Six Irish Poets,* 1962; *Wormwood,* 1966; *Nightwalker and Other Poems,* 1968; *Poems,* 1968 (with Douglas Livingstone and Anne Sexton); *Tear,* 1969; *Butcher's Dozen,* 1972; *A Selected Life,* 1972; *Finistere,* 1972; *Notes from the Land of the Dead and Other Poems,* 1972; *New Poems,* 1973; *Selected Poems, 1956-1968,* 1973; *Vertical Man,* 1973; *The Good Fight: A Poem for the Tenth Anniversary of the Death of John F. Kennedy,* 1973; *One,* 1974; *A Technical Supplement,* 1976; *Song of the Night and Other Poems,* 1978; *The Messenger,* 1978; *Fifteen Dead,* 1979; *One and Other Poems,* 1979; *Peppercanister Poems, 1972-1978,* 1979; *Poems, 1956-1973,* 1979; *One Fond Embrace,* 1981; *Songs of the Psyche,* 1985; *Her Vertical Smile,* 1985; *Blood and Family,* 1988; *Poems from Centre City,* 1991.

Other literary forms

In addition to his own poetry, Thomas Kinsella has published a large body of verse translated from the Irish. This work, which has been going on throughout his career, is most notably embodied in his celebrated version of the eighth century Irish epic *Táin bó Cuailnge (The Tain,* 1969) and in *An Duanaire, 1600-1900: Poems of the Dispossessed* (1981; with Sean O Tuama). ("An duanaire," literally translated, means "the poemery.") An appreciation of the significance which Kinsella attaches to the Irish-language tradition of Irish poetry, and the magnitude of his commitment to it, is crucial to an overall sense of his achievement. His introduction to *The New Oxford Book of Irish Verse* (1986), which he edited, provides convenient access to Kinsella's thinking on the subject of the Irish-language poetic tradition. The attitude expressed in that introduction recapitulates earlier statements contained in the poet's small but influential body of cultural criticism.

Achievements

Kinsella is the most important Irish poet to emerge since the end of World War II. By means of a restlessly experimental formal and aesthetic sense, broadly conceived themes, and relentless self-scrutiny and self-exposure, his work has raised him above all of his Irish contemporaries and placed him in the forefront of his generation of poets writing in English.

In the context of contemporary Irish poetry, his work has an unwonted syntactical density, complexity of imagery, and dramatic intensity. Since modern Irish poetry in English is noted more for lyric grace than for tough-minded plumbing of existential depths, Kinsella's poetry gains in importance because of its originality. Its essential inimitability, in turn, commands respect by virtue of the tenacity of vision it embodies.

In recognition of his uniqueness and commitment, Kinsella has received widespread critical acclaim and has won numerous prestigious prizes and two Guggenheim Fellowships.

Biography

Thomas Kinsella was born in Dublin on May 4, 1928. His family background is typical of the vast majority of native Dubliners—Catholic in religious affiliation, left-tending Nationalist in politics and lower-middle/upper-working-class in social standing: the kind of background detailed with such loving despair by one of Kinsella's favorite authors, James Joyce, in the stories of *Dubliners* (1914). Thomas Kinsella's father worked at the Guinness brewery and was active in labor union matters.

Educated at local day schools, Kinsella received a scholarship to attend University College, Dublin, to read for a science degree. Before graduation, however, he left to become a member of the Irish Civil Service, in which he had a successful career as a bureaucrat, rising to the rank of Assistant Principal Officer in the Department of Finance.

Kinsella left the Civil Service in 1965 to become artist-in-residence at Southern Illinois University. In 1970, he was appointed to a professorship of English at Temple University. He eventually would teach for one semester a year at Temple, spending the rest of the year in Dublin running the Peppercanister Press.

Founded in 1972, Peppercanister is the poet's private press. It was established, in the poet's own words "with the purpose of issuing occasional special items." As well as being a notable addition to the illustrious private and small tradition of Irish publishing, Peppercanister has allowed Thomas Kinsella to produce long poems on single themes and to carry out fascinating exercises in the area of the poetic sequence.

Analysis

From the outset of his career, Thomas Kinsella has shown an unremitting preoccupation with large themes. Love, death, time, and various ancillary imponderables are persistently at the forefront of Kinsella's poetic activity. Such concerns beset all poets, no doubt, as well as all thinking beings. More often than not, Kinsella grapples with these overwhelming subjects without the alleviating disguise of metaphor, and he confronts them without the consolations of philosophy. Their reality consists of the profundity of the poet's human—and hence, frequently baffled and outraged—experience of them.

Even in Kinsella's early love lyrics, it is impossible for the poet merely to celebrate the emotion. He cannot view his subject without being aware of its problematical character—its temporariness and changeability. Thus, to identify Kinsella's themes, while initially informative, may ultimately be misleading. It seems more illuminating to consider his preoccupations, which a reader may label time or death, as zones of the poet's psychic experience, and to recognize that a Kinsella poem is, typically, an anatomy of psychic experience, a rhetorical reexperiencing, rather than a particularly conclusive recounting. Such a view would seem to be borne out by the forms which his poems typically assume. Their fractured look and inconsistent verse patterns (unavoidably but not imitatively reproducing the prosody of T. S. Eliot and Ezra Pound) suggest an idea still developing. As Kinsella writes in "Worker in Mirror, at His Bench": "No, it has no practical application./ I am simply trying to understand something/ —states of peace nursed out of wreckage./ The peace of fullness, not emptiness."

An immediate implication of this approach to poetry is that it owes little or nothing to the poet's Irish heritage. His concerns are common to all humanity, and while the conspicuous modernism of his technique has, in point of historical fact, some Irish avatars (the unjustly neglected Denis Devlin comes to mind), these are of less significance for a sense of Kinsella's achievement and development than the manner in which he has availed himself of the whole canon of Anglo-American poetry. In fact, an interesting case could be made for Kinsella's poetry being an adventitious, promiscuous coalescence of the preoccupations of poets since the dawn of Romanticism. Such a case might well produce the judgment that one of the bases for Kinsella's general importance to the history of poetry in the postwar period is that his verse is a sustained attempt to inaugurate a post-Romantic poetic that would neither merely debunk its predecessor's fatal charms (as perhaps T. S. Eliot desired to do) nor provide them with a new repertoire of gestures and disguises (which seems to have been Ezra Pound's project). The effect of this judgment would be to place Kinsella in the company of the other great Irish anti-Romantic of twentieth century literature, Samuel Beckett.

A more far-reaching implication of Kinsella's technique is that it provides direct access to the metaphysical core of those preoccupations. Often the access is brutally direct. Throughout, Kinsella repeats the refrain articulated in the opening section of "Nightwalker": "I only know things seem and are not good." This line strikes a number of characteristic Kinsella notes. Its unrelieved, declarative immediacy is a feature which becomes increasingly pronounced as his verse matures. There is a sense of the unfitness of things, of evil, of times being out of joint. The speaker is strikingly committed to his subjective view. The line contains a representative Kinsella ambiguity, depending on whether the reader pauses heavily after "seem": Is "are not good" entailed by, or opposed to, "seem"? Readers familiar with Kinsella will hear the line announce a telltale air of threat and of brooding introspection. There is also, perhaps, a faint suggestion of meditative quest in "Nightwalker," which occurs in other important Kinsella poems from the 1960's (such as "Baggot Street Deserta," "A Country Walk," and *Downstream*). Such an undertaking, however, is hardly conceived in hope and does not seem to be a quest for which the persona freely and gladly volunteers. Rather, it seems a condition into which he has been haplessly born.

It is not difficult to understand Kinsella's confession that his vision of human existence is that of "an ordeal." In fact, given the prevalence in his verse of ignorance, darkness, death, and the unnervingly unpredictable tidal movements of the unconscious—all frequently presented by means of apocalyptic imagery—there is a strong indication that the poet is doing little more than indulging his idea of "ordeal," despite the prosodic virtuosity and furious verbal tension which make the indulgence seem an authentic act of soul-baring. Such an evaluation, however, would be incomplete. Also evident is the poet's desire to believe in what he has called "the eliciting of order from experience." Kinsella's verse is a continuing experiment in the viability of the desire to retain such a belief and a commitment to negotiate the leap of artistic faith which alone is capable of overcoming the abyss of unjustifiable unknowing that is the mortal lot. The possibility of achieving that act of composed and graceful suspension is what keeps Kinsella's poetry alive and within the realm of the human enterprise.

Although Kinsella's oeuvre exemplifies, to a dauntingly impressive degree, persistence and commitment in the face of the virtually unspeakable abyss, it has gone through a number of adjustments and modifications. Taken as a whole, therefore, Kinsella's output may be considered an enlarged version of some of its most outstanding moments, a sophisticated system of themes and variations. In the words of the preface to *Wormwood*, "It is certain that maturity and peace are to be sought through ordeal after ordeal, and it seems that the search continues until we fail."

One of the most important adjustments to have occurred in the development of Kinsella's poetic career is its emergence from largely private, personal experience, primarily of love. His early poems, particularly those collected in *Another September* and *Downstream*, seem too often to conceive of experience as the struggle of the will against the force of immutable abstractions. While these poems respect the necessarily tense and tentative character of experience, they seem also to regard mere experience as a pretext for thought. These poems share with Kinsella's later work the desire to achieve distinctiveness through allegories of possibility. Yet their generally tight, conventional forms have the effect of limiting their range of possibilities. In addition, the typical persona of these poems seems himself an abstraction, a man with only a nominal context and without a culture.

By *Downstream*, such isolation was being questioned. The concluding line of this collection's title poem—"Searching the darkness for a landing place"—

may be taken (although somewhat glibly) as a statement emblematic of much of Kinsella's early work. Yet the collection also contains poems which, while painfully acknowledging the darkness, consider it as an archaeological redoubt. One of the effects of this adjustment is that the poet's personal past begins to offer redemptive possibilities. In addition, and with more obvious if not necessarily more far-reaching effects, a generalized past, in the form of Irish history, becomes an area of exploration. It is not the case that Kinsella never examined the past prior to *Downstream* ("King John's Castle" in *Another September* is proof to the contrary). Now, however, to the powerful sense of the past's otherness which "King John's Castle" conveys is added a sense of personal identification.

The poem in *Downstream* which demonstrates this development in Kinsella's range (a development that occurred around the time that the poet was preparing *The Tain*, his translation of an eighth century Irish epic and a major work of cultural archaeology) is "A Country Walk." Here, the persona, typically tense and restless, finds himself alone, explicitly undomesticated, with nothing between him and the legacy of the past discernible in the landscape through which he walks. The poem does not merely testify to the influential gap between present and past (a crucial preoccupation in all modern Irish writing) but also enters into the past with a brisk openness and nonjudgmental tolerance. "A Country Walk" reads like a journey of discovery, all the more so since what is discovered is not subjected to facile glorification. The fact that the past is so securely embedded in the landscape of the poem suggests that history is in the nature of things and that there is as much point in attempting to deny its enduring presence as there is in trying to divert the river which is, throughout the course of the poem, never out of the poet's sight. The poem ends, appropriately, on a note of continuity: "The inert stirred. Heart and tongue were loosed:/ 'The waters hurtle through the flooded night....' "

If anything, the present is circumvented in "A Country Walk." To ensure that the reader is aware of this, Kinsella daringly uses echoes of Yeats's "Easter 1916" to show how counterheroic is contemporary Ireland and to emphasize that the country is still, to paraphrase a line from Yeats's "September 1913," fumbling in the greasy till. This moment in "A Country Walk" prefaces the understandable admission, "I turned away." The interlude, however, draws attention to a noteworthy feature of Kinsella's verse: its satire. From the outset, Kinsella's work was capable of excoriation. The addition of local, often contemporary, Irish subject matter has created the opportunity for some scalding satirical excursions.

Perhaps the most notorious of these sallies is to be found in the long title poem of *Nightwalker and Other Poems*, a poem which, in many ways, is an illuminating counterpart to "A Country Walk." Here, the setting is urban, contemporary Dublin, and the speaker, lacking the briskness of his opposite number in "A Country Walk," refers to himself as "a vagabond/ Tethered." The demoralizing spectacle of modern life is the poem's subject. Nothing is spared. In particular, Kinsella's years in the Civil Service are the basis for a damning portrait of national ideals stultified and betrayed. This portrait goes so far as to include figures from Irish public and political life who, although distorted by the poet's satirical fury, remain eminently recognizable and still occupy the highest positions in the land. Each of the poem's numerous scenarios is exposed as hollow social charades, and in direct contrast to the sense of release felt at the end of "A Country Walk," this poem concludes on a note of anticlimax: The speaker fails to find anything of redemptive value in current conditions.

While Kinsella has by no means forsaken the satirical mode (as *Butcher's Dozen*, Peppercanister's first publication, makes vividly clear), his career has developed more fruitfully through exploring the pretexts and presuppositions of his need that poetry be a salvage operation, acknowledging existence's many disasters and the intimacy of their wreckage, and through acknowledgement saving face. Thus, in *Notes from the Land of the Dead and Other Poems* and *New Poems* the past is personal and the poems seem like diagnoses of memory and origins. Just as the setting for many of these poems is the poet's childhood home, so the poems reveal what has to be internalized for the sake of comprehending one's native land. In these poems, the speaker is the absorbed witness of others' agony, not only the agony of the deathbed but also the equally unrelenting travail described in "Tear": "sad dullness and tedious pain/ and lives bitter with hard bondage."

The poems in *Notes from the Land of the Dead and Other Poems* are also noteworthy for their degree of interaction with one another. Earlier, in *Wormwood*, Kinsella produced a strict yet supple poetic sequence. Now, the idea of sequence reemerges and takes more fluid form, a technique which can be seen embryonically in the interrelated sections of "Nightwalker" and which finds mature embodiment in many of the Peppercanister poems. This greater access to range and flexibility has enabled the poet to be less dependent on the singular effects of the dramatic lyric, where, as noted, there seemed to be a considerable degree of pressure to will experience to denote purpose. As a result of an increasing commitment to formal and metrical variety, Kinsella's voice has become more authentically meditative, its brooding habit engendering a measure of containment rather than disenchantment. This voice is present not only in such important Peppercanister collections as *One, A Technical Supplement*, and *Song of the Night and Other Poems*, but in some of the superb individual poems these books contain, notably, *Finistere (One)* and "Tao and Unfitness at Inistiogue on the River Nore" (*Song of the Night and Other Poems*).

It is not clear, however, that Kinsella established Peppercanister with the expectation that such wonderful poems would result. On the contrary, the press came into being because of the need to publish an uncharacteristic Kinsella production, a poem written for a particular occasion. The poem in question, *Butcher's Dozen*, was written in response to the killing in the city of Derry, Northern Ireland, of thirteen civil rights demonstrators by British troops. This event took place on the afternoon of Sunday, January 30, 1972, a day which will live in infamy in the minds of Irish people. The poem's immediate occasion is the horrifying event, but its subtitle clarifies the line of attack taken by Kinsella. The subtitle, "A Lesson for the Octave of Widgery," names the Lord Chief Justice of the United Kingdom, Lord Widgery, chairman of the essentially whitewashing court of inquiry set up to examine the event. Thus, *Butcher's Dozen* is a critique not only of the troops' action but also of the mind-set such actions denote. The poem's incisive and abrasive couplets enact an alternative language and disposition to that of the Lord Chief Justice's report. While, from an aesthetic standpoint, *Butcher's Dozen* is hardly Kinsella's greatest poem, its significance as a cultural document is indisputable and is reinforced by the explanatory background notes which Kinsella wrote to accompany it.

The other occasional poems contained in the Peppercanister series also have to do with significant deaths. In order of appearance, the poems are *A Selected Life, Vertical Man, The Good Fight: A Poem for the Tenth Anniversary of the Death of John F. Kennedy*, and *The Messenger*. It has become standard practice to regard *A Selected Life* and *Vertical Man* together, two independent but intimately related treatments of the one event, the untimely death of the poet's friend, Seán Ó Riada. Again, the issue of cultural significance arises. Ó Riada, as well as being an accomplished composer of classical music (*Vertical Man* is the title of one of his compositions for orchestra), was also an extraordinary influence on Irish folk musicians. His conception of the rich tradition and important heritage of Irish folk music was the direct inspiration of the internationally acclaimed group The Chieftains. More relevant to the development of Kinsella's career, Ó Riada's scholarly, pleasure-giving rehabilitation of a dormant legacy is an important counterpart to the poet's explorations in Irish-language poetry. As the penultimate stanza of *Vertical Man* has it: "From palatal darkness a voice/ rose flickering, and checked/ in glottal silence. The song/ articulated and pierced."

In the light of the public demeanor assumed in *Butcher's Dozen* and the greater degree of interplay between textural openness and formal control contained in both the Ó Riada poems, Kinsella undertook his most ambitious public poem, *The Good Fight*. Not only is the poem's subject matter ambitious, in particular given how rare it is for Irish poets to seek subjects outside the ambit of their own culture and tradition (a rarity which younger Irish poets such as Derek Mahon would work to dismantle), but also, formally speaking, *The Good Fight* is one of Kinsella's more daring experiments.

As in the case of earlier Peppercanister poems on public themes, *The Good*

Fight has an author's note attached, which begins with the remark, "With the death of Kennedy many things died, foolish expectations and assumptions, as it now seems." In a sense, the poem is a collage of contemporary desires, a view borne out by the numerous allusions to and quotations from Kennedy speeches and other sources from the period. Yet such a view is contradicted by two other features of the poem. The most obvious of these are the various quotations from Plato's *Republic* and *Laws*, which are used to counterpoint the poem's development. This classical reference has the effect of measuring Kennedy's fate against some nominal, yet conventionally uncontroversial, standard of age-old wisdom. This feature in turn is seen in terms of the pervasive sense of unfulfilled aftermath which pervades the poem. It seems remarkable that this achievement is so little known.

The significant death in *The Messenger* is not that of a well-known figure but of the poet's father. This immensely moving document testifies to Kinsella's growth as an artist. The poem's subject, death, has been a constant presence in his work since "A Lady of Quality," in *Poems*, and has been treated variously in such accomplished and representative poems as "Dick King" and "Cover Her Face." *The Messenger*, however, dwells more on celebrating the life that preceded its occasion than on the death, particularly on the public life, on the life of a man desiring to possess his culture: "The eggseed Goodness/ that is also called/ Decency." The poet's redemptive power, and his cultural as well as personal responsibility to discharge it, is seen to consummate effect in this powerful, moving work.

Blood and Family, Kinsella's first publication from a major publisher since the 1979 *Peppercanister Poems, 1972-1978*, is a reprint of more recent Peppercanister publications. This volume is the next place non-Irish readers will have to go for new Kinsella material. The volume contains *The Messenger, Songs of the Psyche, Her Vertical Smile, Out of Ireland*, and *St. Catherine's Clock*. The decision to open the volume with a reprint of *The Messenger* is a good one, given that it sets the cultural tone and prosodic idiom for the remainder of the poems. At the same time, it may be said that this volume consolidates rather than enlarges Kinsella's reputation, not merely because of the familiarity of some of its contents but because of the tension which its title invokes. The sense of belonging to two disjunctive collectives, family and nation, is here articulated thematically but also in terms of form and metrics. The result is an emphatic, diverse restatement of themes of brokenness and incompleteness which have informed the poet's vision from virtually its inception. While these themes are addressed and expressed with Kinsella's typical vehement, tight-lipped energy, the impression remains one of ground being reworked as worked anew, of a poet revisiting old preoccupations in search of unfamiliar nuances.

In the case of *Poems from Centre City*, however, there is evidence of a slightly different Kinsella. The poems in this Peppercanister pamphlet address the state of contemporary Dublin in a much more direct way than hitherto, lacking the range and ambition of, for example, "Nightwalker," and presenting themselves more intimately, as more the products of occasions, than is customary with this poet. Metrically simple and verbally direct, they attempt to come to terms with the decay—physical, moral, and institutional—of Kinsella's native place. Decay as a subject is no stranger to Kinsella's imagination. Yet, despite the comparatively fresh perspective on the poet's concerns that *Poems from Centre City* provides, it should not be assumed that the collection is intended to be thought of as a polemic. The inclusion of a poem on W. H. Auden, one of Kinsella's most permanent influences, may be understood as a caution against the reader's comprehending *Poems from Centre City* as a narrowly activist set of statements on, for example, an environmental theme.

At the same time, the diagnostic—or at least exploratory—thrust of much of Kinsella's work is once again in evidence in this small sampling of his work. The formal range is restricted; the subject matter is largely drawn from the immediacy and adventitiousness of an attentive citizen's experience. A number of the poems are suggested by memory, though all succeed in avoiding either moralizing or sentimentality. In terms of accessibility and immediate effectiveness, *Poems from Centre City* are among the most appealing of Kinsella's late works.

In terms of intensity and commitment, as well as the fascinating odyssey of his development, Thomas Kinsella is clearly a poet worthy of the utmost respect. As to his honesty and artistic integrity, it seems appropriate to allow a verse from the preamble to *The Messenger* to speak for those qualities: "The hand conceives an impossible Possible/ and exhausts in mid-reach./ What could be more natural?"

George O'Brien

Other major works

NONFICTION: *Davis, Mangan, Ferguson? Tradition and the Irish Writer,* 1970 (with W. B. Yeats).

TRANSLATIONS: *The Breastplate of Saint Patrick,* 1954 (revised as *Faeth Fiadha: The Breastplate of Saint Patrick,* 1957); *Longes mac n-Usnig, Being the Exile and Death of the Sons of Usnech,* 1954; *Thirty-three Triads, Translated from the XII Century Irish,* 1955; *The Tain,* 1969 (of *Táin bó Cuailnge*); *An Duanaire, 1600-1900: Poems of the Dispossessed,* 1981 (with Sean O Tuama).

ANTHOLOGY: *The New Oxford Book of Irish Verse,* 1986 (edited).

Bibliography

Harmon, Maurice. *The Poetry of Thomas Kinsella.* Atlantic Highlands, N.J.: Humanities Press, 1974. The author provides an overview of many of Kinsella's achievements, as well as helpful background information. Kinsella's preoccupation with the Irish language is also dealt with, and close readings of the major poems are offered. In addition, the poet's prosodical originality is analyzed. A valuable introductory guide.

John, Brian. "Irelands of the Mind: The Poetry of Thomas Kinsella and Seamus Heaney." *Canadian Journal of Irish Studies 15*, (December, 1989): 68-92. An analysis of the cultural implications of the two most important Irish poets of their generation. Kinsella's severe lyricism is contrasted with Heaney's more sensual verse. The two poets' senses of place, time, and history are also examined. The visions of Ireland produced are important evidence of the contemporary debate about Irish national identity.

Johnston, Dillon. "Kinsella and Clarke." In *Irish Poetry After Joyce.* Notre Dame, Ind.: University of Notre Dame Press, 1985. Kinsella's debt to his most important Irish poetic mentor is discussed. The origins and thrust of Kinsella's satirical tendencies are identified and analyzed. The poet's standing in the tradition of modern Irish poetry is also evaluated. An essential contribution to recent Irish literary history.

McGuinness, Arthur E. "Fragments of Identity: Thomas Kinsella's Modernist Imperative." *Colby Library Quarterly* 23 (December, 1987): 186-205. The poet's debt to, in particular, T. S. Eliot's theory and practice of poetry is considered. Kinsella's prosody is located in the context of Modernism. His emotional timbre is evaluated in the light of the same context. The essay valuably addresses Kinsella's international poetic influences.

O'Hara, Daniel. "An Interview with Thomas Kinsella." *Contemporary Poetry* 4, no. 1 (1981): 1-18. The most comprehensive of the small number of Kinsella interviews. The poet speaks freely about his various artistic concerns, concentrating in his poetic practice. The intellectual atmosphere is bracing. Kinsella's interiority and the question of its formal consequences receive much attention.

_____. "Love's Architecture: The Poetic Irony of Thomas Kinsella." *Boundary 2* 9 (Winter, 1981): 123-135. An elaborate theoretical assessment of Kinsella's achievement. The essay's approach is indebted to the criticism of Harold Bloom. The chief focus is on the metaphysical dimension of Kinsella's lyrics. A rigorous, intense account of Kinsella's art.

RUDYARD KIPLING

Born: Bombay, India; December 30, 1865
Died: Hampstead, London, England; January 18, 1936

Principal poetry

Schoolboy Lyrics, 1881; *Echoes,* 1884 (with Alice Kipling); *Departmental Ditties and Other Verses,* 1886; *Barrack-Room Ballads and Other Verses,* 1892; *The Seven Seas,* 1896; *An Almanac of Twelve Sports,* 1898; *Recessional and Other Poems,* 1899; *The Five Nations,* 1903; *Collected Verse,* 1907; *A History of England,* 1911 (with C. R. L. Fletcher); *Songs from Books,* 1912; *Sea Warfare,* 1916; *Twenty Poems,* 1918; *The Years Between,* 1919; *Rudyard Kipling's Verse: 1885-1918,* 1919; *Q. Horatii Flacci Carminum Librer Quintus,* 1920 (with Charles L. Graves, A. D. Godley, A. B. Ramsay, and R. A. Knox); *Songs for Youth,* 1924; *Sea and Sussex from Rudyard Kipling's Verse,* 1926; *Songs of the Sea,* 1927; *Rudyard Kipling's Verse: 1885-1926,* 1927; *Poems 1886-1929,* 1929; *Selected Poems,* 1931; *Rudyard Kipling's Verse: 1885-1932,* 1933; *The Sussex Edition,* 1937-1939; *Rudyard Kipling's Verse: Definitive Edition,* 1940.

Other literary forms

Rudyard Kipling is best known for his short stories. His *Just So Stories* (1902), *The Jungle Book* (1894), and *The Second Jungle Book* (1895), are favorites with children and are among the most widely read collections of stories in the world. His novel *Kim* (1901) also ranks among the world's most popular books. Kipling's fiction, however, presents a critic with most of the problems that his verse presents, making it difficult to discuss one without the other. The fiction is often thought to be barbaric in content and representative of a discredited imperialistic point of view; too often, critics discuss Kipling's political views (which are often misrepresented) rather than his literary merits. Kipling's contempt for intellectualism makes him unfashionable in most critical circles, and those who admit to having admired him seem to be ashamed of their affection. Not all critics, however, have been ambiguous in their admiration of Kipling's work; especially since the 1960's, critics have made the short stories objects of serious study. In any case, Kipling's fiction has remained immensely popular from the late Victorian era to the present. It has been made into no fewer than thirteen motion pictures, including *Captains Courageous* (1937) and *The Jungle Book* (1942 and 1967). Kipling's fiction has the vigor and passion that appeal to the popular imagination, and a subtlety and brilliant prose style that are worthy of careful study.

Achievements

Henry James called Kipling a genius; T. S. Eliot called him a writer of verse who sometimes ascended to poetry. His *Departmental Ditties and Other*

Verses brought him extravagant praise and fame. Some scholars assert that he was the world's best-known author from the 1890's to his death. Yet, even his admirers have been uncertain of his achievement, particularly in poetry. Kipling often sang his poems while he composed them; they are often ballads or hymns, and all feature clear rhythms that urge a reader to read them aloud. Their surface themes are usually easy to understand; the language is clear and accessible to even casual readers.

Perhaps the accessibility of Kipling's verse is the source of the confusion; twentieth century critics have all too often regarded poetry that is popular among the great unwashed as automatically bad; obscurity has been the hallmark of much of the best of twentieth century poetry. Kipling's verse is informed by the Victorian masters, such as Alfred, Lord Tennyson and Algernon Charles Swinburne. It is out of step with the modernist school, which may be why many readers think of Kipling as Victorian, even though he actively wrote and published into the 1930's; his autobiography appeared in 1937, the year after his death. His harsh views of ordinary people, his angry polemics, political conservatism, and lack of faith in so-called utopian societies, and the Cassandra-like prophecies of war which fill much of his verse, repel many aesthetes and political liberals. Kipling has been portrayed as a philistine. The truth is that he did not understand much of the social change of his lifetime, but he understood people, and in his verse he preserves the thoughts, emotions, hopes, and despairs of people usually ignored by poets. If one approaches his verse with an open mind, one will likely find brilliant prosody, excellent phrasing, surprising metaphors, and a poetic ethos that transcends literary and political fashion.

Kipling won the Nobel Prize for Literature in 1907. The award was, in part, a recognition of Kipling's worldwide appeal to readers; he touched more hearts and minds than anyone else of his generation. His work added phrases to the English language; few today realize that they paraphrase Kipling when they assert that "the female is deadlier than the male," or that "East is East and West is West."

Biography

Joseph Rudyard Kipling was born in Bombay, India, on December 30, 1865. His parents were John Lockwood Kipling and Alice (née Macdonald) Kipling. His father was then a sculptor and designer, and was Principal and Professor of Architectural Sculpture of the School of Art at Bombay, and he later became Curator of the Museum at Lahore. His mother came from a family of accomplished women. John Lockwood Kipling set many of the high standards for literary skill that Rudyard endeavored to match in both fiction and poetry. Both parents encouraged their son's literary efforts and took pride in his achievements.

Except for a brief visit to England, Rudyard Kipling spent his first five years in India. In 1871 he was taken with his sister Alice to England and left with Captain and Mrs. Holloway of Lorne Lodge in Southsea. After several unhappy years in the ungentle care of Mrs. Holloway, he left Lorne Lodge in 1877. In 1878, he was sent to United Services College in Devon. In 1882, he traveled to Lahore, where his father had found him a job as a reporter for the *Civil and Military Gazette*. He had seen little of his parents since 1871. Somewhat to his annoyance, he discovered that his parents had gathered the verses from his letters to them and had them published as *Schoolboy Lyrics* in 1881. In 1887, he joined the staff of the *Pioneer* of Allahabad, which he left in 1889. His experiences in England figure in many of his stories; his experiences as a journalist in India are reflected not only in his fiction, but also in much of his best verse.

In 1888, Émile Édouard Moreau began The Indian Library, primarily to help Kipling and to capitalize on the young writer's talents. The first six volumes of the series consisted of Kipling's work. In 1889 Kipling traveled to Singapore, Hong Kong, Japan, through the United States, and to England. His *Departmental Ditties and Other Verses* was printed in England in 1890, and the response to his poetry moved him from the status of a promising young writer to the forefront not only of English letters, but also of world literature. His writing from 1890 onward brought him wealth and lasting popularity. The initial praise of his work was extraordinary—in 1892, Henry James wrote to his brother William, "Kipling strikes me as personally the most complete man of genius (as distinct from fine intelligence) that I have ever known"—but by the 1900's he would suffer extraordinary abuse at the hands of the critics. Kipling married Caroline Starr Balestier in 1892 and moved to Brattleboro, Vermont, where her relatives lived. While living in the United States he had two daughters. Although he liked his home in Vermont, Kipling left the United States when his enmity with his brother-in-law became public and created a scandal. After some traveling, he returned to visit his mother-in-law; during a stay in New York he and his family fell ill; his wife, younger daughter, Elsie, and baby son, recovered quickly, but he nearly died and his elder daughter, Josephine, did die.

He settled at Rottingdean in England in 1897. His wife took charge of much of his family and social affairs, and A. P. Watt, a literary agent, handled his literary and business affairs. His life in Rottingdean was productive, but isolated; as the years passed, he saw less and less of his literary friends. In 1907, to the chagrin of his detractors, he won the Nobel Prize for Literature. His poetry at the time warned England of impending war and of England's unpreparedness. When war began in 1914, his son, with his father's help, enlisted in the army. In late 1915, John Kipling was killed in a British attack during the Battle of Loos. From the end of World War I to his death, Kipling worked to perfect his literary art and vigorously expressed his opinions on politics and society. At the end of his life he wrote his autobiography and helped prepare the Sussex Edition of his works. He died January 18, 1936, while embarking on a vacation. His ashes were buried in Westminster Abbey's Poets' Corner.

Analysis

Rudyard Kipling's poetry is such a part of the culture of English-speaking people that one is hard put to approach his work without preconceived notions of its quality and content. In his own day, Kipling's poetry outraged many critics and provided handy epithets for politicians of many political leanings. Even today, scholars can be excited by his so-called racial and imperialistic topics. Myths thus abound. Kipling's verse is called racist; in fact, Kipling's verse repeatedly emphasizes that no one can rightfully be regarded superior to another on the basis of race or origin. "The White Man's Burden," he wrote, was to "Fill full the mouth of Famine/ And bid the sickness cease." Although imperialistic, the poem emphasizes not race, but the obligations of Europeans and Americans to the oppressed peoples of the world.

Kipling is said to glorify warfare by devoting much of his poetry to descriptions of the lives of soldiers; in fact, he shows war to be ugly and stupid. In "The Last of the Light Brigade," he portrays veterans of the Crimean War as destitute: "We leave to the streets and the workhouse the charge of the Light Brigade!" In the poem, Kipling calls attention to the differences between Tennyson's poetic description of the ill-fated charge and the degradation that characterized the soldiers' lives. Another myth is that Kipling's poetry is coarse and crude. The subject matter is, indeed, sometimes crude, but not the prosody. Even T. S. Eliot, who admired Kipling's work, asserted that Kipling wrote good verse that occasionally ascended to poetry, but that in general Kipling did not write poetry. Some of the sources of misconceptions about Kipling's poetic achievement seem obvious: casual or careless readings might glean only the surface remarks of subtle poems; Kipling's political poetry was and remains unpalatable to many people who condemn it on no other grounds than political distastefulness; his aggressive dislike of academics and admiration for men of action alienate many of those who would be likeliest to write about his poetry. Some of the negative myths are Kipling's fault. If one writes on the politics of the moment, one invites political interpretations of one's work.

Nevertheless, too much of the criticism of Kipling's poetry is clearly biased. Many rationales for denigrating the poetry seem contrived, as if covering reasons that would not bear exposure. After all, portraits of the hard lives of working people, as well as soldiers, dominate novels from Zola to the present; such novels are often praised for their realism. One of the most highly regarded Anglo-American poets of the twentieth century, Ezra Pound, was a Fascist who made propaganda radio broadcasts from Italy during World War II. His avowed racism is well-known and is as unpalatable to well-informed and compassionate people as anything to be found in the work of Kipling. Indeed, Kipling deplored Nazi Germany and dictatorships in general. Yet Pound was fashionable; Kipling was not.

Kipling's unfashionableness has its origins in two important aspects of his poetry: his versification was clear and usually unadorned, and his subjects were usually plain, working-class people. He began his career in the Victorian era, and his lyrical and narrative poetry has more in common with the styles of Tennyson, Robert Browning, and Swinburne than it has with the styles that have been predominant in a more modern age. One of the important aspects of modernism in poetry was the emphasis on metaphor; metaphors were used to make such works as Eliot's *The Waste Land* (1922) hauntingly remote from casual reading. Critics came to expect good poetry to demand close and sometimes prolonged reading in order for one to understand even the most basic meanings of the verse.

Kipling's approach to his poetry was neither better nor worse than that of his later contemporaries; it was merely different, because he aimed for an audience other than the literary elite. Poetry had been a genre for popular reading; Kipling kept it such. His best poetry will reward close reading by perceptive readers; it will also reward the unskilled or casual reader with a basic surface meaning. For example, "Loot" provides a basic discussion of techniques for looting; the persona—the poem's speaker—says, "always work in pairs—/ It 'alves the gain, but safer you will find." A quick reading elicits the picture of a lowly soldier providing a description of an ugly but realistic aspect of war (and provides ammunition against Kipling for anyone who is determined to misread the poem as somehow glorifying looting). A close reading of the poem, however, reveals a careful use of language; Kipling uses his knowledge of soldiers and their ballads to give his persona an authentic voice. One will also discover a picture of the mindless violence and degradation of war at the level of the common foot soldier. Kipling's style was out of step with the literary movement of his day; it was judged by the wrong standards and often still is.

Poetry has traditionally been regarded as the elite of literary genres. The term *poet* was reserved in the sixteenth, seventeenth, and eighteenth centuries for those who had excelled in literature; it was a term of honor to which writers aspired. Poetry has been thought of as appropriate to high aspirations and great ideas; it has been considered "elevating." The Victorians added the notion that poetry was morally uplifting and that a poet was obliged to discuss high topics in grand language; thus, biblical phrasing and high-sounding archaisms such as "thee" and "thou" lingered in nineteenth century poetry. No matter how much they were involved with the literary revolutions of their time, Kipling's contemporaries were children of the Victorians. Many of the most admired poems of the first three decades of the twentieth century focused on the Arthurian legends or revived Latin poetic traditions.

Kipling's poetry, in contrast, focuses on common people, the active people whose raw manner of dealing with the world most interested him. Soldiers, as the frequent vanguard of the British Empire and the products of the laboring classes, were often subjects of Kipling's poetry; laborers themselves were also often the subject of his verse. Kipling gave these people voices; his keen insight made his language strikingly acute. It is coarse, harsh, and elemental. In addition, the poetry by which he is best known is in the ballad form. The ballad is a lyrical folk song that grows and changes with use and custom; it is heard in bars, at country fairs, and in the barracks of soldiers. Kipling's use of the ballad explains in part Eliot's judgment that Kipling is a verse-writer instead of a poet; the form is believed by some scholars to be beneath poetry.

Thus, elitism has had much to do with negative responses to Kipling; critics seem to believe that Kipling has degraded verse. Even though he was a conservative with some Victorian notions of poetry, Kipling was ahead of his time. Egalitarianism became one of the significant movements in the twentieth century; literacy burgeoned, as did access to literature. Kipling wrote for the broad literate mass of people; he gave voices to people who were generally left out of poetry, and he did not romanticize them. A soldier's achievement is to survive one more day; a laborer's achievement is to feed himself one more day. Their contempt for those who are not physically active fits well with Kipling's own disgust with aesthetes who are out of touch with much that is thought and done by those who provide the foundations for civilization.

Kipling's verse is highly crafted poetry. It uses metaphors and prosody in unusual ways, but this is a strength, not a weakness. Kipling's mastery of metaphor is apparent, for example, in "The Way Through the Woods," which describes an eroded road that was closed some seventy years before. On its surface, the poem offers a wistful description of the encroachment by the wilderness on a road no longer used. It is more than that, however; there is an eeriness in its description of "coppice and heath," "ring-dove broods," and "trout-ringed pools," which all utterly hide a road that makes its presence felt only in echoes of the past. The lost road and the woods that have covered it are metaphors for the passage of time and the transitoriness of human works. The theme of the fragility of human achievements is an important one in poetry; in "The Way Through the Woods," Kipling makes the theme mystical and haunting.

The near futility of human endeavors when confronting time is a common motif of Kipling's work. Although "The Way Through the Woods" is remote in tone and metaphor, Kipling is perfectly willing to be blunt—and still metaphorical. In "Cities and Thrones and Powers" he uses flowers as metaphors:

                         Cities and Thrones and Powers
                         Stand in Time's eye,
                         Almost as long as flowers,
                         Which daily die:

The poem continues and turns tragedy into triumph:

                         But, as new buds put forth
                         To glad new men,
                         Out of the spent and unconsidered Earth
                         The Cities rise again.

Few readers would have trouble understanding the basic metaphor: flowers die but leave seeds that grow into new flowers, and cities do the same. Even Kipling's eccentric phrase "Almost as long as flowers" is within easy reach of the unsophisticated reader: in the vastness of time, cities exist only briefly. The surface meanings of the central metaphor do not preclude subtlety. The transitoriness of "Cities and Thrones and Powers" is a melancholy topic, one that other poets have used to show the vanity of human achievements. Percy Bysshe Shelley's "Ozymandias" is the archetypal expression of the theme; a pedestal alone in the desert bears an almost meaningless inscription: "My name is Ozymandias, king of kings:/ Look on my works, ye Mighty, and despair!" Shelley adds: "Nothing beside remains." A city and civilization are reduced to desert. Kipling takes the same sad theme, attaches it to flowers, making the frail plants bear the weight of civilization, and in flowers he reveals that seeming transitoriness is in fact a cycle of renewal. "Time," he says, "Ordains . . . That in our very death,/ And burial sure,/ Shadow to shadow, well persuaded, saith,/ See how our works endure!" In the deaths of human works are the seeds of new works: one civilization begets another.

     Kipling's interest in the passing and survival of civilizations also extended to current events. In "The Dykes" of 1902, he ponders the dangers to Britain posed by the militancy of Europe. "These are the dykes our fathers made: we have never known a breach," he says. The people of Britain have built protections against their enemies, but through neglect the "dykes" might be broken. "An evil ember bedded in ash—a spark blown west by the wind . . ./ We are surrendered to night and the sea—the gale and the tide behind!" Kipling the prophet uses metaphor to warn of war. "The Dykes" is dynamic and threatening; history has shown its warning to be apt.

     Kipling's narrative poetry is probably his best-known. It includes "Gunga Din" and "The Ballad of East and West," both of which discuss British imperialism and cultural differences and are thus unfashionable. "Gunga Din" is as well-known a poem as exists in English. In it Gunga Din, a water-bearer for British soldiers in India, faithfully serves his masters and saves the life of the poem's narrator—giving up his own life in the process. Kipling uses the rhythm of the ballad form to create strikingly memorable phrases, including the last lines:

> You Lazarushian-leather Gunga Din!
> Though I've belted you and flayed you,
> By the livin' Gawd that made you,
> You're a better man than I am, Gunga Din!

The language is raw and the verse melodic; the combination is powerful. Gunga Din's life is shown to be miserable, and his masters are shown as beastly, but Gunga Din is revealed as having a noble quality that Kipling valued; Gunga Din cares enough for his fellow men to die for them. Thus, the last line summarizes the central theme of the poem; Gunga Din is the better man.

In a similar vein, "The Ballad of East and West" shows that all men can understand one another in the fundamental test of courage:

> Oh, East is East and West is West, and never the twain shall meet,
> Till Earth and Sky stand presently at God's great Judgment Seat;
> But there is neither East nor West, Border, nor Breed, nor Birth,
> When two strong men stand face to face, though they come from the ends of the earth!

Kipling admired men of action and physical courage. He asserted that men can communicate on fundamental levels that transcend the veneer of culture. In "The Ballad of East and West" two strong men are brought face to face, their differences seemingly beyond hope of peaceful resolution. They discover that they are alike and not as different as others would believe. Beginning as enemies, they part as friends.

Kipling dealt with large metaphysical ideas, with the cycles of civilizations and the threats to Western civilization, yet for all his great themes, Kipling was at home with subjects no more lofty than the ordinary person's hope for a better future. In "The Absent-Minded Beggar," for example, Kipling reminds his readers of the hard lot of the dependents of the soldiers who fought in the Boer War. "When you've finished killing Kruger with your mouth,/ Will you kindly drop a shilling in my little tamborine/ For a gentleman in khaki order South?" The poem was written to help raise money for the needs of the families of the soldiers. The tone is sympathetic but honest. The British soldier has "left a lot of little things behind him!" The "little things" include his children—not necessarily legitimate—wives, lovers, girlfriends, and debts. The families will "live on half o' nothing . . . 'Cause the man that earns the wage is ordered out." The soldier is "an absent-minded beggar, but he heard his country call." Kipling's language demonstrates his understanding of his subject. The poem reveals the fundamental Kipling—not imperialist, not prophet, not poet playing with great poetic conceits—but a poet who understands people and cares about them. Few writers can be honestly said to have cared more about their subjects than Kipling.

Long after the politics of his day are forgotten and his polemics have become of interest only to literary historians, Kipling's essential efforts will still have meaning. Readers who approach Kipling's verse with a love for poetry can still declare as did David Masson to his students at Edinburgh in 1890, while holding a copy of "Danny Deever," "Here's Literature! Here's Literature at last!"

Kirk H. Beetz

Other major works

LONG FICTION: *The Light That Failed*, 1890; *The Naulahka: A Story of East and West*, 1892 (with Wolcott Balestier); *Captains Courageous: A Story of the Grand Banks*, 1897; *Kim*, 1901.

SHORT FICTION: *Quartette*, 1885 (with John Lockwood Kipling, Alice Macdonald Kipling, and Alice Kipling); *Plain Tales from the Hills*, 1888; *Soldiers Three: A Collection of Stories*, 1888; *The Story of the Gadsbys: A Tale Without a Plot*, 1888; *In Black and White*, 1888; *Under the Deodars*, 1888; *The Phantom Rickshaw and Other Tales*, 1888; *Wee Willie Winkie and Other Child Stories*, 1888; *The Courting of Dinah Shadd and Other Stories*, 1890; *The City of Dreadful Night and Other Places*, 1890; *Mine Own People*, 1891; *Life's Handicap*, 1891; *Many Inventions*, 1893; *The Jungle Book*, 1894; *The Second Jungle Book*, 1895; *Soldier Tales*, 1896; *The Day's Work*, 1898; *Stalky & Co.*, 1899; *Just So Stories*, 1902; *Traffics and Discoveries*, 1904; *Puck of Pook's Hill*, 1906; *Actions and Reactions*, 1909; *Rewards and Fairies*, 1910; *A Diversity of Creatures*, 1917; *Land and Sea Tales for Scouts and Guides*, 1923; *"They" and the Brushwood Boy*, 1925; *Debits and Credits*, 1926; *Thy Servant a Dog*, 1930; *Humorous Tales*, 1931; *Animal Stories*, 1932; *Limits and Renewals*, 1932; *Collected Dog Stories*, 1934.

NONFICTION: *American Notes*, 1891; *Beast and Man in India*, 1891; *Letters of Marque*, 1891; *The Smith Administration*, 1891; *A Fleet in Being: Notes of Two Trips with the Channel Squadron*, 1898; *From Sea to Sea: Letters of Travel*, 1899; *Letters to the Family*, 1908; *The New Army in Training*, 1914; *France at War*, 1915; *The Fringes of the Fleet*, 1915; *Sea Warfare*, 1916; *Letters of Travel, 1892-1913*, 1920; *The Irish Guards in the Great War*, 1923; *A Book of Words*, 1928; *Souvenirs of France*, 1933; *Something of Myself: For My Friends Known and Unknown*, 1937; *Uncollected Prose*, 1938 (2 volumes); *Rudyard Kipling to Rider Haggard: The Record of a Friendship*, 1965 (Morton N. Cohen, editor).

MISCELLANEOUS: *The Sussex Edition of the Complete Works in Prose and Verse of Rudyard Kipling*, 1937-1939 (35 volumes).

Bibliography

Carrington, Charles E. *Rudyard Kipling: His Life and Work*. 3d ed. London:

Macmillan, 1978. This detailed study of Rudyard Kipling as a man of letters begins and ends by ranking Kipling with Daniel Defoe and Charles Dickens, as a popular writer whose appeal has never waned. Still the standard biography, it contains a chronology, a genealogical chart, a bibliography of printed and unprinted sources, notes, useful appendices, and an index.

Gilbert, Elliot L., ed. *Kipling and the Critics.* New York: New York University Press, 1965. A selection of classic essays about Kipling with a brief but detailed survey of the history of Kipling's criticism. The formidable array of critics includes T. S. Eliot, Bonamy Dobree, and Lionel Trilling. The essays by Eliot and Dobree in particular were responsible for revivals of interest in Kipling.

Harrison, James. *Rudyard Kipling.* Boston: Twayne, 1982. In this useful volume, Harrison divides Kipling's life into three periods; within each, he groups the stories thematically to show Kipling's preoccupations. Harrison sees more poetry in Kipling's prose than in his poetry. The poems' didacticism regarding views many consider outdated and distasteful, he argues, will prevent them from regaining critical regard. The text contains notes and references, a bibliography, and an index.

Tompkins, J. M. S. *The Art of Rudyard Kipling.* 2d ed. Lincoln: University of Nebraska Press, 1965. The best and most comprehensive critical assessment of Kipling's work. Focuses on the timeless human and moral themes in Kipling's fiction and verses, and on his craftsmanship. Supplemented by an index and a list of the tales, essays and verses discussed in this study, along with their dates of publication and the sources in which they appear.

Wilson, Angus. *The Strange Ride of Rudyard Kipling: His Life and Works.* New York: Viking Press, 1977. In this indispensable source, Wilson combines criticism and biography. He argues that while Kipling and his work may have suffered from his fear of self-knowledge, few writers have gone outside the usual range in so many different directions with such skill. References and an index supplement the text.

CAROLYN KIZER

Born: Spokane, Washington; December 10, 1925

Principal poetry

The Ungrateful Garden, 1961; *Knock upon Silence*, 1965; *Midnight Was My Cry: New and Selected Poems*, 1971; *Mermaids in the Basement: Poems for Women*, 1984; *Yin: New Poems*, 1984; *The Nearness of You*, 1986.

Other literary forms

Carolyn Kizer is the author of numerous critical reviews and articles on poetry that have been published in major periodicals. She is a prolific translator of poetry from other languages, including Chinese, Japanese, Urdu, Macedonian, Yiddish, French, and French African. An account of an academic year spent in Pakistan, "Pakistan Journal," is included in her book of poetry translations *Carrying Over* (1988). "A Month in Summer," a prose-poem that mingles four-line haiku with journal entries, appeared in *Mermaids in the Basement*, and an illuminating prose reminiscence of her extraordinary mother, entitled "A Muse," is included in *Yin*. "Dear Bob" in *The Nearness of You*, a letter written in response to a request for information about her late father, is a revealing autobiographical memoir about a formidable parent. She has written several short stories, one of which, "A Slight Mechanical Failure," appeared in *The Quarterly Review of Literature* in 1978, and she was coeditor, with Elaine Dallman and Barbara Gelpi, of *Woman Poet: The West* (1980).

Achievements

When the 1985 Pulitzer Prize for Poetry was awarded to Carolyn Kizer for *Yin*, her admirers considered that appropriate recognition was being given, if belatedly. Many others were undoubtedly asking, "Carolyn who?" because her work has not received a great amount of critical attention, and consequently her name is not well known. At an interview following her winning of the Pulitzer Prize, Kizer offered two explanations for her relative neglect by critics: "For one thing, I think my poems are very clear, so my work lacks the interesting ambiguities that appeal to the critical mind. And I write in so many genres—free verse, formal verse, just about anything—that I can't be pigeonholed." Possibly another reason for critical neglect is that Kizer is a poet of relatively slender output, one who chooses to be known more for the excellence of her work than for the number of her poems. Nevertheless, in the wake of the Pulitzer Prize and with the increasing interest in gender studies on college and university campuses, Kizer is attaining greater recognition as a feminist writer and critic. Some of her writings about women, particularly "Pro Femina," are and have for some time been well known to students of women's poetry.

Although she may not have achieved the name recognition of a Sylvia Plath or an Adrienne Rich, Carolyn Kizer's career as a poet has not been lacking in awards and honors. In the same year that she won the Pulitzer Prize, she was awarded a five-thousand-dollar prize by the American Academy and Institute of Arts and Letters. Among her other honors are the Masefield Prize from the Poetry Society of America in 1983, the Governors Award from the State of Washington and an award from San Francisco Arts Commission, both for *Mermaids in the Basement*, and the Theodore Roethke Memorial Foundation Poetry Award in 1988 for *The Nearness of You*. She is a recipient of the Frost Medal for Lifetime Achievement in Poetry from the Poetry Society of America.

Biography

Carolyn Kizer was born December 10, 1925, in Spokane, Washington, the only child of exceptional parents, Mabel Ashley Kizer and Benjamin Hamilton Kizer. Her mother had earned a Ph.D. in biology from Stanford University in 1904, taught at Mills College and San Francisco State while helping three younger brothers through college, administered the first federally sponsored drug clinic in New York, and worked as organizer for the Industrial Workers of the World. She had been in her mid-forties by the time she met and married Benjamin, a well-established Spokane lawyer and regional planner. Kizer's recollections of her childhood convey ambivalent feelings toward her distinguished but difficult parents. Her father's emotionally remote, authoritarian personality intimidated and disturbed her, yet she feels profound respect for his integrity, self-discipline, and achievements. Her brilliant mother's abandonment of a career for a near-neurotic obsession with her daughter, especially with her daughter's "creativity," also dismayed Kizer. She confesses that her mother's demands and expectations hampered her, and that she could only come into her own as a serious poet after her mother's death. Yet she also pays tribute to her mother as beloved muse: "I wrote the poems for her. I still do."

After receiving a B.A. degree from Sarah Lawrence College in 1945, Kizer began graduate studies at Columbia University, where she became a Fellow of the Chinese Government in Comparative Literature; she traveled to Taiwan, where she lived for one year. Upon her return she studied poetry with Theodore Roethke at the University of Washington and settled in Seattle. From 1948 to 1954 she was married to Charles Stimson Bullitt, with whom she has three children: Ashley, Scott, and Jill. In 1959 she founded the Seattle-based poetry journal *Poetry Northwest*, which she edited until 1965. In 1964-1965 she was a specialist in literature for the United States Department of State in Pakistan. From 1966 to 1970 she was the first director of literature programs for the newly created National Endowment for the Arts, a position in which she aided struggling writers and promoted poetry readings in inner-city schools.

In addition to writing, editing, and translating, she has since 1970 lectured and given readings of her poetry at numerous colleges and universities throughout the United States and Europe. She has been poet-in-residence and visiting professor of poetry at the University of North Carolina at Chapel Hill, Ohio University, University of Iowa, University of Maryland, Stanford University, Princeton University, Washington University, Barnard College, and Columbia University. In 1975 she was married to John Marshall Woodbridge, an architect and planner with whom she lives in Sonoma, California.

The breadth of Kizer's interests in other times, other places, other cultures, other languages and literatures, has made her one of the United States' least provincial poets. Frequently her poems are grounded in the largest contexts of myth, history, and philosophy, so that they are not all as "clear" and easily accessible as she has avowed. An international perspective is evident in many ways in her work, in her love of Oriental forms as well as in her translations. Her worldview is well summarized by her comment on *Carrying Over*, a book of poems translated from Chinese, Urdu, Macedonian, Yiddish, and French African: she refers to the book as "a kind of paradigm of our world as I wish it were, of the United Nations as I pray it might become: all of us, with sharply individual voices, but together—an orchestra!"

Analysis

Although Carolyn Kizer has asserted that her poems are "very clear" and lacking in "interesting ambiguities that appeal to the critical mind," a number of them show considerable complexity of style, tone, and subject. Her poems based on Greek myth are an example of one kind of complexity, a complexity that has irritated at least some readers, who wish that she would express herself directly, without using myth. To this complaint Kizer would undoubtedly respond first by pointing to a large number of her poems in which she does express herself quite directly, and second by observing that not everything can or should be so expressed. As Robert Frost said in a talk titled "Education by Poetry," "Poetry provides the one permissible way of saying one thing and meaning another. People say, 'why don't you say what you mean?' We never do that . . . being all of us too much poets. We like to talk in parables and in hints and in indirections." With characteristic insight, Kizer observes that people need to use metaphor, to speak of one thing in terms of another, because "the metaphor, like love,/ Springs from the very separateness of things." Additionally, she has spoken of the need to transform grim or painful experience by imposing a form on it through imagination and language.

Not all of her poems that use myth are difficult and obscure. The title poem in *The Ungrateful Garden* uses the familiar myth of King Midas and his golden touch to underscore the ironies of human beings' attitude toward nature. Having made nature unnatural, Midas is maddened by the results. Furious to find his eyes blinded by golden flowers, his ears assaulted by "the heavy clang of leaf on leaf," his fingers pricked by golden thorns, his feet cut by golden stubble in his garden, he concludes: "Nature is evil."

At other times, Kizer uses Greek myth to write poems of metaphysical wit, such as "The Copulating Gods." The deities are amused by the way mortals have misunderstood the frank carnality of the gods. Unable to comprehend the gods' sensual pleasure, humans have invented histories for them and made them into a confused religion of "spiritual lust." "The headboard of our bed became their altar," declares a lascivious goddess as she returns to dalliance with her lover:

> Tracing again the bones of your famous face,
> I know we are not their history but our myth.
> Heaven prevents time, and our astral raptures
> Float buoyant in the universe. Come, kiss!
> Come, swoon again, we who invented dying
> And the whole alchemy of resurrection.
> They will concoct a scripture explaining this.

In another poem inspired by Greek myth, "The Dying Goddess," Venus is no longer the revered love goddess. The poem is a witty comment on a degenerate society in which love has been replaced. Some men are looking for mothers, others are taking to drink; still others join "odd cults . . . involving midgets,/ Partial castration, dismemberment of children," but none are worshipers of Venus. In the end, her image disappearing even from her own mirror, "she turns her face from the smokeless brazier." Kizer's attitude toward the modern world frequently conveys a feeling of decline or loss. In "The Old Gods," a lament for the lost splendor of the classical world, Zeus and his pantheon have fallen on hard times, replaced by Christianity ("that God-kissed girl, and her God-given Son") and other "windy deities" of disgusting meekness. The speaker in the poem is ambivalent: "You old Gods, I never cared about you./ I don't feel for the Greeks; I loathe the Romans." Still, the speaker's resentment at what has replaced the old gods rouses him to fight on their side, even knowing it is the losing side in this "battle of the Gods."

In other poems, Kizer uses Greek myth to develop feminist themes. "In "Hera, Hung from the Sky," Hera is punished for having the audacity to dream of sexual equality, to imagine "that woman was great as man." Zeus punishes his wife by hanging her by her heels from the sky: having "lost the war of the air," she is left "half-strangled" in her hair, dangling, "drowned in fire." "Semele Recycled" is a quasi-comic, surreal account of what happened after Semele, a mortal, was burned to ashes when her lover Zeus appeared to her in all of his blazing glory. The scattered parts of her body are horribly degraded, but are magically reassembled at the god's command. God and mortal, their bodies meeting "like a thunderclap/ in mid-day," startling the cattle and bystanders, make love on a compost heap. Besides being a comment on the male god's absolute command over life, death, and rebirth, the poem is interested in the relationship between the "sacred" and "profane" aspects of love. Yeats's perception that "fair and foul are near of kin,/ And fair needs foul" is relevant here, as is Crazy Jane's statement that "Love has pitched his mansion in/ The place of excrement;/ For nothing can be sole or whole/ That has not been rent." Presumably, Kizer's Semele agrees.

In "Persephone Pauses," the goddess Persephone's bondage to Hades and the Underworld is a metaphor for woman's bondage to a sensual desire she is powerless to resist. Persephone's "dolor" and "dower" are the "sweet Hell" of female sexuality. The equivocal tone of the poem is perfectly conveyed when Persephone, realizing that her bondage means that only half of her life is "spent in light," nevertheless descends with an almost cheery "Summertime, goodnight!"

"Pro Femina," which first appeared in *Knock upon Silence*, is Kizer's fullest and most celebrated treatment of feminist themes. It does not use myth, but its form was inspired by classical literature. A three-part witty verse satire about "the fate of women," it turns the tables on Juvenal's Tenth Satire, which attacked women's vices, particularly vanity. Kizer's cunning strategy is to begin by conceding, "We *are* hyenas. Yes, we admit it./ While men have politely debated free will, we have howled for it,/ Howl still. . . ." The poem's catalog of injustices and outrages that women are expected to suffer in a male-dominated culture explains why women are "hyenas." Kizer's honesty compels her to acknowledge in some cases women's complicity in their own suffering—for example, the "cabbageheads" "who, vague-eyed and acquiescent, worshiped God as a man." Far worse are the women who sold out, became "scabs to their stricken sisterhood,/ Impugning our sex to stay in good with the men." Kizer's sardonic comment: how the men "must have swaggered/ When women themselves endorsed their own inferiority!"

With canny eye for telling detail, Kizer loads the poem with examples of the ways women are dehumanized and trivialized, as in the culturally mandated femine concern with "surfaces," with dress and appearance: "So primp, preen, prink, pluck and prize your flesh,/ All posturings! All ravishment! All sensibility!/ Meanwhile, have you used your mind today?" Some women, writers, try to escape marginalization by "aping the ways of the men," smoking cigars, swearing, drinking straight shots, all in hope of receiving the ultimate compliment: "*she writes like a man*!" Others are driven to opposite extremes, going "mad in a mist of chiffon," or become practical feminists such as the poet Sara Teasdale, who wore chiffon over red flannel underwear. Kizer reserves special scorn for the "Quarterly priestesses/ Who flog men for fun, and kick women to maim competition," but she believes that women writers are "emerging from all that, more or less," and perhaps better times for women are at hand.

Finally, having told the reader what she cannot stand, Kizer tells what she wants: free women of steady vision, discipline, and courage. These women, if unmarried, will keep their heads and their pride; if married, they will believe their creative work more important than doing dishes; if mothers, they will neither devour nor be devoured by their children. These women's husbands or lovers prefer and know how to cherish free women. This view in "Pro Femina" accords well with a statement Kizer made in an interview. Defining feminism as "equality with men in every way," she explains what that means to her:

> I don't want women to have to be superwomen. I want them to be able to be talented and good at what they do, and not have to be the perfect wife, the perfect mother, the perfect job-holder, and crochet besides. . . . I want them able to make money commensurate with their efforts. I want them to have flex-time so they can take time off for their children in emergencies. . . . I want them not to get fired if they get pregnant, and to have husbands who help out, not because they have to but because they want to.

Clearly, Kizer is not angry, radical, or separatist in her views, despite the harshly satiric tone of "Pro Femina." "I'm not particularly angry at men," she said. "I don't think anybody likes relinquishing power. If we lived in a matriarchy I wouldn't like to give it up either. The division of power is one of the things that make marriage a very complex relationship—trying to keep things in some kind of reasonable balance. . . . Constant attention has to be paid . . . ."

To the three sections of "Pro Femina" just discussed, Kizer added a fourth section, "Fanny," when "Pro Femina" was reprinted in *Mermaids in the Basement.* ("Fanny" also appeared as a separate poem in *Yin.*) "Fanny," a long poem written in Roman hexameter, purports to be the diary of Frances, the fifty-year-old wife of Robert Louis Stevenson, written in Samoa in 1890 during the last year of his life. It is a singular account of hardship and harvest, triumph and terror. While her famous husband writes, Fanny builds a pig house, bakes bread in the rain, and, earth mother that she is, furiously plants—corn, potatoes, eggplant, pineapple, artichoke, cantaloupe, mangoes, strawberries, pumpkin. Samoa, however, is no Eden. The strawberries and potatoes rot, rats eat and horses trample the corn, the cantaloupe are stolen, and in the leaking and listing house, mildew spreads. Fanny, undaunted, goes on planting while her husband mocks her, calling her a peasant "because I delve in the earth." She broods a bit on this hurtful remark, but the rigors of everyday life leave her little time for such self-indulgence. Living with influenza epidemics, volcanoes, hurricanes, war, headhunters, and—what may be even worse—a vexing mother-in-law, an irritating clergyman, and someone who regularly reads and censors her diary, Fanny survives it all. Her husband dies, but Fanny triumphs: by removing her husband from London's unhealthy climate and nourishing him, she had "kept him alive for eight more years." She feels well satisfied. Yet the reader sees the self-sacrifice and loneliness of a brave woman, which is all the more poignant because it is unconscious.

Possibly Kizer added "Fanny" to "Pro Femina" in order to provide a model of feminine virtue, or possibly she intended it as a negative example of woman as victim. Kizer's own attitude toward her remarkable character creation is not clear. What is clear is that she has written an extraordinary poem; its Keatsian richness of language, its beguiling portrait of Fanny, and its careful control of tone and distance have caused many reviewers to rank it among her best poems.

What impresses even a casual reader of Kizer's works is her mastery of a variety of subjects, styles, forms, and voices. She seems able to write a villanelle such as "On a Line from Sophocles" and free verse with equal ease. Her technical skill is widely acknowledged and at times dazzlingly displayed, as in some of her Chinese "imitations" and in her translations. A case in point is "Seven Sides and Seven Syllables" in *Carrying Over*. As is generally well recognized, poetry translation is itself an act of creation. In translating from French African, her difficult task was to preserve Edouard Maunick's seven-syllable lines while remaining faithful to the original poem's imagery and syntax. Printing the original text and her translation on facing pages, she invites qualified readers to judge the results for themselves.

Kizer has written political, comical, satirical, and lyrical poems. Some are public poems, while others seem more private. Among her personal poems, those about her parents and her children are particularly strong. One of the finest of these is "The Great Blue Heron," dedicated to her mother. A child playing sees a heron standing on the beach, "shadow without a shadow." Chilled by the sight of the spectral bird, the child runs to fetch her mother. They return just in time to see him "drifting/ Over the highest pines/ On vast, unmoving wings." The child suddenly realizes that her mother "knew what he was": the bird is death. Fifteen years later, her mother has died, everything has changed, except one thing: "Now there is only you/ Heavy upon my eye." No summary can convey the power of the poem and its image of the great heron, which becomes for the reader, as for the speaker in the poem, an objective correlative of death.

Another moving personal poem is "Antique Father," in which a speaker unsuccessfully implores a dying father to communicate, to utter some final word, perhaps some "grave secret." The spare, broken lines upon a mostly empty page perfectly reinforce the poem's meaning: the terror as they "gaze into the pit/ eternity," the breathless expectancy and urgency of this ultimate moment, the father's "terrible silence."

Kizer has written two poems for her daughter Ashley, one of which, "The Blessing," celebrates a complex grandmother-mother-daughter relationship. The daughter is self-controlled because the mother is not: "Holding me together at your expense/ has made you burn cool," mother tells daughter. Yet she realizes that she played the same role for her own mother—hence her references to "Daughter-my-mother" and "Mother-my-daughter." Ultimately, images of grandmother, mother, and daughter merge in this warmly autobiographical poem, in which the only certainty is that since there always will be "a hard time" for mother, a loving daughter is indeed a blessing.

Kizer's love poems are as wonderfully various as she is. The witty "Food of Love" takes for its epigraph an observation by Samuel Butler II, "Eating is touch carried to the bitter end," and goes on from there:

> I'm going to murder you with love;
> I'm going to suffocate you with embraces;
> I'm going to hug you, bone by bone,
> Till you're dead all over.
> Then I will dine on your delectable marrow.

Moving to carefully controlled but extravagant metaphors of the Sahara and the Mediterranean Sea, the poem develops its theme of the inexhaustible renewal of love. "You will become my personal Sahara," but "I will be that green" of water and vegetation that transform a dusty desert into a "field in bloom." Then, "I will devour you, my natural food," once again.

"What the Bones Know" is indebted to William Butler Yeats for more than his philosophy of frank sensuality referred to in the poem: "I think that Yeats was right,/ That lust and love are one." The spare imagery (those bones), the rhymes, the rhythms, the conversational tone, all pay homage. The repeated rhymes of death/breath and the variations she plays on them are particularly effective in this concise meditation on sex and death. Kizer's great mentor and friend, Roethke, was also influenced by Yeats. (Can there be many contemporary poets who are not?) A reader catches echoes of Roethke in such images as "frozen brow" and the "shaking sides of lust."

A poem about love in quite a different mode is "The Patient Lovers." Its use of puns, its wordplay, and the extended conceit of love as illness are reminiscent of the Metaphysical poets; John Donne comes immediately to mind. Yet Kizer places her own individual stamp upon whatever she writes. Her own self-assured voice is the one the reader hears. An elegiac poem, "Winter Song," explores the dark winter of the soul when love has failed. Images of tedium and exhaustion convey the truth of proselike assertion: *"Thinking of you, I am suddenly old."* The temptations of sentimentality (which must always be great in a poem on this subject) are resisted. The poem compellingly tells an unromantic truth: "We are separated, finally, not by death but life:/ We can cling to the dead, but the living break away." Some way to live with this melancholy fact is what the poem struggles to find. Surveying the achievements of Carolyn Kizer, one feels impelled to make lists of contraries: she is a poet of passion and control, of intellect and earthiness, of tradition and innovation, of classicism and modernity, of the mythic and the mundane, of the colloquial and the formal, to name a few of the possibilities. Yet what is important in her writing cannot by conveyed by schizophrenic-sounding lists. What is notable is the wise and knowing sense of an authentic self that informs her writing, a self that knows what is genuine and what is not. In an era of increasing fragmentation, incoherence, and tawdriness, it is good to have writers such as Carolyn Kizer to remind the reader of what wholeness, lucidity, and authenticity are all about.

Karen A. Kildahl

Other major works

TRANSLATION: *Carrying Over*, 1988.

EDITED TEXT: *Woman Poet: The West*, 1980 (with Elaine Dallman and Barbara Gelpi).

Bibliography

Fulton, Alice. "Main Things." *Poetry* 151 (January, 1988): 372-377. A perceptive essay-review of *Mermaids in the Basement* and *The Nearness of You*, written with feminist concerns foremost in mind. Fulton scrutinizes some of Kizer's language choices and finds evidence of bias against women. She believes that Kizer's attitude toward women is ambivalent at times, but that overall the poet's strengths greatly outweigh her few weak moments. Along the way, Fulton offers many excellent insights into the poems.

Hampl, Patricia. "Women Who Say What They Mean." *The New York Times Book Review* 89 (November 25, 1984): 36. This essay-review of *Mermaids in the Basement* and *Yin* praises Kizer for having the courage of her early feminism, but finds "Pro Femina" a less satisfying poem than others that are more lyrical and personal, such as "Thrall" and "Where I've Been All My Life." In some of her poems Kizer's humor seems forced and her tone uneven, but in her prose memoir "A Muse," humor and tone are perfectly managed.

Ostriker, Alicia Suskin. *Stealing the Language: The Emergence of Women's Poetry in America*. Boston: Beacon Press, 1986. An indispensable book for the study of women's poetry and for an understanding of the formidable obstacles it still confronts. It offers brief but illuminating references to Kizer's poems, primarily "Pro Femina," but is mainly helpful in providing a cultural context for reading not only Kizer's but any woman's poetry. A selected bibliography of poets, criticism, and feminist theory adds to its usefulness.

O'Connell, Nicolas. *At the Field's End: Interviews with Twenty Pacific Northwest Writers.* Seattle: Madrona, 1987. Kizer discusses the influence of her teacher and mentor Theodore Roethke in her development as a poet and credits him with making her a serious writer. She explains the importance of revision in writing, why reading poetry aloud is of supreme importance to her, why she believes that Oriental influence on Western writers is good, and what being a feminist means. Of additional interest are her comments on the Northwest school of writers and artists with whom she associated.

Skelton, Robin. *Five Poets of the Northwest.* Seattle: University of Washington Press, 1964. The introduction to this collection by a well-known Northwest poet and editor discusses the concept of a regional, Northwest school of poetry. Considering writers as different as Kenneth O. Hanson, Richard Hugo, Carolyn Kizer, William Stafford, and David Wagoner, he argues that what they share is an "awareness of a mixed cultural inheritance." He finds Kizer the most versatile poet of the group and the one whose poetic world most resists summation.

KENNETH KOCH

Born: Cincinnati, Ohio; February 27, 1925

Principal poetry

Poems, 1953; *Ko: Or, A Season on Earth*, 1960; *Permanently*, 1960; *Thank You and Other Poems*, 1962; *When the Sun Tries to Go On*, 1969; *Sleeping with Women*, 1969; *The Pleasures of Peace and Other Poems*, 1969; *The Art of Love*, 1975; *The Duplications*, 1977; *The Burning Mystery of Anna in 1951*, 1979; *From the Air*, 1979; *Days and Nights*, 1982; *Selected Poems, 1950-1982*, 1985; *On the Edge*, 1986.

Other literary forms

In addition to poetry, Kenneth Koch has published one novel, *The Red Robins* (1975), and books of dramatic pieces, including *Bertha and Other Plays* (1966) and *A Change of Hearts: Plays, Films and Other Dramatic Works 1951-1971* (1973). Both Koch's novel and his works for the stage are imaginative and improvisatory in their consistent portrayal of the comic drama of life.

The plays achieve their comic repercussions primarily through the juxtaposition of incongruous situations, and by means of rapid, often unpredictable changes of language, character, and scene. The plays echo and imitate older dramatic forms such as the Elizabethan chronical and the court masque, frequently appropriating the earlier dramatic conventions for comic purposes. *E. Kology* (1973), for example, a five-act play in rhymed verse, is as much masque as play. In it, the main character, E. Kology, persuades various polluters of air and water to abandon their destructive habits. An additional masque element is provided by a troop of young men and women who assist E. Kology, performing a series of celebratory dances as part of the play's action. An even more masquelike play is *The Moon Balloon*, performed in New York's Central Park on New Year's Eve, 1969. *The Moon Balloon* is an entertainment in rhymed verse that makes use of spectacle, celebration, and metamorphosis.

History forms the basis for humor and metamorphosis in Koch's two historical plays, *Bertha* (1959), a historical pageant, and *George Washington Crossing the Delaware* (1962), a chronicle play. Bertha is a Norwegian queen who saves her people from the barbarian menace. She performs this feat regularly, whenever she becomes bored with routine rule. The humor of the play resides in the use of formal Elizabethan language to describe Bertha's idiosyncratic behavior, and in strangely concatenated literary allusions such as the linked references to *Antony and Cleopatra* (c. 1606-1607) and *Alice's Adventures in Wonderland* (1865), Bertha being related to both the tragic queen of Egypt and the mad queen of Wonderland.

George Washington Crossing the Delaware, perhaps Koch's best play, is part myth, part chronicle, part comedy. Its comic incongruities, its colloquial deflation of a more stately heroic language, and its juxtaposition of low comedy and high seriousness serve to make it a surprising and inventive theatrical entertainment.

Achievements

At his best, Koch is a good comic poet and a fine parodist. A poet of limited tonal range yet of a wide and resourceful imagination, Koch's random structures, open forms, and loose meters give his poetry freedom and surprise that occasionally astonish and often delight. Just as often, however, the formlessness of Koch's poems results in slackness and self-indulgence. The tension that one expects in good poetry, deriving largely from exigencies of form, is missing in Koch's poems.

In *The King of the Cats* (1965), F. W. Dupee compared Koch to Marianne Moore. Dupee notes that while both Koch and Moore make poetry out of "poetry-resistant stuff," Koch lacks Moore's patient scrutiny and careful, sustained observation. Preferring to participate imaginatively rather than to observe carefully, Koch often seems more interested in where he can go with an observation, with what his imagination can make of it, than in what it is in itself. At his best, Koch's imaginative facility translates into poetic felicity; at his worst, Koch's freedom of imagination obscures the clarity and lucidity of the poems, frequently testing the reader's patience.

Perhaps the most trenchant and perceptive criticism of Koch's work has been that of Richard Howard in his book on contemporary poetry, *Alone with America: Essays on the Art of Poetry in the United States Since 1950* (1969). Howard suggests that the central poetic problem for Koch is to sustain the interest of the instant, to hold onto the momentary imaginative phrase or the surprising conjunction of dichotomous ideas, experiences, and details. Koch frequently hurries beyond moments of imaginative vitality and verbal splendor; rather than sustaining or developing them, he abandons them. At his best, however, such abandonments lead to other moments that are equally splendid, culminating in convincingly coherent poems.

Some of Koch's most distinctive and successful poems are parodies. His parody of Robert Frost, "Mending Sump," in which he alludes to and satirizes the style and situation of both "Mending Wall" and "The Death of the Hired Man," is one of his most famous. A modestly successful parody, "Mending Sump" does not compare with Koch's brilliant and witty parody of William Carlos Williams' brief conversational poem, "This Is Just to Say." Koch entitles his parody "Variations on a Theme by William Carlos Williams." In four brief stanzas, Koch parodies the occasion, structure, rhythm, and tone of a poet whose work has powerfully influenced his own.

Although in his nonparodistic poetry Koch may not often attempt to imitate Williams, he does try to accomplish what Williams achieved in his best work: the astonishment of the moment; the astonishment of something seen, heard, felt, or understood; the magic and the beauty of the commonplace. Koch, too, can astonish—but not by acts of attention like those of Williams nor by his power of feeling. Koch astonishes by his outrageous dislocations of sense and logic, his exuberant and risk-taking amalgamation of utterly disparate experiences. His achievement, finally, consists of small surprises, delights of image and allusion, phrase and idea; his poems rarely possess the power to move or instruct, but they do entertain.

Biography

Kenneth Koch was born in Cincinnati, Ohio, on February 27, 1925. Although he wrote his first poem when he was five, he did not begin writing seriously until he was seventeen, when he read the novels of John Dos Passos and was thereby stimulated to imitate their particular style of stream-of-consciousness. Koch served as a rifleman in the U.S. Army during World War II. After the war, he earned a B.A. degree from Harvard University in 1948, and a doctorate from Columbia in 1959. At Harvard, Koch was a friend of John Ashbery and Frank O'Hara, poets who held similar views about the nature of poetry. Later, when they had settled in New York, Ashbery, O'Hara, and Koch came to be thought of as principal poets of the New York School.

Koch spent three important years in Europe, mostly in Italy and France. During that time, he was influenced by the humorous, surrealistic verse of Jacques Prévert. In a brief autobiographical account that appeared in *The New American Poetry* (1960, Donald Allen, editor), Koch noted that French poetry "had a huge effect" on his own work. Moreover, he acknowledged that he tried to get into his own writing "the same incomprehensible excitement" that he found in French poetry.

Koch has taught at Brooklyn College, Rutgers University, and The New School for Social Research. He became a Professor of English at Columbia University in 1971; he has been a recipient of Fulbright, Guggenheim, and Ingram Merrill fellowships, and he has been awarded a grant from the National Endowment for the Arts. He lives in New York City.

During the late 1960's and early 1970's Koch began teaching poetry writing at P.S. 61, a grammar school in New York City, and at a neighborhood museum at Brooklyn. A few years later he taught similar classes at a New York nursing home. Out of these experiences came a series of books about the teaching of poetry to children and the aged. The first of these, *Wishes, Lies and Dreams: Teaching Young Children to Write Poetry* (1970), is perhaps the best known. A companion volume, *Rose Where Did You Get That Red?*, followed in 1973. Both are noteworthy for their inventive approach to teaching poetry, especially for the imaginative ways they keep reading and writing poetry together. An additional value of the books, and of two later volumes as well (*I Never Told Anybody: Teaching Poetry in a Nursing Home*, 1977, and *Sleeping on the Wing: An Anthology of Modern Poetry with Essays on Reading and Writing*, 1981), is that all reveal something about Koch's poetic temperament and inclinations. The qualities that Koch encourages in his student's writing animate his own poems. Open forms, loose meter, memory and feeling, joy and humor, colloquial language, imaginative freedom—these reflect Koch's view that "there is no insurmountable barrier between ordinary speech and poetry."

Analysis

Among Koch's long poems are *Ko: Or, A Season on Earth*, a mock-heroic epic in ottava rima about a Japanese baseball player, a poem with a variety of story lines; *The Duplications*, a comic epic about sex that employs trappings of Greek mythology and that in its second part becomes a self-reflexive poem concerned with the poetic vocation; and *When the Sun Tries to Go On*, a poem that goes on for 100 twenty-four-line stanzas, in large part because Koch wanted to see how long he could go on with what was originally a seventy-two-line poem. All three poems are characterized by Koch's infectious humor, his far-fetched analogies, and his digressive impulse.

More interesting and more consistently successful are Koch's shorter poems, ranging in length from a dozen lines to a dozen pages. In the poems included in Koch's best collections, *The Art of Love* and *The Pleasures of Peace*, one encounters Koch at his most graceful and disarming. In the best poems from these volumes (and there are many engaging ones), Koch exhibits his characteristic playfulness, deliberate formlessness, and almost surrealistic allusiveness. The poems are humorous yet serious in both their invitations and their admonitions.

Koch's major poetic preoccupations find abundant exemplifications in his volume *The Pleasures of Peace*. The title poem is divided loosely into fourteen sections, each section describing different kinds of pleasures: of writing, of peace, of pain, of pleasure itself, of fantasy, of reality, of memory, of autonomy, of poetry, and of living. The poem is both a catalog and a celebration of the rich pleasures of simply being alive. Its self-reflexiveness coexists with its Whitmanesque embrace of the range, diversity, and variability of life's pleasures. Another stylistic hallmark evident in this poem is a playful use of literary allusion. In addition to evoking Walt Whitman, Koch alludes directly to William Butler Yeats ("The Lake Isle of Innisfree"), Andrew Marvell ("To His Coy Mistress"), Robert Herrick, Percy Bysshe Shelley, and William Wordsworth. The allusions are surprising: Koch's lines modify and alter the words of the earlier poets as they situate them in the context of a radically different poem.

These observations about "The Pleasures of Peace" fail to account for what is perhaps its most distinctive identifying quality: a wild, surrealistic concatenation of details (pink mint chewing gum with "the whole rude gallery of war"; Dutch-speaking cowboys; the pleasures of agoraphobia with the pleasures of blasphemy; the pleasures of breasts, bread, and poodles; the pleasures of stars and of plaster). Moreover, amidst the litany of the poem's pleasures occur several notes of desperation—for the horrors of war and suffering. Koch seems to find it necessary to remind his readers of the peaceful pleasures of life largely because the horrors of war and the futility of modern life allow them to be forgotten.

Although Sigmund Freud is an obvious influence on Koch's "The Interpretation of Dreams," a zany poem that imitates the syntax of dream in its associative structure, in its dislocations and disruptions of continuity, and in its oddly mismatched characters, Whitman is the dominant voice and force behind most of the other poems in the volume. Whitman's influence is discernible in "Hearing," a rambling play on sounds in which Koch makes music out of the disparate noises of waterfalls and trumpets, throbbing hearts and falling leaves, rain and thunder, bluebirds singing and dresses ripping. The poem, concluding with the words "the song is finished," owes something also to the other American poets it invokes: Ezra Pound, William Carlos Williams, and Wallace Stevens.

It is Whitman, however, who stands behind Koch's "Poem of the Forty-Eight States," especially the Whitman of "On Journeys Through the States"; and it is Whitman who hovers over the incantatory litany of Koch's "Sleeping with Women," especially the Whitman of "The Sleepers" and "Beautiful Women." Perhaps the most successful of Koch's Whitmanesque poems is "Faces," which, while less uniform in tone than "Sleeping with Women," with its hypnotic, anaphoric incantation, and while not as close to Whitman's own tone, nevertheless carries something of Whitman's power of suggestion in its implication that the variety of faces called up in the poem (Popeye and Agamemnon, Herbert Hoover and the poor of the Depression) reflect the life of the speaker of the poem. By implication, Koch seems to suggest that each reader could create a similar yet highly individual and personal collage of faces that, taken together, reflect the range and variety of his experience and that, in a concentrated yet variegated image, sum up his or her life.

Koch's other important volume, *The Art of Love*, while retaining something of the humorous tone of *The Pleasures of Peace* as well as something of its imaginative wit, reaches more deeply in feeling and ranges more widely in thought. Many of the poems are cast in an admonitory mode; others are ironic, while still others include both irony and admonition. "The Art of Poetry" alternates between ironic posture and serious gesture in its descriptions of poetic attitudes, ideals, and practices. The speaker advises poets to stay young even while growing and developing, something that Koch has consistently tried to do. He suggests that a poet should imitate other poets, try on other styles, and try out other voices in an effort to form, paradoxically, his own style. After addressing the problems of beginning a poem, sustaining and ending it (and also revising it), the speaker reminds the poet to absorb himself totally in poetry, for only such a total immersion will enable the poet to see poetry as "the mediation of life." Such is Koch's poetic credo.

This poetic creed notwithstanding, perhaps the most unusual and the most useful advice in "The Art of Poetry" is given in a set of questions and answers that further reveal the direction and impulse of Koch's own poetry: Is the poem astonishing? Is it wise? Is it original? Does it employ cheap effects, tricks, or gimmicks? Does it engage heart and mind? Would the poet envy another's having written it? If the answer is "yes" to all but the fourth question, the poem qualifies, if not for greatness, at least for honesty and integrity, qualities and standards certainly deserving of respect and admiration. In his "The Art of Poetry" Koch seems to have achieved them.

Although not overtly about the art of poetry, "Some General Instructions" can be taken as describing Koch's poems even as it gives more explicit advice about living. One statement in particular suggests the connection between poetry and life: "Things have a way of working out/ Which is nonsensical, and one should try to see/ How the process works." This implies that nonsense ultimately makes sense, that beneath the apparent confusion lies order, purpose, and meaning. The statement provides a helpful gloss on the best of Koch's poems, which often go by way of nonsense to make a final and useful kind of sense.

"Some General Instructions" alternates between aphorism and meditative commentary. Like any set of aphorisms, it bristles with contradictions. Even so, it shines with joy and radiates humor. Koch seems to enjoy juxtaposing serious moral and ethical advice with comic yet practical admonition. He advises, for example, that his readers be glad, that they savor life, love, pleasure, and virtue, and that they not eat too many bananas.

Although a similar tone mixing playful humor with thoughtful advice permeates Koch's lovely and beautiful "On Beauty," a rather different note is struck by two other poems in the volume. In "The Circus," a nostalgic reminiscence about the time he wrote an earlier poem with the same title, Koch wonders about the value of the earlier poem, and then, by extension, about the value of any of his poems, about the value of his poetic vocation. Moving out of a concern with poetry, "The Circus" becomes more somber, turning into a meditation on time, death, and loss, especially the loss of friends. In "The Art of Love," a how-to manual of eroticism, the speaker describes a set of outrageous sadomasochistic procedures. The practical nature of the advice ranges from how to meet and greet a girl, to how to get her to do the things described in the poem. "The Art of Love" ends with a catalog of questions about love, some serious, some humorous. Ludicrous answers are provided to each question. Full of high spirits, erotic fantasies, hyperbole, and insult, the poem needs to be taken ironically if it is not to be considered an offense against decency. Even then, its specificity of reference and particularity of detail make it seem less an ironic poem about the art of love than a degrading if witty description of perverse fantasies.

Koch's 1986 volume *On the Edge* consists of two long poems, the title poem and "Impressions of Africa." The former is a strongly autobiographical work; the latter, as its title suggests, presents images and impressions gathered while the poet was in Africa. Although both present difficulties, with their fragmentations and free associations that attempt to represent experience and memory in Koch's unique way, the structure is not entirely haphazard. More than the usual Koch work, "Impressions of Africa" gives the reader a sense of how a place objectively appears, in lines that sometimes remind one of diary entries transformed into verse. "On the Edge" is harder to grasp. In the poem, events involving Koch and his friends circle an apparently fictional character named Dan. Moments of clarity are scattered among thoughts that interrupt themselves, such as "Our modern— fragmentary—Dan stands up—it's about time—reason." Koch's charm and sense of humor appear throughout, but the landscape of the work frequently exists so deep within the poet's consciousness that it seems indecipherable.

Koch's talent is perhaps best manifested in *The Pleasures of Peace* and *The Art of Love*. While the poems do not range widely in style, theme, and technique, they do offer a distinctive set of pleasures for the accepting and patient reader, the pleasures of engaging an unusual and unpredictable poetic imagination as it reveals itself in a colloquially inflected idiom which is, by turns, earnest and ironic. The deliberate dislocations of logical organization, the profusion of incongruities in image and idea, the exaggeration and far-fetched analogies are all part of Koch's effort to avoid the predictable, the stodgy, and the dull. They are all part of his effort to create a poetry full of fun and surprise, which, even though it only infrequently ends in wisdom, nevertheless very often sustains the delight with which it begins.

Robert DiYanni

Other major works

LONG FICTION: *The Red Robins*, 1975.

PLAYS: *Bertha*, 1959; *George Washington Crossing the Delaware*, 1962; *Bertha and Other Plays*, 1966; *The Moon Balloon*, 1969; *A Change of Hearts: Plays, Films and Other Dramatic Works 1951-1971*, 1973; *The New Diana*, 1984.

NONFICTION: *Wishes, Lies and Dreams: Teaching Young Children to Write Poetry*, 1970; *Rose Where Did You Get That Red?*, 1973; *I Never Told Anybody: Teaching Poetry in a Nursing Home*, 1977; *Sleeping on the Wing: An Anthology of Modern Poetry with Essays on Reading and Writing*, 1981 (with Kate Farrell).

Bibliography
Auslander, Philip. *The New York School Poets as Playwrights: O'Hara, Ashbery, Koch, Schuyler, and the Visual Arts.* New York: P. Lang, 1989. Auslander discusses the plays written by these poets who attended the New York School of Art. Their life in New York affects their artistic endeavors, regardless of their form: poetry, experimental drama, short story, or visual art. This survey is useful as it gives an idea of Koch's competency in varied artistic media.
Carruth, Hayden. "Kenneth Koch." In *Contemporary Poets,* edited by James Vinson and D. L. Kirkpatrick. 4th ed. New York: St. Martin's Press, 1985. Carruth, an outstanding poet in his own right, outlines Koch's background and work. Carruth first covers Koch's apprenticeship with the New York School of Poets in the 1950's, and then discusses Koch's current poetry, which is simpler and more effective than his earlier work. A good introduction for all students.
Hollander, John. "Kenneth Koch." In *Contemporary Poets,* edited by Harold Bloom. New York: Chelsea House, 1986. Hollander wrote this appreciation of Koch's work to celebrate the publication of Koch's *Selected Poems, 1950-1982.* He discusses some early poems, especially *Ko: Or, A Season on Earth,* and touches on *The Art of Love,* noting the shift in "manner" of the later poems.
Howard, Richard. *Alone with America: Essays on the Art of Poetry in the United States Since 1950.* New York: Atheneum, 1969. In his chapter on Koch, Howard discusses his emphasis on the individual moment and (paradoxically) its movement. Howard also notes Koch's ability to be funny, calling him a master parodist, and mentions devices that Koch uses in his "improvisational plays."
Koch, Kenneth. "An Interview with Kenneth Koch." Interview by John Tranter. *Scripsi* 4 (November, 1986): 177-185. In this rare interview, Koch discusses the evolution of his work from his rebellious New York School of Poetry days to his 1980's poetic style. He also talks about his work in the theater, which is experimental and plentiful. For all students.
Lang, Nancy. "Comic Fantasy in Two Postmodern Verse Novels: *Slinger* and *Ko.*" In *The Poetic Fantastic: Studies in an Evolving Genre,* edited by Patrick D. Murphy and Vernon Ross Hyles. Westport, Conn.: Greenwood Press, 1989. This interesting article compares the use of fantasy for fun in Koch's *Ko: Or, A Season on Earth* and Edward Dorn's *Slinger.*
Moss, Howard. *The Poet's Story.* New York: Macmillan, 1973. Moss collects the short stories of twenty writers who are much better known for their poetry. In this collection, Moss includes Koch's short story "A Slight Mechanical Failure." Interesting, for it demonstrates Koch's versatility as a writer.

MAXINE KUMIN

Born: Philadelphia, Pennsylvania; June 6, 1925

Principal poetry

Halfway, 1961; *The Privilege*, 1965; *The Nightmare Factory*, 1970; *Up Country*, 1972; *House, Bridge, Fountain, Gate*, 1975; *The Retrieval System*, 1978; *Our Ground Time Here Will Be Brief*, 1982; *Closing the Ring: Selected Poems*, 1984; *The Long Approach*, 1985; *Nurture*, 1989.

Other Literary Forms

Maxine Kumin's novels include *Through Dooms of Love* (1965), *The Passions of Uxport* (1968), *The Abduction* (1971), and *The Designated Heir* (1974). She has published a collection of short stories, *Why Can't We Live Together like Civilized Human Beings?* (1982), and collections of essays, including *To Make a Prairie: Essays on Poets, Poetry, and Country Living* (1980) and *In Deep: Country Essays* (1987). Kumin has also published numerous volumes of children's literature, several coauthored with Anne Sexton.

Achievements

Most recognized for her rural poems, Maxine Kumin received a Pulitzer Prize in 1973 for her fourth volume of poetry, *Up Country*. She is applauded for her positive tone, her affirmation of life; for this life-affirming quality, her work is often contrasted to that of Anne Sexton and Sylvia Plath, in whose work critics find the negation of life. Among other awards, she has received a National Endowment for the Arts grant (1966), a National Council on the Humanities fellowship (1967), the Eunice Tietjens Memorial Prize from *Poetry* (1972), the American Academy and Institute of Arts and Letters Award for excellence in literature (1980), and an Academy of American Poets fellowship (1986). She has published regularly, throughout her career, in the most prestigious magazines in the country, including *Poetry*, *The New Yorker*, and *The Atlantic*.

Biography

Born of Jewish parents in Germantown, Pennsylvania, in 1925 and educated as a child at a Catholic convent school, Maxine Kumin describes herself as an agnostic who believes passionately in poetry. Kumin's father, Peter Winokur, was a successful pawnbroker. As a teenager, Kumin trained to become an Olympic swimmer, but she abandoned this dream upon entrance to Radcliffe College, which lacked suitable training facilities. She received a bachelor's degree in 1946 and a master's in 1948, both from Radcliffe, but did not begin writing seriously until her late twenties, when, as a suburban housewife with small children, she turned to poetry for self-gratification. She met the poet Anne Sexton at a writing workshop at the Boston Center for Adult Education, and the two women developed a close personal and professional relationship, installing an extra telephone line in each of their homes so they could talk at length.

Kumin began her teaching career in 1958 at Tufts University in Massachusetts and has taught as visiting lecturer at Radcliffe, Columbia University, Amherst College, Princeton University, and Bucknell University, among others. She has been on the staff of the Bread Loaf Conference on numerous occasions, and she served as poetry consultant to the Library of Congress from 1981 to 1982. She prefers to spend much of her time at her horse farm in New Hampshire, where she lives with her husband, Victor Montwid Kumin, whom she married in 1946. They have three children: Jane Simon, Judith Montwid, and Daniel David.

Analysis

The poetry of Maxine Kumin is concerned with loss (particularly loss through death or separation) and surviving such loss. Equally at home with natural and domestic images, Kumin organizes most of her poems into groups of pastoral or tribal poems. These groupings allow her to explore relationships found in nature and also relationships within extended human families. These pastoral and tribal poems connect through Kumin's recurring emphasis on the seasonal patterns of nature and the regenerative cycles of familial generations.

Kumin prefers to write in traditional forms (as opposed to free verse) and often employs exacting syllable counts, set rhyme and stanza patterns, and alliteration. She develops many of her poems with catalogs or extends them through simile, though in her later work simile appears less frequently. Her work has also changed through moving from a very personal, private voice to one that is more public.

Images of the body abound in Kumin's poetry: skin, bone, knees, ribs, and thighs. Swimming recurs as a metaphor with associated water imagery, especially in her first volume, *Halfway*. This first book also shows a concern for the instructor-student relationship and sometimes, as in the opening poem, "Junior Life Saving," explores this relationship within the context of water.

The poem expresses concern with loss by drowning and the desire to prevent such loss. It begins with physical details, describing the young students, an "isosceles of knees," as they sit crosslegged and pick at their peeling sunburns. The lake assumes human powers; as the children enter the water to role-play the drowning victim and the rescuer, the lake seems to be smiling, "turned sudden to a foe." The speaker of the poem, who is aware of danger, gives instructions: "Class, I say, this is/ the front head release." Important is what the instructor, almost in a parental role, does not or can not say: "Class,

I say (and want/ to say, children, my dears,/ I too know how to be afraid)."
Instead, the instructor remains firm and practical: "I tell you what I know:/
go down to save."

The swimmer in "400-Meter Free Style" is again practical. Utilizing
"thrift," he employs no movement that is not needed. This poem emphasizes images of the body, including references to the functionally clean movement of feet, muscle, wrist, heel, mouth, lungs, and heart. Furthermore, the
typography of the poem suggests the movement of a swimmer's laps.

Both "High Dive: A Variant" and "The Lesson" suggest that mastery
through practice can empower. The key word in "High Dive" (a sestina) is,
in fact, "masterful": "Practice has made this come out right" so that "at
peak" the male diver is "a schooled swan, arched and masterful." Although
"The Lesson" (set in a natural body of water rather than a pool) approaches
the theme more subtly, it announces itself flatly: "Eleven. Your hour of danger." The speaker-instructor continues to address the students, showing them
how to do the sidestroke. Her directives are intertwined with observations of
natural life in the water:

> it is the top leg goes forward
> forming the blade of the scissors,
> wherefore the cattails unseaming
> go rattletatat in the marshes,
> seeding the smallest of moments,
> all of us braver by inches.

The instructions seem themselves to cut through the poem and the water as
if this concrete knowledge somehow lessens the danger of the lake. With the
proper instruction, the swimmers learn to move through the water as if to do
so were natural: "Up out and together we glide."

Kumin again explores the instructor-student relationship in "The Young
Instructor in a Winter Landscape." The setting for this poem is a university
campus rather than a body of water, but the poem begins with a reference to
physical movement, reflecting on the fact that many college campuses are
built on hills, so that teachers and students going to and from classes must
exert themselves physically. The poem speaks of physical work and mental
work as complementary: "Hills are warm work in icy weather:/ something
the mind/ can chew on." It ends with a reference to the similarity between
the instructor and his students and alludes to the passage of time in which
they will replace him: "on that all-climbing hill of Sisyphus/ he sees it has
begun to snow/ and all the faces facing him are his."

"Poem for My Son" and "The Journey: For Jane at Thirteen" are precursors of many poems in subsequent volumes on the separation of mothers
and children. Separation in "Poem for My Son" is emotionally difficult; the
mother remembers the oxygen tent that saved her son just after his birth and

cannot force herself now to "unfasten from the boy." She knows that he will "wash away/ to war or love or luck,/ prodigious king, a stranger." It is a separation that she cannot make of her own will, yet by the end of the poem, she yields to the pull of life. "My pulse knit in your wrist/ expands. Go now and spend it."

Relinquishment of the daughter in "The Journey: For Jane at Thirteen" is not only difficult but also perilous: "It is a dangerous time./ The water rocks away under the timber." Luckily, the daughter carries with her, in her purse, magical objects that will protect her, "pale lipstick, half a dozen lotions," and she bears history and mythology texts and wears pennies in her shoes. Ultimately, though, her own self-confidence is most powerful: "You lean down your confident head./ We exchange kisses; I call your name/ and wave you off as the bridge goes under."

The last poem in the volume, "For Anne at Passover," is the first of many poems dedicated to Kumin's friend Anne Sexton. The speaker of this poem, again an instructor, ironically addresses Socrates (rather than Sexton) when she states that "one student says you sinned the sin of pride./ Another consecrates your suicide." This poem alludes to ironies within the women's backgrounds—Sexton's Catholicism and Kumin's Judaism—yet it ends on a note of faith in love and the return of spring:

> we pray and eat tonight in greening weather.
> Time swells the buds. A sharper rain begins;
> we are all babes who suck at love together.

Kumin's poems celebrating love and spring (or summer) are among her most eloquent. Her rhythms soften. For example, in the conclusion of "We Are," from her fourth volume, *Up Country*, she uses enjambment rather than her usual end-stopped lines, allowing her sentences to flow over line and stanza breaks:

> Even knowing
> that none of us can catch up with himself
>
> we are making a run
> for it. Love, we are making a run.

Images of survival are lush and ripe; in "Five Small Deaths in May," for example, the speaker makes plans to bury a much-loved dog "under the milkweed bloom/ where in July the monarchs come/ as spotted as he, as rampant, as enduring." In "Watering Trough," water suggests richness and plenty. A footed Victorian bathtub has been set outside as a trough for farm animals, and the speaker invites "all longnecked browsers" to partake of its "green water for sipping/ that muzzles may enter thoughtful/ and rise dripping."

Kumin uses the image of water similarly in "Morning Swim," one of her most successful poems. Here water serves as nourishment:

> My bones drank water; water fell
> through all my doors. I was the well
> that fed the lake that met my sea
> in which I sang *Abide with Me*.

The speaker of the poem attains this state of immersion "in chilly solitude," and the act of swimming is not actually physical but a movement within the speaker's imagination: "Into my empty head there come/ a cotton beach, a dock wherefrom/ I set out, oily and nude."

The amenities of solitude appear again in Kumin's series of hermit poems. Like Kumin's love poems, several poems in this series are quite sensuous. The sequence opens with "The Hermit Wakes to Bird Sounds": "He startles awake. His eyes are full of white light./ In a minute the sun will ooze into the sky." Kumin's description of night in "The Hermit Has a Visitor" is similar but more richly fertile than her reference to "night fog thick as terry cloth" in "Morning Swim": "Night is a honeycomb./ Night is the fur on a blue plum." For Kumin, blue is a color of ripeness. In "The Hermit Picks Berries," she describes the ripening of blueberries by noting their transformation in color, from "wax white" to "the green of small bruises" to "the red of bad welts": "Now they are true blue."

Kumin is even more sensual in "August 9th," but here she extols the deeper colors of black and purple. The poem revolves around the picking of dewberries, each berry "a black bulge fattening/ under its leaf blanket." The speaker experiences these berries in a purely physical manner, without spiritual overtones, because God is not present:

> in fact I am
> alone in the pasture,
> bending among deerflies
> and the droppings of porcupines.
> I am stripped to the waist.
> The sun licks my back.

But, ironically, the speaker, who seems very close to the hermit persona, uses plurals throughout the poem. It ends in exuberant command: "pinch!/ pull!/ purple your fingers!"

Although Kumin's sixth volume, *The Retrieval System*, is quite different from *Up Country* in subject matter and tone, one of its poems, "Extrapolations from Henry Manley's Pie Plant" recaptures some of the earlier volume's lushness. The poem opens with a description of Henry's rhubarb: "The stalks are thick as cudgels, red/ as valentines."

In contrast to *Up Country, The Retrieval System* is structured thematically.

In this book, Kumin confronts middle age and the loss of parents, children, and her friend Anne Sexton. In "Extrapolations from Henry Manley's Pie Plant" (one of a series of poems centered on Kumin's country neighbor), she reflects on the choices she has made: "I look at my middling self and recognize/ this life is but one of a number of possible lives." She considers some of these possible lives, then describes the one she has chosen: "Instead, mornings I commence with the sun,/ tend my animals, root in the garden/ and pass time with Henry." She does not regret this choice, because it has enabled her to live where the "goldfinches explode/ from the meadow."

In "Henry Manley, Living Alone, Keeps Time," the last and most successful poem of the series, Kumin considers the effects of aging: "Sundowning,/ the doctor calls it, the way/ he loses words when the light fades." Henry often cannot remember the names of those he loves, yet the poet recognizes that he "goes on loving them out of place." She is saddened by the separation of the body and the soul and notes his awareness of how loose his connection to life is becoming. At any moment his soul could slip out of his body, lightly and without warning, like the helium-filled balloon that floated from his grasp when he was a child.

Kumin titles a section of *The Retrieval System* "Body and Soul," and in one poem from this section, "Body and Soul: A Meditation," ponders the soul's physical location. In this poem, she is humorously regretful:

> Body, Old Paint, Old Partner,
> I ought to have paid closer
> attention when Miss Bloomberg
> shepherded the entire fifth grade
> into the Walk-Through Woman.

Though she remembers walking through the various chambers of the heart, she does not remember seeing the woman's soul, "that miner's canary flitting/ around the open spaces." She envisions the body's interior as a pinball machine in which the "little ball-bearing soul" rolls about, reversing direction as it clicks against various bones.

Kumin explores more serious regrets in this volume, confronting losses very specific and real. She refers to them explicitly in "Address to the Angels." These losses include the suicide of Anne Sexton, her father's fatal heart attack, and her daughter's move to Europe. She thinks that if she could go back in time she could prevent these bad occurrences: "I am wanting part of my life back/ so I can do it over./ So I can do it better."

In "How It Is" she wishes again that she could go back in time, this time so she could prevent Sexton's suicide; she thinks of the last day of Sexton's life, "how I would unwind it, paste/ it together in a different collage,/ back from the death car idling in the garage."

Several poems in this volume, which is dedicated to Kumin's daughters, concern the separation of parents and adult children, and particularly the separation of mothers and daughters. "Changing the Children" suggests the painfulness of adolescence and the distance it creates between parents and children. This distance is temporary, but by the time it closes, the relationship has changed: "Eventually we get them back./ Now they are grown up./ They are much like ourselves."

In "Seeing the Bones," Kumin mourns her separation from her world-traveling daughter: "now you're off to Africa/ or Everest, daughter of the file drawer,/ citizen of no return." Again Kumin wishes to return to an earlier time: "Working backward I reconstruct/ you. Send me your baby teeth, some new/ nail parings." Yet in "The Envelope," Kumin, although fearful of her own death, looks forward—to the near-immortality that her daughters will give her: "we, borne onward by our daughters, ride/ in the Envelope of Almost-Infinity."

Sometimes Kumin questions the possibility of surviving all these losses. In "July, Against Hunger," near the end of the book, she exclaims: "There are limits, my God, to what I can heft/ in this heat!"

Assuming a voice more political than personal in her tenth volume, *Nurture*, Kumin frets about the condition of the environment and the actual physical survival of animals. In "Thoughts on Saving the Manatee," she questions the possibility of the manatee's survival, for "experts agree that no matter/ how tenderly tamed by philanthropy/ [their] survival is chancy." The poem ends with a possible solution and a call to action reminiscent of Jonathan Swift's "A Modest Proposal":

> Let's revert to the Catch of the Day
> and serve up the last few as steak marinara.
> Let's stop pretending we need them
> more than they need us.

In this volume, and especially in the animal poems, Kumin displays a recurring concern for mothers and children. In "Thoughts on Saving the Manatee," she notes that the manatee in her area are "mostly cows and their calves." Quite a different scenario is presented in "Catchment," in which the speaker watches a female leopard pounce on a newborn antelope. Here the speaker faces a dilemma and wonders which animal she should root for—the helpless baby antelope or "the big cat, in whose camouflaged lair/ three helpless youngsters wait/ so starved for meat."

In the title poem, "Nurture," Kumin states her motherly interest directly: "I suffer, the critic proclaims,/ from an overabundance of maternal genes." Touched by a televised report of the surrogate parenting of a baby kangaroo, she is willing to open her heart and home to such an orphan—or to a human orphan, however wild: "it is safe to assume,/ given my fireside inked with paw prints,/ there would have been room." Considering the language

she and the orphaned creature would share, Kumin constructs a list of forms
of communication, alternating human and animal forms:

> Think of the language we two, same and not-same,
> might have constructed from sign,
> scratch, grimace, grunt, vowel:
>
> Laughter our first noun, and our long verb, howl.

Kumin again reflects on the language shared by animals and humans in
"Sleeping with Animals." Keeping watch through the night over a mare ready
to give birth, she finds herself and the mare in communion through "a word-
less yet perfect/ language of touch and tremor." What they are saying to
each other has to do with origins, "the wet cave we all/ once burst from
gasping, naked or furred,/ into our separate species." As she meditates on
the wonder of birth, Kumin considers her time with the mare well spent:
"Together we wait for this still-clenched burden."

"Surprises," a "tribal poem," suggests a connection between Kumin and
orphaned animals. Here, the poet, who is celebrating the success of her California peppers after fifteen years of failure, remembers how, when her
mother's thriving roses finally caused the dilapidated trellis to collapse under
their weight, "she mourned the dirtied blossoms more, I thought,// than if
they'd been her children." While her mother "pulled on/ goatskin gloves to
deal with her arrangements/ in chamberpots, pitchers, and a silver urn,"
Kumin was left to watch, "orphan at the bakeshop window."

Kumin moves forward to present time in "We Stood There Singing," which
tells of a drive in Switzerland with her daughter and infant grandson. Kumin
connects the grandson to the "wild child" in "Nurture" by using the verb
"howled," again emphasizing the similarity between humans and animals.
Kumin's grandson reappears in "A Game of Monopoly in Chavannes." Thinking of him, she contemplates the passing of her own generation: "Our sole
inheritor, he has taken us over// with his oceanic wants, his several pass-
ports." This grandson will someday replace her, will learn how to make his
way through life, how to invest himself. Yet Kumin is not yet ready to leave.
Mourning the deaths of her uncles in "Grappling in the Central Blue" makes
her determined to hold on to life:

> Let us eat of the inland oyster.
> Let its fragrance intoxicate us
> into almost believing
> that staying on is possible
> again this year in
> benevolent blue October.

Some of Kumin's most beautiful poems, such as "Magellan Street, 1974," are
about her daughter. Although she is again ruminating on the separation of

mother and daughter, she is not sad, but hopeful. She stands in her daughter's kitchen, bright with potted herbs, and is able to envision how the younger woman's life "will open, will burst from/ the maze in its walled-in garden/ and streak toward the horizon."

Kumin's poetry is endlessly positive, celebrating the sensuousness of physical existence, the naturalness of movement and time. Had she published fewer volumes, choosing poems more selectively, her poetic achievement would have been more honed, her weaknesses less apparent. Yet solitary and social, personal and public, her poetry is a testament of affirmation within the context of painful losses.

Nettie Farris

Other major works

LONG FICTION: *Through Dooms of Love*, 1965; *The Passions of Uxport*, 1968; *The Abduction*, 1971; *The Designated Heir*, 1974.

SHORT FICTION: *Why Can't We Live Together Like Civilized Human Beings?*, 1982.

NONFICTION: *To Make a Prairie: Essays on Poets, Poetry, and Country Living*, 1980; *In Deep: Country Essays*, 1987.

CHILDREN'S LITERATURE: *Sebastian and the Dragon*, 1960; *Spring Things*, 1961; *Summer Story*, 1961; *Follow the Fall*, 1961; *A Winter Friend*, 1961; *Mittens in May*, 1962; *No One Writes a Letter to the Snail*, 1962; *Archibald the Traveling Poodle*, 1963; *Eggs of Things*, 1963 (with Anne Sexton); *More Eggs of Things*, 1964 (with Anne Sexton); *Speedy Digs Downside Up*, 1964; *The Beach Before Breakfast*, 1964; *Paul Bunyan*, 1966; *Faraway Farm*, 1967; *The Wonderful Babies of 1809 and Other Years*, 1968; *When Grandmother Was Young*, 1969; *When Mother Was Young*, 1970; *When Great Grandmother Was Young*, 1971; *Joey and the Birthday Present*, 1971 (with Anne Sexton); *The Wizard's Tears*, 1975 (with Anne Sexton); *What Color is Caesar?*, 1978; *The Microscope*, 1984.

Bibliography

Gioia, Dana. Review of *Our Ground Time Here Will Be Brief. Hudson Review* 35 (Winter, 1982-1983): 652-653. Although short, this review (in contrast to typical, merely descriptive reviews) is valuable for its critical assessment of Kumin's poetic achievement as reflected in a volume containing work from six previous volumes of poetry. Gioia suggests reasons for Kumin's popularity but argues that her poetic facility with language is limited.

Harmon, William. Review of *Our Ground Time Here Will Be Brief. Poetry* 143 (April, 1983): 50-51. This review is valuable in its attention to both Kumin's strengths and weaknesses as a poet. Harmon notes that one of

Kumin's assets is her originality, but that this originality is often weakened by repetition that fails to make use of its possibilities.

Kumin, Maxine. *To Make a Prairie: Essays on Poets, Poetry, and Country Living.* Ann Arbor: University of Michigan Press, 1979. This book-length collection includes five interviews, three lectures on poetic craft, two essays on the origins and revisions of particular poems, and a critical essay on Kumin's "Tribal Poems." Gives the student access to the formal strategies of Kumin's work and biographical information relevant to her poems. Includes a section centered on Kumin's life on her New Hampshire farm, important because of the effect of her farm life upon her work.

Sexton, Anne, and Maxine Kumin. "A Nurturing Relationship: A Conversation with Anne Sexton and Maxine Kumin, April 15, 1974." Interview by Elaine Showalter and Carol Smith. *Women's Studies* 4 (1976): 115-136. In this rather lengthy, informal interview, Kumin and Sexton discuss their friendship and how each of them has influenced the other's work. Although both poets insist that they do not try to influence the other's voice, they do look at each other's work with an eye toward improvement. Of particular interest is Sexton's revelation that she suggested Kumin write a collection of country poems and that it be titled *Up Country.*

Shaw, Robert B. Review of *The Long Approach. Poetry* 148 (April, 1986): 36-38. This relatively lengthy review notes Kumin's narrative skill and also her power of observation. Though Kumin's later work has moved toward political themes, Shaw argues that she has not yet achieved the requisite shift in voice from a private voice to a public one.

STANLEY KUNITZ

Born: Worcester, Massachusetts; July 29, 1905

Principal poetry
Intellectual Things, 1930; *Passport to the War: A Selection of Poems*, 1944; *Selected Poems, 1928-1958*, 1958; *The Testing-Tree: Poems*, 1971; *The Terrible Threshold: Selected Poems, 1940-1970*, 1974; *The Coat Without a Seam: Sixty Poems, 1930-1972*, 1974; *The Lincoln Relics*, 1978; *The Poems of Stanley Kunitz, 1928-1978*, 1979; *The Wellfleet Whale and Companion Poems*, 1983; *Next-to-Last Things: New Poems and Essays*, 1985.

Other literary forms
Stanley Kunitz has published numerous essays, interviews, and reviews on poetry and art. These are collected in *A Kind of Order, a Kind of Folly: Essays and Conversations* (1975) and in *Next-to-Last Things: New Poems and Essays* (1985). In addition, he has made extensive translations of modern Russian poetry, most notably in *Poems of Akhmatova* (1973, with Max Hayward) and *Story Under Full Sail* by Andrei Voznesensky (1974), as well as editing and cotranslating Ivan Drach's *Orchard Lamps* (1978) from the Ukrainian.

Achievements
In nearly sixty years of writing poetry, Kunitz has produced a corpus of work that is notable for its cohesiveness, its courageous explorations of the modern psyche, and its ever-broadening sympathies that adumbrate (with some fierce reservations and caveats) the unity of human experience. In language that has never failed to sustain a high degree of passionate dignity yet has never fallen prey to the hortatory or didactic, Kunitz has boldly knocked again and again upon the doors of his obsessions with family, love, memory, and identity to demand that they surrender their secret meanings.

From the start of his career, Kunitz has paid consummate attention to matters of form, as bespeaking—to use his borrowed phrase—"a conservation of energy." Indeed, Kunitz has on numerous occasions spoken of form as a constant in art, as opposed to techniques and materials, which vary according to time and cultural necessity. Nevertheless, Kunitz's later poems have surprised his readers with their fresh embodiments: journal poems, prose poems, and free verse. At the same time, the poems retain the characteristically impassioned, sometimes bardic, voice of the earlier work, a voice that constitutes an unbroken thread running through his six decades of poetry.

In many ways, Kunitz's work declares allegiance to the "flinty, maverick side" of American literature, the side inhabited by Henry David Thoreau and Walt Whitman, and holds to humanistic values, independent judgment, self-discipline, and a distrust of power in all of its modern manifestations, particularly in the hands of the state. At the same time, the poems bear witness to the individual's spiritual yearnings in an age of decreasing sanctity at all levels. While not explicitly a religious poet ("I'm an American freethinker, a damn stubborn one . . ."), Kunitz wrote poems that, nevertheless, remind readers of the tragic consequences that befall humans at the loss of that dimension. His achievement has been "to roam the wreckage" of his own humanity in a way that is both highly personal and representative and to ennoble that pursuit with the transformative powers of his art, an achievement which won for him the 1987 Bollingen Prize for Poetry.

Biography

The son of immigrants, Stanley Jasspon Kunitz was born July 29, 1905, in Worcester, Massachusetts. Kunitz's father, Solomon, descended from Russian Sephardic Jews, committed suicide shortly before Stanley was born—an event that was to haunt the poet and that stands behind some of his most important and best-known poems. His mother, Yetta Helen, of Lithuanian descent, opened a dry goods store to support herself, her son, and two older daughters and to repay accumulated debts. Reared principally by his sisters and a succession of nurses, Kunitz grew up with his father's book collection, into which, as he put it, he would "passionately burrow." Though his mother shortly remarried, his stepfather, of whom he was fond, died before Kunitz reached his teens.

Educated in Worcester public schools, Kunitz edited the high school magazine, played tennis, and was graduated valedictorian of his class. Winning a scholarship to Harvard, Kunitz majored in English and began to write poetry, subsequently winning the Lloyd McKim Garrison Medal for poetry. He was graduated summa cum laude in 1926 and the following year took his M.A. degree from Harvard. He worked briefly as a Sunday feature writer for the Worcester *Telegram*, where he had worked summers during college. He also completed a novel, which he later "heroically destroyed."

In 1927, Kunitz joined the H. W. Wilson Company as an editor. With Wilson's encouragement, he became editor of the *Wilson Bulletin*, a library publication (known now as the *Wilson Library Bulletin*). While at Wilson, he edited a series of reference books, including *Authors Today and Yesterday: A Companion Volume to "Living Authors"* (1933; with Howard Haycraft and Wilbur C. Hadden), *British Authors of the Nineteenth Century* (1936; with Haycraft), *American Authors, 1600-1900: A Biographical Dictionary of American Literature* (1938), and *Twentieth Century Authors: A Biographical Dictionary of Modern Literature* (1942; with Haycraft).

In 1930, Kunitz married Helen Pearse (they were divorced in 1937) and published his first collection of poems, *Intellectual Things*. The book was enthusiastically received by reviewers. Writing in *Saturday Review of Litera-*

ture, William Rose Benét observed, "Mr. Kunitz has gained the front rank of contemporary verse in a single stride." In 1939, Kunitz married a former actress, Eleanor Evans (from whom he was divorced in 1958), a union that produced his only child, Gretchen.

Kunitz's tenure with the H. W. Wilson Company was interrupted by World War II, during which he served as a noncommissioned officer in charge of information and education in the Air Transport Command. His second collection, *Passport to the War,* appeared in 1944. A reviewer of that volume for *The New York Times Book Review* noted, "Kunitz has now (it seems) every instrument necessary to the poetic analysis of modern experience." Kunitz was awarded a Guggenheim Fellowship in 1945 and began a second career as an itinerant teacher, first at Bennington College, at the behest of his friend, the poet Theodore Roethke, then at a succession of colleges and universities, including the State University of New York at Potsdam, the New School for Social Research, Queens College, Brandeis University, and the University of Washington.

In 1958, Kunitz married the artist Elise Asher, published *Selected Poems, 1928-1958,* which was awarded the Pulitzer Prize for Poetry in 1959, and received grants from the National Institute of Arts and Letters and the Ford Foundation.

During the 1960's, though based in New York City and Provincetown, Massachusetts, Kunitz was a Danforth Visiting Lecturer at colleges and universities throughout the United States. He also lectured in the Soviet Union, Poland, Senegal, and Ghana. In 1964, he edited a volume of the poems of John Keats and two years later translated selections from Russian poet Andrei Voznesensky's *Antiworlds and The Fifth Ace.* He continued to edit for the Wilson Company (with Vineta Colby, *European Authors: 1000-1900: A Biographical Dictionary,* 1967) and coedited a memorial volume of essays on the poet Randall Jarrell. In 1968, along with artist Robert Motherwell and novelist Norman Mailer, he helped found The Fine Arts Work Center in Provincetown, a resident community of young artists and writers, and in 1969 he assumed the general editorship of the Yale Series of Younger Poets.

The Testing-Tree, a volume of poems and translations, appeared in 1971, prompting Robert Lowell to assert in *The New York Times Book Review,* "once again, Kunitz tops the crowd, the old iron brought to the white heat of simplicity." In 1974, Kunitz was awarded one of the nation's top official literary honors when he was appointed Consultant in Poetry to the Library of Congress. In addition to *The Testing-Tree* and the collected volume *The Poems of Stanley Kunitz, 1928-1978,* a book of essays and conversations entitled *A Kind of Order, a Kind of Folly,* as well as three volumes of translations, appeared during the 1970's.

Kunitz published a thematic volume of old and new poems, *The Wellfleet Whale and Companion Poems,* in a limited edition in 1983, with the new poems later incorporated in *Next-to-Last Things: New Poems and Essays*, published in 1985. In recognition of his lifetime achievement, Kunitz was chosen as the first New York State Poet, for the term 1987-1989.

Analysis

Stanley Kunitz has constantly sought to achieve higher and higher ground, both in his thoughtful aesthetic and in his themes. Kunitz's first poems were composed after the initial wave of modernism, led, in poetry, by T. S. Eliot and Ezra Pound, had crested. They resemble, to some extent, the earlier, tightly organized, ironic poems of Eliot, though the influence of the seventeenth century Metaphysical poets, particularly George Herbert (again an indirect influence of Eliot, who was largely responsible for the resurgence of interest in the Metaphysicals), is probably more preponderant. Moreover, by the 1920's, the work of Sigmund Freud had successfully invaded American arts and provided the introspective poet with a powerful tool for the analysis of self and culture.

The poems of *Intellectual Things* sketch many of the themes that will later be subject to elaboration and enrichment: the figure of the regenerative wound that is both the fresh scar of loss and the font of the power to transform experience into art, man's willful capriciousness (the "blood's unreason") and the inevitable cargo of guilt, and the search for the father, which is ultimately the search for identity, authority, and tradition.

Eloquent and formally rigorous, the poems in this first collection show a poet already mature in his medium, writing of his "daily self that bled" to "Earth's absolute arithmetic/ of being." Characterized by paradox and a wish for transcendence (though that wish is frequently denied or diverted to another object), the early poems often poise upon niceties of intellection—though they are also fully felt—and suggest transport by language rather than the transcendence to which they aspire. From the first, Kunitz's poems have typically employed the language and images of paradox. In "Change," the opening poem to his first collection, man is "neither here nor there/ Because the mind moves everywhere;/ And he is neither now nor then/ Because tomorrow comes again/ Foreshadowed. . . ." In more characteristically personal poems, such as "Postscript," the poet observes, in what will develop into one of his ongoing themes, the self's phoenixlike destruction and subsequent regeneration: "I lost by winning, and I shall not win/ Again, except by loss." The losses Kunitz traces in *Intellectual Things* are those of past life (or of a past one that was denied), symbolized by the loss of his father, and the loss of love. In "For the Word Is Flesh" the poet admonishes his dead father: "O ruined father dead, long sweetly rotten/ Under the dial, the time-dissolving urn,/ Beware a second perishing. . . ." The second death is the doleful fate of being erased from the memories of the living. In a memorable passage that presages a later, more famous poem ("Father and Son"), Kunitz writes,

"Let sons learn from their lipless fathers how/ Man enters Hell without a golden bough"—that is to say, uninstructed.

Some of the finest effects attained in *Intellectual Things* can be attributed to a high degree of control over phrasing, combined with the use of rhyme as a tool of force reminiscent of Alexander Pope, as in "Lovers Relentlessly": "Lovers relentlessly contend to be/ Superior in their identity.// The compass of the ego is designed/ To circumscribe intact a lesser mind. . . ." Kunitz uses rhyme also as a vehicle of wit, as in the shorter, three-beat lines of "Benediction": "God banish from your house/ The fly, the roach/ the mouse// That riots in the walls/ Until the plaster falls. . . ."

Passport to the War retains much of the density and bardic resonance of *Intellectual Things*, but the range of subject matter is broader: The self must now take its transformations into account against the background of recent history, for which regeneration is entirely problematic: "One generation past, two days by plane away,/ My house is dispossessed, my friends dispersed,/ My teeth and pride knocked in, my people game/ For the hunters of man-skins in the warrens of Europe." To the question "How shall we uncreate that lawless energy?" the poet can only defer to the determinisms of time: "I think of Pavlov and his dogs/ And the motto carved on the broad lintel of his brain:/ "Sequence, consequence, and again consequence." If the shadow of history casts the representative self in a darker hue, the poet, like Matthew Arnold before him, clings to what is most central to the life of the individual: "Lie down with me, dear girl, before/ My butcher-boys begin to rave./ 'No hope for persons any more,'/ They cry, 'on either side of the grave.'/ Tell them I say the heart forgives/ The World." The strange weapons of intimacy and charity would seem ill-suited as protection in a brutal world, but the sacramental element, the desire to raise the supposed commonplace, remains one of the bolts of a civilization unravaged by history. If history is the inevitable backdrop of our mortality, so do a representative mortal's most private strivings and sufferings themselves constitute a part of its fabric: "What the deep heart means,/ Its message of the big, round, childish hand,/ Its wonder, its simple lonely cry,/ The bloodied envelope addressed to you,/ Is history, that wide and mortal pang."

The visionary "Father and Son," perhaps Kunitz's best-known poem, establishes, in surrealistic images full of longing and regret, the poet's existential fate in the context of history. "Whirling between two wars," he follows "with skimming feet,/ The secret master of my blood . . . whose indomitable love/ Kept me in chains." Addressing his father "At the water's edge, where the smothering ferns lifted/ Their arms . . . ," the poet asks for his father's instruction: "For I would be a child to those who mourn/ And brother to the foundlings of the field . . . / O teach me how to work and keep me kind." Yet the summons brings only a shocking specter of discontinuity: "Among the turtles and the lilies he turned to me/ The white ignorant hollow of his face." One senses that what the poet asks is already, in some way, self-provided, though minus the love so deeply rooted in biology that it has the status of a cultural given. As war and upheaval expose these roots, one senses the poet's implication that, in a metaphorical sense, all are orphans.

"Open the Gates," another well-known visionary lyric, delivered in a grave voice that eerily suggests posthumous utterance, finds the poet "Within the city of the burning cloud," standing "at the monumental door/ Carved with the curious legend of my youth." Striking the door with "the great bone of my death," the poet stands "on the terrible threshold," where he sees "the end and the beginning in each other's arms." The seamless and incestuous image suggests the allegorical figures of Sin and Death in John Milton's *Paradise Lost* (1667), and the allusion holds to the extent that both figures are determinants of human fate. At the same time, the emphasis is less on moral conditioning than on the endlessly reforming fate of the human, as felt from the inside, in contrast with the wholeness of a life, glimpsed, so to speak, from a vantage somehow apart from it. Our lives, as William Shakespeare said, are "rounded with a sleep," and it is a matter of indifference whether one attempts an artificial distinction between the two sleeps, except, of course, that one's only knowledge takes place as human, and forever from the vantage of one looking outward (even when he is looking inward). As for the question of inside versus outside, no other consciousness has yet much to contribute to the subject.

In 1958, after another long hiatus, Kunitz published his *Selected Poems, 1928-1958*, more than a third of which are new poems. The new poems take up the modern subject of otherness, as in "The Science of the Night," in which the speaker contemplates his sleeping beloved "Down the imploring roads I cannot take/ Into the arms of ghosts I never knew." Even if he could track her to her birth, he admits, "You would escape me." He concludes, "As through a glass that magnifies my loss/ I see the lines of your spectrum shifting red,/ The universe expanding, thinning out,/ Our worlds flying, oh flying, fast apart." Always a time-bewitched poet, Kunitz brings to this and other new poems in the volume an added sense of urgency, for they are imbued with a love and desire that is unintentionally but nevertheless increasingly rearranged by the shifting weight of years.

With amiable, if slow, regularity, Kunitz's fourth volume, *The Testing-Tree*, marks a departure from the rhetorical shimmer and elevated diction displayed in the previous collections. Written in a less knotty, more transparent syntax and style, the poems confront the upheavals of the 1960's, the guilt of failed marriage and inadequate parenthood, the ravages of time past ("the deep litter of the years"), and the inexplicable urge to carry on in the face of public and private failures: "In a murderous time/ the heart breaks and breaks/ and lives by breaking." The consolations of this volume, though sparse, strike the reader as all the more authentic for their scrupulous lack of façade, which, however, in no way implies a lessening of charity on the part of the poet.

One of the most notable poems in *The Testing-Tree* is "King of the River," a poem of the skewed hopes and unclear motives that disfigure and sometimes break a life, but which are finally overtaken, with individual life itself transcended and transfigured by the relentless biological urge to perpetuate the species. The poem, whose central symbol is the chinook salmon swimming upstream to spawn, seeks to rebut the materialist's claim that "there is no life, only living things." By addressing the fish throughout as "you," the poet clearly implicates the reader in an allegory of life: "If the water were clear enough,/ if the water were still,/ but the water is not clear . . . If the knowledge were given you,/ but it is not given,/ for the membrane is clouded/ with self-deceptions." The psychological phrase helps swing the pointed finger around to the reader. "If the power were granted you/ to break out of your cells,/ but the imagination fails . . . If the heart were pure enough, but it is not pure . . . ," continues the litany of denial that underpins the allegory. The salmon ("Finned Ego") thrashes to a place of which it has no knowledge, for "the doors of the senses close/ on the child within." The blind, headlong rush to "the orgiastic pool" brings about dreadful change ("A dry fire eats you./ Fat drips from your bones") into something "beyond the merely human," where, despite the "fire on your tongue," promising that "The only music is time/ the only dance is love,/ you would admit/ that nothing compels you/ any more . . . but nostalgia and desire,/ the two-way ladder/ between heaven and hell." At the "brute absolute hour" when the salmon spawns only to die, when "The great clock of your life/ is slowing down,/ and the small clocks run wild," he ("you") stares into the face of his "creature self" and finds "he is not broken but endures," but at a price: he is "forever inheriting his salt kingdom,/ from which he is banished/ forever." The "forever" that rounds the conclusion like a little sleep suggests that the victory of life's mission to perpetuate itself is ironically accomplished at the loss of the human's vaunted objectivity and understanding.

In "Robin Redbreast," Kunitz reveals a similar, but distinct, necessity. In "the room where I lived/ with an empty page" (a room identified in "River Road" from the same volume as one the poet inhabited after his second divorce), the poet hears the squawking of blue jays tormenting a robin, "the dingiest bird/ you ever saw." Going out to pick up the bird "after they knocked him down," in order to "toss him back into his element," he notices the bullet hole that "had tunneled out his wits." The hole, cut so clean it becomes a window, reveals "the cold flash of the blue/ unappeasable sky." The sky's indifference to the poet's sympathy for the bird ("Poor thing! Poor foolish life!") or to his own condition (he lives "in a house marked 'For Sale'") provides the chilling backdrop for a revelation of the necessity for human charity toward all living things. The poem knowingly alludes to a passage in "Father and Son": "For I would be . . . brother to the foundlings of the field/ And friend of innocence and all bright eyes." As with that earlier poem, "Robin Redbreast" finds no consolation in received wisdom, either from a father's love or the heavens. What charity there is exists (as do humans) in what scientists dryly refer to as "terminal structure."

Memory is more directly the subject of "The Magic Curtain," a cultural tour of America during the 1920's. A paean to his nurse, Frieda, the poem affectionately recounts his happy childhood adventures with this blue-eyed, Bavarian maid, while his mother, "her mind already on her shop," unrolled "gingham by the yard,/ stitching dresses for the Boston trade." Frieda, identified as his "first love," in secret complicity with the knowing child, bestows "the kinds of kisses mother would not dream" and serves as his guide to the melodramatic, romantic world of the motion pictures where, during reels of *The Perils of Pauline* (1914), Keystone Kops, and Charlie Chaplin, "School faded out at every morning reel." The films are a hint of the glamorous world beyond for Frieda too, who takes her cue in a cinematic cliché and runs off "with somebody's husband, daddy to a brood." Although the poet's mother never forgives her this abandonment, the older poet, returning to her in the sanctuary of memory, eargerly does, for each has in a different way unknowingly conspired in fulfilling the dreams of the other.

The uneasy subject and situation of parents (and parent figures) weighs heavily, if somewhat obliquely, in the poems of *The Testing-Tree*. In fact, the volume opens with "Journal for My Daughter," a poem in which the poet, in nine free-verse sections, confronts his own hesitations and guilt in the upbringing of his only child. He imagines himself through her eyes as beckoning "down corridors,/ secret, elusive, saturnine." Now that, he hopes, the smoke of these misgivings has cleared, he declares, "I propose/ that we gather our affections." Looking back over his role in her life, he recounts his absence ("his name was absence") but claims, "I think I'd rather sleep forever/ than wake up cold/ in a country without women." He recounts too, drunken nights of bonhomie with his friend, the poet Theodore Roethke, "slapping each other on the back,/ sweaty with genius," while she "crawled under the sofa." While he confesses that he is now "haggard with his thousand years," he declares his solidarity with her 1960's protests: "His heart is at home/ in your own generation," and to prove it he equates her misspelled slogan *"Don't tred on me"* with the *"Noli me tangere!"* he used "to cry in Latin once." Though it seems implausible that one would cry out in Latin anyplace outside the Vatican or a course in Tudor poets, the point is well made. Recalling "the summer I went away," he carries her outside "in a blitz of fireflies" to observe her first eclipse. To this image he adds Samuel Taylor Coleridge's carrying his crying son outside and catching the reflection of stars in each of his suspended tears. The heavens and the natural world are captured, comfortably diminished, and naturalized as a way of sanctioning human folly and love. The reverse of this coin is that it is an illusion, a pint-sized reflection of a placid cosmos that will momentarily evaporate.

The book's title poem, composed in four sections of unrhymed tercets, concerns a ritualistic childhood game of stone-throwing ("for keeps") at a specific oak tree able to confer magic gifts: one hit for love, two for poetry, three for eternal life. In the summers of his youth, searching for "perfect stones," he is master "over that stretch of road . . . the world's fastest human." Leaving the road that begins at school at one end and that at the other tries "to loop me home," he enters a field "riddled with rabbit-life/ where the bees sank sugar-wells/ in the trunks of the maples." There, in the shadow of the "inexhaustible oak,/ tyrant and target," he calls to his father, "*wherever you are/ I have only three throws/ bless my good rightarm.*" In the final section, he recalls a recurring dream of his mother "wearing an owl's face/ and making barking noises." As "her minatory finger points," he steps through a cardboard door and wonders if he should be blamed for the dirt sifting into a well where a gentle-eyed "albino walrus huffs." Suddenly the scene shifts, and the highway up which a Model A chugs becomes the road "where tanks maneuver,/ revolving their turrets." He concludes, "It is necessary to go/ through dark and deeper dark/ and not to turn." With the clear implication that the poet is mindful of his approaching mortal hour, with or without his father's blessing, he cries, "Where is my testing-tree?/ Give me back my stones!"

The Testing-Tree differs from the first three volumes in being composed of nearly a quarter translations, all from postrevolutionary Russian poetry. It was during the 1960's that Kunitz met and befriended two of the Soviet Union's best-known poets, Yevgeny Yevtushenko and Andrei Voznesensky, and, in collaboration with Max Hayward, translated a selection of poems by a third, Anna Akhmatova. Clearly, the poems enabled Kunitz, with the aid of this fortuitous ventriloquism, to take aim at the brutality and inhumanity of the modern political bureaucracy, whether Soviet or American. In Yevtushenko's "Hand-Rolled Cigarettes," for example, the common man's practice of rolling cigarettes in papers torn from *Pravda* and *Izvestia*, the two chief organs of state propaganda, gives rise to a dandy send-up of the bureaucrat's contempt for the common man: "Returning late, the tired fisherman/ enjoys his ladled kvass's tang,/ and sifts tobacco at his ease/ onto some bureaucrat's harangue."

The Poems of Stanley Kunitz, 1928-1978, like *Selected Poems, 1928-1958*, contains a section of new poems, entitled "The Layers." Here, the poet returns to the garden of his obsessions—father, family, time, the wounds of guilt, and memory—in poems of reconciliation and commemoration. In the opening poem, "The Knot," the poet imagines that the knot "scored in the lintel of my door" keeps "bleeding through/ into the world we share." Like a repressed thought, the knot wants more than anything to grow out again, to become a limb: "I hear it come/ with a rush of resin/ out of the trauma/ of its lopping-off." Characteristically, the poet associates the wound with a door, a threshold. It is as though something in nature has had to be tamed in order to effect the domestic tranquillity so delicately limned here, but its desire to return to its true nature is such that it "racks itself with shoots/ that crackle overhead." Identifying a part of his own nature with that of the knot, the poet completes the metaphor: "I shake my wings/ and fly into its boughs."

Kunitz returns to the theme of the lost father in "What of the Night?" and "Quinnapoxet." In the former, the poet wakes in the middle of the night "like a country doctor," having imagined, "with racing heart," the doorbell ringing. It is a messenger (Death) whose "gentle, insistent ring" finds the poet "not ready yet" and realizing "nobody stands on the stoop." Suddenly the poem switches focus from the grown son to the father: "When the messenger comes again/ I shall pretend/ in a childish voice/ my father is not home." His father has, in actuality, never been home, but in a deeper, metaphorical sense, he has never left home. In this light, just as the grown man must receive the messenger at the end of his life, so the son must protect the father in memory from the "second death," the oblivion of forgetting. The poet's task of remembering is obligatory, as his question earlier in the poem recognizes: "How could I afford/ to disobey that call?" "Quinnapoxet" takes place on a mysterious fishing trip where, on a dusty road similar to the one described in "Father and Son," the poet describes a hallucinatory vision of his mother and father "commingling with the dust/ they raised." His mother admonishes him for not writing, and the poet's response is simple: "I had nothing to say to her." Yet for his father who walks behind, "his face averted . . . deep in his other life," the poet, too awestruck to attempt speech, touches his forehead with his thumb, "in deaf-mute country/ the sign for father."

One of the most original of the new poems in this volume is "A Blessing of Women," a prose poem inspired by an exhibit of early American women painters and artisans mounted by the Whitney Museum. In the form of a litany, the poem briefly describes, in dignified understatement, the works and lives of five of the representative women: an embroiderer, a quilter, and three painters, "a rainbow-cloud of witnesses in a rising hubbub." He blesses them and greets them "as they pass from their long obscurity, through the gate that separates us from our history."

"Our history" is again the subject of "The Lincoln Relics," a meditation on Lincoln's passage from the "rawboned, warty" mortal "into his legend and his fame." Written not long after the Watergate trauma during Kunitz's tenure at the Library of Congress, the poem alludes to that episode by invoking the ancient struggle between idealism and materialism, no less fierce in Lincoln's day than in ours: "I saw the piranhas darting/ between the rose-veined columns,/ avid to strip the flesh/ from the Republic's bones." The source of Lincoln's, the sacrificial redeemer's, strength is identified as his "secret wound"—that is to say, "trusting the better angels of our nature." It is this trust, evoked by the humble but talismanic relics—a pocketknife, a handkerchief, a button—found on his person after the assassination, that makes "a noble, dissolving music/ out of homely fife and drum."

The title poem of the new section, "The Layers," looks forward to the possibilities of new art. The poet has "walked through many lives" and from the present vantage sees "milestones dwindling/ toward the horizon/ and the slow fires trailing/ from the abandoned camp-sites." To the question, "How shall the heart be reconciled/ to its feast of losses?" the answer comes "In my darkest night" from a "nimbus-cloud voice" that thunders, "Live in the layers,/ not on the litter." Though the poet admits, "I lack the art/ to decipher it," he concludes, "I am not done with my changes."

Kunitz's work *Next-to-Last Things: New Poems and Essays* makes at least three important additions to his poetic canon. A dream poem, "The Abduction," begins with the image of the beloved stumbling out of a wood, her blouse torn, her skirt bloodstained; she addresses the poet with the mysterious question, "Do you believe?" Through the years, he says, "from bits/ from broken clues/ we pieced enough together/ to make the story real." Led into the presence of "a royal stag,/ flaming in his chestnut coat," she was "borne/ aloft in triumph through the green,/ stretched on his rack of budding horn." In the next verse paragraph, the poet discloses that the episode was "a long time ago,/ almost another age" and muses on his sleeping wife (recalling, with the same image, the theme of otherness in "The Science of the Night"): "You lie in elegant repose,/ a hint of transport hovering on your lips." His attention shifts "to the harsh green flares," to which she is indifferent, that "swivel through the room/ controlled by unseen hands." The night world outside is "childhood country,/ bleached faces peering in/ with coals for eyes." His meditation leads him to realize that "the shapes of things/ are shifting in the wind," and concludes, "What do we know/ beyond the rapture and the dread?" echoing William Butler Yeats's famous question, "How can we know the dancer from the dance?" As a poem of transformation, "The Abduction" does not lend itself easily to interpretation—partly by design— for, at a very basic level, the preternatural images of transformation are rooted in undisclosed biographical events. As a poet of knowledge, however, Kunitz is poignant in his recognition that when people sleep, when they are most themselves, they are also most withdrawn and indifferent to their surroundings, even, or especially, from those they love. Yet by acknowledging, even honoring, the terms of this indifference, one most surely understands the unselfish nature of love.

"Days of Foreboding" begins with the announcement, "Great events are about to happen." The poet has seen migratory birds "in unprecedented numbers" picking the coastal margin clean. Turning to himself, he observes, "My bones are a family in their tent/ huddled over a small fire/ waiting for the uncertain signal/ to resume the long march." He too is migratory, warmed by the small fire of his heart. Presumably, the "uncertain signal" is in some way keyed to the signal by which the migratory birds decide to move on—that is, it is keyed to nature. Moreover, while the signal is uncertain in terms of time and origin, it is nevertheless inevitable. The ultimate phrase, "the long march," sings with historical resonance and the promise of an irreversible transformation at the end. In this poem and in others, Kunitz accepts the awful (literally) fact of mortality, not by making an abstraction of it, but by naturalizing both it and the patch of history that is the bolt of time and circumstance given for its completion. Avoiding the need for consolation, it is a brave and existential view.

Certainly the centerpiece of *Next-to-Last Things* is the five-part meditative elegy, "The Wellfleet Whale," composed, like "The Testing-Tree," in tercets. Kunitz has noted that much of contemporary meditative poetry suffers from "the poverty of what it is meditating on," but this poem, occasioned by the beaching of a finback whale near the poet's home on Cape Cod, is rich in its suggestion that life's secret origins can be, if not revealed, then somehow embodied by the evocativeness of language, which is itself, as the poet notes elsewhere, "anciently deep in mysteries." The poem begins by ascribing to the whale, both Leviathan and deliverer of Jonah, Christ's precursor, the gift of language: "You have your language too,/ an eerie medley of clicks/ and hoots and trills. . . ." That language, to which humans are denied access (just as historical man, exiled from Eden, can no longer hear the Music of the Spheres), becomes only "sounds that all melt/ . . . with endless variations,/ as if to compensate/ for the vast loneliness of the sea." In the second section of the poem, the whale's arrival in the harbor is greeted with cheers "at the sign of your greatness." Unlike man, the whale in its element seems "like something poured,/ not driven," his presence asking "not sympathy, or love,/ or understanding,/ but awe and wonder," responses appropriate to deity. Yet by dawn, the whale is stranded on the rocks, and the curious gather in: "school-girls in yellow halters/ and a housewife bedecked/ with curlers, and whole families in beach/ buggies. . . ." As the great body is slowly crushed by its own weight, the Curator of Mammals arrives to draw the requisite vial of blood, someone carves his initials on the blistered flanks, and sea gulls peck at the skin. The poet asks, "What drew us, like a magnet, to your dying?" and answers, "You made a bond between us." This unlikely company, "boozing in the bonfire night," stands watch during the night as the whale enters its final agony and swings its head around to open "a bloodshot, glistening eye/ in which we swam with terror and recognition." The terror is that of witnessing "an exiled god" and the recognition that the creature, bringing with it "the myth/ of another country, dimly remembered" is "like us,/ disgraced and mortal," like all beings, and "delivered to the mercy of time." Despite the desecrations visited upon the creature, it remains an emissary from that other "country," the country of myth and inspired origin that stands at the beginning of human memory—and thus of identity—and so supervenes upon the noble disenchantment of the poem.

The tension that is everywhere apparent between noble disenchantment and hard-won acceptance demonstrates the ruling dialectic in Kunitz's poems. At the very least, it reveals the long trail of a poetic career (poetic careers have been built on much less); at its most resplendent, this dialectic embodies, through its variously charted interests, experiences, and investigations, a reason for the mind's commitment to the things of this world. Standing simultaneously in their singular and typical natures, they suggest the duality that is both a curse and triumph and lead to an appreciation and understanding, as individuals rebound endlessly between the two, of the transformations that must be endured to ensure survival.

David Rigsbee

Other major works

NONFICTION: *A Kind of Order, a Kind of Folly: Essays and Conversations*, 1975.

TRANSLATIONS: *Stolen Apples*, 1972 (with others, of Yevgeny Yevtushenko's poetry); *Poems of Akhmatova*, 1973 (with Max Hayward); *Story Under Full Sail*, 1974 (of Andrei Voznesensky's poetry); *Orchard Lamps*, 1978 (of Ivan Drach's poetry).

MISCELLANEOUS: *Next-to-Last Things: New Poems and Essays*, 1985.

Bibliography

Henault, Marie. *Stanley Kunitz*. Boston: Twayne, 1980. A good introduction to Kunitz for the beginning reader. Presents biographical detail and criticism of his poetry, discussing his themes, form and techniques, and the "interior logics" of his poems. A sympathetic study lamenting the fact that Kunitz has not received the wide critical recognition he deserves.

Lowell, Robert. "On Stanley Kunitz's 'Father and Son.'" In *The Contemporary Poet as Artist and Critic*, edited by Anthony Ostroff. Boston: Little, Brown, 1964. Analyzes "Father and Son" and takes issue with a number of images in this poem, such as an orange being "nailed." Despite his unfavorable response, Lowell acknowledges that Kunitz has "never published an unfinished and unfelt poem."

Orr, Gregory. *Stanley Kunitz: An Introduction to the Poetry*. New York: Columbia University Press, 1985. A full-length criticism of Kunitz, noting that love and art are the two ways in which this poet seeks his identity. Discusses the key image, which Orr maintains is the single most important element in Kunitz's work. The chapter on *The Testing-Tree* is particularly recommended.

Vinson, James, ed. *Contemporary Poets*. 3d ed. New York: Macmillan, 1980.

The entry on Kunitz, by Michael True, examines his poetry as it retraces the "myth of the lost father." Cites his devotion to craft and the high standards he strove to maintain throughout his work. Notes Kunitz's earlier works as being more intellectual and his later ones as being more oriented toward feelings.

Wagoner, David. "A Review of *Selected Poems*." *Poetry* 93 (December, 1958): 174-178. A sympathetic review acknowledging that Kunitz should have a "place among the very best poets of our time." The only detraction from these poems, Wagoner notes, is that they are neither dated nor arranged chronologically. Praises Kunitz for his "imagination functioning repeatedly at the highest pitch."

Weisberg, Robert. "Stanley Kunitz: The Stubborn Middle Way." *Modern Poetry Studies* 6 (Spring, 1975): 49-57. In this sympathetic article, Weisberg laments that Kunitz's "impressive" canon has aroused little critical interest. In discussing *Selected Poems, 1928-1958*, however, he criticizes Kunitz for being a "reincarnation of John Donne" but praises "The Words of the Preacher" for the energy that his other metaphysical lyrics lack. Includes an analysis of *The Testing-Tree*.

CHARLES LAMB

Born: London, England; February 10, 1775
Died: Edmonton, England; December 27, 1834

Principal poetry

Blank Verse, 1798 (with Charles Lloyd); *Poetry for Children*, 1809 (with Mary Lamb); *The Works of Charles Lamb*, 1818; *Album Verses*, 1830; *Satan in Search of a Wife*, 1831; *The Poetical Works of Charles Lamb*, 1836.

Other literary forms

Charles Lamb began his literary career writing poetry and continued to write verse his entire life. He tried his hand at other genres, however, and is remembered primarily for his familiar essays. These essays, originally published in the *London Magazine*, were collected in *Essays of Elia* (1823) with another collection appearing ten years later, *Last Essays of Elia* (1833). In addition to his poetry and essays, Lamb wrote fiction, drama, children's literature, and criticism. He wrote one novel, *A Tale of Rosamund Gray and Old Blind Margaret* (1798). In 1802, he published his first play, *John Woodvil: A Tragedy*, which was followed shortly by another attempt at drama: *Mr. H.: Or, Beware a Bad Name, a Farce in Two Acts* (1806). In addition to several prologues and epilogues, he published two other dramas: *The Pawnbroker's Daughter: A Farce* (1825) and *The Wife's Trial* (1827). In addition, he wrote (largely in collaboration with his sister Mary) several children's books: *The King and Queen of Hearts* (1805), *Tales from Shakespear* (1807), *Adventures of Ulysses* (1808), *Mrs. Leicester's School* (1809), and *Prince Dorus* (1811). Lamb's criticism appeared in various periodicals but was never systematically collected and published during his lifetime. He did publish copious critical notes to accompany his voluminous extracts from Elizabethan plays, *Specimens of English Dramatic Poets, Who Lived About the Time of Shakespeare, with Notes* (1808).

Achievements

Much of Lamb's literary career was spent in search of an appropriate genre for his particular genius. He wrote poetry, drama, fiction, and criticism, but of these he truly distinguished himself only in criticism. When he happened upon the persona of Elia and the familiar essay, however, these early efforts contributed to his success. As if he had been in training for years preparing to create the *Essays of Elia*, Lamb applied what he had learned from each of the earlier literary forms in which he had worked. Incorporating his knowledge of the importance of rhythm, dramatic context, characterization, dialogue, tone, and point of view, he placed it into the *Essays of Elia* collections and created masterpieces.

Today's literary critics value the essays of Lamb because they embody and reflect in prose the Romantic predisposition found in the great poetry of the day. These familiar essays have a biographical impulse, organic form, symbolic representation, syntactic flexibility, and occasional subject matter. The popularity of Lamb's essays, however, does not depend upon their historical or theoretical relevance. The *Essays of Elia* collections were as celebrated in Lamb's day as they are in modern times and for the same reason: the character of Elia that Lamb creates is one of the most endearing personae in English literature. Elia's whimsical reminiscences may border upon the trivial, but that is insignificant, because the character of the speaker preempts the content of his speech. The personality of Elia becomes the focal point of the essay. His sentimentality, tempered by irony, elevates these pieces to the status of art, conferring upon them their timeless appeal.

Just as the character of Elia is essential to the success of the essays, Lamb's personality overwhelmed his accomplishments in his own day. No discussion of Lamb's achievements would be complete without mention of his many friends, who provided the essential ingredient for his famous nights at home and his fascinating correspondence. A list of his friends is a roster of the major figures of English Romanticism: Samuel Taylor Coleridge, Robert Southey, William Wordsworth, William Godwin, William Hazlitt, Thomas De Quincey, George Dyer, and Benjamin Robert Haydon. His midweek parties from 1801 through 1827 assembled writers, artists, actors, and critics for both frivolous and serious discussion. Port, mutton, cards, and tobacco made the following work day the longest of the week for Lamb. What the success of his weekly gatherings suggests, his correspondence corroborates: Lamb was an honest critic, a sensitive friend, and a sympathetic confidant. When he mentioned his many friends, he assumed his usual tone of self-deprecation, claiming that they were "for the most part, persons of an uncertain fortune." When talking of Lamb, his friends were less diffident. Henry Crabb Robinson epitomizes the opinion of Lamb's friends when he characterized Lamb as "of all the men of genius I ever knew, the one the most intensely and universally to be loved."

Biography

Charles Lamb was born in London to poor parents. His father was a servant and clerk to Samuel Salt, Esquire, of the Inner Temple, and his mother was Salt's housekeeper. Like his older brother John, Lamb went to Christ's Hospital School when he was seven, sponsored by Salt. There he met Coleridge, who was to become his friend for life. Because of a stutter, Lamb did not follow Coleridge to Cambridge on scholarship. Instead, at the age of fourteen, with his education complete, he went to work. His first two apprenticeships came to nothing. In 1792, however, he took a position as an accountant in the East India House, where he remained until his retirement in 1825. Lamb often complained about his position at the East India House, claiming that the work was boring and unimaginative. In fact, the routine about which he complained was a settling and stabilizing influence that his temperament needed and his art exploited. Lamb received an adequate income for a modicum of work, and, though not rich, he was comfortable by the standards of his day. Two other events in his life, however, diminished the happiness offered by this financial security.

Among celebrated bachelors, Lamb is one of the most famous. His unmarried status, however, was not of his own choosing. Sometime around 1792, he fell in love with Ann Simmons, a Hertfordshire neighbor of his maternal grandmother Field. Mrs. Field is said to have discouraged the relationship by pointing out that there was insanity in the Lamb family, and Ann married a London pawnbroker and silversmith named Barton. Lamb's poetry, letters, and essays testify to the sorrow he felt over his loss. Thirty years later in "Dream Children," Elia would fantasize about the woman he never married and the children he never fathered, who instead "call Bartram father." Mrs. Fields's warning may have been a self-fulfilling prophecy. At the end of 1795, in despair over "another Person," Lamb committed himself to Hoxton Asylum for six weeks. In a letter to Coleridge dated May 27, 1796, he explains his condition: "I am got somewhat rational now, & *don't bite any one*. But *mad I was*—& many a vagary my imagination played with me."

The second unhappy event that crucially influenced Lamb's life was also related to madness. On September 22, 1796, his sister Mary went mad and fatally stabbed their mother with a kitchen knife. She was tried in the courts, found insane, and remanded to Lamb's custody for life, at his request. Because of his devotion to Mary, his life was altered permanently. Lamb and Mary had always been close, but now they became inseparable, except, that is, when Mary felt her madness coming on. Then the two could be seen walking hand in hand—crying and carrying Mary's straitjacket—to Hoxton Asylum where she would stay until she was well again. To make up for the family that neither of them had, they both cultivated a great number of friends. Stories abound concerning Lamb's remarkable personality, his charming wit, quick sallies, pointed puns, and clever ripostes. It was this engaging personality that Lamb managed to translate into his depiction of Elia. Elia first appeared in the *London Magazine* in August, 1820, with the essay "Recollections of the South-Sea House." Elia is, of course, a mask, but a mask sharing many of Lamb's traits and experiences.

In 1825, Lamb sent his last Elia essay to the *London Magazine*, and in that year he retired from the East India House. His retirement, eagerly awaited, proved disappointing. He missed the routine, the motivation, the camaraderie of the office. Worse was the frequent illness of Mary that left him alone more and more often. Lamb was not a man able to cope with loneliness, and his drinking increased. With the death of Coleridge in July of 1834, Lamb seemed to lose interest in life. On Saturday, December 27, 1834, he died in his home at the age of fifty-nine. He is buried in Edmonton churchyard, outside of London.

Analysis

Charles Lamb's attitude toward poetry evolved as he matured. As a young man, he considered himself an aspiring poet. He experimented with rhythms, modeled his diction after Sir Philip Sidney and his sentiment after William Lisle Bowles, discussed theory with Samuel Taylor Coleridge, and took pleasure in criticizing his own and others' work. In his early verse, there is little of the humor, irony, or modesty that typify his later writing. Lamb is not only serious but also self-consciously so, dealing with weighty topics in an elevated style. His early poems are heavy with melancholy and despair, even before Mary killed their mother. The poems are also personal and confessional and suggest an adolescent indulgence in emotion. Writing to Coleridge in 1796, Lamb explained, "I love my sonnets because they are the reflected images of my own feelings at different times."

Following Mary's disaster, Lamb's reality became as tragic as he had previously imagined. He wrote to Coleridge, "Mention nothing of poetry. I have destroyed every vestige of past vanities of that kind." This was the first of several renunciations of poetry made by Lamb throughout his life, but—like similar renunciations of liquor and tobacco—it was temporary. In a few months, he was sending Coleridge new verses, but the subject matter was altered. Lamb turned to poetry for solace and consolation, composing religious verse. His interest in poetry had revived, but the sensational occurrences that influenced the rest of his life encouraged him to become one of the least sensational of poets. From this new perspective, he counseled Coleridge to "cultivate simplicity," anticipating William Wordsworth's "Preface" to *Lyrical Ballads* (1798). In his next letter to Coleridge, he praised Bowles and Philip Massinger and said he favored "an uncomplaining melancholy, a delicious regret for the past." Lamb's early sentimentality had been displaced by real tragedy, and his poetry changed accordingly.

With the healing passage of time, Lamb's literary interests shifted. In the years 1800 and 1805, he wrote several poems, but for the most part these middle years of his literary career were spent as a journalist. Around 1820, Lamb again began to write poetry, but of a completely different sort. The last period of his poetic production had been spent writing album verse and other occasional poems. As he matured, Lamb outgrew his earlier confessional mode and turned to people and events around him for subjects. He used his imagination to a greater degree, coloring reality, creating fictions, and distancing himself from his subject. His poetry changed with him, and it came to reflect a fictitious personality similar to the Elia of the essays. Like the Elian essays, Lamb's later poetry contains many autobiographical elements, but they are cloaked and decorous. In place of self-indulgent confessions is a distance and control not found in the early verse.

Lamb wrote and published most of his serious verse—that which today is most often anthologized—in the period between 1795 and 1800. His best and worst poems are among these efforts, which are autobiographical and despondent. They mourn the loss of love, of bygone days, and of happier times. They vary greatly in form, as Lamb experimented with different meters and structures. He was most successful in tight and traditional verse forms, and least successful in blank verse. In fact, his blank verse is bad, a surprising situation since his strength in more structured forms is in the control and variation of meter and rhythm.

A favorite form of Lamb's throughout his life was the sonnet, which he began writing early in his career. Appropriately enough, two of his earliest and best poems are English sonnets, published in Coleridge's *Poems on Various Subjects* (1796). This first significant publication by Lamb shows the influence of the Elizabethans on his poetry. His syntax, imagery, and diction suggest the practice of two centuries earlier. One of these sonnets, "Was it some sweet device of Faery," mourns a lost love "Anna" and is clearly a response to the loss of Ann Simmons. The poem's sophisticated rhythm, with frequent enjambment and medial stops, transcends its commonplace subject. Here, as often in Lamb's poetry, the handling of rhythm turns what might be a mediocre effort into an admirable poem. His use of rhetorical questions in this sonnet is skillful, too. Unlike the stilted tone that such questions often provide, in this sonnet the questions actually help to create a sense of sincerity. Another sonnet from the same volume, "O, I could laugh to hear the midnight wind," also treats the subject of lost love. The poem is nicely unified by the images of wind and wave, and it reflects the Romantic idea of the unity of man and cosmos. It also presents another Romantic concept, the value of the imagination and the powerful influence of memory. This poem is a reminder that much of Wordsworthian theory was not unique to Wordsworth. The ideas that the poem considers may be Romantic, but the style is that of an earlier day. The diction is antique, the imagery tightly unified, and the sonnet form itself conventionally developed. Lamb's prosody is pleasant but not novel.

In 1797, Coleridge's book of poetry went into a second edition, but with an amended title, ". . . to which are now added Poems by Charles Lamb." Lamb had already contributed four poems to the earlier edition, but now there appeared fourteen of his poems. The additional ones are, on the whole, inferior to the initial four; seven are sonnets written about the same time as those that Coleridge had already published. Of interest is one addressed to Mary and written before her tragedy, "If from my lips some angry accents fell." The closing lines give a sense of the personal nature of these verses:

> Thou to me didst ever shew
> Kindest affection; and would oft times lend

An ear to the desponding love-sick lay,
Weeping with sorrows with me, who repay
But ill the mighty debt of love I owe,
Mary, to thee, my sister and my friend.

The other poem of note in this volume was published in a Supplement at the end of the edition. Lamb was signaling its inferiority, and his judgment was correct. "A Vision of Repentance" is an experiment in Spenserian stanza. It opens with a vision, "I saw a famous fountain, in my dream." The fountain turns out to be the waters of redemption that have attracted "Psyche" as well as the speaker. A dialogue between the two ensues, and Psyche reports that she has forsaken Jesus and given "to a treacherous WORLD my heart." After some further conversation, the speaker leaves Psyche with the wish, "Christ restore thee soon." The poem is one of several by Lamb that deal with Christianity. Like his other religious verse, it is flawed: didactic, prolix, and unrhythmical.

Lamb's failure with the Spenserian stanza is paralleled by his experiments in blank verse. In 1798, he and Charles Lloyd published a volume entitled *Blank Verse*. Lacking the direction given by a tight form or a controlling convention, Lamb's blank verse is verbose, clumsy, and unsure. His autobiographical subject matter and confessional intent are uncomfortably couched in an elevated style reminiscent of John Milton. The two are not compatible. The volume, however, does contain one work by Lamb worthy of his talent. "The Old Familiar Faces," though not in blank verse, is Lamb's best-known poem. The subject is typical of this period in Lamb's career; it is a lamenting revelation of intense personal grief and loss. Its power, however, lies not in its subject matter, but in the skillful way in which Lamb manipulates the prosody. The poem evokes man's essential isolation and loneliness in the dolorous tolling repetition of the phrase, "All, all are gone, the old familiar faces." The form of the poem creates the effect. Rather than blank verse or the thumping rhymed verse of which he was too fond, Lamb chose a three-line stanza that replaced rhyme with the repetition of the title line. In this way, he gained form without the convoluted syntax of the padded line that rhyme often demanded. The rhythm of the line is that used by Coleridge in "Christabel," and it is agreeable to think that it was Lamb who suggested this meter to his friend. The poem is justly often anthologized; its rhythm is perfectly suited to the subject. Ian Jack in the *Oxford History of English Literature* (1963) suggests that the success of the meter conflicts with the other poems in the volume. He concludes, "It is hard to say how far the effect of the poem is due to metrical sophistication, and how far to a felicitous awkwardness."

By 1800, the self-indulgent moroseness of Lamb's early verse was beginning to be displaced by a greater sense of reserve and control. These years saw less poetic activity by Lamb, but the poems he wrote are, on the whole, more

able. An excellent example of the newfound discipline displayed by Lamb
occurs in "Hester." The poem again deals with the subjects of loss, death,
and despair, but he handles them with a new and previously uncharacteristic
restraint. The tight rhyme scheme and the concluding hypermetrical iambic
dimeter line provide Lamb with a form he uses well: a short line, a varied
rhythm, and a regular stanza:

> A springy motion in her gait,
> A rising step, did indicate
> Of pride and joy no common rate
> That flush'd her spirit

"Hester" is not one of the immortal poems in the English language, but it is
a solid achievement worthy of a young poet. Ian Jack has compared it favor-
ably with the lyrical ballads of Wordsworth.

Another poem from this period breaks the morbidity of Lamb's previous
verse and prefigures the wit and urbanity found in *Essays of Elia*. Lamb wrote
"A Farewell to Tobacco" in what he called "a stammering verse" because he
used tobacco to retard his own stammering. Once again he turned to the
short line, in this case an irregular eight-syllable trochaic line with rhyming
couplets, and it well served his comic intent. Gone is the gross subjectivity;
instead, the poem humorously indicts tobacco, while admitting that the habit
is unbreakable. Good-natured wordplay and clever burlesque make the poem
one of Lamb's most enjoyable. The comic tone established in "A Farewell
to Tobacco" appears again in 1812 when Lamb composed one of his few
political poems. "The Triumph of the Whale" gently ridicules the Prince
Regent by comparing George with a leviathan. He satirizes the Regent's girth,
appetite, retinue, and failed constancy. The poem exists mainly, however, for
the pun on which it ends: "the PRINCE of WHALES."

The last noteworthy poem of this period is a sonnet that illustrates Lamb's
mature, relaxed, and personal style. "Written at Cambridge" is an autobiographical whimsy that details how the poet feels as he walks around the
university. A note of disappointment begins the poem because the speaker
regrets that he had been unable to attend such an institution. This sense of
loss disappears, however, with the speaker's slightly foolish but nevertheless
touching portrait of his imaginative usurpation of Cantabrigian wisdom while
strolling its grounds. This poem is worthy of "gentle Charles."

Of the original poems published in the posthumous collection, *The Poetical
Works of Charles Lamb*, almost half are from his last period, 1820 to 1834.
Most of these are "album verse," a popular form in the 1820's. These occasional verses—written at the request of and about the album's owner—are
humorous and light, built around epigrams, puns, and acrostics. Most of this
album verse, while representative of the genre, is hardly memorable, with
two exceptions. "On the Arrival in England of Lord Byron's Remains" is a

good example of Lamb's mature tone, and it reveals his opinion of Byron: "lordly Juan, damned to lasting fame,/ Went out a pickle, and came back the same." A more serious work which arrives at unpleasant conclusions is "In My Own Album," a poignant comparison of life to an album. The poem returns to the theme of self-reproach that colored so much of Lamb's early verse, but there exists a distance and a universality that was not at work before. Rhymed tercets provide Lamb the form in which he worked best, and his iambic hexameters are smooth and graceful. The music of his verse complements his rhythm and meter.

Two of Lamb's best poems, both products of this late period, nicely exemplify his mature serious and comic styles. Both were written after Lamb had won recognition as an essayist, when he no longer felt he had to prove himself as a poet. Freed from the necessity of competing with Edmund Spenser, John Donne, and Milton (not to mention Coleridge, Robert Burns, and Robert Southey), Lamb discovered his own rhythm and voice. These, his finest verses, are the products of his natural strengths, and not those borrowed from another time or another artist. Relaxed and self-assured, Lamb mastered the short line and the comic effect of rhyme. He cultivated forms that worked for him and his voice. "On an Infant Dying as Soon as Born" deals with loss and death in a poignant and moving way. The maudlin, pathetic tone is gone. In its place is an elegant lament for the state of all men, an elegy that transcends the single occasion, a threnody whose language and figures are worthy of Andrew Marvell or Henry Vaughan. The dead child, addressed as "Riddle of destiny," presents to the speaker an insoluble problem, the suffering of innocent men. The speaker concludes that "the economy of Heaven is dark" and that even the "wisest clerks" are unable to explain why an infant dies while

> shrivel'd crones
> Stiffen with age to stocks and stones;
> And crabbed use the conscience sears
> In sinners of an hundred years.

The poem closes with a traditional, but guarded, optimism.

Lamb's longest and last poem published during his life, *Satan in Search of a Wife* (1831), consists of two books of thirty verses each. It is usually said that Lamb never valued this poem because he wrote his publisher not to mention that the "damn'd 'Devil's Wedding'" was written by the author of the *Essays of Elia*. Nevertheless, he thought highly enough of the poem to have it published. The ballad is Lamb at his best: light, jocular, ironic, punning, occasional, and personal. It begins with an echo of Lord Byron's *The Vision of Judgment* (1822) in reverse. Instead of St. Peter grown bored, the devil is out of sorts:

> The Devil was sick and queasy of late,
>   And his sleep and his appetite fail'd him;
> His ears they hung down and his tail it was clapp'd
> Between his poor hoofs, like a dog that's been rapp'd—
>   None knew what the devil ail'd him.

The tale continues, telling of the Devil's love for a tailor's daughter, his successful wooing of her, and the joyful wedding. Lamb's autobiographical propensity shows up even here, for lurking behind all the fun are serious complaints about bachelorhood, about women as lovers, women as mothers, and even women who murder, with the speaker concluding that "a living Fiend/ Was better than a dead Parent." The poem is, however, anything but maudlin. It is an energetic and fancy-filled romp which spoofs the devil, marriage, foreigners, and the Christian idea of hell. It is vintage Lamb: genteel, a bit cynical, but kind and sincere. The essays of Lamb will continue to earn him fame, but poems such as *Satan in Search of a Wife* have been too long neglected.

John F. Schell

Other major works

LONG FICTION: *A Tale of Rosamund Gray and Old Blind Margaret*, 1798.

PLAYS: *John Woodvil: A Tragedy*, 1802; *Mr. H.: Or, Beware a Bad Name, a Farce in Two Acts*, 1806; *The Pawnbroker's Daughter: A Farce*, 1825; *The Wife's Trial*, 1827.

NONFICTION: *Specimens of English Dramatic Poets, Who Lived About the Time of Shakespeare, with Notes*, 1808; *Essays of Elia*, 1823; *Last Essays of Elia*, 1833.

CHILDREN'S LITERATURE: *The King and Queen of Hearts*, 1805; *Tales from Shakespear*, 1807 (with Mary Lamb); *Adventures of Ulysses*, 1808; *Mrs. Leicester's School*, 1809 (with Mary Lamb); *Prince Dorus*, 1811.

MISCELLANEOUS: *The Works of Charles and Mary Lamb*, 1903-1905 (7 volumes), 1912 (6 volumes); *The Letters of Charles Lamb*, 1935 (3 volumes).

Bibliography

Barnett, George Leonard. *Charles Lamb*. Boston: Twayne, 1976. This volume is an excellent introduction to Lamb. Barnett supplies a biography interwoven with an analysis of Lamb's major works. Supplemented by a chronology of Lamb's life and work, an index, and a bibliography. Suitable for all students.

Cornwall, Barry. *Charles Lamb: A Memoir*. Boston: Roberts Brothers, 1866. Serious students of Lamb will find this old book essential, as it was written only thirty-two years after Lamb's death by a contemporary who knew him well. Lamb was astonishingly well loved, and his work held in high esteem by his contemporaries. It is interesting to see that the reputation of his work remains good today.

Hine, Reginald Leslie. *Charles Lamb and His Herfordshire*. London: J. M. Dent & Sons, 1949. Lamb was born in London, in town, but his heart was in his adopted home in the country, in Herfordshire. This book sheds valuable light on Lamb's personality, which was shaped by his attachment to country life. Contains paintings and drawings of Lamb and Herfordshire, a bibliography, and an index.

Howe, Will David. *Charles Lamb and His Friends*. Indianapolis: Bobbs-Merrill, 1944. Lamb was a lovable man and had many friends who wrote about him. Howe has stitched together many of these reminiscences and allowed the modern reader to see how Lamb's friends viewed him, and how he saw himself. Contains an index and a bibliography.

Lucas, Edward V. *The Life of Charles Lamb*. 5th ed. 2 vols. London: Methuen, 1921. This book remains the standard biography on Lamb. It is built on information gathered from Lamb's writings. Lucas provides a great deal of facts about Lamb's life but little critical analysis of his work. Valuable for all students.

WALTER SAVAGE LANDOR

Born: Warwick, England; January 30, 1775
Died: Florence, Italy; September 17, 1864

Principal poetry

The Poems of Walter Savage Landor, 1795; *Gebir: A Poem, in Seven Books,* 1798; *Poems from the Arabic and Persian,* 1800; *Poetry by the Author of Gebir,* 1800; *Gebirus, Poema,* 1803; *Count Julian* (a verse drama), 1812; *Idyllia Nova Quinque Heroum atque Heroidum,* 1815; *Idyllia Heroica Decem Librum Phaleuciorum Unum,* 1820; *Andrea of Hungary,* 1839 (verse drama); *Giovanna of Naples,* 1839 (verse drama); *Fra Rupert: The Last Part of a Trilogy,* 1840 (verse drama); *The Siege of Ancona,* 1846 (verse drama); *The Hellenics Enlarged and Completed,* 1847; *Poemata et Inscriptiones,* 1847; *Italics of Walter Savage Landor,* 1848; *The Last Fruit off an Old Tree,* 1853; *Heroic Idyls, with Additional Poems,* 1863; *The Poetical Works of Walter Savage Landor,* 1937 (Stephen Wheeler, editor).

Other literary forms

Walter Savage Landor's reputation rests primarily on his poetry, but he was a skilled writer of prose as well. His political writings are notable for their anger and his criticism for its insight into the mechanics of writing. All of his prose is witty; it is frequently satirical. As with his poetry, Landor's prose works are carefully phrased and sometimes more perfect in their parts than their wholes. Ranking as one of the most important practitioners of nonfiction prose in the nineteenth century, he is viewed by critics as one of the outstanding prose stylists of the English language.

Achievements

Landor's poetry has never had a wide readership. Much of its appeal is in its near-perfect phrasing and versification; such an appeal of skill almost inevitably attracts admirers among other poets, the fellow practitioners of a demanding art. Landor remains admired for the variety of poetic forms that he mastered and for the clarity of his phrasing; he is often faulted for the detached tone of his work—for the lack of emotional response to his subjects. His poetry often seems crystalline and fragile, as if unable to withstand the burden of a large audience. Fine prosody and marvelously apt phrasing when combined with the distant tone of much of his verse makes ranking him among poets a difficult task. Compounding the difficulty are his poetry's classical characteristics, which seem in conflict with the Romantic and Victorian eras during which he wrote. His poetry lacks the emotional vigor of Percy Bysshe Shelley's work but compares well with the beauty of John Keats's odes and is superior to George Gordon, Lord Byron's verse in ingenuity. He cannot match William Wordsworth in importance to the history of poetry, although many poets have valued his contributions to the understanding of prosody. Taken by itself, apart from its era and influence, Landor's poetry is equal in melodic beauty and economy of phrasing to much of the best in English poetry. As a poet, Landor might fairly be ranked behind Wordsworth and Robert Browning in overall achievement and behind Keats in imagery; he is second to none in phrasing and prosody.

Biography

Walter Savage Landor was a man given to fierce passions; he could burst out in either anger or generosity almost without warning. He was egotistical and given to romantic notions about life; this combination caused him much unhappiness and yet underlies much of his best writing. He was born on January 30, 1775, in Warwick. In 1780, he began his schooling at Knowle; in 1783, he was sent to study at Rugby. After eight years of annoying his teachers and antagonizing others with his satirical sense of humor, he was sent home. Landor, however, remembered Rugby fondly; while there, he developed his taste for poetry and demonstrated a precocious skill in composing verse. Reverend William Langley, of Ashbourne, Derbyshire, became Landor's tutor in 1792. The next year, Landor entered Trinity College, Oxford. While at Oxford he punctuated a political dispute by shooting at a neighbor's shutters; suspended from college for two terms, he left Oxford in 1794, never to return. He moved to London and had his poetry published under a grand title for a mere twenty-year-old, *The Poems of Walter Savage Landor* (1795). The volume brought him a small but loyal following among other writers and readers who had a taste for fine literature.

When his father died, Landor inherited a large fortune. This he spent on a large estate in Wales and on outfitting his own regiment to fight in Spain against the French. After the French left Spain, Landor's regiment disappeared, and he hastened home. In Wales, he tried to improve the lives of the peasants and to introduce enlightened methods of managing an estate. No one seemed to appreciate his efforts, and after losing much money, he abandoned the effort.

In 1811, in one of his grand gestures, he married an attractive woman who was beneath him in both wealth and social station. Far from being grateful, his bride, Julia Thuillier, repeatedly cuckolded Landor and made his life unpleasant. She did not appreciate her husband's generous nature, his intellect, or his interests. Although she is often portrayed as a nasty and cruel woman, she and Landor seem to have had enough truces to produce a daughter and three sons. In 1814, Landor toured the Continent, where he was eventually joined by his wife. From 1816 to 1818, he stayed in Como, Italy, and in 1818 his first son was born. His daughter followed in 1820, while he was in Pisa. From 1821 to 1828, he lived in Florence, where his second and third sons were born in 1822 and 1825. By 1835, his family life was unbearable;

his wife dedicated herself to embarrassing him publicly and committing adultery privately. Landor had doted on his children and spoiled them; nevertheless, when he left his wife and returned to England, they chose to remain with her, although in the 1840's his two eldest sons and his daughter visited him for months at a time. During the years of unhappy marriage, Landor continued to write, building a loyal following of admiring friends, including Ralph Waldo Emerson and John Forster.

Landor's trenchant wit and attacks on the misdeeds of public officials frequently involved him in trouble. In 1857, old but still fiery, he published attacks on a Mrs. Yescombe, whom he saw as a villainess because of an injustice visited on a young woman. Convicted of libel in 1858, he left England in 1859 to seek refuge from litigation in Fiesole, where he had maintained his family since 1835. Rejected by his family, he wandered to nearby Florence, where Robert Browning offered him a home. He died on September 17, 1864. He had wanted to be buried near Bath in England but was interred instead at Florence. He had wanted an epitaph that mentioned his closest friends but instead received one that mentions his wife and children.

Analysis

The poems of Walter Savage Landor are like fragile crystals, the clarity of which disguises their masterfully crafted form. The meaning of Landor's verse often seems transparent; he believed in clarity as a poetic virtue. The seeming ease with which his verse can be understood belies the strenuous efforts Landor made to pare down his phrases and to present his ideas with near-perfect economy. Much of his success in economical phrasing comes from his mastery of a host of meters and poetic subgenres, chief among which were the verse drama, the dramatic scene, the heroic poem, and the Hellenic poem. Landor had a restless mind, requiring activity; he had a voracious appetite for ideas. Writing poetry provided him with relief from such intellectual demands. Poetry was thus more of a hobby than a career; Landor wrote verse for recreation, and the complexity of his prosody and the pureness of his language originate in part from this recreational aspect of his versifying. His poetry represented an effort to find peace of mind, to discharge some of his extraordinary intellectual energy. The literature of ancient Greece and Rome had a long history of amateur scholarly study and had inspired and informed the neoclassical period in England that was just ending when Landor was born, and he found ready materials for such agreeable study in a host of commentaries on form and style. The Greeks supplied him with ideas about life and human relationships; the Latin poets supplied him with high standards for poetic composition and style. He sometimes wrote in Latin, perhaps to capture the elegance and sense of sweet phrasing that typifies much of the best of the poetry of the classical Romans.

Landor's use of classical materials has long created problems for literary historians. His life spans the Romantic era and ends when the Victorian era was well under way. Although some Romantic poets—notably Percy Bysshe Shelley—used classical myths as subjects, they rarely employed classical forms. A classicist can be identified by his use of the standards of the ancient poets: an emphasis on phrasing, good sense, and logical order. A classicist restrains his emotions in favor of clarity of expression and tends to use classical works as models for his own. The Romantics, on the other hand, reacted to the preceding neoclassical age by emphasizing mysticism, nature, and traditional English poetic forms such as blank verse and the sonnet.

In his tastes and models, Landor was every inch a classicist and had more in common with Alexander Pope and Samuel Johnson than with Wordsworth or Shelley, but in his subjects he turned to nature as an ideal, somewhat as Wordsworth did and even more as did the Renaissance poet Sir Philip Sidney, and he wrote blank verse with a facility that had been alien to many of his neoclassical forebears. He had in common with his contemporaries a vast enthusiasm for poetry, but, whereas his contemporaries lived for their art, Landor's art was his servant. Emotional outbursts were reined in, uncontrolled poetic fervor was not for Landor. His spirit was as restless as Lord Byron's, but where Byron turned his restlessness into a poetic ideal, Landor used poetry to subdue his own restlessness. Thus, the determined and hard self-control evident in Landor's verse sets him apart from the poets of his time. Some critics call him a Romantic, though seemingly more for the age in which he lived than for the qualities of his work. He actually was the son of the neoclassical age; he followed a poetic path that was a logical extension of what the neoclassicists had achieved, while Wordsworth and the Romantics followed a poetic path that was a logical reaction against the neoclassicists. Landor was a classicist in a Romantic age.

As a good student of the classical authors, Landor believed in poetic simplicity. His verse dramas reveal at once the strengths and weaknesses of the simplicity that gives his poetry its crystalline character. Although not the best of his dramatic efforts, perhaps the best known of his dramas is the tragedy of *Count Julian* (1812). The play resembles a child's perception of tragedy— all loud voices and grim visages. The characters exclaim instead of converse; each word seems meant for the ages. The welter of "Ohs!" and other short exclamations are sometimes more risible than dramatic. Even so, the subject of *Count Julian* has much potential for good drama. A Spanish warrior who has driven the Moors from Spain avenges the rape of his daughter by his king by leading the Moors back into his country, with disastrous consequences. The play's blank verse is austere, remote from the characters and their emotions. Landor had hoped that *Count Julian* might be performed, but its poetry is more important than its drama; it is now regarded strictly as a closet drama. *Andrea of Hungary* (1839) and its sequels *Giovanna of Naples* (1839) and *Fra Rupert: The Last Part of a Trilogy* (1840) are dramatically and poetically more successful. Blank verse and character blend well in these plays; the scenes between Andrea and Giovanna in the first of them are relaxed, revealing two interesting personalities. Landor cared little for plot, which he called "trick"; thus, the sequence of events in his trilogy of plays is predictable and has few twists. Andrea is murdered, probably at the instigation of the ambitious Fra Rupert; Giovanna remains a paragon of virtue through three marriages and is eventually murdered; Fra Rupert commits suicide and his villainy is revealed. Landor uses the plot as a vehicle for some of his notions about power and politics and his blend of apt phrase, characterization, and good verse is often moving.

Landor's dramatic scenes also feature blank verse, though they are only short conversations. In "Essex and Bacon," for example, Landor shows the Earl of Essex meeting with Francis Bacon after the Earl's condemnation to death for treason. Landor's interest in ambition and the abuse of power provides the scene's depth. Essex sees himself as greater than Bacon because he took a glorious chance by opposing Queen Elizabeth, and he cannot understand how his friend can call him "lower than bergess or than churl." Essex declares, "To servile souls how abject seem the fallen!/ Benchers and message-bearers stride o'er Essex." He dismisses Bacon with contempt. When alone, Bacon is allowed the last word, which, in summary, says that ambition is often mistakenly thought to be great by those who allow it to run their lives, when, in fact, it is arrogance. The dramatic scenes generally reflect Landor's concern with the abuse of power; "Ippolito di Este" perhaps makes Landor's feelings clearest. This short drama introduces the audience to the brothers Ferrante, Giulio, and the Cardinal Ippolito di Este. Ferrante has the misfortune to have his eyes admired by a woman whom his brother the Cardinal desires; the Cardinal has Ferrante's eyes removed. The dramatic scene is truly horrible, even if Ferrante is too saintly to be palatable.

Of Landor's heroic poems, his first (and his first important poem, written when he was perhaps twenty years of age), *Gebir*, is probably the best known. Gebir is king of Gades (Cadiz); he conquers Egypt and the heart of Queen Charoba, then is assassinated. The poem takes him through heroic adventures, including a trip to the underworld. *Gebir* reveals Landor's extensive scholarship, based as it is on Arabian history. The verse is spare, already featuring Landor's emphasis on succint phrasing; its scenes are dramatic and resemble the tragedies in structure. Unfortunately, the language of the poem is too remote for successful characterization; Gebir, who is a strong, dynamic young man, talks like an ancient Greek god. His love, Charoba, is more accessible to readers, although she, too, often merely declaims. *Gebir* displays much fine poetry; it may not always succeed, but it is good enough by itself to establish Landor's claim to poetic importance. Admired by contemporary critics and poets, including Robert Southey, the poem established Landor as a significant poet.

Landor's so-called Hellenics are poems that are informed by ancient Greek myths and history. They encompass blank verse, lyrics, sonnets, and conversations. The best of these, such as "Coresos and Callirhöe," "The Altar of Modesty," "Acon and Rhodope," "Pan," and "The Marriage of Helena and Menelaos," are exquisite gems of the poet's art. Each is representative of Landor's classical principles; the poems are simple in form, their clarity of language being the result of much revision, and they reflect intelligent observation. They focus on characters and generally deliver homilies on love and life. In "Pan and Pitys," for instance, Pitys is loud in her derogation of Boreas, her suitor. Boreas hears her, and he drops a large rock on her. The exchanges between Pan and Pitys are loud and boisterous; her foolishness and insensitivity are also loud; perhaps she should have spoken more kindly of her suitor. In "Acon and Rhodope," a man loses sight of what is important in his life and loses all he cares for. The verse is thick with colors and odors that represent a mixture of life and death; apple trees have "freckled leaves" and oleanders have "light-hair'd progeny." The effect of the Hellenic poems is one of another world that is somehow part of the common one. The characters have thoughts, emotions, and problems, much like those that are common to humanity, but their world is richer, more intense than common experience. Such intensity is well evoked in "The Marriage of Helena and Menelaos," in which the sixteen-year-old Helena faces her husband-to-be and the prospect of adulthood for the first time. The gibes of siblings, the fears of appearing foolish, the sense of losing youth too soon, condense into a poignant, short series of events. "The Marriage of Helena and Menelaos" is a product of the mature Landor; it is alive with ideas, focused on a dramatic moment, and deceptively simple on its surface.

Although Landor strove to use elevated language and to create clear, often austere, verse, his poetry contains much variety and life. Works such as "Homer, Laertes, Agatha" and "Penelope and Pheido" not only feature Landor's classicism but feature high poetry and are lively as well. Landor brings humanity to his poetry; he focuses on the difficulties people have when faced with problems larger than themselves. As with other poets who lived long lives, Landor's verse changed over the years; it began by being brash and noisy, as in *Gebir* and *Count Julian*, grew to reflect his thoughts on politics and power, as in *Fra Rupert*, and attained a blend of erudition and humanity that bring sensitivity to "The Marriage of Helena and Menelaos," written when Landor was eighty-nine. Among his most sensitive and interesting works is the verse drama *The Siege of Ancona* (1846). Typical of Landor's work, it is known to only a few critics and admirers of poetry. Its verse is clear and its tone is heroic, without the declamatory faults of *Count Julian*; its psychology is subtle and its values those of a classicist who was nevertheless a part of the Romantic period. The Consul of Ancona asserts that "the air/ Is life alike to all, the sun is warmth,/ The earth, its fruits and flocks, are nutriment,/ Children and wives are comforts; all partake/ (Or may partake) in these" (III, ii, lines 48-52). Like Wordsworth, Landor found a universal metaphor in nature; unlike Wordsworth, he made his natural world Arcadian in the manner of English Renaissance poets. He labored at the classical ideal of spare verse and detached tone; he yielded to the Romantic desire to express his innermost spirit. At its best, his poetry is clear and crystalline, maintaining a warmth and sensitive empathy for the common joys, miseries, and confusions that people face in their daily lives.

Kirk H. Beetz

Other major works
LONG FICTION: *The Pentameron and Pentalogia*, 1837.
SHORT FICTION: *Dry Sticks Fagoted*, 1858.
PLAYS: *Count Julian*, 1812; *Andrea of Hungary*, 1839; *Giovanna of Naples*, 1839; *Fra Rupert: The Last Part of a Trilogy*, 1840; *The Siege of Ancona*, 1846.
NONFICTION: *Imaginary Conversations of Literary Men and Statesmen*, 1824-1829 (5 volumes); *Citation and Examination of William Shakespeare*, 1834.
MISCELLANEOUS: *The Complete Works of Walter Savage Landor*, 1927-1936. (Thomas E. Welby and Stephen Wheeler, editors; 16 volumes).

Bibliography
Dilworth, Ernest. *Walter Savage Landor.* New York: Twayne, 1974. An excellent critical introduction for those unfamiliar with Landor's work. The author points out the poet's aims and achievements as well as his shortcomings in style and substance. Frequent quotations support the text and a chronology, notes, references, and an excellent select bibliography are included.
Elwin, Malcolm. *Landor, a Replevin.* London: Macdonald, 1958. This is a rewriting of a book originally published in 1941 specifically for publication in England. The author's goal is to save the poet's reputation and work from misrepresentation and neglect. Written in a very personable style, he quotes both Landor's and others' letters extensively. Supplemented by a scholarly bibliography and a chronology.
Landor, Walter Savage. *Walter Savage Landor: Selected Poetry and Prose.* Edited by Keith Hanley. Manchester, England: Carcanet Press, 1981. This selection contains almost two hundred samples of poetry from Landor's entire career including some published posthumously. Helpful notes are appended along with a select bibliography. An introduction by the editor discusses Landor's role as a neoclassicist, the art of imitation, the classical structure of feeling, and his poetic style.
Pinsky, Robert. *Landor's Poetry.* Chicago: University of Chicago Press, 1968.

This analysis of about twenty poems explores, among other things, Landor's repeated use of subjects and gives a fair picture of his poetic artistry. The author defends Landor and makes a case for the intellectual content of the poems. He shows some of the lesser verse to have real artistry behind it. Special attention is paid to an analysis of Landor's use of rhythms. Omitted in the discussion are Landor's tributes to other writers.

Super, Robert H. *Walter Savage Landor: A Biography.* New York: New York University Press, 1954. This lengthy, definitive biography replete with accurate detail includes material and documents hitherto ignored or undiscovered. The author corrects previous carelessness, errors in chronology, and other distortions. This fine example of biographical scholarship includes an index and an extensive system of notes and references displaying the meticulous accuracy seen throughout.

WILLIAM LANGLAND

Born: Cleobury Mortimer(?), Shropshire, England; c. 1332
Died: London(?), England; c. 1400

Principal poetry
The Vision of William, Concerning Piers the Plowman, 1362 (A Text), c. 1377 (B Text), c. 1393 (C Text); *Richard the Redeless,* c. 1395 (attributed).

Other literary forms
William Langland wrote only poetry.

Achievements
Apparently, in its own day, *The Vision of William, Concerning Piers the Plowman* was a very popular work. More than fifty manuscripts of the poem in its various versions still exist. The poem's four printings before 1561 are evidence of its continued popularity. The audience of *Piers Plowman* was not, as it was for most poems of the alliterative revival, a small group of provincial nobles; rather, as J. A. Burrow (*Anglia,* LXXV, 1957) has shown, the poem would have been read by a broadly based national public of parish priests or local clergy whose tastes favored purely didactic literature. In addition, Burrow connects the poem with a growing lay public of the rising bourgeoisie, whose tastes were still conservative and generally religious. The didactic content of the poem, then, was its chief appeal in its own time.

By the sixteenth century, however, with the rise of Protestantism, William Langland's poem became acclaimed for its aspects of social satire. This strain in the poem had been underlined even in the fourteenth century, when John Ball, in a letter to the peasants of Essex during the revolt of 1381, mentioned Piers the Plowman. Possibly because of this mention, the very orthodox Catholic Langland came, ironically, to be associated with Lollardy, and to be looked upon as a bitter critic of the Roman Church and a precursor of Protestantism.

By the late sixteenth century, Langland's western Midland dialect had become too difficult for any but the most ardent reader, and so no new edition of *Piers Plowman* appeared until 1813. Though nineteenth century readers deplored Langland's allegory, they could still, like the readers before them, admire *Piers Plowman* as social satire, and, in addition, they could appreciate and admire the stark realism in such scenes as the confession of the seven deadly sins in Passus V (B Text). Their chief interest in Langland was historical: they viewed the poem as a firsthand commentary on the fourteenth century.

Modern criticism has begun to concentrate, for the first time, on the artistry of the poem. Elizabeth Salter (*Piers Plowman,* 1962) has pointed out how, with the return of so many modern poets to the free accentual verse similar to Langland's, readers are now more able to respond to the verse of *Piers Plowman*. Further, with the contemporary conviction that everyday themes and language are valid subjects for poetry, readers have become more sympathetic to some of Langland's finest passages, which treat everyday experiences in the vocabulary of the common man.

Yet it seems, ultimately, that the first readers of *Piers Plowman* were most correct: the poem's basic intent is didactic, and, for Langland, all artistry was secondary to the message he was trying to convey. Perhaps his greatest achievement is the theme itself, which is at once as simple and as complex as any in literature. Beginning as the Dreamer's simple question in Passus II (B Text), "How may I save my soul?," the theme turns into a multilayered search for individual salvation, for the perfection of contemporary society, for a mystical union with God, and for a way to put mystical vision to practical use in perfecting society. These searches are set against varied landscapes ranging from the contemporary world to the inner world of the soul, across biblical history, through hell to Armageddon. For contemporary critics concerned largely with structure in literature, Langland's most remarkable feat is his ability, in spite of real or apparent digressions and inconsistencies, to put a poem of the encyclopedic range and depth of *Piers Plowman* together into a structured whole.

Biography

Virtually nothing is known of the poet who wrote *Piers Plowman*. At one time, in fact, there was some debate about whether a single author or perhaps as many as five were responsible for the three separate versions of the poem. That controversy has since ended, and scholarship has established a single author for all three versions.

That author's name was almost certainly William Langland. Two fifteenth century manuscript notes attribute the poem to Langland, and there is a line in the B Text which seems to be intended as a cryptogram of the poet's name: "'I haue lyued in londe', quod [I], 'my name is longe wille.'" One manuscript declares that Langland was the son of a certain Stacey (Eustace) de Rokayle, who later held land under the Lord Despenser at Shipton-under-Wychwood in Oxfordshire; in all likelihood, Langland's father was a franklin. It has been conjectured that Langland was illegitimate, but the difference in surname is no real reason to assume this, such differences being common in the fourteenth century. Langland was not born in Oxfordshire but rather in Shropshire, at Cleobury Mortimer, some eight miles from the Malvern Hills which serve as the setting for the first two visions in *Piers Plowman*. Because the B Text is dated with some accuracy c. 1377, and because the poet in the B Text declares himself to be forty-five years old, the date of Langland's birth has been set at about 1332.

Whatever else is "known" about the author's life is conjectured from passages in the poem which describe the narrator's life, and is based on the assumption that the narrator, "Will," and the poet Langland are one and the same. In the C Text, the poet speaks of having gone to school, and most likely he was educated at the priory of Great Malvern in Worcestershire. He would have gone through the usual training for the priesthood, but, according to evidence in the poem, the deaths of his father and friends left him without a benefactor and forced him to abandon his studies before taking holy orders. He would have been unable to advance in the Church, having left school with only minor orders, partly because of his incomplete education and because, as the poet writes, he was married—a right permitted only to clerks in orders below subdeacon.

Because of these apparent facts, E. Talbot Donaldson assumes that Langland was an acolyte, one of the poor, unbeneficed clergy who had no official way of making a living within the Church hierarchy. Certainly he was poor, but he seems to have claimed exemption from manual labor by virtue of his being a tonsured clerk. W. W. Skeat conjectures that Langland may have earned some money as a scribe, copying out legal documents, since the poem displays a close knowledge of the form of such documents. Perhaps he was able to pick up odd clerical jobs here and there in the city of London, where, according to an apparently autobiographical account in the C Text, he went to live at Cornhill with his wife, Kitte, and daughter, Callote. According to this passage, Langland seems to have earned money by going about singing the office of the dead, or other prayers for the living, and making regular monthly rounds to the homes of his wealthy patrons.

Langland describes himself, though perhaps with some ironic hyperbole, as a singular character, apparently very tall and lean (his nickname is "Long Will"), wandering about dressed as a beggar, showing little respect for the wealthy who liked to parade their own importance, and spending time scribbling verses. Some considered him mad. Certainly it is true that he spent a good deal of time writing and rewriting *Piers Plowman*. He seems to have labored some thirty years, refining the poem, and perhaps was still revising it at his death: the last two passus of the C version show little change from those of the B Text, suggesting that Langland may have died before he finished the last revision. To be sure, the date of Langland's death is even less certain than that of his birth; it is unlikely that the poet survived his century. If, as has often been disputed, Langland was the author of the poem *Richard the Redeless*, he was still alive in 1395.

Analysis

Piers Plowman is a difficult poem. One is not likely to find a more complex poem, nor one which poses quite so many problems. An entrance to the poem might best be achieved by an examination of those problems—problems of text, of form, of structure, and of interpretation—one at a time.

First, the poem exists in three totally different versions. The earliest version, known as the A Text, must have been written, or at least begun, about 1362, since it alludes to such things as the plague of 1361 and a certain great wind storm known to have occurred in January, 1362. This first version is a poem of some 2,500 lines, consisting of a prologue and eleven books or "passus." In the second, or B Text, William Langland revised his poem and added nine new passus, expanding *Piers Plowman* to more than 7,200 lines. This version must have been written about 1377, since the fable of the cat and mice in the prologue seems to allude to events which occurred in the parliament of 1376-1377. Langland thoroughly revised the poem one more time, increasing its length by another hundred or so lines, and this final version is known as the C Text. It contains no prologue but twenty-three passus. W. W. Skeat dated the C Text about 1393, believing that it reflected the differences which began in 1392 between the citizens of London and the king. An earlier date may be more accurate, however, since Thomas Usk seems to refer to the C version of *Piers Plowman* in his *Testament of Love* (1387), and Usk died in 1388. In the C version the poet often attempts to clarify ambiguities, and at times eliminates some of the social criticisms. He also eliminates some of the more dramatic scenes in B, such as Piers's tearing of Truth's pardon in Passus VII. Although the C Text may represent the author's ultimate intent, and although accurate critical texts of the C Text have made it more universally available, the vast majority of scholars and readers have preferred the B version, and so all references to the poem in this analysis are to George Kane and E. Talbot Donaldson's edition of the B Text.

Having established the B version as the poem, however, one is not at all sure what sort of poem it is. *Piers Plowman* falls simultaneously into several categories, none of which defines it completely. It is, first, a poem of the alliterative revival. Poetry in English had originally been alliterative, and followed strict metrical rules. When English verse began to appear once more in the west and north in the mid-fourteenth century, poets attempted to follow this native tradition. The Middle English alliterative line, however, was much freer than it had been in Old English: lines had no fixed syllabic content, the number of stressed syllables was not always four, as in classic alliterative verse, but might be three, five, or six, and the alliterated sound was not always governed by the third stressed syllable, as in classic alliterative verse. The alliterative poets did, however, tend to rely on a special poetic diction and to decorate their poetry with elaborate rhetorical figures recommended by the poetic manuals of the time, such as that of Geoffrey of Vinsauf. Langland, however, differed markedly from other alliterative poets. Possibly because his audience was not the aristocracy, he had no interest in elaborate rhetoric or poetic diction, but rather used simple vocabulary and employed only those figures of speech which involved repetition, since his goal was to get his message across clearly. Langland did, however, continue and even furthered the trend toward a freer alliterative line, employing various rhythmic patterns as they suited the tone of his poem, sometimes alliterating a different sound in the second half-line than he had in the first, sometimes not alliterating at all, and often tossing in Latin quotations as nonalliterating half-lines. The overall tendency of Langland's verse, despite the Latin, is toward a naturalness of vocabulary and rhythm.

Piers Plowman also has a great deal in common with sermon literature. G. R. Owst saw Langland as drawing primarily from the pulpits of England his message of social reform, justice for the poor, condemnation for those who pervert the great institution of the Church, and a recommendation of love and work as opposed to revolution. Elizabeth Salter sees Langland's emphasis on teaching rather than fine writing, and his use of metaphors and imagery in a purely functional manner to illustrate his material, as consistent with sermon literature; however, Piers Plowman, in scope and complexity, goes far beyond even the most elaborate sermons, so again the label "sermon in verse" is inadequate.

The poem also takes the form of a dream vision. For the Middle Ages, influenced as they were by the biblical stories of Joseph and Daniel and by Macrobius' famous commentary on the Dream of Scipio, dreams were profoundly important, and could often take on oracular significance. Thus, beginning with Jean de Meung's thirteenth century Romance of the Rose, there arose a genre of poetry containing a dreamer-narrator who relates his vision, which may be full of signs which the reader must interpret. Once again, however, Piers Plowman transcends the bounds of the form, for Langland writes not of one vision but of many. There are, in fact, ten separate visions in the poem, two of which are represented as dreams within dreams. Moreover, in contrast with the more typical medieval love visions, Langland seriously presents the visions as divine revelations. Perhaps Morton Bloomfield is more accurate, then, in describing Piers Plowman as an apocalypse: a literary work in the form of a vision revealing a divine message and deeply criticizing contemporary society.

A knowledge of its genre may help to explain some of the confusion in the structure of the poem. Anyone reading Piers Plowman for the first time must be struck by the bewildering plunges into and out of scenes, the unannounced and unexpected comings and goings of a multitude of new characters, the apparently unrelated sequence of events which seem to follow no cause-and-effect relationships. It could be argued that a dream vision would follow the logic of dream—of association and symbol rather than induction and deduction; this may be a partial answer. One could also say that the poem is not intended to be a narrative, which would follow a cause-and-effect pattern. It has, rather (like a sermon), a thematic unity. The Dreamer asks in the beginning, "What must I do to save my soul?," and the theme which unites the poem is the answer to that question. Essentially, the unifying motif is the quest for the answer, a quest which becomes a pilgrimage of the individual to God. Significantly, Langland calls the divisions of his poem *passus*, or *steps*—each new incident is another step toward the goal of the quest.

Structurally, the poem is divided into two sections, the *Visio* and the *Vita*. The *Visio* section depicts the world as it is, introduces the main themes, and prepares the way for the search which follows in the *Vita*. The narrator, Will (a persona for William Langland, but also a personification of the human will), falls asleep and relates his dream of a "fair field full of folk"—the people of Middle Earth as they work out their lives between heaven (a Tower of Truth) and hell (a dark dungeon). The Holy Church appears to Will as a lady and discourses on the fall of Lucifer and on love as the way to Truth. When the Dreamer asks how he may recognize falsehood, he is shown a series of scenes involving Lady Meed and her proposed marriage, first to Falsehood, then to Conscience. Lady Meed is the representation of *cupiditas*, the opposite of love: she is the love of earthly reward, and when she is driven out by Conscience and Reason, it represents the possibility of man's controlling his desire for worldly wealth by following the dictates of reason and conscience. In Will's second dream, Reason gives a sermon inspiring the people to repent, and there follows Langland's noted portrayal of the confession of the seven deadly sins. The people then begin a pilgrimage in search of Truth; here Piers the Plowman makes his first appearance, offering to guide them to Truth. First, however, Piers must plow his half-acre. The implied moral is that the needs of the body must be taken care of, but that the will should desire no more than what is of material necessity.

The pilgrimage to Truth never takes place. Truth sends Piers a pardon, saying that those who do well will be saved. When a priest tells Piers that this is no pardon at all, Piers tears up the paper in anger. The point of this scene seems to be lost in obscurity. Robert Worth Frank considers the scene an attack on papal indulgences: the true "pardon" is God's command to do well. The priest, on the other hand, supports the idea of papal indulgences, which Piers angrily rejects by tearing the parchment, symbolically tearing up paper pardons from Rome. In a later interpretation, Denise N. Baker denied that Piers's pardon is a pardon at all. The scene, according to Baker, reflects the Nominalist-Augustinian controversy of the fourteenth century, which concerned man's ability to do good works. The Augustinian position was that man was unable to do good works without God's grace, and Piers's tearing up of the pardon is Langland's emblem of man's dependence on God's gift of grace. Whichever interpretation is correct, Piers decides to leave plowing and begin a life of prayer and penance in order to search for Do-Well.

The *Vita* section of the poem is divided into three parts: the lives of Do-Well, Do-Better, and Do-Best. With the abandonment of the people's search for Truth, it is apparent that society cannot be reformed corporately, but only on an individual basis. Will goes on an individual quest for the three degrees of doing well, for three grades of Christian perfection. The life of Do-Well is confusing: in the third dream, Will confronts his own faculties (Thought, Intelligence, Imagination), as well as guides such as Study, Clergy, and Scripture. In the meantime, Will has a dream within a dream wherein he follows Fortune for forty-five years. After he wakes, Will falls asleep again, and in a fifth vision, led by Patience and Conscience, he meets Haukyn, the Active Man, whose coat (his soul) is terribly stained with sin.

The sixth vision, the life of Do-Better, begins with Will's discourse with Anima, who rebukes Will for vainly seeking knowledge and extols the virtue of charity. Will falls into another, deeper, vision, in which he sees Piers Plowman as guardian of the Tree of Charity; sees Abraham, Moses, and the Good Samaritan as the personifications of Faith, Hope, and Charity; and learns about the Holy Trinity. In the eighth vision, the climax of the life of Do-Better and of the poem, the Dreamer witnesses the passion of Christ, sees Christ jousting in the arms of Piers Plowman, witnesses the Harrowing of Hell, a debate between the four daughters of God, and the resurrection.

The two final dreams present the life of Do-Best. Piers Plowman is now Christ's vicar on earth. The Holy Spirit descends, bestowing gifts on the Christian body, enabling Piers to plow the field of the world. Conscience, seeing the Antichrist preparing to attack, directs all Christians to build a fortress, the Church of Unity, but the Christians are unprepared for battle. In the final vision, the Antichrist attacks. Conscience makes the mistake of letting a Friar into Unity, whose easy confessions corrupt the Church, and the people lose all fear. Conscience then vows to become a pilgrim and search for Piers Plowman to help in the fight, and the quest begins anew as the Dreamer awakes.

The poem is unified by the repetition of various themes. Salter gives the example of the recurring themes of the nature and function of sin, which is introduced in the section on Lady Meed, expanded upon in the confession of the seven deadly sins, restated in the picture of Haukyn's coat, and returned to again as the sins assist the Antichrist in the final attack on Unity. Even so, the nature and function of love in the universe, as it pertains to personal salvation and the reform of society, is the chief theme of the poem; and that theme is inextricably linked with the chief unifying motif of the poem, Piers the Plowman in his many incarnations.

Deciding precisely what Piers signifies is part of the last and largest problem of the poem, that of interpretation. It is obvious that Langland's chief vehicle of expression in *Piers Plowman* is allegory, but it is unclear precisely how to read the allegory. Robert Worth Frank calls the kind of allegory which is typical of Langland "personification-allegory," which, he says, generally involves a single translation of the character's *name* (such as "Study," "Reason," "Scripture") into the abstract quality which it denotes. In this sense, the characters are "literal." It is a mistake to read more into the allegory than the form allows. In practice, however, this does not seem to work. "Sloth," for example, is simply sloth—one need inquire no further; but the more important characters, such as Do-Well, Do-Better, and Do-Best, are obviously much more complicated, and seem to have multiple meanings.

An alternative approach to the allegory is that of D. W. Robertson and Bernard Huppé, who, in applying medieval exegetical criticism to literary texts, see a fourfold interpretation of the allegory. In discussing the complex symbol of the Tree of Charity, for example, they say that it allegorically represents the just; anagogically, Christ on the cross; and tropologically, the individual Christian. The difficulty with this approach is its rigidity: some things are simply meant to be taken literally, while others may have multitudes of meanings far beyond these four.

A more beneficial approach to the meaning of these symbols is Salter's, which emphasizes a more open and flexible reading; here the reader is receptive to various sorts of significations, not necessarily in any exact order or category. The two most puzzling and multifaceted allegorical symbols are the three lives and Piers himself.

Do-Well, Do-Better, and Do-Best have been most often identified with the active, the contemplative, and the mixed lives. This may make more sense to modern readers if they realize, as T. P. Dunning notes, that the active life in the Middle Ages denotes, not manual labor, but rather the active practice of virtue, the works of prayer and devotion to which Piers devotes himself at the end of the *Visio*. This is the active life conceived of as the first stage of the spiritual life, and in the *Vita* it involves, first, the Dreamer's search through his own faculties, the emergence from intellectual error, and then, with the repentance of Haukyn, the rejection of moral disorder. Do-Better would then represent the contemplative life, in which the Dreamer actually experiences a kind of union with God in a firsthand vision of Christ's passion. Do-Best, however, represents the mixed life, in which the individual must return to life in the world and, with the assistance of the Holy Spirit, work for the reform of society: charity is not limited to love of the individual for God, but includes love for others as well.

At the same time, the three lives may suggest the mystical theme of the soul seeking God, where Do-Well represents the purgative state, and Do-Better the stage at which the mystic, like the Dreamer, achieves his illumination in a direct vision of God. For the mystic, however, there is no final unity in this world; he, like Conscience in the end, must continue the search and work toward another partial union. Do-Best reveals the practical results of illumination, which are in the service of others.

The three lives, then, suggest at least these things, and more, but Piers's meaning is more obscure. He appears in the poem only occasionally, but his presence dominates the action at crucial points. In the *Visio*, after the confession of the sins, Piers steps in, announcing that he is a friend and servant of Truth, and offering to lead all on a pilgrimage to Him. First, however, he must plow his half-acre, and he organizes all of the people to help with the work, thus establishing an ordered society in this world. At the end of the *Visio*, he receives the pardon from Truth for himself and his followers, which he tears up, pledging to leave his plow and search for Do-Well.

In the Do-Well section, Piers is mentioned by Clergy (Passus XIII) as one who preaches the primacy of love as opposed to learning. In Do-Better (Passus XV), Anima identifies Piers with Christ by means of a cryptic Latin comment about "Peter, that is Christ." In Passus XVI, Piers is warder of the Tree of Charity, which he explains to the Dreamer. The tree's fruit, identified as the patriarchs and prophets, is stolen by the devil, whom Piers chases, armed with a stave symbolizing Christ. Piers is then shown teaching Jesus the art of healing. At the climax, Christ fights for the souls of men, the fruit of Piers the Plowman, clad in Piers's arms.

In Do-Best, Piers returns to the poem. First the Dreamer sees a confused image in which Christ himself seems to be Piers, stained with blood and bearing a cross. The Holy Spirit then makes Piers the Plowman his vicar on earth, and Piers founds the Church, dispensing grace in the form of the eucharist, behaves like God in his charity to all, and then disappears.

All of this presents a confused figure who seems at times to be the symbol of moral integrity, at times Christ himself, and at the end perhaps the ideal pope whom conscience searches for to restore the corrupt and divided Church of the fourteenth century. The eminent literary historian Nevill Coghill thought that Piers personified Do-Well, Do-Better, and Do-Best successively. Later, Barbara Raw showed that Piers's career in the poem depicts the restoration of the divine image in man, somewhat distorted with the Fall but still present, and restored at Christ's incarnation. According to Augustine and Aquinas, the restoration of this image took place in three stages, which may parallel Do-Well, Do-Better, and Do-Best. In Do-Better, Piers becomes the image of Christ because Christ has taken human form, Piers's arms. In Do-Best, Piers embodies the restored image of God in man: he has become like God. Salter sees Piers similarly: when Piers describes the way to Truth in Passus V, he declares that people will find Truth's dwelling in their own hearts. Piers represents this divine element in man, the Truth of God as it exists in man, and as the poem reaches its climax, it is revealed that God *is* to be found in man, as the man Piers becomes Godlike. This, then, is Langland's ultimate message, which in spite of all the problems with *Piers Plowman* can still be stated with some certainty: human beings bear the stamp of the image of God, and can, through Christ, achieve Do-Best with Piers the Plowman.

Jay Ruud

Bibliography
Alford, John A., ed. *A Companion to Piers Plowman.* Berkeley: University of California Press, 1988. Contains nine essays on such subjects as the historical and theological context of Langland's *Piers Plowman*, literary and intellectual influences on the poet, and the text and language of the poem. Also includes an excellent introduction to the poem and its shape. Most essays provide good general overviews of the various scholarly opinions on the subjects covered and each essay includes abundant bibliographical details.
Hussey, S. S., ed. *Piers Plowman: Critical Approaches.* London: Methuen, 1969. An excellent collection of twelve essays on a wide variety of aspects of Langland's work. Includes discussions of theme, structure, allegory, Christian theology, and satire in *Piers Plowman*, as well as more focused examinations of particular aspects such as the role of the Dreamer, Langland's understanding of "the Good Life," and a particularly interesting assessment of the "tearing of the Pardon" scene.
Krochalis, Jean and Edward Peters, eds. *The World of Piers Plowman.* Philadelphia: University of Pennsylvania Press, 1975. An interesting examination of the historical, intellectual, and social context in which Langland wrote. The editors provide a multitude of Middle English primary sources, from sermons to statutes to royal proclamations, as illustrations of Langland's world. Each general section, and many of the individual works, are prefaced with informative introductory passages. Not all spellings are modernized, and, despite marginal glosses, some texts may be difficult for the beginner. Still, this work offers valuable insight into the currents of thought in Langland's day.
Langland, William. *Piers Plowman: An Alliterative Verse Translation.* Edited and translated by E. Talbot Donaldson. New York: W. W. Norton, 1990. Donaldson's translation of *Piers Plowman* into modern English retains the alliterative qualities of Langland's verse while making it easily accessible to the reader with little or no knowledge of Middle English. Contains helpful glosses and margin notes and a useful list of suggestions for further reading.
_____. *The Vision of Piers Plowman: A Complete Edition of the B-Text.* Edited by A. V. C. Schmidt. London: J. M. Dent & Sons, 1978. Although this is primarily an untranslated edition of one version of Langland's great work, the concise but thorough and accessible introduction and the excellent, copious commentary make this a valuable tool for the student of Langland. Commentary is divided into two sections: textual/lexical and literary/historical. Marginal glosses of words and phrases within the text are generous and will be enormously helpful to the student interested in a close examination of the text.
Martin, Priscilla. *Piers Plowman: The Field and the Tower.* London: Mac-

millan, 1979. The author focuses on irony and allegory in *Piers Plowman* and on the difficulties and paradoxes that result for both Langland and the reader as a result of the use of these literary devices. A good examination of Christian allegory is included.

Vasta, Edward, ed. *Interpretations of Piers Plowman*. Notre Dame, Ind.: University of Notre Dame Press, 1968. This volume offers important essays on religious allegory, structure, and philosophy in *Piers Plowman* and some interesting comment on the "Three Lives" as set forth by Langland. Although this is an older collection, it contains several seminal essays of historic critical importance by prominent Langland scholars.

SIDNEY LANIER

Born: Macon, Georgia; February 3, 1842
Died: Lynn, North Carolina; September 7, 1881

Principal poetry:
Poems, 1877; *Poems*, 1884 (Mary Day Lanier, editor).

Other literary forms

Although Sidney Lanier is remembered primarily as a poet, he wrote in a surprising variety of genres. His *The Science of English Verse* (1880) is a handbook of prosody which is still valuable as a discussion of poetic theory and technique despite its overemphasis on the importance of sound. It was originally meant to be a textbook for Lanier's students at The Johns Hopkins University, and in fact his lecture notes were collected and published posthumously as *The English Novel* (1883) and *Shakspere* [sic] *and His Forerunners* (1902). Lanier's first book, however, was an autobiographical novel entitled *Tiger-Lilies* (1867), which drew upon his Civil War experiences and his reading in the German Romantics. His second published volume was *Florida: Its Scenery, Climate, and History* (1875), a travel book commissioned by the Atlantic Coast Line Railway and the standard guide to Florida for many years. Lanier was especially successful at revising classics, such as *The Boy's King Arthur* (1880) for juvenile audiences—a literary endeavor which appealed to his strong romantic sensibility while providing a welcome source of income. Finally, Lanier produced a remarkable number of essays, including "Retrospects and Prospects" (1871) and the four "Sketches of India" (1876), which were originally published in magazines. Lanier's writings are most readily available in the *Centennial Edition* (1945).

Achievements

Lanier was the first distinctively Southern poet to achieve a truly national recognition and acceptance. This is an honor usually accorded to Edgar Allan Poe (1809-1849); but unlike Poe, who was born in Boston, spent several of his formative years in Britain, and did much of his literary work in the Northeast, Lanier was a Georgian by birth who spent his entire life in the South. Nevertheless, by virtue of such works as "The Centennial Meditation of Columbia" and "Psalm of the West," Lanier came to be regarded as a spokesman for the American, rather than only the Southern, experience; yet, by one of those paradoxes of literary history, at the same time that he achieved this national status, Lanier won for Southern writers a degree of respect and credibility which was unprecedented in American literature and which is still evident today.

Lanier was one of the earliest American poets to use dialect in his verse, most notably the "Georgia cracker" speech utilized in "Thar's More in the Man Than Thar Is in the Land." In this regard, Lanier was an early practitioner of "local-color" writing, that literary movement which flourished at the end of the nineteenth century. Imbued with a strong social conscience, Lanier was noted for his poetic treatment of current economic difficulties. In poems such as "The Symphony," he pleaded that love and music be used as antidotes for the miseries generated by "Trade" (read "industry and commercialism"), and in "Corn" and "Thar's More in the Man Than Thar Is in the Land" he offered a practical solution to the economic problems of the postwar South: the cultivation of corn and grain instead of cotton. Lanier was also a tireless poetic experimenter. He is to be recognized for his ambitious attempts at metrical innovation (see "The Revenge of Hamish," an experiment in the use of logaeodic dactyls), as well as his attempts to achieve heightened musical effects in his verse (see, for example, "Song of the Chattahoochee"). He also is remembered for his *The Science of English Verse*, a textbook which is still interesting and perceptive, despite Lanier's unfortunate attempt to formulate a "science" of prosody which is analogous to musical notation.

Lanier is frequently cited as an example of a writer who could have achieved a great deal had he lived longer. There is no question that at the time of his death at age thirty-nine, his career was just getting under way. As Charles Anderson observes, Lanier wrote 164 poems; of these, 104 were written in two periods of intense creativity (1865-1868; 1874-1878), with the latter period producing his best work—fifty-eight major poems. At the time of his death Lanier had made plans for at least three more volumes of poetry, as is clear from the so-called "Poem Outlines" (see the *Centennial Edition*).

Biography

Sidney Clopton Lanier was born on February 3, 1842, in Macon, Georgia, a small city which was at the time the thriving center of the cotton industry. Both his parents were of good, long-established Virginia families who had settled comfortably into the urban, middle-class life-style of antebellum Macon. His father, Robert Sampson Lanier, was a graduate of Virginia's Randolph-Macon College and a practicing attorney; his mother, Mary Jane Anderson Lanier, was a devout Scottish Presbyterian who fostered in her children a deep appreciation for the writings of Sir Walter Scott. Sidney was the eldest child, with a sister Gertrude (born 1846), and a brother Clifford (born 1844) who occasionally collaborated with Sidney and who earned a minor literary reputation with the publication of his novel *Thorn-Fruit* (1867).

Lanier was a happy, bookish child noted for his good behavior and piety as well as for his love of literature, including works by Edward Bulwer-Lytton, John Keats, and the perennially popular Scott. He also demonstrated exceptional musical ability at a very early age and eventually became expert at playing the violin, guitar, organ, and flute. In certain respects, Lanier's musical talent was unfortunate: the distinctive musicality of his verse too often over-powers the meaning, and his desire to become a professional musician often diverted his time and energies away from his career as a poet. At any rate, music was an integral part of his formal education. Evidently, Macon had no public-supported schools during Lanier's youth, so he was educated at private academies run by local clergymen. It is unclear how solid an education he received in this fashion, but at a time when only one out of thirteen adult white Southerners could read or write, it was certainly adequate to gain him admittance into a relatively new Presbyterian college, Oglethorpe University. Lanier matriculated at the age of fifteen: he was a good student, being espe-cially adept at mathematics, and was named covaledictorian of his class. He returned to Oglethorpe in the fall after his graduation to serve as a tutor, a position secured for him by Professor James Woodrow. Woodrow (the uncle of Woodrow Wilson) possessed a degree of open-mindedness and cosmo-politanism which was unusual for Oglethorpe and something of a revelation for Lanier.

Before Lanier could explore the new worlds opened to him by Woodrow, however, the Civil War broke out. Lanier joined the Confederate Army in June, 1861, serving first as a private with the Macon Volunteers and later in the Mounted Signal Service. In 1864, while on signal duty on a blockade-runner, Lanier was captured and sent to a prison camp at Point Lookout, Maryland. Although Lanier was able to solace himself by playing his flute (which he had smuggled into prison inside his sleeve) and translating German poetry, the months spent at Point Lookout in 1864 and 1865 activated the latent tuberculosis which eventually killed him.

In 1867, Lanier married Mary Day, whom he had met while on furlough in 1863. It was not love at first sight: Lanier, a ladies' man of sorts, did not seem to notice Day until after his current sweetheart, one Gussie Lamar, jilted him. Day, an invalid, reportedly was advised by her physician that a marriage would improve her health (apparently it did: she outlived her hus-band by half a century, dying in 1931 at the age of eighty-seven). Despite the inauspicious circumstances surrounding the wedding, the marriage was a good one, and Lanier spent much of their fourteen years together attempting simultaneously to support his growing family (four sons), to satisfy his creative urges, and to find relief from his tuberculosis. From 1868 to 1873, he read law and clerked in his father's law office, an occupation for which he was temperamentally ill-suited, and which was all the more intolerable because of his worsening health and the frustration of having no time to write. He spent the winter and spring of 1872 to 1873 in Texas, and the trip which had been undertaken because of his health proved beneficial in another way. The Germans who played such a prominent role in San Antonio's cultural life encouraged him to pursue a career in music.

In 1873, with financial assistance from his brother Clifford, Lanier began his career as first flautist with the Peabody Orchestra of Baltimore. An extraordinarily talented player, Lanier was able to maintain his position with the orchestra intermittently for the next seven years. When his musical engagements were completed in the spring of 1874, he went to Sunnyside, Georgia, to spend a few months, and there he was deeply impressed with the region's cornfields. This led to the composition of "Corn," and his career as a poet began in earnest. "Corn," published in *Lippincott's Magazine* in 1875 after a devastating rejection by the *Atlantic Monthly*, was so successful that it resulted in commissioned work (including the guidebook *Florida*) and the opportunity to meet the writer-diplomat Bayard Taylor and Gibson Peacock, the editor of the Philadelphia *Evening Bulletin*, both of whom helped to further Lanier's career. In the first half of 1876, Lanier worked on two long poems: "The Centennial Meditation of Columbia," an assignment for the Philadelphia Centennial Exhibition, secured through the influence of Taylor, and "Psalm of the West," commissioned by the editor of *Lippincott's Magazine*. They are not among his best works ("The Centennial Meditation of Columbia" in particular was roundly criticized for its obscurity), but they did gain Lanier national attention.

In the summer of 1876, the exhausted Lanier moved with his family to a farm in West Chester, Pennsylvania, where he wrote a series of pot-boiling essays. That fall his health broke completely, and the generous Peacock financed a three-month vacation for Lanier in Tampa. While in Florida, Lanier felt sufficiently well to write eleven poems, including "The Stirrup-Cup"; but, homesick for Georgia, he left Tampa in April, 1877. Unsuccessful in his bid for a position in the U.S. Treasury, Lanier attempted to support his wife and children by borrowing from his brother and selling the family silver. He was fortunate enough, however, to be able to resume his position with the Peabody Orchestra. A few months later, in March, 1878, he began an intensive study of English literature at the Peabody Library in Baltimore in the hope that it would lead to a teaching position at The Johns Hopkins University. For once his hope was realized, and in the fall of 1879, he began to teach poetry and the English novel at the new Baltimore university.

The last few years of his life (from approximately 1877 to 1881) were remarkably full and productive. In addition to his research and teaching, Lanier was writing his best-known poems (including "Song of the Chattahoochee" in November, 1877, and "The Marshes of Glynn" in 1878), *The Science of English Verse*, and the series of books for children known as "The Boy's Library of Legend and Chivalry." He also had published in 1877 his first and only book of verse, *Poems*, a slim volume (ninety-four pages; ten poems) issued by *Lippincott's Magazine*. The attempt to compress a lifetime's work into a few months was, however, ultimately self-defeating: Lanier's final bout with tuberculosis began late in 1880, and he died in the mountains of North Carolina in September, 1881.

Analysis
Although literary historians are correct in maintaining that Sidney Lanier had only minimal influence on other writers, that influence is most apparent in the post-Civil War interest in the recording of regional dialects. Perhaps taking his cue either from James Russell Lowell's satirical, *The Biglow Papers* (1848, 1867) or Augustus Longstreet's humorous *Georgia Scenes* (1835), Lanier wrote several propagandistic poems in Southern dialect, in which humor was incidental rather than integral. Works written in dialect, yet serious in intent, were an innovation in American literature, and one of the first such works was Lanier's "Thar's More in the Man Than Thar Is in the Land." Written sometime between 1869 and 1871, the poem was originally published in the Macon *Telegraph and Messenger* on February 7, 1871, and thereafter in newspapers throughout the South and Midwest. Lanier reworked a local story into a serious statement of what he personally felt was the soundest strategy for the survival of the postwar South: resist the temptation to emigrate, and diversify crops. The poem itself (despite the challenges of the dialect) is unusually straightforward for a work by Lanier, not only because of the paucity of imagery, but also and more important, because of Lanier's uncharacteristic avoidance of sentimentality. Written in ten sestets, it recounts how a man named Jones (appropriately enough a resident of Jones County, Georgia) was a failure as a farmer. Jones sold his farm to a man named Brown for $1.50 an acre and moved to Texas where ostensibly "cotton would sprout/ By the time you could plant it in the land." The redoubtable Brown "rolled up his breeches and bared his arm" and within five years had become a prosperous farmer, "so fat that he wouldn't weigh." One day while Brown was sitting down to "the bulliest dinner you ever see," Jones showed up, having literally walked back to Georgia to try to find work. Brown fed him and provided the moral of the poem: "'whether men's land was rich or poor/ Thar was more in the *man* than thar was in the *land*.'"

In a region of the United States which was still suffering from a deep depression fully five years after the war, Lanier's little parable must have been a breath of hope and encouragement. The poem, however, is far more than a paean to the advantages of working hard and staying in Georgia. It is the emphatic statement of an economic reality: instead of continuing to raise "yallerish cotton" like Jones, one must grow corn and wheat. Thanks to crop diversification, Brown avoided the economic stranglehold which the Northern markets had on King Cotton (and, consequently, on the entire South), while enjoying the self-reliance that comes with raising a crop which one could literally consume. Whether or not the Southern audience noticed the poem's horticultural/economic message, they certainly admired "Thar's More in the Man Than Thar Is in the Land," and its immense popularity was due in part to its qualities as a poem. By virtue of its sing-songy rhythm, the familiar dialect, the predictable rhyme (generally aabbbc; the *c* invariably was the word "land"), and the surprisingly subtle humor (such as the broken rhyme "hum-/ Ble in stanza nine), it was ideally suited to essentially rural, semiliterate readers who were accustomed to a rich oral tradition and who frequently found themselves in situations comparable to that of the unfortunate Jones.

Even the most cursory glance at his letters, poems, and essays reveals that Lanier sincerely regarded poetry as a noble calling, and he resisted the temptation to write broadly popular, potentially remunerative verse. He preferred producing poems which appealed to the finer aspects of individual, regional, or national character, or which expressed his personal views on economic or political matters. There was no affectation inherent in these twin didactic conceptions of poetry, and they were at least partly responsible for the cool reception which his poems often received in his lifetime. Still, Lanier's poems occasionally did manage to achieve some popularity, and only a few years after the regional success of "Thar's More in the Man Than Thar Is in the Land," Lanier received his first national attention with "Corn."

"Corn" is a reiteration of the ideas presented in "Thar's More in the Man Than Thar Is in the Land," but the two poems are handled in strikingly different ways. Lanier apparently began the composition of "Corn" in July, 1874, while he was staying in the hamlet of Sunnyside, Georgia. Evidently he was especially impressed by the extensive corn fields and the terrain. Unlike "Thar's More in the Man Than Thar Is in the Land," this poem was definitely not intended for a semiliterate, rural Southern audience. In format, it is a sterling example of a Cowleyan ode. Unlike the technically rigid "Thar's More in the Man Than Thar Is in the Land," "Corn" is irregular in stanza length, line length, and rhythm. It is so heavily enjambed that at first one may not even be conscious of the extraordinary degree to which Lanier relies on rhyme to give his poem coherence. The rhyming couplets and tercets, the eye rhyme ("hardihood"/"food"), and the leonine rhyme ("Thou lustrous stalk, that ne'er mayst walk nor talk") are testimonies to Lanier's fascination with sound—a fascination which, unfortunately, was largely responsible for the charges of obscurity, sentimentality, and even banality which have been leveled against Lanier's poetry throughout the last century.

One need not look beyond the first stanza of "Corn" to understand what these critics have in mind. The persona passes through some woods before he encounters the field of corn, but the little forest, as is typical of Lanier, has been personified and emotionalized to such an embarrassing degree that the first stanza sounds like a sentimentalized psychosexual dream. The leaves which brush the persona's cheek "caress/ Like women's hands"; the "little noises" sound "anon like beatings of a heart/ Anon like talk 'twixt lips not far apart"; and the persona clearly has abandoned himself to the pleasures of the sensuous forest.

The persona proceeds through the concupiscent forest until finally, in stanza three, he encounters the corn itself, which Lanier had intended to be the controlling image of the poem. In one of his more fortunate metaphors, Lanier likens the field of corn to an army; and although at times that metaphor is strained (one stalk functions as the "corn-captain"), what makes it especially appropriate is that there are in fact three "battles" going on in this poem: the corn stalks are competing for soil with the sassafras and brambles, the ante-bellum "King Cotton" economy is clashing with the new diversified crop system, and Lanier is positing life as a battle with The Poet as its hero and the "corn-captain" as his symbol. It is apparent, then, that Lanier is attempting to make the battle metaphor operate on at least three levels; although it is an interesting concept and Lanier makes a noble effort to realize it, in the final analysis it simply does not work. Instead of being mutually enriching, the various images result in a confusing clutter. This fundamental technical problem and a host of others are readily apparent to even the most sympathetic reader of "Corn."

In stanza four, the "fieldward-faring eyes" of the persona do not simply look at the corn, but harvest it in his heart. It is characteristic of Lanier that he favors the use of rather grotesque metaphors. What tends to make the metaphor a bit less dubious, however, is that Lanier is not as interested in the physical corn as he is in the abstract qualities which he believes the corn embodies. Much as people can learn industriousness from bees and content-ment from cows, Lanier felt that the cornstalk could teach readers about virtuous living.

One may reasonably question how a technically and thematically weak poem such as "Corn" could possibly attract a national audience. Part of the answer lies in the very matter of technique: at the time he was writing, Lanier was sufficiently innovative to generate interest. The second part of the answer is more a matter of sociology than of poetics. During the Reconstruction period, and in particular during the 1870's when Centennial enthusiasm was running high, there was an impulse toward reconciliation in the United States—an impulse which frequently took the form of Northern readers responding enthusiastically to any piece of writing from, or about, the South. Even though Lanier initially had some difficulty finding Northern periodicals which would publish his work, the fact is that these journals were far more receptive to Southern writers after the Civil War than they were at any time before it. Lanier's career actually came during an ideal time, for he was clearly, insistently a Southern writer, and nowhere is his Southern influence more apparent, perhaps, than in his two best-known poems, "Song of the Chattahoochee" and "The Marshes of Glynn."

"Song of the Chattahoochee" was written in Baltimore at the end of November, 1877, and its first verifiable publication (December, 1883) was in the *Independent*, a New York-based weekly paper with a wide circulation. It became so popular that for decades it was a staple of elementary school reading books, the only poem by Lanier with which many people were even vaguely familiar. That distinction is a dubious one, for in fact, "Song of the Chattahoochee" is not one of Lanier's better efforts; and yet the very qualities which tend to weaken it were those responsible for its popularity. In typical Lanierian fashion, its most striking feature is its sound. Ostensibly the Chattahoochee River itself is speaking the poem (an earlier version reprinted by F. V. N. Painter in his *Poets of the South*, 1903, is in the third person), and this provides a golden opportunity for Lanier to utilize diction which conveys the sound of moving water. Words featuring liquid consonants and alliteration are so common that at times the poem reads like a tongue-twister: "The willful waterweeds held me thrall,/ The laving laurel turned my tide." This effect is compounded by Lanier's heavy reliance on repetition, not only of individual words but also of phrases: each of the five stanzas both begins and ends with some variation of the opening couplet, "Out of the hills of Habersham, Down the valleys of Hall." Clearly Lanier is seeking to depict moving water onomatopoeically, and to a certain extent he succeeds, but in such a short poem (fifty lines) one simply does not need the phrases "the hills of Habersham" and "the valleys of Hall" repeated ten times each. The effect of soothing musicality which Lanier was trying to create becomes monotonous. It is so overwhelming that the reader may very well fail to detect either the structure of the poem or the theme.

The "Song of the Chattahoochee" begins with the river explaining how it rises in Habersham County (in northeastern Georgia) and travels through Hall County on its way to "the plain." In stanza two, the speaker/river provides a catalog of the various small plants which attempt to delay it; stanza three is a catalog of the trees which seek to distract the river; stanza four reveals the rocks and minerals which try either to retard the flowing of the river or to dazzle it with their beauty. Then in stanza five, readers learn why the river resists these sensuous distractions: compelled by a strong sense of Duty (with a capital *d*), it must both make itself useful through "toil" and allow itself to "be mixed with the main." It is possible to infer that the personified river represents a human being whose life is purposefully active and who willingly acknowledges the "rightness" of death (here conveyed as the merging of one's identity with the vastness of the ocean—an idea explored more fully in "The Marshes of Glynn"); but if this analogy were central to Lanier's purpose, he certainly did not handle it well, and as a result the depiction of the river as "dutiful" seems to be nothing more than a romantic imposition on the part of Lanier.

Despite its didactic impulse, Lanier's poem retained its popularity in elementary schools for many years and, consequently, among several generations of Americans. Brief and strikingly musical, it is ideally suited to introducing poetry to youngsters. "Song of the Chattahoochee" also had the dubious but undeniable advantage of posthumous publication: to be frank, Lanier's career was never stronger than in the years immediately following his early death.

Even so, he did enjoy some nationwide popularity in his lifetime, most notably with "The Marshes of Glynn."

It is unclear when Lanier began the composition of "The Marshes of Glynn," although it is possible that it had been evolving over at least a three-year period before Lanier actually wrote it in the summer of 1878. The "Glynn" of the title is Glynn County, Georgia, noted for its salt marshes near the coastal village of Brunswick, a favorite haunt of the Lanier family for many years. As with "Corn," "The Marshes of Glynn" had its origins in Lanier's personal response to a specific element of the Georgia landscape, but it is notably more private and esoteric than that early effort. Both as an artist and a man, Lanier had changed significantly during the four years following the composition of "Corn." For one thing, he had discovered Walt Whitman. Although Lanier (despite the distinctive sensuality of his imagery), was singularly reticent about sexual matters, he nevertheless was deeply impressed with Whitman's work, even going so far as somehow to amass the requisite five dollars and order a copy of *Leaves of Grass* (1855) from the Good Gray Poet himself. In a letter to Bayard Taylor in February, 1878, Lanier described that book as a source of "real refreshment" to him, and likened its effect, significantly, to "rude salt spray in your face." It is probably no coincidence that Lanier made that comparison only a few months before the composition of "The Marshes of Glynn," for the poem can justifiably be termed Whitmanesque in its remarkable range and sweep.

Lanier also had changed as a result of his discovery of Ralph Waldo Emerson. During his stay in Tampa in the winter of 1877, Lanier apparently read Emerson in earnest, an undertaking at least partly attributable to the precarious state of his health. By the late 1870's, Lanier was finally beginning to admit to himself that the tuberculosis with which he had struggled for a decade would probably kill him within a very few years, as indeed it did. This admission of imminent death, coupled with his lack of orthodox religious faith, apparently generated his interest in Emerson and fostered significant changes in the themes and techniques of his poems. These changes are especially evident in "The Marshes of Glynn," which shows Lanier in far better control of his material than was the case in "Corn."

The two poems begin in a similar fashion with an extensive catalog of the elements one encounters while walking through a forest, but in "The Marshes of Glynn" Lanier has carefully pruned the embarrassingly overwritten sensual passages which are so striking in the opening of "Corn." True, he mentions "Virginal shy lights/ Wrought of the leaves to allure to the whispers of vows," but this is as purple a passage as one finds in the opening of "The Marshes of Glynn." Then with remarkable skill, the orientation is shifted from the association of the forest with love to that of religious faith, and from this point on, the rather long ode is devoted to spiritual matters. Unlike the irrelevant opening of "Corn," that of "The Marshes of Glynn" almost immediately presents Lanier's two concerns: the traditional belief that Nature is the great refresher of men's souls, and the contemporary Emersonian view that one may find the true God in the natural world. The intimate relationship between nature (specifically the forest) and the persona (transparently Lanier himself) is first overtly presented in line 20, and it is at this point that the reader realizes that the previous nineteen lines were actually an exceptionally elaborate apostrophe to the forest. The persona's love for the beauties and mysteries of the wood is palpable, and that love is conveyed through Lanier's characteristic compound adjectives ("myriad-cloven"), alliteration ("beautiful-braided"), and assonance ("oaks"/"woven").

It is made abundantly clear, however, that the forest experience represents merely a phase in the persona's life which has now passed, a phase which was associated with "the riotous noon-day sun." It is impossible to determine whether this represents a point in the persona's maturation (most likely his young manhood) or an earlier moment in his shifting orientation (when his concerns were more material or "earthly" than spiritual), or a combination of the two; but perhaps this is a moot point. What matters is that one phase of his existence (represented by the forest) is over, and that a new one (represented initially by the marshy beach) has begun. In keeping with the previous association of the forest with noon, the new locale is associated with the setting sun, whose "slant yellow beam" seems "Like a lane into heaven." That this sunset is to be associated with an overwhelming spiritual experience (most likely death) is clear from the persona's observation that "now, unafraid, I am fain to face/ The vast sweet visage of space"—a space which a few lines later is depicted, significantly, as the "terminal" sea. Although the persona finds himself "drawn" to "the edge of the wood . . ./ Where the gray beach glimmering runs," he willingly submits and soon finds himself "Free/ By a world of marsh that borders a world of sea."

There is nothing even remotely frightening about the beach: it is gray (reportedly Lanier's favorite color), and it forms the transitional zone between something the persona has voluntarily rejected and something which he deeply desires. The Emersonian element of the poem is most evident as the persona reacts to the new freedom of the beach. At this point, the persona conveys his reaction to his spiritual freedom through two similes. First, "As the marsh-hen secretly builds on the watery sod,/ Behold I will build me a nest on the greatness of God," and he also will fly as she does; second, "By so many roots as the marsh-grass sends in the sod/ I will heartily lay me a-hold on the greatness of God." The two metaphors are perfect in their appropriateness and simplicity, and they usher in the third movement of the poem: the shift from sunset to night, and from marshy beach to ocean. Much as the persona's identity was blurred with that of the beach as he likened himself to the bird and grass, the identity of the beach is blended with that of the ocean as the tide rises, until finally "the sea and the marsh are one" and "it is night." The poem has progressed so steadily to this climax that the final stanza sounds almost like a postscript. It is unfortunate that Lanier did not live long enough to complete the series of projected "Hymns of the Marshes" of which "The Marshes of Glynn" was to be only a small part. Experimental in subject, scope, and technique (note the logaoedic dactyls and the long, loose Whitmanesque lines), "The Marshes of Glynn" is one of Lanier's best poems, revealing an intellectual maturity and a technical expertise which, had they been allowed to flower, might well have placed him among the foremost American poets of the nineteenth century.

Alice Hall Petry

Other major works

LONG FICTION: *Tiger-Lilies*, 1867.

NONFICTION: "Retrospects and Prospects," 1871; *Florida: Its Scenery, Climate, and History*, 1875; "Sketches of India," 1876; *The Science of English Verse*, 1880; *The English Novel*, 1883; *Shakspere* [sic] *and His Forerunners*, 1902.

CHILDREN'S LITERATURE: *The Boy's King Arthur*, 1880.

Bibliography

De Bellis, Jack Angelo. *Sidney Lanier*. New York: Twayne, 1972. De Bellis examines Lanier's growth by analyzing his growing awareness of the ways to make poetry express the morality of feeling. "The Symphony" is treated as a poem in which Lanier discovered how to symbolize the conflict between feeling and thought, and how to inject great feeling into the poem via the musicality of his verse. "The Marshes of Glynn" and "Sunrise" are shown to be rhythm experiments. Supplemented by indexes.

Gabin, Jane S. *A Living Minstrelsy: The Poetry and Music of Sidney Lanier*. Macon, Ga.: Mercer University Press, 1985. This study maintains that Lanier is unique in American literature because he is the only poet who is both active and accomplished in music. Gabin believes his poetry developed as a direct result of his pursuit of musical interests and that his achievements and innovations came as a direct result of his exposure to innovation in musical composition. Includes a bibliography and an index.

Mims, Edwin. *Sidney Lanier*. 1905. Reprint. Port Washington, N.Y.: Kennikat Press, 1968. Mims's study relies heavily on Lanier's letters and stresses his modernity. He suggests that the advances the poet made in "The Marshes of Glynn" and *The Science of English Verse* were negated by his weak health and short life. Supplemented by an introduction and illustrations.

Parks, Edd Winfield. *Sidney Lanier: The Man, the Poet, the Critic*. Athens: University of Georgia Press, 1968. Originally delivered as a Lamar Lecture at Wesleyan College. "The Man" provides a biographical sketch that adheres to authenticated facts. "The Poet" suggests obstacles that prevented Lanier from becoming a major poet, although his later poems are seen to override these weaknesses. "The Critic" reveals his inconsistencies as a critic by discussing his moralistic view of fiction.

Starke, Aubrey Harrison. *Sidney Lanier: A Biographical and Critical Study.* New York: Russel & Russel, 1964. Starke interprets all Lanier's work in the factual context of his life. He maintains that Lanier was sensitive to the development of the "New South" and was therefore a forerunner of the Fugitive-Agrarian writers, who responded to the ways materialistic society had replaced a traditional way of life. Starke says that in his poems, Lanier finds refuge by responding to music and nature. Supplemented by full notes, a documentation, and a bibliography.

PHILIP LARKIN

Born: Coventry, England; August 9, 1922
Died: Hull, England; December 2, 1985

Principal poetry
The North Ship, 1945, 1966; *The Less Deceived*, 1955; *The Whitsun Weddings*, 1964; *High Windows*, 1974; *Collected Poems*, 1988.

Other literary forms
Although Philip Larkin is thought of today primarily as a poet, his first literary successes were novels: *Jill* (1946, 1964) and *A Girl in Winter* (1947). The two were widely acclaimed for their accomplished style, accurate dialogue, and subtle characterization. *Jill* was valued highly for its intimate look at wartime Oxford. The protagonist in each is an outsider who encounters great difficulty in attempting to fit into society, and the two novels explore themes of loneliness and alienation to which Larkin returns time and again in his later poetry. Larkin wrote comparatively little about literature and granted few interviews. His literary essays were collected into *Required Writings: Miscellaneous Pieces, 1955-1982* (1984). He also wrote extensively on jazz, chiefly in his reviews for the *Daily Telegraph*, and a number of those pieces appear in the volume *All What Jazz* (1970). His opinions of those works were frequently instructive for the reader who wishes to understand his views on poetry, particularly his comments on what he saw as the "modernist" jazz of Charlie Parker, which, like all modernism, concentrates on technique while violating the truth of human existence. True to his precepts, Larkin eschewed, throughout his career, technical fireworks in favor of a poetic that reflects the language of the people. He edited *New Poems, 1958*, with Louis MacNeice and Bonamy Dobrée, and he was chosen to bring out *The Oxford Book of Twentieth-Century English Verse* (1973).

Achievements
Few poets succeeded as Larkin did in winning a large audience and critical respect for such a small body of poetry, and indeed his success may be attributable in part to the rate at which he wrote poems. Because he brought out, according to his own estimate, only three to five poems a year, he could give each one the meticulous attention required to build extremely tight, masterful verse. As a result, each of his slim volumes contains numerous poems that immediately catch the reader's attention for their precise yet colloquial diction.

His chief contribution to British poetry may well be his sustained determination to work in conventional forms and colloquial, even vulgar and coarse, language. In this attempt, as in his ironic self-deprecation and his gloomy outlook, he resembles Robert Frost. Also like Frost, he worked consciously against the modernist poetics of Wallace Stevens, T. S. Eliot, Ezra Pound, and their heirs, the poetics of disjunction and image. Most of Larkin's poetry demonstrates a distrust of symbolic and metaphorical language, and a reliance instead on discursive verse. His insistence on plain language reflects a belief in the importance of tradition, a faith in the people who remain in touch with the land, and a suspicion of modern society, urban development, and technological advancement. Larkin stands as the chief example among his contemporaries of the line of counter-modernist poetry running not from William Butler Yeats and the Symbolists but from Thomas Hardy and Rudyard Kipling, for both of whom he had great admiration.

Larkin's popularity also results, in part, from his speaking not only as one of the people but for them as well. For all its bleakness and irony, or perhaps because of it, his poetry represents the attitudes of a segment of the British population that found itself with greatly diminished expectations following World War II; institutions were losing their traditional value and function, and the problems of empire (the crowning achievements of those institutions) were rushing home to roost. His poetry represents a search for meaning within the bewildering complexity of the twentieth century.

Biography

The Englishness of Philip Larkin's poetry is decidedly provincial; his England does not revolve around London, and in fact, there is a marked suspicion of the capital and the cosmopolitan urbanity it represents. From his diction to the frequency with which his speakers are seated in cars or trains traveling through the countryside, his poems reflect the provincialism of his life. Larkin was born August 9, 1922, in Coventry, where his father served as City Treasurer throughout his childhood. He described his childhood as a bore and not worth mentioning, suggesting that no biography of him need begin before he turned twenty-one. Although he was not a particularly good student at the King Henry VII School in Coventry, he matriculated at St. John's College, Oxford, in 1940, hoping to get in a year of school before he was called into the military. As it eventually turned out, he failed his Army physical and stayed in college, graduating with first-class honors in 1943. His time at Oxford had a profound effect upon the youthful Larkin; in the Introduction to *Jill*, he suggests that the war radically diminished the students' grand view of themselves, and this sense of reduced importance has stuck with him in his poetry. Perhaps even more crucial to his development, though, were his friendships with budding writers Bruce Montgomery (Edmund Crispin) and Kingsley Amis. The Amis-Larkin friendship seems to have influenced both men, and their early writings share many attitudes and themes.

While at the university, Larkin published poems in the undergraduate magazines and in the anthology *Poetry in Wartime* (1942). (He had had one poem published in the *Listener* in 1940.) Fortune Press took notice and asked him to submit a collection; he did, and *The North Ship* was published in 1945. The poetry in that collection is heavily influenced by Yeats's work, to which he was introduced by the poet Vernon Watkins, who read and lectured at the English Club at Oxford and with whom Larkin subsequently developed a friendship.

After graduation, Larkin took a post as librarian in Wellington, Shropshire. He claimed that while there he began to read Thomas Hardy's poetry seriously, which allowed him to throw off the Yeatsian influence. He subsequently worked as a librarian in Leicester, in Belfast, and, after 1955, as head librarian at the University of Hull. His attitudes toward his work vacillated, and that ambivalence is displayed in his poems, particularly in "Toads" and "Toads Revisited." Nevertheless, he remained at his position as librarian and eschewed the life of poet-celebrity. He died in Hull on December 2, 1985.

Analysis

If Rudyard Kipling's is the poetry of empire, then Philip Larkin's is the poetry of the aftermath of empire. Having lived through the divestiture of England's various colonial holdings, the economic impact of empire-building having finally come home, together with the ultimate travesty of imperial pretentions and the nightmare of Nazi and Soviet colonization in Europe, Larkin was wary of the expansiveness, the acquisitiveness, and the grandeur implicit in the imperial mentality. Many features of his poetry can be traced to that wariness: from the skepticism and irony, to the colloquial diction, to the formal precision of his poems.

Indeed, of all the writers who shared those ideals and techniques and who came to be known in the 1950's as The Movement, Larkin most faithfully retained his original attitude and style. Those writers—Kingsley Amis, Donald Davie, John Wain, Elizabeth Jennings, Thom Gunn, among others—diverse though they were, shared attitudes that were essentially empirical, antimodernist, skeptical, and ironic. Most of those views can be understood as outgrowths of an elemental alienation from society and its traditional institutions. Amis' Jim Dixon is the outstanding fictional embodiment of these attitudes; although he desperately wants and needs to be accepted into university society and the traditional power structure it represents, his contempt for the institution and those in it, bred of his alienation, carries him into situations that border on both hilarity and disaster. *Lucky Jim* (1954) is *the* Movement novel.

Isolation and alienation figure prominently in both of Larkin's novels, as well; yet it is in his poems that they receive their fullest development. The speakers of his poems—and in the great majority of cases the speaker is the poet himself—seem alienated from their surroundings, cut off from both people and institutions. While that alienation normally shows itself as distance, as irony and wry humor, it can sometimes appear as smugness, complacence, even sneering judgment. Larkin turns his sense of isolation, of being an outsider or fringe observer, into a position of centrality, in which the world from which he is alienated seems to be moving tangentially to his own sphere. In his best poems, that distance works two ways, allowing the poet to observe the world in perspective, as if viewing it through the wrong end of a pair of binoculars, so that weighty matters seem less momentous, while at the same time reminding the poet that he, too, is a figure of little consequence. When his poems fail, the poet risks very little of his own ego as he sits back in safety, judging others across the frosty distance.

Larkin gains his perspective in large measure through his belief that nothing lies beyond this world, that this existence, however muddled it may be, is probably the only one. His skepticism is thoroughgoing and merciless; he rarely softens his tone. In some writers such belief might provoke terror or a compulsion to reform the world. In Larkin, it gives rise to irony. He examines the feeble inhabitants of this tiny planet surrounded by the void and asks if it can all be so important.

The resulting sense of human insignificance, including his own, leads him to several of the characteristic features of his work. He rejects "poetic" devices in favor of simpler, more mundane vehicles. His diction, for example, is nearly always colloquial, often coarse, vulgar, or profane. His distrust of a specialized diction or syntax for poetry reflects his distrust of institutions generally. Similarly, he shies away from the intense poetic moment—image, symbol, metaphor—in favor of a discursive, argumentative verse. While he will occasionally resolve a poem through use of an image or a metaphor, particularly in *High Windows*, he more commonly talks his way through the poem, relying on intellect rather than emotion or intuition.

This rejection of the stuff of poetry leads him to a problem: if overtly poetic language and poetic devices are eschewed, what can the poet use to identify his poems *as* poems? For Larkin the answer lies in the external form of the poems: scansion, rhyme schemes, stanzaic patterns. The tension and the power of a Larkin poem often result from the interplay of common, unexceptional language with rigorously formal precision. "The Building," from *High Windows*, is an example of such tension. The poet meditates upon the function of the hospital in modern society and the way in which it takes over some of the duties traditionally performed by the Church, all in very ordinary language. The poem, however, is stretched taut over not one but two sophisticated units: a seven-line stanza and an eight-line rhyme scheme (abcbdad). Rhyme pattern and stanzaic pattern come together at the end of the eighth stanza, but the poem does not end there; rather, the poet employs another rhyme unit, a stanza plus a line, as a means of resolving the poem. Even here Larkin's shrewd distrust of the intellectual viability of poetic forms displays itself: ending neatly on the fifty-sixth line would be too neat, too pat, and would violate the poem's ambivalence toward the place. Similarly, although his rhyme schemes are often very regular, the same cannot be said for the rhymes themselves: speech/touch, faint/went, home/welcome. If Larkin recognizes his need for traditional forms in his poems, he recognizes also the necessity of altering those forms into viable elements of *his* poetry.

Finally, there is in Larkin a sense of an ending, of oblivion. For all his distrust of the "new apocalypse crowd," many of his poems suggest something similar, although with a characteristic difference. Where the "crowd" may prophesy the end of the world and everything in it, he, working out of his alienation, more commonly seems to be watching the string run out, as if he were a spectator at the edge of oblivion.

Larkin's first volume of poetry, *The North Ship*, went virtually unnoticed at the time of its original publication and would be unnoticed still were it made to stand on its own merits. It has few. The poems are almost uniformly derivative Yeatsian juvenilia, laden with William Butler Yeats's imagery but shorn of its power or meaning; this is the verse of a young man who wants to become a poet by sounding like a known poet. No one has been more critical, moreover, of the volume than the poet himself, characterizing it as an anomaly, a mistake that happened when he did not know his own voice and thought, under the tutelage of Vernon Watkins, that he was someone else. That he allowed the republication of the work in 1966, with an introduction that is more than anything else a disclaimer, suggests a desire to distance the "real" poet from the confused adolescent.

Despite his objections, the book can be seen as representative of certain tendencies in his later verse, and it is enlightening to discern how many features of his mature work show themselves even when buried under someone else's style. A major difference between Larkin's poems and Yeats's lies in the use of objects: while the younger poet borrows Yeats's dancers, horses, candles, and moons, they remain dancers, horses, candles, and moons. They lack transcendant, symbolic value; objects remain mere objects.

There is also in these early poems a vagueness in the description of the phenomenal world. Perhaps that generality, that vagueness, could be explained as the result of the Yeatsian influence, but it is also a tendency of Larkin's later work. One often has the impression that a scene, particularly a human scene, is typical rather than specific.

One of the things clearly missing from this first work is a suspicion of the Yeatsian symbols, attitudes, and gestures, almost none of which the mature Larkin can abide. His assertion that it was his intense reading of Hardy's poetry that rescued him from the pernicious influence of Yeats may have validity; more probably, time heals youthful excess, and during the period when he was outgrowing the poetry of *The North Ship*, he began a salutary reading of Hardy.

A striking development in Larkin's second book of poems, *The Less*

Deceived, is his insistence on the mundane, the unexceptional, the commonplace. In "Born Yesterday," a poem on the occasion of Sally Amis' birth, for example, he counters the usual wishes for beauty or brilliance with the attractive (for him) possibility of being utterly unextraordinary, of fitting in wholly by having nothing stand out. This wish he offers, he says, in case the others do not come true, but one almost has the sense that he wishes also that the others will not come true, that being average is much preferable to being exceptional.

He makes a similar case for the ordinary in the wickedly funny "I Remember, I Remember," which attacks the Romantic notions of the writer's childhood as exemplified in D. H. Lawrence's *Sons and Lovers* (1913). In other places he has described his childhood as boring, not worthy of comment, and in this poem he pursues that idea vigorously. In the first two stanzas, he comes to the realization that he does not recognize the Coventry station into which the train has pulled, although he used it often as a child. When his traveling companion asks if Coventry is where he "has his roots," the poet responds in his mind with a catalog of all the things that never happened to him that supposedly happen to writers in their youth, "the splendid family/ I never ran to," "The bracken where I never sat trembling." Through the course of that list, he recognizes that the place looks so foreign now because it never gave him anything distinctive, that there is nothing that he carries with him that he can attribute to it. Then, in a remarkable about-face, he realizes that the location has very little to do with how his childhood was spent or misspent, that life is largely independent of place, that the alienation which he senses is something he carries with him, not a product of Coventry.

The poem at first seems to be an honest appraisal of his youth in contradistinction to all those romanticized accounts in biographies and novels, but the reader is forced finally to conclude that the poet protests too much. There is no childhood in which *nothing* happens, and in insisting so strongly on the vacuum in which he grew up, Larkin develops something like the inverse of nostalgia. He turns his present disillusionment and alienation back against the past and views it from his ironic perspective. Larkin is often the victim of his own ironies, and in this poem his victim is memory.

His irony, in this poem as in so many, is used defensively; he wards off criticism by beating everyone to the punch. Irony is in some respects safer than laying oneself open for inspection. In many of his finest poems, however, he drops his guard and allows himself to think seriously about serious subjects. The foremost example in *The Less Deceived* is "Church Going." The title turns out to be marvelously ambiguous, appearing at first blush to be a mere reference to attending church, but then becoming, as the poem progresses, an elliptical, punning reference to churches going out of fashion.

The first two stanzas are curtly dismissive in a manner often encountered in Larkin, as he describes his stop from a bicycle trip at a church that is apparently Ulster Protestant. Neither he (since he stops for a reason he cannot name and acts guilty as he looks around) nor the church (since it is not at all out of the ordinary) seems worthy of attention. He leaves, thinking the church "not worth stopping for." In the third stanza, however, the poem shifts gears in a way typical of Larkin's finest work: the dismissive attitude toward mundane existence, the wry observations give way to serious contemplation. "Church Going," in fact, contains two such shifts.

In stanzas three through seven Larkin reflects on the fate of churches when people stop going altogether—whether they will become places which people will avoid or seek out because of superstition, or become museums, or be turned to some profane use—and wonders, as well, who will be the last person to come to the church and what his reasons will be. Larkin has a sense, conveyed in a number of poems, that he and his generation of skeptics will be the end of religion in England, and in this poem he wonders about the results of that doubting. The final stanza contains yet another shift, this one rather more subtle. As if the "serious house on serious earth" were forcing the poet to be more serious, he shifts away from his musings about its fate, which are after all only another kind of dismissal, and recognizes instead the importance of the place. He suggests, finally, that the shallowness and disbelief of modern man cannot eradicate the impulse to think seriously and seek wisdom that the Church, however outmoded its rituals, represents.

The two finest poems in Larkin's succeeding volume display similar movements of thought. In the title poem, "The Whitsun Weddings," the movement takes on further embellishment; not only does the poem move from dismissiveness to contemplation, but also the language of the poem moves from specificity toward generality in a way that mirrors the theme. The poem also contains one of Larkin's favorite devices: the use of a train ride (occasionally a car ride) to depict the movement of thought.

The poem opens with the concern for specificity of someone who, like the speaker, is late; when the train leaves the station at "one-twenty," it is "three-quarters-empty." He catches glimpses of scenery along the way, none of it very interesting, much of it squalid and polluted. Not until the third stanza (suggesting the incompleteness of his detailed observation) does he notice the wedding parties at each station. Even then, it is with the dismissive attitude of someone who, as a professional bachelor and alienated outsider, rather scorns the tackiness of the families gathered on the platforms to see the couples off, as well as that of the unreflective couples with whom he shares the coach. His ironical, detailed description takes up most of the next five stanzas.

Toward the end of stanza seven, however, he undergoes a change, has a moment of vision in which the postal districts of London appear as "squares of wheat." That image leads him, in the final stanza, to see the couples as symbols of fertility, so that finally the slowing train inspires in him an image of arrows beyond the scope of his vision, "somewhere becoming rain." That he loosens the reins of his vision, so that he can describe not merely what he sees but also what he can only envision, is a major development in his attitude from the beginning of the poem. It demonstrates a breaking down, however slight or momentary, of his alienation from the common run of existence and of his resistance to recognizing his own relationship with these others. The poem may ultimately be judged a failure because of the brevity of that breaking down, but the image it spawns of fertility and life just beginning is magnificent.

"Dockery and Son" displays a similar movement and is a stronger poem because the poet is forced to lower his defenses much earlier and reveal himself more fully during the course of his meditation. An offhand comment by the Dean that a fellow student now has a son at school sets the speaker's mind in motion. His first musings on the train home are again mundane, dismissive, of the "you-never-know-do-you" sort, and so boring that he falls asleep. On reconsideration, though, the poet experiences the shock of being brought up hard against the reality of having missed, irrevocably, what is for most men a major part of life—familial relations. Even this reflection remains thin and unsatisfactory, and he moves on to explore the nature of unquestioned and unquestioning belief and its source, deciding that it results not from wisdom or truth but from habit and style grown sclerotic. Yet those beliefs are what a man's life turns on, producing a son for Dockery and nothing for the poet.

At this point, very late in the poem, Larkin develops one of his marvelous reversals on the word "nothing." For most, it connotes an absence, a negation, a nonentity, but for Larkin "nothing" is a positive entity, a thing or force to be reckoned with, "Nothing with all a son's harsh patronage." The line suggests that the poet has had to wrestle with this "nothing" he has created even as a father, such as Dockery, has had to wrestle with the problems brought on by having a son. The similarity, however, does not stop there; the poet goes on to recognize the common fate that awaits not only Dockery and himself but everyone as well. Most commentators read the final phrase, "the only end of age," as meaning death, and certainly that meaning is there. Nevertheless, to understand it as *merely* meaning death is to lose some of the force it holds for the speaker. Rather, it must be read back through the stanza and the poem as a whole, so that the emphasis on nothingness informs that certain knowledge of death. That the poet not only knows he will die, but also that he has already tasted the nothingness he knows, as an unbeliever, that death entails, makes the experience of that knowledge the more poignant. As is so often true in Larkin's work, that poignancy, which could border on self-pity, is tempered by the understanding that he at least comprehends, and there lies behind the poem's ending an unstated irony aimed at those such as Dockery who engage life so fully as to obscure that reality.

Again, that constant strain of alienation insinuates its way into poem after poem. Throughout *The Whitsun Weddings* the poet feels himself cut off from his fellow humans, often struggling to retrieve a spirit of community with them, sometimes simply wondering why it is so. The volume, while it represents little change from its predecessor, renders a picture of a man in middle age who feels life passing him by, and who sees more and more clearly the inevitable. Settings are close, small; lives are petty, insignificant; society is filled with graffiti and pollution. In "The Importance of Elsewhere," he finds comfort in being a foreigner in Ireland, since at least he can explain his estrangement from his fellow inhabitants there. In England, ostensibly at home, he has no such excuse.

A number of the poems in *High Windows* display that estrangement, often in unsettlingly smug tones. "Afternoons," in the previous book, shows Larkin at his judgmental worst, picking out nasty little details of petty lives and common tastes. In this volume, "The Old Fools," a poem that is often praised for its unexpected ending, displays a similar attitude. After railing against the infirmity and senility of the elderly throughout the poem, the tag line of "Well, we shall find out" rings false, sounding too much like an attempt to dodge inevitable criticism.

"Going, Going" presents some of the same problems, yet it implicates the poet in his critique in a way that "The Old Fools" does not. What is going is England itself, and that entity, it turns out, is place, not people. People have ruined the landscape and the architecture, reducing everything to rubbish. The poem redeems itself through its linguistic implication of its creator. The piece remains polemical throughout, avoiding the impulse to resolve through metaphor, as if the misanthropic, gloomy sensibility demands a crabbed style distrustful of the richness of figurative language and, perhaps, mirroring the destruction of English literature: if "carved choirs," echoing as they do William Shakespeare's "bare ruined choirs where late the sweet birds sang," are ruined and replaced with "concrete and tyres," then this poem's language is the replacement for Shakespeare's. Everywhere the poet turns, he finds traditional institutions, including poetry, degraded into mundane modern forms.

A much finer expression of that discovery is to be found in "The Building," which brings together numerous themes and ideas from throughout Larkin's canon. Like "Dockery and Son," it is a meditation on the foretaste of death; like "Going, Going," a consideration of the degradation of institutions in the modern world; like "Church Going," a questioning of what man shall do without churches.

The first two stanzas examine the ways the building in which the speaker sits resembles so many other modern buildings—high-rise hotels, airport lounges—although there is something disturbingly unlike them, as well. Not until the end of the second stanza does he reveal that it is a hospital. What unites people here is the common knowledge of their own mortality; even if they are not to die immediately, they are forced by the place to confront the fact that they will die eventually. The inescapability of that knowledge tames and calms the people in the building, as once the knowledge of death and its aftermath quieted them in church.

The recognition of this similarity grows slowly but steadily throughout the poem. The words keep insinuating a connection: "confess," "congregations," a "locked church" outside. The reaction people have in the hospital also suggests a function similar to that of the Church; outside they can hide behind ignorance or refusal to face facts, while inside the hospital those illusions are stripped away and reality is brought into the clear, sharp light, the unambiguous clarity of hospital corridors. This growing realization culminates in a final understanding that unless the modern hospital is more powerful than the traditional cathedral (and Larkin, suspicious of all institutions, does not think it is), then nothing can stop the ineluctable fate that awaits humanity, although (and now the similarities are overwhelming) every night people bring offerings, in the form of flowers, as they would to church.

A remarkable poem such as "The Building" can overcome a score of "Afternoons," and what is more remarkable about it is the way Larkin overcomes his initial alienation to speak not only at, but also to and even for, his fellow humans and their very real suffering. His finest poems end, like this one, in benedictions that border on the "Shantih" of T. S. Eliot's *The Waste Land* (1922), giving the reader the sense that a troubling journey has reached a satisfying end.

The publication of his *Collected Poems* (1989) brought to light scores of poems previously uncollected, long out of print, or unavailable to the general reading public. These poems will not significantly alter Larkin's reputation, other than to expand the base on which it rests. For fans of his work, however, the additions prove quite valuable, showing as they do the movement from juvenilia to maturity. The early work displays even more clearly than, say, *The North Ship* the various influences on the young poet: Yeats and Auden. A work such as "New Year Poem" demonstrates a remarkable prescience, dated as it is the day before (and written an ocean away from) Auden's famous "New Year Letter" of 1941; both poems look at the future and consider the social and spiritual needs in a time of crisis.

Larkin, ever parsimonious, wrote very few poems during the last decade of his life: *Collected Poems* reveals a mere seventeen. Many of those concern themselves with his standard topics—the ravages of age, the sense of not being in step with the rest of society, the approach of death. In "The Mower," for example, he ruminates on having run over a hedgehog in the tall grass, killing it. From this experience, he takes away a feeling of responsibility for the death, a sense of the loss of this fellow creature, and the reflection that, given our limited time, we should be kind to one another. This slight poem (eleven lines) sums up much of Larkin's thought in his later years: death is a complete cessation of experience, not a transmutation but a blankness, an end, while life itself is a vale of unhappiness, and people therefore owe it to themselves and one another to make the way as pleasant as possible.

In "Aubade," perhaps the most substantial of the late poems, Larkin writes of the approach of death, now another day closer because it is a new morning. He declares that we have never been able to accept death, yet are also unable to defeat it. Once religion offered the consolation of afterlife; for Larkin, that promise is no longer valid. What people fear most, he asserts, is the absence of sensation, of affect, that is death, as well as the absolute certainty of its coming. His "morning poem" is really a poem of the dark night of the soul. The fifth, and final, ten-line stanza brings the light of day and the unmindful routine of the workaday world, the routine that acts as a balm by taking our minds off our ultimate problem. Indeed, the poem's closing image presents those representatives of the mundane, postal carriers, going among houses like doctors, their daily rounds offering temporary solace.

These two poems present Larkin's typically ironic approach to the literary tradition. "The Mower" is a highly unconventional garden song. While its title recalls Marvell's poems "The Garden" and "The Mower, Against Gardens," it shares none of their pastoral innocence or coyness. It finds death, not life, in the world of nature. Similarly, he subverts the traditional use of the aubade form to discuss not the coming day but also a coming night. In both cases he undermines traditionally upbeat forms. Yet these poems also point to the playfulness of which Larkin was capable even in his bleakest moments, finding amusement in poems of abject despair. That may prove to be his great gift, the ability to face darkness fully, to take it in, and still to laugh, to be ironic even about last things.

Thomas C. Foster

Other major works
LONG FICTION: *Jill*, 1946, 1964; *A Girl in Winter*, 1947.
ANTHOLOGY: *New Poems*, 1958 (edited with Louis MacNeice and Bonamy Dobrée).
MISCELLANEOUS: *Required Writings: Miscellaneous Pieces, 1955-1982*, 1984.

Bibliography
Brownjohn, Alan. *Philip Larkin*. Harlow, England: Longman, 1975. This little book (34 pages with select bibliography), the first to deal with all four major volumes, is written with a poet's sensitivity to Larkin's verse. It includes a brief biographical section, followed by chronological discussion of the poems and concluding with an examination of the novels. A handy

starting point for the student.

Day, Roger. *Philip Larkin.* Philadelphia: Open University Press, 1987. As one in the series of Open University Guides to Literature, this volume takes teaching as its primary focus. While the result holds little new for specialists, the focused questions and resulting commentary point students toward the important features of the poems and toward confidence in reading the poetry on their own, offering them suggestions for further reading and a select bibliography.

Hartley, Jean. *Philip Larkin, the Marvell Press, and Me.* Manchester, England: Carcanet, 1989. This memoir by the cofounder of the Marvell Press gives interesting insights into its most famous author. While the book deals with Hartley more than Larkin, it shows the exciting period of creative activity leading to and resulting from the publication of a truly important work, *The Less Deceived,* and it chronicles the lifelong friendship that resulted.

Hassan, Salem K. *Philip Larkin and His Contemporaries: An Air of Authenticity.* Basingstoke, England: Macmillan, 1988. Well-researched, this volume places Larkin within the context of his Movement colleagues of the 1950's: John Wain, Thom Gunn, Kingsley Amis, and D. J. Enright. The first part discusses Larkin's poetry book by book. Part 2 devotes a chapter to careers of his four contemporaries, discussing their work in terms of his. The text also includes a select bibliography of primary and secondary sources, notes, and an index.

Motion, Andrew. *Philip Larkin.* London: Methuen, 1982. A volume in Methuen's Contemporary Writers Series, this short work (ninety-two pages including index, notes, and bibliography) provides a handy, if incomplete, introduction to the man and his work. The book offers thematic and literary-historical overviews, although only one chapter on the poems themselves.

Rossen, Janice. *Philip Larkin: His Life's Work.* New York: Simon & Schuster, 1989. This intelligent and highly readable overview traces Larkin's development through the first two books, then looks at his lyric impulse, his firmly rooted Englishness, his sexual ambivalence, his use of vulgarity, and his struggle with mortality. The study ties in the poetry with the novels, jazz criticism, and literary criticism to develop a total view of the context of the poetry.

Timms, David. *Philip Larkin.* Edinburgh: Oliver & Boyd, 1973. The first book on Larkin, although somewhat dated, still proves useful for its understanding of his early development. Timms is particularly useful on the significance of Larkin's association with the Movement for his work, and he places the novels in the context of his poetic development.

D. H. LAWRENCE

Born: Eastwood, Nottinghamshire, England; September 11, 1885
Died: Villa Robermond, Vence, France; March 2, 1930

Principal poetry
Love Poems and Others, 1913; *Amores,* 1916; *Look! We Have Come Through!,* 1917; *New Poems,* 1918; *Bay,* 1919; *Tortoises,* 1921; *Birds, Beasts and Flowers,* 1923; *Collected Poems,* 1928; *Pansies,* 1929; *Nettles,* 1930; *The Triumph of the Machine,* 1931; *Last Poems,* 1932; *Fire and Other Poems,* 1940; *Phoenix Edition of Complete Poems,* 1957; *The Complete Poems of D. H. Lawrence,* 1964, 1971 (Vivian de Sola Pinto and Warren Roberts, editors).

Other literary forms
D. H. Lawrence's productions reflect his artistic range. Accompanying his considerable body of poetry, the eleven novels published during his lifetime include *Sons and Lovers* (1913), *The Rainbow* (1915), *Women in Love* (1920), *The Plumed Serpent* (1926), and *Lady Chatterley's Lover* (1928). He wrote almost continuously for literary periodicals in addition to publishing five volumes of plays, nine volumes of essays, and several short story collections including *The Prussian Officer and Other Stories* (1914), *England, My England* (1922), *The Ladybird* (1923), and *The Woman Who Rode Away and Other Stories* (1928). His final works, including *Apocalypse* and *Etruscan Places,* appeared between 1930 and 1933, and more poetry, essays, and drafts of fiction have since been collected in *Phoenix* (1936) and *Phoenix II* (1968). Several of Lawrence's works, as well as his biography, *The Priest of Love,* have been adapted for the screen. The *Phoenix Edition of D. H. Lawrence* was published in 1957; Viking has printed *The Complete Short Stories of D. H. Lawrence* (1961) and *The Complete Plays of D. H. Lawrence* (1965). The definitive *The Cambridge Edition of the Letters and Works of D. H. Lawrence* began appearing in 1979.

Achievements
Lawrence's work has consistently appealed to the adventurous and the perceptive. Ford Madox Ford, editor of the progressive *English Review,* printed Lawrence's earliest poems and short stories there in 1911, recognizing beneath their conventional surfaces potent psychological and emotional undercurrents previously unexplored in British letters. Before Freud's theories were widely known, Lawrence's *Sons and Lovers* daringly probed the dangerous multilayered mother-son-lover triangle he had experienced in his own life. After his elopement, itself a scandal, Lawrence produced *The Rainbow,* seized by Scotland Yard in 1915 and publicly condemned for obscenity. Lawrence's subsequent self-exile from England and his growing artistic notoriety

came to a climax in the censorship trials of *Lady Chatterley's Lover*. Behind the alleged pornography, however, critics soon grasped Lawrence's genuine ability to convey what T. S. Eliot called "fitful and profound insights" into human behavior. Lawrence's admirers also included Edward Garnett, John Middleton Murry, Richard Aldington, Amy Lowell, and Rainer Maria Rilke, although Virginia Woolf perhaps illustrated her generation's ambivalence toward Lawrence most pungently: "Mr. Lawrence has moments of greatness, but he has hours of something quite different." Lawrence's own critical studies, particularly his pseudonymous *Movements in European History* (1921), and *Studies in Classic American Literature* (1923), reveal a singular blend of historical perspective and instinctive understanding appreciated only after his death. Once the laudatory memoirs and abusive denunciations had died out, Lawrence's artistic reputation grew steadily, attributed generally to the craftsmanship of his short fiction and the uncompromisingly honest investigations of sexuality in his novels. As readers young in spirit increasingly observe, however, Lawrence's greatest gift, his affirmation of life, shines most brightly in his poetry.

Biography

David Herbert Richards Lawrence was born in Eastwood, Nottinghamshire, England, on September 11, 1885. His mother, Lydia Beardsall, had come from a fiercely religious middle class family reduced in circumstances since the depression of 1837. Lydia, "a superior soul," as her third son called her, had been a schoolteacher, sensitive and musical, six years younger than her husband, to whom she was distantly related by marriage. His family had also lost money and position, and Arthur Lawrence, the proud possessor of a fine physique and a musical soul, had gone down into the mines as a child to work. Lydia's disillusion with her marriage, her husband's alcoholic degeneration, and the continual marital strife that haunted her son's childhood provided much of the conflict at the heart of Lawrence's work.

Out of hatred for her husband and a desperate resolve that her children should not sink to his level, Lydia used them as weapons against him. Much later, Lawrence regretted and in part redressed the unfavorable portrait of his father in his autobiographical "colliery novel," *Sons and Lovers*, which exhibits his mother's domination and his own fragile opposition through his love for Jessie Chambers, the "Miriam" whom he loved and left in literature as well as life.

Obedient to his mother's demands, Lawrence took a teaching position at Croydon, near London, in 1908. He was devastated by the ugly realities of urban life, disgusted by his savage pupils, and frustrated by the young women in his life. His mother's lingering death from cancer in late 1910, not long after he had laid an early copy of his first novel, *The White Peacock*, in her hands, sent him into a "heavy, bitter year," from which he emerged physically shaken by near-fatal pneumonia, unable to progress with his writing, and bent on leaving England. In the spring of 1912 he became smitten with "the woman of a lifetime," his former language professor's wife, the Baroness Frieda von Richthofen. Upon their elopement that May, they left behind them Frieda's children and Lawrence's England forever, except for a few brief and mostly unhappy intervals.

Lawrence then had to live by his pen, and he increased his output dramatically, pouring out not only fiction and poetry but also criticism and travel essays. After a painful stay in Cornwall during World War I, shunned because of Frieda's German connections and his own antiwar sentiments, Lawrence, shocked by British repression of *The Rainbow*, began the worldwide wandering which lasted the remainder of his life.

Lawrence almost realized his ambition of writing a major novel on each continent. After visiting Ceylon and Australia, he settled for a time with Frieda and a few friends near Taos, New Mexico, devoting himself to the idealization of primitivism as a vehicle for modern man's regeneration. Working on his novel *The Pluméd Serpent* in Mexico in late 1924, he was struck simultaneously with harsh psychic and physical blows; he realized that his artistic position was untenable and went down "as if shot" with a combination of typhoid and the long-standing illness diagnosed then for the first time as tuberculosis.

Slowly recuperating on his ranch, Lawrence regained his creative equilibrium in a play, *David*, and a lovely fragmentary novel, "The Flying Fish," written, he said, "so near the borderline of death" that its spell could not be recaptured "in the cold light of day." There he proclaimed the belief in "regenerate man" to which he dedicated the rest of his short life. He returned in thought at least to England with *Lady Chatterly's Lover*, written on a sunny hill in Italy, a "novel of tenderness" that awakened violent protests and lawsuits, driving him even further into his metaphysical contemplation of human destiny. Very ill, holding to life through the strange bond of creativity alone, Lawrence worked out his conclusions on personal immortality in his *Last Poems*, until on March 2, 1930, in a sanatorium on the French Riviera aptly called "Ad Astra," "once dipped in dark oblivion/the soul ha[d] peace, inward and lovely peace."

Analysis

D. H. Lawrence had written poetry all of his creative life, but he did not set his poetic theory down until 1923. His poetry, as with nearly everything that he wrote, is uneven; and he knew it, distinguishing between his early self-conscious verse and the "real poems" that his "demon" shook out of him, poems he called "a biography of an emotional and inner life." In a preface to another man's poetry, Lawrence defined the process by which he himself transmuted "inner life," the core of his work, into art: "a bursting of bubbles of reality, and the pang of extinction that is also liberation into the roving, uncaring chaos which is all we shall ever know of God." Lawrence's poetry is thus best seen in the context of his life and through the painful paradox of his creativity, rooted in his most profound basic concept, the theory of human regeneration that he conveyed so often in the image of Paradise Regained.

As Richard Hoggart has observed, Lawrence's inner life spoke with both "the voice of a down-to-earth, tight, bright, witty Midlander" and "the voice of a seer with a majestic vision of God and life and earth." The Midlands voice first announced the major themes that Lawrence never abandoned: class, religion, and love. Lawrence very early felt the strictures of a workingman's life and the humiliation of poverty as keenly as he felt the happiness he shared at the Chambers' farm, among birds, beasts, and flowers threatened by encroaching industrialism. His *Rhyming Poems* also reflect his youthful love, quivering between the extremes of idealistic "spirituality" pressed upon him by his mother and Jessie Chambers, so fatally alike, and a powerful sexual drive crying out for satisfaction. At sixteen he abandoned his mother's harsh Congregationalism, though the "hymns of a man's life" never lost their appeal for him, and from 1906 to 1908 he was affected deeply by his experience of Arthur Schopenhauer's "Metaphysics of Sexual Love," which places sex at the center of the phenomenal universe, and Friedrich Wilhelm Nietzsche's works, probably including *The Birth of Tragedy*, which sees Greek tragedy as the result of creative tension between Apollonian rationalism and Dionysian ecstasy. Lawrence's prophetic voice had begun to whisper.

While his mother's slow death gradually disengaged him from her domination, Lawrence tried to weave his early concerns of class, love, and religion into an organic whole. Once he recovered from his own severe illness late in 1911, he looked toward new physical and creative horizons, and after his elopement with Frieda he at last was able to complete *Sons and Lovers* in a new affirmation of life. There were, however, characteristic growing pains. Frieda's aristocratic connections in Germany afforded him the social position that he, like his mother, had always envied while decrying its values, and he delighted in using his wife's baronial stationery at the same time that he was undergoing inevitable agonies at her cavalier disregard for sexual fidelity. The first book of Lawrence's *Unrhyming Poems*, *Look! We Have Come Through!*, records the resolution of his complicated marital relationship in a form completely liberated from Georgian poetic convention. During World War I, Lawrence tried to locate man's vital meaning in a balance of power between love and friendship, replacing the God he had lost with the human values promised by his *The Rainbow* and the four-part sexual harmony of *Women in Love*.

After the debacle of *The Rainbow*, Lawrence's social message became more strident. From 1917 to 1925, rapt in his dream of human regeneration—now fixed upon the figure of a patriarchal political leader—Lawrence went to the ends of the civilized earth. The fiction that he produced during that period urges progressively more primitivistic reorganizations of society, culminating in a faintly ridiculous neo-Aztec pantheon imposed upon Mexico in *The Plumed Serpent*, a novel embedding Lawrence's highest hopes in stubbornly incantatory verse and sometimes turgid prose.

At the midpoint of his career, a substantial conflict was brewing between Lawrence's urge for social reform and his prophetic sense of responsibility. The religious voice was clear in the poems of *Birds, Beasts and Flowers*, where, as Vivian de Sola Pinto has observed, "the common experience is transformed and invested with mythical grandeur." Such a stirring transmutation proved incompatible with the "down-to-earth Midlands voice" calling for political answers to social questions. By 1923, possibly with memories of Nietzsche and Schopenhauer, Lawrence had defined his "simple trinity" as "the emotions, the mind, and then the children of this venerable pair, ideas." Lawrence also insisted that God's traditional position relative to human beings had changed, so that Christ could no longer serve as the pathway to the Father; the Holy Ghost would have to lead human beings to a "new living relation," nothing less than the spiritual regeneration that Lawrence hoped to bring to mankind from the wreckage of modern Western civilization.

When Lawrence collapsed upon completing *The Plumed Serpent*, he was forced to abandon his old dream of social rebirth through politically enforced primitivism. In the poetic "The Flying Fish" he announced that the Indian's "primeval day" and the white man's mechanism "nullified each other." Now, as de Sola Pinto remarked, Lawrence's "ecstasy controlled by the rational imagination" produced memorable poetry in *Birds, Beasts and Flowers*, foreshadowing the affirmation of life eternal that Lawrence finally was to achieve.

Lawrence's irritation with Western materialism erupted once more late in his life in the angry little poems that he called his *Pansies* and *Nettles*, glimpses of man's stupidity, conceit, and boorishness encapsulated in stinging doggerel. Hardly his finest poetic achievement, these poems nevertheless represent more than a sick man's impatience with human frailty. They also demonstrate a quality of Lawrence's insight that he called "quickness," "the breath of the moment, and one eternal moment easily contradicting the next eternal moment."

By 1928, already gravely ill, Lawrence had turned almost completely to examining "the pang of extinction that is also liberation," the paradox, as he saw it, of physical death. His prophetic voice far outstripped the satiric note as he painted and wrote in the familiar archetypes of the Garden of Eden, regained, he felt now, through the apocalypse of death. His three original themes had coalesced into a great hymn of man's essential renewal, the "religion of wonder" that he had glimpsed in the Etruscans: "The whole universe lived; and the business of man was himself to live amid it all." Lawrence paid a heavy price for restoring man to Paradise, the unification of his Midlands voice and his prophetic voice in the acceptance of death as life's necessary other half. At last he was able to create a convincing myth as he had created all his work, from the ideas born of his own mind and emotions. Lawrence's *Last Poems*, like Rainer Maria Rilke's terrible and beautiful angels, burst the bubbles of reality, and Lawrence closed his poems, like his life, upon the noble vision of resurrection.

Lawrence's "biography of an emotional and inner life" begins with his *Rhyming Poems*, written between 1904 and 1912. Those he called "imaginative or fictional" he reworked twenty years later, mostly in his Midlands voice, "to say the real say," because "sometimes the hand of commonplace youth had been laid on the mouth of the demon." The subjective poems of his early years, "with the demon fuming in them smokily," were unchangeable.

One of the lessons that Lawrence had had to learn as a young poet was when to leave his "demon" alone. "Discord in Childhood," a pain-filled record of the elder Lawrences' marital combat, had originally been a long poem, and, he said, a better one. Frightened by his own creativity, Lawrence burned the first poem as a young man, although he later worked the scene into *Sons and Lovers*. Characteristically, even the preserved version connects violent human emotion with nature and its forces: "Outside the house an ash-tree hung its terrible whips," while within, "a male thong" drowned "a slender lash whistling she-delirious rage" in a "silence of blood."

A similar sensuous absorption in brutal natural forces appears in the "Miriam" poems, darkening the mood of "Renascence," which celebrates "The warm, dumb wisdom" that Lawrence learned from his "Eve." The woman was to provide his pathway to creativity, the means to his apprehension of nature, and the viewpoint of sensitivity, but for now Lawrence only received "Strange throbs" through her, as when "the sow was grabbing her litter/ With snarling red jaws"; and, as in "Virgin Youth," "We cry in the wilderness."

Later, when he lived in Croydon, Lawrence saw violent urban deformation of nature, and it nearly shattered him; in "Transformations," beauty spills continuously into decay before him as men, "feet of the rainbow," are "twisted in grief like crumpling beech-leaves," and Lawrence is left to wonder at humanity's destiny: "What are you, oh multiform?"

He began to sense an answer looming in the growing recognition of his prophetic mission. In the poem "Prophet," he proposed "the shrouded mother of a new idea . . . as she seeks her procreant groom," using familiar biblical symbolism to stress the religious aspect of his utterance. Before the "shrouded mother," "men hide their faces," the fear bred of artificial social pressures forcing them to deny the powerful enriching role of sexuality in their lives. At last, in "Dreams Old and Nascent," Lawrence called for violent social action: "to escape the foul dream of having and getting and owning." For the first time, he attempted to define his affirmation of the vital impulse: "What is life, but the swelling and shaping the dream in the flesh?"

Lawrence shaped the dream of his own "crisis of manhood, when he marrie[d] and [came] into himself" in the cycle *Look! We Have Come Through!*, attempting in these highly personal poems a crucial connection between the lives of the flesh and the spirit. Greeting physical love in intimate Imagist lyrics like "Gloire de Dijon," he passed through "the strait gate of passion" in "Paradise Re-entered," in which his typically fierce human love must be "Burned clean by remorseless hate." His religious sense, too, had already departed materially from orthodox Christianity. In the same poem, he abandoned both God and Satan "on Eternity's level/ Field," and announced, "Back beyond good and evil/ Return we," with a distinctly Nietzschean echo suggesting his burgeoning preoccupation with spiritual evolution.

From the same nontraditional quarter came the promise that Lawrence incorporated into "Song of a Man Who Has Come Through," one of the closing poems of this cycle. Lawrence willingly yielded himself up to "the wind that blows through me," "a fine wind . . . blowing the new direction of Time." The wind of his prophetic aspect, to prove at times tempestuous, was the vehicle that Lawrence hoped to use "to come at the wonder" he sensed in the act of being, and with it he fashioned the personal experiences recorded in this set of poems into *The Rainbow* and *Women in Love*.

The major poetic work of Lawrence's middle years was *Birds, Beasts and Flowers*, which R. P. Blackmur called "a religious apprehension" and de Sola Pinto has described as an "exploration of what may be called the divine otherness of non-human life." The social criticism that Lawrence vented in this volume is chiefly directed at America, "lurking among the undergrowth/ of Many-stemmed machines." Lawrence plainly confirmed his simultaneous fascination with and repulsion for "Modern, unissued, uncanny America" in "The Evening Land": "And I, who am half in love with you,/ What am I in love with?" Although Lawrence distrusted the American reliance on the machine, he saw "Dark, aboriginal eyes" in the American "idealistic skull," a "New throb," which, like his dramatic character David, he finally concluded was "the false dawn that precedes the real." The aspect of humanity that had always most repelled him, inflexible will, was even less acceptable to him in America than it had been in Europe, as he noted in "Turkey-Cock," "A raw American will, that has never been tempered by life." In several pieces of fiction, including "The Woman Who Rode Away" and *The Plumed Serpent*, he attempted to subdue that will by sheer force of primitive emotion and even compulsive self-sacrifice. Reversing that position in "Eagle in New Mexico," Lawrence candidly acknowledged the necessity of opposition to bloodthirsty will, negating his own proposal of primitivism as a remedy for modern civilization: "Even the sun in heaven can be curbed . . ./ By the life in the hearts of men." Finally, Lawrence unleashed considerable venom at "The American Eagle," which he had come to consider the symbol of civilization's disaster, "The new Proud Republic/ Based on the mystery of pride." Contradicting the very concept of political dominance by an "aristocracy of the spirit" that he had advocated for so long, Lawrence denounced the "bird of men that are masters,/ Or are you the goose that lays the . . . addled golden egg?"

None of the rancor of Lawrence's American-directed diatribes is present in the finest poetry of *Birds, Beasts and Flowers* in which de Sola Pinto finds "an affirmation of the grandeur and mystery of the life of nature." Working from a mundane incident, a visit by a poisonous Sicilian snake to his water trough on "a hot, hot day," "Snake" illustrates Lawrence the poet at his most capable, commanding a deceptively simple style, ordinary speech, and a consummate adaptation of rhythm to meaning. The resulting interior monologue evokes a passionate mythopoeic response. The snake "had come like a guest in quiet," and Lawrence described himself as "afraid," but "honoured still more/ That he should seek my hospitality." In one of Lawrence's flashes of intuitive perception, the snake "looked around like a god" before retreating through a cranny in the wall. Lawrence's "voices . . . of accursed human education" impelled him to toss a log at the creature, a petty act that he shortly regretted profoundly: "And so, I missed my chance with one of the lords of life." "Snake" realizes a striking balance between mind and emotion, penetrating the mystery of civilized man's destruction of nature and eclipsing the conventional Christian symbolism of Evil Incarnate. In the snake's deathly potential, too, is the premonition that "the lords of life are the masters of death," an insight not developed fully until Lawrence had returned to Europe.

Still closer than "Snake" to expressing man's most archetypal need, the yearning after life renewed, Lawrence's "Almond Blossom" opens "a heart of delicate super-faith/ [in] . . . The rusty swords of almond-trees." Much of Lawrence's poetry has been assailed for supposed incoherence of utterance and Whitmanesque repetitiousness, but in "Almond Blossom," de Sola Pinto notes, Lawrence is "thinking in images." Lawrence's old Christian path to God, "The Gethsemane blood," bursts now into "tenderness of bud," a splendid annunciation of "A naked tree of blossom, like a bridegroom bathing in dew." The "new living relation" of man with God which Lawrence was proclaiming in his philosophical essays now assumed fulfillment in an emboldened image that merged social consciousness, love, and religion: "Think, to stand there in full-unfolded nudity, smiling,/ With all the snow-wind, and the sun-glare, and the dog-star baying epithalamion."

There is a marked shift in tone from *Birds, Beasts and Flowers* to the following volumes of poems, *Pansies* and *Nettles*. In *Pansies*, Lawrence was immediately accused of obscenity for using "the *old* words [Lawrence's italics], that belong to the body below the navel." Those who knew him intimately, like Frieda, often referred to him as a puritan in sexual matters, and a purpose far different from obscenity motivated both his *Pansies* and *Nettles*; he had a stern, almost Calvinistic urge to destroy what he considered genuine pornography, "the impudent and dirty mind[s]" that had condemned *Lady Chatterley's Lover*. Lawrence had never been a patient man, and his Introduction to *Pansies* is one of his most savage jeremiads: "In the name of piety and purity, what a mass of disgusting insanity is spoken and written." Such social "insanity" was his greatest enemy, and he fought the mob "in order to keep sane and to keep society sane." His chief weapon was a hard-edged Swiftian wit that did not shrink from the scatological to make a point. In *Pansies*, Lawrence assailed most of the sacred cows of his time: censorship, "heavy breathing of the dead men"; "our bald-headed consciousness"; "narrow-gutted superiority"; the "Oxford cuckoos"; "ego-perverted love"; even "elderly discontented women."

His short series of *Nettles* must have stung his detractors even more viciously. In "13,000 People," a poem on the public reaction to the brief exhibition of his paintings abruptly terminated by British police, he flailed the "lunatics looking . . . where a fig-leaf might have been, but was not." He even figuratively neutered his "little Critics": "brought up by their Aunties/ who . . . had them fixed to save them from undesirable associations."

Despite his ferocity when assaulting social "insanity," the unhealthy forces of repression and censorship, Lawrence was still approaching a positive solution for modern man's woes in both *Pansies* and *Nettles*. In the little poem "God" in *Pansies*, he declared: "Where sanity is/ there God is," linking his own beliefs to the Supreme Being. He also dedicated several of the longer *Pansies* (*pensées*, or even heartsease, he had suggested in the Introduction) to the Risen Lord, the new subjective path to God by which man could serve as his own Savior: "A sun will rise in me,/ I shall slowly resurrect." In "More Pansies," a still later group, Lawrence came even nearer the mystery of man's being, identifying the Holy Ghost as "the deepest part of our own consciousness/ wherein . . . we know our dependence on the creative beyond." Finally, as Lawrence struggled both in his poems and in his philosophic essays with the immensity of his apocalyptic vision, his satiric voice became only an overtone of the religious message he was attempting to enunciate. That message sprang from his "strange joy/ in a great [new] . . . adventure."

None of the poetry that Lawrence wrote during his life became him more than the *Last Poems*, which he wrote while leaving it. In his final prose work, *Apocalypse*, he was still clinging to the physical life he had celebrated so long and so rapturously, but in the *Last Poems* Lawrence was setting out gladly into a new country whose borders he had glimpsed in *Etruscan Places*, his vivid sense of place even capturing the paradoxical "delight of the underworld" in ancient tombs, "deep and sincere honour rendered to the dead and to the mysteries."

In "Bavarian Gentians," Lawrence powerfully enlarged the mythic role of nature's archetypes of resurrection as he descended into the "new adventure": "Reach me a gentian, bring me a torch!" Previously concentrating on Eve as man's mediatrix with Paradise Regained, Lawrence now saw woman as symbolic Persephone, "a voice . . . pierced with the passions of dense gloom." The image of biblical mystical marriage could satisfy him no longer, and

Lawrence now looked toward the mythic "splendour of torches of darkness, shedding darkness on the lost bride and her groom."

With the relatively minor exceptions of poems dealing with the symbols of his *Apocalypse* and a few more prickly observations on man's social vicissitudes, *Last Poems* represents the birth pangs of Lawrence's incomplete poetic masterpiece, "The Ship of Death." He had seen a little model ship in an Etruscan tomb and it had carried his imagination toward the possibility of one long poetic testament, where, as Richard Aldington suggests, "suffering and the agony of departure are turned into music and reconciliation." The extant fragments of Lawrence's radiant vision center on a new concept in his stormy artistry, the peace of a soul fulfilled at last in its greatest adventure: "the long and painful death/ that lies between the old self and the new." Lawrence's long struggles with the nightmares of man's collective insanity were finally over, and he had "come through" his early preoccupations with the stresses of class and love and even religion, finding again within himself the possibility of a new dimension of human perception. At last body and mind, life and death had become one for him, "filling the heart with peace."

Lawrence's poetic development from conventional Georgian verse to mythopoeic vision spanned only the first thirty years of the twentieth century, yet his ultimate vision approaches the universal. In his "moments of greatness," far from a willfully obscene *Weltbild*, he opens a breathtaking vista of the potential of the human condition in its entirety, not only body, not merely soul, but a creativity as vital as the Greek tragedy that Nietzsche had earlier proclaimed as the result of Apollonian-Dionysian tension. Lawrence's occasional Midlands lapses from literary propriety seem a small enough price to pay for the validity and vitality of his finest poetry, described best in the tenderly honest words of his fellow poet Rainer Maria Rilke: "act[s] of reverence toward life."

Mitzi M. Brunsdale

Other major works

LONG FICTION: *The White Peacock*, 1911; *The Trespasser*, 1912; *Sons and Lovers*, 1913; *The Rainbow*, 1915; *Women in Love*, 1920; *The Lost Girl*, 1920; *Aaron's Rod*, 1922; *Kangaroo*, 1923; *The Boy in the Bush*, 1924 (with M. L. Skinner); *The Plumed Serpent*, 1926; *Lady Chatterley's Lover*, 1928; *The Virgin and the Gipsy*, 1930; *Lady Chatterley's Lover*, 1932 (abridged); *The First Lady Chatterley*, 1944; *John Thomas and Lady Jane*, 1972 (second draft of *Lady Chatterley's Lover*); *Mr. Noon*, 1984 (wr. 1920-1922).

SHORT FICTION: *The Prussian Officer and Other Stories*, 1914; *England, My England*, 1922; *The Ladybird*, 1923 (in the United States, *The Captain's Doll*); *St. Mawr: Together with The Princess*, 1925; *The Woman Who Rode Away*, 1928; *The Escaped Cock*, 1929 (later *The Man Who Died*); *Love Among the*

Haystacks, 1930; *The Lovely Lady and Other Stories,* 1933; *The Tales,* 1933; *A Modern Lover,* 1934; *The Complete Short Stories of D. H. Lawrence,* 1955, 1961; *The Escaped Cock,* 1973 (with new material).

PLAYS: *The Widowing of Mrs. Holroyd,* 1914; *Touch and Go,* 1920; *David,* 1926; *The Plays,* 1933; *A Collier's Friday Night,* 1934; *The Complete Plays of D. H. Lawrence,* 1965.

NONFICTION: *Study of Thomas Hardy,* 1914; *Twilight in Italy,* 1916; *Movements in European History,* 1921; *Psychoanalysis and the Unconscious,* 1921; *Sea and Sardinia,* 1921; *Fantasia of the Unconscious,* 1922; *Studies in Classic American Literature,* 1923; *Reflections on the Death of a Porcupine and Other Essays,* 1925; *Mornings in Mexico,* 1927; *Pornography and Obscenity,* 1929; *Assorted Articles,* 1930; *A Propos of Lady Chatterley's Lover,* 1930; *Apocalypse,* 1931; *Etruscan Places,* 1932; *The Letters of D. H. Lawrence,* 1932 (Aldous Huxley, editor); *Phoenix: The Posthumous Papers of D. H. Lawrence,* 1936 (Edward McDonald, editor); *The Collected Letters,* 1962 (2 volumes; Harry T. Moore, editor); *Phoenix II: Uncollected, Unpublished and Other Prose Works,* 1968 (Harry T. Moore and Warren Roberts, editors); *The Cambridge Edition of the Letters and Works of D. H. Lawrence,* 1979 and continuing.

Bibliography

Balbert, Peter, and Phillip L. Marcus, eds. *D. H. Lawrence: A Centenary Consideration.* Ithaca, N.Y.: Cornell University Press, 1985. Balbert and Marcus gather a collection of essays of leading scholars on concerns that Lawrence's writings continue to raise. Includes a chronology and directions for further reading.

Burgess, Anthony. *Flame into Being: The Life and Work of D. H. Lawrence.* London; Heinemann, 1985. Although primarily a novelist, Burgess has also written studies of other writers. Because he begins from a writer's point of view, his approaches are extraordinarily accessible and readable. This is the best single work on Lawrence, full of incisive insights. Contains no index, and the bibliography is limited to the memoirs.

Kermode, Frank. *D. H. Lawrence.* New York: Viking Press, 1973. In this study, a major literary critic presents an introduction that far surpasses most volumes of this type. Kermode surveys Lawrence's life and provides introductions to all the major works that are both informative and illuminating. A good first reference. Includes a complete index and a good introductory bibliography.

Meyers, Jeffrey. *D. H. Lawrence: A Biography.* New York: Alfred A. Knopf, 1990. This excellent "popular" biography covers all aspects of Lawrence's life and times and opens up new areas of investigation, especially as far as Lawrence's personal relationships are concerned. Augmented by a full index and a detailed bibliography.

Moore, Harry T. *The Priest of Love.* Rev. ed. New York: Farrar, Straus &

Giroux, 1974. Although rather scholarly in some respects—the literary discussions are sometimes sophisticated—Moore's work is a solid biography that is particularly effective in examining Lawrence's working-class background. It offers a substantial index and a bibliography, but it is especially useful for the supplementary material in the appendices, illustrations, and maps.

Sagar, Keith. *A D. H. Lawrence Handbook.* New York: Barnes & Noble Books, 1982. Although not the standard literary handbook, this study is an unusually useful reference book. In addition to the customary bibliography and directions for further readings, it offers materials on mining regions and practices, social background, chronology in relation to world events, films and sound recordings, dialects, and maps.

Squires, Michael, and Keith Cushman. *The Challenge of D. H. Lawrence.* Madison: University of Wisconsin Press, 1990. Gathered in this volume are fifteen essays by leading scholars who were asked to provide fresh responses to recurrent topics in Lawrence's criticism. The essays cover most of the major issues in his life and work, and are regularly thought-provoking.

LAYAMON

Born: Unknown. Flourished, probably in North Worcestershire, England;
c. 1200
Died: Unknown

Principal poetry
Brut, c. 1205.

Other literary forms
Layamon is known only as the author of the partially translated poetic
chronicle known as Layamon's *Brut*.

Achievements
Layamon's *Brut*, which J. S. P. Tatlock describes as "the nearest thing we
have to a traditional racial Epic," is the first major literary work in Middle
English, and the first version in English of the stories of King Arthur and of
King Lear. Assessing Layamon's achievement is difficult because his *Brut* is
a much expanded translation of Wace's *Roman de Brut* (c. 1155), itself an
Anglo-Norman translation and expansion of Geoffrey of Monmouth's *Historia regum Britanniae* (c. 1136, *History of the Kings of Britain*). Consequently,
it is necessary first to briefly describe these earlier versions and the influence
they are known to have exerted.

Geoffrey of Monmouth, writing in Latin in about 1136, constructed a pseudo-
history of the British (as opposed to the Anglo-Saxon) kings of England, beginning with the legendary Brutus (a grandson of Aeneas), continuing through
the celebrated reign of King Arthur, and ending with the last British kings in
the seventh century. The primary effect of Geoffrey's *History of the Kings of
Britain* was to stimulate international interest in the legends of Arthur, which
previously had been well-known only to the Welsh and Breton peoples. Geoffrey's *History of the Kings of Britain* and the *Prophecies of Merlin* which
make up its seventh book were translated in places as far away as Iceland.
Centuries later, in Elizabethan times, Geoffrey's *History of the Kings of Britain* would be rediscovered by the Tudor kings, who wished to stress their
ancient Welsh claims to the throne. As part of this new interest, the *History
of the Kings of Britain* would provide subject matter for Edmund Spenser
and William Shakespeare. Spenser devotes a canto of *The Faerie Queene*
(1590, 1596, Book II, Canto X) to a "Chronicle of British Kings," based on
Geoffrey and derivative histories, such as Raphael Holinshed's *Chronicles*
(1577). For his tragedy of *King Lear* (c. 1605-1606), Shakespeare consulted
both Holinshed's and Spenser's versions. There he found the basic plot outline, including the opening love test, Lear's progressive humiliation by Goneril
and Regan, and his eventual redemption (restoration in Geoffrey's *History of*

the Kings of Britain) by Cordelia and the duke of France. To these elements Shakespeare added the parallel subplots of Gloucester, Kent, and the Fool, and he rearranged the ending in a masterful fashion typical of his treatment of source materials.

The influence of Geoffrey's *History of the Kings of Britain* on medieval Arthurian literature was primarily by way of the Anglo-Norman translation by Wace. Wace's courtly version in octosyllabic couplets motivated and stylistically influenced his immediate successors, Chrétien de Troyes, Marie de France, and Thomas of Britain. More substantial use of his subject matter was made by fourteenth century prose romancers, in the Vulgate *Merlin* and the *Morte Arthure*. The latter work was a major source for Thomas Malory's *Le Morte d'Arthur* (c. 1469), and thus one can trace a circuitous route from the first to the last of the great Middle English Arthurians. Malory also made use of the alliterative *Morte Arthure*, perhaps the Arthurian work closest in spirit and substance to Layamon's *Brut*. Even this product of the alliterative revival, however, is thought to be based not on Layamon but on Wace, or perhaps on the fourteenth century translation of Wace by Robert Mannyng of Brunne. Among medieval works, only Robert of Gloucester's chronicle (in its later recension, c. 1340) can confidently be said to have made direct use of Layamon's *Brut*.

Even though his chronicle, which survives in only two manuscripts, represented something of a dead end in the development of Arthurian legend, Layamon has been rediscovered in the nineteenth and twentieth centuries. Both Alfred, Lord Tennyson and Ezra Pound made demonstrable use of Layamon's poetic style. Linguists continue to study the *Brut*'s early, more highly inflected dialect, and stylistic critics remain fascinated by its poetic form, which lies somewhere between the formulaic, alliterative meter of Anglo-Saxon poetry and the developing meter of the Middle English rhymed romances. This century's major contribution to Layamon scholarship, however, is the new edition by G. L. Brook and R. F. Leslie. Interested readers would be well advised to consult the introduction and notes to this edition when the third and final volume appears.

Biography

All the known details concerning Layamon's life are derived from the opening section of his *Brut*, the first five lines of which read as follows (in Madden's translation, which includes the significant manuscript variants):

> There was a priest on earth, (or in the land,) who was named Layamon; he was son of Leovenath (Leuca),—may the Lord be gracious to him!—he dwelt at Ernley, at a noble church (with the good knight,) upon Severns bank (Severn),—good (pleasant) it there seemed to him—near Radestone, where he books read.

The author's name, which has been spelled in a number of ways, is Scandinavian in origin, and is cognate with modern English "Lawman." The recorded variant spellings of his father's name are less confusing when one realizes that the scribe often writes "u" for "v"; "Levca" can then be seen as a shortened form of "Leovenath." Tatlock hypothesizes, in light of the familiarity with Ireland that Layamon exhibits in his poem, that perhaps Leovenath went to Ireland with the Norman invading force, married a Scandinavian Irishwoman (there having been a sizable Viking population in Ireland at that time), and later returned to England with his son. In any case, the only residence Layamon himself mentions is a church at "Ernley" on the banks of the Severn near "Radestone." These details accord well with a village variously referred to as Lower Areley, Areley Kings, and Areley Regis, not far from Worcester and the Welsh border. The books that Layamon mentions as having read (line 5) have usually been taken to be service books that he used in his role as a priest. Despite attempts to find the man behind these few details, however, Layamon remains little more than a name, an occupation (priest and translator), and a place-name. Even the time in which he "flourished" is derived from the supposed date of composition of the *Brut*, which is itself undergoing a reevaluation.

Analysis

In order to analyze Layamon's *Brut*, it is first necessary to continue the discussion of his sources. As mentioned above, Layamon's main source was Wace's *Roman de Brut*, which in the edition that Madden consulted consisted of 15,300 lines, as opposed to the 32,350 lines in his edition of Layamon's *Brut*. Granted that Madden's lines (now termed half-lines) are shorter than the lines in Wace, it is still apparent that Layamon considerably expanded his main source. It has been suggested that Layamon may have used an already expanded version of Wace, which had been conflated with an earlier chronicle (now lost) by Gaimar. As this suggestion cannot be verified, however, most critics have looked elsewhere for supplementary sources. One recent modification in this matter of primary sources is the discovery that some of the material previously considered original in Wace derives instead from an extant "variant version" of Geoffrey. Furthermore, additions occurring in a Welsh version of Geoffrey are paralleled in Layamon.

Layamon in his Preface mentions two works in addition to Wace: "the English book that Saint Bede made," and another book "in Latin, that Saint Albin made, and the fair Austin." Bede's best-known work, and the work potentially of the most use to Layamon, is his *Historia Ecclesiastica Genta Anglorum* (c. 732, *Ecclesiastical History of the English Peoples*), written in Latin and later translated into Anglo-Saxon. Albinus (d. 732) reportedly helped Bede to gather source materials, and so a number of critics have assumed that Layamon erroneously attributed the Old English translation to Bede, and Bede's Latin original to Albius (and to the great apostle to the

English, "Austin" or Augustine of Canterbury, d. 604). Layamon claims both to have "compressed" these three books (including Wace) into one and to have used the latter two books "as a model." This second statement is closer to the truth, for Layamon did not in fact make any incontestable use of Bede. He was probably acting in a tradition of vague citation to a previous authority; Geoffrey before him had claimed access to a certain "most ancient" source book. Nor can Layamon be shown conclusively to have drawn upon Geoffrey in the original Latin, upon classical authors, upon French Arthurians (besides Wace), or upon Welsh records. Recent evidence does suggest, however, that he was familiar with late Anglo-Saxon homiletic literature, and may even have read classical Anglo-Saxon verse in manuscript.

Presumably the forthcoming notes to Brook's edition will supplant Madden in indicating where Layamon drew neither on Wace nor on any known source; it is in these passages that one would then look for Layamon's most original work. This is not to say that these are the only passages of interest, for there is much in Layamon's retelling that adds quite a different tone to the material in Wace; such considerations will be reserved for the discussion of style, below.

The best known of Layamon's additions are those that contribute new material to Arthurian legend. Wace had made the first recorded reference to the Round Table, to which Layamon adds an account of the quarrels over precedence which led to its institution (11360ff.) To Arthur's biography, Layamon adds an account of the elvish gifts at his birth (9608ff.), a premonitory dream of his final misfortunes in the battle with Molred (13982ff.), and an expanded version of Arthur's mysterious departure to Avalon (14277ff.) Arthur as a character seems less a romance hero than a stern and successful king, feared and respected by all the kings and great knights of Europe. (Perhaps it should be noted that the better-known exploits of some of Arthur's knights, such as the Lancelot affair and the quest for the Holy Grail, do not appear in Geoffrey, Wace, or Layamon.) As for Merlin, Layamon reports more of his prophecies than Wace had done, and adds an account of his stay in the wilderness (9878ff.) that can be compared with the Welsh tales of Merlin Silvestris. A long list of Layamon's minor Arthurian additions can be found in R. H. Fletcher, *The Arthurian Material in the Chronicles* (1906).

C. Friedlander discusses additions from other parts of Layamon's *Brut* in her examination of five of its longer episodes: those of Leir, Belin and Brennes, Vortiger, Colgrim and Childric, and Penda. Here Layamon invents dialogue (as Wace had also done), adds characters and scenes, interjects comments, introduces stylistic devices, and manifests what according to Friedlander is a predominant theme: a concern with reversal in personal and national fortunes. Of the Leir episode, for example, Friedlander remarks, "The demonstration of Leir's folly and gradual enlightenment, the emphasis on materialistic values, and the pervasive consciousness of reversals in human fortune are all Layamon's contributions." Friedlander's basic contention is that the theme of reversal, the focus on a few major episodes, and the repeated use of stylistic formulas all contribute to lend to the *Brut* a greater sense of structure than is usual for the chronicle genre.

C. S. Lewis characterized Layamon as "more archaic and less sophisticated" than Wace, adding that "Wace's characters are knights and courtiers; those of the *Brut*, heroes and thanes." As an illustration he cites an interesting Arthurian passage, in which Wace's knights ascend a tower and joke gaily about the relative merits of wartime and peace. Layamon, on the other hand, first characterizes the "ancient stonework" of the tower (12419), in a motif that recalls the older Anglo-Saxon elegies. The gay debate becomes a tense exchange or "flit" (12459) that recalls the "flytings" of Anglo-Saxon and Old Icelandic narrative verse. Another "Saxon echo" frequently alluded to is found in the description of Loch Ness (10848ff.), which is populated with the same sea-creatures ("nicors") mentioned in *Beowulf* (c. 1000).

Lewis also finds Layamon "fiercer but kinder" than Wace; Tatlock comments on a pervasive delight in crushing enemies, and sees therein echoes of Irish saga literature. Also suggestive of Irish influence is Layamon's greater emphasis on the marvelous and on appearances from the world of "faery." Layamon's additions concerning Arthur's weapons and the elvish smith who forged them evoke equally Anglo-Saxon and Irish legends. Finally, Tatlock also mentions Layamon's technical familiarity with matters of seamanship, which, together with other details from medieval life, contributes to the personal stamp that Layamon puts on his material.

Layamon achieves a further degree of originality simply by virtue of the poetic form he employs. Geoffrey's *History of the Kings of Britain* is in prose, and Wace's *Roman de Brut* is in octosyllabic couplets; Layamon's *Brut* is written in a combination of alliterating and rhyming half-lines. The presence of alliteration suggests an inheritance from Anglo-Saxon verse, though not without some attendant changes. Metrically, Layamon's lines favor an iambic-trochaic rhythm rather than the predominantly trochaic rhythm of Anglo-Saxon verse. This change leads to a greater proliferation of unstressed syllables at either end of the half-line. Furthermore, alliteration seems to be more an ornament than a strictly regulated requirement in Layamon's verse.

In these aspects of form, Layamon's *Brut* resembles a few other Early Middle English poems, including some late poetic entries in the Anglo-Saxon chronicle, the "Worcester fragments," "The Grave," and "The Proverbs of Alfred." Tatlock remarks how these poems also all lack the understatement, parenthesis, and periphrasis that characterized Anglo-Saxon verse. To account for these developments, scholars have hypothesized that a less strict, more popular form of alliterative verse may have existed alongside the more refined Anglo-Saxon compositions, such as *Beowulf*, which were committed to manuscript. It may be that the tradition degenerated (partially as a result of changes in the language itself), or, again, it may be that Layamon and the others, perhaps additionally influenced by the "rhythmic alliteration" of Anglo-Saxon prose, imperfectly revived the old forms. Such a revival (variously explained) did occur in the later Middle Ages, yielding, for example, the alliterative *Morte Arthure* mentioned above.

Another feature that Layamon's *Brut* shares with the earlier Anglo-Saxon poetry is the presence of repeated lines and half-lines called *formulas*. Examples have been collected by Tatlock and Herbert Pilch, who also lists formulas that the *Brut* shares with Anglo-Saxon verse and with roughly contemporary verse. Formulas are present in much of the world's traditional narrative poetry, the recurrent epithets in Homer perhaps being the best-known examples. Earlier in the twentieth century, the Homeric scholar Milman Parry, supplementing his research with fieldwork on contemporary Yugoslavian oral epic, developed what is known as oral-formulaic theory to account for this widespread appearance of formulas. According to Parry and his student Albert Lord, formulas are learned by apprentice poets as a means whereby they may improvise long oral narratives. This theory has since been applied to Old English and some Middle English verse, even though many of Parry's original statements have had to be modified considerably. For example, Layamon as a translator is not improvising but rather working in close conjunction with a written text (even if he probably worked more "in his head" than modern poets tend to do). Why, then, would he have a need for ready-made formulas? He may instead have been using formulas ornamentally, in imitation of the earlier models, or there may have been other factors at work which made formulas desirable. Layamon seems to have been constrained to avoid ending his sentence units with the first half-line (as had often been the case in the earlier poetry). Formulas, which are more frequent in his second half-lines, may have represented a useful way to "pad out" the whole line, acting somewhat like the "rhyme tags" in metrical romances. Layamon's use of formulas differs in other ways from Anglo-Saxon practice. Fixed epithets, such as "athelest kingen" for Arthur, are more common, as are formulas that recur in similar situations, such as "wind stod an willen," often used in sea voyage descriptions.

Rhyme was likewise employed ornamentally in the Early Middle English poems mentioned above, prompting some scholars to hypothesize that rhyme was developing independently in England, probably under influence from Latin hymns. Surely the example of Wace strengthened this tendency toward the couplet, which would become the norm in rhymed romances. There may also be an Irish influence at work in Layamon's unusual rhyming by consonant classes and on contrasting stresses. Here are some sample rhyme-pairs, modernized from the episode of Arthur's final dream (13971ff.): bestride/ride; tiding/king; son/welcome; fair knight/fare tonight. The first rhyme is exact; the second example rhymes an unstressed with a stressed syllable as does the third; yet here the consonants *m* and *n* do not match, but are related instead by way of a shared phonological class ("nasals"). The last example ingeniously interweaves homonyms and rhymes.

One final stylistic element distinguishing Layamon from his Anglo-Saxon predecessors is his use of the extended simile. Arthur's pursuit of Colgrim, for example, is compared (for eight lines, 10629ff.) to a wolf hunting down a mountain goat. Most of Layamon's extended similes, in fact, occur in this part of the Arthurian section, leading scholars to suppose that a single source may be responsible for this stylistic feature. Here, as elsewhere, however, the question of sources should not be allowed to overshadow Layamon's unique achievement. The *Brut* can and should be read for its own merits, as a poem and not simply as "Arthurian matter" divorced from its particular form.

Paul Acker

Bibliography
Layamon. *Layamon's Arthur: The Arthurian Section of Layamon's Brut.* Edited by W. R. J. Barron and S. C. Weinberg. Austin: University of Texas Press, 1989. This edited translation of lines 9229-14297 of the *Brut* includes an introduction with textual notes and commentary. The editors have added modern punctuation and spelling in the literal translation. Sources are reviewed, as well as the social context of the poem and the structure. A discussion of the Arthur character as hero and the *Brut* as a national epic are revealing and interesting. Includes a bibliography.

——————————. *Selections from Layamon's Brut.* Edited by G. L. Brook. Oxford, England: Clarendon Press, 1963. The selections specifically include the events preceding Arthur's birth, his marriage, the accession and victories over the Scots, Saxons, and Irish, the origin of the Roman War and the Morte. Includes notes, an excellent glossary, an index of names, and a select, short bibliography. The short introduction and biographical note is by the noted scholar and author, C. S. Lewis.

——————————. *Layamon's Brut.* Translated by Donald G. Bzdyl. Binghamton, N.Y.: Center for Medieval and Early Renaissance Studies, 1989. This prose translation of the *Brut* is accompanied by an excellent bibliography that includes many articles and related studies. The introduction gives a good survey and appreciation of Layamon and the poem.

Le Saux, Francoise H. M. *Layamon's Brut: The Poem and Its Sources.* Cambridge, England: D. S. Brewer, 1989. This study characterizes Layamon as more than the simple parish priest, as he is so often seen. Le Saux looks at many possible sources and traditions that inform the poem. She sees Layamon as a mixture of Welsh and English cultures—the allies against the Norman invaders. Previous scholarship is reevaluated and the thematic and stylistic relationship to the sources is examined. An exhaustive bibliography is also appended.

Wace, and Layamon. *Arthurian Chronicles.* Translated by Eugene Mason. London: J. M. Dent & Sons, 1970. The introduction by Gwyn Jones traces the roots of the poems to Geoffrey of Monmouth and looks at the spread of the Arthurian legend in the twelfth century. It also contains a short biographical sketch of Layamon and a commentary on the *Brut.* A scant bibliography cites several useful chapters on the poem in survey collections.

EDWARD LEAR

Born: Holloway, England; May 12, 1812
Died: San Remo, Italy; January 29, 1888

Principal poetry

A Book of Nonsense, 1846, 1861; *Nonsense Songs, Stories, Botany and Alphabets,* 1871; *More Nonsense, Pictures, Rhymes, Botany, etc.,* 1872; *Laughable Lyrics: A Fourth Book of Nonsense Poems, Songs, Botany, Music, etc.,* 1877; *Nonsense Songs and Stories,* 1894; *Queery Leary Nonsense,* 1911 (Lady Strachey, editor); *The Complete Nonsense of Edward Lear,* 1947 (Holbrook Jackson, editor); *Teapots and Quails,* 1953 (Angus Davidson and Philip Hofer, editors).

Other literary forms

Edward Lear's verse collections include three prose stories and three prose recipes called "Nonsense Cookery." A few of his fanciful botanical drawings are accompanied by whimsical texts. Like his poems, these pieces show Lear at play with language, blithely disregarding common sense.

Two volumes of letters, most of them to Chichester Fortescue, were published in 1907 and 1911. Enlivened by riddles, cartoons, and bits of verse, they demonstrate Lear's fascination with the sound and meaning of words. He uses puns and creative phonetic spellings; he coins words and humorously distorts existing ones. A cold January day in Corfu is so "icicular" that it "elicits the ordibble murmurs of the cantankerous Corcyreans." He complains of the proliferation of tourists, especially "Germen, Gerwomen, and Gerchildren," around his property in San Remo. Although he often revealed his loneliness and depression, Lear characteristically found something to laugh about—if not in his situation, then in his response to it: he called himself "savage and black as 90,000 bears," and wished he were "an egg and was going to be hatched." In 1883 he wrote, "I sometimes wish that I myself were a bit of gleaming granite or pomegranite or a poodle or a pumkin"; at seventy-one and in ill health, Lear's imperishable delight in wordplay pulled him out of self-pity.

He kept journals of his painting excursions; these were later published with his own illustrations. Lacking the warmth and spontaneity of the letters, these topographical and travel books are valuable to readers who relish pictorial description and wish to know the conditions of travel in the nineteenth century.

Achievements

Lear thought of himself as a topographical landscape painter, but he is best known for the verses and cartoons he created to entertain children. He popularized the form which came to be known as the limerick. His innovative comic drawings have influenced many artists, notably James Thurber. Lear's ornithological drawings are highly regarded, and students of nineteenth century painting also admire his watercolor drawings—pen or pencil sketches executed out-of-doors and later elaborated and colored. Even so, his reputation as an author has overshadowed his painting. Known as the father of nonsense literature, Lear has never been surpassed in that genre. Charles L. Dodgson (Lewis Carroll) had the opportunity to learn from Lear, and Lear may have learned from him; however, Carroll's nonsense verse is much different: funnier, more intellectual, and less musical. Lear was a true poet, keenly sensitive to the sounds and "colors" of words. His poems have lasted not only because they are amusing and melodious but also because they express the innocence, melancholy, and exuberance of Lear himself.

Biography

Edward Lear was the twentieth of twenty-one children born to Jeremiah and Ann (Skerrett) Lear. Financial difficulties led to the dispersal of the family; although the Lears were later reunited, from 1816 Edward was looked after by his oldest sister, Ann. She was devoted to him and encouraged his interest in reading and painting, but the near-sighted, homely, rather morbid child brooded over being rejected, as he saw it, by his mother. His diary alludes mysteriously to another early trauma, perhaps a homosexual assault. His inclination to isolate himself grew after the onset of epilepsy (he called it his "demon") when he was five years old. He always felt that he was not like other people.

At fifteen he was earning his own living as a draftsman. Within five years, his skill in drawing birds brought him to the attention of Lord Stanley (later the thirteenth Earl of Derby), who invited him to Knowsley to make drawings of his private menagerie. There he made acquaintances who would become lifelong patrons and began to create comical verses and drawings to amuse his host's children.

In 1837, the Earl sent him to Italy to recover his health and to study landscape painting. From that time England was no longer his permanent home. Lear traveled throughout the Mediterranean world and lived in several places, explaining his wandering by saying that his health required a temperate climate, that he needed to make sketches as "studies" for his oil paintings, and that he must support himself by making his work available to wealthy tourists. His restlessness also suggests that he was searching for, and perhaps trying to avoid, something: an all-consuming interest.

Amazingly industrious even by Victorian standards, Lear generally spent most of his day sketching or painting; in leisure hours he read widely and taught himself a half-dozen languages. Hard work seemed to help ward off depression and epileptic attacks but did not prevent his being lonely. For thirty years his only constant companion was his Albanian servant, Giorgio

Kokali, to whom Lear showed extraordinary kindness and loyalty. While busily preparing one set of illustrations for a travel book and another for a volume of natural history, he decided to publish the series of limericks he had begun at Knowsley. His painting gave him less satisfaction than his nonsense verse, which he wrote for the children of friends and for other youngsters he met in hotels and aboard ships. His verse became a vehicle for self-expression, while painting all too often meant drudgery and frustration. Upon receiving a legacy at the age of thirty-seven, he studied for a time at the Royal Academy, as if hoping to win recognition as a serious artist. Lear apparently had small regard for the watercolor drawings he produced by the hundreds: they were "pot-boilers" and "tyrants" that required much time yet brought little money. Although he sometimes sold large landscapes in oil and received modest sums for his books, he often worried about his finances and had to rely on the patronage of wealthy friends.

Lear tried to be independent, but he constantly suffered from loneliness. He maintained a voluminous correspondence with scores of friends, sometimes rising early to write as many as thirty-five letters before breakfast. Occasionally he expressed wonder that "this child," an odd, moody fellow, should have so many friends. He confided in a few—Chichester Fortescue, Franklin Lushington, and Emily Tennyson (his ideal woman)—but even to them he could not reveal his dark memories or speak of his "demon." More than once he considered marriage but could never bring himself to propose, despite evidence that Augusta Bethell would have accepted him. Terrified of rejection, this charming and lovable man told himself and his confidants that he was too crotchety, ugly, poor, and sickly to be a good husband. Another impediment of which he may have been conscious was his tendency to homosexuality. His response to Lushington, a kind but undemonstrative person, can only be called passionate; for several years he fretted over Lushington's inability to give and receive affection. Emotional and spiritual intimacy were what he most craved, however, and his relationship with Lushington eventually became mutually satisfying. Throughout his adult years, Lear seems to have been happiest in the company of children.

Haunted by a sense of failure and determined to put an end to his wandering, in 1871 he moved into a house he had built in San Remo. Yet he traveled to India after his sixtieth birthday, making hundreds of drawings, and talked of going a second time. His last years were darkened by loneliness, illness, and a series of disappointments. He finally lost the will to work when his eyesight failed and he was near collapse. None of his friends was with him when he died.

Analysis

According to Edward Lear himself, he adopted the form for his limericks— or "nonsense rhymes," as he called them—from "There was a sick man of

Tobago," published in *Anecdotes and Adventures of Fifteen Gentlemen* (c. 1822). Most of them begin with this formula: "There was an Old Man [or Old Person, Young Lady] of [place name]." The last line is nearly the same as the first, with Lear typically using an adjective (sometimes appropriate, sometimes whimsical) before the character's designation. Each limerick is accompanied by a cartoon of its main character in action—riding a goose, sitting in a tree, refusing to respond sensibly to a sensible question. More than three-quarters of the limericks concern old people; even some of those called "young" in the texts appear elderly in the drawings. Most of Lear's folk are eccentrics. One old man runs through town carrying squealing pigs; another will eat nothing but roots. Physical oddities such as very long legs or huge eyes are common. Several characters with noses even more prodigious than Lear's deal variously with that handicap: one hires an old woman to carry it, another allows birds to roost on it, while a third adamantly denies that his nose is long. Lear's intended audience, children of the Victorian age, were surely amused not just by his characters' oddness but also by the fact that these laughable people were supposed to be "grown-ups."

Lear often found humor in incongruity and arbitrariness. An old man of Dunrose, "melancholy" because his nose has been "seized" by a parrot half as large as himself, is said to be "soothed" upon learning that the bird's name is Polly. A few characters suffer terrible ends—drowning, suicide, choking on food, death from despair, being baked in a cake. Yet even their situations are amusing; either the text indicates that these people somehow deserve their fate, or the poem or cartoon indicates that they are not distressed by it. For example, the "courageous" Young Lady of Norway, flattened by a door, asks, "What of that?"

Lear's avowed purpose was to write "nonsense pure and absolute" for the amusement of "little folks." Consciously or not, he also dramatized the conflict between the individual and society. Even children must have noticed how often the limericks' heroes and heroines were at odds with the people around them. In Brill, Melrose, Parma, Buda, Columbia, and Thermopylae, and other real-world settings specified by Lear, "they"—representatives of Respectable Society—stare, turn aside, express disapproval, offer unwanted advice, and punish. A man who "dance[s] a quadrille with a Raven" is "smashed" by his countrymen; so is the fellow who constantly plays his gong. A fat man is stoned by the children of Chester. The reader is not surprised that one old man has "purchased a steed, which he rode at full speed,/ And escaped from the people of Basing." Aldous Huxley called Lear a "profound social philosopher" for his portrayal of the consequences of nonconformity (*On the Margin*, 1928). Lear's touch, however, was always light; even the limericks containing violence or death are not sad or horrific.

The eccentrics are more likely to be friendly with animals than with other human beings. They live with birds, ride bears, play music for pigs, and try to teach fishes to walk—but they can also be attacked by insects, bulls, and dogs (Lear was terrified of dogs). Apparently, being truly alive is a lonely, risky affair. Accidents, physical and mental afflictions, and rejection by others, all in the nature of things, seem especially likely for the person who is different from his neighbors. Yet, unpredictably, "they" are sometimes solicitous and considerate, inquiring about the comfort of some irascible characters, warning others of imminent danger. "They" treat a depressed man by feeding him salad and singing to him; "they" glue together a hapless fellow "split quite in two" by a fall from a horse. Lear's society, then, is committed to maintaining order and the general well-being—if necessary, at the expense of people who behave in ways "they" do not approve and cannot understand. This is the world we know. Without the preachiness of much contemporary children's literature—or rather, literature written for the edification of children—the limericks convey that civil, mannerly behavior is expected. From Lear's perspective, as from the child's, adult judgments appear arbitrary. For some reason, or no reason, "they" are delighted with a girl named Opsibeena who rides a pig; "they" seem less likely to appreciate innovation than to encourage decorum, however meaningless: one man ingratiates himself with his neighbors by sitting in his cellar under an umbrella.

The nonsense songs are set in an imagined world in which animals and objects talk, sing, and dance with one another. Some of these characters are heroes; others are bored and lonely misfits. Like Lear, an early admirer of Lord Byron, they seek happiness in love, companionship, and travel. Odd friendships and courtships, mysterious events, and unexpected reversals abound. Lear has created a world in which anything wonderful may happen. The rules of decorum do not apply, do not exist. An owl marries a pussycat, and the Poker woos the Shovel. The title characters in "The Daddy Long-Legs and the Fly," unwelcome in polite society, sail away to "the great Gromboolian Plain," where they spend their days at "battlecock and shuttledoor." Disgusted with idleness, a Nutcracker and a Sugar-tongs ride off on stolen ponies, never to return—ignoring the protests of their household companions. Less adventurous, a perambulating table and chair ask some friendly animals to lead them safely home. Most successful in their quest are the Jumblies of the green heads and blue hands. Despite the warnings of "all their friends" (akin to the limericks' "they"), the Jumblies go to sea in a sieve, discover "the Lakes, and the Torrible Zone,/ and the hills of the Chankly Bore," and return home after twenty years to be lionized by their neighbors. Unlike most of Lear's songs, "The Jumblies" has no undercurrent of melancholy or dread.

A wanderer for most of his life, Lear often wished for (but doubted that he really wanted) a home with a wife and children. His "laughable lyrics," which sometimes poke fun at the conventional sex roles, courtship rituals, and marriage, reveal that he was ambivalent about committing himself to a woman. As George Orwell remarked in his essay "Nonsense Poetry," "It is easy to guess that there was something seriously wrong in [Lear's] sex life" (*Shooting an Elephant and Other Essays*, 1950). More recent critics, reading nonsense literature as a manifestation of the author's repressed emotions, have noted that it is the pussycat, not the owl, who proposes matrimony; judging by Lear's cartoon, the owl is somewhat afraid of his bride. Again, a duck (a cigar-smoking female) talks a rather effeminate kangaroo into letting her ride around the world on his tail. Deserted by the girl he loves, the sorrowful title character in "The Dong with a Luminous Nose" wanders in lonely frustration; at night his great red nose, illuminated by a lamp "All fenced about/ With a bandage stout," is visible for miles. In pre-Freudian times this poem was surely "laughable" in a simpler way than it is now. The hero of "The Courtship of the Yonghy-Bonghy-Bò" proposes to a married woman; when she regretfully refuses him, he flees to "the sunset isles of Boshen" to live alone. Remaining in Coromandel, "where the early pumpkins blow," the lady "weeps, and daily moans." So romantic and comical an ending would have been impossible if the Bò had offered himself to a woman who was free to marry him. "The Courtship of the Yonghy-Bonghy-Bò," one of the songs for which Lear composed a piano accompaniment, uses the verbal music of repetition, assonance, and alliteration. Indeed, in this and other songs he achieves a lyricism reminiscent of the Romantic poets. Parodying the Romantic manner as he made verse out of personal concerns and fantasies, he was looking for a way to deal with his emotions. He once burst into tears while singing the song, written while he struggled to make up his mind about marrying "Gussie" Bethell.

To the Nutcrackers and Sugar-tongs, domesticity—perhaps the most sacred of Victorian ideals—is a "stupid existence." Home is sweet only to the timo-rous table and chair, the phobia-ridden Discobboloses, and the cautious Spikky Sparrows. Mr. and Mrs. Sparrow don human clothing, ostensibly to protect themselves from catching cold but actually, it seems, to "look like other people." Lear does portray some happy and admirable couples. In "The Pelican Chorus," King and Queen Pelican sing of their present joys and recall their daughter's courtship by the King of the Cranes. They are content, even though they realize that they will probably never see Daughter Dell again. A less skillful poet would have allowed the song to become maudlin or merely ridiculous, but Lear maintains a balance of melancholy, nostalgia, and humor. He reveals the singers' pride in their "lovely leathery throats and chins" and pleasure in the "flumpy sound" their feet make as they dance. (This kind of music is impossible for the crane who, it is whispered, "has got no webs between his toes.") They complacently visualize Dell's "waddling form so fair,/ With a wreath of shrimps in her short white hair." The old pelicans' confusion—or fusion—of past and present is at once amusing and poignant; each stanza ends with this refrain:

> Ploffskin, Pluffskin, Pelican jee,

We think no Birds so happy as we!
Plumpskin, Ploshkin, Pelican jill,
We think so then, and we thought so still!

"Mr. and Mrs. Discobbolos," another poem about a family, ends with what must be described as an entertaining catastrophe. For twenty years this couple lives in peaceful isolation atop a wall—because they are afraid of falling off. Then, quite suddenly, the wife begins to fret because their "six fine boys" and "six sweet girls" are missing the pleasures and opportunities of social intercourse. Disgusted, perhaps driven mad, Mr. Discobbolos slides to the ground and dynamites home and family "into thousands of bits to the sky so blue." One feels that he has done the right thing, even though his action is surprising and mysterious. Possibly he cannot endure mixing once again with conventional society or thinking that any of his children may marry such a "runcible goose" as his wife. Perhaps the poet is once again exploding the myth of the happy home. The attempt to make sense out of exquisite nonsense is part of the pleasure of reading Lear.

No doubt he exposed more of his hopes and fears than he intended. Some of the songs, especially those written late in his life, involve the emotions in a way that the limericks do not. Since the poet sympathizes with the pain and joy of these creatures of fantasy, so does the reader. Two works published posthumously are clearly autobiographical. Lear's last ballad, "Incidents in the Life of My Uncle Arly," is a formal imitation of "The Lady of Shalott" which tells of the wanderings and death of a poor and lonely man. At last "they" bury him with a railway ticket (representing Lear's freedom and rootlessness) and his sole companion, a "pea-green Cricket" (symbolic, perhaps, of the poet's inspiration to make music of his own experience). Lear, the "Adopty Duncle" of many children, states four times that the hero's shoes are "far too tight." Among the many afflictions of the poet's last years were swollen feet. Arly's tight shoes may represent any of the constraints on the poet's happiness. Thomas Byrom has pointed out that Lear, like UncLE ARly, was a homeless traveler for more than forty years before building a villa in Italy (*Nonsense and Wonder*, 1977). Sad without being pessimistic, the poem characterizes a man whose life was lonely yet rich in experience.

Lear's "Eclogue" is the product of his capacity for making fun of his sorrows and his tendency to self-pity and grumbling. In this parody of a classical genre, the singing contest between shepherds, Lear and John Addington Symonds catalog their woes; the latter's wife, Catherine, finally judges whose miseries are greater. The "Eclogue" is laughable, but the reader of Lear's correspondence sees how truly it reflects his assessment of himself and his career; but *A Book of Nonsense* saw thirty editions in his lifetime.

Lear's pleasure in his verse is expressed most clearly in "The Quangle Wangle's Hat." Wearing a beaver hat one hundred and two feet wide, the title character sits sadly in a Crumpetty Tree, wishing (like Lear in San Remo) that someone would come to visit. Then he is approached by a series of exotic animals, some of them (like the Quangle Wangle himself) familiar from Lear's other writings. When they ask for permission to live on his hat, the hero welcomes each one. Enjoying a simple yet profound comradeship, an assembly of Lear's creatures blissfully dances "by the light of the Mulberry moon"—"and all [are] as happy as happy could be." Here in microcosm is Lear's imagined world, singularly free of conflict. The real world is not like this, but Lear persuades readers to imagine that it might be. Friendship and sharing of oneself offer the best hope of contentment in the fantasy world, as in the real one. The Quangle Wangle is Edward Lear.

Mary De Jong

Other major works

NONFICTION: *Illustrations of the Family of Psittacidae: Or, Parrots*, 1832; *Views in Rome and Its Environs*, 1841; *Illustrated Excursions in Italy*, 1846; *Journals of a Landscape Painter in Albania, etc.*, 1851; *Journals of a Landscape Painter in Southern Calabria, etc.*, 1852; *Views in the Seven Ionian Islands*, 1863; *Journal of a Landscape Painter in Corsica*, 1870; *Lear in Sicily*, 1938; *Indian Journal*, 1953 (Ray Murphy, editor); *Edward Lear in Southern Italy*, 1964.

Bibliography

Byrom, Thomas. *Nonsense and Wonder: The Poems and Cartoons of Edward Lear.* New York: E. P. Dutton, 1977. A full-length, sympathetic study of Lear that discusses his poetry in depth. The author has been generous in providing extracts of Lear's long poems, as well as reproductions of Lear's sketches accompanying his limericks. Possibly the most comprehensive literary criticism available on Lear's poetry.

Chitty, Susan. *That Singular Person Called Lear.* London: Weidenfeld & Nicholson, 1988. A biography of Lear, recommended for its appreciation of Lear, as well as for the breadth of knowledge about him. Discusses Lear's life and early development, his poetry, and his paintings. Essential background reading for Lear scholars.

Hark, Ina Rae. *Edward Lear.* Boston: Twayne, 1982. A useful introduction to Lear examining his nonsense poetry and its parallels with his life. The critical commentary covers his limericks, nonsense poems, and longer poems.

Noakes, Vivian. *Edward Lear: Selected Letters.* Oxford, England: Clarendon Press, 1988. A thoroughly researched volume, containing an important selection of letters by Lear. Recommended reading for insight into Lear's thinking and inspirations for his works. Included among the letters are drawings by Lear.

Vinson, James, ed. *Great Writers of the English Language: Poets.* New York:

St. Martin's Press, 1979. The entry on Lear gives a brief overview of his life and lists his works. Notes the irony that although Lear's nonsense poems originated as a diversion from his professional career as an artist, they were to become the key to his fame and influence. Acknowledges the strength of Lear's visual and linguistic playfulness.

DENISE LEVERTOV

Born: Ilford, Essex, England; October 24, 1923

Principal poetry

The Double Image, 1946; *Here and Now*, 1957; *Overland to the Islands*, 1958; *Five Poems*, 1958; *With Eyes at the Back of Our Heads*, 1959; *The Jacob's Ladder*, 1961; *O Taste and See: New Poems*, 1964; *City Psalm*, 1964; *Psalm Concerning the Castle*, 1966; *The Sorrow Dance*, 1967; *A Tree Telling of Orpheus*, 1968; *A Marigold from North Vietnam*, 1968; *Three Poems*, 1968; *The Cold Spring and Other Poems*, 1969; *Embroideries*, 1969; *Relearning the Alphabet*, 1970; *Summer Poems 1969*, 1970; *A New Year's Garland for My Students: MIT 1969-1970*, 1970; *To Stay Alive*, 1971; *Footprints*, 1972; *The Freeing of the Dust*, 1975; *Chekhov on the West Heath*, 1977; *Modulations for Solo Voice*, 1977; *Life in the Forest*, 1978; *Collected Earlier Poems, 1940-1960*, 1979; *Pig Dreams: Scenes from the Life of Sylvia*, 1981; *Wanderer's Daysong*, 1981; *Candles in Babylon*, 1982; *Poems, 1960-1967*, 1983; *Oblique Prayers: New Poems with Fourteen Translations from Jean Joubert*, 1984; *The Menaced World*, 1984; *Selected Poems*, 1986; *Breathing the Water*, 1987; *Poems, 1968-1972*, 1987; *A Door in the Hive*, 1989.

Other literary forms

The Poet in the World (1973) gathers prose articles, reviews, criticism, statements to the press, and tributes to fellow poets. *Light Up the Cave* (1981), Denise Levertov's second volume of prose pieces, includes three short stories; articles on the nature of poetry and politics; speeches and political commentary; and memoirs and notes on other writers—Hilda Morley, Michele Murray, Bert Meyers, Rainer Maria Rilke, and Anton Chekhov. Of particular interest are the pages on dream, memory, and poetry and the details of her arrest and imprisonment experience as a war protester.

Levertov has also written a novella *In the Night: A Story* (1968), and the libretto for an oratorio, *El Salvador: Requiem and Invocation* (1983). With Kenneth Rexroth and William Carlos Williams, she edited *Penguin Modern Poets 9* (1967). She has produced translations of other poets' works, including *In Praise of Krishna: Songs from the Bengali* (1967, with Edward C. Dimock, Jr.), *Selected Poems*, by Eugene Guillevic (1969), and *Black Iris*, by Jean Joubert (1988).

Achievements

Levertov's first book of poems, *The Double Image*, was published in England in 1946. It brought her to the attention of British and American critics and poets such as Kenneth Rexroth and Robert Creeley. Eleven years later, her first American book was published, followed by many volumes of poems and several translations of other poets' work. She has taught at many institutions, including Vassar College, Drew University, City College of New York, University of California at Berkeley, Massachusetts Institute of Technology, Brandeis University, Tufts University, and Stanford University. As the poetry editor of *The Nation* in the 1960's, she influenced the critical reception of new poets. She was elected to the American Academy of Arts and Letters. Her many awards include a Guggenheim Foundation Fellowship in 1962, the Lenore Marshall Poetry Prize in 1975 for *The Freeing of the Dust*, and the Elmer Holmes Bobst Award in 1983.

Biography

Born near London, England, in 1923, Denise Levertov was reared in a multicultural environment: Welsh and Russian, Jewish and Christian. On her mother's side, her lineage was Welsh. Beatrice Spooner-Jones, her mother, was a daughter of a physician and great-granddaughter of a tailor, teacher, and preacher, Angell Jones, made famous by Daniel Owen, "the Welsh Dickens," in the novel *Hunangofiant Rhys Lewis* (1885). Beatrice Spooner-Jones had a beautiful singing voice and a stock of stories to tell of Welsh life. She loved to travel, and in Constantinople, where she was a teacher in a Scottish mission, she met a young Russian Jew, Paul Peter Levertoff, who had converted to Christianity. They were married in London, where he was ordained to the Anglican priesthood. His great passion in life was reconciliation between Christians and Jews. A daughter, Olga, was born to the couple, and seven years later, a second daughter, Denise.

In some ways, Denise felt like an only child. She never attended a public or private school; her mother, her only teacher, read many classic works of fiction to her. She visited museums and libraries in London and studied ballet for many years; for a time she considered a career in dance. When World War II came, she entered nurse's training and worked in a number of London public hospitals caring for children, the aged, and the poor. She had been writing poems since childhood and published her first volume of poems in England shortly after the war.

Levertov met and married an American writer, Mitchell Goodman, who was studying abroad. They lived in Europe until 1948, returning to Europe from New York for a period in 1950-1951. Her son Nikolai was born in 1949. In 1956, she became an American citizen. For the next thirty years, she published more than a dozen volumes of poetry with the same publisher, New Directions. During the Vietnam era, she wrote and spoke passionately against the war; in 1972, with Muriel Rukeyser and Jane Hart, she traveled to Hanoi. In the years of nuclear bomb testing in the air, she participated in the movement toward a test-ban treaty and the elimination of nuclear weapons altogether. Later, she vigorously supported protests against American involvement in civil wars in El Salvador, Honduras, and Nicaragua. She lived in

Mexico for a number of years: indeed, her mother grew to love Mexico and remained with a family in Oaxaca for twenty years before her death in 1977. Currently, Levertov maintains a residence in Massachusetts but teaches at Stanford during the academic year.

Analysis

Many major lyric poets who live a full, long life produce a body of work that encompasses between six and nine hundred poems. Denise Levertov has published about six hundred poems. Yet despite this large number of works, her poems revolve around a few preoccupations and questions that continue to engage her attention: the meaning of life, the issues of justice that have arisen in the twentieth century, and more personal concerns that have to do with friendships, family relationships, and immediate thoughts and feelings. Since the lyric poem captures a moment of intense feeling and thought (it is the most compressed form of literature), chronological analysis of Levertov's work gives access to a record of the poet's unfolding life. Levertov seems to have been uniquely placed in her family and time to inherit two great streams of lyric power—the Welsh gift of song and speech and the profound religious thought of her priest father's Jewish-Christian search for truth.

With such a combination of parental influences, the themes that prevail in Levertov's poetry—the nature and form of poetry, and the moral obligations of the poet to society—are hardly surprising. She has said that the Hasidic or mystical beliefs in her father's Jewish heritage gave her an ease and familiarity with spiritual mysteries. For the purpose of analysis, one can study these three areas of her concern—poetry, morality, and mystery—but in her poems they often appear not separately but together, coloring the mosaic of her words. She combines the skills of a craftsman and an artist, the vision of moral integrity and spiritual insight.

A young poet must establish her voice and style. Levertov learned from modernistic poets such as Charles Olson and William Carlos Williams, who used concrete, everyday words and familiar settings and events to convey profound truths. She drew also from Welsh hymn-singing lines. Lines and line breaks are essential to the sound quality of her poetry. Some of her inspiration comes from dreams, images, and dream sounds. Naturally, the technical apparatus of poetry making absorbs her interest as a poet and teacher of poetry writing: How should journals be used? How should a poet revise drafts? How does one evaluate poetry and distinguish what is good from what is bad? Who are the great poets of the twentieth century?

As to the second preoccupation in Levertov's poetry, the integrity of moral vision, the twentieth century has provided abundant evidence of the human capacity for sin as well as visionary leadership in the fight against evil. The age-old oppression of Jews by Christians flared into monstrous proportions as millions of innocent women, children, and men were gassed in death camps in Europe. The shock of this discovery in 1945 as World War II came to a close must have been intense for the young poet-nurse whose father was both Jew and Christian. In later decades, she felt an imperative to protest the horror and injustice of war. The effort to end the Vietnam War brought women together before the women's movement had gathered full force. The sight of children mutilated and burned by napalm aroused the conscience of many "unpolitical" people. Levertov's actions and her words expressed the outrage of many citizens. She explored the relevance of poetry to politics and questioned the moral responsibility of the poet in a time of peril. What use should be made of the gift of speech?

Early in her career, Levertov expressed her vision of unity in the physical and spiritual worlds. "Taste and See," the title poem of her seventh volume, has a biblical sound. Insisting that one cannot know a divinity apart from what is given to the senses, she probes the meaning of physical experience— a life affirmation—and considers its relationship to religious values. Decades before the general public awakened to the need to respect the physical world, Levertov spoke of the mystery in the objects people taste, touch, and see: the moon, food, a glass of water. She found both happiness and wisdom in the realization of mystery. Increasingly, in her later poetry, the value of mystical and religious experience becomes her theme.

Levertov links the imagination with truth in poetry; thus the poem has a religious significance. As "religion" literally means "binding anew," she finds connections to be the essence or truth of imagination. In the poem "A Straw Swan Under the Christmas Tree," she writes, "All trivial parts of/ world-about-us speak in their forms/ of themselves and their counterparts! . . . one speech conjuring the other." The human emotion of sympathy depends on understanding the connections in animate and also inanimate life. "May the taste of salt/ recall to us the great depths about us," she writes in "The Depths." The principle of interrelated form applies even in the extreme case of the Nazi leader, Karl Adolf Eichmann. In "During the Eichmann Trial," she says that if we look accurately into another face, or into a mirror, one sees "the other," even Eichmann. This oneness is a mystery, and something Eichmann did not know: "We are members/ one of another."

One should not conclude, however, that the truth of imagination Levertov seeks is an intellectual truth. Unlike the poet Dante, who moves from love and care in the physical world to a spiritual and intellectual understanding of love, Levertov remains firmly based in the physical realm, however far along the mystical path she may travel. Perhaps in the modern age the presence of evil within and without is so strong that the poet dares not abandon her mooring in the physical "real" world that needs so much assistance. Humanity is "a criminal kind, the planet's nightmare" (as she quotes Robinson Jeffers in the poem "Kith and Kin"). The truth she continually explores remains the connection in the patterns of human and natural life. Courage is a necessity, and models of courage may be found in her lean, economical poetic voice.

A "speaking-voice" quality in Levertov's poems results from the open form of uneven line lengths. In keeping with the tone of a human voice in natural and varied cadences, her diction neither startles nor challenges the reader with rare and exotic words in the manner of Marianne Moore or Edith Sitwell. She "tunes up" or increases the vibrancy of her poems by making them "tight," with no excess words or phrases. She often omits subjects and verbs, punctuating a fragment as though it were a sentence, and alternates or intersperses fragments with complete sentences. Another skill is accuracy in word choice, using the best word to evoke the scene, the object, the person, or the feeling she is describing. She can change the feeling of a line by inserting words from another collocation—sets of words often found together. For example, in a late poem, "Those Who Want Out," from *A Door in the Hive* (1989), she describes people who are designing permanent colonies in space—their optimism, their love of speed and machines that are "outside of nature." Then a closing line judges them with icy and stern tone in six one-syllable words with biblical power: "They do not love the earth." This use of sparse, plain Anglo-Saxon English for a "stopper" of great power is found frequently in William Shakespeare.

Along with devices of diction, poetic speech uses images to convey truth. Levertov's images are most frequently from the natural world—plants, animals, and landscapes—and of everyday household objects. "In the Unknown" takes the reader to the poet's home: "As if the white page/ were a clean tablecloth,/ as if the vacuumed floor were a primed canvas." In "To the Muse" she describes the body as the house one lives in and the place to find one's inner poetry. There are many rooms in this house, and when the Muse seems to have departed, she is hiding, like a lost gold ring. One has forgotten to make a place for her, and to bring her back, one needs to attend to the house, find some flowers to decorate it, and be alert to the Muse with all of one's senses. Images of caves, mirrors, water, cloud, shadow, and moon fill her poems to make her feelings and ideas accessible to the common reader.

In harmony with her use of diction and form, Levertov has expressed a modest view of the poet: a person who can articulate feeling through the medium of language. She refuses the exalted aura of a supersensitive person whose feelings are beyond the reach of ordinary human beings. Glorification by "temperament" has never been attractive to her and is as suspect as misplaced romantic adulation—not a twentieth century ideal. It is the process of writing, not the result, that fascinates her. She sees poems as structures of meaning and sound that convey feelings accurately. The poet must revise and polish until the poem is complete. Technical skill with diction, form, rhythm, syntax, and sound—above all, sound—raise a poem from mediocrity to perfection. As a teacher, she has much experience to share. From her essays and articles on the subject of poetry one can gain information about many technical aspects of her craft. Her poems are more readily understood when one is familiar with these principles.

Like many young poets, Levertov experimented in her early writings with various rhyme schemes, tones, and forms. A 1946 poem, "Folding a Shirt," uses Dante's interlacing *terza rima* rhyme pattern for six stanzas: aba bcb cdc ded efe fgf. "Midnight Quatrains" rhymes the second and fourth end words of each stanza. There are dramatic poems in dialogue form and ballads. Typically, however, Levertov's poems have no end rhyme or regular meter. (The lack of regular rhyme and stressed beats in most modern poetry has been attributed to the chaos and irregularity in the twentieth century— poetry reflects life.) Her rhythm is subtle, moving with the line break. Uneven lines are the rule, not the exception. The placement of words and indentations create rhythmic ebb and flow, abrupt interruptions, slow pauses, and dramatic suspense. The eye follows a varied typography that signals rhythm with blank space and black ink, like a design for reading aloud. The "melos" or song quality of such an open form comes from the rightness of the line length—the line's appropriate length in the poem's internal system of meanings.

As well as obtaining rhythm by a masterful use of line breaks, Levertov excels in the construction of sentences within the poem. Often a poem is built like an argument: a proposition followed by a rebuttal, in the way of a sonnet. The poem's syntax often matches the idea of the poem. In "The Prayer," the poet is praying to Apollo at Delphi for the flame of her poetry to be maintained. As if the poem were the flame, it keeps going until the poet breaks the sentence when she begins to wonder whether the god is mocking her. The sentence ends at the same time that her belief in the god falters. The second sentence, a reprise, says that the flame is flickering, and perhaps it is some other god at work. In a very sensual poem, "Eros at Temple Stream," she pictures lovers bathing near a river, soaping each other with long, slippery strokes—their hands as flames. The poem's syntax—one long sentence with no punctuation at its close—mirrors the meaning.

In Levertov's narrative and dramatic poems, she sets the stage quickly. A mini-play, "Scenario," opens bluntly: "The theater of war. Offstage/ a cast of thousands weeping." A poem about animal life at the dump begins, "At the dump bullfrogs/ converse as usual." Often these poems begin with brief noun phrases, as in "A Hunger": "Black beans, white sunlight." Levertov's impulse for story and drama has resulted in a number of long poem sequences and poetic plays. "Staying Alive," with its prologue and four parts with entr'actes, vividly recalls events and feelings at the height of the Vietnam War protests and the People's Park struggle in Berkeley, California, in 1969. In 1983, an oratorio, *El Salvador: Requiem and Invocation*, was performed at Harvard University; the text by Levertov was set to music by the composer Newell Hendricks. Using the structures of the Johann Sebastian Bach passions and George Frideric Handel and Franz Josef Haydn oratorios, Levertov wrote voices for a narrator, Archbishop Oscar Romero, a questioner, nuns, and a chorus. She studied the speeches of the murdered archbishop and quoted his words as well as passages from Mayan prayers. The work was given to help fundraising efforts of relief organizations active in Central America.

That the poet should be also a political person came as an early and natural revelation to Levertov. Her first published poem, "Listening to Distant Guns" (1940), tells of hearing "a low pulsation in the East" that "betrays no whisper of the battle scream." She actually heard the guns of World War II from the south coast of England, to where she, along with many young people, had been evacuated from the city of London. She herself was safe, but the war was very near. She describes the dismal feelings of the English people in "Christmas 1944," when no celebration could hide the blackout curtains on the windows, the knowledge of "fear knocking on the door" of so many Europeans. She gives a welcome: "Come in, then poverty, and come in, death:/ This year too many lie cold, or die in cold." During her impressionable teens and early twenties, she was surrounded with war. Although two decades would pass before her active involvement in the American antiwar movement, she had already expressed her grief at the mass destruction war brings.

In "On the Edge of Darkness: What Is Political Poetry?" (originally a lecture delivered at Boston University in 1975), Levertov defends the idea that a lyric poem can be simultaneously intimate, passionate, and political. Indeed, there is a long history of poets speaking out their political ideas—generally, though not always, in defense of liberty and peace. Contemporary "political" poets usually participate actively in the struggles of which they write. Specific issues give rise to topical poetry on race, class, environment, and gender problems. These poems, like the songs associated with the struggles, change the feelings of the listeners and readers; they alter the awareness of a community. The standards of aesthetic value apply to this poetry as to all other; it should arouse the whole being of the listener: mind, senses, and spirit.

By 1966, Levertov was writing poems about the war in Vietnam. The most influential and famous of these is probably "Life at War." Speaking for her contemporaries, she tells of war's pervasive influence in her century— "We have breathed the grits of it in, all our lives"—and then begins a long lament over the damage war has done to people's imaginations. The modern imagination, she argues, is "filmed over with the gray filth of it," because humankind (and here she lists wonderful and praiseworthy achievements and powers of human beings) "whose language imagines *mercy* and *lovingkindness*," can schedule the burning of children's bodies. "Burned human flesh/

is smelling in Vietnam as I write." As a former nurse, Levertov can bring her sensual awareness into her passionate denunciation of modern war. The poem closes with a statement that humankind needs the "deep intelligence" that living at peace can give. The violence to human imagination from war comes from its insult to intelligence.

Other antiwar poems were composed in the form of dialogues such as questions and answers about Vietnamese people or a narrator questioning a bomber pilot. Levertov's poems also protest the false language of war communiqués. She pays tribute to the young men and women antiwar activists— those who die, those who live, those who go to jail. One poem honors her friend and fellow poet Muriel Rukeyser, who went to Vietnam with her in 1972. Both women were rearing sons at the time—teenagers who were in line for a future military draft.

Family life, and in particular marriage, has inspired many of Levertov's most memorable poems. In keeping with her insistence on the beauty of sensual experience, she celebrates the joy of marriage. The short poem "Bedtime" puts the contentment of fulfilled love in natural terms: "We are a meadow where the bees hum,/ mind and body are almost one." "Hymn to Eros" praises the "drowsy god" who quietly circles in "a snowfall hush." Two beautiful poems to her son, Nikolai, are spaced years apart—one before his birth, "Who He Was," and one, "The Son," as he becomes a man. The first tells of his conception, gestation, and birth, and the second of skills he has gained.

The death of love and the contemporary difficulties in male-female relationships also provide subjects for notable poems. The much-quoted "About Marriage" begins with a cry for freedom, "Don't lock me in wedlock, I want/ marriage, an/ encounter," and concludes, "I would be/ met/ and meet you/ so,/ in a green/ airy space, not/ locked in." As the women's movement and the antiwar movement seemed to merge, the desire for peace and independence became the message of many women writers and poets. "The Ache of Marriage" compares marriage to Jonah's life in the belly of a whale; the poet and her spouse are looking for joy, "some joy/ not to be known outside it." Marriage is not discarded as an ideal, but its confinement brings problems to women who feel an urge to work in a wider field. In "Hypocrite Women" Levertov tells women that they should not be ashamed of their "unwomanly" traits but should admit boldly the truth of their lives.

The nature of another woman-to-woman relationship is explored in the "Olga poems." Levertov's sister, older by seven years, was estranged from her family for many years. Her death brought a recollection and definition of the two lives that were linked in dream and memory but separated by behavior, circumstances, and distance. The gaze of her sister's eyes haunts the poet: "eyes with some vision/ of festive goodness in back of their hard, or veiled, or shining,/ unknowable gaze." Poems to her mother and father join poems to other poets as Levertov continually seeks and writes about the connections in her life. Rilke, Rukeyser, Boris Pasternak, Robert Duncan, and Pablo Neruda are some of the poets she has addressed in poems.

Reflecting the world consciousness typical of Americans in the second half of the twentieth century, Levertov traveled widely. Many of her poems describe the people and places she visited in Europe, Mexico, the United States, and Asia. Distant places remain alive in memory with sensual evocations— dreamscapes. The perfume of linden trees in blossom in an ancient European town is recalled in "The Past." Feelings of comfortable married happiness mingle with the beauty of the setting. The poem "In Tonga" describes the life of sacred bats hanging in their caves, squeaking in night flight. The poet muses about them, "If they could think/ it would not be of us." "Poem from Manhattan" builds a prayer and invocation to New York City through its power, energy, and hope—"city, act of joy"—to its desolation—"city, gesture of greed." Moral and spiritual awareness accompanies the poet's sensory connections to the world.

The mystical and religious tones of Levertov's poetry can be traced from their beginnings to their full flowering in the poems of the 1980's collected in two volumes, *Breathing the Water* and *A Door in the Hive*. The daughter of a clergyman who was steeped in mystical Jewish Hasidism, Levertov showed her familiarity with religious texts in early poems. "Notes of a Scale" gives four moments of wonder; its reference note directs the reader to Martin Buber's *Tales of the Hasidim: The Early Masters* (1975). The poem "Sparks" includes passages from the Old Testament book of Ecclesiastes. In this work, Levertov moves easily from the ancient Hebrew text to the circumstances of a modern life. Not only Jewish mysticism but also Christian tradition inspired her poetry. Later poems take as their themes the annunciation to Mary, Jesus' parable of the mustard seed, and the path of Calvary.

Levertov's religious poetry is deeply imbued as well with thoughts on the lives and works of religious saints and writers. Saint Thomas Didymus, Julian of Norwich, William Blake, William Everson, and W. H. Auden are evoked in various poems. One should remember, also, that she translated religious poetry of the Bengali Vaishnava faith. Collaborating with the scholar Edward C. Dimock, Jr., she published this fascinating poetry under the title *In Praise of Krishna: Songs from the Bengali*. The warm emotional and erotic content of these poems has a kinship to Levertov's sensual approach to religious mysticism.

Access to religious symbols often comes in dreams. The immensely influential biblical accounts of dream visions (those of Ezekiel, Daniel, and John of Patmos, among others) echo in texts from every century. Many of these dream visions were part of Levertov's own home educational fare. She has written of two childhood dreams: One consisted of a violent transformation from a rustic scene of happiness to a scene of burning and devastation. The other recurring dream was of a large country house made of a warm pink stone; its name was Mazinger Hall. These two dreams, like the later ones she used in poems, carry emotional content of joy and sorrow, gain and loss, security and terror. Gradually, her dream material has been transformed into poems that evoke similar feelings in her readers.

In Levertov's early dream-based poems, the process of transferring a dream to a poem involved describing the dream content. The poet has explained that later, after analytical work on her dreams, she abandoned that objectivity and gave her images stronger and clearer emotional force to present the dream content more directly to the reader. A third stage in this process came with the realization that the dream needs a literary form that cannot be imposed but must be listened for. Several times she found that a dream worked only as a prose tale. The stories "Say the Word" and "A Dream" began as poems that she transformed to a rhythmic prose. The experience of using dream material for a work of art teaches the poet that the poem must be not only visually clear but also morally or emotionally significant for the reader. An expression that is too private does not make an effective poem.

Another kind of dream poem may result from an auditory message received in a dream state, or as a combined visual and auditory dream. Levertov has experienced each type and has made poems of them. In "The Flight," she retells a vision of the poet and mystic William Blake, who spoke the words, "The will is given us that we may know the delights of surrender." She waited several years before composing a poem about that experience, to avoid a too-literal transcription. Again, an auditory message was received in a dream about the Russian poet Boris Pasternak. The visual scene disappeared from memory, but the words remained. In both instances, as Levertov explains, the quality of the resulting poem came from the poet's willingness to recognize and absorb a hidden quality that lay beyond the superficial appearances. Some dream images may indicate the questions or problems present at that moment in the poet's life. In that case, the truth of the life and the truth of the dream provide an interplay that makes a powerful poem.

The religious message that hums (a favorite Levertov verb) throughout her poetry is the oneness of all life: all human beings, animals, trees, and the great elements of earth, air, fire, and water. The vision of air and water blended comes in poems about bees, honey, and ocean currents that hold "my seafern arms." The cleansing properties of honey in the hive, she writes in "Second Didactic Poem," neutralize even the poison of disease organisms. That hive with its transforming power may be the same as human activity— "honey of the human." Transformation may also move in the opposite direction, from a joyful morning self-confidence to a rapid pace that diminishes the person ("Remembering"). These apparent divisions between good and evil in a person's emotional life can be harmonized from a point of view that is wide enough to encompass the other side, or opposite, in what is experienced.

Certain lines of Denise Levertov's poetry shine as lighthouse beacons across the restless waters of human experience: for example, "We are one of another" ("A Vision"), the lovely love song "We are a meadow where the bees hum" ("Bedtime"), and "To speak of sorrow/ works upon it" ("To Speak"). Why do these lines hum in the mind years after they are first encountered? In them one finds three qualities that characterize Levertov's poetic work: music, morality, and mysticism. Her best poems are true lyrics—songs, in their flowing rhythms and enchanting sound patterns of vowel and consonant combinations. Moreover, she teaches the lessons modern Americans need to hear, about respect for natural life and for unprotected, helpless human beings, especially children and the elderly. Then there is the wonder she shares in the magic of common things—the "gleam of water in the bedside glass" ("Midnight Gladness") and the moonlight crossing her room ("The Well"). Levertov says, "There is no magic, only facts"; her magic is found in accurate and loving observation of everyday shapes, colors, and sounds.

Yet beyond her mastery of the poem's form and even beyond the thought content, Levertov's poetry can be appreciated for the qualities of the poet herself. During the 1960's, before the women's movement had strengthened the fragile position of women poets, when a cult of death followed the suicides of Anne Sexton and Sylvia Plath, Denise Levertov lamented their loss, not only because they were fine poets but also because their deaths would confirm a popular conception of the poet as abnormally sensitive, often on the edge of madness. For her, alcoholism and nervous breakdowns were not signs of poetic talent. Creativity, she wrote, belongs to responsible, mature adults who take citizenship seriously. In the late 1960's and 1970's, she put this antiromantic view to the service of the peace and women's liberation movements—marching, protesting, speaking against social injustices. She called attention to the political poets imprisoned in many countries. In the 1980's, she produced poetry of great beauty on the human and material sources of her spiritual inspiration. She has shown that a poet in the United States can support herself economically. Generously and with humor, she shares with students the fruits of her years of practicing her craft. In all these ways, she has modeled a high standard for both poetry and the poet.

Doris Earnshaw

Other major works

LONG FICTION: *In the Night: A Story*, 1968.

NONFICTION: *The Poet in the World*, 1973.

TRANSLATIONS: *In Praise of Krishna: Songs from the Bengali*, 1967 (with Edward C. Dimock, Jr.); *Selected Poems*, by Eugene Guillevic, 1969; *Black Iris*, by Jean Joubert, 1988.

EDITED TEXT: *Penguin Modern Poets 9*, 1967 (with Kenneth Rexroth and

William Carlos Williams).
MISCELLANEOUS: *Light Up the Cave*, 1981; *El Salvador: Requiem and Invocation*, 1983.

Bibliography

Felstiner, John. "Poetry and Political Experience: Denise Levertov." In *Coming to Light: American Women Poets in the Twentieth Century*, edited by Diane Wood Middlebrook and Marilyn Yalom. Ann Arbor: University of Michigan Press, 1985. In this brief but valuable study, Felstiner shows that Levertov awakens human sensitivity—male and female—by insisting on the sacramental quality of all physical presence. In poetry, she finds hope while facing the horrors of war in Central America, in Vietnam, and in American cities. Felstiner's words on the oratorio *El Salvador: Requiem and Invocation* are particularly worthwhile.

Lacey, Paul A. "Denise Levertov: A Poetry of Exploration." In *American Women Poets*, edited by Harold Bloom. New York: Chelsea, 1986. Lacey considers the influence of Hasidism in Levertov's poetry: She treats the miraculous in a matter-of-fact tone. Her weakness in the early poetry, Lacey says, stemmed from an inability to deal seriously with evil in the world. Later, however, she grew into the political consequences of what it means to be, as she says, "members one of another."

Marten, Harry. *Understanding Denise Levertov*. Columbia: South Carolina University Press, 1988. The most important study of Levertov in book form, Marten's analysis covers four decades of poetry. Individual chapters give an overview, a history of the earliest poetry, an analysis of the volumes that established her reputation, a consideration of her public voice, and a discussion of spiritual dimension in her later development. The annotated bibliography of critical articles is particularly helpful.

Pope, Deborah. "Homespun and Crazy Feathers: The Split Self in the Poems of Denise Levertov." In *A Separate Vision*. Baton Rouge: Louisiana State University Press, 1984. In Levertov's poems, divisions of the self appear in images of passivity and sleeping on one hand and cold, dark violence on the other. Her central concern for the woman artist becomes an effort to harmonize oppositions. In her later poetry, Levertov celebrates the freedom and power of a new role, the "wise woman."

Wagner-Martin, Linda. *Denise Levertov*. New York: Twayne, 1967. Although written when Levertov was in midcareer, Wagner's biography, survey of poems, and bibliography provide an excellent introduction to the poet's life and work. Seven chapters discuss Levertov's family and education in England, her poetic themes and forms, and influences from modernist poets. Includes a chronology and notes.

PHILIP LEVINE

Born: Detroit, Michigan; January 10, 1928

Principal poetry

On the Edge, 1963; *Not This Pig*, 1968; *Thistles*, 1970; *5 Detroits*, 1970; *Pili's Wall*, 1971; *Red Dust*, 1971; *They Feed, They Lion*, 1972; *1933*, 1974; *On the Edge and Over*, 1976; *The Names of the Lost*, 1976; *Ashes: Poems New and Old*, 1979; *7 Years from Somewhere*, 1979; *One for the Rose*, 1981; *Selected Poems*, 1984; *Sweet Will*, 1985; *A Walk with Tom Jefferson*, 1988.

Other literary forms

Philip Levine has published a collection of interviews, *Don't Ask* (1981), in the University of Michigan's "Poets on Poetry" series.

Achievements

Levine's most important achievements are the two books of poetry *Not This Pig* and *They Feed, They Lion*. In the best poems of these two books, he reflects the influence of the surrealist and political poets of Spain and South America and takes on the subject of the city with a remarkable vitality. Along with James Wright, Allen Ginsberg, Denise Levertov, and Robert Bly, Levine has managed to incorporate politics into his poetry, going far beyond the immediate protest reaction to the Vietnam War. He writes about the working poor without condescension and with an empathy that puts him clearly in the tradition of Walt Whitman and William Carlos Williams; these poems are often about survivors, people who have suffered, but who are courageous and do not quit.

Biography

Philip Levine was born in Detroit of Russian-Jewish immigrant parents; his experiences of the Depression and World War II in that city play a central role in his poetry. In an interview Levine has said that he spent most of his childhood fighting against people who attacked him because he was a Jew. His father died when he was young (apparently in 1933, according to the poem entitled "1933"), and both his parents often appear in his many poems that explore the past. According to Levine, the workers he knew as a child and as a young man had a great effect on him, and various immigrant anarchists had a lasting effect on his politics. He married Frances Artley in 1954, and they have three sons, Mark, John, and Theodore.

Since Levine often writes from personal experience, it is possible to draw a picture of him and his relationship from his poems. There are many poems about his grandparents, parents, brother, sister, wife, and each of his three sons. Not all of the "facts" in his work, however, may necessarily be true.

The poems do reveal much about the writer, but the poet's tendency to fictionalize must be kept in mind.

After a number of jobs, including working in a foundry, Levine attended Wayne State University, where he studied under John Berryman, receiving a B.A. degree in 1950 and an M.A. in 1955. He refused to serve in the Korean War, and although this was clearly a political protest on his part, he was declared 4-F for psychological reasons. He received a Master of Fine Arts in Creative Writing from the University of Iowa in 1957 and won a fellowship to attend Stanford University. He has taught at California State University, Fresno, since 1958. He has won a number of awards for teaching. He has given readings of his poetry throughout the United States, often revealing a comic side of his character that is not obvious in his poetry. He has won a number of poetry awards, most significantly the Lenore Marshall Award for *The Names of the Lost*, the National Book Critics Circle Award for *Ashes and 7 Years from Somewhere*, and the American Book Award for *Ashes*.

He was actively opposed to the Vietnam War, and his first trip to live in Spain in the late 1960's was taken, in part, to escape from America. In Spain the Levines lived near the Catalan city of Barcelona, the stronghold of the anarchists during the Civil War, a city that Levine has said reminds him of the Detroit of his childhood. He has had an interest in the Spanish Civil War for many years, sympathizing with the losing Republicans but identifying with the anarchists rather than the Communists or Socialists, and he has made Spain and that war the subject of some of his most memorable poems.

Analysis

When Philip Levine issued a new version of his first book *On the Edge*, he added to the title the words *and over*, declaring the direction of his dark and fierce poetry. His poems examine a world of evil, loneliness, and loss, where a poem entitled "Hymn to God in My Sickness" can only be a cry of unbelief. Paradoxically, there is a strong faith in human nature running throughout Levine's work. His is a poetry of community that at times holds out some distant but powerful dream of a better society. Often this is dramatized in the lives of the anarchists of the Spanish Civil War, celebrating their nobility and courage. His work expresses admiration for those who suffer but do not give in, those who fight against prejudice and pain. Many of his poems employ a second-person voice, and although they often have specific addressees, they are also addressed to the reader as a brother or sister to say "Your life is mine."

Levine is one of the most overtly urban poets in America today. His hometown of Detroit—its factories and foundries, its dead-end jobs, its dirt and smoke, its dying lives—plays a central part in his imagination. It is the city he escaped from—or tried to—to Fresno, California, a place often depicted by him as lonely and sad, a silent place where "each has his life/ private and sealed." Then there is the third city—Barcelona, Spain, where Levine often seems most at home, where he feels a greater sense of community and history, even though he carries what he sees as the political burden of America with him.

The second poem in Levine's first book, *On the Edge*, "Night Thoughts over a Sick Child," sets off a central image and theme of his work, presenting the speaker helpless before the boy's suffering, with no faith in the efficacy of prayer. He finds the situation intolerable and refuses to justify it in any way:

> If it were mine by one word
> I would not save any man,
> myself or the universe
> at such cost: reality.

There is nothing for him to do but to face "the frail dignity/ of surrender." The mixture of suffering and helplessness, anger and sadness, points toward many of Levine's later poems.

In this early volume Levine is writing rather formal poetry, metrical or syllabic, with rhymes or off-rhymes. In poems about World War II and the Algerian War, he shows his concern for the public causes of suffering. In "Gangrene" he draws an ugly picture of torture, "the circus of excrement," and ends with a self-righteous address to the reader as being secretively thrilled by these descriptions of torture even though he fakes boredom. In later volumes Levine achieves a more satisfactory tone of identification with suffering of this kind.

Probably the best poem in *On the Edge* is "For Fran," a picture of the poet's wife as gardener, an image that appears also in later poems. She is seen preparing the flower beds for winter, and she becomes for the poet the person who bears the promise of the future: "Out of whatever we have been/ We will make something for the dark." These final lines can be taken as a kind of motto for Levine's later poetry, his attempt to make something in the face of the dominant darkness.

Levine's second volume, *Not This Pig*, is the key work in his development as a poet. There are some poems that are like the tightly ordered style of *On the Edge*, but a number of them indicate a new direction—more open, riskier, and more original. The fact that he is moving away from syllabics and rhyme— as did most poets of his generation in the 1960's—is not the main source of this originality; but a more daring language is in evidence, opening his work to a wider and deeper range.

His poem "The Midget," drawing on his experiences in Spain, is a fine example of this new range. In a café where the anarchists planned the burning of the bishop of Zaragoza, the speaker sits on a December day—off-season, no tourists—amidst the factory workers and other laborers. A midget in the bar begins to sing of how he came from southern Spain "to this terrible/ Barcelona," telling them all that he is "big in the heart, and big down/ here, big where it really counts." The midget confronts the speaker with talk of his sexual prowess and insists that he "feel this and you'll believe." The speaker tries to turn away from him, buy him off with a drink, but the midget insists, tugging at him and grabbing his hand. The midget ends up sitting in his lap, singing of "Americas/ of those who never left." The others in the bar turn away in disgust, and then the drunken speaker begins to sing to the midget. In the final section, the poem goes beyond anecdote, stepping off into an eerie, mysterious world where the midget and the speaker merge in their opposition. They are both singers, old world and new, both strangers and outcasts. They come together in the brotherhood of freaks, the pain of being human.

The title of this volume comes from a brilliant tour de force, "Animals Are Passing from Our Lives," a poem told from the point of view of a pig. At first the pig seems complacent, going off to market "suffering children, suffering flies,/ suffering the consumers." He has no intention, however, of giving in, playing the human fool as the boy who drives him along believes he will. He will not "turn like a beast/ cleverly to hook his teeth/ with my teeth. No. Not this pig." This can be taken as a kind of slogan for the entire book, Levine's "Don't tread on me." In a somewhat similar vein is the poem "Baby Villon," about a 116-pound fighter who was robbed in Bangkok because he was white, in London because he was black; he does not give in—not this pig—he fights back. Different as they are, the poet and Villon become one: "My imaginary brother, my cousin,/ Myself made otherwise by all his pain."

Levine identifies with these tough losers, even though he admits that their pains are greater than his, their toughness surpassing his. His attitude toward suffering can be summed up in his often-anthologized poem, "To a Child Trapped in a Barbershop." In mock seriousness he tells the six-year-old that his case is hopeless, advising him not to drink the Lucky Tiger because "that makes it a crime/ against property and the state." "We've all been here before," he informs the boy: we have all suffered the fears of the barbershop and the sharp instruments, but "we stopped crying." The boy should do the same; that is, welcome the world of experience, its difficulties, fears, and pains.

In his next full-length volume, *They Feed, They Lion*, and in the chapbooks *Red Dust* and *Pili's Wall*, Levine pushes further the discoveries that were made in poems such as "The Midget." As he said in his statement in *Contemporary Poets of the English Language*, he was influenced by the surrealistic Spanish and South American poets Miguel Hernández, Rafael Alberti, Pablo Neruda, and César Vallejo. These poets, as well as showing the way to a greater freedom of language, were political poets, all of them affected deeply by the Spanish Civil War. Possibly, though, the greatest reason for the renewed vigor of Levine's work is the discovery of his hometown, Detroit, as a subject for his poetry. This city is at the heart of *They Feed, They Lion*, and it provides the starting point for some of the finest of Levine's poems.

When Levine returns to the city in 1968 in the poem "Coming Home," he finds it an affront to nature, a riot-torn city with "the eyes boarded up," the auto factories' dirt and smoke dominate the hellish landscape: "We burn this city every day." In "The Angels of Detroit" sequence, however, the poet again and again expresses his sympathy for the workers, people such as Bernard:

> His brothers are factories and
> bowling teams, his mother is the
> power to blight, his father
> moves in all men like a threat,
> a closing of hands, an unkept
> promise to return.

Out of such beaten lives comes Levine's most remarkable poem, the title poem, "They Feed, They Lion." As that title illustrates, the poem breaks away from conventional language and syntax. It is a chant celebrating the workers who come "out of burlap sacks, out of bearing butter . . . out of creosote, gasoline, drive shafts, wooden dollies." "They lion grow," the refrain proclaims, "From 'Bow Down' come 'Rise Up.'" It is a cry of and for the workers, in praise of their resiliency and courage.

In the poem "Salami" Levine draws on his Spanish experience to praise the sausage and the culture it comes from. The poet draws a picture of a Spanish man rebuilding an old church all by himself, caring for his retarded child, and praying each night with "the overwhelming incense/ of salami." Then the poem returns to the speaker—so different from the old man— waking from a nightmare, full of guilt, fear, and chaos. He discovers his son sleeping peacefully, feeling that each breath of the boy carries a prayer for him, "the true and earthly prayer/ of salami." The salami gathers the figures of the poem into a community and draws from Levine an expression of reverence. It is an "earthly prayer," a praise of life in all its harshness and the beauty that, at times, comes from it.

After Levine had established his distinctive voice, he continued in a series of volumes—five in seven years—to mine the ore he had discovered in *They Feed, They Lion*. None of these later volumes have quite the excitement and explosiveness of the earlier ones, yet all of them contain excellent poems. During this period, Levine often moves back and forth between personal and political poems, although sometimes the personal and political merge.

Despite the difficulties of his life, despite encounters with prejudice and brutality, he often looks back with pleasure to the child who thought he could be happy. Now he knows that the earth will "let the same children die day/

after day." There is nothing one can do except "howl your name into the wind/ and it will blow it into dust." Everything is ashes and the best wish a man can make is to become "a fine flake of dust that moves/ at evening like smoke at great height/ above the earth and sees it all."

In the meantime, the poet seems to say, one can travel, looking for landscapes of greater beauty and intensity than the bombed-out cities of America. In the poem "7 Years from Somewhere," Levine speaks of an experience, apparently in Morocco, where he was lost and a group of laughing Berber shepherds came to help him, even though they did not share a common language. One of the shepherds took his hand in an effort to communicate with him. After traveling on to "Fez, Meknes, Tetuan, Ceuta, Spain, Paris, here," he awakens to a world where no one takes his hand, and he remembers the shepherd's gesture:

> as one holds a blue egg
> found in tall grasses
> and smile and say something
> that means nothing, that
> means you are, you
> are, and you are home.

Human touch represents the hope that resides at the heart of many of Levine's best poems, and these poems show the way toward his directly political poetry. The poet Robert Bly, in "Leaping Up into Political Poetry," the Introduction to *Forty Poems Touching on Recent American History* (1970), argues that one has to be an inward poet to write about outward events successfully, that "the writing of political poetry is like the writing of personal poetry, a sudden drive by the poet inward." Levine fits this notion of political poetry better than almost any other modern American poet, often exploring his own life while at the same time exploring the lives of the Spanish anarchists of the Civil War. He admits that someone else "who has suffered/ and died for his sister the earth" might have more to say than he, yet he feels the necessity to speak for those who have no other spokesman.

In "For the Fallen" Levine visits the graves in Barcelona of the leading anarchists who were executed during the war. After describing the sight of the graves amidst the noise of the city, he remembers himself as a schoolboy in Detroit going on with his own life at the same time that the heroes were killed. The boy and others trudging home from their dreary jobs knew, in some mysterious way, that there was an important relationship between them and the men in Barcelona. After all these years the feeling the poet has for these men can "shiver these two stiff/ and darkening hands."

In his volumes *Sweet Will* (1985) and *A Walk with Tom Jefferson* (1988) Levine began a subtle but important shift in his poetry. Overall, the tough bitterness appears less often and a quieter, more meditative element begins to dominate the feeling of these longer poems. Reviewers have been about equally divided in either regretting this change or praising it.

The poems often still have a strong narrative quality as Levine draws on events of his past or creates other speakers to reflect on their pasts. The harsh world of Detroit's neighborhoods and factories has become even more central to his work, but the poems sometimes end on surprisingly quiet notes. This is still, however, the work of Philip Levine; the horizons of hope remain darkened by storm clouds.

Levine has sometimes taken to turning the speaking roles in his poems over to others to tell their stories. The speaker in "Voyages" spent his early life working on ships on the Great Lakes, but one day he impulsively jumps ship and makes his way to another life. He settles for a middle-class existence and in the final lines insists—too strenuously—that he does not miss what he left behind:

> Not once has the ocean wind changed
> and brought the taste of salt
> over the coastal hills and through
> the orchards to my back yard, Not once
> have I wakened cold and scared
> out of a dreamless sleep
> into the dreamless life and cried
> and cried for what I left behind.

The speaker in "Buying and Selling" spends his life traveling the country buying and selling automotive parts but once, at the age of twenty, he "wept in the Dexter-/ Davison branch of the public library/ over the death of Keats in the Colvin/ biography." The successful buying day ends on the note of sadness, a sadness for his lost youth, like "the sadness of children/ themselves, who having been abandoned believe/ their parents will return before dark."

When the poems are spoken by the poet himself, a sad note of acceptance becomes the dominant tone. In the ironically titled "I Sing the Body Electric" Levine pictures himself crossing the continent to bring audiences poems about the wars of which they never heard. In "Picture Postcards from the Other World," however, he imagines a reader, like himself, a middle-aged man or woman who "lost whatever faiths he held goes on/ with only the faith that even more/ will be lost." He hopes to bring such a reader his gift of language, even if it comes down to saying "nothing and saying it perfectly."

In the 1980's, Levine's meditative narratives became lengthier, and in the title poem of *A Walk with Tom Jefferson* he moved on to his largest canvas. Tom Jefferson is an elderly black Detroit factory worker, but his famous namesake drifts like a ghost at the heart of this ambitious poem. The narrator walks with Tom through his bombed-out landscape of Detroit's inner city, blocks left to rot since the riot of 1967. Tom's family came from Alabama when he was a child to work in the automobile industry for five dollars a day, but Tom still often remembers the world of his childhood. The narrator muses on the lives destroyed by this industrial system that could not match their "ordinary serviceable dreams" and views the landmarks of the city with hatred—the Renaissance Center that "Ford built/ to look down on our degradation" and the auto plant "where he broke first our backs/ and then the rest." Tom Jefferson, however, still plants his vegetable garden every year, a habit brought from Alabama, and the garden flowers amid the wreckage of the ghetto. Tom is a believer, and his refrain of "That's Biblical" helps him interpret the sufferings of his life. The American Dream of the other Jefferson, the poem suggests, ended in the ugliness of cities like Detroit, but this Jefferson continues to survive and believe.

Philip Levine remains a prolific and ambitious poet. He found his essential subject—the suffering world of the industrial city—rather early in his poetic career, but he has managed to keep it vivid and vital through the decades by the depth of his talent and the seriousness of his commitment.

Michael Paul Novak

Other major works

NONFICTION: *Don't Ask*, 1981.

Bibliography

Holden, Jonathan. *Style and Authenticity in Postmodern Poetry*. Columbia: University of Missouri Press, 1986. In the concluding section of this analysis of contemporary poetry, Holden singles out a poem by Levine, "Milkweed," for special praise. He feels that it combines the attention to the world with the ability to make value judgments, the characteristics of postmodern poetry according to Holden.

Jackson, Richard. "The Long Embrace, Philip Levine's Longer Poems." *The Kenyon Review* 11 (Fall, 1989): 160-169. This is a detailed analysis of three long poems of Levine: "Letters for the Dead: (*1933*, 1976)," "A Poem with No Ending (*Sweet Will*, 1985)," and "A Walk with Tom Jefferson," the title poem of the 1988 volume. He singles out the most recent poem as the most successful in sustaining intensity throughout a long poem.

Mariani, Paul. "Keeping the Covenant." *The Kenyon Review* 11 (Fall, 1989): 170-171. This is an extensive review of *A Walk with Tom Jefferson*; Mariani compares Levine to Walt Whitman and William Carlos Williams, among others, in this laudatory essay. He concludes that his poetry has kept its covenant with the dispossessed.

Mills, Ralph. *Cry of the Human*. Urbana: University of Illinois Press, 1975. This is the clearest analysis of Levine's early work. Mills singles out "They Feed, They Lion" and "Angel Butcher" as remarkable achievements and concludes his analysis by calling Levine one of the best poets writing in English today.

Smith, Dave. *Local Assay: On Contemporary American Poetry.* Urbana: University of Illinois Press, 1988. Despite the fact that Smith feels that the work is sometimes marred by polemics, he states that Levine is a master in depicting daily life. He praises the work for its honesty and accessibility and finds the theme of communion at the heart of Levine's poetry.

Vendler, Helen. "All Too Real." *The New York Review of Books* 28 (December 17, 1981): 32-36. This is an all-out attack on Levine's poetry, an exception to the usual praise heaped on it. Vendler criticizes the metrics, the anecdotal subjects, and what she calls the sentimentality of the poetry. She states that Levine has too limited a notion of the real.

JANET LEWIS

Born: Chicago, Illinois; August 17, 1899

Principal poetry

The Indians in the Woods, 1922; *The Wheel in Midsummer*, 1927; *The Earth-Bound, 1924-1944*, 1946; *The Ancient Ones*, 1979; *The Birthday of the Infanta*, 1979; *Poems Old and New, 1918-1978*, 1981; *Late Offerings*, 1988.

Other literary forms

Janet Lewis is best known for her four historical novels, critical and popular successes published between 1932 and 1959. The first and least acclaimed, *The Invasion: A Narrative of Events Concerning the Johnston Family of St. Mary's* (1932), shared with her early poems an interest in Native American life and the American wilderness. Three others, of which *The Wife of Martin Guerre* (1941) and *The Trial of Soren Qvist* (1947) are probably the best known, deal in a lucid, documentary style with historic cases of circumstantial evidence. Lewis' fictional prose reflects her apprenticeship in Imagistic poetry —a narrative style that, in her own words, is "supposed to be transparent."

Lewis also published a novel with a contemporary setting, *Against a Darkening Sky* (1943), and a collection of contemporary short stories, *Good-Bye, Son, and Other Stories* (1946), as well as children's books. She adapted *The Wife of Martin Guerre* as an opera, produced in 1956 by the Juilliard School of Music and subsequently at other schools. She wrote two other opera librettos, *The Swans* (1986) and *The Legend* (1987).

Achievements

Lewis' poetic output is slight but distinguished. The ninety-four lyrics in her collected poems, many of them brief, show a remarkable stylistic evolution through her career of more than sixty years. A reviewer of the volume for *Poetry* described Lewis' poetic gift as "slight—I mean, both delicate and minor." Her husband, poet-critic Yvor Winters, praised her as a "stylist of remarkable native gift" but regretted her penchant for "domestic sentiment, which sometimes goes all the way to sentimentality."

Whatever the merits of these limiting remarks, Lewis remains important as a verse stylist and as a participant in—and transcender of—modern literary quarrels regarding the use of traditional forms. Her first book of poems, perhaps one of the best collections in the strict Imagist mode, was published in 1922 in a series which included William Carlos Williams and Marianne Moore. Two books later, in 1946, she had evolved into openly philosophical verse in traditional forms, and she won the Shelley Memorial Award for poetry in 1948. Her newer poems, a group begun when she was seventy-two years old, expand her reputation and answer the complaints of sentimentality and dry formalism sometimes lodged against her work of the 1930's and 1940's.

Lewis' collected poems appeared at a time when fashion had caught up with her lifelong interests. The American Indian, the Sun Belt, and the lives of women had become, in the words of a *Parnassus* reviewer, "radical chic." In her eighties, Lewis achieved long-postponed recognition for decades of lyrical vision and craftsmanship.

Biography

Janet Lewis was born on August 17, 1899, in Chicago, Illinois, the daughter of Edwin Herbert Lewis, a poet, novelist, and English teacher. In the summer, the family lived in northern Michigan, where Lewis came to know the Ojibwa Indians, the subjects of her first book. She published her first poem in *Poetry* when she was twenty-one, a book when she was twenty-three. Earning an A.A. at the Lewis Institute in 1918 and a Ph.B. at the University of Chicago in 1920, Lewis worked for the American consulate in Paris, for *Redbook* magazine in Chicago, and finally, for the Lewis Institute in Chicago, where she taught until stricken with tuberculosis in 1922. She moved for her health to Santa Fe, New Mexico, and became a friend of Yvor Winters, another Chicago poet convalescing in the West. On June 22, 1926, when Lewis was still in frail health, they were married and in 1927 moved to Stanford University in California, where her husband pursued his doctorate and began teaching in 1928.

The direct effect of Winters, Janet Lewis' famous husband, on her career is not easy to assess. They remained devoted to each other until his death in 1968, and her poetic style evolved in a way harmonious with his published critical stance. Both strict Imagists in the 1920's, Winters and Lewis began, in the 1930's, to work in traditional verse forms and with paraphrasable morals—a position hostile to the high modernist mode of T. S. Eliot and Ezra Pound and closer to the writing of Thomas Hardy than to any other major modern poet.

Meanwhile, writing in the mornings when the family was "off to school," Lewis established a national reputation as a novelist and published in 1946 what was to be for more than thirty years her last volume of poetry. It won for her the Shelley Memorial Award for poetry in 1948. Writing her books and assuming the public role of housewife in Los Altos, California, near Stanford University, Lewis apparently settled into a peaceful uniformity of life suggested in her poem "No-Winter Country." A Guggenheim Fellowship in 1950-1951 to do research in Paris for her novel *The Ghost of Monsieur Scarron* (1959) was perhaps the most significant interruption in her routine until her husband died of cancer in 1968.

In 1971, still living in Los Altos, Lewis began writing poetry again, and her style again differed from what had gone before. The new work, in a more expansive and intimate voice, reestablished her reputation as a poet. For some years before and after her husband's death, Lewis taught writing at Stanford University. In 1976, she visited Indian ruins in northern Arizona, making the last part of the journey on horseback and by foot, and her experiences on this pilgrimage back toward the Indian themes of her earlier work resulted in some of her strongest new poems, a thin volume entitled *The Ancient Ones*. In the 1980's, she continued to write, publishing *Late Offerings* in 1988.

Analysis

During a literary career spanning more than sixty years, Janet Lewis has produced a small body of well-crafted poetry in styles evolving through three distinct stages: compact Imagism in the 1920's, formal lyricism in the 1930's and 1940's, and, after a twenty-five-year hiatus, a free incantatory style in the 1970's and 1980's. The first two stages paralleled the career of Winters, who began as a strict and respected Imagist and became in the 1930's the leader of a self-styled "reactionary" return to traditional rhyme and accentual meter. Opinion is divided as to whether Lewis' formalist turn was well advised—whether her middle poems moved toward sentimentality and dryness or whether she wrote rich and finely crafted work in the tradition of Thomas Hardy and earlier English verse.

Her collected volume, *Poems Old and New, 1918-1978*, was received with almost universal praise, critics differing only about which poems to single out. In this book, Lewis collected her best poems in a wide range of styles, including the 1918 poem which won for her entrance into the Poetry Club at the University of Chicago. The most recent works in the volume, written after 1971, are a synthesis and extension of the styles which preceded them— returning to the free verse and Indian subjects of her Imagistic period but exploring the powers of a complex, discursive long line. Without the Imagistic restrictions against abstract statement and paraphrasable content, Lewis displays more freely her feeling for nature, her lyricism, and her sense of history.

The lyrics in her 1922 volume, *The Indians in the Woods*, average less than twelve lines and, with haikulike compression, suggest the closeness between the lives of the Ojibwa Indians and the processes of nature, particularly the cycle of the harsh northern seasons. The poems are rigorously Imagistic, expunged of nearly all general statement or transition—each a sequence of evoked sensations and elemental feelings. Central to the sequence is the god whose return is celebrated in the spring; even without this underpinning of myth, however, the poems function individually as icons of time's destructive passage, the promise of rebirth, and the muted joy of participation in natural process. The narrator is repeatedly identified as female, at times a wife, at times a grandmother, so that the poems are genuinely feminocentric, with a male god playing the role of mysterious natural Other. In most of the poems, the god could as well be a mortal lover, the seasons as well figurative as literal, and the forest as well suburban as primeval. The reversal of literary gender roles—particularly in 1922—is reason alone to reread these poems. If stripped of their bibliographic history, they might as readily be attributed to the 1970's as to the 1920's. Like William Carlos Williams' poems in *Spring and All* (1922), which they antedate and resemble, the lyrics are spare and evocative; short lines play occasional run-ons against the expected pause at line's end. What the Ojibwa poems lack in range, they make up for in polished intensity.

Actually, though Imagism stands at the beginning of Lewis' collected poems, it was not her first style. "The Freighters," her earliest published poem, uses traditional accent and meter and describes trees along a bank as singing "with moving branches/ Songs of eternity." This is the sort of generalization which Lewis, as an Imagist, excluded from the 1922 volume, but to which she would return in her post-Imagist work after 1930. Between 1922 and 1927, the years of her convalescence, Lewis was evolving toward a softer, more traditional style without sacrificing the Imagistic virtues of sensation and compression. Some of her most memorable short poems are from this transitional period. Generally domestic in subject, the poems often use traditional lyric forms but have compact images in the foreground. Some, like the title poem to her second book, "The Wheel in Midsummer," are stylistically similar to the Ojibwa poems. Among the best works from her convalescent period are "The Reader," "Girl Help," and "Remembered Morning," which chart the direction in which her art was to evolve. "The Reader" is a delicately descriptive poem about a reader lost in a book, as the sun, the fire, and the leaves clamor ineffectually to recall him to sensory reality—all this shown with Imagistic directness. Then a newborn "creature"—presumably a moth—is at the screen door, "heaving damp heavy wings." Lewis' readers are left with the nascent symbol, no explanation. Less cryptic but equally delicate is "Girl Help," a three-quatrain rhyming poem in which a servant is shown to pause and smell lilacs scented with promise. "Remembered Morning" succeeds with perhaps an even less promising subject, the remembrance of a happy summer's day in childhood. Yet Lewis' spare, evocative description rescues the poem from its conventional versification and a line such as "O happy early stir!" Less successful experiments with traditional verse include "Love Poem," "The Candle Flame," "The Manger," and "The Tennis Players," which fall into the mannerisms of turn-of-the-century magazine verse.

After her marriage and move to California, Lewis' style changed decisively, probably encouraged by her husband, who had recently made a sharp theoretical turn against "experimental" modern poetry and was already developing the position he would expound in his controversial critical books.

Lewis' poems between 1927 and 1944 were in a style that adapted traditional prosody and direct paraphrasable purpose to the needs of twentieth century life. Some are flawed, at least from the mainstream perspective, by archaisms, inversions, predictable rhymes, and hackneyed similes—dangers deliberately courted by a reformed Imagist who knew what she was doing. The best are effective as beautifully crafted antiques newly made, and that was clearly Lewis' intention. Among the best is "Time and Music," a philosophical poem in octameter couplets which uses its very formality as an extension of its content: the suggestion that willed form is life; its absence, death. "Country Burial" works in a more emotional mode, describing vividly a funeral procession across a flowery field, then turning away from the numbing, discomforting vision of a Heaven without the wetness and color of earth. In this, and in "Baby Goat"—a poem saved from preciousness by the visual exactness of Lewis' descriptions—she contrasts the world of changing, doomed colors with the mysterious colorless world of Heaven, or unchanging form. This theme was implicit even in the "The Freighters" and the Ojibwa poems, but the best of the middle poems gain intellectual and moral density by making it explicit.

In the poems written between 1930 and 1944, Lewis has clearly accepted the aim expressed in her husband's criticism and adopted by a school of California poets: to fuse fully realized descriptive detail with expressed abstract meaning through exertion of the conscious will in traditional verse. "Lines with a Gift of Herbs," "The Hanger at Sunnydale," "In the Egyptian Museum," and "Helen Grown Old" are successes in this effort, all reflecting on the contrast between particulars which change and universals which inhere through this change—the scent in dry herbs, the steel hanger of a lost dirigible, the jewelry of a dead civilization, and the mystery of Helen of Troy's unmemorialized old age. Though the verse, again, is sometimes too dry, too mannered for some modern tastes, these poems do seem to work through the willed fusion of image and explicit moral called for by Winters' theory. Nevertheless, despite the critical success of these poems, Lewis ceased writing poetry altogether between 1944 and 1971.

When she took up verse again, it was free verse without rhyme or with casual rhyme in the manner of Ezra Pound or William Butler Yeats, and her lines set up a biblical narrative cadence not as free as Walt Whitman's but clearly in the same tradition. This was a clear break from the formalism of the middle years, though it is not a return to Imagism, for abstract statement and reasoning mix freely with description. Also, Lewis returns to the domestic and Indian subjects of her pre-California lyrics. Here the interplay between the transient and the eternal receives its most serene and poignant treatment in poems such as "For the Father of Sandro Gullota," "The Anasazi Woman," "The Ancient Ones: Betátakin," "In a Convalescent Hospital," and "Geometries." Though Lewis maintains a recognizable voice through all of her changes, in the later poems she seems to draw the reader closer, sharing her empathy with a child dying of leukemia, with the mummy of an Indian woman, with a ruins of pre-Navajo people moved by universals of water and beauty, with a once-vital woman dying alone, and with geometric shapes replicated eternally in nature. The later poems in her collected volume are not uniformly her best, but they are a triumphant summation, suggesting or incorporating the best of what came before.

William H. Green

Other major works

LONG FICTION: *The Invasion: A Narrative of Events Concerning the Johnston Family of St. Mary's*, 1932; *The Wife of Martin Guerre*, 1941; *Against a Darkening Sky*, 1943; *The Trial of Soren Qvist*, 1947; *The Ghost of Monsieur Scarron*, 1959.

SHORT FICTION: *Good-Bye, Son, and Other Stories*, 1946.

OPERA: *The Wife of Martin Guerre*, 1956 (libretto; adaptation of her novel); *The Swans*, 1986 (libretto); *The Legend*, 1987 (libretto).

Bibliography

Crow, Charles L. *Janet Lewis.* Boise, Idaho: Boise State University Press, 1980. This excellent study of Lewis' life and work provides careful, insightful, and detailed attention to her novels. Supplemented by an index and a bibliography.

Davie, Donald. "The Historical Novels of Janet Lewis." *The Southern Review* 2 (January, 1966): 40-60. Specific attention is given to novels of Lewis, although other works are briefly discussed. Davie provides a very useful definition of the historical novel. His analysis is insightful and detailed.

Ingles, Fred. "The Novels of Janet Lewis." *Critique: Studies in Modern Fiction* 7 (1964/1965): 47-64. This excellent introduction to the novels of Janet Lewis compares Lewis' prose with the prose of various historians. Her work is also discussed in terms of her husband's work with historiography and historical novels.

Killoh, Ellen. "Patriarchal Women: A Study of Three Novels by Janet Lewis." *The Southern Review* 10 (April, 1974): 342-364. A very careful and thought-provoking analysis of three novels, with an emphasis on how the novels concern themselves with the conventional roles of women. This easy-to-read study pays specific attention to *The Wife of Martin Guerre*.

Steele, Trimpi. "The Poetry of Janet Lewis." *The Southern Review* 18 (April, 1982): 251-258. Provides a fine and detailed examination of the poetry of Lewis in terms of themes, symbols, and influences. Steele's analysis is well conceived and readable and provides an excellent introduction to Lewis' poetry.

VACHEL LINDSAY

Born: Springfield, Illinois; November 10, 1879
Died: Springfield, Illinois; December 5, 1931

Principal poetry

The Tramp's Excuse and Other Poems, 1909; *Rhymes to Be Traded for Bread*, 1912; *General William Booth Enters into Heaven and Other Poems*, 1913; *The Congo and Other Poems*, 1914; *The Chinese Nightingale and Other Poems*, 1917; *The Golden Whales of California and Other Rhymes in the American Language*, 1920; *The Daniel Jazz and Other Poems*, 1920; *Collected Poems of Vachel Lindsay*, 1923, 1925; *Going-to-the-Sun*, 1923; *Going-to-the-Stars*, 1926; *The Candle in the Cabin*, 1926; *Johnny Appleseed and Other Poems*, 1928; *Every Soul Is a Circus*, 1929; *Selected Poems of Vachel Lindsay*, 1931 (Hazelton Spencer, editor); *Selected Poems of Vachel Lindsay*, 1963 (Mark Harris, editor); *The Poetry of Vachel Lindsay*, 1984-1986 (3 volumes; Dennis Camp, editor).

Other literary forms

Adventures While Preaching the Gospel of Beauty (1914) and *A Handy Guide for Beggars* (1916) are autobiographical accounts of Vachel Lindsay's walking tours, narratives that simultaneously articulate the populist ideals of his life and identify the sources for much of his poetry, the themes and characters that preoccupied him in the years before his great success. These and other prose works and designs are collected in *Adventures: Rhymes and Designs* (1968, Robert Sayre, editor); *Letters of Vachel Lindsay* (1979, Marc Chénetier, editor) offers a fair sampling of Lindsay's correspondence with the literary community after his fame was established. Lindsay produced quantities of broadsides and pamphlets on topics ranging from workers' rights in the mines, to racial injustice, to his own peculiarly passionate brand of Christianity. These, frequently set in frames of hieroglyphs of his own design or scrawled sketches vaguely in the style of *art nouveau*, suggest both his wide-ranging ambition and his lack of focus, his mercurial temperament.

Achievements

Lindsay's achievements have always been measured by the size, enthusiasm, and attention of his audiences. The great recitals of the "higher vaudeville" poems of the 1910's aroused such enthusiasm that good critics responded with varying assessments: John Masefield, after meeting him in Indianapolis in 1916 and hearing him read in England in 1920, said flatly that Lindsay was "the best American poet," whereas Ezra Pound, polite at first, finally dismissed Lindsay with the observation that one could write such stuff "as fast as one scribbles." Poets as various as William Butler Yeats, Robert Graves, Stephen Vincent Benét, and Theodore Roethke all saw Lindsay's work as

Masefield did, whereas Amy Lowell, Conrad Aiken, and many others not so politely scorned him. The difference of opinion, finally, has less to do with Lindsay's style than with the two basic ways of perceiving poetry: hearing and reading. Lindsay's accomplishment was that he could write good poetry that could be read aloud well. The language, themes, and implications of his verse were profoundly American; they canvassed American culture clearly, affectionately, and critically. He built his poetry on his "tramps" through the land as well as in the city, "tramps" which taught him to see, as Walt Whitman, Robert Frost, and Carl Sandburg did, the particulars of American life that defied sentimentality and generalization. When he invoked the gods, they were American heroes, the names that the folk he met knew and revered, both successes and failures: Abraham Lincoln, John Peter Altgeld, William Jennings Bryan, and John Chapman (Johnny Appleseed). Just as important, however, his poetry sang; it moved those who sounded it and those who heard it. His British audiences in 1920 heard the unfamiliar cadences of American speech in song and were astounded. His American audiences heard the rhythms and voices of their own culture, normally absent from the esoteric world of the "New Poetry." This balance of theme and song, of creed in distinctive rhythm, is Lindsay's most durable accomplishment. With it he achieves what Whitman seemed to predict for the twentieth century American poet. Masterpieces like "General William Booth Enters into Heaven," "Santa Fe Trail," "Chinese Nightingale," "Flower-fed Buffaloes," and others will remain among the classics of twentieth century American poetry, for they perfectly express the sounds and concerns of a complex moment in American history.

Biography

Nicholas Vachel Lindsay was born and died in his father's house next to the Governor's Mansion in Springfield, Illinois. His father, Dr. Vachel Thomas Lindsay, was a general practitioner whose home and financial stability made possible his son's slow progress toward a self-sustaining career as a poet. His mother, Esther Catharine Frazee Lindsay, a college mathematics teacher and instructor of painting before she married Dr. Lindsay, had the spirit and endurance to continue hopefully to support their son as he ambivalently moved from college (leaving Hiram College in June of 1900 without a degree after three years), to the Art Institute in Chicago, and on to New York to try to market his skills as an artist. His father may have hoped that his son would join his practice and settle down, but both parents were trampers and travelers in their own way. They had courted each other in the art galleries of Europe in the summer of 1875, and had taken the family to Europe in the summer of 1906, immediately after Lindsay's first American walking tour. In the spring of 1906, Lindsay had walked from Florida back north through the Okefenokee swamp to Atlanta, lecturing (on the Pre-Raphaelites), singing his poems ("The Tree of the Laughing Bells") all the way to Grassy Springs, Kentucky, and the home of relatives. The immediate leap to Europe, the Louvre, and the tomb of Napoleon was in some ways shocking, but Lindsay was comfortable in both milieux, marking the range of his experience, the talents and interests of his parents, and the end of the era of art and design as his principal interests.

His next "tramp" (in 1912) led directly to publication. He had tried "poem-peddling" in New York in the spring of 1905 without success, but now set out to trade rhymes for bread as he walked from Illinois to California. He caught the Santa Fe trail in Kansas and felt charged with poetic material and enthusiasm. That the trip was hard was undeniable; there was less room for self-delusion or self-indulgence than in any other episode of his life. When he "gave up" and took the train from Wagon Mound, New Mexico, to Los Angeles, he felt defeated; but here, after gloom and despair, came the inspiration for "General William Booth Enters into Heaven." Booth of the Salvation Army had died almost a month earlier, but as Lindsay walked the city at night, the poem flashed into being.

"General William Booth Enters into Heaven" was his making, and, because it was such a showpiece to read, perhaps his unmaking as well. Lindsay's career has been divided into sections of composition and recital, with the transitional stage between the publication of *General William Booth Enters into Heaven and Other Poems* by Kennerley in 1913 and *The Chinese Nightingale and Other Poems* by Macmillan in 1917. After this period, regardless of his own interests and enthusiasms, he was seen as a reciter of his own verse, a performer, an actor. His livelihood depended on the income generated from such recitals, and the verse he wrote later (with several notable exceptions) does not match the standard of the poetry of the 1910's.

It is important to note that Lindsay saw his public readings as the best way to reach the largest audience of American readers of poetry. If they all wanted to hear "The Congo," he would read it, repeatedly, even though he knew it was not representative of his best work. "I have tried to fight off all jazz," he said. He knew that it was he (as much as his verse, or more) who charmed or conjured his audiences; *he* had to read his work to have it go. He termed his reciting style and material a "higher vaudeville" and knew that in reaching new audiences he would have to alienate older or more traditional ones. In his day, however, academe did not scorn him: Yale, Wellesley, Oxford, Cambridge, all invited him to read, and they sat spellbound. Robert Graves, who introduced him to the circle of Oxford dons and students with the notion of showing off an American curiosity, was astonished at Lindsay's success. It is hard to reconstruct the experience: it depended on the power of Lindsay's delivery, but he asserted that the energy was there in the lines. In his passionate, reverent attention to his audience, his desire for its conversion, he poured himself out. Thus, in his reciting tours, Lindsay saw himself as no less than the Christian-democratic poet, a man who could, by the power of his poetry and personality, revive the artistic and moral sensibility of the nation.

Lindsay seemed more showman than troubadour, a performer, not a poet, primarily because he was more interested in speaking to America than to literary critics. The poets who supplanted him in American poetry anthologies consciously and particularly addressed themselves to the scholar-reader, the literary elite, the would-be student of literature. There is more to the contrast than this: Lindsay may have felt that he could not impress that literary elite beyond the first shock of amazement and delight at his readings: he may have doubted his staying power, his ability to follow "General William Booth Enters into Heaven" and "The Chinese Nightingale" with more of the same. Although Dr. Paul Wakefield (his brother-in-law) finally got him to the Mayo Foundation in Rochester, Minnesota, in June, 1924, for a diagnosis of his nervous condition, Lindsay must have feared the worsening of his serious physical and nervous disorder all his adult life. The word "epilepsy" was not mentioned until Eleanor Ruggles' biography (1959), but the severe seizures were public knowledge.

Celibate and unmarried until his mid-forties, but in love with a series of remarkable women who rejected his proposals, Lindsay married Elizabeth Conner on May 19, 1925, without revealing the secret of his seizures until after the ceremony. Paranoia, "morbid fancies," as Ruggles painfully documents them, insulting and insane accusations of family and stranger alike: these multiplied in the late 1920's, and gave Lindsay's career a kind of lurid richness that tempts readers to consider the pathological case and not the poet. Lindsay drank a bottle of Lysol at home, upstairs, early in the morning of December 5, 1931, killing himself quickly but painfully. In the past decade he had read triumphantly in England, married a young, bright, determined wife, and was known internationally for poems many could recite from memory, but fear of the increased frequency of epileptic attack, financial anxieties, anger with critics who wanted "more of the same," and despair that he was tied to the task of reading to audiences that would not read him—these concerns, and doubtless others, resulted in suicide.

Analysis

Music and message, rhythm and truth, Vachel Lindsay's best poetry offers extraordinary examples of the absolute interdependence of sound and sense. Lindsay finds ways of presenting on the page effects as various as the thump, whistle, and wheeze of a calliope ("The Kallyope Yell"), the staggered, percussive rattle of native dancing ("The Congo"), the smooth, mournful music of prairie birds singing in counterpoint to highway traffic ("The Santa Fe Trail"), and the unexpected brevity of a tall tale's punch line ("The Daniel Jazz"). Masterful as these effects are in themselves, they also illustrate Lindsay's affection for the details and the personality of his Midwestern world.

The gaudy steam calliope which blasted the fairgrounds with its din, the communities of blacks moving north to Illinois with their brand-new tempos of jazz music, the individual note of a bird called the Rachel Jane, the black servant's power in the household ("The Daniel Jazz") are all hard facts in his verse, keeping the dreams and generalizations, the hopes and fears of his populist idealism, rooted in the actual.

When, for example, Lindsay plucks General Booth out of his British setting for a tribute in a dream vision, marching deadbeats cruise around the courthouse in downtown Springfield. Here Lindsay harnesses the melting-pot theory of American meliorism to serve an evangelical cause, and where better to link the two powerful processes of social equality and salvation than on the courthouse steps that Abraham Lincoln climbed? The courthouse still dominates countless Midwestern town squares, a kind of secular temple: Lindsay recognized its power as a symbol. The paradoxical quality of the courthouse is carried on in the paradox of "Booth the Soldier," the tension derived from the "salvation" army, almost oxymoronic, however Pauline and familiar, from Protestant hymns. Again secular power and spiritual grace unite in a specific figure.

Lindsay revered the ideals of the courthouse and the Salvation Army, but the poem really celebrates the transformation of the "blear review." When all are made new, the "blind eyes" which are opened are not specifically identified as Booth's, because *all* gaze on "a new, sweet world." Lindsay's concern for a mass of people is evident in this poem; the variety of their disabilities, their instruments, their crimes, all fascinate him. Their energy is captured in the way the lines begin—trochees and spondees abound and alliteration provides speed and percussion. The principal accents are often just two, forcing the reading voice to pace on as it makes sense of the line.

In "General William Booth Enters into Heaven," Lindsay's technical genius can be appreciated; his belief in the new life of grace is given authority by the rippling power of the verse. In the first stanza, the alliteration and repeated stress at the start and finish of the first line exemplify Booth's confidence; the fact that he was blind makes this parade all the more bravely led. The undercurrent of the parenthesis "(Are you washed in the blood of the Lamb?)" changes the meter with its anapestic feet, implying the smooth confidence of the saint's question, but also slowing or interrupting the raucous motion of the parade. The couplet rhymes are remarkably appropriate as an organizing frame for this disorderly procession, but "the blood of the Lamb" never has its rhyme completed. Even in the last line of the poem, when the question is stripped of parentheses and quotation marks, when it comes straight to the reader/hearer, it has no echo, for it is Lindsay's unanswered, unanswerable question.

In the second stanza ("Every slum had sent . . .") Lindsay continues to move the reader/hearer through contradictory feelings: delight with the visual splendor of the scene (banners blooming and "transcendent dyes" in "the golden air") and awe or apprehension at the human forms that are here collected ("Bull-necked convicts," "Loons with trumpets"). The diction suggests salvation ("bloomed with glory," "transcendent," "upward thro' the golden air") while the subjects are clearly fallen, and likely to remain so.

The poem almost halts, therefore, caught by this paradox of evangelistic passion in fallen men, in the opening accounts of the third stanza with its three slow beats: "Booth died blind. . . ." Lindsay picks up the rhythm with uncharacteristic iambs: "and still by faith he trod," thus metrically emphasizing the miracle—dying blind but walking on. Lindsay hides the actual moment of transition here, as he does when the "blear review" is "in an instant" made new. In the middle of the stanza, with no italicized directions for music, Lindsay seems to lose the moment of salvation, and emphasizes instead the continuation of the parade of the purified host as it accompanies Booth to heaven.

Lindsay balances the familiar with the mystical perfectly. The parade of deadbeats playing musical instruments as they circle the town square becomes Booth's contribution to his world of slum victims, a metaphoric representation of his collected good works, and a fantastic vision of the heavenly scene.

It is easy to see that the italicized passages of advice ("Sweet flute music") are meant to invite the reader/hearer to change attitude, to prepare for a new meter, to modulate tone. Lindsay's stage directions are meant to aid readers, not to stage shows or revise the verse. Lindsay structured his verse with care, setting lines on the page in groups indented or flush, with headnotes or numerical demarcation, always trying to slow the reader's headlong rush through a poem.

Much more sober and conventional but no less successful is the trio of poems united under the title "The Gospel of Beauty." Lindsay sang the sections of this poem on his walking tours, and it is not hard to imagine the farmers of the plains listening with some pleasure to this celebration of their past and future. Once again, Lindsay's characteristic concerns emerge from the lines, although there is little of the jazzy movement of the Booth poem in these thoughtful stanzas. "The Proud Farmer" (the title of the first segment) was Lindsay's mother's father, whose town, church, fields, and cemetery he knew well. The poet sees the heroic accomplishments of the rural life and the failure of the town to grow and prosper according to his grandfather's design: "They sleep with him beneath the ragged grass . . ./ The village withers, by his voice unstirred." The poet, "a sturdy grandchild," is empowered by the meditation, this time admiring the characteristic American pioneer hero, the man who worked by day, read by night, preached the word, and sired a family to spread to the ends of the earth. Frazee, like Booth, was a hero, capable of converting and saving, and Lindsay feels his inheritance and expresses it in the run-ons of the last stanza. The inversions ("furtive souls and tame") and archaisms ("he preached and plowed and wrought") are not meant to ape the formal diction of poetic recollection; they are gestures of respect to a man of an earlier age, whose language was formed by biblical study. The second section, "The Illinois Village," reminds the reader of Lindsay's preoccupation with Springfield as a holy and aesthetically charged place. *The Golden Book of Springfield* (1920) and *The Village Magazines* (which he published several times at his own expense) were documents of his vision of Springfield as a site for political and spiritual rebirth, a new American life to start in the fields of Illinois. The three parts of "The Gospel of Beauty" move from one man on the land, to a village with promise, to a visionary city of the ideal future. "The Illinois Village" is Springfield in its youth, with the "village church by night" the image of "Spirit-power." Commerce is de-emphasized in favor of artful decoration ("fountain-frieze" and painters and poets); the church is the moral and cultural center. Lindsay's image of the church in moonlight and veiled by trees at dusty noon again places the fact between mere observation and fantasy, like the courthouse in "General William Booth Enters into Heaven": "The trees that watch at dusty noon/ Breaking its sharpest lines, veil not/ The whiteness it reflects from God."

"On the Building of Springfield" closes the work, its prophetic tone sharply in contrast to the meditative observations of the first two sections. Lindsay's dream here is like that of any booster of an "All-American city"; he wishes his city to claim its place with Athens, Oxford, and Florence. But his terms and rhythms are unique and defy casual description. "The Proud Farmer" saw the house of God and the farm to be one; in "The Illinois Village," the church organizes a square of town land, wreathed by trees; now a city is laid out in aisles, not streets, "where Music grows and Beauty is unchained." The renaissance of Springfield is larger than a religious conversion or a chamber of commerce scheme; it demands aesthetic appreciation, a vision beyond the practical payoff. Lindsay sees the danger of boosterism and calls Springfield "Ninevah" and "Babylon" unless it heeds his call, the proud farmer's heritage. Nature returns to assert its power when "Maple, Elm and Oak" are capitalized to suggest both the trees and the streets (as they are named in Springfield and almost every other American town); the trees again are the images of germinating genius in a town which tends to ignore the power of its own symbols. "Attics" are places to store rummage, not "sacred tears," as Attics of Athens might have shed. The curious choice of the verb form in the repeated line ("A city is not builded in a day.") reminds the reader/hearer of the process of the action, not its completeness: the open end of the trochee suggests both the incompleteness of the building and the hope for more.

Thus Lindsay continues to combine vision and fact, myth and reality, all set in a form whose sound and meter supports and explains the message. This pattern is still evident, on a larger scale, in "The Chinese Nightingale," a poem with its roots in the great tradition of nightingale poetry (Ovid, Samuel

Taylor Coleridge, John Keats, Thomas Hardy, William Butler Yeats) and in the fairy tale (Hans Christian Andersen's tale of the bird and the emperor). Typically, Lindsay starts with a metrical and literary joke: the "How, how," of Chang is the musical salutation in Chinese which the reader/hearer understands only in English. Lindsay's sister and brother-in-law in China provided accurate images and diction for this poem. The question in reply to "How?" reminds the reader/hearer of William Wordsworth's silly questions to the leech gatherer, but instead of a lament over lost greatness and present drudgery, the artful objects that surround Chang conjure up the beauty of a civilization gone, like Yeats's piece of lapis lazuli. The nightingale, the joss, and the lady all sing with appropriate imagery and rhythm, to create the tapestry of sound that makes up the poem. The introduction of the lady's song, for example, is effected with a couplet of lifting iambs, ending with a double-rhyme that has an unaccented final syllable, a feminine ending: ("aflower . . . bower"), while Chang is solid in iambs at the lines' ends (his "countenance carved of stone/ ironed and ironed, all alone"). The living figure petrifies as the icons come alive: Keats would have approved, and Yeats did. The repetitions in the lady's song are mesmerizing, with their alterations ("bright bronze breast" and "bronze-brown wing") suggesting her accuracy, an accuracy which deteriorates in Chang's responses to short-line generalizations and visions of his San Francisco world. The Chinese laundryman is, like Keats, called back to his sole self after the nightingale's voice is stilled, but his memory of the dialogue between lady and joss whispers, hinting at evocative details, the remains of inspiration.

The tones of the song are distinct: the nightingale is the medium, the muse, whose brief invitation and occasional punctuation of the tale are done with almost nonsensical repetition. The lady sings gently, with fewer explosive consonants and more iambs at line-starts, dotting her lines with more anapestic feet ("I had a silvery name") than the "great gray joss" whose tone is more belligerent and stylized:

> Hear the howl of the silver seas,
> Hear the thunder.
> Hear the gongs of holy China
> How the waves and tunes combine
> in a rhythmic clashing wonder, . . .

A comparison of the speaking voices here with Yeats's later "Byzantium" poems will reveal how many of the images are shared, and how differently the poems sound. Lindsay's details are, literally, taken from the laundryman's shelf, as Yeats's stone in "Lapis Lazuli" was from his own desk, but the integrity of the speaking voices and the metrical effects are pure Lindsay.

Whether Lindsay impersonates a joss or a calliope, or celebrates heroes like Pocahontas, Altgeld, Bryan, or Lincoln, the theme is frequently one of measured loss, hopes unrealized, populist dreams evaporating, death before accomplishment. In this regard, "General William Booth Enters into Heaven" and "The Daniel Jazz" form a jolly retelling of a familiar tale. The "Kallyope" runs out of steam and will not, finally, convert the proud, but it *has* insisted on the equation of "the gutter dream" and "the golden dream." The senseless notes that *is* sounds at the poem's close are invitations to enjoy pure body rhythm, which cannot succeed on the page or with the ear. Lindsay was fascinated by the loss of the dream and the bittersweet recollections of the promise once imagined. From "The Last Song of Lucifer," which he worked on in college, to "The Flower-fed Buffaloes," published in *Going-to-the-Stars* in 1926, Lindsay seems to understand and accept the cycle of creation and destruction, hope and despair. This last poem, fifteen short lines, perfectly embodies the cycle in its music and diction.

The poem opens with the title's descriptive phrase, evoking the perfect pastoral, then quickly turns to the song of the locomotive in the third line. Like Henry David Thoreau, Lindsay did not see the railroad as an evil force; both poets allowed their trains to sing. Still, the flowers that sustained the buffalo "lie low" under the ties, just as the "perfumed grass" gives way to the wheat. Although flowers and grass have been replaced by railroad tracks and wheat farms, the spring "still is sweet"; Lindsay is not cheaply nostalgic or willing to falsify his experience. Nevertheless, something is gone, not just the buffalo, but the tribes that fed on the species. Lindsay surprises the reader/ hearer with the intrusion of the Blackfeet and the Pawnees "lying low, lying low."

The savagery of the past age is captured in the diction describing the buffaloes' behavior ("They gore . . . they bellow . . . they trundle . . .") and the reader suddenly glimpses the vigor and violence of that age. Perfect pastoral? Not at all, but assuredly gone. The sibiliant *s*'s the aspirate *f*'s and *wh*'s, and the lingering *l*'s create a mood that the bellowing and goring only briefly interrupt, for the spring *is* sweet, and the wheels of the harvesting machines and the railroad cars sweep through the prairie contentedly. Lindsay's point is to note the transition and loss and savor the memory, but not to hope for restoration.

Lindsay was an optimist, aware of history as creator as well as destroyer. His poetry urges the reader/hearer to hear and read: to know how we sound, where we came from, and "what to make of a diminished thing," that is, our future. When Frost used that phrase in "Oven Bird," he preceded it with "the highway dust is over all"; Frost, too, had "tramped" the American countryside in isolation and even despair. Frost and Lindsay represent different views of American culture, Frost so subtle and indirect, Lindsay so brassy; Frost so New England, Lindsay so plain; Frost so academically ironic, Lindsay so insistently proletarian. Lindsay exercised his power by singing, Frost be reflecting, but the two believed in a moral life, in which the poet's power to distinguish between what appears to be and what is, was supremely important.

John Chapman Ward

Other major works

SHORT FICTION: *The Golden Book of Springfield*, 1920.

NONFICTION: *Adventures While Preaching the Gospel of Beauty*, 1914; *The Art of the Moving Picture*, 1915; *A Handy Guide for Beggars*, 1916; *The Litany of Washington Street*, 1929; *Letters of Vachel Lindsay*, 1979 (Marc Chénetier, editor).

MISCELLANEOUS: *Adventures: Rhymes and Designs*, 1968 (Robert Sayre, editor).

Bibliography

Chénetier, Marc, ed. *Letters of Vachel Lindsay*. New York: Burt Franklin, 1979. Chénetier's fine introduction focuses on Lindsay's vision of himself as a prophet leading the masses to an understanding of America and American art. Lindsay emerges not as a character from a modern folktale but as a serious thinker and scholar. The foreword is by Lindsay's son, Nicholas.

Flanagan, John T., ed. *Profile of Vachel Lindsay*. Columbus, Ohio: Charles E. Merrill, 1970. This collection of essays deals with Lindsay's life and work. The essays are grouped into three approaches: reactions of critics during Lindsay's lifetime, reactions immediately after his death and specialized critical articles written during the 1950's and 1960's. The book contains a chronology of the poet's life.

Massa, Ann. *Vachel Lindsay: Fieldworker for the American Dream*. Bloomington: Indiana University Press, 1970. Attempts to take all Lindsay's writings —poetry, prose, short stories, and articles—and describe their basic underlying philosophy. Explores Lindsay's life and his career as a public performer in the context of American thought at the time. Contains illustrations, including drawings by Lindsay, and a brief bibliography.

Masters, Edgar Lee. *Vachel Lindsay: A Poet in America*. New York: Charles Scribner's Sons, 1935. Masters was himself a poet and a longtime friend of Lindsay, and he wrote this biography only a few years after Lindsay's death, at the request of Lindsay's widow. In spite of several factual errors, this is an important critical study.

Ruggles, Eleanor. *The West-Going Heart: A Life of Vachel Lindsay*. New York: W. W. Norton, 1959. This frankly admiring but quite accurate biography presents Lindsay as something of an American legend, a larger-than-life figure in the tradition of Johnny Appleseed. Excerpts from the poems are used to illustrate Lindsay's life and ideas, but are not critically analyzed. Sixteen photographs are included.

THOMAS LODGE

Born: London(?), England; 1558(?)
Died: London, England; September, 1625

Principal poetry
Scillaes Metamorphosis, 1589; *Phillis*, 1593; *A Fig for Momus*, 1595; *The Complete Works of Thomas Lodge*, 1875-1888 (Sir Edmund Gosse, editor, 4 volumes).

Other literary forms
Thomas Lodge wrote widely in genres other than poetry. His first prose work was *A Reply to Gosson* (1580), an answer to Stephen Gosson's *School of Abuse*. His prose romances include *The Delectable Historie of Forbonius and Prisceria* (1584), *Rosalynde* (1590), *Euphues Shadow* (1592), and *A Margarite of America* (1596). Other prose works encompass miscellaneous subject matter: a biography, *The Famous, True, and Historicall Life of Robert Second Duke of Normandy* (1591); an invective in dialogue form, *Catharos* (1591); and a historical narrative, *The Life and Death of William Long Beard* (1593). *An Alarum Against Usurers* (1584), an exposé of contemporary money lenders, has the strong moral message of *A Looking Glasse for London and England* (1594), the play that Lodge wrote with Robert Greene. In about 1586, *The Wounds of Civill War*, another play he had written, was produced. His pamphlets on philosophical and religious topics include *The Divel Conjured* (1596), *Prosopopeia* (1596), and *Wits Miserie and The Worlds Madnesse* (1596). His later works are translations (*The Flowers of Lodowicke of Granado*, 1601; *The Famous and Memorable Workes of Josephus*, 1602; *The Workes of Lucius Annaeus Seneca*, 1614; *A Learned Summary upon the Famous Poeme of William of Saluste, Lord of Bartas*, 1625) and medical works (*A Treatise of the Plague*, 1603; *The Poore Mans Talentt*, 1621).

Achievements
Lodge's poetry displays a facility in versification that, by itself, would mark him as a poetic talent. His experiments with verse forms—quatrains and couplets in *Scillaes Metamorphosis*; sonnets of ten to thirty-two lines ranging from tetrameters to hexameters in the poems appended to *Scillaes Metamorphosis*; poems mixing long and short lines in the miscellanies; and iambic pentameter couplets in the satires—show him to be much concerned with the craft of poetry, even when his experiments are not successful. He shows the same eagerness in trying new types of poems and subject matter, and his works range from sonnets to verse epistles, complaints, satires, eclogues, lyrics, and Ovidian narrative. His debt to the Romans in his verse epistles, satires, and Ovidian narrative is one that later writers also incurred, and Lodge to a great extent introduced these literary forms into English. Not all

of his works are equally successful, and his facility at versification and image-making sometimes produces trivial or precious poems; nevertheless, he did point the way to later poetic development in English literature.

Biography

Thomas Lodge's biography is sketchy. The existing evidence prompted early biographers to portray him as a dissolute rake—disinherited by his family and jailed for debts—but more recent writers have been kinder. While his mother was apparently worried about Lodge's stability, she also favored him in her will above her other sons. Furthermore, even though there are ample records of suits and countersuits involving Lodge and various creditors, some of his problems seem to have been caused by naïveté, such as neglecting to get receipts and then being sued for ostensibly unpaid debts.

Lodge was born probably in 1558, since on taking his bachelor's degree in 1577 he would most likely have been eighteen or nineteen. Moreover, in a lawsuit with his brother William in 1594, he lists his age as being about thirty-six. In *A Treatise on the Plague*, he talks about London as if it were his birthplace, and presumably it was. His father was a prosperous grocer who became city alderman and, in 1562, Lord Mayor of London. As a child, Thomas Lodge may have been a page in the household of Henry Stanley, fourth Earl of Derby: *A Fig for Momus* opens with a dedication to Stanley's son, William, and reminds him of the time his "noble father in mine infancie . . . incorporated me into your house." If this reference is to a lengthy period of time spent in Stanley's household, he surely would have met the famous people of his day and acquired the attributes—and education—of a gentleman.

Lodge's affluence, however, was not to continue. By the time his father had finished his term as Lord Mayor he declared bankruptcy, a victim of financial problems caused by England's war with France and the 1563 outbreak of the plague. When Thomas Lodge entered the Merchant Taylor's School in 1571, he was one of a group of students who were admitted as the sons of poor men, paying reduced tuition. In 1573, Lodge entered Trinity College, Oxford. After taking his degree, he entered the Inns of Court in 1578.

His relationship with his parents at this period is problematical. When his father died in 1584, Thomas Lodge was not mentioned in his will. By this time Lodge had written pamphlets—his *A Reply to Gosson*—and perhaps had converted to Catholicism. Trinity College, which had been founded during Mary's reign, still reflected strong Catholic influences, and Lincoln's Inn also had strong Catholic affinities, numbering among its members many recusants. In 1581, Lodge had been called before the Privy Council to answer charges, perhaps stemming from his religion. His literary activity and new religion might have displeased his father enough to cause him to disinherit his son; on the other hand, his mother's will, made in 1579, had already left him a large estate, which perhaps accounts for his father's reluctance to leave him any more. Yet even his mother's intentions are open to speculation. She stipulated that Lodge was not to receive his bequest until he was twenty-five, prompting some biographers to believe that she doubted her son's stability. She also included a proviso that Lodge would receive a yearly allowance only if he stayed at Lincoln's Inn and conducted himself "as a good student ought to do." If his behavior displeased her executors, they were to distribute his bequest among her other sons; Lady Anne seems to have felt the need to exercise special control over this particular son. Early biographers tended to see Lodge at this period as a profligate and debt-ridden young man. This view, however, is based partly on Gosson's attack on Lodge's character, which is hardly a credible source. Lodge's youthful degeneracy seems to have been exaggerated in early accounts of his life.

Sometime between 1585 and 1588, Lodge made a sea voyage, a venture he was to repeat in 1591 with Sir Thomas Cavendish. This latter voyage shows the perils to which the Elizabethan sense of adventure could lead: the expedition was plagued with bad weather, a mutinous crew, and widespread disease. Throughout his life, Lodge had published regularly, no matter what he did on a day-to-day basis; in 1597, however, he turned to the study of medicine and from then on produced only translations or works on medicine. He took his medical degree from the University of Avignon and probably practiced for a while in Belgium. He later returned to England and, in 1602, had his degree from Avignon registered at Oxford, a formality that would, perhaps, have attracted English clients. During the plague of 1603, Lodge worked tirelessly, even publishing a treatise on the disease with the intent of discrediting quack doctors who were profiting from people's fear and ignorance.

In 1604 Lodge married the widow of an Elizabethan spy who had formerly been a Catholic working for the Pope. Although this man eventually became an atheist, his wife remained loyal to her religion, receiving a pension from Gregory XIII. Lodge's marriage to her—along with his own earlier conversion—apparently brought him under suspicion by the government, and the Royal College of Physicians denied him permission to practice in London. By 1605, Lodge was again practicing in Belgium. Finally, with the help of the English ambassador to France, he was allowed to return to England and, in 1610, entered the Royal College of Physicians. The plague again swept through London in 1625 and Lodge was made plague-surgeon. He died in 1625, presumably a victim of that disease.

In many ways Lodge's life exemplifies the variety of experience that a Renaissance man might have. While born to wealth, he was often involved in litigation over debts, whether incurred through real want or only through carelessness. A writer of delicate sonnets, he was also an adventurer who undertook two sea voyages. Although he was not persecuted for his religion as actively as some, his fortunes still rose and fell as his beliefs changed.

Finally, the rather heedless young man acquired over the years a moral depth that caused him to work assiduously as a doctor throughout the plague years while others were fleeing London.

Analysis

Perhaps Thomas Lodge's most famous work is the prose romance *Rosalynde*, the source for William Shakespeare's *As You Like It* (1590-1600) and a lively piece of writing by itself. While the prose narrative of *Rosalynde* lies outside the bounds of this analysis, it does contain lyrical poems that, for their excellence, rival the best of Lodge's work. Their beauty was appreciated by Lodge's contemporaries, and many reappeared in *England's Helicon* (1600). Containing simple and even homely images and language, they explore the paradoxes of the Petrarchan lover without being excessive; as usual, Lodge is a master of metrics and many of these lyrics are presented as songs. "Rosalynds Madrigal" is an especially good example of Lodge's success as a lyricist. The poem alternates long and short lines in the first quatrain of each stanza; the stanzas close with four consecutive rhyming lines and a final line which may or may not rhyme with one of the lines in the first or second quatrain. Lodge's craftsmanship is evident in the way he can alternate long and short lines and use intermittently rhyming final stanza lines to achieve a musical effect. The homely images—love builds a "neast" in Rosalynd's eyes—also give the poem a certain lightness of tone. Many of the poems he wrote for the miscellanies show the same light touch and metrical skill:

> My bonnie Lasse thine eie,
> So slie,
> Hath made me sorrow so:
> Thy Crimsen cheekes my deere,
> So cleere,
> Hath so much wrought my woe.

When Lodge's lyrics fail they do so because they lack lightness and are not really profound enough to carry their serious, heavy tone; often they simply catalog the complaints of the Petrarchan lover and use balanced euphuistic lines to achieve a stately emphasis. Such emphasis seems misplaced, however, since the situations Lodge describes are often derivative. The sonnets in *Phillis* vary in quality. Some of them have the light touch of *Rosalynde*, although even in these Lodge is not consistent. Sonnet XIII opens by comparing Cupid to a bee:"If I approch he forward skippes,/ And if I kisse he stingeth me." The images describing love become more conventional as he goes along— tears, fire—and the poem ends with a conventional statement of constancy: "But if thou do not loue, Ile trulye serue hir,/ In spight of thee, by firme faith deserue hir." Sonnet XXXVII, containing heavy hexameter lines, lacks even the intermittently light tone of Sonnet XIII.

The *Phillis* sequence closes with a long medieval complaint, "The Complaint of Elstred." While hardly an inspired poem, it does show Lodge's affinities with pre-Renaissance verse. "Truth's Complaint over England" is also medieval in feeling and recounts Truth's lament over the condition of Lodge's England. Lodge's concept of satire seems mixed in his early works. "Truth's Complaint over England" achieves its social criticism through moralizing sentiments reminiscent of medieval complaint; Lodge's *A Reply to Gosson*, however, seems to show an awareness of different satiric possibilities. Confusing the etymology of *satire* and *satyr*—as most Renaissance writers did—Lodge gives a history of drama in which he asserts that tragedy evolved from satyr plays. The widely accepted Renaissance belief was that these plays allowed the playwright to scourge his audiences for their vices by having a satyr denounce them. In this way English writers came to think of satire as a harsh, uncouth form: Juvenal as opposed to the more urbane Horace. Lodge himself follows *Scillaes Metamorphosis* by a poem entitled "The Discontented Satyr," a paean to discontent, the best emotion one can feel in a corrupt age.

By the time he wrote *A Fig for Momus*, Lodge seems to have adopted this harsher Juvenalian mode of satire. This series of poems opens with a satire of flatterers and hypocrites, and Lodge is at his best in the imaginary characters and situations he evokes. Meeting an innkeeper with "a silken night-cap on his hed," the narrator is told that the man has had "An ague this two months." The narrator comments sardonically that "I let him passe: and laught to heare his skuce:/ For I knew well, he had the poxe by Luce." Lodge's second satire— incorrectly labeled the third—urges parents to set good examples for their children. The piece owes a special debt to Juvenal's Satire XIV on the same subject, and, if much of it seems simply moral preaching, the sheer number of vices which he catalogs keeps the poem moving. Perhaps Lodge's fourth satire offers his most memorable and bitter character study: a miser, old and decrepit, but still concerned with amassing a greater fortune. The gruesomely realistic description of the man shows Lodge at his best. His fifth satire opens with a paraphrase of Juvenal's Satire X, although his debt to Horace is also apparent in his description of the contented life. If this satire is less bitter and harsh than his others, it is perhaps because of the influence of Horace. In addition to introducing Juvenal into English literature, Lodge made one other lasting contribution to English satire: he was the first to use the epigrammatic pentameter couplet.

If *A Fig for Momus* does not seem, as a whole, the bitter invective that the satiric elements might lead one to expect, it is because Lodge has interspersed other genres: eclogues and verse epistles. His eclogues offer little new to English literature—Alexander Barclay, Barnabe Googe, Edmund Spenser, and Michael Drayton had already worked in this form—and their general theme of human corruption is not developed in an interesting way. Furthermore, their poetry, compared to Spenser's masterpiece in this genre, is noticeably deficient. Lodge's verse epistles, however, were the first to appear in English and, although they are uneven, the best of them have a lightness and wit that are typical of Lodge. The epistle "To his Mistress A. L." opens with a buildup in the first two lines which the following ones humorously deflate: "In that same month wherein the spring begins,/ And on that day when Phoebe left the twinnes/ (Which was on Saturday, the Twelfth of March)/ Your servant brought a letter seal'd with starch." The letter turns out to be a request for information on how to lose weight and the epistle cites various learned authorities on the subject, concluding that it is better to be "fat, slicke, faire" than "leane, lancke, spare." The epistle entitled "In praise of his Mistris dogge" opens wittily enough with a request that his mistress "for a night . . . grant me Pretties place," and then proceeds to a canine history, ending with a pun: "Thus for your dog, my doggerell rime hath runne."

If Lodge introduced the verse epistle into English, he was also one of the first to write Ovidian narrative, a literary type that would later appear in Christopher Marlowe's *Hero and Leander* (1598), Shakespeare's *Venus and Adonis* (1593), Drayton's *Endimion and Phoebe* (1595), and John Marston's *The Metamorphosis of Pygmalion's Image and Certain Satires* (1598). Ovid had, of course, been known before Lodge: Arthur Golding's translation of the *Metamorphosis* (1567) was a standard Elizabethan treatment of the Roman poet. Yet Golding allegorizes Ovid to make his eroticism acceptable; Lodge is far from finding any allegory in his source. *Scillaes Metamorphosis* is noteworthy for its elaborate images and conceits: Lodge has taken Ovid's 143 lines and expanded them to nearly eight hundred. To the original story of Glaucus' love for the disdainful Scilla, Lodge adds an opening frame story in which the narrator, also a rejected lover, walks along the shore "Weeping my wants, and wailing scant reliefe." Finally he meets Glaucus, the sea god, and hears his story. As Glaucus recounts Scilla's disdain to a group of nymphs, Venus appears with Cupid. Cupid cures Glaucus' lovesickness with an arrow and then shoots Scilla, who immediately falls in love with Glaucus, who now rejects her. Knowing her case to be hopeless, Scilla finally curses all men, whereupon she is beset by the personifications *Furie*, *Rage*, *Wan-hope*, *Dispair*, and *Woe*, who transform her into a flinty isle.

If one could sum up Lodge's handling of Ovid in one word, it would be *embroidery*. Whenever he can stop for a lengthy and sensuous description, he does. Some of these are very successful, such as the description of Venus after she has found the wounded Adonis: it ends with Lodge's touching lines "How on his senseless corpes she lay a crying,/ As if the boy were then but new a dying." The story of Venus and Adonis itself shows Lodge's leisurely narrative pace, since it is interpolated in the main story of Glaucus. Glaucus' description of Scilla is also leisurely and sensuous. Ovid simply says that she was *sine vestibus* when Glaucus saw her; Lodge's Glaucus minutely recounts her physical beauty, dwelling on her hair, cheeks, nose, lips, neck, breasts, and arms.

The flaws in Lodge's poem—and it is by no means of uniform quality— have to do in part with this massing of description and detail. Lodge does not seem to have any awareness that his poem cannot sustain the same high pitch stanza after stanza: Glaucus' laments, for example, all begin to sound alike. Lodge has partially dealt with this problem in the frame story at the beginning of the poem, the very place where the reader is unlikely to need a rest from the high pitch of the poem. Nevertheless, Lodge does offer an interesting double perspective on Glaucus that the rest of the poem might have done well to develop. After the narrator spends four stanzas crying and groaning over an unrequited love, Glaucus appears and berates the narrator's love-sickness in stanzas that almost bristle with moral advice. After counseling the narrator, however, Glaucus falls into exactly the same error and even faints while describing his own hopeless love. This humorous contradiction between Glaucus' words and actions lends an ironic perspective to the story which the rest of the poem does not explore. Indeed, the personifications from medieval allegory who transform Scilla seem totally out of place in Lodge's poem, as if he had not really decided what the dominant tone of Ovidian narrative should be.

His verse form is also ill-chosen, although he does the best he can with it. Composed of stanzas consisting of a quatrain (abab) and a couplet (cc), the poem has difficulty moving forward: the couplets are always stopping the flow of action. In one sense this hardly matters, since Lodge is more concerned with leisurely description than with fast-paced narrative action. The poem, nevertheless, is a narrative, however leisurely, and the recurring couplets do present a problem. Lodge almost seems to feel that this is so and usually manages to begin a new clause as the couplet begins, avoiding at least the awkwardness of the self-contained couplet having to continue the lines before it.

Hardly any of Lodge's long poems are unqualified successes, although they all have striking passages and show much facility of versification. That he was an experimenter is evident in the number of new poetic forms he introduced into English; experimenters cannot always produce perfect products. Nevertheless, music and lightness of tone mark many of Lodge's best works and make him a considerable figure in the development of Renaissance poetry.

Carole Moses

Other major works

FICTION: *The Delectable Historie of Forbonius and Prisceria*, 1584; *Rosalynde*, 1590; *Euphues Shadow*, 1592; *A Margarite of America*, 1596.

PLAYS: *The Wounds of Civill War*, c. 1586; *A Looking Glasse for London and England*, 1594 (with Robert Greene)

NONFICTION: *A Reply to Gosson*, 1580; *An Alarum Against Usurers*, 1584; *The Famous, True, and Historicall Life of Robert Second Duke of Normandy*, 1591; *Catharos*, 1591; *The Life and Death of William Long Beard*, 1593; *The Divel Conjured*, 1596; *Prosopopeia*, 1596; *Wits Miserie and the Worlds Madnesse*, 1596; *The Flowers of Lodowicke of Granado*, 1601 (translation); *The Famous and Memorable Workes of Josephus*, 1602 (translation); *A Treatise of the Plague*, 1603; *The Workes of Lucius Annaeus Seneca*, 1614 (translation); *The Poore Mans Talentt*, 1621; *A Learned Summary upon the Famous Poeme of William of Saluste, Lord of Bartas*, 1625 (translation).

Bibliography

Alexander, Nigel, ed. *Elizabethan Narrative Verse.* Cambridge, Mass.: Harvard University Press, 1968. Besides collecting eleven of the most important verse narratives, Alexander prefaces them with a twenty-six-page introduction that establishes the Ovidian background of these poems and comments on them individually. Contains interpretative and documentary notes, as well as a useful bibliography.

Donno, Elizabeth Story. "The Epyllion." In *English Poetry and Prose, 1540-1674*, edited by Christopher Ricks. New York: Peter Bedrick Books, 1986. A leading authority on Elizabethan narrative poetry, Donno illuminates the conventions and qualities which characterize the forms. Places Lodge clearly against his cultural background. The thorough index demonstrates Lodge's manifold activities, and the bibliography covers all major works.

Hulse, Clark. *Metamorphic Verse: The Elizabethan Minor Epic.* Princeton, N.J.: Princeton University Press, 1981. Hulse's book is the modern authoritative study of the minor epic genre. Covers the field thoroughly, although much of the material is technical and sophisticated. The bibliography and index are complete.

Muir, Kenneth. *Introduction to Elizabethan Literature.* New York: Random House, 1967. Muir is a major literary historian with unrivaled knowledge of this period. As a result, his commentaries are unusually insightful and learned. He brings out clearly Lodge's diverse interests and accomplishments. The bibliography, though dated, is useful; the notes and index offer significant help.

Ostriker, Alicia, and Leslie Dunn. "The Lyric." In *English Poetry and Prose, 1540-1674*, edited by Christopher Ricks. New York: Peter Bedrick Books, 1986. Ostriker and Dunn divide the field here, the former taking verse written independently, the latter lyrics written for music—a division first made during the Elizabethan period. Lodge is covered in both categories. The index demonstrates more of his diversity, and the bibliography collects the primary sources.

Rae, Wesley D. *Thomas Lodge.* New York: Twayne, 1967. This 128-page book covers all aspects of Lodge's diverse activities, bringing them together in a common light—which does not often happen. It approaches Lodge's work chronologically, showing how his life sheds light on the writings. Includes a chronology, notes and references, an index, and a dated select bibliography.

Sisson, Charles J., ed. *Thomas Lodge and Other Elizabethans.* 1933. Reprint. London: Frank Cass, 1966. This volume collects five biographical studies, of which Sisson's, on Lodge, comprises more than 150 pages. The discussion devotes chapters to Lodge's father, his brothers, and Lodge himself, through painstaking reference to contemporary documents. A geneological chart of the Lodge family is appended.

Tenney, Edward Andrews. *Thomas Lodge.* Ithaca, N.Y.: Cornell University Press, 1935. Another biography of Lodge, this one supplements and updates that by Sisson.

JOHN LOGAN

Born: Red Oak, Iowa; January 23, 1923
Died: San Francisco, California; November 6, 1987

Principal poetry

Cycle for Mother Cabrini, 1955; *Ghosts of the Heart,* 1960; *Spring of the Thief,* 1963; *The Zig-Zag Walk,* 1969; *The Anonymous Lover,* 1973; *Poem in Progress,* 1975; *Aaron Siskind: Photographs/John Logan: Poems,* 1976; *The Bridge of Change,* 1979; *Only the Dreamer Can Change the Dream,* 1981; *John Logan: The Collected Poems,* 1989.

Other literary forms

Because John Logan's reputation stems from his poetry, his fiction has, for the most part, been overlooked. Logan's most sustained attempt at fiction, *The House That Jack Built: Or, A Portrait of the Artist as a Sad Sensualist* (1984), celebrates the discovery and sheer joy of language. Concerned with the poet's young life, the book offers childhood experiences, relationships, and images which reveal the intellectual and emotional development of Logan's poetic sensibility. Eighteen of Logan's stories, including five previously unpublished, are gathered in *John Logan: The Collected Fiction* (1991). Also a teacher and critic, Logan contributed essays, interviews, forewords, and reviews to numerous magazines and books, most of which are collected in *A Ballet for the Ear: Interviews, Essays, and Reviews* (1983), edited by A. Poulin, Jr. This volume demonstrates Logan's wide-ranging scholarship and his dedication to the life of the poet. He explores with enthusiasm and keen insight such contrasting figures as Herman Melville and E. E. Cummings, and he develops provocative explanations for his own writing, his personal poetics, and the work and poetics of many contemporary writers. The passion of Logan's literary life, however, is best understood after hearing the poet read; his performances were often described as "spellbinding." Logan reads from his work on a recording from the Watershed Foundation entitled *Only the Dreamer Can Change the Dream.*

Achievements

Often and incorrectly described as a confessional poet (a misnomer in Logan's vocabulary since good confessional poetry confesses the reader), John Logan was one of the few truly personal poets to come to prominence in the twentieth century. James Wright tells an anecdote which best summarizes Logan's influence:

> I once stopped a fistfight between two of the best living poets I know, and I did it by reading aloud to them a poem by John Logan. . . . He is a genius of love in my lifetime, and, to my mind, one of the three or four masters we have to give to the world.

James Dickey placed Logan's work alongside the poetry of Robert Lowell, and Robert Bly wrote that "John Logan is one of the five or six finest poets to emerge in the United States in the last decades." Logan's reputation as a teacher equaled his reputation as a poet, and some of his noteworthy students, including Marvin Bell, have written at length about Logan's "humanistic" workshops. Logan received the Miles Modern Poetry Prize from Wayne State University in 1967, a Rockefeller Foundation grant in 1969, the Morton Dauwen Zabel Award from the National Institute of Arts and Letters in 1973, a Guggenheim Fellowship in 1979, a grant from the National Endowment for the Arts in 1980, and the Robert Hazel Ferguson Award from the Friends of Literature, Chicago, 1982. He served as poetry editor for both *The Nation* and the *Critic*, and he was also the founder and editor of *Choice*, a magazine of poetry and photography.

Despite winning critical acclaim and the respect of his peers, Logan has never enjoyed a wide readership. The reasons are many, but most important is the fact that, like Walt Whitman, Logan is an intensely personal poet who demands an ultimate commitment from his reader. Logan's poetry transcends the ordinary form of things and transforms those things into something more real, more useful, than conventional reality. Consequently, the reader of a Logan poem cannot in any way remain passive; instead, he must confront the shadow or inarticulate counterself that exists within. Logan's commitment to this type of self-searching was absolute, and while such intensity may alienate some readers, his insistent demands lend power, depth, and psychological complexity to the poems. At his best, Logan explores the inner self without moral judgment, conceit, sentimentalism, or self-pity. Instead, he uncovers what at first seems threatening and perhaps grotesque in order to reveal what is finally beautiful in all living things.

Biography

The speaker in John Burton Logan's poetry is a wanderer, due, in part, to Logan's belief that poets are constant, spiritual travelers, but also because of the fact that Logan's life cannot be identified with any one particular place. The outward search for home, a place of rest, combined with Logan's inward search, gives the poems their universal appeal.

Logan was graduated magna cum laude from Coe College in 1943 with a B.A. in biology. In 1945, he married; it was a union that produced nine children but that finally ended in divorce. He received his M.A. in English in 1949 from the State University of Iowa, and in the years following, he did occasional graduate work in philosophy at Georgetown University and the University of Notre Dame. Beginning in 1947 and proceeding chronologically, Logan taught at St. John's College in Maryland, Notre Dame, St. Mary's College in California, the University of Washington, San Francisco State College, and, after 1966, the State University of New York at Buffalo. Logan served as resident writer for countless poetry workshops and colonies, and because of his popular and distinctive reading style, he maintained a busy schedule of public appearances.

Logan was reared as a Protestant but converted to Catholicism after his marriage. His early work reflects a clear and strong religious orientation that takes the Christian God very seriously. After the early books, however, religious allusions eventually disappear, and only in a few later poems did Logan return to religious themes. He died in San Francisco, California, on November 6, 1987.

Analysis

John Logan built a personal poetry from his own obsessions: grace, the search for more than anonymous love, the friend or lover as rescuer, the father-son relationship, death, and poetry as rebirth.

"Poem for My Brother," a characteristic Logan poem, dramatizes the desire for acceptance and reconciliation between brothers that have grown apart. The younger of the two feels intimidated—or at least awkward—around his more athletic elder sibling and wants desperately to identify with him. This sense of physical and emotional alienation pervades Logan's poetry, paralleling a similar alienation in his career as a writer.

In "Poem for My Brother," Logan explains the many differences between the poet and his elder brother, but always with a desire for identification. The contrasts between the two remain sharp (as illustrated by the brothers' colors, blue and brown), and this is what gives the poem its natural power. A capsulized history of the color blue included in the poem explains that many societies still do not have a word other than "dark" for this "last of the primary colors to be named." "It's associated with black. . . ." Blue, for Logan, represents the *other*, the society of *other lovers* to which Logan seeks admission—a place where, were he to gain access, he could not stay. Logan realizes that the redemption and grace of being accepted and forgiven is only temporary since any person soon finds himself alone again as he began, arguing only with himself, and being accountable, in the final analysis, only to himself. The tension between desire for the *other* and the knowledge that the consequent redemption is only temporary fuels much of Logan's poetry.

Grace, in Logan's own words, is the escape from anxiety through supernatural means—the sacraments and divine redemption—or through natural means: art and love. Logan's need for forgiveness and its subsequent grace motivated his outward and inward search, and his poems often show that such rare and precious gifts are not easily won. Indeed, implicit in Logan's poetry is the necessity for taking risks. Even in the early *Cycle for Mother Cabrini*, Logan charged his poems with a nervous energy that thrives on the anticipation of danger. At the same time, the volume overflows with classical allusions, establishing Logan as an extension of the poetic tradition that he revered. He carried on "The Lives of the Poet," the first poem in *Ghosts of the Heart*, both figuratively and literally; that is, the book begins a tradition of poems celebrating the lives of other poets, Arthur Rimbaud and Lord Byron, that continues with E. E. Cummings, John Keats, James Joyce, and Dylan Thomas, to name only a few, through several of the other books. These homages, tributes, and elegies not only reassert the presence of literary figures in the reader's consciousness, but they often reveal a great deal about Logan's own feelings and position as a poet.

Spring of the Thief deals primarily with the need for spiritual and physical change through imagination or uncanny transformation: the dread of stagnation suddenly transformed by new realization. This theme, however, does not fully mature until *The Zig-Zag Walk*. Although rich with translations of Georg Trakl and Tibor Tollas, the tone of *The Zig-Zag Walk* is more informal and the poetry less academic. Here Logan freed himself to explore personal relationships without the encumbrance of a superimposed poetic structure. Love becomes the central meaning of life, and it is love that saves the poet from his own self-destruction: "... as you reached for me/ ... it was my self you hauled/ back from my despair." These lines from "The Rescue" resonate with lines from several poems, including the recent "Medicine Bow," in which the poet, shaking and losing his energy, is shocked back into life when he brings a handful of snow to his mouth. Such rescues always occur when the poet is on the edge, and, by their somber moods and continuing recurrence, the reader understands the transience of both rescue and relief.

Not until *The Anonymous Lover* is there any realization that the poet is also responsible for himself, that he is capable of self-rescue (as dramatized in "Medicine Bow"), and that he, indeed, must find or build his own refuge. In *Poem in Progress* (first published as a chapbook and then reprinted in *The Bridge of Change*), Logan manages to transcend many of the limitations that his younger obsessions seem to embody. He takes up with authority the wealth he has learned and constructs the world of his imagination (his fear of death and the desire for rebirth) around an in-depth study of the father-son relationship.

Throughout *Poem in Progress*, the poet appears variously as friend, brother, son, father (teacher), and lover, recapitulating many of the roles already established in Logan's poetry. (When Logan shifts his role, companions also change their position. In "Lines for Michael in the Picture" from *The Zig-Zag Walk*: "... that transforming island fire/ that seems to fade in your eyes in the picture./ It makes you brother, friend, son, father.") From the poet's shifting viewpoint, *Poem in Progress* explores a series of personal relationships which, to some degree, originate in erotic attraction creating homoerotic overtones and suggesting incestual fantasies. Some critics have made much of the text's "atmosphere" and have dwelled unnecessarily on what appear to be unfulfilled homoerotic confrontations. The characters in any one situation are of no importance to the total effect of the poem since love is fulfillment, even redemption, and love is not preferential about partners: "love in Plato's 'Phaedrus' is not thus: the need of man/ for woman, or of man for man, woman for woman;/ instead, it is the love that will be felt as fulfill-/ ment." Love that relieves human anxiety cannot be limited by predetermined judgments and prejudices. It must be accepted when offered and appreciated, for, as Logan knows all too well, its effects will not last.

Here, as in most of Logan's work, the poet is on an endless journey or search for the means to achieve grace. Moments of love and acceptance offer only brief respite from the continuing frustration of grace that eludes. For example, the poet in "IV Rescue in Florida: The Friend," feeling insecure and childlike before a reading, takes strength from a stranger sitting in the audience. This unknown person will soon receive the poet's love, and so, for that moment, the poet is not isolated or *anonymous*. The stranger, again, performs a temporary rescue.

The word *anonymous* recurs several times in *Poem in Progress*, and working at the center of this one-word refrain is Pablo Neruda's idea that poetry is "an exchange between strangers," a token of thanks, perhaps, for what is given unknowingly. For example, the young lovers in section five give the poet a wooden figurine in thanks for what his poetry has given them. This gesture is unexpected, and the poet as traveler identifies with the figure of the old Colombian man, sack over his back, with "fifty-year-old-hands." Yet, more than merely identification, the gesture of the gift returns to the poet some of what he has given: ". . . the breath/ he as breathed into it—or it has blown inside him—/ is given back again." Once more, Logan dramatizes the respite from the search, the rest in the middle of the journey.

Art, however, like love, offers only a temporary rest, and the friends, sons, brothers, students, and lovers who rescued Logan from time to time on his journey could not offer what the poet ultimately sought—a permanent state of grace. Like Edgar Allan Poe, Logan was frequently subject to spiritual vertigo; just as Poe feared chaos and entropy, feared falling into the maelstrom or being sucked into the whirlpool, so Logan feared the ultimate falling away of his gifts and powers. This fear is evident in Logan's images of his youthful sons and friends—godlike and indestructible—and the poet's own admissions, even guilt, over his slowly diminishing powers: "(. . . but my Greek is no longer sure)." What saves Logan's poetry at this level is that the narrator is not morose about his insecurities and fears. His offhand comments about his slipping abilities and his celebration of youth and confidence come as the natural components of Logan's total embrace. *Poem in Progress* portrays the lost, searching, sometimes fragile poet at odds with the various roles thrust upon him, but a poet still reveling in a sea of anonymous lovers provided by the Mardi Gras where the heat of the sculptor's kiln consumes the outer coverings of both the poet and his friends leaving them

". . . stark naked there as for making love or art."
"Believe It," the last poem in *The Bridge of Change*, is all at once a celebration of life's diversity and absurdity, an acknowledgement of fear concerning the loss of power and ability, the reassertion of the poet as a lifelong and
constant traveler, and, finally, the reaffirmation of life and giving—an invitation to all the anonymous lovers that they are free to come and partake of
the poet's joys.

Joseph Coulson

Other major works
FICTION: *The House That Jack Built: Or, A Portrait of the Artist as a Sad
Sensualist,* 1984: *John Logan: The Collected Fiction,* 1991.
NONFICTION: *A Ballet for the Ear: Interviews, Essays, and Reviews,* 1983.

Bibliography
Chaplin, William. "Identity and Spirit in the Recent Poetry of John Logan."
The American Poetry Review 2 (May/June, 1973): 19-24. Chapman does
not attempt to validate specific events and places in Logan's poetry; instead, he asserts that everything worth knowing is in the poems themselves. As a result, he examines the pattern of feelings that emerge from
the poems to gain insights into Logan's life and aesthetics. An important
analysis that questions the conventional view of Logan's poetry as being
confessional.
Dickey, James. *Babel to Byzantium.* New York: Farrar, Straus & Giroux, 1968.
A highly personal and enlightening reading of Logan's poetry by an equally
impressive novelist and poet. Dickey convincingly argues that Logan is
one of the finest American Poets ever. He offers important insights into
the religions and literary influences that shaped Logan's work.
Hilgers, Thomas, and Michael Molloy. "A Conversation With John Logan."
The Iowa Review 10 (Spring/Summer, 1980): 221-229. An excellent overview of Logan's life and work as told by the poet himself. Logan discusses
the European locales that served as inspirations for many of his works,
the influence of Rainer Maria Rilke, and the history behind many of his
poems and his prose work, *The House That Jack Built: Or, A Portrait of
the Artist as a Sad Sensualist.*
Petrosky, Anthony. "In and Out of John Logan's Workshops." *Ironwood* 15
(Fall, 1987): 97-101. A fascinating and illuminating personal account of
Logan as a teacher, a poet, and an acquaintance, based on Petrosky's friendship with him. These recollections are a vivid study of Logan's personality, aesthetics, interests, and tastes. The numerous anecdotes—from Bach
concerts to poetry workshops and meetings with other poets—offer valuable insights into Logan and his poetry.

Waters, Michael. *Dissolve to Island: On The Poetry of John Logan.* Houston: Ford-Brown, 1984. This first book-length critical study of Logan's poetry includes essays by Tama Baldwin, Marvin Bell, and Peter Makuck and is supplemented by selected poems. This valuable resource also contains bibliographic and biographical information.

HENRY WADSWORTH LONGFELLOW

Born: Portland, Maine; February 27, 1807
Died: Cambridge, Massachusetts; March 24, 1882

Principal poetry

Voices of the Night, 1839; *Ballads and Other Poems*, 1841; *Poems on Slavery*, 1842; *The Belfry of Bruges and Other Poems*, 1846; *Evangeline*, 1847; *The Seaside and the Fireside*, 1850; *The Golden Legend*, 1851; *The Song of Hiawatha*, 1855; *The Courtship of Miles Standish* 1858; *Tales of a Wayside Inn*, 1863; *Flower-de-Luce*, 1867; *The Divine Comedy of Dante Alighieri*, 1867-1869 (translation); *The New England Tragedies*, 1868; *The Divine Tragedy*, 1871; *Three Books of Song*, 1872; *Christus: A Mystery*, 1872; *Aftermath*, 1873; *The Hanging of the Crane*, 1874; *The Masque of Pandora and Other Poems*, 1875; *Kéramos and Other Poems*, 1878; *Ultima Thule*, 1880; *In the Harbor*, 1882; *Michael Angelo*, 1883.

Other literary forms

Besides his poetry, Henry Wadsworth Longfellow produced a variety of works, most of them connected with his scholarly duties as Professor of Modern Languages and Literature at Bowdoin College (1829-1835) and at Harvard College (1837-1854). He created his own grammars: *Elements of French Grammar* (1830) and *Manuel de Proverbes Dramatiques* (1830). He wrote a series of scholarly articles in linguistics and literature for *The North American Review*, most of them reprinted in his collection, *Drift-Wood* (1857), and several other prose works. *Outre-Mer: A Pilgrimage Beyond the Sea* (1833-1834) was an account of his first European tour; *Hyperion* (1839) was an account of his second, highlighted by an autobiographical reshaping of his romance with Fanny Appleton, whom he married three years later. *Kavanagh: A Tale* (1849) was his only attempt at writing a novel. He edited four anthologies of poetry: *The Poets and Poetry of Europe* (1845) contained selections from four hundred poets from ten different countries; *The Waif: A Collection of Poems* (1845) and *The Estray: A Collection of Poems* (1847) gathered together antislavery verses; and the thirty-one volumes of *Poems of Places* (1876-1879), one of the largest anthologies of poetry ever assembled. As the leading American poet of his age, Longfellow carried on a voluminous correspondence, writing more than five thousand letters, many of which have been published as *The Letters of Henry Wadsworth Longfellow* (1966-1974) by Harvard University Press. George T. Little reissued twenty-seven poems written during Longfellow's college days in an edition entitled *Longfellow's Boyhood Poems* (1925).

Achievements

Longfellow was the most popular English-language poet of the nineteenth century. In both England and the United States, volumes of his poetry outsold all other verse and most fiction for nearly fifty years. When he died, more than a million copies of his poetry had been sold. He was granted private audiences with Queen Victoria, honorary degrees from Oxford and Cambridge, and a memorial in the Poets' Corner of Westminster Abbey, a distinction hitherto reserved for only the greatest of England's own poets. In America, a national holiday was proclaimed to celebrate his seventy-fifth birthday. From the late nineteenth century to the mid-twentieth, nearly every school-age child in the United States and most of those in Britain were required to read some of his lines. Apparently, few poets of any age had shown themselves better able to articulate the values, beliefs, and aspirations of their readership. The body of Longfellow's work can be seen as an index to some of the newly industrialized world's deepest self-images. Contemporaries praised "the sentiments of tenderness" in *Hyperion*, admired the "unexaggerated truthfulness" of *Evangeline*, and the "accuracy" of *The Song of Hiawatha*. They extolled the way he "obeyed the highest humanity of the poet's calling" in *The Golden Legend* and repeatedly singled out the universal appeal of his voice: "force of thought" for the old, "melody" for the young, "piety" for the serious, and a "slight touch of mysticism" for the imaginative.

Longfellow was decidedly the most popular of a concentrated group of American poets that helped shape one another's stylistic response to the demands of such an audience. The group included James Russell Lowell, John Greenleaf Whittier, and William Cullen Bryant, all of whom catered primarily to a mass readership. They have frequently been called "Fireside Poets," meaning that they wrote not by but rather for the family hearth. They specialized in polite, sentimental, and traditional homilies for readers trying desperately to reaffirm some of their oldest and most cherished values during a period of unsettling and apparently chaotic change. Longfellow specifically imagined that each of his lines would be read aloud after dinner around the family circle, with young and old profiting by his every word. For them, he tried to picture a world where an omniscient God was still in control, where the human soul was still immortal, where death remained only "a beginning, not an end," where noble and courageous acts could still affect the outcome of a crisis, where the first duty of all was to sustain their spirituality by concentrating on the good, the beautiful, and the true, and where the duty of poets was to help their readers in this concentration on the sublime.

Longfellow was lionized for supporting these pieties in the nineteenth century and has been largely ignored because of them during much of the twentieth. A literate, scholarly, and compassionate man, Longfellow's verses probably merit neither critical extreme. At his worst, he could write prosaic and long-winded verse which seemed to aim principally at giving his audience the sentimentality they came to demand of him. At his best, he could struggle with his own and his age's doubts forthrightly; he could write movingly of the passing of traditional agrarian society and Christian ideals. Stronger minds than Longfellow's were puzzled by the abrupt changes which industrialization, urbanization, and political revolution had brought to their world. If he remained unsure of the qualities which the new world needed, he articulated with precision those qualities from the old which had been lost. There was an elegiac suppleness in his affirmations which created a tone of frailty and a sense of transience that often contradicted the superficial optimism which his readers demanded of him.

Biography

Henry Wadsworth Longfellow, the second of eight children, was born into an old and distinguished New England family. Stephen Longfellow, his father, was a prominent lawyer who had served as a representative in Congress and who could count among his ancestors New England patriarchs such as Samuel Sewell. His mother, Zilpah, could trace the Wadsworth name back through a Revolutionary War general to seventeenth century Plymouth Puritans such as John Alden. Schooled at the Portland Academy and Bowdoin College, Longfellow finished his formal education in 1825, graduating in a class which included Nathaniel Hawthorne. From the beginning, he had been expected to carry on the traditions of his two family groups: "You must adopt a profession which will afford you subsistence as well as reputation," his father had counseled him just before graduation. During his collegiate years, Longfellow had shown so much aptitude for foreign languages that Bowdoin actually offered him a newly established professorship in modern languages. The trustees of the college, however, insisted that their new professor travel to Europe at his own expense to round out his language training.

Accepting the offer, Longfellow toured Europe from 1826 to 1829, dividing his time between France, Spain, Italy, and Germany. By August 11, 1829, he was back at Bowdoin, preparing lecture notes and writing his own grammars and study texts. For the next six years, his scholarly duties at the college and his academic writing in linguistics and literature occupied most of his professional life. He did, however, find time to renew an interest in creative writing. His only book during the stay at Bowdoin, *Outre-Mer: A Pilgrimage Beyond the Sea*, was a prose account of his European travels, modeled on Washington Irving's *The Sketch Book of Geoffrey Crayon, Gent.* (1819-1820). Settling more comfortably into academic life, Longfellow married Mary Storer Potter on September 14, 1831, and devoted himself to extending his reputation by publishing literary criticism. Three years later, Harvard College was impressed enough with the quality of his academic writing to offer him the Smith Professorship of French and Spanish Languages, again contingent on his willingness to travel to Europe for further study.

He and his wife, Mary, sailed in April, 1835, to visit England, Denmark, Sweden, and Holland. In October, tragedy overtook the couple; Mary lost the child she was carrying and, in November, died from complications from the miscarriage. It took a year of grieving, studying, and falling in love again—this time with Fanny Appleton, the daughter of a prominent Boston family whom he had met in Switzerland—for Longfellow to recuperate fully from the loss. By the fall of 1836, he had returned to Harvard to continue his scholarly writing. By 1842, he had also finished *Hyperion*, a highly autobiographical account of his unrequited love for Fanny, and three volumes of original poetry. By 1843, he had apparently achieved enough recognition for Fanny to consent to marriage. The stay at Harvard marked the beginning of the most productive period of Longfellow's career, and his home life, with six children, was apparently a happy one. His creative writing blossomed: he issued three more volumes of poetry. His scholarly endeavors continued to absorb him, and he added to his academic bibliography two major collections of verse. By 1854, his poetry had gained so much recognition that he could afford to resign his professorship and devote himself to writing full-time. In the next seven years, he produced his most popular works: *The Seaside and the Fireside*, *The Golden Legend*, *The Song of Hiawatha*, *The Courtship of Miles Standish*, and *Tales of a Wayside Inn*. The flowering of Longfellow's productivity was again interrupted by personal tragedy: the death of his second wife in 1861. While sealing some letters with hot wax, Fanny set herself on fire and burned to death in the family living room. Longfellow himself was badly burned trying to rescue her. He never completely recovered from the loss, although he tried to lose himself in an ambitious verse translation of Dante's *The Divine Comedy* (c. 1320), in some passionate and realistic poems about the horrors of the Civil War, and in a dramatic narrative of the life of Christ.

Throughout the next decade, Longfellow devoted most of his flagging energies to reissuing previously published poetry, writing sequels to previously successful poems, and experimenting with a few new forms which he did not intend for publication during his lifetime. Much of his mature thought and many of his penetrating personal reflections were invested in an uncompleted drama about the life of Michelangelo. His health began to fail before the work was completed and he died from peritonitis after a short illness, on March 24, 1882, less than a month after his seventy-fifth birthday had been celebrated all over America.

Analysis

Henry Wadsworth Longfellow worked in two entirely different poetic forms: short lyrical sketches which tried to point out similarities between passing, subjective emotions and lasting, objective settings or locations and long historical narratives which aimed at celebrating inspirational events. Like other Fireside Poets, Longfellow tailored both kinds of verse to an audience which, he envisioned, would read them aloud in front of the family hearth.

He once defined the persona for most of these public works as "no unwelcomed guest," who, he "hoped, would have [his] place reserved among the rest" at "your warm fireside." Appropriately, his subjects were often chosen so that young and old might be elevated by his treatment of traditional values. They stressed home, family, romantic love, dutiful children, quiet acceptance of suffering and death, and the appreciation of nature, God, and country. He wrote in traditional metrical patterns which would be easy for his readers to follow. He selected a solemn, sometimes archaic, diction which might add a devotional tone to the after-dinner recitations. He characteristically kept his symbols and images simple, so that even his youngest listeners might understand his homilies at first hearing. After the shocking death of his second wife, it became more difficult for Longfellow to confine himself to the expectations of such an audience and to such a rigid series of poetic restrictions. Yet the progress of his work showed a single-minded commitment to continue fulfilling the dictates of this public role, long after he himself had outgrown them. Increasingly, Longfellow's later lyrics and narratives showed a quiet subversion of the subjects and styles which his adoring audience expected of their laureate. The later poems proposed the same simple formulas in the same simple intonations as the earlier works had, but they seemed to waver, often undercutting themselves with a quiet pessimism which directly contradicted their superficial cheeriness.

In the last lyric he wrote, "The Bells of San Blas," Longfellow seemed to reevaluate his poetic career and to dismiss it as belonging to a "dreamer of dreams" to "whom what is and what seems" were frequently "the same." Like the bells of the decaying Catholic Church, he claimed that the voice of his public persona had tried "to bring us back once more" to the "vanished days of yore," when the world was still "filled with faith, with zeal." But like many a nineteenth century artist, Longfellow concluded that such sounds were probably "in vain": the past could not successfully be called back again. The struggle to affirm publicly traditional values while privately doubting their efficacy provided the central tension in much of his poetry. Even the twenty-seven short poems he composed during his college days and published in a variety of little magazines and academic journals were prophetic of the difficulties that Longfellow would encounter whenever he attempted to bring together the spirituality of the past with the progress of the present. Like "The Bells of San Blas," they were tinged with a solemn, mournful sense of desperation, rueful that the traditions, values, and wisdom painfully accumulated over mankind's previous three thousand years of history no longer offered much guidance to the present. The young Longfellow examined the deaths of a variety of heroic Indians, stoic ship captains, and brave infantrymen who had given their lives for some noble cause. He concluded sadly that such nobility produced little lasting effect: theirs had been moments of brightness darkened by an unappreciative and uncaring present. In *Voices of the*

Night (1839), a slim collection of nine short poems, Longfellow amplified the melancholy and focused it through a spokesman who was both confused and troubled by "life's deep storm." While striving to balance his images of life's forms, which could bring both "sorrow and delight," and life's sounds, which could both "soothe or affright," the collection kept straying to the darker, more negative pole.

Each of the nine major collections of lyrics which followed these tentative beginnings sustained his sense of confusion and foreboding. In *Ballads and Other Poems*, Longfellow examined the traditional life-styles of a Viking warrior, a New England sea captain, and a simple village blacksmith with the same effusive sentimentality he had employed on a similar grouping during his undergraduate years. He characterized these simple lives as an accumulation of "toiling and rejoicing and sorrowing," emphasizing heavily "the sorrowing," and dismissed them as incapable of providing workable models for surviving the modern world. The tone of the collection was established by the resignation inherent in "The Goblet of Life," whose brim, Longfellow concluded, tended too often to overflow "with bitter drops of woe." The best anyone could hope for, given such pessimism, was the "strength to bear a portion of the care" which "crushes one half of humanity with despair."

This pessimism was repeated throughout *The Belfry of Bruges and Other Poems*, whose title piece forced a tenuous metaphorical comparison between the "sweet sonorous clangor" of a city's bell tower and the poet's own "airy chimes," anticipating the image he would execute with greater skill in "The Bells of San Blas" almost forty years later. In 1845, Longfellow could only claim that the sounds from "the belfry of his brain" were, like the city's bells themselves, "scattered downward, though in vain" to a world no longer moved by "the hollow sound of brass." He complained that producing such irrelevant music might only "overburden his brain" and fill him with a sense of weariness and pain. He ended the collection with a downtrodden portrait of a morose poet, despondent because his book was "completed and closed." Painfully, he sensed that "dim" would "grow its fantasies"; soon "forgotten" they would "lie, like coals in the ashes . . . darken and die." Such abjection, Longfellow suggested, could only partially be relieved with a night which grew "darker and darker" as the "black shadows fall" and with the troubled observation that shortly "sleep and oblivion will reign over all."

Longfellow was never exactly sure which names or shapes to give the fears which haunted his early lyrics. It is true that the undifferentiated anxiety seldom paraded itself in his more frequently read historical narratives, but the fears had much to do with his sense that traditional solutions were failing to answer modern questions. In *The Seaside and the Fireside*, he conjured up a slightly paranoid image of a fisherman's daughter staring dumbly "out into the night" from behind the window of her family's cottage, hoping to see "some form arise." The child remained incapable of discerning what "tales the roaring ocean and the night wind, bleak and wild" might have to tell. But at the poem's end, those projected fears could beat "at the heart" of the child's mother and "drive the color from her cheek." It was more than a child's fascination mingled with fear of night mysteries which colored much of Longfellow's lyricism; it was a vague but omnipresent fear that something was dreadfully wrong with the direction of modern civilization. Keener minds than Longfellow's remained similarly mystified, unable to articulate the questions which by the twentieth century would evolve into a systematic pattern of *Angst*.

The "Birds of Passage" sequence, which he distributed throughout many of the later collections of lyrics, confronted these fears as directly as Longfellow could. The poems purported to reproduce the sounds of modern life, "murmurs of delight or woe" and the "murmurs of pleasures and pains and wrongs" which comprised his polarized judgment. Like his earlier efforts, however, these dwelt on the negative side, frequently echoing "the only sound we can discern," the "sound of lament." Even these, "all this toiling for human culture," he worried, might prove to be "unavailing." The sequence showed Longfellow at his best: his lines filled with sophisticated internal rhymes, with sometimes startling end rhymes ("Flanders" and "commanders," "unafraid" and "cannonade," "mountbanks" and "tan and planks"), with easy musical rhythms.

The "Birds of Passage" sequence is representative of Longfellow at the height of his powers, groping sometimes toward a Whitmanesque mysticism which might redeem his early fears and negativities. "All the houses where men have lived and died are haunted houses," he offered as the cornerstone of his belief-system in one poem in the sequence: "The spirit world around this world of sense floats like an atmosphere." In the lyrics which transcended his sense of despair, Longfellow began to avow his own personal, haphazard mixture of New England mysticism, Bostonian New Thought, spiritualism, numerology, astrology, and staid Unitarianism, hoping to offer some redemptive spirituality to a world which frequently defined itself as a "dark abyss." "To the dark problems, there is no other solution possible," he wrote to James Russell Lowell, "except the one word, Providence."

The last collections of lyrics wavered between the knowledge of how darkly a people tended to live their lives and the hope of how brightly those lives could be lived. The poems tended to deal more directly with the paradoxical ambiguities which had provided many of the tensions in the "Birds of Passage" sequence. They turned on life and death, daylight and moonlight, the heart of man, "blithe as the air is, and as free" and the heart of man so burdened "by the cares of yesterday" that "each today" was "heavier still." A view of the world in which defeats frequently turned out to be victories in disguise and the lowest ebbs were often only "the turn of tides" bound together *The Masque of Pandora and Other Poems, Kéramos and Other Poems,* and

Ultima Thule. These collections suggested a more peaceful and accepting stance toward the dynamic balance of opposites which, Longfellow believed, characterized all of life.

In the later poems, the destructive forces which men could unleash were being quieted by the vaguely meditative and heartfelt notion that "God is All." His last lyrics, though never completely shaking the sense of despair, transience, and futility which had dogged his poetic vision, showed a Longfellow who was coming to terms with evil and who was growing surer with hope. In the complex polarities of "Victor and Vanquished," Longfellow seemed to suggest that even the worst of life could lead to the best. The victim, harried into a corner and confronted with certain death, could still stand unmoved and unafraid, taunting the victor with the chivalric challenge, "Do with me what thou wilt." Such spirit, Longfellow insisted, could make even "the vanquished here," the "victor of the field." Whenever "a noble deed is wrought" or "spoken is a noble thought," Longfellow articulated his redemptive code of hope: "our hearts, in glad surprise to higher levels rise." In *Ultima Thule*, he was explaining the presence of evil with the time-honored formula that "noble souls" inevitably "rise from disaster and defeat, the stronger." The effort would make them more conscious of "the divine with them." For these traditional platitudes, Longfellow could, at his best, often find fresh and moving imagery.

The collections of late lyrics were probably his most enduring works. They chronicled a troubled soul, torn with the doubts of his age, groping to articulate a sense of mystery, awe, and spirituality which might bring hope to a culture too concerned with its own certitudes and material advances. It was not these lyrics, however, but rather his long historical narratives which had brought him acclaim from his contemporaries. Neither the profound doubts nor the genuine hopes which animated his lyrics could be found in these more saccharine celebrations of traditional values. At their worst, *The Spanish Student* (1843), *Evangeline*, *The Song of Hiawatha*, *The Courtship of Miles Standish*, *The Divine Tragedy*, *The Golden Legend*, and *The New England Tragedies* were dull prosaic narratives which have done much to discourage modern readers from discovering the strengths of Longfellow's talents. *The Spanish Student* was an infelicitous three-act verse comedy intended for the stage. It found no one willing to venture the capital necessary for producing it. *Evangeline* was the work which first won a mass audience for Longfellow. It was a simple tale, first spun by the clergyman, H. L. Conolly, while he dined with Longfellow and Nathaniel Hawthorne. Longfellow seized the story line, picked a formal, though not always formally kept, dactylic hexameter metrical pattern for it, and composed a long tale of the French Arcadienne, Evangeline, as she wandered through the forests of eighteenth century New England looking for her kidnaped lover. It was a cliché-ridden effort whose descriptive powers ran to portrayals of Evangeline as "living at peace with

God and the World," to summaries of her relationship with her betrothed as "their two hearts, tender and true," and to a plot which described her quest for him as searches "in want and cheerless discomfort, bleeding, barefooted, over the shards and thorns of existence." When at the poem's and her own life's end Evangeline finally located her long-lost fiancé, the best Longfellow could fashion for an ending was to have her "meekly bow" her head and "murmur, 'Father, I thank Thee'" just before she died. The popularity of the poem probably revealed more about the tastes of Longfellow's readers than about his own talents.

The same audience responded even more enthusiastically to *The Song of Hiawatha*. With its two-footed lines vaguely resembling the alliterative verse of traditional northern European epics like the Finnish *Kalevala*, with its heavy borrowings from Henry Rowe Schoolcraft's two volumes on North American Indians, and with its upbeat ending, the appeal of *The Song of Hiawatha* was quick and widespread. The tale borrowed the grandiose proportions of the European epic, picturing a Hiawatha whose every stride measured "a Mile," whose canoe needed no paddles "for his thoughts as paddles served," whose father was "the west wind," and whose true love was Minnehaha, daughter of the god of arrow makers. The poem's rhythmic devices could sometimes be interesting. Especially when read aloud, the Indian material could lend a freshness to the overworked conventions of the epic, and Longfellow's battle scenes, pitting Hiawatha against a variety of mythic creatures, were frequently well-paced. All this technical virtuosity, however, could not hold together the disconnected elements of the plot or prepare the reader for the arbitrarily imposed ending in which Hiawatha vacates his native village so that his fellow Indians might be more inclined to listen to the redeeming gospel of Christianity brought to them by European missionaries. The same muddle of values and formlessness of plot marred *The Courtship of Miles Standish*. The poem returned to the dactylic hexameters of *Evangeline* and to the romantic love angle shared between two recognizably human historical figures. Set in seventeenth century Puritan New England, *The Courtship of Miles Standish* wavered between sustaining a heroic view of the Plymouth Colony and a lighthearted glance at the foibles of its founders. Longfellow could never quite make up his mind whether to emphasize the "strong hearts and true" of the pilgrims or to satirize the quirky leader who could lock himself in his room and cheer himself with passages from Julius Caesar: "Better be first, he said, in a little Iberian village/ Than be second in Rome, and I think he was right when he said it."

With *The Divine Tragedy*, an epic about the life of Christ, *The Golden Legend*, a retelling of the Faust story, and *The New England Tragedies*, an unfinished grouping about Christianity in the New World, Longfellow began to lose the mass audience he had so carefully cultivated. These works marked the same kind of transition to a tentative but serious spirituality which had characterized his later collections of lyrics. These poems, far more earnest than his early narratives, constituted reevaluations of two thousand years of Western religious thought through which Longfellow hoped to sift beliefs which might still have meaning to his contemporaries. He originally planned a chronicle of the triumph of religious progress in the ancient, medieval, and modern worlds. But his own lack of conviction in doctrinaire Christianity and his own unshakable doubts led him to undercut the tales of triumph by dwelling on those moments in which the purity of the original doctrines were perverted by fallible man. *The Divine Tragedy* set out to recapture the original message, but neither Longfellow's scattered theology nor his limited talents lent themselves to a subject of Miltonic proportions. His Christ blandly mouthed excerpts from the King James Bible; his apostles turned out to be featureless; his plot was a pastiche of New Testament incidents only vaguely related to one another; and his ending was an inconclusive recitation of the Apostles' Creed, with each of the twelve taking turns uttering the lines. "Poor sad humanity," St. John says, summarizing the effort, "turns back with bleeding feet by the weary road it came." With Longfellow's growing need to explain the tragedies which had befallen him, the turning back took the form of *The Golden Legend* and *The New England Tragedies*. Both sought to examine the storehouse of Western religious traditions and decide which "messages" from the "world of the spirits" could still animate contemporary man. "Death is the chilliness that precedes the dawn," he would declare in *Michael Angelo*, "then, we awake in the broad sunshine of the other life."

In *The Golden Legend*, Longfellow used the character of Prince Henry to examine how that belief in the other life came to be abandoned. His reshaping of both medieval and modern Christianity questioned, not the validity of the original doctrines, but the applications through which their adherents distorted them. His Faust figure in *The Golden Legend* was tempted by a sophisticated and worldly Lucifer, often disguised as a village priest, who counseled his charge not toward sin but toward a more modern point of view. Prince Henry was led to accept the belief in progress, materialism, the priority of the senses, and the certainty of the here and now. Lucifer eased his conscience. His temptations ran not to rejecting formal Christianity, but to ignoring its underlying sense of the mystical. In *The New England Tragedies*, this temptation was accepted with fewer questions. "O silent, sombre, and deserted streets," says a forlorn John Endicott, noting the emphasis on progress instead of spirituality: "To me, ye're peopled with a sad procession and echo only to the voice of sorrow." Where Prince Henry had placed too much faith in the powers of the intellect, the New Englanders had overemphasized the social mission of Calvinism. Both, Longfellow maintained, had lost sight of the underlying mystery and awe evident in the original testament espoused in *The Divine Tragedy*. Late in his last two narratives, Longfellow came to recommend the same kind of inchoate spirituality which had displayed redemptive powers in the most hopeful of his lyric poems. He was not enough of a theologian to formulate a systematic creed, nor enough of a zealot to recommend one path over another; and he was too much of a symbolist not to believe that all religious systems were only rough approximations of the same underlying unity. Nevertheless, a direct, experiential contact with the mysticism in man and the mysticism in nature could, Longfellow felt, explain much of the darkness of life.

Philip Woodard

Other major works
LONG FICTION: *Kavanagh: A Tale,* 1849.
PLAY: *The Spanish Student,* 1843.
NONFICTION: *Elements of French Grammar,* 1830 (translation); *Manuel de Proverbes Dramatiques,* 1830; *Outre-Mer: A Pilgrimage Beyond the Sea,* 1833-1834; *Hyperion,* 1839; *Drift-Wood,* 1857; *The Letters of Henry Wadsworth Longfellow,* 1966-1974 (Andrew Hilen, editor, 5 volumes).
ANTHOLOGIES: *The Poets and Poetry of Europe,* 1845; *The Waif: A Collection of Poems,* 1845; *The Estray: A Collection of Poems,* 1847; *Poems of Places,* 1876-1879.

Bibliography
Buell, Lawrence. *New England Literary Culture.* Cambridge, England: Cambridge University Press, 1986. Buell notes Longfellow's strong interest in New England life, a fact that many critics have neglected. His *The New England Tragedies* are the most comprehensive portrayal of the region by any nineteenth century poet. Longfellow's interest in religious epics is also stressed: the poet regarded *Christus: A Mystery* as his crowning achievement. Longfellow's religious vision was Unitarian, and he was worried by the possibility that religion is only a human projection.
Pearce, Roy Harvey. *The Continuity of American Poetry.* Middletown, Conn.: Wesleyan University Press, 1987. The earlier edition (1961) of this work is a standard critical survey of American poetry. Pearce adopts a dismissive tone toward Longfellow. He lived in a closed world, constantly intent on proving that life is not an empty dream. His work was a constant and misguided search for certainty. In spite of his wide acquaintance with world literature and history, Longfellow was narrowly provincial in outlook. Preoccupied with his own thoughts, he was unable to see objects as they really are.
Suchard, Allen. "The Nineteenth Century: Romanticism in American Poetry." In *American Poetry.* Amherst: University of Massachusetts Press, 1988. In spite of Longfellow's reputation as a celebrator of the American

way of life, he, in fact, was possessed by a gloomy vision. Cosmic abandonment is constantly present in his work. In "Hymn to the Night," he welcomes night and death as a release from life. His dark side became more prominent after the death of his second wife. The brooding quality of his verse is its best feature. Longfellow's sonnets have been unduly neglected: he is one of the foremost American masters of this verse form.

Turco, Lewis P. *Visions and Revisions of American Poetry*. Fayetteville: University of Alabama Press, 1986. Turco views Longfellow as a derivative poet of minor importance. He imitated the English Romantics, and, in spite of the bulk of his output, almost none has endured. "Ropewalk" is his greatest poem, and his Civil war carol "Christmas Bells" also ranks as outstanding. The greatness of the poem to a large extent consists of the fact that it illustrates pessimism, while ostensibly supporting a sunny outlook.

Waggoner, Hyatt H. "Five New England Poets." In *American Poets: from the Puritans to the Present*. Baton Rouge: Louisiana State University Press, 1984. Longfellow was the saddest of all American poets. His dominant theme is that time is man's enemy. He was unwilling to face his own vision and made constant efforts to cheer himself up. In his most famous poem "Psalm of Life," his message is that life must be worth living, but we do not know why. Waggoner contends that Longfellow was unintelligent and that his poems are often incoherent.

AUDRE LORDE

Born: New York, New York; February 18, 1934

Principal poetry

The First Cities, 1968; *Cables to Rage*, 1970; *From a Land Where Other People Live*, 1973; *New York Head Shop and Museum*, 1974; *Between Our Selves*, 1976; *Coal*, 1976; *The Black Unicorn*, 1978; *Chosen Poems, Old and New*, 1982; *Our Dead Behind Us*, 1986.

Other literary forms

The Cancer Journals (1980) is a personal account of Audre Lorde's struggles with breast cancer. *Zami: A New Spelling of My Name* (1982), which Lorde has called a "biomythography," is a retrospective narrative of her emerging sexuality. *Sister Outsider* (1984) and *A Burst of Light* (1988) are collections of essays and speeches on poetry, feminism, lesbianism, and racism.

Achievements

Lorde received a National Endowment for the Arts grant and was a poet-in-residence at Tougaloo College in Jackson, Mississippi, in 1968. Since then, she has received other recognitions, including the Creative Artists Public Service grant (1972 and 1976) and the Broadside Poets Award (1975). She has called herself a "black lesbian feminist warrior poet." At the heart of her work as poet, essayist, teacher, and lecturer lies an intense and relentless exploration of personal identity. Beyond the stunning portrayals of her deepest insights and emotions, her work is filled with powerful evocations of universal survival. The substance of her poetry and essays always reaches beyond the individual self into deep concerns for all humanity. Progressively, her work reveals an increasing awareness of her West Indian heritage in relation to her place in American society and its values.

Biography

Audre Lorde's parents emigrated from Grenada to New York City in 1924. Lorde, the youngest of three girls, was born in 1934. She has recounted many of her childhood memories in *Zami*, identifying particular incidents that had an influence or effect on her developing sexuality and her later work as a poet. She attended the University of Mexico (1954-1955) and received a B.A. from Hunter College (1959) and an M.L.S. from Columbia University (1961). In 1962, she was married to Edwin Rollins, with whom she had two children before they were divorced in 1970.

Prior to 1968, when she gained public recognition for her poetry, Lorde supported herself through a variety of jobs, including low-paying factory work.

She has also served as a librarian in several institutions. Since her first publication, *The First Cities*, Lorde has worked primarily within American colleges and free presses. She was an instructor at City College of New York (1968-1970), an instructor and then lecturer at Lehman College (1969-1971), and a professor of English at John Jay College of Criminal Justice (1972-1981). Since 1981, she has been a professor of English at Hunter College and poetry editor of the magazine *Chrysalis*. She is a contributing editor of the journal *Black Scholar* and a founding member of SISA (Sisterhood in Support of Sisters in South Africa) and Kitchen Table: Women of Color Press. She has also served on the board of the National Coalition of Black Lesbians and Gays.

Analysis

All Audre Lorde's poems, essays, and speeches are deeply personal renditions of a compassionate writer, thinker, and human being. Indeed, she draws much of her material from individual and multifaceted experience; she renders it in writing that seeks to reveal the complexity of being a black feminist lesbian poet. She expresses the feelings of being marginalized in an American society that is predominantly white, male, heterosexual, and middle-class. Her writings reflect the changing constitution and perspective of American life, but she never relents to an easy optimism, nor does she make uninformed dismissals of society's ills. Her personal experiences have made her compassionate toward those who suffer under oppressive regimes all over the world. By drawing from the history and mythology of the West Indies, she is able to refer to the racism and sexism that exist in other cultures.

In her early collections of poetry, *The First Cities* and *Cables to Rage*, Lorde expresses a keen political disillusionment, noting the failure of American ideals of equality and justice for all. When Lorde uses the pronoun "we" in her poetry, she speaks for all who have been dispossessed. In "Anniversary," for example, she writes, "Our tears/ water an alien grass," expressing the separation between those who belong and those who do not. In poems such as "Sowing," the poet reveals the land's betrayal of its inhabitants by showing images of destruction juxtaposed to personal rage: "I have been to this place before/ where blood seething commanded/ my fingers fresh from the earth."

She also demonstrates a concern for the children of this earth in "Bloodbirth": casting about to understand what it is in her that is raging to be born, she wonders how an opening will come "to show the true face of me/ lying exposed and together/ my children your children their children/ bent on our conjugating business." The image of the warrior, the one who must be prepared to go about the business of existing in an unjust world, signifies the need to take care of those not yet aware of unfulfilled promises.

If the rage in her early poems appears "unladylike," Lorde is setting out to explode sexual typecasting. Certainly, there is nothing dainty about her sharp images and powerful assessments of social conditions. As she confronts harsh realities, the portrayals must necessarily be clamorous. Yet the poet's rage does not lead to a blind rampage. In "Conversation in Crisis," the poet hopes to speak to her friend "for a clear meeting/ of self upon self/ in sight of our hearth/ but without fire." The poet must speak honestly and not out of false assumptions and pretenses so that real communication can occur. The reader and listener must heed the words as well as the tone in order to receive the meaning of the words. Communication, then, is a kind of contractual relationship between people.

In the collections *From a Land Where Other People Live* and *Between Our Selves*, Lorde uses a compassionate tone to tell people about the devastation of white racism upon African Americans. She mixes historical fact with political reality, emphasizing the disjunction that sometimes occurs between the two. In "Equinox," Lorde observes her daughter's birth by remembering a series of events that also occurred that year: she had "marched into Washington/ to a death knell of dreaming/ which 250,000 others mistook for a hope," for few at that time understood the victimization of children that was occurring not only in the American South but also in the Vietnam War. After she heard that Malcolm X had been shot, she reread all of his writings: "the dark mangled children/ came streaming out of the atlas/ Hanoi Angola Guinea-Bissau . . . / merged into Bedford-Stuyvesant and Hazelhurst Mississippi."

From the multiplicity of world horrors, the poet returns to her hometown in New York, exhausted but profoundly moved by the confrontation of history and the facts of her own existence. In "The Day They Eulogized Mahalia," another event is present in the background as the great singer Mahalia Jackson is memorialized: six black children died in a fire at a day care center on the South Side; "firemen found their bodies/ like huddled lumps of charcoal/ with silent mouths and eyes wide open." Even as she mourns the dead in her poems, the poet is aware of both the power and the powerlessness of words to effect real changes. In the poem, "Power," Lorde writes,

> The difference between poetry and rhetoric
> is being ready to kill
> yourself
> instead of your children.

Once the event has occurred, one can write about it or one can try to prevent a similar event from occurring; in either case, it is not possible to undo the first event. Therefore, as a society, people must learn from their errors and their failures to care for other people. Lorde even warns herself that she must discern and employ this crucial difference between poetry and rhetoric; if she does not, "my power too will run corrupt as poisonous mold/ or lie limp and useless as an unconnected wire."

For Lorde, the process of learning all over again how to transform thought into action begins with the awareness of her personal reality. In the collections *Coal, The Black Unicorn,* and *Our Dead Behind Us,* the poet addresses more specifically the individual human beings in her life, creating vignettes of her relationships with other people. In particular, she returns again and again to images of her mother, Linda Belmar Lorde, whose relatively light-colored skin is mentioned in many of the poems. In "Outside," she links her mother's lightness to the brutal faces of racism: "Nobody lynched my momma/ but what she'd never been/ had bleached her face of everything." When Lorde questions, "Who shall I curse that I grew up/ believing in my mother's face," she is echoing the anger that also appears in the poem "Sequelae." There she states explicitly the rage that evolved from the mother's lies, white lies: "I battle the shapes of you/ wearing old ghosts of me/ hating you for being/ black and not woman/ hating you for being white." (*Zami* elaborates many of the specific events to which Lorde refers in her poems about her mother.)

The return to childhood allows the poet to come to new terms with her mother. In several of her poems, she also returns to even deeper roots constituting her identity. In "Dahomey," she refers to the African goddess Seboulisa, "the Mother of us all" or the creator of the world. In embracing the mother goddess, the poet is able "to sharpen the knives of my tongue." Because the subjects of her poetry are painful ones, Lorde empowers her own speech by always calling attention to the dangers of remaining silent. In "A Song for Many Movements," she states simply and precisely the project of her poetry: "Our labor has become/ more important/ than our silence."

The title of one of her essays is especially appropriate to describing her work as a poet, "The Transformation of Silence into Language and Action." In a self-characterization when she was a poet-in-residence at Tougaloo College, Lorde said, "I became convinced, anti-academic though I am, that all poets must teach what they know, in order to continue being." Her insistent drive to exist according to the terms of her individual desires and powers is the focal point of many of her speeches and essays. Lorde is also active on the lecture circuit, and she has been invited to speak to women writers in the Soviet Union and in Berlin. She has documented many of her insights into various cultures and places in essays and poems.

The various forms of her writing provide many pieces to the whole picture that makes up Lorde's life and work. She is unsentimental in naming the people who have been a part of her life and in evaluating the events that make up her experiences. Her parents and her sisters are addressed with some frequency in her poems. A girlhood friend, Genevieve, appears in *Zami,* and Lorde eulogizes her death in a poem entitled "Memorial II." Many women are treated in several different poems, sometimes in cycles—for example, Martha and Eudora. In these ways, Lorde documents the people and the course of her life as she charts the changes and the progress that occur; at each turn, she seeks to understand more deeply the situation and to learn which detours to take next.

When she was in her forties, Lorde was diagnosed as having breast cancer. *The Cancer Journals* and the essay "A Burst of Light: Living with Cancer" are important pieces of personal writing that record her uncertainties, fears, and doubts about her mortality. Writing mostly in the form of a diary, Lorde allows the reader to enter into her most private thoughts and emotions, with the hope that others may be encouraged to fight cancer. Out of her determination to survive, Lorde has converted her struggles with cancer into energy for battling in behalf of other humanitarian concerns.

She has set out rigorously to combat racism, sexism, heterosexism, and homophobia in her work. At times she deals with the issues separately, but more frequently she speaks of the whole gamut, since she perceives that each stems from human blindness about the differences among people. What is remarkable about Lorde's insights is the balance that she seeks in presenting her views. Overtly political in intent and social in content, the essays and speeches ask all individuals to understand more deeply the ways in which human lives are organized. She then beckons people to take charge of their lives, to confront the tasks at hand, and to take responsibility for making changes.

Much of Lorde's mature work has evolved from her identity as a black feminist lesbian poet. These terms are essential conjunctions that express her existence and her vision. In the essay "The Master's Tools Will Never Dismantle the Master's House," Lorde makes no apologies or defenses for her choices. She writes, "For women, the need and desire to nurture each other is not pathological but redemptive, and it is within that knowledge that our real power is rediscovered." For Lorde, the power to exist and be alive comes from her love—in all senses of the word—for women.

In her most often cited essay, "The Uses of the Erotic: The Erotic as Power," Lorde dislodges some of the negative assumptions that have sprung up around the terms "erotic" and "power," and offers new perspectives on how an individual must use her power and ability to love. For Lorde, the erotic is "a resource within each of us that lies in a deeply female and spiritual plane, firmly rooted in the power of our unexpressed or unrecognized feeling." Through a redefinition of the terms, Lorde shows how societal oppression numbs a woman's ability to feel and act deeply. Often the two—emotion and action—are in conflict with the values of a "racist, patriarchal, and anti-erotic society." Before individual human beings can come together as one society, each person must be in touch with his or her own feelings and be willing to express and share with others. These are the necessary first steps to effecting real political change.

Lorde contends that the need to share is a fundamental one that all people feel. Unfortunately, the prevailing attitudes of American society preclude true expression of individualism: if people do not fit into the norms or expectations of the dominant system of values, they are deemed "not normal" or deviant. Lorde argues against the hypocrisy of American values: where is freedom if any forms of expression considered "unfit" are excluded? How might one such as herself, who is on the margins of all that is "normal," empower herself to take effective action?

These are the kinds of difficult questions Lorde has raised from the beginning of her work as a writer and poet. She has made efforts to answer them anew in much of what she has produced. She has emphasized the necessity of listening to others and teaching what she herself has learned in the course of her work. Always receptive to the notion of difference that exists among all people, Lorde sets out to consider the meaning of her own experiences first, before she attempts to convey to others what those experiences might mean in the larger context of existence. On the one hand, her work is intensely personal; it may even be considered self-absorbed at times. Yet on the other, she has managed to transform her deeply private pains and joys into universal and timeless concerns.

Cynthia Wong

Other major works

NONFICTION: *The Cancer Journals*, 1980; *Zami: A New Spelling of My Name*, 1982; *Sister Outsider*, 1984; *A Burst of Light*, 1988.

Bibliography

Avi-Ram, Amitai F. "*Apo Koinou* in Lorde and the Moderns: Defining the Differences." *Callaloo* 9 (Winter, 1986): 193-208. *Apo koinou* comes from a Greek phrase meaning "in common." This original and ambitious essay discusses the uses of eroticism and the importance of a political consciousness in Lorde's work. The author situates Lorde's work in the context of other modernist poets. The argument is sophisticated and learned; its stimulating premise derives from a familiarity with literary history and Western philosophical thought.

Brooks, Jerome. "In the Name of the Father: The Poetry of Audre Lorde." In *Black Women Writers (1950-1980): A Critical Evaluation*, edited by Mari Evans. Garden City, N.Y.: Doubleday, 1984. This brief chapter deals with a topic to which Lorde gives little direct attention in her own essays—the death of her father. It is a useful analysis of a focused topic that clarifies the meaning of some of the poems in which the figure of the father appears.

Hull, Gloria, T. "Living on the Line: Audre Lorde and *Our Dead Behind Us*." In *Changing Our Own Words: Essays on Criticism, Theory, and Writing by Black Women*, edited by Cheryl A. Wall. New Brunswick, N.J.: Rutgers University Press, 1989. This is a thoughtful essay on one of Lorde's collections of poetry. While it refers to some contemporary critical theory, it is an engaging and accessible study that traces the trajectory of Lorde's work. Hull also assesses various critical reviews of the collection.

Lorde, Audre. "Sadomasochism: Not About Condemnation." Interview by Susan Leigh Star. In *A Burst of Light.* Ithaca, N.Y.: Firebrand Books, 1988. Lorde talks energetically about her sexuality, setting the discussion in the context of her life's work. This interview is the first in a series of private meditations centered on her bouts with cancer.

Lorde, Audre, and Adrienne Rich. "An Interview: Audre Lorde and Adrienne Rich." In *Sister Outsider: Essays and Speeches.* Trumansburg, N.Y.: Crossing Press, 1984. The two poets speak about a wide range of topics such as power, knowledge, and eroticism. Lorde also discusses her views on the uses of prose and poetry, focusing on the process of perception.

Martin, Joan. "The Unicorn is Black: Audre Lorde in Retrospect." In *Black Women Writers (1950-1980): A Critical Evaluation*, edited by Mari Evans. Garden City, N.Y.: Doubleday, 1984. This is a useful compendium of Lorde's work up to 1984, focusing on the collection entitled *The Black Unicorn.*

RICHARD LOVELACE

Born: Woolwich, England, or Holland; 1618
Died: London, England; 1656 or 1657

Principal poetry

Lucasta: Epodes, Odes, Sonnets, Songs, &c. to Which Is Added Aramantha, a Pastorall, 1649; *Lucasta: Posthume Poems of Richard Lovelace, Esq.*, 1659; *The Poems of Richard Lovelace*, 1925 (C. H. Wilkinson, editor, 2 volumes).

Other literary forms

Apart from the lyrics published in the two volumes of his poetry, Richard Lovelace wrote two plays, neither of which appears to be extant. The youthful *The Scholar* or *The Scholars*, a comedy, may have been produced at Gloucester Hall, Oxford, in 1636, and repeated later at Whitefriars, Salisbury Court, London. The prologue and epilogue appear in *Lucasta* (1649). A second play, a tragedy entitled *The Soldier* (1640), was written during the second Scottish expedition in 1640 but was never produced, according to Anthony à Wood, because of the closing of the theaters. Lovelace also wrote commendatory verses for a number of volumes published by friends or associates, versions of which appear in the collected editions of his poems. In addition, he wrote some lines, engraved under the portrait of Vincent Voiture, prefixed to the translation of the *Letters* by John Davies in 1657.

Achievements

Although chiefly remembered for a handful of exquisite lyrics celebrating what Douglas Bush called the Cavalier trinity of beauty, love, and honor, Lovelace has gradually risen to critical attention. Written for the most part against the somber landscape of England during the Civil War and Interregnum, Lovelace's poetry asserts more complex concerns and more authentic attitudes than those usually attributed to that "mob of gentlemen who wrote with ease." Decidedly a literary amateur in the Renaissance tradition of the courtier, Lovelace's sensibilities were deepened and roughened by the calamities that befell him, his cause, and his king. "To Althea, from Prison," and "To Lucasta, going to the wars" are justly admired along with a few other frequently anthologized pieces, but the achievement is considerably larger than their slight number and scope might suggest. In his ode "The Grasshopper," for example, written to his friend Charles Cotton, Lovelace fashions from an emblematic examination of the fate of that "poor verdant fool" an affirmation of human friendship that transcends particular circumstance and achieves an authentic tragic tone. In the lines written "To my worthy friend Mr. Peter Lely, on that excellent picture of his Majesty and the Duke of York, drawn by him at Hampton Court," Lovelace evokes the "clouded majesty" of King Charles the First, transforming a typical genre piece describing a painting into a somber elegiac on human dignity and courage in the face of adversity.

Like most of his fellow Cavalier poets, Lovelace was indebted to the poetry of Ben Jonson and John Donne. To Jonson he owed what graciousness and form he achieved, especially in the choice of classical models. To Donne he owed some degree of intellectual toughness and delight in what ingenious conceits he could master. To the limitations of both, in different ways, he was indebted for those infelicities of style that came with too much striving and too much care. Among his immediate contemporaries he was, no doubt, influenced by his relative, the translator Thomas Stanley, who may have helped him in more substantial matters than verse. Other poets with whom Lovelace shared stylistic affinities and thematic concerns were Robert Herrick, Sir John Suckling, and Andrew Marvell.

Biography

The broad outlines of Richard Lovelace's life are easy enough to sketch; but when it comes to filling in the details, much remains conjectural. Born in 1618 either at the family manor of Bethersden, Woolwich, Kent, or in Holland, Lovelace was the eldest son of Sir William Lovelace and his wife Anne (Barne). (The Woolwich church register does not commence until 1663.) His mother spent some time in Holland, where his father served under Sir Horace Vere and was later killed at the siege of Groll in 1627. Her references to her son Richard in her will make it seem likely that he was born while she was with her husband in the Low Countries.

Richard had four brothers, Thomas, Francis, William, and Dudley (the last of whom was responsible for seeing *Lucasta: Posthume Poems* through the press after his brother's death), and three sisters, Anne, Elizabeth, and Johanna. There are no records of Lovelace's childhood. In January, 1630, Lady Lovelace married Jonathan Brown or Browne of London, Doctor of Laws, and it may be presumed that the family's fortunes were enhanced as a result. The poet was educated at Charterhouse and entered Gloucester Hall, now Worcester College, Oxford, as a gentleman commoner in 1634.

By all accounts, the young scholar was handsome and amiable. In his second year, according to Anthony à Wood, a not very reliable authority in the case of Lovelace, he attracted the attention of an eminent Lady of the Queen, who prevailed upon the Archbishop of Canterbury, then Chancellor of the University, to have him awarded a Master of Arts, though he was only of two years' standing. The following year Lovelace was at Cambridge University, where he met several young men then in residence who were to contribute commendatory verses to *Lucasta* twelve years later; among them was Andrew Marvell.

Upon leaving the university, Lovelace joined the court, where he attracted the attention of George, Lord Goring, later Earl of Norwich, and was sent by him as an ensign in the first expedition against the Scots in 1639, under the Earl of Northumberland. During the second of these ineffectual campaigns, he was commissioned captain. Although he apparently wrote the tragedy entitled *The Soldier* during the second campaign, the only direct reference to the Scottish campaigns is the drinking song "To General Goring, after the pacification of Berwick." Among those who rode northward with Lovelace was the poet Sir John Suckling, whose "Ballad upon a Wedding" is traditionally thought to address Lovelace, although there is little, if any, substantive evidence for the attribution.

Following the Scottish campaigns, Lovelace returned to Kent and took possession of the family estates. In late April, 1642, he helped deliver the Kentish Petition to the House of Commons, for which he was confined in prison for perhaps as long as two months. The petitioners could not have hoped for any response less severe, especially as a similar petition of the previous month on behalf of the bishops and the liturgy had been ordered burned by the common hangman. In June, Lovelace was released on bail from his confinement, provided he remain in close communication with the Speaker of the House. Although he was forbidden to take an active role in the struggle between the King and Parliament, he outfitted his brothers Francis and William with men and money to aid the royalist cause and arranged for his younger brother, Dudley, to study tactics and fortification in Holland.

Lovelace probably spent the greater part of the years 1643-1646 in Holland and France. His departure may have occasioned the lyric "To Lucasta, going beyond the seas." In Holland he presumably learned the language and acquired an appreciation of the world of art then flourishing with Rembrandt at the height of his powers. Lovelace was present at the siege of Dunkirk in 1646, where he was wounded. A year later he was back in London and was admitted with the Dutch-born portraitist Peter Lely to the Freedom of the Painters' Company. In 1648 he and his brother were taken as prisoners to Peterhouse in London, possibly as a precautionary measure because of their past activities and the turbulent state of affairs in Kent at the time. It was during this second confinement, apparently, that he prepared his lyrics for publication in 1649. He was discharged on April 10, 1649, some ten months after his incarceration. During the year Lovelace sold what remained of his family estates, including the family portraits, among which was one of himself by an unknown artist. These later came to Dulwich College.

Virtually nothing is known of Lovelace's activities in the years preceding his death, which occurred sometime before October, 1657, the date of the publication of Eldred Revett's *Poems*, which contained an elegy on Lovelace. Wood provides an account of Lovelace's last days and death. It has achieved popularity as suiting the legend of the man, but that Lovelace died a miserable death in utter poverty seems less than likely. Fifteen months prior to his death he wrote "The Triumphs of Philamore and Amoret" for the celebration of the marriage of his friend Charles Cotton. The poem, itself, may account for Wood's version of Lovelace's wretched end. Its references to Cotton's aid, however, "when in mine obscure cave/ (Shut up almost close prisoner in a grave)/ Your beams could reach me through this vault of night," would seem not to call for Wood's exaggerated description of the event. That Lovelace's fortune and fortunes were gravely reduced by the end seems clear. He would hardly have been alone in facing such hardships. There were friends to help, and it is unlikely that such abject poverty would not have been hinted at, had it occurred, in the various elegies occasioned by the publication in 1659 of *Lucasta: Posthume Poems*. The community of lettered friends was closely knit and evidence exists that discounts the implications of Wood's narrative. The poet Thomas Stanley, Lovelace's kinsman, had helped several needy and deserving poets and royalists, among them Sir Edward Sherburne, John Hall, and Robert Herrick. Cotton clearly assisted Lovelace in his time of need, and it is well known that Marvell tirelessly aided Milton in the early years of the Restoration. These are examples of the kind of support that surely would have been available to such an important gentleman and poet. Lovelace's place of burial, in Wood's account, was "at the west end of the Church of Saint Bride, alias Bridget, in London, near to the body of his kinsman William." The church was completely destroyed in the Great Fire along with any records that could verify the place of burial.

Analysis

Richard Lovelace's name has epitomized the supposed values of the world he inhabited, while its later link with Samuel Richardson's villain in *Clarissa* (1747-1748) has added guilt by association. The poet was, however, neither villain nor fop. Whatever glitter or romance touched his poems was incidental to a career dominated by darkness and despair, against which he strove with considerable stoicism. Indeed, although the themes of love, friendship, and retirement appear frequently in his poems (along with an informed and highly cultivated notion of the role of the arts of music, painting, and literature in relation to the good life), a pervasive sense of disillusionment and tragic isolation gives the best of them a keen edge. More than one critic has noted a claustrophobic sense of entrapment that is never far from the surface of his work. The traditional themes of what Earl Miner calls the "social mode of cavalier poetry" celebrate the good life, the ruins and remedies of time, the ordering process of art set against the disorder of the age, and the special values of love and friendship in the face of loss. Yet the cavaliers were forced increasingly to survive in a winter world, like that characterized by Lovelace in "The Grasshopper," a poem which has received considerable critical attention in recent years.

In this poem, as in "The Snail," "The Ant," and "A Fly Caught in a

Cobweb," Lovelace turns to the emblems of nature for lessons that bespeak the necessary fortitude of all life faced with the inevitable process of mutability. He shares his desire to fashion ethical and political statements of an allegorical kind by means of a microscopic examination of the natural world with other poets of his time, particularly Andrew Marvell, although the Anacreontic strain was most fully exploited by the royalist writers Thomas Stanley, Robert Herrick, and Abraham Cowley. Of the various reasons for examining the tiny creatures of the natural world, foremost was the wish to draw comparisons with the world of affairs amounting to little more than thinly veiled subversive propaganda. Although Lovelace and his fellow royalists were fascinated by the delicate craftsmanship that art shared with nature, "The Grasshopper" emerges as both a political and an ethical warning, as well as a pattern for refined artistry. The dual impulses in the poem, indeed, threaten its unity. In the end, it is only by recourse to paradox that Lovelace holds the disparate elements together.

In their enterprise to reinforce the royalist position by examples drawn from the world of nature, Lovelace and his fellow poets could not claim a monopoly on the material. Rebellion employed its own arguments from nature in support of human rights. When all else failed, the royalists found that their best alternative was a return to the nature found on what country estates were left to them, where they accepted a life of enforced retirement with whatever solace they could find. For Lovelace this last refuge from the political realities was no longer available.

The best known of Lovelace's lyrics are those that celebrate love, honor, and truth, especially "To Lucasta, going to the wars" and "To Althea, from prison," the latter set by John Wilson for John Playford's *Select Airs and Dialogues* (1659). It is one of a number of royalist dungeon pieces which may be indebted to Vincent Voiture's *Dans la prison*, although prison philosophy was certainly something of a Cavalier convention. For all of Lovelace's asseverations that "iron bars do not a prison make," a sense of lost conviction lingers about the poem like Althea's whispering to her loved one "at the grates." While the poet extravagantly claims his right to lie "tangled" in his mistress' hair and "fettered to her eye," a feeling of suffocating doom weighs heavily on the poem. In comparison, the joyous, almost Elizabethan "Gratiana, dancing and singing," creates a world of exuberance, excitement, and courtly fascination, defining an atmosphere that exists, like Izaak Walton's trout-filled streams, in a world forever vanished. The theme of mutability sparkles through the verse like the golden tresses of Amarantha, that flower of another poem, which when loosened and shaken out will "scatter day."

In truth, for Lovelace it is sorrow that scatters his days, along with the realization that "joys so ripe, so little keep." Though the popular lyric "The Scrutiny" flaunted that brand of cynicism and masculine arrogance learned from John Donne through Thomas Carew and Sir John Suckling, the richer imaginative strain is the note that sounds touching true worth irretrievably lost. The general slightness of Lovelace's lyrics is, in one sense, a measure of what has vanished; and the brief attention span that shows itself in many of the poems, such as "Gratiana, dancing and singing," which disintegrates after the brilliance of the opening four stanzas, may be as much the result of distracted or shattered sensibilities as it is of limited poetic skills. The lyrics frequently end in fragments of broken vision or imaginative exhaustion. There are debts, as well, to the courtier poet Thomas Wyatt, whose verse, like Lovelace's own, was often crabbed and tortured but could rise to take the measure of a tawdry world.

Perhaps because he was an amateur poet and a connoisseur of art, Lovelace saw very clearly the value of restoring the ruins of time. Like many of his contemporaries, particularly Stanley, an indefatigable translator, Lovelace went to continental as well as classical models for his verse, including that fantastic lyricist of the previous generation, Giambattista Marino. It may be assumed that the Petrarchan themes employed by Marino and his followers fascinated the royalist imagination, both by their sensuousness and by the brilliance of their metaphorical transformations. If poetry could change things, such linguistic strategies as the Marinisti presented in search of the marvelous might be enlisted by the Cavaliers in support of the royalist vision. After all, in the King they were accustomed to see poetically and politically the divinely linked agent of the miraculous. Beyond this, translation became for the poets of the time a means both to enrich their own meager gifts and to reinforce the realm of humane letters that was, they believed, the special preserve of the royalist writers.

From Marino, Lovelace borrowed the ideas and images for a number of his better poems. In "Elinda's Glove," working from Marino's *Il Guanto*, "Gli occhi di foco e'l sen di ghiaccio armata," Lovelace developed the images of sexual passion and feminine cruelty into an emblem that combined its sexuality with a social statement, transforming the intensely private into the mode of social convention and sophisticated tolerance, with tinges of mockery. Lovelace's "Song: To Amarantha, that she would dishevel her hair" develops one of Marino's favorite themes, while the complimentary verses of "Gratiana, singing and dancing" paraphrase the sonnet of Giovanni Leone Sempronio, "La bella ballerina," and Lovelace's lyric "The Fair Beggar" employs a motif developed in the poem "Bellissima Mendica" by the Marinist Claudio Achillini.

While much of his poetry written to celebrate friends and fellow artists was mere compliment, Lovelace often struck a note of sincerity that swept aside cant and allied human dignity with the longer life of art. On occasion these poems may owe something to models drawn from Marino's *La Galeria* (1619), but mere ingenuity gives way to the demands of authentic history and personal tragedy. In this regard, his poems written to Lely deserve a place in any appraisal of his accomplishments as a poet. In "Painture" (1659) he displays a fairly comprehensive understanding of painting and its particular fate in England, where the indifference of the average Englishman to anything but family portraits had troubled painters from Holbein on. With Lely, Lovelace shares a sense of the importance of painting and seeks, by that bond, to establish an alliance against philistinism: "Now, my best Lely, let's walk hand in hand,/ And smile at this un-understanding land," where men adore merely ' their "own dull counterfeits."

Like his "Fly Caught in a Cobweb," as a poet and courtier Lovelace may seem to be a "small type of great ones, that do hum/ Within this whole world's narrow room." His vision as a minor poet, however, may display more clearly the age that produced him than do the more majestic tones of genius that rise above the humble chorus of voices from the land. In his "Advice to my best brother, Colonel Francis Lovelace," he counsels that "to rear an edifice by art so high/ That envy should not reach it," one must inevitably "build low." The lessons of humanity lie close to the surface of his poetry, more visible than the treasures of his wit. In the analysis of his poetry, that shallow part has satisfied most inquirers. Many have failed even to look that closely.

In his own day Lovelace's poetry achieved little serious recognition. A few poems were known and recognized, but he did not enjoy a reputation such as Suckling did, for example. By the eighteenth century he seems to have been almost forgotten. Had it not been for Bishop Thomas Percy, who reprinted his two most famous lyrics in his *Relics of Ancient English Poetry* (1765), he might easily have completely faded from sight. From his friend and benefactor Cotton he received a suitable estimate in an elegy written for *Lucasta: Posthume Poems*:

> In fortune humble, constant in mischance,
> Expert in both, and both served to advance
> Thy name by various trials of thy spirit
> And give the testimony of thy merit;
> Valiant to envy of the bravest men
> And learned to an undisputed pen.

Galbraith M. Crump

Other major works
PLAYS: *The Scholar(s)* 1636(?); *The Soldier,* 1640.

Bibliography
Allen, Don Cameron. "Richard Lovelace: 'The Grass-Hopper.'" In *Seventeenth-Century English Poetry: Modern Essays in Criticism,* edited by William R. Keast. New York: Oxford University Press, 1962. Examines the rich tradition embodied in the image of the grasshopper, at once the spend-

thrift, the poet-singer, and the King. Concludes that the indestructible kingdom created at the end of the poem is an inner one created by the poem.

Marcus, Leah S. *The Politics of Mirth: Jonson, Herrick, Milton, Marvell, and the Defense of Old Holiday Pastimes.* Chicago: University of Chicago Press, 1986. Marcus couples Lovelace and Marvell, contemporaries whose poetry concerned cultural survival, and finds *Lucasta* a treasury of Cavalier political beliefs that Marvell later modified in his own poetry. Marcus accords only one of Lovelace's poems, "The Grasshopper," an in-depth analysis, but that discussion is followed by a treatment of Marvell's Mower poems, which rewrite Lovelace's original poem.

Miner, Earl. *The Cavalier Mode from Jonson to Cotton.* Princeton, N.J.: Princeton University Press, 1971. Uses the emblem tradition to explicate Lovelace's "The Grasshopper," a poem that summarizes Lovelace's attitude to the "Grasshopper King." Miner's lengthy analysis also places the poem within another "mode," that of friendship, for the poem is addressed to his "Noble Friend, Mr. Charles Cotton."

Skelton, Robin. *Cavalier Poets.* London: Longmans, Green, 1960. Skelton's monograph contains a chapter on Lovelace, the model of the Renaissance man but a poet whose lack of spontaneity and tendency to moralize are shortcomings. For Skelton, Lovelace is primarily concerned with the ideal and the idyllic and is also prone to rely on the pastoral manner.

Wedgwood, C. V. *Poetry and Politics Under the Stuarts.* Cambridge, England: Cambridge University Press, 1961. Wedgwood traces the disintegration of the defeated Cavaliers through her reading of Lovelace's famous "To Althea, from Prison," a poem that prompted many imitations by other Cavalier poets.

AMY LOWELL

Born: Brookline, Massachusetts; February 9, 1874
Died: Brookline, Massachusetts; May 12, 1925

Principal poetry

A Dome of Many-Coloured Glass, 1912; *Sword Blades and Poppy Seed*, 1914; *Men, Women and Ghosts*, 1916; *Can Grande's Castle*, 1918; *Pictures of the Floating World*, 1919; *Legends*, 1921; *Fir-Flower Tablets*, 1921 (translation with Florence Ayscough); *A Critical Fable*, 1922; *What's O'Clock*, 1925; *East Wind*, 1926; *Ballads for Sale*, 1927; *Selected Poems of Amy Lowell*, 1928 (John Livingston Lowes, editor); *The Complete Poetical Works of Amy Lowell*, 1955 (Louis Untermeyer, editor); *A Shard of Silence: Selected Poems of Amy Lowell*, 1957 (G. R. Ruihley, editor).

Other literary forms

In addition to collections of poetry, Amy Lowell published translations, criticism, and a literary biography. Her output was prodigious, fourteen of her books being published within a thirteen-year span. In addition, she wrote numerous essays and reviews and kept up an active correspondence, much of it concerning literature. Lowell edited three anthologies of Imagist poetry: *Some Imagist Poets* (1915), *Some Imagist Poets*, Vol. II (1916), and *Some Imagist Poets*, Vol. III (1917). Her three critical works were *Six French Poets* (1915), essays drawn from her lectures on the postsymbolist poets; *Tendencies in Modern American Poetry* (1917), essays also drawn from lectures on contemporary poetry and six poets in particular, including two Imagists; and *Poetry and Poets* (1930), essays compiled from her lectures and published posthumously. Although she did other translations (of operettas and verse dramas), Lowell's only published translations, with the exception of those in the appendix to *Six French Poets*, were those in *Fir-Flower Tablets* (1921), a collection of ancient Chinese poetry done in collaboration with Florence Ayscough. Lowell's monumental two-volume biography, *John Keats*, appeared in 1925, shortly before her death. A sampling of Lowell's letters can be found in *Florence Ayscough and Amy Lowell: Correspondence of a Friendship* (1946).

Achievements

During her lifetime, Lowell was one of the best-known modern American poets. This reputation had as much to do with Lowell the person and literary spokesperson as with Lowell the poet, though her work was certainly esteemed. Today her place in literary history as a whole is still to be determined, but her importance in the limited field of early twentieth century American letters is undisputed.

In her day, as F. Cudworth Flint has said, both Lowell and poetry were "news." Between 1914 and 1925, she spoke out for Imagism, free verse, and the "New Poetry" more frequently, energetically, and combatively than any of its other promoters or practitioners. She took on all comers in Boston, New York, Chicago, and any other city where she was invited to speak. "Poetry Society" meetings were often the best show in town when Lowell was on the platform.

Lowell's art probably suffered as a result of her taking on the role of promoter as well as producer of the new poetry, but she unquestionably helped to open the way for younger poets among her contemporaries and for free expression and experimentation in poetic form and theme. T. S. Eliot's *The Waste Land* (1922), which Lowell did not admire, might not have had such an immediate impact on the development of modern poetry had Lowell not helped to prepare for its reception.

Critical opinion on Lowell's own poetry is divided. Her detractors argue that she lacks passion and feeling; that she is concerned only with the surfaces of things; that she is imitative, an assimilator without any original creative force. Some even say that she never really understood the new poetry she so tirelessly advocated, that she was temperamentally grounded in the conservatism and sentimentality of the nineteenth century.

Her supporters, on the other hand, cite the enormous variety of her subject matter; the breadth of forms she employed and the extent to which she developed rhythmical variation in her polyphonic prose; the freshness and vitality of many of her lyrics, particularly her poetry dealing with love; her brilliant and vivid sensory perceptions; the intelligence that complemented emotion in her poetry; and the range of emotions that her verse expressed. Contemporary feminist critics, in particular, in their revisionist readings of Lowell, have found her worthy of greater prominence than literary criticism has generally accorded her.

What most critics would probably agree on is that Lowell wrote at least a handful of excellent poems worthy of inclusion in any anthology of American poetry. There would also be general agreement that she played a paramount role in the poetic renaissance of the early twentieth century.

Biography

Amy Lowell was born in the family home (named "Sevenels" after her birth because there were then seven Lowells) in Brookline, Massachusetts, just outside Boston. Both of her parents were from distinguished and wealthy Massachusetts families. Her father, Augustus Lowell, was a member of the wealthiest branch of the Lowells, the prominent family who had come to America in 1639 and later had become a major force in the intellectual and industrial history of Massachusetts. The mill town of Lowell, Massachusetts, was named for the family. Lowell's mother, Katherine Bigelow Lawrence, was the daughter of Abbot Lawrence. The Lawrences were also an old American family, and another Massachusetts mill town was named for them.

Although the Lowells also owned a town house for the winter months, most of Lowell's childhood was spent at Sevenels, and she continued to live there, with the exception of summers in New Hampshire and abroad, until her death. After her parents' deaths, her mother's in 1895 and her father's in 1899, Lowell settled into Sevenels and made it her own, remodeling and refurnishing it extensively. The gardens there were the source of much of Lowell's imagery.

Lowell had two brothers and two sisters. Both brothers distinguished themselves, each in a different area. The elder, Percival, after ten years in the Orient and the publication of two books on the Far East, went to Flagstaff, Arizona, where he founded the Lowell Observatory and made discoveries concerning Mars. The younger brother, Abbott Lawrence, became president of Harvard University in 1909.

Lowell's formal education was limited. She was a mischievous pupil who was easily bored and a challenge to her teachers. Although she received a private school education, she did not attend college. Her own comment on her formal education was that "it really did not amount to a hill of beans." Most of her real education came from her avid reading in her father's library and in the Boston Athenaeum, a building she later wrote about and saved from razing. Her future profession was foreshadowed when she discovered Leigh Hunt's *Imagination and Fancy* and read it through and through. She was particularly taken with John Keats, about whom she later wrote a biography. Hunt's ideas about poetry were those of an earlier time, however, and were responsible, in part, for Lowell's unsuccessful first volume of rather old-fashioned poetry.

Because of a glandular condition, the five-foot-tall Lowell became obese in her adolescence and remained so, eventually weighing about 250 pounds. In spite of such corpulence, she was a successful debutante, having some sixty dinners given for her. Suitors, however, were few. Those who did appear were interested chiefly in her family connections. Lowell rejected two proposals of marriage and then accepted a third, only to be rejected later by her fiancé.

Eventually reconciled to spinsterhood, though not without much suffering, including a nervous breakdown requiring several years of convalescence, Lowell finally turned to poetry as a focus for her life. It also seemed to serve as a substitute for the orthodox Christian faith of her childhood, which she had rejected. Lowell had always been fascinated by the theater and was a creditable performer. Many thought that had she not been heavy, she would have become a professional actress. Her interest in theater, and indeed in all of the arts, continued throughout her life. Perhaps not so coincidentally, then, it was an actress, the great Eleanor Duse, who inspired Lowell to become a poet. It was 1902, the third time that she had seen Duse perform. Lowell later said that watching her "loosed a bolt in my brain and I knew where my true function lay." Having little training in poetry, Lowell began a long period of study and writing, with Hunt as her primary tutor. It was eight years before she published her first poems and ten before her first book appeared. During those years, she gradually withdrew from her many civic activities in order to concentrate on poetry. She received much support and encouragement throughout this period from Carl Engel, a young composer who also introduced her to new music.

On March 12, 1912, she met the person who was later to become her companion, critic, supporter, and confidante for life, Ada Dwyer Russell, an actress whom Lowell eventually coaxed into retirement. Many of Lowell's poems were inspired by, or written for, Mrs. Russell.

On October 12, 1912, her first collection of poems, *A Dome of Many-Coloured Glass*, was published to uniformly bad reviews, including one by Louis Untermeyer, who was later to become her friend and eventually to edit her collected poems. The year 1912 was an important one in American poetry. Harriet Monroe launched her new magazine *Poetry* in that year, a journal to which Lowell contributed both money and poems. The early issues of *Poetry* alerted Lowell to a group of poets in England who called themselves Les Imagistes and who were led by Ezra Pound and T. E. Hulme. Recognizing her own poetic tendencies in what she read, Lowell sailed for England, in the summer of 1913, to meet with Pound and the other poets and learn more about Imagism. She returned enthusiastic about what she had learned and about her own future. Within a year, Pound was in the center of a new movement, Vorticism, though he had recently edited a small anthology called *Des Imagistes*. Lowell traveled to England again in 1914, meeting, among others, D. H. Lawrence, who was to become a close friend and whose talent Lowell immediately recognized. During that summer, Lowell and Pound parted in disagreement over the editorial policy of the next edition of *Des Imagistes*, and Lowell, with many of the poets on her side, took over the editorship of the anthology. She also took over the leadership of the Imagist movement and of the battle in America for the new poetic forms. Pound later dubbed the American movement "Amygism."

Lowell had learned much in two years, and *Sword Blades and Poppy Seed* was published in 1914 to great success, although only about a fourth of the poems were actually written in free verse. Lowell herself, in a short preface to the volume, used the term "unrhymed cadence." Three of the poems were written in what she called "polyphonic prose," a technique that she explained in the preface to a later book, *Can Grande's Castle*.

In 1915, 1916, and 1917, Lowell published the three volumes called *Some Imagist Poets*, picking up where Pound's *Des Imagistes* had left off and presenting seven to ten poems by each poet. Also in 1915, she published the successful *Six French Poets*, a book that brought her numerous speaking and reading engagements. From 1915 to 1918, Lowell was indefatigable. She gave countless lectures and readings, often traveling long distances on behalf of her own verse and of the New Poetry. She also wrote essays and reviews and produced several books. Always she was a friend to good writing and good writers, crusading tirelessly for others as well as for herself.

Men, Women and Ghosts, her next collection of poems, followed her French study. Next came another critical work, *Tendencies in Modern American Poetry*, followed by another volume of verse, *Can Grande's Castle*, her virtuoso production in polyphonic prose.

In 1916, Lowell injured herself lifting a carriage out of a ditch, causing the hernia which would eventually necessitate four operations and contribute to her death.

Her next publications were *Pictures of the Floating World*, reflecting her long study of the Orient, *Legends*, and *Fir-Flower Tablets*, translations of Chinese poetry done in collaboration with Florence Ayscough. A *Critical Fable* followed, and then Lowell began work on the book that was to be the culmination of a lifetime devotion to a single poet, John Keats. *John Keats* appeared in 1925; Lowell, driving herself to accomplish the task, became physically weaker and weaker during the course of its writing.

On May 12, 1925, she saw the side of her face droop while looking in a mirror, and in that moment, according to Damon, she "recognized her death." She died less than two hours later.

On August 25, *What's O'Clock* was published, and the following spring it won the Pulitzer Prize for Poetry.

Analysis

In its entirety, Amy Lowell's work is, as Flint has observed, a history of the poetry of her time. Born in the 1870's, she died just three years after the publication of *The Waste Land*.

Although her first published work owed much, in both theme and form, to the Romantics and the Victorians, by her second book Lowell was planted more firmly in the twentieth century and, more specifically, in what has come to be known as the Poetic Renaissance. She herself used this term in her critical work, *Tendencies in Modern American Poetry*. It was a time of experimentation in all of the arts, in America as well as abroad. Lowell took control in America of the movement to revolutionize and modernize poetic forms and, by the end of her life at fifty-one, she was largely responsible for the acceptance in America of the "New Poetry." Poetry was popular in Lowell's day, and Lowell made it even more so. Though both her poetry and her ideas about it often enraged her audience, they never failed to elicit responses, and Lowell was such a dynamic saleswoman that she usually had the final word. Not a highly original thinker or writer, Lowell was able, nevertheless, to absorb the best of what was going on around her and build on it.

Lowell's work, though often faulted for being focused on externalities and devoid of emotion, is psychologically revealing, both of her own emotional states and, in some poems, of the ideas of Sigmund Freud and modern psychology. Many of her poems reveal her own experiences and emotions, and much of her imagery derives from her own life. Lowell's childhood at Sevenels, at least into adolescence, when she became very heavy, was largely a happy one, and one of her greatest joys was her father's garden, later to become hers. Her knowledge and love of flowers, gardens, and birds permeates her work. The imagery is not all joyful, however, for Lowell lived out her life at Sevenels and her life also had its great disappointments and pain. Her obesity was probably responsible for her failure to marry and have a family, and, in disillusionment, she embraced poetry, almost as a spouse. Disillusionment about her work also occurs in the poems. In all, there is a tremendous amount of psychological as well as intellectual energy in her poems, partly a result of Lowell's driving need to achieve and compensate for what she had lost or never had. There is also peace in many of the poems, inspired by the security and contentment she found during the last eleven years of her life with Mrs. Russell. Many of the poems centering on love and devotion were inspired by Mrs. Russell.

Lowell's poetic subjects were wide-ranging. She wrote narratives on subjects as disparate as the frustration of a violinist's wife and the attempted rape of the moon by a fox. She wrote lyrics on such traditional subjects as love, disillusionment, artistic inspiration, and gardens, but she also wrote poems on buildings, cities, and wars. She wrote quasiepics that encompassed different centuries and countries, and dialect tales set in rural New England.

Glenn Richard Ruihley finds these diverse subjects unified by Lowell's transcendentalism, her search for the "Numinous or Divine" residing in all people and things. It was, according to Ruihley, the possibility of transcendence that she recognized that night while watching Duse act.

Her technical virtuosity was as great as her thematic range. Her use of metaphors and symbols was extensive. According to Ruihley, the only way to understand much of Lowell's work is through a study of "her chosen symbols." Though an outspoken advocate of poetic experimentation, she wrote in traditional forms as well as in free verse and polyphonic prose, often ranging through several forms in a single poem. Her virtuosity was unquestioned, but, like most virtuosity, it was exhausting as well as dazzling. She exhausted not through sheer variety of poetic forms but through a prolixity, particularly in much of her polyphonic prose, that left the reader drugged with sheer sensation and unable to absorb more.

Though she professed to be an Imagist, at least in her early work, and was the movement's leader in America, Lowell was never contained or restrained enough in her work to be truly Imagistic in the sense that the movement is usually defined. She was too expansive. In many of her poems, however, sometimes only in individual groups of lines, she did achieve what is usually thought of as Imagistic expression.

One of the recurring themes in Lowell's poetry is her disillusionment, self-doubt, and even despair. A representative poem in this vein is "On Looking at a Copy of Alice Meynell's Poems: Given Me Years Ago by a Friend" (*Ballads for Sale*). When Lowell learned of Meynell's death in November, 1922, she turned again to the volume of Meynell's poems given to her twenty-five years earlier by Frances Dabney. In that year, 1897, Lowell had had her marriage engagement broken off by her young Bostonian suitor. Hoping to alleviate her grief, Dabney had given her the poems. In rereading the poems on Meynell's death, Lowell found little to admire, but the poems did renew her feelings of despair and bitterness.

Written in a rhyming, metered, and regular stanzaic form, the poem records Lowell's present and past reflections on Meynell's book. She evaluates it both as a gift and as a work of art. As she reads again the "whispered greeting" inscribed by Dabney, the memories surface, "dim as pictures on a winking wall," but vivid enough in the illumination of the moment to revive her emotions. Dabney's gift, intended "to ease the smart," was instead a painful "mirror," reflecting Lowell's own tragic lack of fulfillment, yet Lowell remembers how she once "loved to quote" these lines.

From her present perspective, Lowell wonders at both her own and Dabney's judgment. She distances herself from her memories as she contemplates the changes brought by time. Both Dabney and Meynell are dead, and the verses that once seemed so brilliant now seem merely "well-made." Lowell has "lived the almanac" since that time and still has "so much to do." Though Meynell's and Lowell's old griefs seem insignificant now and Lowell refuses to linger any longer with them, she is still sympathetic to the pain, a sympathy tempered, however, by her awareness of old age and death and the ultimate futility of fame and happiness. These feelings are briefly captured in the magnificent and poignant third-from-the-last stanza: "So cried her heart, a feverish thing./ But clay is still, and clay is cold,/ And I was young, and I am old,/ And in December what birds sing!" Lowell cannot allow herself to remain in this mood, and in the final two stanzas, she returns the book to its shelf where "dust" will again cover the pain. For Ruihley, "Lowell's incompleteness" and "longing for wider satisfactions" are shared in some measure by everyone, albeit for varying reasons and in varying degrees. Her poem, then, transcends her own experience in its applicability and appeal.

A second theme running throughout Lowell's work, and one that is suggested rather than directly stated, is the relationship between human beings and material forms. Lowell's pictorialism is brilliant and abundant, but rather than representing only surface effects as it was often unfairly accused of doing, it has its origin in sympathetic feeling and reveals a passionate heart. A beautiful example of this theme (and the poem which was most often requested at Lowell's frequent readings) is "Lilacs" (*What's O'Clock*). "Lilacs" expresses clearly the relationship between things or places and people, a relationship indivisible and full of emotion. The poem expansively chronicles the spatial and temporal domain of the lilac. It is a list that finally incorporates the poet herself until she and New England and history and time and the lilac are one. Throughout the poem, the lilac is an active participant in its settings, playing many roles—conversing, watching, settling, staggering, tapping, running, standing, persuading, flaunting, charging, and calling. Having originated in the East, the lilac beckons to those who sail in from China, but it has become most fully itself in the soil of New England. The flower is both in its settings and of its settings, and finally it becomes its settings as it mingles with places and lives and takes on a significance far beyond that of any of its individual manifestations:

> You are the great flood of our souls
> Bursting above the leaf-shapes of our hearts,
> You are the smell of all Summers,
> The love of wives and children,
> The recollection of the gardens of little children,
> You are State Houses and Charters. . . .

In the last stanza, Lowell identifies herself directly with the lilac as it embodies her own soil, New England ("Lilac in me because I am New England"). Her litany of reasons for such a union, underscored by repetitive structures, serves to emphasize the force and passion of her feelings.

Another example of the emotional import of material forms in Lowell's work is the popular "Meeting-House Hill." The scene portrayed is a simple one. The poet, from the eminence of "a squalid hill-top," observes a quiet scene: "the curve of a blue bay beyond a railroad track" and "a white church above thin trees in a city square." The scene itself is unremarkable except as it affects the poet, who suggests that she must be "mad, or very tired." The bay seems to sing to her and the church "amazes . . . as though it were the Parthenon." The imagination and emotion of the poet give movement to the scene until it is transformed into the final arresting image, which occupies ten of the poem's twenty-five lines. The spire of the church becomes the mast of a ship just returned from Canton. As the ship enters the bay carrying "green and blue porcelain," the poet sees a "Chinese coolie leaning over the rail/ Gazing at the white spire." It is a vivid scene and the reader moves within the imagination of the poet so that the reader too feels the emotion of the moment and sees the transformation.

The "coolie" is both of the spire (the mast of his ship) and gazing at it, both passive object of contemplation and active contemplator, so that the two worlds of reality and imagination merge fully. This is far from a mere portrayal of the surfaces of things. Objects, landscapes, flowers, and birds are emblems in Lowell's work and are always portrayed with feeling.

A third dominant theme in Lowell's poetry is that of love and devotion. It is "love in its combined physical and spiritual totality," as Jean Gould points out, that is celebrated in Lowell's work. Poems on this theme take many forms and honor many subjects, but the greatest are those inspired by Eleanor Duse and Mrs. Russell. Among those written for Russell are several of Lowell's most popular and enduring lyrics: "Madonna of the Evening Flowers," "Venus Transiens," "A Sprig of Rosemary," and "A Decade," all from *Pictures of the Floating World;* "In Excelsis" (*What's O'Clock*); and "The Taxi" (*Sword Blades and Poppy Seed*).

The scene in "Madonna of the Evening Flowers" is again simple. Lowell, tired from her day's work, calls for Russell. She is answered only by the wind and the sun shining on the remnants of her companion's recent activity—her books and her sewing implements. Though Lowell impatiently continues the search for her friend, the scene above has foreshadowed for the reader the simple domestic setting in which Russell will eventually be found. When finally spotted, Russell is "Standing under a spire of pale blue larkspur,/ With a basket of roses on [her] arm." The rest of the poem records Russell's practical responses to Lowell and Lowell's concomitant reflections. Lowell's attitude is worshipful, in contrast with the secularity of Russell's concerns, and the natural and human scene merges with the divine as Lowell hears the imagined "*Te Deums* of the Canterbury Bells."

"In Excelsis" again strikes a worshipful note and one full of rapture. In it, Lowell sees Russell as both the creator of the natural world and the embodiment of it. It is Russell whose movements control the processes of nature and Russell who is herself the "air—earth—heaven" of Lowell's universe. As in "Madonna of the Evening Flowers," the poet's impulse is to kneel before such glory, but she restrains herself from excesses: "Heaven" is not a "boon deserving thanks." She will accept the life that Russell brings to her; her poems will be her thanks, "rubies" set in "stone."

"The Taxi" has a different tone. Probably written during one of Lowell's separations from Russell, the poem speaks of the pain of separation. The images are vivid and startling, hauntingly modern in their metaphors. In the loved one's absence, the world turns hostile to the poet. The streets "wedge" Russell away from Lowell, and the city lights "prick" Lowell's eyes. The night has "sharp edges" that "wound."

Other love poems are more tranquil, projecting neither the rapturous adoration of "Madonna of the Evening Flowers" and "In Excelsis" nor the fearful tension of "The Taxi." The poet is often at peace in her love, admiring the beauty of her friend as if she were Botticelli's Venus ("Venus Transiens"), reflecting on the restfulness of her hands and voice ("A Sprig of Rosemary"), and savoring the simple nourishment of her presence ("A Decade").

Lowell's importance as a force in American literary history is undisputed. Her crusading efforts on behalf of modern poetry and poets had a formative influence on the development of American poetry in the twentieth century. The place of her own poetry is not as solidly determined. An untiring experimenter in verse forms, she was not a great poet, but she did write a few enduring poems which, it seems likely, will find a permanent place in the literary canon of her time.

Elaine Gardiner

Other major works
NONFICTION: *Six French Poets,* 1915; *Tendencies in Modern American Poetry,* 1917; *John Keats,* 1925; *Poetry and Poets,* 1930; *Florence Ayscough and Amy Lowell: Correspondence of a Friendship,* 1946.
ANTHOLOGIES: *Some Imagist Poets,* Vols. I-III, 1915-1917.

Bibliography
Benvenuto, Richard. *Amy Lowell.* Boston: Twayne, 1985. Aims to give a fair and detailed reading of Lowell's poetry in order to suggest the strengths and limitations of her art, as well as to acquaint the reader with poems that, in Benvenuto's opinion, should not be neglected any longer. Besides being an erratic and uneven writer, Lowell was, Benvenuto argues, one of the most important literary figures of her time. Includes an annotated bibliography.
Flint, F. Cudworth. *Amy Lowell.* Minneapolis: University of Minnesota Press, 1969. This forty-eight-page pamphlet devoted to Lowell's life and work contains useful information about Lowell's participation in the Imagist movement. Addresses the question of how Lowell was able to achieve what Flint calls a "para-literary" eminence so quickly. Contains a bibliography.
Gould, Jean. *Amy: The World of Amy Lowell and the Imagist Movement.* New York: Dodd, Mead, 1975. This lengthy volume views Lowell's work in its historical context. Gould asserts that Lowell was one of the outstanding influences in the literary art of her time and focuses his discussion on her role in creating the Imagist movement. In her campaign for modern freedom of expression in poetry, Gould portrays Lowell as a vociferous advocate of revolutionary rhythms and free verse. Includes a bibliography.
Gregory, Horace. *Amy Lowell: Portrait of the Poet in Her Time.* Edinburgh, N.Y.: Thomas Nelson, 1958. Purports not to be a conventional biography but a portrait of the poet. The interpretative historical essay attempts to place Lowell among other poets of her day. Gregory sees Lowell as an archetypal "romantic" and discusses her role as advancer of the New Poetry.

Hughes, Glenn. "Amy Lowell: 'The Success,'" In *Imagism and the Imagists: A Study in Modern Poetry*. Stanford, Calif.: Stanford University Press, 1931. In this dated but excellent study of Lowell's life and work, Hughes, interested in the new effects of Lowell's work, discusses the polyphonic aspects of her poetry. Examines both her contribution to American poetry and her influence on it. Passages from individual poems are analyzed.

Ruihley, Glenn R. *The Thorn of a Rose: Amy Lowell Reconsidered*. Hamden, Conn.: Archon Books, 1975. One of the most useful critical studies on Lowell, this book assesses Lowell's rightful place in American literature. In attempting to redress the balance of critical opinion in her favor, the author argues that it is necessary to understand the inner character of Lowell's life and work—for example, the philosophical framework of her poetry. Focuses on the art of Lowell's middle and late periods. Contains a bibliography.

JAMES RUSSELL LOWELL

Born: Cambridge, Massachusetts; February 22, 1819
Died: Cambridge, Massachusetts; August 12, 1891

Principal poetry

A Year's Life, 1841; *Poems,* 1844; *Poems: Second Series,* 1848; *A Fable for Critics,* 1848; *The Biglow Papers,* 1848; *The Vision of Sir Launfal,* 1848; *The Ode Recited at the Harvard Commemoration,* 1865; *The Biglow Papers: Second Series,* 1867; *Under the Willows and Other Poems,* 1869; *The Cathedral,* 1870; *Three Memorial Poems,* 1877; *Heartsease and Rue,* 1888; *Last Poems of James Russell Lowell,* 1895; *The Complete Poetical Works of James Russell Lowell,* 1896; *The Uncollected Poetry of James Russell Lowell,* 1950.

Other literary forms

Besides thirteen volumes of poetry, James Russell Lowell published during his lifetime ten collections of essays, most of which had already been printed in periodicals. The ten collections centered themselves on literary criticism, arising from his scholarly duties as Professor of Modern Languages and Literature at Harvard University (1855-1886), and political theory, arising from his contact with the Republican party and his role as American ambassador to Spain (1877-1880) and England (1880-1887). The criticism—*Conversations on Some of the Old Poets* (1845), *Among My Books* (1870), *My Study Windows* (1871), *Among My Books: Second Series* (1876), *The English Poets: Lessing, Rousseau* (1888), *Latest Literary Essays and Addresses* (1891), and *The Old English Dramatists* (1892)—shows a fluid, informal style grounded on few theoretical principles. The early works tend toward a vaguely Romantic approach, emphasizing the authors whom Lowell found inspirational. The later volumes are more conservative, based on more formal aesthetic principles. The same movement can be detected in Lowell's political theory. In *Fireside Travels* (1864) Lowell collected informal, chatty essays on Italy, Maine, and Cambridge. His *Democracy and Other Addresses* (1887) and *Political Essays* (1888) display a much more systematic approach to cultural commentary.

Since most of the thirteen volumes of poetry and ten volumes of prose were first printed in magazines and newspapers, Lowell's primary audience was found among periodical readers and editors. He helped to shape many of the major American magazines of the nineteenth century. He was a contributing editor to short-lived literary magazines such as *The Pioneer* and *The Dial*, to abolitionist magazines such as the *Pennsylvania Freeman* and the *National Anti-Slavery Standard*, and to major publications such as *The Atlantic Monthly* and the *North American Review.* Much of the work that he did for these publications was reprinted in *Early Prose Writings of James Russell Lowell* (1902) and *Anti-Slavery Papers of James Russell Lowell* (1902). Lowell saved some of his best prose for his personal friends, and the two-volume edition of his *Letters of James Russell Lowell* (1894, Charles Eliot Norton, editor) deserves to be more widely read.

Achievements

For Lowell, writing poetry was but one of several careers that he managed to sustain successfully and simultaneously. His first volume of poetry was composed during 1840 and 1841 while he was also trying to open his own law practice. His second was written while he was helping to launch a new magazine, *Pioneer: A Literary and Critical Journal*. After the magazine failed in 1843, Lowell threw himself into writing propaganda for the antislavery movement, accepting the post of editorial writer for the Philadelphia *The Freeman* and *Anti-Slavery Standard* simultaneously. From 1845 to 1848 he was also supplementing his meager income by writing literary criticism for *Graham's Magazine*. Despite the demands and prestige of the three assignments, he also found time to write three of his longest and best poems—*A Fable for Critics*, *The Biglow Papers*, and *The Vision of Sir Launfal*—all by 1848.

Lowell sustained such division of energy and interest throughout his career. In the 1850's, he mixed the publication of scholarly criticism, teaching at Harvard, and editing the newly founded *Atlantic Monthly* with his poetry. For good measure, he also started a novel. In the 1860's, he tried to edit the *North American Review*, keep his post at Harvard, issue collections of his prose works, and still write poetry. In the 1870's, he added a political career to his publishing, academic, and creative endeavors, campaigning to reform the Republican party and accepting appointments as the nation's ambassador to Spain in 1877 and to Great Britain in 1880. He broadened the base of his readership and reputation by publishing a great deal of political commentary as well. In addition to being a poet, he was, said one of his admirers, "our acknowledged, foremost man of letters." Diplomat, journalist, critic, academic, and poet, Lowell's life was divided among a variety of interests, none of which seemed capable of holding his attention for very long.

This multiplicity of interests proved to be both the greatest strength and the greatest weakness of his literary career. It injected into the corpus of his poetry a fresh stream of ideas, moving them from stilted and derivative lyrics to bitter abolitionist verse, biting satire, political commentary, cultural meditation, and warm-hearted regional description. The division of his energies, however, also robbed his poetry of the singularity of voice and consistency of tone that frequently mark poets of the first rank. Technically facile and frequently erudite, Lowell's poetry too often seemed to flow or ebb with the vagaries of his employment or the shifts in popular taste. His contemporaries thought that his poetry—which eventually filled 650 double-columned pages in the memorial edition of his work—was among the best their era had produced. He was generally acknowledged to be one of the two or three major American poets of the century. Twentieth century readers have not been so receptive, branding his ideas as commonplace, his style as derivative, and his voice as inconsistent. Lowell's poetry lacked the intensity to merit the praise it was given in the nineteenth century, but it deserves a more careful reading than it has been given by most twentieth century readers. With his range of tone, the fluidity of his cadences, the breadth of his intellect, the wit of his satire, and the accuracy of his depictions of nineteenth century American thought, Lowell's poetry remains much more than a historical curiosity.

Biography

James Russell Lowell was born into an important New England family that had been playing a prominent role in Massachusetts history ever since a wealthy merchant from Bristol, Percival Lowell, had helped to found the town of Newbury. Lowell's grandfather was a lawyer, a leading member of the Continental Congress. The poet's uncle, Francis Cabot Lowell, was one of the leading industrialists of the age, having given the family name to a factory town on the banks of the Merrimac River. His cousin was founder of Boston's Lowell Institute, and descendants of these Lowells, the poets Amy and Robert, kept the family name before readers well into the twentieth century. To be born into such a family meant that Lowell was outfitted for success from birth. His parents had him reading before he was four, translating French before he was ten, studying Latin and Greek in the small classical school run by William Wells, and gaining admission to Harvard by the time he was fifteen.

The youngest of six children, Lowell never quite outgrew the advantages his family so willingly bestowed on him. As it turned out, he lived and died in the same familial mansion, Elmwood, in which he was born. His father helped to subsidize his first three volumes of poetry. In 1854, his cousin helped to launch his academic career by paying him to deliver a series of lectures at the Lowell Institute. The lectures turned out well enough to convince a close family friend, Henry Wadsworth Longfellow, to campaign to have him appointed to a professorship at Harvard the following year. Another cousin, James Elliot Cabot, as well as Longfellow and Ralph Waldo Emerson, recommended him for the editorship of the newly established *Atlantic Monthly* in 1867. The Lowell name and fortune, together with the conservative political commentary that he wrote for the *Atlantic Monthly* and the *North American Review*, proved to be influential enough to launch him eventually on a diplomatic career. By 1877, his support of President Hayes had netted him an appointment as the American ambassador to Spain. By 1880, he had moved up to become the country's ambassador to England.

From the start, Lowell abetted these advantages with his own hard work, his serious commitment to the craft of writing, and his enviable record for accomplishing nearly everything he set out to do. The Lowell name may have opened for him many a door, but his own steady performance guaranteed that he would be offered positions of increasing importance and influence. Yet the same hard work and the responsiveness to the traditions and duties of his family kept him from finding the real James Russell Lowell. From the time when his Harvard classmates elected him to write and read their class poem during the 1839 commencement to the posthumous publication of *Last Poems of James Russell Lowell* in 1895, Lowell could be counted on to write what was expected of him rather than what he expected of himself. To gain the approval of his fellow graduates, Lowell could satirize the militancy and zeal of the abolitionist movement. To gain the approval, five years later, of his fiancée—Maria White was a protégée of Margaret Fuller and a militant abolitionist—he could turn his talents to editing the same abolitionist journals he had poked fun at in his commencement poem. When she died in 1853, Lowell lost either his interest in or sense of duty toward the abolitionist movement. Yet another family commitment, a contract to deliver thirteen lectures on the English poets for his cousin's Lowell Institute, moved him from his bent toward satire, his involvement in reform, and his formal lyric poetry to a career as a literary critic.

Lowell spent nearly fifty years as an apologist for institutional America, articulating clearly and sometimes passionately the principal social, aesthetic, and political beliefs of the educated upper class of America's Atlantic seaboard. It was a community of readers for whom his family, his friends, his training, and his temperament had made him a perfect spokesman. Beneath the public success, however, Lowell privately grew more despondent about spending his life as a publicist for the country's most influential periodicals, prestigious universities, and reputable literary circles. "I feel that my life has been mainly wasted," he complained only a few years before his death: "that I have thrown away more than most men ever had." His confession that he was "never quite pleased with what I do," that he had "spent most of my life" pursuing "the muse, without ever catching up to her," hinted at an underlying frustration. Lowell invested so much of his energy in meeting the obligations of his station that he never quite settled on who he wanted to be or what he wanted to write. Retired from his diplomatic appointments, Lowell spent the last two years of his life at Elmwood, living with his daughter and grandchildren, rearranging and rewriting his volumes for a "collected" edition of his works, and lamenting occasionally that his poetry seemed "to me, just like all the verses I read in the papers." He died at home on August 12, 1891.

Analysis

Much of James Russell Lowell's poetry does not deserve as harsh a judgment as he himself accorded it. Partially, Lowell's sense of failure came from his inability to settle on what kind of verse he was most suited to write. He could pose as a lyric poet who was facile in dressing up contemporary ideas in traditional verse forms with appropriately suitable diction in the manner of the Fireside School. He could pose as a writer of light verse who could supply the periodical audience with historical romances such as *The Vision of Sir Launfal* or warmhearted, local-color sketches of New England eccentrics. He could pose as a satiric poet who could capture the foibles of the political and academic establishments. He could pose as a philosophical poet in the manner of William Wordsworth or Samuel Taylor Coleridge. Yet none of his four most frequently employed poetic stances seemed to be the genuine voice of James Russell Lowell. His regret that he had never "really caught up" to his muse was a complaint that many of his severest critics would echo. "In Mr. Lowell's prose works," a reviewer pointed out in 1848, "we have before observed a certain disjointedness." With his new *A Fable for Critics*, the "looseness," the "rambling plot," the "want of artistic finish," the "lack of polish" characteristic of his criticism had spilled over into his approach to poetry, the critic continued. In 1952, one of Lowell's ablest biographers branded his work as lacking the kind of "coherent personality" that could make his words endure.

Unable to find a voice of his own, too distracted by the various employment opportunities that came his way to spend much time rewriting or repressing the worst of his poetry, and betrayed by his own prodigious talents, which enabled him to dash off verses quickly and fluently, Lowell had produced by the end of his life much undistinguished poetry. In each of his four characteristic modes, however, individual poems can be found that display a high degree of craftsmanship, a quick wit, a sharp eye for detail, an easy, natural cadence, and a steady and thoughtful mind.

Six of Lowell's thirteen collections of verse were anchored by traditional odes, sonnets, and lyrics dressed up in a style that one of Lowell's contemporaries praised as a "masterful" blend of all "the chords of a lyre," sounding in "loud, but harmonious concert." In *A Year's Life*, the 1844 and the 1848 editions of *Poems*, *Under the Willows and Other Poems*, *Heartsease and Rue*, and *Last Poems of James Russell Lowell*, Lowell struggled with the poetic conventions of his day. Frequently, he lost. Imitating alternately the voices of John Keats, Wordsworth, Longfellow, and Alfred, Lord Tennyson, Lowell created a series of random reflections that stitched together pat phrases, formulaic ideas, long Latinate constructions, and overly generalized descriptions. These were the least successful of his four stylistic poses. They reworked well-worn subject matter: his love for Maria White in the earlier volumes and his awe of the New England countryside in the later ones. Frequently, they were derived not from his actual life experiences but from secondary reactions to some other art form: a review of "The Mona Lisa" or "On Hearing a Sonata of Beethoven Played in the Next Room" or his sonnet sequences to Keats or Wordsworth. Many of these poems managed to sound "Poetic" without displaying much originality or passion. They could offhandedly summarize Keats's poetry as "serene and pure, like gushing joy of light." They could describe Lowell's fiancée as a "maiden whose birth could command the morning-stars their ancient music make." They could explain the duty of the poet: "his nobleness should be God like high" so that "his least deed is perfect as a star."

On occasion, however, he could infuse even these traditional forms with a freshness of diction, a naturalness of rhythm, a precision of image, and an economy of language showing that when he found the time to write, he could write very well indeed. In *Under the Willows and Other Poems* and *Heartsease and Rue*, Lowell's facility at turning a phrase could frequently redeem his conventional material by unconventional animation. His skies could be "sweet as a psalm." A scorned lover, "walking alone where we walked together," could discover "in the grey autumnal weather" that "the leaves fade, inconstant as you." His philosophy of life could be compressed into the pithy "not failure, but low aim, is the crime."

When Lowell aimed his poetry lower, however, he frequently achieved greater success. His conventional lyrics, which were aimed at a cultivated audience who demanded conventional ideas in a conventional style, frequently deadened Lowell's enthusiasms. When he wrote down to a less educated readership with the aim of persuading, delighting, or entertaining, he often gave his natural wit full rein and created a series of lighthearted poems having the suppleness, spontaneity, and mischievousness of Mark Twain's prose or Ogden Nash's verse. His first three volumes contained few of these newspaper or magazine pieces, but *Under the Willows and Other Poems* and *Heartsease and Rue* were in the main collections of periodical pieces first printed in the *Atlantic Monthly*, the *Century Illustrated Monthly Magazine*, *The Nation*, and the *New York Ledger*.

"The Unhappy Lot of Mr. Knott," which first appeared in *Graham's Magazine* in 1851, typified this happier Lowell with its sharp-edged portrait of the more shallow aspirations of New England's middle classes. His description of Knott's daughter's wedding, complete with its digressive and gratuitous advertisement, was characteristic of the stylistic pyrotechnics he sustained throughout the thousand-line cultural portrait:

> Accordingly, this artless maid
> Her father's ordinance obeyed,
> And, all in whitest crape arrayed,
> (Miss Pulsifer the dresses made
> And wishes here the fact displayed
> That she still carries on the trade,
> The third door south from Bagg's Arcade.)

His control of rhyme, rhythm, and narrative showed a technical virtuosity that he seldom duplicated in his more serious poetry. His "Fitz Adams' Story," published in the *Atlantic Monthly* in 1867, displayed several additional devices in his arsenal of skills. Primary was Lowell's command of regional dialect. Ezra Weeks, the proprietor of the country inn where Fitz Adams was staying, could summarize his approach to cooking game birds this way:

> Wal, them's real nice uns, an'll eat A 1,
> Ef I can stop their bein' overdone;
> Nothin' riles me (I pledge my fastin' word)
> Like cookin' out the natur' of a bird . . .
> Jes scare 'em with the coals,—thet's my idee.

Lowell also exhibited a keen eye for detail and an even keener mind for universalizing the details he found. Above Weeks's mantel was this portrait of his parents:

> Mister and Mistress W. in their youth,—
> New England youth, that seems a sort of pill . . .
> Bitter to swallow, and which leaves a trace
> Of Calvinistic colic on the face.

Its breezy, iambic pentameter rhythm, accented with rhyming couplets, showed a playfulness and an experimental approach to metrics that kept the poem's cadences fresh for almost all of its 632 lines. In "The Flying Dutchman" and "The Voyage to Vinland," Lowell discovered that he could make the same informal approach to purely historical subjects. In his light verse, he seemed to find the freedom to overcome the deadening conventions that marred his more serious poetry. Yet his own sense of self-worth and his traditional attitudes toward what poetry should be prevented him from writing much verse in this, his happiest of styles. He had frequently proven that he was good at the pose, but he never quite let himself believe that the pose was good enough for him.

On occasion, Lowell could turn the warmhearted humor of his lighter verses into cool, even bitter, invective. Some of his satiric poetry managed to be as biting as some of Jonathan Swift's best prose and as angry as Alexander Pope's least charitable couplets. The most famous of his satires, and the most often anthologized, was his *A Fable for Critics*, which first appeared in 1848. It was a long, loosely structured narrative that gave Lowell the opportunity to demean most of the major and many of the minor writers in America. To a gathering of the gods on Olympus is summoned a critic who "bolts every book that comes out of the press/ Without the least question of larger or less." He was asked to review the careers of his fellow writers and find among them, "a rose." After ripping apart Bronson Alcott, Orestes Brownson, Theodore Parker, William Cullen Bryant, John Greenleaf Whittier, Richard Henry Dana, Edgar Allan Poe, and James Fenimore Cooper, the critic concluded that the best American has to offer Greece was but a thistle. If Lowell's critical summaries of rival authors tended toward brutality, he managed to leaven the tone of the whole by using the same playfulness he would later use in "Fitz Adams' Story." He filled *A Fable for Critics* with puns, condemning, for example, prophets who "got their name of augurs, because they were bores." He tightroped his way around the downright silly with an array of surprising rhymes. In one breathless sequence, he strung twelve feminine rhymes together: rely on, scion, ply on, try on, eye one, zion, buy one, fie on, lion, spy on, wry on, and die on.

What *A Fable for Critics* did for American letters, the two series of *The Biglow Papers* did for American politics. Prompted by Lowell's conservative reaction against the imperialism of the Mexican-American War, the first series of satires appeared in 1848 along with *A Fable for Critics*. The papers consisted of a series of letters, essays, poems, and commentaries supposedly written by a variety of New England eccentrics. They indicted recruiters (with "twenty rooster tails stuck onto their hats and eenamost enuf brass a bobbin' up and down"), soldiering ("Ninepence a day for killin' folks comes kind o' low for murder"), American conformity ("for one might imagine America to have been colonized by a tribe of those nondescript African animals the Aye-Ayes, so difficult a word is 'No' to us all"), jingoistic politicians in general, General Winfield Scott and Senator John Calhoun in particular, and hawkish newspaper editors ("the name 'editor' is [derived] not so much from *edo*, to publish, as from *edo*, to eat. . . . They blow up the flames of political discord to boil their own pots"). Lowell's satires could be telling displays of a lifetime accumulation of stored anger: at writers who did not take themselves as seriously as he did, at politicians more swayed by popularity than by principle, at the general thickheadedness of the American public, and especially, perhaps, at his own failures to confront these concerns in his own serious writing.

On the few occasions when Lowell allowed himself to tackle serious thought with what he took to be serious verse, he produced a group of uneven reflections, sometimes brilliant, sometimes banal. In *Under the Willows and Other Poems*, *The Cathedral*, "The Ode for the 100th Anniversary of the Fight at Concord Bridge," "The Ode for the Fourth of July, 1876," "Agassiz," and *The Ode Recited at the Harvard Commemoration*, Lowell tried to compress a lifetime of thought. Together, these poems show his growing conservatism, a rigidity of mind and form that bears little resemblance to the inventiveness of his lighter verse. In *Under the Willows and Other Poems*, he moodily reflects on the glories of nature without garnering much glory for his subject or for his treatment of it. Its nearly four hundred lines do little more than recommend being gentle on and with New England's best June days. In *The Cathedral*, probably his best philosophical poem, he centers on a visit to Chartres and explores with precision, depth, and compassion some of the material only briefly touched on in "Under the Willows." Man's relationship with nature, so fuzzily treated in the early poem, is amplified in *The Cathedral* as a mixture of the objective and the subjective. Whether inspecting willows on a hot

June day or building a monument, "graceful, grotesque, with ever new surprise," man seeks always, Lowell claims, some sort of synthesis between his interior consciousness and his exterior environment. For him, the cathedral becomes "Imagination's very self in stone." Like many a nineteenth century author, Lowell's visit occasioned a regret-filled commentary on the lack of the spiritual and the mystical in contemporary life. Whether in communing with nature or constructing edifices to religious aspirations, "this is no age to get Cathedrals built." Instead, modern man seems more likely to demean the efforts of the past, asking questions such as: "Did Faith build this wonder? Or did Fear, that makes a fetish and misnames it God?" In blotting "out life with questions marks," in unduly relying on "secular conclusions," in its own hyperconsciousness of "earth's comedy," modern civilization has failed to realize, he claims, that "each age must worship its own thought of God." His own age has been unable to find a satisfactory image of this transcendental impulse and thus remains a world of "incompleteness" where "sorrow" is "swift, consolation a laggard." The sense of faith and purposefulness, displayed so extravagantly at Chartres, suggests answers of a sort desperately needed by modern man. Lowell tries to end the rumination optimistically: "Faith and wonder and the primal earth," he asserts, "are born into the world with every child." As much as Emerson or Walt Whitman, Lowell believed that the godly was still available to contemporary man; he was simply less sure than his forebears how it should be attained.

Lowell vaguely recognized that his culture seemed to lack the sense of idealism that had driven previous civilizations. His was an era content with pat answers from the past and blind optimism regarding the future. This awareness filled his satiric poetry with hard-edged bitterness, but in his philosophical poetry Lowell never quite found the right voice to articulate his concerns, nor the courage to betray the commitments of his public voice.

Philip Woodard

Other major works

NONFICTION: *Conversations on Some of the Old Poets*, 1845; *Fireside Travels*, 1864; *Among My Books*, 1870; *My Study Windows*, 1871; *Among My Books: Second Series*, 1876; *Democracy and Other Addresses*, 1887; *Political Essays*, 1888; *The English Poets: Lessing, Rousseau*, 1888; *Latest Literary Essays and Addresses*, 1891; *The Old English Dramatists*, 1892; *Letters of James Russell Lowell*, 1894 (Charles Eliot Norton, editor); *Early Prose Writings of James Russell Lowell*, 1902; *The Anti-Slavery Papers of James Russell Lowell*, 1902.

MISCELLANEOUS: *The Complete Writings of James Russell Lowell*, 1904 (16 volumes).

Bibliography

Beatty, Richmond Croom. *James Russell Lowell.* Knoxville: University of Tennessee Press, 1942. Reprint. Hamden, Conn.: Archon Books, 1969. Beatty's study is based on a thorough examination of Lowell's manuscripts and heavily criticizes the poet's political judgments at times. Includes bibliographical references.

Duberman, Martin B. *James Russell Lowell.* Boston: Houghton Mifflin, 1966. This well-researched biography is based mainly on manuscript materials and refers to the poetry and criticism of Lowell throughout. It provides a historian's evaluation of Lowell's political writings and activities. Supplemented by thorough notes, bibliographies, and an index.

Hudson, William Henry. *Lowell and his Poetry.* 1914. Reprint. New York: AMS Press, 1972. This volume of the Poetry and Life series is a reprint of a 1914 edition originally published in London. Hudson focuses on the poetry, not the life. In the course of his discussion, he quotes the full text of nine poems, which are listed in the beginning of the book. This brief study includes "The Changeling," "The First Snowfall," "After the Burial," and *The Ode Recited at the Harvard Commemoration.*

McGlinchee, Claire. *James Russell Lowell.* Twayne's United States Authors series 120. New York: Twayne, 1967. The first chapter looks at Lowell in the context of nineteenth century American literature, and the second and third chapters offer a chronological account of Lowell's life through 1860. The following six chapters are devoted to his early poems, his criticism, details on his careers as professor, diplomat, and editor, his political verse (*The Biglow Papers*), and his later poetry (*The Cathedral* and the odes). Contains notes, an annotated bibliography, and an index.

Wagenknecht, Edward. *James Russell Lowell: Portrait of a Many-Sided Man.* New York: Oxford University Press, 1971. This book supplements Martin B. Duberman's more definitive biography by providing a less formal character portrait. Wagenknecht's facts are, however, authentic. (Duberman checked his manuscript.) Discussions of the poetic influences on Lowell and his approach to poetry make up two chapters, "Storing the Well" and "The Creative Life." Complemented by notes, a selective bibliography, and an index.

ROBERT LOWELL

Born: Boston, Massachusetts; March 1, 1917
Died: New York, New York; September 12, 1977

Principal poetry

Land of Unlikeness, 1944; *Lord Weary's Castle,* 1946; *Poems 1938-1949,* 1950; *The Mills of the Kavanaughs,* 1951; *Life Studies,* 1959; *Imitations,* 1961; *For the Union Dead,* 1964; *Near the Ocean,* 1967; *Notebook 1967-68,* 1969; *Notebook,* 1970; *The Dolphin,* 1973; *History,* 1973; *For Lizzie and Harriet,* 1973; *Selected Poems,* 1976, 1977; *Day by Day,* 1977.

Other literary forms

Besides his free translations or rewritings of poems by writers from Homer to Boris Pasternak that constitute *Imitations* and the similar translations of Roman poems in *Near the Ocean,* Robert Lowell translated Jean Baptiste Racine's *Phaedra* (published in 1961, premiered at Wesleyan University in 1965) and *The Oresteia of Aeschylus,* which was published posthumously in 1979. *The Old Glory,* a trilogy of plays (*Endecott and the Red Cross, My Kinsman, Major Molineux,* and *Benito Cereno*) based on stories by Nathaniel Hawthorne and Herman Melville, was originally published in 1965; the latter two plays were premiered at the American Place Theater in 1964, winning for Lowell an Obie Award. A revised edition, with an expanded version of *Endecott and the Red Cross,* was issued in 1968, and *Endecott and the Red Cross* had its first performance at the American Place Theater in the same year. *Prometheus Bound,* Lowell's only other dramatic work, was presented at Yale in 1967 and published in 1969. Lowell also published a number of reviews and appreciations of writers; his *Collected Prose* was published in 1987.

Achievements

Lowell's poetry gives uniquely full expression to the painful experience of living in modern America; he speaks personally of his own experience as son, husband, lover, father, and mentally troubled individual human being, and publicly of American policy and society as a morally and spiritually troubled inheritor of Western cultural and Christian spiritual values. All the diverse kinds of poetry that Lowell wrote over a career in which he repeatedly transformed his art—religious, confessional, public—share a high degree of formal interest, whether written in traditional metrical forms or in free verse. Indeed, it was Lowell's ceaseless formal invention that enabled him to articulate, in so many different voices, the experience of modernity.

Biography

Robert Traill Spence Lowell, Jr., the only child of Commander Robert

Traill Spence Lowell, a naval officer, and Charlotte Winslow Lowell, was joined by birth to a number of figures variously prominent in the early history of Massachusetts Bay and in the cultural life of Boston. On his mother's side he was descended from Edward Winslow, who came to America on the Mayflower in 1620. His Lowell ancestors included a Harvard president, A. Lawrence Lowell, and the astronomer, Percival Lowell, as well as the poets James Russell Lowell and Amy Lowell. His ancestors' prominent roles in the early history of Massachusetts and its culture made him feel implicated in the shames of that history—such as the massacre of the native Indians—and the failings of the Puritan culture that became the ground out of which a money-centered American industrial society grew. His sense of his family's direct involvement in the shaping of American history and culture was conducive to the conflation of the personal and the public that is one of the distinguishing features of his poetry.

The poet had a childhood of outward gentility and inner turmoil. He had his schooling at Brimmer School in Boston and St. Mark's Boarding School in Southborough, Massachusetts. His parents had limited means relative to their inherited social position, and his ineffectual father and domineering mother filled the home with their contention. Richard Eberhart, then at the beginning of his poetic career, was one of Lowell's English teachers at St. Mark's, and at Eberhart's encouragement he began to write poetry, some of which was published in the school magazine. In 1935 Lowell entered Harvard, intent on preparing himself for a career as a poet. He was disheartened by the approach to poetry of his Harvard professors, however, and frustrated in his search for a mentor. He was at a nadir of confidence, thrashing about for direction and desperate for encouragement, when an invitation to visit Ford Madox Ford, whom he had met at a cocktail party at the Tennessee home of Allen Tate, brought him to Tate's poetry and to Tate himself, who was to be a formative influence. Lowell was then torn between traditional metrical forms and free verse, and Tate brought him down, for the time being, on the side of the former. What Tate advocated was not bland mechanics but rather an intense struggle to apprehend and concentrate experience within the confines of form, depersonalizing and universalizing experience and revitalizing traditional forms.

His intimacy with Tate led to Lowell's immersion in the world and values of the traditionalist Southern agrarian poets who constituted the Fugitive group. After spending the summer of 1937 at the Tates' home, Lowell transferred from Harvard to Kenyon College to study with John Crowe Ransom, who had just been hired at Kenyon, which he would turn into a center of the New Criticism. At Kenyon, Lowell met Randall Jarrell, with whom he began a personal and literary friendship that ended only with Jarrell's suicide in 1965. While apprenticing himself as a poet, Lowell studied Classics, graduating *summa cum laude* in 1940.

Also in that year, he married the young Catholic novelist Jean Stafford and converted to Roman Catholicism. He did a year's graduate work in English at Louisiana State University, studying under Cleanth Brooks and Robert Penn Warren, and then worked as an editorial assistant at Sheed and Ward, a Catholic publishing house in New York City. Then he and his wife spent a year with the Tates, a year in which Lowell and Allen Tate both did a great deal of writing under each other's inspiration. For Lowell, the year's output became the poems of his first book, *Land of Unlikeness* (1944), about half of which were subsequently revised and included in *Lord Weary's Castle* (1946), the book that launched his poetic career, winning him the Pulitzer Prize. Also during this period Lowell, having earlier tried to enlist, refused to serve in the army in protest against Allied bombing of civilian populations and served time in prison for this failure to comply with the Selective Service Act. In 1948, Lowell's marraige to Jean Stafford ended in divorce, and the following year he married the essayist and fiction-writer Elizabeth Hardwick.

The late 1940's saw the reemergence of Lowell's respect for William Carlos Williams' free verse. Lowell admired the unpoetical language of Williams' "American idiom," and developed a close friendship with the older poet, who succeeded Tate as his mentor. The impact of Williams' work and ideas is reflected in the free verse form of the poems in the last of the four sections of *Life Studies* (1959). From 1950 to 1953, Lowell and his wife were in Europe. Returning to the United States in 1953, he taught at the University of Iowa, where one of his students was W. D. Snodgrass; the younger poet, along with the older Williams, helped Lowell to develop the "confessional" mode pioneered in *Life Studies* and in Snodgrass' *Heart's Needle* (1959). Lowell's mother died in February, 1954, in Italy; "Sailing Home from Rapallo" (*Life Studies*) tells of his trip bringing her coffin, on which "Lowell" had been misspelled "LOVELL," back for her burial in the Winslow-Stark graveyard in Dunbarton, New Hampshire. From 1954 to the end of the decade, Lowell and his wife lived on Marlborough Street in Back Bay, Boston, while he taught at Boston University. His students included Sylvia Plath and Anne Sexton. His daughter Harriet was born in 1957. In 1959, *Life Studies* won Lowell the National Book Award for poetry, while Snodgrass' *Heart's Needle* took the Pulitzer Prize.

In 1960, Lowell moved with his wife and daughter to New York City. *Life Studies* was followed in 1961 by a volume of *Imitations*, translations of European poets intended to represent what the poets might have written had they been alive in contemporary America, and arranged not chronologically but in an expressive sequence of Lowell's own. From 1963 to 1977 he taught at Harvard. During the 1960's Lowell became active in the movement against American involvement in Vietnam. In June, 1965, in an open letter to President Lyndon Johnson, published in *The New York Times*, he refused an invitation to participate in the White House Festival of the Arts in protest against American foreign policy. He participated in the Pentagon March protesting American bombing and troop activities in Vietnam in October, 1967, and was active in Eugene McCarthy's campaign for the Democratic nomination for the Presidency in 1967-1968, becoming a warm personal friend of McCarthy. His political experiences are recorded in *Notebook 1967-68* and the subsequent revisions of that book.

At the beginning of the 1970's, Lowell moved to England. He was a Visiting Fellow at All Soul's College, Oxford, in 1970, and taught at Essex University from 1970 to 1972. His book *The Dolphin* records the breakdown of his marriage of more than twenty years to Elizabeth Hardwick and his developing relationship with the English novelist Caroline Blackwood. While the emotional realities—entangled passion, fear, and joy in the relationship with Caroline, a period of mental breakdown, the pull of his old life and wife and their daughter Harriet—are vividly represented in the poetry, the events, except for the birth of Lowell's son to Caroline, are not always clear. In 1972 he was divorced from Elizabeth Hardwick and married to Caroline Blackwood.

By the late 1970's, Lowell was commuting back and forth between Ireland, where he and Caroline had a house, and America, where he was teaching a term each year at Harvard. His experience at that time, including the trouble into which his third marriage was falling and the experience of having a son late in life, is rendered in the poems of *Day by Day*, the title of which reflects its closeness to the recordings and reflections of journal-writing. In the spring of the last year of his life, he took a trip to Russia. In September, he died of a heart attack in a taxicab in New York City, shortly after he had returned from Ireland.

Analysis

American and European history and historical figures—military, political, and religious—and other writers and their works were very much present in Robert Lowell's consciousness. This influence is reflected in all of his poetry, although the learning is worn more lightly after *The Mills of the Kavanaughs.* As evident in his poetry as his historical sense and awareness of literary tradition is the intensity of his mental and emotional life, expressed indirectly through the vehicles of historical and fictional personae in his early poetry, and in undisguised, if more or less fictionalized, autobiography, beginning with *Life Studies.* Lowell's is a poetry in the symbolist tradition; its symbols, whether used to convey religious significance (as in his first two books) or to express psychological realities (as in his subsequent works) are remarkable for their irreducible ambiguity. Ambiguity is indeed an essential feature of Lowell's mature vision. Symbolic resonance is accompanied in his work by a wealth of named particulars of the represented world; Norman Mailer has aptly described Lowell's language as "particular, with a wicked sense of names, details, places." His craftsmanship in prosody is remarkable in his early metrical verse, with its complex stanzaic forms and tension between the syntactical and the metrical structures. It is equally remarkable, albeit less flamboyant, in his later poetry, whether metrical or free verse. A gristly texture, partly the product of heavy alliteration, is characteristic of the sound of Lowell's verse. Also contributing to this characteristic choppiness is a syntax in which the subject-verb-adjunct sequence is frequently deferred or interrupted, especially by strings of adjectives, or broken off, leaving fragments interspersing the sentences.

Lowell's poetic career is remarkable for the number of times and the extent to which he transformed his art and for the frequency with which he revised his poems in public, publishing successive versions of a poem or different treatments of a single subject in successive volumes or incorporating passages from earlier pieces in new ones.

Lowell's voice in *Lord Weary's Castle* is that of a Catholic convert raging against the spiritual depravity of the Protestant and secular culture of New England, of which his own family was so much a part, and that of a conscientious objector decrying the waging of war. A note reveals that the book's title comes from an old ballad that tells of "Lambkin," a good mason who "built Lord Weary's castle" but was never paid for his work; in Lowell's poems, the mason Lambkin becomes a figure for Christ and Lord Weary for the people who wrong God in their lives. The verse of this early collection is in strict metrical forms, which are strained by features in tension with the metrical pattern, such as terminal caesura followed by violent enjambment. Prominently heavy alliteration also helps to weave its characteristically rough texture.

Of the poems in this book, "The Quaker Graveyard in Nantucket," an elegy for Lowell's cousin Warren Winslow, whose ship had disappeared at sea in the war, has been the most frequently anthologized and extensively discussed. The poem is in seven parts, all in rhymed iambic pentameter verse, varied, except in parts II and V, by occasional trimeter lines. Part I is a dramatic account, with much vivid and grotesque physical detail, of the recovery and sea burial of the drowned sailor's body, derived not from actual experience (Lowell's cousin's body was apparently never found), but, as Hugh Staples has shown, from Henry David Thoreau's *Cape Cod* (1865). It presents the sea as implacable in its power and the loss of life as irrevocable. Parts II to IV elaborate on the power of the sea and view the newly dead sailor as joining dead generations of Quaker whalers who foolishly dared the sea's and the whale's might; Lowell takes his imagery from Herman Melville's *Moby Dick* (1851) and associates the fatal presumption of the Quaker sailors with Ahab's obsessive and fatal quest of the white whale. The whale in whose pursuit the earlier generations of sailors lost their lives is multivalent in its symbolic associations—at once the wrathful, inscrutable Jehovah of the Old

Testament and the merciful Christ of the New. In Part III, "only bones abide/ There . . . where their boats were tossed/ Sky-high, where mariners had fabled news/ of IS, the whited monster" alludes, Staples suggests, both to such a biblical passage as Exodus 3:14—("And God said unto Moses, I AM THAT I AM: and he said, Thus shalt thou say unto the children of Israel, I AM hath sent me to you"—and to Christ under the epithet "*Iesus Salvator*." Lowell's dead cousin, who joins the whalers in their "graveyard," is implicated in their guilt, together with the war-waging society of which he was a member. Part IV closes with the question, "Who will dance/ The mast-lashed master of Leviathans/ Up from this field of Quakers in their unstoned graves?"— ambiguously alluding at once to Ahab and to the Christ whom the whalers are seen as having crucified again in their slaughter of the whale, as the contemporary soldier/sailors do in their killing in war. Part V presents a horrific scene of whale-butchering as a sort of vision of apocalypse; drawing on the exegetical tradition that sees Jonah as a prefiguration of Christ, Lowell concludes this section with a prayer to the hacked, ripped whale, in the richness of its symbolic associations, "Hide,/ Our steel, Jonas Messias, in Thy side." The scene then switches abruptly from the violence of the sea to the pastoral serenity of the Catholic shrine of Our Lady of Walsingham in England, destroyed in the Reformation but recently restored. Yet, while the first of Part VI's two stanzas presents an attractive landscape, the Virgin Mother in the second stanza offers no accessible comfort: "There's no come-liness/ At all or charm in that expressionless/ Face . . ./ This face, . . ./ Expressionless, expresses God." The final part returns the reader to the death-dealing sea, closing with a vision of Creation in which, even as "the Lord God formed man from the sea's slime," "blue-lung'd combers lumbered to the kill." After this formulation of the implacability and inscrutability of God's will, the poem closes with the line, "The Lord survives the rainbow of His will," offering, despite its recollection of the covenant at the end of the flood, no reassurance to the individual human creature who sins and dies, but only an assertion of an ultimate abiding that may or may not prove gracious to him.

The inscrutability and violence of God's ways in "The Quaker Graveyard in Nantucket" as well as the crassness and violence of the ways of men are typical of *Lord Weary's Castle*. This poem is also representative as a family elegy, a subgenre that was to become one of Lowell's most characteristic and successful. "At the Indian Killer's Grave" is another poem in which the poet confronts his dead ancestors, again censoriously. The cenotaph of his ancestors John and Mary Winslow is mentioned as one of the monuments in the grave-yard behind King's Chapel, where the poet's persona meditates amid "baroque/ And prodigal embellishments," that are in vain against the grime and noise of the impinging city (a subway "Blacker than these black stones" lies beneath the graveyard, and its train "grinds . . ./ And screeches").

Unmentioned by name, but part of the public history to which the poem makes reference, is another ancestor, Josiah Winslow, who was noted as an Indian fighter and served as Governor of Plymouth during the war against the Indian leader King Philip. The conquered Indian was beheaded and his head set on a pole in Plymouth. In Lowell's poem, King Philip's head "Grins on a platter" and delivers a jeremiad to his and his people's buried killers, the poet's ancestors, evoking "nature and the land/ That fed the hunter's gashed and green perfection" in implicit contrast to the urban scene that has been sketched earlier in the poem, mocking the Puritans' notions of election as of no avail to save them. In the last of the poem's five rather long verse-paragraphs, the persona of the poet "ponder[s] on the railing" of the grave-yard, wondering who the remote ancestor was "Who sowed so ill for his descent." The poem closes with paradise-garden imagery to answer the image at the beginning of the poem of the cemetery as fallen garden, and, in accord with Lowell's Catholic belief of the time, with an image of Mary conceiving Christ by the divine "Bridegroom," presumably suggesting divine mercy for both victims and victors.

Lowell's next significant collection, *The Mills of the Kavanaughs*, marks a sharp departure from the style and the outlook of *Lord Weary's Castle*. The long title poem and the other six poems of this volume are all at least partially dramatic monologue, and they deal mostly with situations of extremity—incest, madness, death—in the personal lives of their characters. They seem to follow from "Between the Porch and the Altar," a multipart poem of adulterous love in *Lord Weary's Castle*, with a third-person narrative section and a section of dramatic monologue by a woman, "Katherine's Dream." The Catholicism of the earlier book is gone, however; neither Christ nor Mary comes to offer the people of these poems a way to transcend the ills of their worlds. While *Lord Weary's Castle* is densely interlarded with biblical allusions, *The Mills of the Kavanaughs* draws heavily on classical literature. The allusions here are significantly different in their operation from those in the earlier book: while the apparatus of Catholic symbols was imposed on events by the poet in his interpretation of them, the myth of Persephone is very much a part of Anne Kavanaugh's consciousness and, as Richard Fein has pointed out, enters into her own efforts to interpret her situation, and the *Aeneid* (c. 29-19 B.C.) is similarly familiar to the old man in "Falling Asleep over the Aeneid," who assimilates his personal life to his literary experience. Randall Jarrell has remarked that the title poem is an unremitting succession of nightmares and nightmarish visions all at the same high level of intensity, and several reviewers of the book objected to its monotonous violence. With hindsight, subsequent critics have seen the characters of the poems here as vehicles for Lowell to convey experiences of his own, including that of madness, that he would speak of straightforwardly in the first person in *Life Studies*. Certainly one acquainted with the poet's life will recognize autobiographical elements in "The Mills of the Kavanaughs"—the morally problematic heritage and the declining vitality and fortunes of an eminent family (the Kavanaugh family emblem, "Cut down we flourish," is that of the Winslows), Lowell's father's failed military career, and his own mental illness. Anne Kavanaugh seems to combine elements of Lowell's mother and of his wives. One of the remarkable features of the poem, indeed, is the extent to which it sympathetically conveys a woman's experience of a man who fails her; in this it is heralded by "Katherine's Dream" and anticipates " 'To Speak of Woe That Is in Marriage' " in *Life Studies*, the poems given to painfully moving quotations of Elizabeth Hardwick's letters in *The Dolphin*, and many other later poems.

After an eight-year silence, Lowell published *Life Studies*. The book is in four parts: the first consists of four poems close in form and mode (two are dramatic monologues) to Lowell's previous work, although the poem that opens the book, "Beyond the Alps," definitely announces a change of stance from the Catholicism of *Lord Weary's Castle*; the second is an autobiographical prose piece on the poet's childhood; the third consists of four poems on writers who influenced Lowell (Ford Madox Ford, George Santayana, Delmore Schwartz, and Hart Crane); and the fourth, which gives the book its title, "Life Studies," contains the poems that drew the epithet "confessional."

"Beyond the Alps" is actually a sequence of three sonnets, each with a different complex rhyme scheme. The speaker is on the train going from Rome to Paris in 1950, the year the Pope proclaimed the dogma of Mary's bodily assumption. At the end of the octet of the first sonnet, the speaker says, "Much against my will/ I left the City of God where it belongs"; in the sestet he characterizes the figure who has ruled there in his time, Benito Mussolini, as "one of us/ only, pure prose." The central sonnet treats the proclamation of Mary's Assumption as dogma, undercutting it by a description of the Pope listening to the crowds in St. Peter's Square that implies he too is "pure prose": "His electric razor purred,/ his pet canary chirped on his left hand." In the final sonnet, the "mountain-climbing train had come to earth," and the speaker somewhat ruefully owns that "There were no tickets for that altitude/ once held by Hellas."

In the third and fourth parts of this volume Lowell turns from the accentual-syllabic metrics of his previous poetry to free verse rhythms much closer to those of conversation and, especially after the first part, from the relative impersonality and obliqueness of the earlier poetry to the confessional mode that *Life Studies* helped to pioneer. If the artifice is no longer obtrusive and the verse relatively transparent in Part IV, however, the poetry is no less artful in its construction: rhyme and half-rhyme, used occasionally rather than systematically, help to make the lines perceptible as units and to bind together stanzas; and alliteration continues to give the language a gristly texture. In imagery as well as in sound, these poems—sequences as well as individual poems—are unified.

The poems in the first section of Part IV, arranged in order of the chronology of their events in the poet's life, focus successively on Lowell's grandfather (the first three), his father (the next three), his mother (a further three), and an adult mental breakdown of his own (the final two). The last two in the first section take place in the world of Lowell's adult married life, and there is a continuity between their imagery of place and that of the poems in the second section, which focus on the writer's present, even if that present is preoccupied with memories (in "Memories of West Street and Lepke"). In "Man and Wife" and "To Speak of Woe That Is in Marriage" in the second section, Lowell's marriage, in the background in "Waking in the Blue" and "Home After Three Months Away" at the end of the first section, comes into the foreground. The particulars of decor, attire, and gesture with which these poems are richly furnished serve not to invoke an anagogic level of meaning, but at once to create a sense of actual experience in all its centrifugal detail and to convey character and psychological fate.

"Skunk Hour," the poem that closes the book, while highly particular in its dramatized situation, nevertheless has, more than any of the rest of these confessional pieces, a degree of independence from temporal succession, which, besides its power, has probably been a factor in the frequency with which it has been chosen to represent Lowell in anthologies. The eight six-line stanzas of "Skunk Hour" carry the speaker from detached, amusingly sharp observations of the foibles and failings of fellow residents of his New England summer resort town and the "illness" of its season to direct, mordantly sharp confession of his own neurotic behavior and his mind's and spirit's illness, and finally to the richly ambiguous image of vitality and survival in the face of the town's enervation, the season's fading, and the speaker's despair that concludes *Life Studies*. The first four stanzas are devoted to social observation—of "Nautilus Island's hermit/ heiress" who is "in her dotage" and "buys up all/ the eyesores facing her shore,/ and lets them fall"; of the disappearance of the "summer millionaire,/ who seemed to leap from an L. L. Bean/ catalogue," and the sale of his yacht; of the "fairy/ decorator [who] brightens his shop for fall," but finds "no money in his work" and would "rather marry." Significantly, where the first person pronoun appears, it is in the plural ("our summer millionaire," "our fairy decorator"); the poet speaks as a townsman, one of a community (albeit a derelict one). By the fifth stanza, however, he has ceased to be one of the people; now, apart from them, he tells the reader that he "climbed the hill's skull," where "I watched for love-cars." In a scene of anguished isolation suggestive of St. John of the Cross's "dark night of the soul," he declares, "My mind's not right." By the end of the sixth stanza, his voice has come to echo that of Milton's Satan: "I myself am hell;/ nobody's here." From this nadir, his attention swings to be arrested, in the final two stanzas, by "a mother skunk with her column of kittens" that "march[es] . . . up Main Street," "swills the garbage pail . . . / and will not scare." If her crassness is appalling, her vitality is indeed a "rich air" against the town's stale atmosphere and the speaker's self-constructed cell. The significance of the image is as intractable in its ambiguity as its subject is stubborn in her determination to feed on the sour cream in the garbage.

In *For the Union Dead*, Lowell's poetry continues to speak in the personal voice that emerged in *Life Studies*. Poems such as "Eye and Tooth" and "Myopia: A Night" are of the eye turned inward, focused on the "I," its tormenting memories and self-hatred. Others, notably "The Old Flame," "The Scream," "The Public Garden," and "Returning," revisit scenes of the poet's past as child or lover; interestingly, both "The Old Flame" and "The Public Garden" incorporate passages from poems in *The Mills of the Kavanaughs*, where the experiences in question were ascribed to dramatic characters rather than to the poet's self. A difference from the *Life Studies* poems is that these are separate lyrics and do not fit together into sequences. The theme of the cultural heritage of New England, treated in *Lord Weary's Castle*, is again treated here in a poem that speaks of Nathaniel Hawthorne and one that addresses Jonathan Edwards in intimate tones and with great sympathy. (A similar intimacy and sympathy inform the poem addressed to Caligula, by whose name Lowell had been called by his classmates at St. Mark's.) There is, besides, a new element in this book: the poet deals with contemporary society and politics, not, as he had in *Lord Weary's Castle*, in Christian terms, as features of a world for which apocalypse was imminent, but with the same keen, painful observation and moral concern he had, since *Life Studies*, been bringing to bear on his personal life; he deals with them, indeed, as part and parcel of his personal experience.

The title poem, "For the Union Dead," revisits the old Boston Aquarium that the poet had gone to as a child, even as "The Public Garden" revisits that old "stamping ground" of Lowell and his wife. The difference is that while in the latter "[t]he city and its cruising cars surround" a private failure to "catch fire," in "For the Union Dead" the Aquarium is presented not as part of a personal landscape only, but, closed, its fish replaced by "giant finned cars," as emblematic of the course of Boston's, New England's, and America's culture. The other complex emblem in the poem is the monument to Colonel Shaw, friend and in-law to the poet's Lowell ancestors, who led the first regiment of free blacks in an attack on a fort defending Charleston harbor, in which he and about half of his black soldiers were killed. The poem is in a sense another of Lowell's family elegies, but it opens beyond family history to national history. As the Aquarium's fish have been replaced by finned cars, the monument to the Civil War hero is now "propped by a plank splint" as support against the "earthquake" produced by excavation for a parking garage, and it has come to "stick like a fishbone/ in the city's throat."

In a city of giant cars and parking garages, the martyred leader, "lean/ as a compass-needle," who "seems to wince at pleasure," is "out of bounds"; such firm sense of direction and such ascetism are no longer virtues the populace is comfortable contemplating or moved to emulate.

The poem is not, however, a sentimental one of pure nostalgia for an earlier period of the society's life or of the poet's, for the heroism of war before the World Wars or for the lost Aquarium and the child's pleasure in it. The fish that lived in the Aquarium tanks are described as "cowed, compliant," and the child's eagerness was "to burst the bubbles/ drifting from their noses." Colonel Shaw is said to have enjoyed "man's lovely,/ peculiar power to choose life and die"—hardly an unequivocal good, albeit preferable to the power to choose "a Mosler Safe, the 'Rock of Ages'/ that survived the blast" at Hiroshima to safeguard one's material wealth. Nor is the contemporary landscape presented as wholly desert; the steamshovels that excavate for the parking garages are "yellow dinosaur steamshovels . . . grunting/ as they cropped up tons of mush and grass," creatures not without appeal. Indeed, the attractiveness of martyrdom, as Lowell presents it, may not be that far removed from the appeal of fish behind glass or steamshovels behind barbed wire: "I often sigh still," says the poem's speaker, "for the dark downward and vegetating kingdom/ of the fish and reptile." There is, finally, an irreducible ambiguity in the poem's treatment of past and present, Aquarium and garage, Union soldier and contemporary Bostonian.

The title sequence of *Near the Ocean* consists of five numbered poems. The first two of these ("Waking Early Sunday Morning" and "Fourth of July in Maine") and the last ("Near the Ocean") are composed in rhymed couplets of iambic tetrameter lines, arranged in eight-line stanzas. This is the stanza form of Andrew Marvell's "The Garden" and *Upon Appleton House*, a formal resemblance that may be taken to link Lowell's efforts to mediate between the private and the public realms of experience with the similar achievement of his seventeenth century predecessor. Of the remaining poems in the sequence, the third ("The Opposite House") is in nine-line stanzas of unrhymed short-line free verse; the fourth ("Central Park") is in iambic tetrameter couplets grouped in verse paragraphs. One cannot help being struck at the relative traditional formality of this verse after the free verse of *Life Studies* and *For the Union Dead*. Also very striking in the stanzaic verse is the fact that every one of the long stanzas is closed, giving each a tendency toward autonomy and setting the poem trembling with centrifugal forces. The blockiness and relative independence of these individual stanzas that yet for the most part do not stand quite free anticipates the fourteen-line blank verse units that will constitute *Notebook*.

Another striking feature of *Near the Ocean*—speaking, now, of the whole book—is that it consists partly of original poems, partly of translations (of Horace, Juvenal, and Dante). Lowell said in an interview that his translation enabled him to bring into English something that he would not dare write in English himself although he wished he could; thus, even where the translations are close, they are, to an important extent, expressions of Lowell's sensibility. If the translations are, thus, more of Lowell himself than one might at first take them to be, the original poems turn out to engage his poetic predecessors as significantly as do the translations. "Waking Early Sunday Morning" has its meaning in relation to Wallace Stevens' "Sunday Morning"; "Central Park" similarly evokes and responds to the "Sunday in the Park" section of William Carlos Williams' *Paterson* (1946-1958). The title poem of the sequence can be interpreted as a sort of Lowellian "Dover Beach."

While the poet of "Sunday Morning" was content that earth should turn out to "Seem all of paradise that we shall know," the poet of "Waking Early Sunday Morning" finds no "heavenly fellowship/ Of men that perish and of summer morn" (Stevens) to supersede the failed fellowship of "the Faithful at Church," where the Bible is "chopped and crucified/ in hymns we hear but do not read." Lowell finds instead that "Only man thinning out his kind/ sounds through the Sabbath noon," and instead of the vision of earth as a paradisal garden with deer, whistling quail, ripening berries, and flocks of pigeons that closes Stevens' poem, Lowell sees the planet as a joyless "ghost/ orbiting forever lost," its people "fall[ing]/ in small war on the heels of small/ war." The world of Lowell's poem is a more complicated one than that of Stevens' in that it has a political aspect; the state with its monstrous militarism and the vulgarity of its leader, which is seen as "this Sunday morning, free to chaff/ his own thoughts with his bear-cuffed staff,/ swimming nude, unbuttoned, sick/ of his ghost-written rhetoric," is part of what the speaker here must assimilate. Furthermore the spiritual yearning of the speaker in Lowell's poem is more complex than Stevens'. The poem opens with his cry, "O to break loose," but not simply "to break loose"; rather "to break loose like the chinook/ salmon" that overcomes the current to reach its river birthplace "alive enough to spawn and die." The release longed for is the release of suicide. This is not all, though. Further on, the speaker voices an exclamation: "O that the spirit could remain/ tinged but untarnished by its strain!" This cry is preceded by a passage describing a glass of water fuzzed with condensation that looks silvery in the light of the sky; when it is seen from a shifted perspective, with brown wood behind it, the wood comes "to darken it, but not to stain." Salmon and glass of water, like key images in other Lowell poems, are profoundly ambiguous; there is no claim for objectivity in the anatomy of his world by a speaker who looks upon it through the dark glass of his own psychology—which is itself part of the world that the poem presents.

In his next book, *Notebook 1967-68*, Lowell again effects a striking formal transformation. The fourteen-line pieces in blank verse that Lowell used to register his various preoccupations—his marriage, wife and daughter, love affairs; his dreams; the Vietnam War, the Pentagon March, Eugene McCarthy's campaign for the Democratic presidential nomination, other political events by which he was affected or in which he was involved; other writers, both his friends among contemporaries and the predecessors who contributed to the literary tradition that he inherited; figures of history—were, he said in his "Afterthought" to *Notebook 1967-68*, "written as one poem." The organization of the pieces is partially according to Lowell's order of composition/experience, partially according to subject, setting, or season. Individual poems do, however, resist being subsumed in the whole book, either the original or the expanded edition of *Notebook*, in part because they are sonnetlike in more than number of lines and meter. In particular, Lowell's tendency to epigrammatic conclusions helps endow individual poems with an autonomy stronger than the centripetal force exerted by a loosely seasonal organization.

Despite the frequency of the memorable concluding line or couplet, however, and despite the fact that these poems often embrace what Lowell called "the themes and gigantism of the sonnet," they do not have the sort of logical structure characteristic of the traditional sonnet. Their movement is typically associative, sometimes obscurely so; their phrases frequently do not join into complete sentences. The first poem in the section called "October and November" in *Notebook 1967-68*, "Che Guevara," can be taken as representative in its technique and in the spheres of reference—contemporary public affairs, the poet's personal life, the historical past—that it telescopes. Beginning with the notation, "Week of Che Guevara," it sketches Che's assassination and conveys Lowell's attitude toward it (as an instance at once of violence begetting violence and of a spirit having a certain grandeur being done in by meaner ones) in a series of participles and absolute constructions taking the first five lines. The scene then switches, by the mere transition of an "as" (which disappears in subsequent revision) indicating temporal simultaneity, to the poet's autumn in Manhattan, presented first through features indicating the season and evoking a mood—still-green leaves "burn to frittered reds," an oak tree "swells with goiters"—then through ones adumbrating the socioeconomic realities of the city—its "high white stone buildings over-/shadow the poor"—then sliding through progressive subordination to the personal—"where our clasped, illicit hands/ pulse." Abruptly the final couplet first returns readers to the public event with which the poem began; then, taking up an association of the mentioned oak tree, the final couplet throws it into historical perspective, in a resonant, memorable conclusion: "Rest for the outlaw . . . kings once hid in oaks,/ with prices on their heads, and watched for game."

Both the heterogeneity of material treated as readers move from poem to poem, section to section, and the quick shifts within individual poems that are characteristic of their style (Lowell at one point makes explicit reference to this stylistic trait, saying, in the second poem of the "Harvard" section,

"My mind can't hold the focus for a minute./ A sentence? A paragraph? . . ./ Flash-visions . . ."), create the impression of a mind besieged by an unremitting succession of disparate experiences that cannot be checked in their passing. When, in the second poem of *Notebook 1967-68*, the poet, killing a fly that has been "wham[ming] back and forth across" his daughter's bed, says "another instant's added/ to the horrifying mortmain of/ ephemera," he strikes a keynote for the whole book.

The succession of experiences do not, of course, all come from external events, but also from Lowell's reading and memory. The order in which subjects appear from poem to poem reflects his mental associations and the tensions in his thought as much as the flux of events in his life. In two poems on the Pentagon March, Lowell expresses his ambivalence toward pacifism and military valor. In the first, he compares the marchers he is among to "green Union Army recruits/ for the first Bull Run" and characterizes the soldiers who face them by a series of images, "the Martian, the ape, the hero,/ his new-fangled rifle, his green new steel helmet," conveying a profound ambivalence, confounding the two groups even as he distinguishes them and simultaneously both exalting and deflating each of them. The second poem on the March, which closes with Lowell helped staggering to his feet to "flee" the soldiers, is followed by an elegy on his ancestor Charles Russell Lowell, a "Union martyr," a cavalry officer who, struck and dying, "had himself strapped to the saddle . . . bound to death." It all seems to add up to the coexistence in Lowell's mind of pacifist convictions and an admiration for military heroism, which, Richard Fein has remarked, could not be more tellingly displayed.

"Obit," the poem that Lowell uses to end his book, looks toward the ending of the flux of experience in death, toward "the eternal return of earth's fairer children" (that has been adumbrated in the seasonal basis of the book's structure and in its attention to the poet's growing daughter), and back toward the onset and passage of moments of consciousness, as lovers' "unconquered flux, insensate oneness, their painful 'it was. . . .'" The question that constitutes the final couplet is not the typical rhetorical question. "After loving you so much, can I forget/ you for eternity, and have no other choice?" asks Lowell, while the accumulated context of this poem and of the whole book that precedes it indicate that his intellect would answer yes, his inclination, no.

Lowell did not stay satisfied with either the pieces or the whole of *Notebook 1967-68*. First, he revised poems and added to sections to produce the expanded *Notebook*; then, he separated the poems dealing with his marital life into *For Lizzie and Harriet* and rearranged the rest into a sequence following the chronology of history, filling in gaps with new poems and sometimes turning what began as autobiographical poems into poems associating the same attitudes or experiences with historical or mythological figures; this revised sequence constitutes the volume Lowell entitled *History*. While the arrangement of *History*, as contrasted with that of *Notebook*, might at first seem superficial, the book has a thematic focus for which the ordering of poems in accord with the dates of their subject is appropriate. Stephen Yenser has pointed to the section called "The Powerful" in *Notebook*, an expanded version of that called "Power" in *Notebook 1967-68*, as the germ of *History*'s structure and theme. The poem that originally ended the chronological sequence of poems on historical figures in this section becomes, slightly revised, the conclusion of the whole book. It is a summational poem that articulates the relationship among the book's principal subjects—the mythical and legendary heroes and villains, the historical political and military leaders, the writers, and Lowell himself as writer and as a citizen and public man. Originally entitled "New Year's 1968," it is, significantly, retitled "End of a Year." In a book dominated by the elegiac mode, it is an elegy of elegies. From an opening couplet that declares, "These conquered kings pass furiously away/ gods die in flesh and spirit and live in print," it moves to qualify that continued "life" in print as one of misquotation, then to look at the poet's writing of a run-out year "in bad, straightforward, unscanning sentences," the year's "hero" the poet himself, of unsound mind (*"demens"*), his story, given in the imagery of the stories of "conquered kings," one of running his ship on the rocks. From the image of the foundering ship, the text slides to the scene present to the poet, where slush-ice in the Hudson "is rose-heather in the New York sunset"; then, dispensing with the requirements of complete clauses, the poem concludes abruptly and hauntingly with a juxtaposition of images of the landscape before the poet and the carbon that inks copies of his typescript (earlier in the poem compared to a Rosetta Stone): "bright sky, bright sky, carbon scarred with ciphers."

The thread of personal life that was drawn out of the weave of *Notebook* to constitute *For Lizzie and Harriet* is continued in *The Dolphin*, a slim volume which continues the use of the fourteen-line blank verse form. A feature that significantly differentiates *The Dolphin* from those others is the use of a central symbol, accreting in complexity and ambiguity over the course of the book. The dolphin, with variants (mermaid, "baby killer whale") and in its various attractive and fearsome aspects (graceful, playful swimmer; powerful predator), is associated with Caroline, and the contradictory connotations of Lowell's symbol reflect his ambivalence toward her. In the course of the book, Caroline is progressively mythicized and becomes a gigantic, ambiguous, and disturbing character set forth in the image of the dolphin, while Elizabeth, the wife Lowell is waveringly leaving, becomes an ever clearer, ever more human voice, presented principally through quotation from her letters.

"Fishnet" and "Dolphin," respectively the opening and closing poems of the book and serving as its frame, have become the best-known pieces of this collection. "Fishnet" begins with one of the series of nominals detached from any predication common in Lowell's poems of the *Notebook* form: "Any clear thing that blinds us with surprise,/ your wandering silences and bright trouvailles,/ dolphin let loose to catch the flashing fish." Already in its initial appearance, the dolphin symbol is ambiguous, associated with the appealing image of the "bright trouvailles," but presented as catching "the flashing fish" rather than as a flashing fish itself. In other poems the reader will find dolphin-Caroline presented both as a fish that the poet angles for and as a creature that may devour him. After its opening catalog of images, this first poem turns to reflect on the fates of poets: they "die adolescents, their beat embalms them." After several years of writing in the same verse form, Lowell was conscious that it was risky to continue with it any longer. (In a 1971 interview, he said of the form, "I mustn't tempt it.") The conclusion of the poem is affirmative in some of its diction, but ambivalent in its imagery. The poet presents his activity as a writer as "knotting, undoing a fishnet of tarred rope," the "undoing" presumably being a reference to his habitual revising and recasting of his previous work. In the closing couplet the product of this work is presented as surviving, but hardly in the manner in which, say, Elizabethan sonneteers spoke of their poetry as surviving: "the net will hang on the wall when the fish are eaten,/ nailed like illegible bronze on the futureless future." It seems that Lowell foresees a time when his poetry will have ceased not only to be part of a life being lived, but even to be intelligible.

The final poem addresses "My Dolphin" as a guide, guiding "by surprise," "surprise" being conspicuous as the last word of the first line in each of the "frame" poems. The language in which the dolphin's activity is described is again ambivalent: she "made for my body/ caught in its hangman's-knot of sinking lines," the fishnet of the opening poem turned against its maker, become at once noose and weight. Focusing on his own making, the poet indicates that in his use of his life in his art, both in what he has altered and in what he has told as it was, he has done injury to others and to himself, and he calls the book that is ending "an eelnet made by man for the eel fighting," the ambiguity of "for" pointed up by the inversion of normal word order in the participial phrase. Ambiguity of reference is particularly insistent in the final line, "my eyes have seen what my hand did," which points at once to the poet's registering of his life in his poems and to his awareness of what his writings have done with and to his life. Such ambiguity is appropriate to the complexities of experience and of language.

In his last book of poems, *Day by Day*, Lowell left the fourteen-line blank verse form in which he had been working for nearly a decade to write poems in a free verse more transparent and less marked with features such as sound repetition than that of *Life Studies* or *For the Union Dead*. The syntax has the looseness of the poems of *Notebook* and its progeny, without the tightness of their metrical form to resist its centrifugal pressures. Although lacking a single central symbol such as that of *The Dolphin*, this book has a central and insistent theme: age, the fear of aging and pain, the prospect of death. This theme is introduced in the first poem, "Ulysses and Circe"; in Lowell's interpretation of Ulysses' story, the old veteran of the Trojan wars, leaving a troubled affair with the young Circe, returns to Ithaca to find his wife "well-furnished with her entourage" and himself superfluous. Humiliated, cuckolded, his infuriated mind is set on the murder of Penelope's lovers. The situation of the aged lover and husband, here presented through the retelling of a much-retold tale, is presented through autobiographical poetry in the rest of the book.

The bulk of the book, its third part, bearing the title of the book, stays exceedingly close to a journal's day-by-day record of events and emotions. This final part is itself divided into three sections. The first covers a summer in England with Caroline, her daughters, and Lowell's son whom she bore. There is a measure of detachment and a certain urbanity in the reflections on the fate of England's great houses in poems such as "Domesday Book" and *"Milgate."* These poems of summer's fullness are all haunted, however, by intimations of coming emptiness; every subject becomes an occasion for meditation on infirmity and mortality. Most poignant, perhaps, is the edge given to the poet's sense of his age and apprehension of his death by his observation of his young son; a poem named for him, "Sheridan," finds its way to that ancient image of death, the scythe, presented, as is usual in Lowell's poetry, as a particular in the represented scene: "High-hung/ the period scythe silvers in the sun,/ a cutting edge, a bounding line,/ between the child's world and the earth." The second section of "Day by Day" covers a stay in Boston without Caroline, framed by poems of Caroline's departure and her return. This interlude is one for reencounter with figures and events of the past: a poem "To Mother" ends, "It has taken me the time since you died/ to discover you are as human as I am . . ./ if I am"; there is an imaginary dialogue with his father; his grandfather looms in two poems. A terrible memory from his St. Mark's days is told—being taunted to tears by his classmates and possibly having deserved it, having made a habit of harping on the defects of other boys to their friends; Lowell comes to a harsh self-judgment that "even now/ my callous unconscious drives me/ to torture my closest friend."

The third and final section, the most wrenching, records living with Caroline, ill from an old spinal injury, and a mental breakdown and then recovery. Lowell envisions himself and Caroline bound together as "seesaw inseparables," always "one up, the other down," represents her as experiencing "my sickness only as desertion." In sickness, his fear of sickness and expectance of death evoke nostalgia for his lost Catholic faith: "The Queen of Heaven, I miss her,/ we were divorced." Voices and memories crowd upon Lowell in this section, which begins, in "Turtle," with an invocation to memory. In that poem, a memory of hunting snapping turtles turns into a nightmare of death. In "Unwanted," words from an article on John Berryman, remembered words from a family psychiatrist with an ambiguous relation to his mother, and remembered words of his mother converge on his consciousness to bring home the recognition of his having been an unwanted child and of the impact of that on his psychological development—"to give my simple autobiography a plot," as the poet says wryly. The last three poems bring the book to a gentle conclusion. "The Downlook" turns back with nostalgia to the previous year in Lowell's and Caroline's love, evoked in pastoral imagery as a time when "nothing dared impede/ the flow of the body's thousand rivulets of welcome"; such turning back in memory is a conclusion in "days of the downlook." The penultimate poem is a "Thanks for Recovery"; the last is an "Epilogue" that is an apologia, in which the poet regrets that "Those blessed structures, plot and rhyme," have been no help to him in this book, complains that his writings seem to him snapshots, neither fully true to life nor truly imaginary, but concludes by accepting and justifying his work as a response to the fact of mortality, giving "each figure in the photograph,/ his living name."

Eleanor von Auw Berry

Other major works
PLAYS: *Phaedra*, 1961 (translation); *The Old Glory*, 1964 (*Endecott and the Red Cross, My Kinsman, Major Molineux*, and *Benito Cereno*); *Prometheus Bound*, 1967, 1969 (published); *The Oresteia of Aeschylus*, 1979 (translation). NONFICTION: *Collected Prose*, 1987.

Bibliography
Cosgrave, Patrick. *The Public Poetry of Robert Lowell*. New York: Taplinger, 1970. While Lowell is usually seen as a "Confessional" poet, many of his greatest poems were on public issues. Cosgrave brings out that dimension in his poetry and locates it in the traditions of public poetry and modernism. Unfortunately, the book was published in 1970 and does not discuss Lowell's *Notebook*, a central text of Lowell's politics.
Hamilton, Ian. *Robert Lowell: A Biography*. New York: Random House, 1982. This book is occasionally sensational, but it is the best biography available. It traces Lowell's fascinating life in great detail and provides the contexts and occasions for many of his poems, which help readers understand them better.
Perloff, Marjorie G. *The Poetic Art of Robert Lowell*. Ithaca, N.Y.: Cornell University Press, 1973. The best book available on the specifics of Lowell's art. Perloff investigates with acuteness the images and syntax of many of Lowell's poems. She is especially helpful on the Winslow elegies and the

sound patterns of the poems.

Rudman, Mark. *Robert Lowell: An Introduction to the Poetry.* New York: Columbia University Press, 1983. A brief overview of Lowell's poems useful for beginning readers of Lowell. It is a disappointing book, however, for anyone who knows Lowell well.

Wallingford, Katherine. *Robert Lowell's Language of the Self.* Chapel Hill: University of North Carolina Press, 1988. Wallingford uses psychoanalytic criticism to investigate the poems. She finds that Lowell knew Sigmund Freud and applied many of his analytic methods in his poems. Lowell's poetry invites this type of criticism, and this is the fullest use of it available.

Williamson, Alan. *Pity the Monsters: The Political Vision of Robert Lowell.* New Haven, Conn.: Yale University Press, 1974. Williamson discusses the violence as well as the political vision of Lowell. He is one of few critics to fully discuss *Near the Ocean* and *Notebook* (later published as *History*).

JOHN LYDGATE

Born: Lydgate, England; 1370(?)
Died: Bury St. Edmunds, England; 1451(?)

Principal poetry

Translation of Aesop; *Complaint of the Black Knight*, c. 1400; *The Lyf of Our Lady*, c. 1409; *The Pilgrimage of the Life of Man*, c. 1426; *Guy of Warwick*, c. 1426; *Ballade at the Reverence of Our Lady, Qwene of Mercy*, c. 1430; *St. Edmund and Fremund*, c. 1433; *The Lyfe of Seint Albon and the Lyfe of Saint Amphabel*, 1534; *Queen Margaret's Entry into London*, c. 1445; *The Secrees of Olde Philosoffres*, c. 1451; *The Falle of Princis*, 1494; *The Storye of Thebes*, c. 1500; *The Historye, Sege, and Dystruccyon of Troy*, 1513 (better known as *Troy Book*); *The Testament of J. Lydgate*, 1515; *Daunce Macabre*, 1554.

Other literary forms

John Lydgate wrote only one significant piece of prose, *The Serpent of Division*. Scholars are uncertain as to its exact date of composition, but Walter Schirmer, in his *John Lydgate: A Study in the Culture of the Fifteenth Century* (1961), suggests the year 1422. Drawing on Lucan's *Pharsalia* (c. A.D. 80) and Vincent of Beauvais' *Speculum Historiale*, Lydgate here presents the first comprehensive account of the rise and fall of Julius Caesar ever written in English. As in other writings, Lydgate uses this story as an *exemplum*, a story used to teach morality. Here Lydgate's lesson had to do with civil war.

Certain of Lydgate's poems are very intimately connected with later English dramatic forms, especially the *masque*. His "mummings" were meant to accompany short pantomimes or the presentation of *tableaux vivantes*. For example, in 1424 *Mumming at Bishopswood* was presented at an outdoor gathering of London's civic officials. A narrator presented the verses while, at the same time, a dancer portrayed the Goddess of Spring with various gestures and dance steps. The lesson of the poem is conveyed through allegory, where immaterial entities are personified. Here Spring represents civil concord, and Lydgate argues that just as the joy, freshness, and prosperity of Spring replace the heaviness and trouble of winter, so too the various estates, the nobles, the clergy, and the commoners, should throw off their discord and work together in their God-given roles. Success in these "mummings" probably helped prepare Lydgate for his part in the preparation of the public celebrations for the coronation of Henry VI in 1429, and for the triumphant entry into London of the same king with his new queen, Margaret, in 1445.

Achievements

Lydgate was one of the most prolific writers in English, with 145,000 lines of verse to his credit. To match this, one would have to write eight lines a day, every day, for about fifty years. Further, almost every known medieval poetic genre is represented in the Lydgate canon.

Once the uncrowned Poet Laureate of England, Lydgate was appreciated by kings, princes, and nobility. Today, however, he is unknown to the general English-speaking public and often disparaged by literary scholars. Critics have charged that his poetry is dull, long-winded, and poorly wrought. Not all of these charges will stand scrutiny, however, and one could argue that Lydgate's fall is due primarily to a shifting of tastes in poetry rather than to poor craftsmanship on his part.

It is true that Lydgate's poetry consistently frustrates the modern reader, who expects poetry to be compressed and concise; Lydgate's poems are generally voluminous. Instead of irony or ambiguity, Lydgate usually assumes a rather prosaic straightforwardness. On the other hand, instead of ordinary words in their natural order, Lydgate uses obscure terms in complicated syntax. Far from writing "art for art's sake," Lydgate consistently insists on teaching sound doctrine and morality. Finally, in place of a uniquely personal vision and style, Lydgate always writes as a conventional public poet.

If one reads Lydgate through "medieval spectacles," however, these characteristics seem not only normal but praiseworthy as well. Lydgate saw himself as a rhetorician and thus felt it necessary to be both "sweet and useful" in his writing. Poetical art, to the medieval mind, was the application of rhetorical know-how to traditional themes and stories. Thus, he was first a craftsman, not a prophet or seer. He would not have considered his personal emotions or insights worthy of remembrance.

It is ironic, therefore, that Lydgate the careful craftsman has developed the reputation of being a poor versifier. If one assumes that his lines were supposed to be strictly iambic pentameter, this opinion may be justified. Fortunately, beginning with C. S. Lewis in 1939, certain scholars have suggested that Lydgate's line was based on a slightly different model, one which blends the French tradition of decasyllabic verse with the native tradition of balanced half-lines, thus allowing a variable number of stresses and syllables. In the light of these scholarly studies, Lydgate's verse seems consistently good.

Some critics, such as Schirmer (in *John Lydgate*) and Alain Renoir (in *The Poetry of John Lydgate*, 1967), argue that Lydgate is important as a poet of transition, since they find the seeds of Renaissance humanism in some of his work. While it would be foolish to discount their insights completely, however, the more traditional reading, expressed by Derek Pearsall in his *John Lydgate* (1970), still seems more satisfactory: "Looking for signs of humanism in Lydgate is an unrewarding task, because the whole direction of his mind is medieval." Lydgate will best be understood, therefore, if read as a medieval poet *par excellence*.

In any case, for hundreds of years the English literary public regarded Lydgate's achievement as equal to that of Geoffrey Chaucer or John Gower.

Indeed, the three writers were generally grouped together into a conventional triad of outstanding English poets. George Ashby's praise in 1470 is typical:

> Maisters Gower, Chaucer & Lydgate,
> Primier poetes of this nacion,
> Embelysshing oure Englisshe tendure algate
> Firste finders to oure consolacion.

Further, Lydgate was the glass through which his contemporaries understood and appreciated Chaucer, whom they considered a rhetorician, not a realist, the writer who finally formed English into a suitable vehicle for poetry, philosophy, and learning. In the end, perhaps Lydgate's greatest achievement was to consolidate this new status for his native tongue.

Biography

John Lydgate was born into turbulent times. His life spanned seventy years of the Hundred Years' War with France, and, when he died, the Wars of the Roses were about to begin. In 1381, he witnessed the Peasants' Revolt; in 1399, he saw Richard II deposed. The earlier years of his life were those of the Great Western Schism, with popes in both Avignon and Rome. At the same time the anticlerical Lollards were stirring up trouble for the Church in England. Even nature seemed to conspire against the peace, for, beginning in 1349, the plague struck regularly, killing large portions of the English population.

Born of peasant stock, Lydgate was reared in the quiet village of Lydgate, far from the civil turmoil which raged elsewhere. He must have had a fairly normal childhood, for he later wrote: "Loth to lerne [I] loved no besyness,/ Save pley/ or merth . . . Folowyng alle appetytes longyng to childhede" (*Testament*, 11). His serious side prevailed, however, and perhaps as early as 1385 he joined the Benedictine monastery at Bury St. Edmunds, about sixty-five miles northeast of London. Bury St. Edmunds was one of the richest of England's monasteries, with eighty monks, twenty-one chaplains, and 111 servants. Here Lydgate received much of his formal education, although it is likely that he also spent a few years at Oxford, where he may have begun his literary career by writing his *Translation of Aesop*, the first book of fables written in Middle English. If Oxford was a good place to begin writing, however, the magnificent library of Bury St. Edmunds was just the place to nourish such a career, for it is thought to have contained about two thousand volumes, at the time making it one of the finest in England.

By the time he was ordained a priest in 1397, Lydgate probably had begun building a modest literary reputation. Indeed, John Bale, a sixteenth century biographer, suggests that Lydgate had already started a school of rhetoric for the sons of noblemen. Although some scholars are dubious about this, it is certain that Lydgate at this time began to make friends among the aristocracy, many of whom were later to become his literary patrons.

As a matter of fact, Lydgate soon came to the attention of Prince Hal, later Henry V, who in 1409 charged him with writing a life of the Blessed Virgin Mary. Thus Lydgate wrote his first saint's legend, *The Lyf of Our Lady*. This was to be the start of a long and fruitful relationship between Lydgate and the Lancastrian dynasty, a dynasty which both the poet and his brother monks saw as a strong bulwark of Catholic orthodoxy against the Lollards.

Henry V was more interested in battle, conquest, and deeds of chivalry than in piety, however, and by October, 1412, he conceived a different sort of project for Lydgate's talent: a retelling of the popular story of Troy. It took Lydgate eight years, relying mostly on Guido delle Colonne's *Historia Troiana* (c. 1285), to construct this long epic of thirty thousand lines. His taste for versifying history, however, was hardly sated by this massive work, for very soon after completing *Troy Book* (1513), Lydgate set out on another long poem: *The Storye of Thebes* (c. 1500). He found the frame for this tale in Chaucer's works; he presents the work as a continuation of *The Canterbury Tales* (1387-1400). Thus the pilgrim "Daun John" Lydgate himself tells the Thebes story—at length. In the Prologue Lydgate shows his sense of humor, ironically contrasting his own appearance, "so pale, al devoyde of blode," to that of Chaucer's strong, lusty monk.

Lydgate's admiration for his master, Chaucer, knew no bounds; for Lydgate, Chaucer was the "lodesterre" of English letters. Although he probably never met the older poet, Lydgate was a very close acquaintance of Chaucer's son, Thomas, who was a wealthy country gentleman in Oxfordshire. A glimpse of the closeness of this relationship is seen in Lydgate's *Ballad to Thomas Chaucer* (1417).

In 1423, Lydgate moved closer to the circles of power at Windsor; he was given charge of the priory at Hatfield in Essex, a post which he retained, at least nominally, until 1434, when he was granted a *dimissio*, or formal written permission to return to Bury St. Edmunds "to seek the fruit of a better life." In fact, Lydgate probably resided at Hatfield only until 1426. It seems that in that year Lydgate was sent to Paris to take up a senior post on the staff of John of Lancaster, Duke of Bedford. Here, among other things, he wrote *Guy of Warwick*, an adaptation of an old epic poem glorifying a mythical English hero who saves England from the Danes by overcoming their champion, Colbrand.

While in France Lydgate met Thomas de Montacute, the fourth Earl of Salisbury, who was the second husband of Alice Chaucer, the granddaughter of the poet. Montacute had a great interest in letters and commissioned Lydgate's translation of Guilliam de Deguileville's popular *Pèlerinage de la vie humaine* (1330-1331), a long allegorical romance concerning the "pilgrimage" of man through this earthly existence.

It can be assumed that in Paris Lydgate mixed with people of the highest tastes and education, both English and French, for these years were produc-tive ones for him, during which he wrote many of his satires and religious poems. He was inspired, for example, by one of the most popular themes of fifteenth century art, the *danse macabre*. Both in painting and in verse, this motif portrays the skeletons of men and women of all social classes dancing together as equals—in death. Lydgate's *Daunce Macabre* is a fairly close translation of verses which he discovered written on the colonnade surround-ing the cemetery of the Église des Innocents in Paris.

In 1429, Lydgate returned to London for the coronation of the seven-year-old Henry VI. By this time, he was the premier poet of England, and thus he was commissioned to write an official *Roundel for the Coronation*, setting forth Henry's hereditary claim to the throne. Lydgate also had a hand in the planning of the official public celebrations for the event. He did the same in 1432 when Henry triumphantly returned to London from his coronation in Paris as King of France.

The Falle of Princis (1494), Lydgate's most important work, was commis-sioned in May, 1431, by Henry V's brother, Humphrey, Duke of Gloucester, then Warden of England. In some thirty-six thousand lines the poet chroni-cles the continual movement of the Wheel of Fortune, raising up and then casting down men and women of power and wealth. It took him eight years to complete, while he increasingly felt his powers being drained by age.

In 1433, the King spent four months at Bury St. Edmunds and in com-memoration of the event Lydgate was asked to write a life of the monas-tery's patron, St. Edmund, for presentation to the monarch. Later, in 1439, Lydgate wrote his final piece of hagiography, *The Lyfe of Seint Albon and the Lyfe of Saint Amphabel.*

Lydgate received a lifelong pension from the King in 1439, but he was not left in peace at Bury St. Edmunds to enjoy it. In 1445, he was again given responsibilities for the planning of a public celebration, this time for the ar-rival in London of Henry VI's new queen, Margaret, daughter of King René of Anjou. For this occasion he wrote *Queen Margaret's Entry into London*, a work that no longer exists in its entirety.

In 1448, the poet, suspecting that his life was almost over, began his ver-sified *Testament*, perhaps his most intensely personal poem. In it he de-nounces, somewhat conventionally, the levity of his youth, but he later pro-claims in very moving terms his personal devotion to the name of Jesus. The tone and range of subject matter in Lydgate's *Testament* are much different from those of the more famous *Testament* written less than a decade later by François Villon.

Lydgate must have passed his last few years with some sadness over his country's fortunes. The Hundred Years' War was winding down, but not in England's favor. Further, the internal political turmoil which would eventually lead to the Wars of the Roses was growing in England. Lydgate's final work, which he left unfinished, is another attempt to offer wise counsel to the country's leaders. *The Secrees of Olde Philosoffres* is a translation of the *Secreta Secretorum*, supposedly written by Aristotle for his pupil Alexander. Benedict Burgh, who completed the work, relates that just after Lydgate wrote verse 1,491, "deth al consumyth," the pen dropped from his hand, and the much-honored poet passed into history.

Analysis

Much of what can be said about John Lydgate's art in the *Complaint of the Black Knight* can be applied very readily to the bulk of his writings, so it is a fitting piece with which to begin. The poem, written about 1400, is a conventional Love Complaint, a very popular genre of the age, of ninety-seven Chaucerian stanzas (stanzas of seven pentameter lines rhyming ababbcc). It begins with the poet, sick at heart, journeying out into the May morning to find some succor for his pain. He encounters birds singing, beautiful trees and flowers, a clear river, and a fountain which provides him water to refresh his spirits. All of a sudden, the poet discovers an arbor in which a handsome knight, dressed in black, sits moaning as if sick. After hiding, the poet discreetly listens to the lover's complaint.

The centerpiece of this poem is the highly artificial soliloquy which follows. Here the knight first confesses that he is tortured with overwhelming love; second, protests that his lady, because of false rumors about his conduct, disdains him; third, remonstrates with the God of Love, who, he claims, is unfair to honest lovers and rewards only the false; and fourth, offers his life to his lady: "My hert I send, and my spirit also,/ What so-ever she list with hem to do." Moved to tears by this complaint, the poet prays to the rising Venus, asking that she will have pity on this true lover. He then prays that all lovers will be true and that they will enjoy one another's embraces. Finally, he sends his poem off to his princess, hoping that this "little book" will speak eloquently of his pain in love.

The whole poem, in Derek Pearsall's words, is "a tissue of borrowings," not only from Geoffrey Chaucer's *Book of the Duchess* (c. 1370), Lydgate's main source, but also from many of the poems of the French allegorical school. Borrowing, however, is normal procedure for medieval poets, for, as Robert Payne has shown in his *The Key of Remembrance* (1963), they considered their primary task to be not poetic invention but rather the reordering and the embellishment of traditional truths or literary works. Lydgate here is true to his times, and he works as a craftsman, not a seer. His main talent, then, lies squarely within the confines of rhetoric.

The landscape in the *Complaint of the Black Knight*, for example, is not constructed from personal observation or experience, but is taken directly from conventional descriptions of nature which Lydgate found in "old books." He tries to construct a *locus amoenus*, an idealized natural site fit for idealized lovers, both successful and frustrated. Thus, he uses all the details, the May morning, the flowers, the birds, the clear stream, that the sources stipulated. Moreover, Lydgate borrows not only descriptions of nature but also many other traditional themes, images, and literary postures, making the poem entirely conventional.

After selecting his genre, his themes, and his sources, Lydgate, working methodically, amplifying, contracting, or rearranging parts according to his own tastes, next fashions a fitting structure for them. Finally, he adds the embellishment, the literary "colors," such as alliteration, antithesis, chiasmus, echoing, exclamation, parallelism, or repetition. Thus, in lines 232 to 233 the Knight describes his woes with an elaborate chiasmus, reminiscent of Chaucer's *Troilus and Criseyde* (1382), I, 420: "Now hote as fire, now colde as asshes dede,/ Now hote for colde, now colde for hete ageyn." In lines 400 to 403, Lydgate adapts an exclamation from *Troilus and Criseyde*, V, 1828-1832:

> Lo her the fyne of loveres servise!
> Lo how that Love can his servantis quyte!
> Lo how he can his feythful men dispise,
> To sle the trwe men, and fals to respite!

Lydgate regularly protests that he has no literary "colors," but this too is a conventional literary pose. On the contrary, one finds "colors" used carefully and continuously throughout the Lydgate corpus.

In fact, Lydgate is so much interested in the surface decoration of his poetry that he sometimes seems to neglect its deeper significance. The elaborate descriptions of nature in the literature of courtly love, for example, were meant to have a purpose beyond that of mere ornamentation; they were supposed to carry an allegorical meaning. In Chaucer's *Romaunt of the Rose* (c. 1370), from which Lydgate borrowed some of his landscape, the fountain of Narcissus represents the Lady's eyes, the garden represents the life at court, and the rose-plot is the mind of the lady wherein personified fears and hopes do battle. C. S. Lewis discusses these allegorical meanings at length in *The Allegory of Love* (1936), but he could not do the same for Lydgate's version of the garden, for here the long description of the garden is not integrated with the rest of the poem. Once the Knight begins his soliloquy, Lydgate seemingly forgets the garden, whose description is thus solely a piece of rhetorical virtuosity. Indeed, that which is of most value in the poem is the part which is most intrinsically rhetorical: the formal complaint of the Knight. In Lewis' words, "The slow building up and decoration, niche by niche, of a rhetorical structure, brings out what is best in the poet."

In this context Lydgate's famous predilection for florid Latinate diction makes sense. The poet himself coined the term *aureate* to describe both a highly wrought style and an elevated diction. In *The Falle of Princis* he describes his task in the following way: "Writying of old, with lettres aureat,/ Labour of poetis doth hihli magnefie." The medium here fits the message, for Lydgate cannot resist twisting normal English word order. Moreover, the influence of Lydgate's style upon his successors was great indeed, for the use of "aureat lettres" came to dominate fifteenth century verse. It was not until the nineteenth century, when William Wordsworth began to attack "poetic diction," that "aureate" came to have pejorative connotations.

Lydgate, however, felt that, just as the host of the Holy Communion was encased in a highly decorated monstrance for public adoration, so too religious matter should be placed in a suitably ornate poetic vehicle. His invocations to Mary in the *Ballade at the Reverence of Our Lady, Qwene of Mercy*, are often cited as prime examples of this suitably ornate diction. After invoking the "aureat licour of Clyo" to enliven his dull wit, Lydgate compares Mary to the stars, precious jewels, various birds, a red rose, and to many other things in a riot of exotic images expressed in extravagant terminology. Lines 36 through 39 are a good example:

> O closid gardeyn al void of weedes wicke,
> Cristallyn welle of clennesse cler consigned,
> Fructifying olyve of foilys faire and thicke,
> And redolent cedyr most derworthly ydyned.

These images certainly were not original with Lydgate; they are doubtless echoes of the *Song of Songs*, but Lydgate has presented them in fittingly sonorous language, filled with alliteration. Ian Robinson, in *Chaucer's Prosody: A Study of the Middle English Verse Tradition* (1971), summarizes the matter well when he remarks: "Material enters the Lydgate factory mud and leaves it terracotta.

Not surprisingly, a great body of Lydgate's verse is explicitly religious, and nowhere is he more representative of his times than when he writes his saints' lives. Christian saints were the heroes of the medieval Catholic Church, and there was a great thirst on all levels of society for knowledge about them. Very early in the Christian era short narratives about the deaths of martyrs, *passiones*, or about the lives of confessors, *vitae*, began to be composed. These were meant to be read during the liturgy or the Divine Office. In the High Middle Ages, vernacular legends began to be written for the common folk, and, especially with the advent of the friars, these were used for public preaching. The legends, however, were viewed primarily as a literature of edification rather than as objective history or biography. Thus, "successful" structures, incidents, and even historical details were exchanged freely among the various legends. Generally speaking, then, medieval legend can be considered a type of popular formulaic literature.

In honor of the visit, in 1433, of Henry VI to Bury St. Edmunds, Abbott William Curteys commissioned Lydgate, who had written a number of *vitae* earlier, to write *St. Edmund and Fremund* for presentation to the King. Lydgate's response was an "epic legend," in which the life of Edmund, the former king of East Anglia (d. 870), is retold in a suitably long (3,693 lines) narrative.

The work is divided into three sections. Books I and II recount the life, death, and burial of Edmund; Book III treats the life of Fremund, the King's nephew and avenger; and, finally, an appendix records several of Edmund's posthumous miracles. Most of the work is in Chaucerian stanzas.

Lydgate, using the Latin *Vita et Passio cum Miraculis Sancti Edmundi*, Bodlian Ms. 240, as his primary source, incorporates many of the standard characteristics of the *passio*. Thus, Edmund's birth is miraculously foretold by a strange widow when Alkmund, his Saxon father, is on a pilgrimage in Rome. In his youth, Edmund is pious and mature well beyond his years, so much so that his distant relative, Offa, chooses him as his successor to the East Anglian throne. After Offa dies, Edmund governs wisely and moderately, but despite his ability as a warrior, he comes to realize that bloodshed is hateful in the sight of God and repudiates warfare. Therefore, to protect his people from the marauding Danes, he offers his own life in return for their safety. When brought before the violent Hyngwar, leader of the Danes, Edmund refuses apostasy in the standard interrogation. Hyngwar loses self-control, as is typical of "evil judges," at Edmund's aggressive retorts and orders the King's execution. After undergoing a sustained round of tortures with superhuman endurance, Edmund is finally beheaded, but not before he sings out a long panegyric to God in which he asks to die as God's "true knight." The head of the slain king, although hidden, is miraculously protected by a wolf until it is found by Edmund's subjects. Other miracles follow before Fremund is introduced in Book III.

In this legend Lydgate uses his sources freely, carefully choosing incidents that serve his own purposes. The posthumous miracles, for example, are chosen to illustrate his theme that tyrants and other prideful people are eventually punished by God. His arrangement of those miracles indicates concern for symmetry, balance, and artistic control. In short, Lydgate's contribution to the history of the Edmund legend is that of a masterful rhetorician who fitted the legend into an elegant structure, added rhetorical flourishes such as prologues, prayers, and epilogues, and finished the surface with the appropriate sonorous diction.

The literary cousin to the saint is the fallen prince, for one can fashion an *exemplum* from each. If medieval audiences could be edified by the courage of the former, they could be taught detachment and humility from the life of the latter: for example, from the lives of Priam and Saul, Alexander and Caesar, Arthur and King John of France.

The theme of the world's transitoriness was another medieval commonplace, but Giovanni Boccaccio's *De Casibus Illustrium Virorum* (1358) treated the theme in a systematic and comprehensive way for the first time. In this work, all of the kings just mentioned, and many more besides, pass before the Italian poet and complain of their downfalls. Boccaccio's work became extremely popular and was translated into French in 1409 by Laurent de Premierfait. In 1431, Duke Humphrey of Gloucester commissioned Lydgate to translate it into English, and this free translation was entitled *The Falle of Princis*. The task took Lydgate eight years.

Working from the French translation, Lydgate expands Boccaccio's work even more, filling in abbreviated stories, adding missing ones, inserting exhortations, and writing envoys for the end of each chapter. The result is a massive medieval history book (36,365 lines), a mirror for princes, an encyclopedia of world biography. Lydgate follows his medieval penchant for inclusion rather than concision, and thus the sheer bulk of the work is both a positive attribute—it contributes to an impression of weight and solemnity—and a fault—Boccaccio's fine structure seems completely lost.

The Falle of Princis may be called a book of tragedies, for the medieval definition of tragedy was much simpler than Aristotle's: "For tragedie, as poetes spesephie,/ Gynneth with ioie, eendith with adversite:/ From hih estate [Men] caste in low degre." Lydgate follows both Boccaccio and Laurent in deprecating the blind goddess Fortune, a personification blamed as the fickle distributor of both tragedy and good luck. In the Prologue to Book I, Lydgate describes her as "transitory of condicioun," "hasty & sodeyne," since "Whan men most truste, than is she most chaungable." One often encounters medieval representations of the Wheel of Fortune, where one sees the blindfolded goddess spinning a wheel to which various men are attached. Those on the top, the rulers, enjoy the favors of good fortune, whereas those on the bottom, paupers or prisoners, are in misery. Figures on either side, however, the rising courtier or the falling prince, emphasize that the wheel is never static, and that both kingdoms and rulers pass away.

There were several common reactions to these lessons in mutability. First of all, they inspired sorrow over time's passing. Thus the *Ubi sunt?* (Where are they?) theme is found in much of medieval poetry, from the Anglo-Saxon *Wanderer* to the "Ballade des dames du temps jadis" ("Ballad of the Ladies of Bygone Times") of Villon. Poets using this theme complain that everything beautiful, noble, or great in this world eventually passes away. Lydgate repeats this theme often and at length in *The Falle of Princis*. In the Envoy to Book II, Lydgate ponders the fate of Rome. "Where be thyn Emperours, most sovereign of renown?" he asks. "Where is now Cesar"; where "Tullius?" His answer is not as poetic as Villon's "But where are the snows of bygone years?" for he states directly that "Off alle echon the odious ravyne of time/ Hath be processe the brought to ruyne."

If, on one hand, time brings everything to an end and princes are brought low by Fortune's variability, on the other hand, a good Christian ought to see

God's Providence working through Fortune, punishing pride or arrogance. Thus, by pondering tragedy, men of power can learn meekness, detachment, and humility, and place the highest value on spiritual things. "Ley doun thi pride," cries Lydgate; "Cri God merci, thi trespacis repentyng!" For the Romans, of course, it is too late, but it is not too late for Lydgate's contemporaries.

One wonders how many medieval princes read completely through all nine books of Lydgate's *exempla*. Even the Knight from Chaucer's *The Canterbury Tales*, for example, could stand only so many of the similar tragedies told by Chaucer's Monk: "good sire, namoore of this!" he cries, for "litel hevyness/ Is right ynough to muche folke" (*Prologue to the Nun's Priest's Tale*). Even Lydgate himself grew tired of his forced march through the ruins of history, for he complains about his fatigue in the Prologue to Book VIII. Moreover, Lydgate expanded on his sources less and less with each succeeding book.

All this has led Pearsall to speculate that perhaps the best way to read *The Falle of Princis* would be to read only extracts of the best passages, which "are too good to miss." The structure of the work is basically inorganic and encyclopedic, since Lydgate, again being true to the aesthetics of his age, seems to have expanded on his sources to include in his work all "useful knowledge" rather than critically selecting and editing his material to allow an organic structure to emerge. Moreover, Pearsall remarks that probably Lydgate's contemporaries more often read the poem in extracts than as a whole, since parts of the work often appear detached from the rest in surviving manuscripts. Practicality supports this view, for there is much repetition and dull elaboration in the poem which most people would rather avoid; but, on the other hand, more detailed work needs be done on the poem's structure before it can be said that here Lydgate completely lacked structural control.

The versifying in *The Falle of Princis*, as in most of Lydgate's work, has traditionally given critics problems. Although most of his lines can be scanned as rather regular iambic pentameter, a large number cannot, and these have in the past led certain writers to call Lydgate a bungling versifier. Recent critics have been fairer to the poet, however, and for good reason. First, medieval scribes were notoriously free in "correcting" their copy, adding or deleting words or changing spelling according to regional pronunciations. Especially with regard to the final *-e*, the sounding of which had probably ceased by the fifteenth century, scribal practices varied widely. Second, for all the current philological sophistication, medievalists are still not sure how Lydgate's contemporaries would have pronounced their native tongue. In short, all scansion of Lydgate's poetry is tentative at best.

The best approach to Lydgate's line seems to be that of Ian Robinson. He claims that Lydgate wrote a "balanced pentameter" line, a line which was meant to work both in half-lines and as a full line of five metrical feet. The

English metrical line was in transition at the time, and this means that there were two sometimes conflicting traditions competing in the art not only of Lydgate but also of Chaucer. The first was the rather recently adopted French decasyllabic line, later to evolve into the English iambic pentameter of William Shakespeare. The oldest English tradition of verse, however, revived in the thirteenth and fourteenth centuries, constructed lines based on stress and alliteration rather than on syllable count. Thus the opening lines of *The Vision of William, Concerning Piers the Plowman*, a poem of the fourteenth century Alliterative Revival, run as follows: In a sómer séson // whan soft was the sónne/ I shópe me in shróude*s* // as I a shépe wére." Although one generally finds four stressed syllables per line (the first three of which were usually alliterated), the total number of syllables per line, stressed and unstressed, varied widely. That is why it makes no difference, metrically speaking, whether the final unstressed syllables italicized above were pronounced or not. In either case these lines are good alliterative verse since both read smoothly in rhythmic half-lines.

So too with Lydgate. If his verse is read with a strong medial caesura, letting the stresses, whether two or three per half-line, fall where they are most natural, the lines hardly ever seem awkward. On the contrary, they are generally easy to scan. Some lines, especially the "broken-backed" variety— lines with only four stressed syllables—seem to fit the English side of the tradition a bit more, whereas others, being to the modern sensibility more "regular," favor the French side. Line 4,465 from Book II, for example, "Off slaúhtre, móordre // & outráious róbbyng," even offers a hint of alliteration in the stressed syllables. On the other hand, lines such as "Thĭ bildyng gán // off fáls dĭscéncĭouń" can be seen as favoring the French side of the tradition, although it still breaks easily into two smooth half-lines.

In the end, one must rightly conclude that Lydgate, wholehearted monk, sometime administrator, and laureate versifier for kings and princes, wrote poetry representative of his times and proper for someone of his position: sometimes prolix, often dull, but everywhere sincere, decorous, well-crafted, and worthy of remembrance.

Gregory M. Sadlek

Other major works

NONFICTION: *The Serpent of Division*, 1422(?).

Bibliography

Ebin, Lois A. *John Lydgate*. Boston: Twayne, 1985. This concise yet thorough book-length study serves as a useful introduction to the Lydgate canon and contains chapters on his courtly poems, moral and didactic poems, and religious poems. Includes a chronology of Lydgate's life, complete notes, including a list of secondary sources, references, and an index.

Edwards, A. S. G. "Lydgate Scholarship: Progress and Prospects." In *Fifteenth Century Studies*, edited by Robert F. Yeager. Hamden, Conn.: Archon Books, 1984. Edwards' bibliographic essay examines twenty-five years of scholarship devoted to the works of John Lydgate. While this study includes brief, insightful accounts of book-length studies and editorial work concerning Lydgate, its primary value is found in its extended bibliographic notes.

_____. "Lydgate Scholarship: Some Directions for Future Research." In *Manuscripts and Readers in Fifteenth Century England: The Literary Implications of Manuscript Studies*, edited by Derek Pearsall. Cambridge, England: Cambridge University Press, 1983. Discusses Lydgate's work in terms of audience and provenance. Devotes its attention to textual criticism of illuminated manuscripts and the identification of scribes in regard to Lydgate. Contains good notes and serves as a guide for the gaps in the study of Lydgate's works.

Lawton, David. "Dullness and the Fifteenth Century." *English Literary History* 54 (Winter, 1987): 761-799. The primary purpose of this lengthy article is to expose the treatment of humility in Lydgate's works. It is important because it provides a good comparison of Lydgate's works in this regard with those of George Ashby and Thomas Hoccleve. Illuminates the sources of these works as being partly from Geoffrey Chaucer and John Gower. Contains specific notes and references.

Lawton, Lesley. "The Illustration of Late Medieval Secular Texts with Special Reference to Lydgate's *Troy Book.*" In *Manuscripts and Readers in Fifteenth Century England: The Literary Implications of Manuscript Studies*, edited by Derek Pearsall. Cambridge, England: Cambridge University Press, 1983. As the title implies, this work is devoted to the role of illustrations in medieval texts, especially Lydgate's *Troy Book*. Here, the relationships of the illustrations to the text are examined as they relate to the work's structure and its audience. Provides an interesting account of this often neglected idea and is supplemented with notes.

GEORGE MacBETH

Born: Shotts, Scotland; January 19, 1932

Principal poetry

The Broken Places, 1963; *A Doomsday Book*, 1965; *The Colour of Blood*, 1967, 1969; *The Night of Stones*, 1968; *A War Quartet*, 1969; *The Burning Cone*, 1970; *The Orlando Poems*, 1971; *Collected Poems: 1958-1970*, 1971; *Shrapnel and a Poet's Year*, 1973, 1974; *In the Hours Waiting for the Blood to Come*, 1975; *Buying a Heart*, 1978; *Poems of Love and Death*, 1980; *Published Collections*, 1982; *Poems from Oby*, 1982; *The Long Darkness*, 1983; *The Cleaver Gardens*, 1986; *Anatomy of a Divorce*, 1988; *Collected Poems: 1958-1982*, 1989.

Other literary forms

In addition to his numerous volumes of poetry, George MacBeth has published a great many poetry pamphlets, chapbooks, and limited-edition books since the early 1960's. Although these have usually been printed in small numbers and reached only a limited audience, many of them have become parts of larger books and been incorporated into the mainstream of MacBeth's work. MacBeth has also published children's books, numerous novels, and an autobiography, and has edited several volumes of poetry, including *The Penguin Book of Sick Verse* (1963), *Poetry 1900-1965* (1967), and *The Falling Splendour* (1970), a selection of Alfred, Lord Tennyson's poetry. The sheer volume of MacBeth's production reveals his almost obsessive dedication to writing and the breadth of his interests. Among his publications other than poetry, the autobiography *My Scotland* (1973) probably holds the greatest interest for the reader of his poetry because of the insights it offers into his background and development. MacBeth himself has described the book as a nonlogical, non-narrative, massive jigsaw of autobiographical bits, a collection of about two hundred short prose pieces about being Scottish.

Achievements

MacBeth is arguably the most prolific poet writing in Great Britain today, and, in terms of his total output, he has few rivals in the United States. Volume alone has not made him a significant poet; rather, he has gained stature because of the diversity of his writing. He is, in the best sense of the word, an "experimental" poet. He seems absolutely fearless in his willingness to attempt new forms and take on unusual subjects, and yet at the same time he is fascinated by traditional meter and rhyme, as well as by material that has fueled the imagination of poets for centuries. *Poems of Love and Death* contains poems ranging from the dangerously romantic "The Truth," with its didactic final stanza which includes the lines "Happiness is a state of mind,/

2110 Critical Survey of Poetry

And grief is something frail and small," to the satiric "The Flame of Love, By Laura Stargleam," which mocks the dime novel plot-line that it exploits. MacBeth is as likely to write about a missile commander as about evening primroses, and the reader familiar with his writing is not at all surprised to find these disparate topics dealt with in a single book, in this case *Buying a Heart.* In fact, it is the sense of discovery and the vitality of MacBeth's imagination that attract a great many readers.

Biography

Born in Scotland near Glasgow, George Mann MacBeth lived the greater part of his life in England. This circumstance has had a substantial impact on his poetry, because it has led him to view himself as something of an exile. Although he feels comfortable in England, he does not regard himself as English and has remarked on the sensation of detachment, of living and working in a foreign country. The Scotland he left as a child remains in his mind as a lost world, a kind of Eden which can never be regained, and his sense of loss has helped to make him in his own evaluation, "a very retrospective, backward-looking poet." Perhaps more significantly, his detachment, or rootlessness, has enabled him to embrace a larger part of the world than is available to most writers.

Another significant element of MacBeth's life was his long-term association with the British Broadcasting Corporation, where he worked as a producer of poetry programs. This position bought him into contact with the leading poets in England and around the world and exposed him to everything that was happening in poetry. MacBeth himself has acknowledged that his close work with a broad variety of poets over the years influenced his writing, particularly in the areas of technique and structure. Always careful not to become too involved in purely "English" writing, he has consciously tried to keep in touch with poetic developments in the world at large, and his accomplishments as a poet can be measured most accurately if they are considered in the context of this endeavor.

By the late 1980's MacBeth had moved to Ireland, continuing to work there as a free-lance broadcaster, a teacher, and a writer, and traveling frequently to give readings of his poetry abroad.

Analysis

George MacBeth has remarked that he considers the word "experimental," which is often used to describe his work, to be a term of praise. While he acknowledges the possibility of failing in some of his excursions into new forms and new subjects, he obviously feels that the risk is justified. His strongest impulse as a writer is to test the bounds of poetry and, wherever possible, to extend them. This daring push toward the very limits of his craft is nowhere better revealed than in the fourth section of his *Collected Poems:*

1958-1970, where MacBeth employs his no-holds-barred approach and enjoys doing it. Indeed, the sense of pleasure that MacBeth manages to communicate, his pure delight in the shape of language on the page, is essential to the reader because it helps to carry him through poems which at first glance may repel rather than attract.

Two such forbidding poems which challenge the analytical mind in satiric fashion are "Two Experiments" and "LDMN Analysis of Thomas Nashe's 'Song.'" The first of these poems, divided into two sections, presents a "Vowel Analysis of 'Babylonian Poem' from the German of Friederike Mayröcker" and a "Numerical Analysis of 'Brazilian Poem' from the German of Friederike Mayröcker." If the ponderous and unlikely subtitles are not enough to warn the reader not to be too serious, the actual text should be sufficiently illuminating. The first section is a listing of vowels, ostensibly from the Mayröcker poem, presented in the following fashion: "U EE-EI A I AE-IIE-EIE UE EOE U EI; E." Thus runs the first line, and the second section begins in the following way: "(. .2 2 6 2 3 5: 2 3 3-6 3 8: 3." Clearly, these representations are meaningless, but they do make a point, not a very positive point, about the analytical approach to poetry: that critical analyses of poetry may make no more sense than these vowel and number analyses. A similar statement is made in "LDMN Analysis of Thomas Nashe's 'Song,'" which offers an arrangement of *L*'s, *D*'s, *M*'s, and *N*'s, presumably as they might be extracted from the Nashe poem.

As might be expected, the response to such experimentation has not been universally positive, and a number of readers have questioned whether such strategies can properly be called poetry. Ironically, this may be the very question that MacBeth wants the reader to ask, the ultimate critic's question: "What is poetry?" MacBeth himself is as sincere as any reader in his search for an answer, for he offers no dogmatic views of his own; he merely tosses out experiments in an effort to determine where the boundaries lie.

Other poems that are somewhat less eccentric but nevertheless experimental are "The Ski Murders" and "Fin du Globe." The first is an "encyclopaedia-poem" consisting of twenty-six individual entries, one for each letter of the alphabet. The entries themselves are written in a prose style that might have been taken from a spy novel, and the reader is invited to construct his own story by piecing the vignettes together in whatever fashion he wishes. The second poem is presented as a game containing fifty-two "postcards" and four "*fin du globe*" cards. The players (the readers) are instructed to deal out the cards as in an ordinary deck and to read, in turn, the brief postcard message printed on each. When a *fin du globe* card is turned up, the game is over. Again, the question arises—Is this poetry?—and once again MacBeth is challenging the reader while exploring the limits of his craft and trying to extend his artistic territory. Even the most skeptical reader can, if he allows himself, find pleasure in these and similar experiments, for they are clever and entertaining, and one can sense the pleasure that MacBeth himself must have experienced in giving free rein to his imagination.

Among MacBeth's most successful comic poems is "A Poet's Life," which first appeared in *In the Hours Waiting for the Blood to Come* and has since developed into a kind of serial poem published in various installments. In its original form, the poem consists of twelve episodes focusing on various aspects of the poet's life. The point of view is third person, to permit MacBeth as much distance as possible from his subject, himself. The result is a poem, which avoids the gloomy seriousness of typical introspection and yet focuses on some serious themes, showing the poet to be as human as anyone else. The first section of the poem is representative of MacBeth's technique; it shows the poet at home, trying to write and jotting down the following lines: "today I got up at eight, felt cold, shaved,/ washed, had breakfast, and dressed." The banality here reflects a larger tedium in the poet's life, for nothing much happens to him, except in his imagination. It is not surprising, then, when his efforts to write lead nowhere and he turns to the television for an episode of the *Avengers*, a purely escapist adventure show.

Viewed almost as a specimen or as a caged animal might be viewed, the poet is an amusing creature, sipping his "peppermint cream" and sucking distractedly on his pencil; and yet he is also pitiable. There is, in fact, something of the fool about the poet, something reminiscent of Charlie Chaplin's little tramp, for although he evokes laughter or a bemused smile there is something fundamentally sad about him. The poignancy comes from the realization that the poet, no matter how hard he tries to blend into the common crowd, must always remain isolated. It is the nature of his craft; writing poetry sets him apart. Consequently, when he goes to the supermarket, dressed in "green wranglers" to make himself inconspicuous, he still stands out among the old women, the babies, and the old men. He is "looking/ at life for his poems, is helping/ his wife, is a normal considerate man," and yet his role as poet inevitably removes him from the other shoppers and from the world at large.

Technically, "A Poet's Life" is rather simple and straightforward, but several significant devices work subtly to make the poem successful. The objective point of view enables MacBeth to combine the comic and the pathetic without becoming maudlin or self-pitying; this slightly detached tone is complemented by MacBeth's freewheeling, modernized version of the *Don Juan* stanza. It is typical of MacBeth to turn to traditional forms for inspiration, to borrow them and make them new.

Not a poet to break the rules without first understanding what the rules are, MacBeth is fascinated by traditional forms as well as by those that are new and experimental. It is a measure of his poetic temperament that he is able to take a traditional form and incorporate it into his general experimentation. The reader often encounters regular rhyme and meter in Mac-

Beth's work and occasionally recognizes something like a sonnet or sestina. Invariably, though, the standard form is modified to conform to MacBeth's urge to experiment. "How to Eat an Orange" is as nearly a sonnet as it can possibly be without actually being one. It has fourteen lines and a Shakespearean rhyme scheme, including the final couplet; but it lacks the iambic pentameter. In fact, it has no regular meter at all, although the iambic does surface from time to time like a theme played in the background. Form, then, is not an end in itself but a means to an end, and MacBeth employs whatever forms he finds useful, including the traditional, in communicating his ideas.

MacBeth's attitude toward form is captured most provocatively in a poem entitled "What Metre Is." A tour de force of technique, this poem stands as the poet's manifesto. The controlling idea is that the poem itself will provide examples of various poetic devices while they are being discussed. For example, when alliteration is mentioned, it appears in the context of the following passage: "leaping/ long lean and allusive/ through low lines." The uses of prose are considered in this fashion: "Prose is another possibility. There could be three/ sentences in the stanza. This would be an example of/ that." Other aspects of metrics discussed and illustrated in the poem are syllabics, free verse, word and interval counting, internal rhyming, rhythm, assonance, and finally, typography, "its mos/ t irrit/ ating (perhaps) manif/ estation." Irritating and mechanical it may be, representing the voice of the typewriter and the "abdic/ ation of insp/ iration," but still the poet feels compelled to say "I li/ ke it." He likes it because it is "the logica/ l exp/ ression o/ f itsel/ f." Having gone through his paces, the way a musician might play the scale or some well-known traditional piece just to prove he can, MacBeth turns finally to the experimental, which, despite its flaws, holds some irresistible attraction for him. He can manage traditional metrics, and he illustrates this ability in the poem, but he can also handle the riskier, less traditional devices. This poem, then, embodies on a small scale the range of poetic techniques one is likely to encounter in MacBeth's poetry: the traditional, often with modifications, and the experimental, always with MacBeth's own particular daring.

If MacBeth takes chances with the form of his poems, he also takes considerable risks with the content. Many of his poems are violent or sexually explicit, and some readers have found his subject matter objectionable. Perhaps the chief characteristic of the content of his poetry is a fascination with fear and violence, which MacBeth feels can be traced to his childhood. As a boy during World War II, MacBeth lost his father and experienced the bombing of his house. He collected shrapnel in the streets after air raids, spent night after night in the shelters, and grew up surrounded by physical violence and the threat of death. This kind of environment affected him strongly, and MacBeth feels that it led ultimately to a kind of obsession with violence that finds an outlet through his poetry.

The connection between his childhood experience of the war and such poems as "The Sirens," "The War," and "The Passing Ones" is obvious because these poems are explicitly about that experience, about "those bombed houses where/ I echoed in/ The empty rooms." Other poems, such as "Driving West," with its apocalyptic vision of a nuclear war, are less concerned with the actual experiences of World War II than with the nightmare vision it instilled. MacBeth's childhood fear of bombs has been translated into an adult's vision of the end of the world: "There was nothing left,/ Only a world of scrap. Dark metal bruised,/ Flung soup of blood, anchors and driven screws." This is the inheritance of Hiroshima and Nagasaki, a vision of the potential that man has to destroy himself and the entire planet.

The same influences are operating, though less obviously, in "The Burning Poem," which ends with the following passage: "Burning, burning,/ and nothing left to burn:/ only the ashes/ in a little urn." Here the violence has been freed of its war context with only a passing reference to suggest the connection: "rice paper, cartridge-paper,/ it was all the same." The merging of art, as represented by the rice paper, and war, represented by the cartridge paper, suggests the relationship between MacBeth's experiences of the war and his poetry. He is, in effect, "Spilling petrol/ on the bare pages." There is a sense in which many of MacBeth's poems are burning with the effects of remembered violence.

Inevitably, the violence loses its war context entirely and becomes associated with other things, just as it must have been absorbed into MacBeth's life. In "A Confession," for example, the topic is abortion, and the woman who has chosen to abort her child remembers the procedure as "the hard cold inrush of its killer,/ Saw-teeth, threshing fins, cascading water,/ And the soul spat like a bubble out of its head." The act was not clinical or antiseptic but personal and highly violent. The woman, in the course of her dramatic monologue, reveals an obsessive guilt and an inability to deal with what she has done. She wonders, finally, what her punishment might be "For crucifying someone in my womb." In this case MacBeth is somewhat removed from the poem because he uses the persona of the woman, but in "In the Hours Waiting for the Blood to Come" and "Two Days After" he approaches the topic of a lost or aborted child in a much more personal way, considering the impact of the death on the people involved in the relationship. In "Two Days After" the couple make love but the act has less to do with love than with guilt and a kind of spent violence.

Often, MacBeth's images seem designed specifically to shock the reader, to jolt him out of complacency. It is important, however, to realize that MacBeth employs violent and sexually explicit passages for more than merely sensational purposes. He wants to consider the darker side of human nature; violence and fear are alive in the world, and acknowledging their existence is a first step toward coming to terms with them.

It would be a mistake to regard MacBeth as merely a poet of sex and violence, for he has more dimensions than those. MacBeth himself seems bothered by the attention that has been given to the more sensational aspects of his poetry to the exclusion of other elements, and has remarked that he does not find his poetry any more violent than anyone else's. In terms of his total body of work, he is right, but the shocking and explicit poems inevitably call more attention to themselves than those that are more subdued in tone and subject matter, especially the very fine children's poems and MacBeth's engaging forays into the fantastic or surreal.

"The Red Herring" is a good illustration of MacBeth's poetry for children. The elements of the poem are a dried red herring, a bare wall, a ladder, and a man with a hammer, a nail, and a long piece of string. After the man has tied the red herring to the string suspended from the nail in the top of the wall and gone away, the poet addresses the question of why he would bother to make up such a simple story: "I did it just to annoy people./ Serious people. And perhaps also/ to amuse children. Small children." Undoubtedly, a child could take pleasure in this poem, but it is not entirely limited to the child in its appeal. The adult who is able to put off his seriousness for a moment or two will find himself smiling at the poem because of its saucy tone and at himself because he was probably gullible enough to enter the poem with a serious mind, even though the title itself warned him that things were not what they seemed. The playfulness here is characteristic of MacBeth's sense of humor, and, as usual, it is designed to make a serious point as well as to please.

Related to the children's poems are MacBeth's trips into the fantastic, as reflected in "Scissor-Man." The speaker, a pair of scissors used to cut bacon rind, contemplates his position in life, grousing about being kept under the draining-board rather than in the sink unit. Further, he worries about what might be going on between the nutcrackers and the carrot grater and vows that if he should "catch him rubbing/ those tin nipples of hers/ in the bread-bin" he will "have his/ washer off." Clearly, this is not meant to be children's poetry, but it is, perhaps, a kind of children's poetry for adults, for it engages the imagination in the same way that nursery rhymes and fairy tales do. In this case, MacBeth's humor seems designed to be an end in itself, an escape into the purely fanciful.

If one were to compile a list of adjectives to describe MacBeth's poetry, he would include at least the following: experimental, traditional, humorous, serious, violent, compassionate. The fact that these adjectives seem to cancel one another is significant, for MacBeth is possessed of a vital desire to encompass everything. In all his diversity, MacBeth is an original and important contemporary poet, a risk-taker who is continually trying to extend the boundaries of his art.

Neal Bowers

Other major works

LONG FICTION: *The Transformation*, 1975; *The Samurai*, 1975; *The Survivor*, 1977; *The Seven Witches*, 1978; *The Born Losers*, 1981; *A Kind of Treason*, 1982; *Anna's Book*, 1983; *The Lion of Pescara*, 1984; *Dizzy's Woman*, 1986.

PLAYS: *The Doomsday Show*, 1964; *The Scene-Machine*, 1971 (music by Anthony Gilbert).

NONFICTION: *My Scotland*, 1973.

ANTHOLOGIES: *The Penguin Book of Sick Verse*, 1963; *Penguin Modern Poets VI*, 1964 (with J. Clemo and E. Lucie-Smith); *The Penguin Book of Animal Verse*, 1965; *Poetry 1900-1965*, 1967; *The Penguin Book of Victorian Verse*, 1968; *The Falling Splendour*, 1970; *Poetry for Today*, 1983.

CHILDREN'S LITERATURE: *Noah's Journey*, 1966; *Jonah and the Lord*, 1969; *The Rectory Mice*, 1982; *The Book of Daniel*, 1986.

Bibliography

Dooley, Tim. Review of *Collected Poems, 1958-1982*. *The Times Literary Supplement*, January 26, 1990, p. 101. According to Dooley, the poems in the volume under review reveal a healthy development: "Formal scrupulousness replaces formal daring and self-examination replaces self-regard." Dooley praises the "new tenderness" that has accompanied MacBeth's increasing attention to form.

Ries, Lawrence R. "George MacBeth." In *Poets of Great Britain and Ireland Since 1960: Part 2, M-Z*, edited by Vincent B. Sherry, Jr. Vol. 40 of *Dictionary of Literary Biography*. Detroit: Gale Research, 1985. A judicious appreciation that calls attention to MacBeth's black humor and dexterity as a "trickster." Some biographical facts are given, but the piece is primarily a survey of the achievements (and disappointments) of MacBeth's poetry through *Poems from Oby*. The references cited at the end reveal that MacBeth's work gets reviews but very little extended critical attention.

Rosenthal, Macha Louis. *The New Poets: American and British Poetry Since World War II*. New York: Oxford University Press, 1967. Rosenthal discusses Macbeth in the context of all English language poets in the last half of the twentieth century. Macbeth is one of the most prolific and experimental poets writing today. He defines his times as well as being a product of them. Contains a bibliography.

Schmidt, Michael, and Grevel Lindop. *British Poetry Since 1930: A Critical Survey*. Oxford, England: Carcanet Press, 1972. A useful overview that places MacBeth's poetry in context. MacBeth gives shape to the alienation of modern life by being one of the most fecund and experimental of modern poets. Useful for all students who seek a broad view of modern poetry and an understanding of where Macbeth fits in.

Thwaite, Anthony. *Twentieth-century English Poetry: An Introduction*. New

York: Barnes & Noble, 1978. Discusses MacBeth as a member of "The Group," with only a very brief characterization of his poetry itself but providing an overview of the twentieth century British poetry that can serve as a context for a student of MacBeth. Contains a bibliography and an index.

HUGH MacDIARMID
Christopher Murray Grieve

Born: Langholm, Scotland; August 11, 1892
Died: Edinburgh, Scotland; September 9, 1978

Principal poetry

A Moment in Eternity, 1922; *Sangschaw,* 1925; *Penny Wheep,* 1926; *A Drunk Man Looks at the Thistle,* 1926; *The Lucky Bag,* 1927; *To Circumjack Cencrastus: Or, The Curly Snake,* 1930; *First Hymn to Lenin and Other Poems,* 1931; *Scots Unbound and Other Poems,* 1932; *Selected Poems,* 1934; *Stony Limits and Other Poems,* 1934; *Second Hymn to Lenin and Other Poems,* 1935; *A Kist of Whistles,* 1947; *In Memoriam James Joyce,* 1955; *The Battle Continues,* 1957; *Three Hymns to Lenin,* 1957; *Collected Poems of Hugh MacDiarmid,* 1962; *A Lap of Honour,* 1967; *Complete Poems, 1920-1976,* 1978 (two volumes).

Other literary forms

Hugh MacDiarmid wrote prolifically through most of his life. His more than seventy books include social criticism, political polemics, autobiography, and literary criticism. He edited earlier Scottish poets such as William Dunbar and Robert Burns and several poetry anthologies, and he founded and edited a number of Scottish periodicals.

Achievements

Only slowly has MacDiarmid come to be recognized as a major twentieth century poet. He spent most of his life laboring in one way or another for Scotland and won his earliest acclaim there. He was a founder, in 1927, of the Scottish Center of PEN, the international writers' organization, and of the National Party of Scotland the following year, although his always radical political views led him into the Communist Party in the 1930's. Despite his extreme social and political views, his friends were legion. He once observed that few other people could boast of friendships with William Butler Yeats, T. S. Eliot, *and* Dylan Thomas, and the circle of his admirers extended worldwide. After many years of promoting, usually undiplomatically, Scotland and Scottish culture, he was awarded a Civil List pension in 1950, and although his criticism of Scottish education continued unabated, Edinburgh University awarded him an honorary Doctor of Laws degree in 1957.

Not until the 1960's, however, did MacDiarmid's poetry begin to appear in British and modern poetry anthologies. Despite a general awakening to his greatness since that time, reliable commentary of his work remains largely in the hands of Scottish critics. It is safe to say that the study of his poetry to date represents a tiny portion of what will emerge in the years and decades to come. As an innovator in modern literature, MacDiarmid deserves to be ranked with Eliot, James Joyce, and Samuel Beckett.

Biography

Christopher Murray Grieve was born on August 11, 1892, in Langholm, Scotland, near the English border. His father's side of the family worked mostly in tweed mills, while his mother's people were farmers; throughout his life, Hugh MacDiarmid championed the working class. His father, who was a rural postman, died while Christopher was still a teenager. Educated at Langholm Academy and Broughton Junior Student Center, Edinburgh, the young man worked thereafter as a journalist and became active in politics. In World War I, he served in the Royal Army Medical Corps in Salonika, Italy, and France.

In 1918, MacDiarmid was married, and he settled after the war in Montrose, Angus, where he continued as a reporter, local politician, and contributor to the Scottish Renaissance and Nationalist movements. Adopting the pen name Hugh MacDiarmid in the early 1920's, he continued to write prose under his given name for years afterward. He lived in England most of the time between the years 1929 and 1932, working at temporary jobs, perfecting his antipathy to the English, and suffering the breakup of his marriage.

After being remarried in 1932, MacDiarmid returned to Scotland, worked briefly in Edinburgh, and from 1933 to 1941 lived in Whalsay in the Shetland Islands, where he developed the geological interest which permeates his poems of this period. He performed factory and merchant tasks during World War II, after which he traveled considerably, including trips to Communist nations. As late as 1964, when he was seventy-two, he stood as Communist candidate for Parliament in the district of Kinross and West Perthshire, insisting as always that his Communist and Nationalist commitments in no way conflicted. The publication of *Collected Poems of Hugh MacDiarmid* in the United States in 1962, while omitting many good poems, brought him to the attention of a wider reading public, and in his final years, he was acknowledged as one of Scotland's greatest poets. He died at the age of eighty-six on September 9, 1978.

Analysis

When Hugh MacDiarmid began writing poetry seriously after serving in World War I, the Scots literary tradition had reached one of its lowest points. In the century following the deaths of Robert Burns, Sir Walter Scott, and Lord Byron, Scottish poetry consisted largely of enervated and sentimental effusions which imitated the surface mannerisms of Burns's lyrics. Under the circumstances, it is hardly surprising that MacDiarmid wrote his earliest poems in standard English. Although his style was reminiscent of English Romanticism, it had from the start more vigor and individuality than the work of most of his contemporaries. The best of these early poems, *A Moment in Eternity*, first appeared in MacDiarmid's *Annals of the Five Senses* (1923), which contained chiefly experimental prose. This poem establishes his essentially Romantic disposition, "searching the unsearchable" in quest of God and immortality. Although his style and technique were to change radically, these ambitions remained with him, and "eternity" remained to the end of his career one of the most frequent words in his poetic vocabulary. His rhythms in this early poem are supple, varied, but basically iambic; his diction, pleasant but rather conventional.

It was not long, however, before he began to write under his pseudonym in a vocabulary forged from various local Scottish dialects and words from literary Scots dating as far back as the late medieval period of Scottish literary glory, when Robert Henryson, William Dunbar, Gavin Douglas, and others overshadowed the best English poets. He charged this "synthetic Scots" with a surprising vitality in two early books of lyrics, *Sangschaw* and *Penny Wheep*. The poems were about God, eternity, the Scottish countryside, love, and other subjects. Because he broke with the stereotypes of recent Scottish poetry and because he challenged his traditionally literate countrymen with a diction reaching back to a time of Scottish literary ascendancy, MacDiarmid was basing his strategy on an appeal to the best in his readers.

Before the publication of the second of these works, he was already shaping another book. *A Drunk Man Looks at the Thistle*, also issued in 1926, proved a much more ambitious work: a sequence of lyrics and meditative poems making up one long, symbolically unified poem. Although MacDiarmid was to write many long poems, he would never find a structural principle more effective than the one he used here. While some critics have objected to the titles of the fifty-nine poems as interfering with the unity of the book, anyone reading through the sequence will have no trouble perceiving its integrity. The first title, "Sic Transit Gloria Scotia," signals the poet's concern with the cultural and literary decline of his native land and suggests his intention of arresting that decline personally. *A Drunk Man Looks at the Thistle* has come to be recognized as more than a regional achievement, though MacDiarmid took several risks which probably delayed recognition of the scope of his achievement.

In the first place, the title, while accurate, is an odd one for an ambitious literary work, as it seems to lack seriousness and in fact to cater to the common perception of the Scottish peasantry as whiskey-guzzling ne'er-do-wells. His employment of a Scots vocabulary also posed problems. The vocabulary threatened to repel English readers, who expected poets to clothe respectable verse in literary English. The numerous dialect words required heavy use of a specialized dictionary. Even if willing to wrestle with the words, however, such readers were likely to associate Scots with feeble imitations of Burns. MacDiarmid appeared unconventional and frivolous not only in choosing a drunkard as the poem's speaker but also in choosing the lowly thistle, rather than a more "worthy" flower such as a rose, as his central symbol. Who else had made anything of such a homely weed since the rhetorical question of Matthew 7:16: "Do men gather grapes of thorns, or figs of thistles?"

Nevertheless, MacDiarmid had reasons to hope for a harvest. His format permitted him a series of lyrical, comical, and satirical reflections in a variety of meters and stanzas, both rhymed and unrhymed, with the concomitant advantage of showing off his technical versatility. He could also expect that his more extravagant poetic flights, being merely the dreams of a drunken man, would not reflect on him. Apparent digressions were no problem, either, for everyone expects a drunken man to meander. Therefore, while his character indulged in a leisurely display of reactions to all that ailed him and Scotland, the poet could carefully guide his inebriated speaker along a purposeful path.

The drunkard begins by complaining of the difficulty of keeping up with his drinking partners, especially since the Scotch does not compare with the old-time variety, thereby establishing that everything Scottish now seems to be "destitute o'speerit," including the appalling poetry now produced by supposed devotees of Burns. An immediate dilemma presents itself: How can one be a good Scot yet shake off the Scottish lethargy and mediocrity? Interestingly, MacDiarmid's method involves the occasional incorporation of translations and adaptations from French, Belgian, German, and Russian poets, and two original lyrics addressed to Fyodor Dostoevski. MacDiarmid obviously considered the great Russian novelist a kindred spirit in the struggle to repossess imaginatively a stubbornly recalcitrant homeland. To be a good Scot meant, among other things, to accept competent assistance wherever available.

In a poem called "Poet's Pub," based on a poem by Alexander Blok, the drunkard resists the idea of going home to his wife, Jean, who is sure to nag him. Instead, he hopes to discover the truth said to be in wine, especially those truths ordinarily dark to him and to his cronies. He catches sight of a "silken leddy" in the pub, but she soon fades from sight, and eventually he stumbles outside to begin his homeward trek. The fourth poem of the sequence introduces the thistle and the image with which MacDiarmid customarily pairs it, the moonlight: "The munelicht's like a lookin'-glass,/ The thistle's like mysel,'" he observes, one of the resemblances being that he needs a shave.

In the poems that follow, the symbolic values of thistle and moonlight proliferate. A poem adressed to "The Unknown Goddess"—again adapted from Blok—presumably refers to the mysterious lady of the pub, who may represent his muse but is certainly the opposite of Jean. The drunkard's attention alternates between depressing reality ("Our Educational System," "The Barren Fig," "Tussle with the Philistines") and inspired visions ("Man and the

Infinite," "Outward Bound," "The Spur of Love"). The drunken man is not sure of much: "And yet I feel this muckle thistle's staun'in'/ Atween me and the mune as pairt o' a Plan." He regards himself as his nation's "soul" and thus free to appropriate the humble thistle: In one of his flights he compares his homeward course to the wanderings of Ulysses; in another he sees himself "ootward boond" toward eternity. The thistle may serve to unite man and the infinite, or it may simply take off on its own and leave man nothing but the hole in which it was once rooted. Periodically his thoughts return to Jean, who "ud no' be long/ In finding whence this thistle sprang," for it is in her absence that the plant has grown for him.

The man's thoughts oscillate between Scotland—materialistic, Philistine, ill-educated, yet worth redemption—and himself as representative of the more general human condition—earthbound and mortal yet aspiring to eternity. The thistle has, despite its general ugliness, the capacity to flower, to put out at its tip a "rose" that permits MacDiarmid the traditional associations of that flower in a different context. In "The Form and Purpose of the Thistle," the speaker reflects on the "craft" that produced the odd, prickly stalk capable of breaking into flowers "like sudden lauchter," a craft of puzzling contrarieties. In "The Thistle's Characteristics," the poet ranges over man's illusions and presumptions. "For wha o's ha'e the thistle's poo'er/ To see we're worthless and believe 't?" Later he employs the Norse myth of Yggdrasill, the ash tree which binds together Earth, Heaven, and Hell; in this case, however, man is a "twig" on a giant thistle that, far from uniting creation, "braks his warlds abreid and rives/ His heavens to tatters on its horns." The Yggdrasill poem insists on man's suffering and ends by seeing humans as so many Christs, carrying their crosses "frae the seed," although as the drunkard slyly puts it, most feel it far less than he "thro' bein' mair wudden frae the stert!" Such satiric thrusts at his countrymen occur frequently in the work as a whole. However painful the life, the soul will soar in its "divine inebriety." Intoxication, then, is also a metaphor in this poem, standing for the poetic imagination that can rise above, and gain solace by reflecting on, mankind's common "Calvary."

The drunken man contemplates the oppressive English rule over an exhausted and often foolish Scotland, but even more often, his thoughts wind between Heaven and Earth, between the aspirations of the rose and the limitations of the rooted stalk. He longs for the mysterious lady, then is gripped by the recollection of practical Jean at home. Near the end of the work, he sees himself, God, the Devil, and Scotland all on a great cosmic wheel which sums up Scotland's and man's slow journeys through history. Pondering Scottish resistance to change and new ideas, he wonders if he must "assume/ The burden o' his people's doom" by dying heroically for his recalcitrant fellows. He falters over the decision, not exactly rejecting heroism but choosing to return to Jean's arms. The last lyric of the poem pays eloquent tribute to what he has left of his vision: silence. The conclusion is a joke, for he imagines what Jean will say to that: "And weel ye micht,/ . . . efter sic a nicht!"

The final lines of the poem are consistent with the whole work: Despite his insistence on the dignity of human imagination, the drunken man is always aware of the indignity of human circumstances and his inability to grasp the meaning of life. Only a drunk—that is, only a person intoxicated by life generally and the life of the mind particularly—would bother with such a spiritual quest.

MacDiarmid's next book of poetry, *To Circumjack Cencrastus*, is more of a miscellany, but one stanza of the poem aptly titled "MacDiarmid's Curses" holds a particular irony:

> Speakin o' Scotland in English words
> As it were Beethoven chirpt by birds;
> Or as if a Board school teacher
> Tried to teach Rimbaud and Nietzsche.

Although these lines do not precisely deny the possibility of a shift to "English words," they scarcely foretell the fact that within a few years MacDiarmid would virtually cease to write in his Scottish amalgam, even when "speakin' o' Scotland." By the middle 1930's, he would be creating a very different sort of poetry using standard English.

In the meantime, MacDiarmid continued to employ Scots for his first two "hymns to Lenin." Many intellectuals of the time shared his hope, but few his enduring faith, in the efficacy of Communism. It remains difficult to read objectively the "First Hymn to Lenin," in which the Soviet leader is hailed as a successor to Christ, or to appreciate it as poetry. MacDiarmid seems to have traded metaphysical doubts for political assurance, and the exchange does not enhance his poetry. He was always extreme in his enthusiasms, but from this point on, his polemical voice invaded his poetry more frequently. Within *First Hymn to Lenin and Other Poems*, however, is found "At My Father's Grave," with its eight lines of flexible blank verse meditating hauntingly on his father, as if from "across a valley."

With *Stony Limits and Other Poems*, MacDiarmid moved into a new phase of his poetic career. He still included poems in Scots, notably a group called "Shetland Lyrics," but he was now working in a literary English that differed markedly from that of his very early poetry. The English poems were at this point more discursive, somewhat less concrete, and considerably more formal. The title poem, in nine ten-line stanzas, pays tribute to Charles Doughty, a poet, geologist, and travel writer who delighted in the lonely occupation of studying the soil and rock formations of remote regions, his most famous book being about the Arabian desert. Gregarious himself, MacDiarmid could respond enthusiastically to Doughty's serenity, his indifference to the crowd, and his capacity for appreciating realms of silence. When this book appeared, MacDiarmid had retreated to the Shetland Islands, where, without ceasing his political involvements, he had begun to study the geology of this northern outpost. He created a new difficulty for his reader, for "Stony Limits" is peppered with terms such as "xenoliths," "orthopinacoid," "striae," and "microline." The geological terminology signals his camaraderie with Doughty and also a growing love of precision quite distinct from the passion for suggestiveness which created the thistle and moonlight images in *A Drunk Man Looks at the Thistle*. This elegy is quiet, almost reverent, but without the defiant tone of his hymns to Lenin.

He carries his scientific enthusiasm further in a longer poem in the same collection, "On a Raised Beach." The poem begins "All is lithogenesis—or lochia," a line hardly calculated to appeal immediately to the laity, but since the first term signifies rock formation and the second the discharge from the womb after childbirth, the line immediately juxtaposes the contrasting elements of the poem, stones and human life. Actually, the first twenty-four of the poem's more than four hundred lines teem with technical geological terms, most of which cannot be found in an ordinary desk dictionary. Anyone who braves this formidable initial barrier, however, discovers an arresting meditation on the human situation vis-à-vis that of the stones, which "are one with the stars."

MacDiarmid points out that specific terms can be given to scientific phenomena, but man finds more difficulty in expressing his convictions and preferences. The permanence of stone emphasizes the transience and impatience of man. Early in the poem, he compares man unfavorably to the one other creature stirring on the beach, a bird whose "inward gates" are, unlike man's, "always open." MacDiarmid argues that the gates of stones stand open even longer. The poet's admiration for these enduring veterans of a world older than man can easily imagine resembles Henry David Thoreau's for living nature, and a number of the lines have a Thoreauvian ring to them—for example, "Let men find the faith that builds mountains/ Before they seek the faith that moves them." As in Thoreau, nature teaches the perceptive person humility. Life is redundant, says MacDiarmid, but not stones. Human culture pales before the bleak but beautiful sentinels of time on a scale beyond man's ordinary comprehension.

As the stately free verse moves on, MacDiarmid alludes to various stones with human associations: the missile that David hurled at Goliath, pebbles with which Demosthenes filled his mouth, the rock that guarded Christ's tomb. Human culture is like Goliath, doomed to fall, and no orator can hope to rival the lithic earth in eloquence. Stones not only draw men back to their beginnings but also lead them on to their end. No stone can be rolled aside like the "Christophanic" one to release death, but death is not on that account to be feared, because dying is less difficult than living a worthwhile life.

Despite the weightiness of "On a Raised Beach," despite its rather sepulchral tone, the poem does not oppress but conveys a breath of caution, a salutary deflation of human arrogance. The poem might have benefited from a beach more specifically evoked, like Matthew Arnold's Dover Beach, but it nevertheless communicates effectively the "capacity for solitude" by which MacDiarmid strives to imitate the great stones.

The virtual disappearance of Scots lyrics after *Stony Limits and Other Poems* seems to be not a repudiation of the poet's earlier theory but an acknowledgment that after several hundred poems in that medium he needed to test the linguistic possibilities of English. Like Burns before him, MacDiarmid could sing best in Scots and create more comedy and humor than he ever seemed to have tried in literary English. Advocates of his poetry (many of whom are Scottish) have tended to prefer the Scots poems, but the best of his English poems have their own excellence, and it is of a sort appropriate to an older man. They are sober, thought-provoking, and reflective of the intensity of a poet deeply committed to his art and alert to the world about him. Like Yeats and Eliot, he changed his style in middle age to produce a kind of verse in sharp contrast to that which gained for him his initial audience.

Not until the publication of his autobiography, *Lucky Poet*, in 1943 did MacDiarmid formulate in detail his prescription for the poetry he had been attempting to practice for a decade. This book contains several previously unpublished poems, one of which, "The Kind of Poetry I Want," sets forth vigorously the theory that he had been developing. The diction and rhythms of this long poem are prosaic, and its topical allusions date it severely, but it rings with conviction. Probably no poem ever written realizes all of its specifications. According to MacDiarmid, the poet must be a polymath who can base his or her work on "difficult knowledge" in many fields, including the sciences, and must be technically accomplished and equipped with "ecstasy." Poetry must reflect closeness to and knowledge of nature. The poet must know the countryside and the technological order and must deploy linguistic and historical learning. Poetry must be factual and still illuminate values, argues MacDiarmid; it must integrate the knowledge of its various sources and—as a crowning touch—must reflect a poet uninterested in personal success. At one point, MacDiarmid concedes that such poetry must await social reorganization, presumably along communistic lines.

MacDiarmid was better equipped than most to pursue his poetic ideal. By mid-career, his poetry bristled with learned allusions to Russian, Hebrew, Turkish, Chinese, Greek, and Gaelic poetry, to name a few. Not all the poems in *Lucky Poet* are learned, but they are all provoking. Two of them excoriate the cities of Edinburgh and Glasgow for their bourgeois sins, and the good humor of his earlier social criticism has vanished. Clearly, he is less willing than ever to cater to merely conventional taste and expectations.

By the time of *In Memoriam James Joyce*, MacDiarmid was brewing a poetry in some ways like Joyce's prose, packed with recondite allusions, quotations in many languages, puns, technical vocabulary, and an often tortuous syntax. The tone was more likely to be oracular and insistent. How many of his poetic tenets he was then fulfilling is disputable, but he clearly was not integrating knowledge, and perhaps he was inadvertently demonstrating the impossibility of such integration in the second half of the twentieth century, with its myriad specialists. Reminiscent of his previous work is the poem "We Must Look at the Harebell." MacDiarmid is at his best when "looking" rather than persuading, and this poem has fresh observations not only of the harebell but also of the pinguicula or butterwort (a small herb), the asphodel, the parsley fern, and other flora to be found by a person willing to climb rocks and descend into bogs. The plants he observes are interesting, but even more interesting is his determination to reveal the prospects of nature.

MacDiarmid appears to have written relatively little new poetry after the publication of *In Memoriam James Joyce*, but because *Collected Poems of Hugh MacDiarmid* omitted a number of his earlier poems, the volume *A Lap of Honour*, which appeared five years later, when the poet turned seventy-five, was an important addition. It contained some poems that had appeared only in periodicals and others from books difficult to obtain in 1967. One of the most important inclusions was "On a Raised Beach," only a short extract of which had appeared in the 1962 collection. There were several, by then welcome, Scots poems from an earlier day. Thus, this volume made accessible to many readers for the first time a sampling of MacDiarmid's work over the decades of his greatest vitality, the 1920's, 1930's, and 1940's.

The innovations of his later poetry have an importance beyond the success of individual poems. In an age when many poets knew little about science and even affected to despise it, MacDiarmid was trying to widen the range of the poet's expertise. While the scientific knowledge of even an amateur such as MacDiarmid is bound to seem inadequate to a well-trained scientist, he was often able to enhance his subjects with metaphors drawn from science. Thus, in "Stony Limits," he compared his projected poem in praise of Doughty to the process of crystallization in rocks and to the growth of lunar formations, and in "Crystals Like Blood," he could liken the memory to the extraction of mercury from cinnabar. Such metaphors doubtless have very little effect on a scientifically illiterate reader, but his fear was of a poetry that failed by appealing only to the badly educated. His aspiration to the precision of the exact sciences was probably unrealistic, but he was doing his part to integrate the "two cultures" at a time when many intellectuals were dividing into mutually antagonistic and uncomprehending camps. His efforts to apply the discoveries of modern linguistics to poetry were unsuccessful, but there is no telling what they may have suggested to younger poets. He carried allusion and quotation beyond what many readers would consider tolerable limits, but he did not shrink from challenging those who were able and willing to follow him. Like Eliot, MacDiarmid was trying to use tradition creatively, and like Ezra Pound, he often moved outside the Western tradition favored by Eliot. Few poets have worked so diligently for so long to widen the possibilities of poetry.

By a curious irony, MacDiarmid's poems in English, because of their high density of technical words and obscure quotations and allusions, present greater difficulties than his earlier ones in Scots. Lacking the humor and lyricism of the early poems, his English poems often repay the reader's careful attention with their insight into the natural world and their challenge to conventional ways of looking at the world and of expressing the results of such observations. Nevertheless, his early mission to rescue Scottish poetry by creating a composite dialect out of folk and literary sources and to speak to a materialistic generation of the possibilities of a richer culture and authentic spiritual life was doubtless his greatest accomplishment. Even without consulting the glossary of *Collected Poems of Hugh MacDiarmid*, the English-speaking reader can take pleasure in the energy and lyrical buoyancy of *A Drunk Man Looks at the Thistle*, and with very little trouble the full meaning is available to all. It has been suggested that this poem is the modern equivalent of the medieval dream vision. Undoubtedly, only a poet steeped in literary tradition could have written it. Taking advantage of a form that allows a comprehensive and uninhibited vision, MacDiarmid fashions a poem that is highly original because it reflects a modern, skeptical sensibility, and is readily understandable because it is made from the materials of everyday life. While aiming at universality in his later poetry, he achieved it most fully in his odyssey of a drunken cottager beneath the Scottish "mune."

Robert P. Ellis

Other major works

NONFICTION: *Albyn: Or, Scotland and the Future*, 1927; *The Present Condition of Scottish Music*, 1927; *At the Sign of the Thistle: A Collection of Essays*, 1934; *Scottish Eccentrics*, 1936; *The Islands of Scotland*, 1939; *Lucky Poet*, 1943; *Burns Today and Tomorrow*, 1959; *David Hume: Scotland's Greatest Son*, 1961; *The Company I've Kept*, 1966; *Scotland, 1968: Selected Essays of Hugh MacDiarmid*, 1969 (edited by Duncan Glen).

ANTHOLOGIES: *Northern Numbers, Being Representative Selections from Certain Living Scottish Poets*, 1920-1922 (three volumes); *The Golden Treasury of Scottish Poetry*, 1940.

MISCELLANEOUS: *Annals of the Five Senses*, 1923.

Bibliography

Bold, Alan. *MacDiarmid: The Terrible Crystal.* London: Routledge & Kegan

Paul, 1983. A full-length study of MacDiarmid's poetry. In addition to critical commentary of his works, Bold compares him to other writers, particularly those who influenced him, and discusses both the political and mystical elements in his works.

Buthlay, Kenneth. *Hugh MacDiarmid.* 1964. Rev. ed. Edinburgh, Scotland: Scottish Academic Press, 1982. A comprehensive and lively introduction to MacDiarmid, expanded and revised from the first edition in 1964. This study is an illuminating account of MacDiarmid's development as a poet, with critical examination of individual poems and technical devices.

Gish, Nancy K. *Hugh MacDiarmid: The Man and His Work.* London: Macmillan, 1984. A critical appraisal of MacDiarmid's work, with emphasis given to such poems as *A Drunk Man Looks at the Thistle, Stony Limits and Other Poems,* as well as the later long poems. Includes a glossary for "On a Raised Beach." The author interviewed MacDiarmid for this work, which provides much important background information on the poet and his thinking.

Glen, Duncan, ed. *Hugh MacDiarmid: A Critical Survey.* Edinburgh, Scotland: Scottish Academic Press, 1972. A collection of essays, all but one previously printed, affirming the significance of MacDiarmid's poetry. This useful volume offers solid literary criticism of MacDiarmid's work from his early poetry to his later poems.

_____. *Hugh MacDiarmid and the Scottish Renaissance.* London: W. & R. Chambers, 1964. Considered the definitive introduction to MacDiarmid's life and work by a notable scholar of the poet. This thoroughly researched volume places MacDiarmid among Scottish writers who revived Scottish traditions.

Scott, P. H., and A. C. Davis. *The Age of MacDiarmid: Essays on Hugh MacDiarmid and His Influence on Contemporary Scotland.* Edinburgh, Scotland: Mainstream Publishing, 1980. An important collection of essays from eminent scholars of MacDiarmid. The first group of essays is largely autobiographical in nature; the second group addresses themes such as MacDiarmid's nationalism, politics, and the language problem in his work.